For Our Good Always

For Our Good Always

Studies on the Message and Influence of Deuteronomy in Honor of Daniel I. Block

Edited by

Jason S. DeRouchie, Jason Gile, and Kenneth J. Turner

WIPF & STOCK · Eugene, Oregon

Wipf and Stock Publishers
199 W 8th Ave, Suite 3
Eugene, OR 97401

For Our Good Always
Studies on the Message and Influence of Deuteronomy in Honor of Daniel I. Block
By DeRouchie, Jason S. and Gile, Jason
Copyright © 2013 by DeRouchie, Jason S. All rights reserved.
Softcover ISBN-13: 979-8-3852-3165-2
Hardcover ISBN-13: 979-8-3852-3166-9
eBook ISBN-13: 979-8-3852-3167-6
Publication date 9/6/2024
Previously published by Eisenbrauns, 2013

Contents

Contributors ix
Foreword xi
    Peter J. Gentry
Preface xv
The Publications of Daniel I. Block: Overview and Bibliography. . xxi
    Charlie Trimm
Tributes from the Block Family xxxiii

PART 1
The Message of Deuteronomy

Deuteronomy and Ancient Hebrew History Writing in
    Light of Ancient Chronicles and Treaties 3
    Alan Millard

"Because of the Wickedness of These Nations" (Deut 9:4–5):
    The Canaanites—Ethical or Not? 17
    Richard S. Hess

Admonitory Examples in Hittite and Biblical Legal Contexts . . . 39
    Harry A. Hoffner Jr.

"These Are the Words Moses Spoke": Implied Audience
    and a Case for a Pre-Monarchic Dating of Deuteronomy . . 61
    Peter T. Vogt

Laws and Ethical Ideals in Deuteronomy 81
    Gordon J. Wenham

Counting the Ten: An Investigation into the Numbering
    of the Decalogue. 93
    Jason S. DeRouchie

"Keep These Words in Your Heart" (Deut 6:6):
    A Spirituality of Torah in the Context of the Shema 127
    J. Gordon McConville

The Rhetoric of Theophany: The Imaginative Depiction
    of Horeb in Deuteronomy 9–10 145
    Jerry Hwang

v

For Your Good Always: Restraining the Rights of the Victor
    for the Well-Being of the Vulnerable (Deut 21:10–14) 165
    Rebekah Josberger

Deuteronomy's Theology of Exile. 189
    Kenneth J. Turner

PART 2

The Influence of Deuteronomy

The Impact of Deuteronomy on the Books of the
    Deuteronomistic History. 223
    Michael A. Grisanti

Deuteronomy and Isaiah 251
    H. G. M. Williamson

The Enduring Word of the Lord in Deuteronomy
    and Jeremiah 36 269
    Michael Graves

Deuteronomy and Ezekiel's Theology of Exile 287
    Jason Gile

The "Revealed Things": Deuteronomy and the
    Epistemology of Job. 307
    Christopher B. Ansberry

"Fear God and Keep His Commandments"(Eccl 12:13):
    An Examination of Some Intertextual Relationships
    between Deuteronomy and Ecclesiastes. 327
    Richard Schultz

The Influence of Deuteronomy on Intercessory Prayers in
    Ezra and Nehemiah. 345
    Gary V. Smith

Testing God's Son: Deuteronomy and Luke 4:1–13 365
    Grant R. Osborne

Paul's Reading of Deuteronomy: Law and Grace 389
    Douglas Moo

PART 3

The Lasting Significance of Deuteronomy

Making the Ten Count: Reflections on the Lasting Message
of the Decalogue. 415
   Jason S. DeRouchie

Welcoming the Stranger: Toward a Theology of Immigration
in Deuteronomy 441
   M. Daniel Carroll R.

Sermonizing in Deuteronomy, Jeremiah, and the 21st Century . . 463
   Elmer A. Martens

The Prophet Who Is Like and Greater Than Moses:
A Sermon on Deuteronomy 18:15–22. 485
   Daniel L. Akin

Stealing Souls: Human Trafficking and Deuteronomy 24:7 495
   Myrto Theocharous

The Book of the Torah as a Gospel of Grace: A Synthesis of
Daniel I. Block's Biblical Theology of Deuteronomy 511
   Thomas H. McClendon Jr.

Indexes
   Index of Authors 535
   Index of Scripture 545
   Index of Ancient Sources 569

Contributors

DANIEL L. AKIN
President and Professor of Preaching and Theology
Southeastern Baptist Theological Seminary

CHRISTOPHER B. ANSBERRY
Tutor in Old Testament
Oak Hill College, London, England

M. DANIEL CARROLL R.
Distinguished Professor of Old Testament
Denver Seminary

JASON S. DEROUCHIE
Associate Professor of Old Testament
Bethlehem College and Seminary

PETER J. GENTRY
Professor of Old Testament Interpretation
The Southern Baptist Theological Seminary

JASON GILE
Affiliate Professor of Old Testament, Northern Seminary
Adjunct Professor of Old Testament, Olivet Nazarene University

MICHAEL GRAVES
Associate Professor of Old Testament
Wheaton College

MICHAEL A. GRISANTI
Professor of Old Testament
The Master's Seminary

RICHARD S. HESS
Earl S. Kalland Professor of Old Testament and Semitic Languages
Denver Seminary

HARRY A. HOFFNER JR.
The John A. Wilson Professor of Hittitology Emeritus
University of Chicago

JERRY HWANG
Assistant Professor of Old Testament
Singapore Bible College

REBEKAH JOSBERGER
Assistant Professor of Hebrew and Old Testament
Multnomah Biblical Seminary

ELMER A. MARTENS
Professor Emeritus of Old Testament and President Emeritus
Fresno Pacific Biblical Seminary

THOMAS H. MCCLENDON JR.
Senior Pastor
Farmville Baptist Church, Auburn, AL

J. GORDON MCCONVILLE
Professor of Old Testament Theology
University of Gloucestershire, England

ALAN MILLARD
Emeritus Rankin Professor of Hebrew and Ancient Semitic Languages and Honor Senior Fellow
University of Liverpool, England

DOUGLAS MOO
Kenneth T. Wessner Professor of New Testament
Wheaton College

GRANT R. OSBORNE
Professor of New Testament
Trinity Evangelical Divinity School

RICHARD SCHULTZ
Blanchard Professor of Biblical Studies and Professor of Old Testament
Wheaton College

GARY V. SMITH
Adjunct Professor of Old Testament
Bethel Seminary

MYRTO THEOCHAROUS
Professor of Old Testament and Hebrew
Greek Bible College, Athens, Greece

CHARLIE TRIMM
Assistant Professor of Biblical and Theological Studies
Talbot School of Theology

KENNETH J. TURNER
Professor of Bible
Bryan College

PETER T. VOGT
Professor of Old Testament
Bethel Seminary

GORDON J. WENHAM
Professor Emeritus of Old Testament, University of Gloucestershire, England
Tutor in Old Testament, Trinity College, Bristol, England

H. G. M. WILLIAMSON
Regius Professor of Hebrew
University of Oxford, England

Foreword

Peter J. Gentry

Although my area of research has not permitted a contribution to the focus on Deuteronomy in this Festschrift, I am delighted to join colleagues, friends, and students of Dan Block to honour a beloved friend, mentor-scholar-teacher, and above all, a brother in Christ. I came to know Dan relatively recently compared to some—spring of 1999. When I was hired, he was the Associate Dean, Scripture and Interpretation, at the Southern Baptist Theological Seminary. During the hiring process, he casually asked me about my approach to the book of Judges. I had no idea he was writing a major commentary on Judges at the time. After a moment of thought, I replied, "Well there's an excellent article in *Westminster Theological Journal*. I forget who wrote it, but it's about 'Echo Narrative Technique in Hebrew Literature.' I like the approach taken there." This turned out to be an article by Dan who had influenced me through his writings before we met!

Humility is a *huge* indicator of greatness. During my early days in Louisville, I was always amazed at Dan's willingness to entertain and encourage the ideas of a much younger colleague like myself and even to back down when he was confronted by evidence from the biblical text. Like iron sharpening iron, we would go after each other, hammer and tongs, by the hour. He was always willing to stop everything and talk about the Bible. Yet he could be quiet too. In his church in Louisville, he attended an adult Sunday school class on Ezekiel taught by a layman. This was while Dan was finishing his commentary on Ezekiel, but he never disrupted the class and always supported the teacher. He always sought opportunities to support young preachers, pastors, Sunday school teachers, and, above all, his students.

Dan is known for his bold courage in seeking truth. He is not afraid to put all the evidence on the table, including his own presuppositions. His conviction that Jesus Christ is the Lord of all truth has spurred him to disciplined and industrious scholarship and to follow the evidence wherever it leads. For his commentary on Ezekiel, he originally produced 4,000 pages, of which only some 1,800 were published, and for his commentary on Deuteronomy a similar stack of paper was finally reduced after much editorial pain to 880 pages. Dan's work on Ezekiel brought lecturing opportunities and contact with scholars worldwide, yet he was always a model of graciousness in interacting with differing viewpoints. He has always had a burden for the wider academy in the hope that everyone will see the Living Word. At the same time, the standards of excellence that he expected of his students were set first and foremost for himself. And Dan is focused: when he sets his mind to do something, you can be assured it will happen.

Students of Dan such as Greg Smith and Kenneth Turner remember his opening prayers in class as "legendary." It was not uncommon for students to admit that, when tempted to skip class, they went in order to hear the opening prayer. Likewise, many came out of class saying that the opening prayer was the best part. Admittedly, Dan's unique accent was attractive. But as he prayed, all felt that they were no longer in a classroom but before the throne of grace. Dan had no embarrassment in confessing his own sin, or in weeping, as he talked with God. Those prayers set the tone, even when the subject matter for the class became heady.

Professor Block has given new meaning to the phrase "syllabus shock." His syllabi have often been over 300 pages long! Students soon realise that this is due to his concern that they have every word of his lectures and that they understand the information correctly. Although he has often read word for word from his course notes, he has a passion and cadence that does not allow this to come across as dry or boring. Most have finished his courses very appreciative to have these notes in hand. I myself have turned to these materials time and again for my own study and preparation for preaching and teaching. Dan is passionate about making the Scriptures, and in particular the Old Testament, live for students. He still has an enthusiasm for the first day of classes as if he were just starting first grade. One of the greatest joys of Dan's teaching career has been the opportunity to lecture in other countries. He has taught in Russia, Denmark, England, Hong Kong, Singapore, Kenya, China, Columbia, Greece, and, of course, Canada, his homeland.

Dan and Ellen have often opened their home to colleagues, church friends, and students. A glimpse of the man behind the curtain demonstrates the reality of his profession. He is an avid fan of baseball, curling, and most other sports, and despite his pacifist position, he was known to shoot a squirrel or two in his yard! Another favorite quote: "I am a pacifist, but if you touch my wife, I will pass a fist!"

Anyone who knows Dan knows his love of gardening. His Sabbath "rest" usually consists of intensive labour in his garden at home, which might well have been featured in *Better Homes & Gardens*. More to the point, one time Dan stepped up at his church to revamp the whole landscape. Laypeople were amazed that this amazing scholar and preacher was happy to serve by tending the ground and beautifying the whole place. He sees gardening not only as a project to use his creativity, but a time of relaxation and rest. Mowing the lawn is not on his "work list"; it is something to be enjoyed! His creativity is evident not only in his scholarship and gardening but also in drawing pictures or doing projects with his grandchildren.

Of all biblical scholars, Gary Smith has had the most extended collegial association with Dan, working ten years with him in Winnipeg and twelve years with him at Bethel. With this in mind, I asked him for some personal reflections. He recollected a number of details, including Dan's great enthusiasm for the NLT (New Living Translation) project and his strong yet unsuccessful appeal to make Hebrew required at Bethel Seminary. Then he recalled:

> Dan was always at his best preaching in chapel and was always someone you could count on for dealing seriously with the challenges and theology of the text itself. I have never had another colleague that I felt so close to in spirit and in theological convictions. He is a man of God, a wonderful friend, and a great spokesman for the practical significance of the Old Testament. He has had a significant impact on me and on many others who have worked with him and sat under his teaching.

In summary, Dan has lived up well to his own stated aims:

> The paradigm for my own research and ministry is set by Ezra, as described in Ezra 7:10: He committed himself to the study the Torah of Yahweh, to put it into practice, and to teach his revealed will in Israel. This means constantly asking serious questions of the Scriptures: What does the text say? Why does the text say it like that? What did the text mean to the original audience? What does the text have to say to me today? In order to answer these questions we need to understand both the worlds out of which the biblical texts arose and the worlds in which we moderns live.[1]

It is an honour to dedicate this volume to such a man.

---

1. http://www.wheaton.edu/Academics/Departments/Theology/Faculty/Daniel-Block.

Preface

No other book colors the tapestry of biblical thought like Deuteronomy. Its theological significance can scarcely be overstated, for it synthesizes pentateuchal theology, provided Israel a constitution for guiding their covenant relationship with Yahweh in the promised land, and served as a primary lens for later biblical authors to interpret Israel's covenant history.

In recent years, Deuteronomy scholarship has developed in significant ways. Many once held views are being questioned, as developments in biblical interpretation and world history are creating new queries and opening doors for fresh discovery and original proposals. Advances in rhetorical criticism and discourse analysis are proving useful for understanding the meaning of many passages and for assessing both diachronic and synchronic readings of the book. Deeper understanding of ANE literature, ideology, and historiography is drawing attention to Deuteronomy's content and raising new questions about its date and provenance. The sustained debate over the New Perspective on Paul has forced many to rethink old paradigms about law and gospel. Heightened interest in final form analysis, canonical criticism, and biblical theology has identified new vistas for viewing the message and role of the whole in Christian Scripture. In contemporary culture and history, increased environmental crises and devastations due to terrorism, abortion, poverty, sex trafficking, and the like have forced fresh assessment of ethical questions. The time seems right for a new study from evangelical scholars that wrestles with Deuteronomy from historical, literary, theological, and canonical perspectives.

Few OT scholars have worked so ably, carefully, and intentionally as Daniel I. Block to help the church and academy grasp the message of Deuteronomy. For well over a decade, he has devoted the bulk of his academic research to properly hearing the life-giving gospel of Moses in Deuteronomy. In the process, he has guided dissertations on the book, taught and preached the deuteronomic torah all over the world, and written numerous essays on the topic, which have now been collected into two accessible volumes: *How I Love Your Torah, O Lord! Studies in the Book of Deuteronomy* (Eugene, OR: Cascade, 2011); and *The Gospel according to Moses: Theological and Ethical Reflections on the Book of Deuteronomy* (Eugene, OR: Cascade, 2012). Block has also published an 800-page "pastoral" commentary titled *Deuteronomy* in Zondervan's NIVAC series (2012), and he is considering a more developed two-volume Deuteronomy commentary that would in many respects rival his earlier two-volume commentary on *The Book of Ezekiel* in Eerdman's NICOT series.

In the sea of OT studies, Daniel Block's scholarship has been a beacon for many, guiding the developing student, the alert pastor, and the thoughtful scholar safely into the harbor of God's life-giving word. Block's studies always exhibit a unique balance of exegetical rigor, literary and theological awareness, and pastoral care—all for the glory of God. And it is because this man has set his heart to study, practice, and teach God's word so faithfully within his home, the church, and the academy (Ezra 7:10) that we honor him with this volume on the occasion of his 70th birthday.

An Overview of the Book

With a title adapted from Moses' statement in Deut 6:24, *For Our Good Always* is a collection of new essays on the message of Deuteronomy and its influence on Christian Scripture. These studies from a range of evangelical perspectives come from an international group of specialists made up of Daniel Block's colleagues, friends, and former students. Many contributors are leaders in their areas of interest, and this volume has allowed them to show how their specializations overlap with the study of Deuteronomy. Other scholars are younger, some Block's former students, who are here summarizing or building upon their previous work for the benefit of the broader world. All who have contributed to this project (and others who were unable) are delighted to honor Daniel Block with this volume and are so grateful to God for the way this man has served as a steward of God's grace into our lives and into the broader world (1 Pet 4:10–11).

Part 1: The Message of Deuteronomy

The first of this volume's three parts includes ten essays that address the message of Deuteronomy proper. The initial five studies deal with foundational issues related to the book's interpretation. Alan Millard, Daniel Block's doctoral father, opens the collection by comparing Deuteronomy's history writing to ancient chronicles and treaties, and his observations provide provocative implications for the book's dating. Richard S. Hess then relates the biblical portrait of the Canaanites with extra-biblical evidence in order to provide a balanced understanding of the nature of the Canaanite wickedness that Deuteronomy views as the ground for Yahweh's divine judgment. Harry A. Hoffner Jr. identifies several examples of admonitions within Hittite legal material in order to show that the pentateuchal literature follows contemporary practice in mixing anecdotal accounts of defiance and divine response with legal and judicial data. Peter T. Vogt then provides a new argument for a pre-monarchic dating of Deuteronomy by considering the implications of implied audience within the book. Next, Gordon J. Wenham assesses the tension within Deuteronomy between that which is ethically or theologically desirable and that which the law can realistically enforce; along the way he shows how the penal sanctions defined for ancient Israel what was tolerable behavior.

The remaining five essays in Part 1 address specific texts or themes in Deuteronomy but do so in a way that sets trajectories for broader reflection on the message and significance of the book as a whole. Jason S. DeRouchie reassesses the proper enumeration of the Decalogue and argues that a modified Catholic-Lutheran model is most faithful to the discourse grammar and finds support from the perspective of style, semantic content, and cantillation. J. Gordon McConville then explores the meaning and life-encompassing implications of God's external words being "kept in the heart" (Deut 6:6). Next, Jerry Hwang provides a rhetorical study of Deuteronomy 9–10, reflecting on the ideological purposes that guided the imaginative depiction of Horeb and considering what implications this reinterpretation has for the literary relationship between Deuteronomy and the narratives in Exodus. Rebekah Josberger places Deut 21:10–14 within its cultural and literary context, and argues that, rather than endorsing the abuse of subjugated women in the context of war, it actually seeks to restrict the rights of the head of household in order to safeguard the weaker members of society. Finally, Kenneth J. Turner carefully synthesizes Deuteronomy's theology of exile and unpacks how it provides the necessary framework for understanding the book's eschatological vision of restoration as Israel's resurrection from the dead.

Part 2: The Influence of Deuteronomy

With nine essays, Part 2 investigates the influence of Deuteronomy on specific texts or whole books within the Prophets, Writings, and New Testament. Michael A. Grisanti overviews the development of and challenges to the concept of the "Deuteronomistic History," and then proceeds to summarize the linguistic and thematic influence

Deuteronomy had on the Historical Books of Joshua, Judges, Samuel, and Kings. H. G. M. Williamson then analyzes the possible linguistic and ideological influence of Deuteronomy on Isaiah, assuming the standard higher-critical views on the history and composition of both books. Michael Graves explores how the account of the burning of Jeremiah's scroll (Jeremiah 36) builds on Deuteronomy's theology of writing, particularly that the authority of the written word is dependent upon the internalization of the word of Yahweh. Jason Gile then considers the image of scattering as a motif for exile in Deuteronomy and Ezekiel and argues for the priority of Deuteronomy with respect to the direction of dependence.

In the unit on the Writings, Christopher B. Ansberry argues that the deuteronomic torah likely influenced Job's ethical vision in light of the distinctive sources of knowledge within the Joban dialogue and the apparent role of deuteronomic thought in Job's epistemology. Richard Schultz then utilizes recent approaches in intertextuality to show that the outlook of Ecclesiastes, including that of Qoheleth the sage and of the final editor, is compatible with the theology of Deuteronomy. Next, Gary V. Smith focuses on the theological impact of Deuteronomy on the prayers of Ezra (ch. 9) and Nehemiah (ch. 1), showing that both Ezra's more pessimistic outlook and Nehemiah's more optimistic outlook are based on Deuteronomy's multifaceted portrayal of covenant relationship.

Grant R. Osborne examines the so-called "temptation narrative" in Luke 4:1–13 and demonstrates how its backdrop—the larger context of Deuteronomy 6–8—invites us to see Jesus as both victor over cosmic powers and exemplar for disciples to follow. Finally, Douglas Moo focuses on two Pauline quotations of Deuteronomy (Deut 27:26 in Gal 3:10; Deut 30:12–14 in Rom 10:6–8), showing that the apostle finds larger theological contours of law and grace in the words of Moses.

Part 3: The Lasting Significance of Deuteronomy

Part 3 provides six trajectory-shaping essays that consider the lasting significance of Deuteronomy for Christian preaching and ethics. Jason S. DeRouchie follows up his earlier essay on the Decalogue with a sequel: a passionate and pastoral plea for Christians to reflect theologically on and apply practically the Ten Words in light of the work of Christ. In consideration of various approaches to applying OT law to Christian ethics, M. Daniel Carroll R. proposes a theology of immigration based on Deuteronomy's view of the sojourner. Elmer A. Martens then reflects on the sermons in Deuteronomy 4 and Jeremiah 7 in order to highlight rhetoric and themes that ought to be emulated by preachers today. Daniel L. Akin's sermon on Deut 18:15–22 considers this text's relevance and application for biblical prophets and modern preachers, but points to Jesus as the ultimate fulfillment of "the prophet like Moses." Myrto Theocharous, who herself is involved with fighting human trafficking in Greece, provides a sensitive, provocative, and timely application of the kidnapping prohibition in Deut 24:7 to the church's fight against this modern evil. Finally, with the expected warmth of a former student, Pastor Thomas H. McClendon Jr. synthesizes Daniel Block's understanding of the theology of Deuteronomy by rehearsing Block's writings on Deuteronomy's vision in four areas: word, worship, leadership, and missions.

Words of Thanks

This Festschrift would not have been possible without the backing of many others. We wish to thank Jim Eisenbraun for his enthusiastic support of this project. His admiration for Dan made this a fitting partnership. We are grateful to Ellen Block, who supported the project at many stages. Even more, we admire her life-long, faithful devotion to Dan and her relentless support of all his endeavors. We also acknowledge our families, who have graciously helped us balance our commitments to them with our teaching, writing, and church commitments. Finally, we pray that this volume expresses our appreciation to Daniel Block, for modeling what it means to be a godly scholar, teacher, husband, and father. May our God, who has worked enduring good for us in Jesus Christ, use this volume for his glory and for the advancement of his kingdom.

Jason S. DeRouchie
Jason Gile
Kenneth J. Turner

July 2013

The Publications of Daniel I. Block
Overview and Bibliography

CHARLIE TRIMM

Daniel I. Block is loved and admired by scholars, students, and laypeople alike for much more than his prolific scholarly career. Indeed, it is his personal character, exuberant personality, and commitment to the church and individuals that commends his writings. He is a man who has modeled his life after the priest-scribe Ezra, "who determined to study and obey the Law of the LORD and to teach those decrees and regulations to the people of Israel" (Ezra 7:10 NLT).

Besides his teaching career at some of the most prominent evangelical institutions in North America, Block has kept busy teaching adult Sunday school classes, preaching in churches, and speaking at retreats, sharing his joy on topics like worship and the importance of the Old Testament for the church. He has taught seminars and classes all over the world, including Columbia, Russia, England, Denmark, China, Greece, Singapore, Hong Kong, Kenya, and Canada (his home country). Perhaps his greatest influence outside the academy has been his work with the translation and revision of the New Living Translation, where he served as the general reviewer of the NLT Pentateuch and the co-translator for Exodus and Ezekiel. He delights to hear stories of people who first understood the Bible when they read the NLT.

Block began his post-secondary study at Bethany Bible Institute in Hepburn, Saskatchewan, Canada, where he received a Diploma in Biblical Studies in 1965. He then went on to receive a BEd in General Education in 1968 from the University of Saskatchewan in Saskatoon. In 1968 he pursued Foreign Studies in German and Geistesgeschichete at Friedrich Alexander University, Erlanger, Germany, and in 1969 he was awarded the BA in History and German from the University of Saskatchewan. He received his M.A. in Old Testament in 1973 from Trinity Evangelical Divinity School in Deerfield, IL, and then went on to study in England with Alan Millard at the University of Liverpool's School of Archaeology and Oriental Studies, where he earned his DPhil in Semitics: Classical Hebrew in 1982.

The study of the ancient Near East has been an important part of Block's scholarly career, the groundwork of which was laid by his doctoral dissertation, *The Foundations of National Identity: A Study in Ancient Northwest Semitic Perceptions*. Although part of this expansive work was released as the monograph *The Gods of the Nations: Studies in Ancient Near Eastern National Theology*, the majority remains unpublished.

Along with his interest in the ancient Near East, Block has made significant contributions to topics like creation care, worship, David and the Messiah, eschatology, and preaching the Old Testament. These areas, however, have only supplemented and fueled his principal focuses, which have progressed in three main phases, each roughly associated with one of his long-term teaching positions.

After years of ministry in his homeland at Providence College near Winnipeg, Manitoba, his shift to Bethel Theological Seminary in Saint Paul, MN, was accompanied by a heightened focus on the book of Ezekiel. His research in Ezekiel began with an interest in how the prophet's presence in a foreign land would influence the book he produced. This fourteen-year study resulted in a series of journal articles (now reprinted in two volumes) and culminated in a detailed and comprehensive two-volume commentary in the New International Commentary on the Old Testament series that has become a standard work in the field.

After his magisterial study on Ezekiel, some might have expected him to focus his research on the prophets. However, Block turned his attention to Judges during his time at the Southern Baptist Theological Seminary in Louisville, KY. In an early essay titled "The Period of the Judges: Religious Disintegration under Tribal Rule" he had formulated his "Canaanization of Israel" thesis, and he developed it more fully in his New American Commentary on Judges and Ruth. By showing how the narrator depicts the gradual metamorphosis of Israel into Canaan, he argued against the views that the book was simply pro-David propaganda and that the judges were moral examples for us to follow today.

During his later years at Southern Seminary and his present post at Wheaton College Graduate School in Wheaton, IL, he has lived with Moses in the plains of Moab and meditated on his Deuteronomic sermons. This has resulted in many journal articles (now reprinted in two volumes) and a recently published commentary on Deuteronomy in the NIV Application Commentary series. In contrast to the common assessment of the "law of Moses" as sub-Christian or even anti-Christian, Block focuses on the grace found in the "gospel of Moses" and demonstrates its powerful relevance for Christian life today.

Block has not restricted his academic work to his own research and writing. He has been a long-time active member of the Society of Biblical Literature, the Evangelical Theological Society, and the Institute for Biblical Research, and he served as President of the Institute from 2002–2005. He has edited multi-author books and stands as the general editor of Zondervan's new "Hearing the Message of Scripture Commentary Series." He served as a member of the executive committee of the Hexapla Institute from 2001–2006, stood on the editorial board of *The Southern Baptist Journal of Theology* from 1996–2001, and participated on the steering committee for the Ezekiel consultation of the Society of Biblical Literature from 1989–1997. Most directly, he has poured himself into his doctoral students, mentoring them in life, teaching, and writing. Block always challenges his students to read the biblical text closely, not only questioning what the text says and how it is relevant for life today, but also asking, "Why does the text say it like that?" Block's scholarly acumen is paired with a loving and kind heart. It is an honor to have been taught and mentored by such a gifted and godly man.

Books, Edited Volumes, Dissertation, and Thesis[1]

An Historical Analysis of the Worship of Baal in Israel. M.A. thesis, Trinity Evangelical Divinity School, Deerfield, IL, 1973.

The Foundations of National Identity: A Study in Ancient Northwest Semitic Perceptions. Ph.D. diss., University of Liverpool, Liverpool, 1982.

The Gods of the Nations: Studies in Ancient Near Eastern National Theology. Evangelical Theological Society Monograph 2. Jackson, MS: Evangelical Theological Society, 1988. 2nd edition; Evangelical Theological Society Studies. Grand Rapids: Baker, 2000. 3rd edition; Eugene, OR: Wipf & Stock [forthcoming].

Ezekiel 1–24. New International Commentary on the Old Testament. Grand Rapids: Eerdmans, 1997.

Ezekiel 25–48. New International Commentary on the Old Testament. Grand Rapids: Eerdmans, 1998.

Judges, Ruth. New American Commentary 6. Nashville: Broadman & Holman, 1999.

Israel: Ancient Kingdom or Late Invention? Editor. Nashville: Broadman & Holman, 2008.

Keeping God's Earth: The Global Environment in Biblical Perspective. Edited with Noah J. Toly. Downers Grove, IL: InterVarsity, 2010.

How I Love Your Torah, O LORD! Studies in the Book of Deuteronomy. Eugene, OR: Cascade, 2011.

---

1. I thank Carmen Imes and Austin Surls for their help compiling bibliographic data for the most recent publications.

The Gospel according to Moses: Theological and Ethical Reflections on the Book of Deuteronomy. Eugene, OR: Cascade, 2012.
Deuteronomy. NIV Application Commentary. Grand Rapids: Zondervan, 2012.
Ezekiel's Hope: A Commentary on Ezekiel 38–48. Jacob Milgrom and Daniel I. Block in Conversation. Eugene, OR: Cascade, 2012.
By the River Chebar: Historical, Literary, and Theological Studies in the Book of Ezekiel. Eugene, OR: Cascade, 2013.
Beyond the River Chebar: Studies in Kingship and Eschatology in the Book of Ezekiel. Eugene, OR: Cascade, 2013.
For the Glory of God: Recovering a Biblical Theology of Worship. Grand Rapids: Baker, forthcoming.
Obadiah: The Kingship belongs to YHWH. Hearing the Message of Scripture Commentary Series. Grand Rapids: Zondervan, forthcoming.

Essays and Articles

"BNY 'MWN: The Sons of Ammon." *Andrews University Seminary Studies* 22 (1984) 197–212.
"'Israel'—'Sons of Israel': A Study in Hebrew Eponymic Usage." *Studies in Religion/Sciences Religieuses* 13 (1984) 301–26.
"The Role of Language in Ancient Israelite Perceptions of National Identity." *Journal of Biblical Literature* 103 (1984) 321–40.
"Israel's House: Reflections on the Use of *BYT YŚR'L* in the Old Testament in the Light of its Ancient Near Eastern Environment." *Journal of the Evangelical Theological Society* 28 (1985) 257–75.
"In Praise of Fig Leaves: A Study on Nudity from a Biblical Perspective." *Bethel Journal* (1985).
"Gog and the Pouring Out of the Spirit: Reflections on Ezekiel xxxix 21–9." *Vetus Testamentum* 37 (1987) 257–70. Reprinted in pages 144–57 in *Beyond the River Chebar*.
"The Period of the Judges: Religious Disintegration under Tribal Rule." Pages 39–57 in *Israel's Apostasy and Restoration: Essays in Honor of Roland K. Harrison*. Edited by A. Gileadi. Grand Rapids: Baker, 1988.
"Text and Emotion: A Study in the 'Corruptions' in Ezekiel's Inaugural Vision (Ezekiel 1:4–28)." *Catholic Biblical Quarterly* 50 (1988) 418–42. Reprinted in pages 199–226 in *By the River Chebar*.
"The Prophet of the Spirit: The Use of *RWḤ* in the Book of Ezekiel." *Journal of the Evangelical Theological Society* 32 (1989) 27–49. Reprinted in pages 141–68 in *By the River Chebar*.
"Echo Narrative Technique in Hebrew Literature: A Study in Judges 19." *Westminster Theological Journal* 52 (1990) 325–41.
"Ezekiel's Boiling Cauldron: A Form-Critical Solution to Ezekiel xxiv 1–14." *Vetus Testamentum* 41 (1991) 12–37. Reprinted in pages 227–52 in *By the River Chebar*.
"Beyond the Grave: Ezekiel's Vision of Death and Afterlife." *Bulletin for Biblical Research* 2 (1992) 113–42. Reprinted in pages 169–98 in *By the River Chebar*.

"Chasing a Phantom: The Search for the Historical Marduk." *Archaeology in the Biblical World* 2 (1992) 20–43. Reprinted in pages 108–40 in *By the River Chebar*.

"Gog in Prophetic Tradition: A New Look at Ezekiel xxxviii 17." *Vetus Testamentum* 42 (1992) 154–72. Reprinted in pages 126–43 in *Beyond the River Chebar*.

"Deborah among the Judges: The Perspective of the Hebrew Historian." Pages 229–53 in *Faith, Tradition, and History: Old Testament Historiography in Its Near Eastern Context*. Edited by A. R. Millard, James K. Hoffmeier, and David W. Baker. Winona Lake, IN: Eisenbrauns, 1994.

"Bringing Back David: Ezekiel's Messianic Hope." Pages 167–88 in *The Lord's Anointed: Interpretation of Old Testament Messianic Texts*. Edited by P. E. Satterthwaite, R. S. Hess, and G. J. Wenham. Grand Rapids: Baker, 1995. Reprinted in pages 74–94 in *Beyond the River Chebar*.

"'O Death, Where is Thy Sting?' Reflections on Hosea 13:1–6." *The Standard* (April 1995).

"Reviving God's Covenant with Levi: Reflections on Malachi 2:1–9." *Reformation and Revival* 4 (1995) 121–36.

"Empowered by the Spirit of God: The Holy Spirit in the Historiographic Writings of the Old Testament." *The Southern Baptist Journal of Theology* 1 (1997) 42–61.

"Gog and Magog in Ezekiel's Eschatological Vision." Pages 85–116 in *Eschatology in Bible and Theology: Evangelical Essays at the Dawn of a New Millennium*. Edited by Kent E. Brower and Mark W. Elliott. Downers Grove, IL: InterVarsity, 1997. Reprinted in pages 95–125 in *Beyond the River Chebar*.

"Will the Real Gideon Please Stand Up? Narrative Style and Intention in Judges 6–9." *Journal of the Evangelical Theological Society* 40 (1997): 353–66.

"Unspeakable Crimes: The Abuse of Women in the Book of Judges." *The Southern Baptist Journal of Theology* 5 (1998) 46–55.

"Divine Abandonment: Ezekiel's Adaptation of an Ancient Near Eastern Motif." Pages 15–42 in *The Book of Ezekiel: Theological and Anthropological Perspectives*. Edited by Margaret S. Odell and John T. Strong. Society of Biblical Literature Symposium Series 9. Atlanta: Society of Biblical Literature, 2000. Reprinted in pages 73–107 in *By the River Chebar*.

"Training Scribes and Pastors in the Tradition of Ezra." *The Southern Seminary Magazine (The TIE)* 67.2 (2000) 3–6.

"Handel's Messiah: Biblical and Theological Perspectives." *Didaskalia* 12 (2001) 1–23.

"Recovering the Voice of Moses: The Genesis of Deuteronomy." *Journal of the Evangelical Theological Society* 44 (2001) 385–408. Reprinted in pages 21–67 in *The Gospel according to Moses*.

"Why Deborah's Different." *Bible Review* 17.3 (June 2001) 34–40, 49–52.

"Old Testament Commentaries: Psalms–Daniel." *Catalyst* 28.3 (March 2002) 6–8.

"Marriage and Family in Ancient Israel." Pages 33–102 in *Marriage and Family in the Biblical World*. Edited by Ken M. Campbell. Downers Grove, IL: InterVarsity, 2003. Translated into Italian as *Matrimonio e famiglia nell'Antico e nel Nuovo Testamento*. With A. Köstenberger. Studi di teologia biblica 01. Rome: Edizioni GBU, 2007.

"My Servant David: Ancient Israel's Vision of the Messiah." Pages 17–56 in *Israel's Messiah in the Bible and the Dead Sea Scrolls*. Edited by Richard S. Hess and M. Daniel Carroll R. Grand Rapids: Baker, 2003.

"Recipe for Revival." Pages 352–54 in *The Minister's Manuel*. Edited by J. W. Cox. San Francisco: Jossey-Bass, 2003.

"Tell Me the Old, Old Story: Preaching the Message of Old Testament Narrative." Pages 409–38 in *Giving the Sense: Understanding and Using Old Testament Historical Texts: Essays in Honor of Eugene Merrill*. Edited by David M. Howard and Michael A. Grisanti. Grand Rapids: Kregel, 2003.

"How Many Is God? An Investigation into the Meaning of Deuteronomy 6:4–5." *Journal of the Evangelical Theological Society* 47 (2004) 193–212. Reprinted in pages 73–98 in *How I Love Your Torah, O Lord!*

"In Search of Theological Meaning: Ezekiel Scholarship at the Turn of the Millennium." Pages 227–39 in *Ezekiel's Hierarchical World: Wrestling with a Tiered Reality*. Edited by S. L. Cook and C. L. Patton. Society of Biblical Literature Symposium Series 31. Atlanta: Society of Biblical Literature, 2004.

"The Old Testament on Hell." Pages 43–65 in *Hell Under Fire: Modern Scholarship Reinvents Eternal Punishment*. Edited by Christopher W. Morgan and Robert A. Peterson. Grand Rapids: Zondervan, 2004.

"Other Religions in Old Testament Theology." Pages 43–78 in *Biblical Faith and Other Religions: An Evangelical Assessment*. Edited by David W. Baker. Grand Rapids: Kregel, 2004. Reprinted in pages 200–36 in *The Gospel according to Moses*.

"The Grace of Torah: The Mosaic Prescription for Life (Deut. 4:1–8; 6:20–25)." *Bibliotheca Sacra* 162 (2005) 3–22. Reprinted in pages 1–20 in *How I Love Your Torah, O Lord!*

"The Joy of Worship: The Mosaic Invitation to the Presence of God (Deut. 12:1–14)." *Bibliotheca Sacra* 162 (2005) 131–49. Reprinted in pages 99–118 in *How I Love Your Torah, O Lord!*

"The Burden of Leadership: The Mosaic Paradigm of Kingship (Deut. 17:14–20)." *Bibliotheca Sacra* 162 (2005) 259–78. Reprinted in pages 119–40 in *How I Love Your Torah, O Lord!*

"The Privilege of Calling: The Mosaic Paradigm for Missions (Deut. 26:16–19)." *Bibliotheca Sacra* 162 (2005) 387–405. Reprinted in pages 141–62 in *How I Love Your Torah, O Lord!*

"What has Delphi to do with Samaria? Ambiguity and Delusion in Israelite Prophecy." Pages 189–216 in *Writing and Ancient Near Eastern Society: Papers in Honour of Alan R. Millard*. Edited by Piotr Bienkowski, Christopher Mee, and Elizabeth Slater. Library of Hebrew Bible/Old Testament Studies 426. London: T & T Clark, 2005.

"Preaching Old Testament Apocalyptic to a New Testament church." *Calvin Theological Journal* 41 (2006) 17–52.

"Preaching Old Testament Law to New Testament Christians." *Hiphil (Scandinavian Evangelical E-Journal)* 3 (2006) 1–24. Reprinted in three parts in *Ministry* 78.5 (2006) 5–11; 78.7 (2006) 12–16; 78.9 (2006) 15–18 and in pages 104–36 in *The Gospel according to Moses*.

"When Nightmares Cease: A Message of Hope from Daniel 7." *Calvin Theological Journal* 41 (2006) 108–14.

"Israel – Ancient Kingdom or Late Invention?" Pages 1–8 in *Israel: Ancient Kingdom or Late Invention?* Edited by Daniel I. Block. Nashville: Broadman & Holman, 2008.

"All Creatures Great and Small: Recovering a Deuteronomic Theology of Animals." Pages 283–305 in *The Old Testament in the Life of God's People: Essays in Honor of Elmer A. Martens*. Edited by Jon Isaak. Winona Lake, IN: Eisenbrauns, 2009. Reprinted in pages 174–99 in *The Gospel according to Moses*.

"Judges." Pages 94–241 in *Zondervan Illustrated Bible Backgrounds Commentary*. Edited by John H. Walton. Grand Rapids: Zondervan, 2009.

"Preaching Ezekiel." Pages 157–78 in *Reclaiming the Old Testament for Christian Preaching*. Edited by Grenville J. R. Kent, Paul J. Kissling, and Laurence A. Turner. Downers Grove, IL: InterVarsity, 2010. Published in England as pages 157–78 in *'He Began with Moses. . .' Preaching the Old Testament Today*. Edited by G. J. R. Kent and P. J. Kissling. Nottingham: InterVarsity, 2010. Reprinted in pages 1–24 in *By the River Chebar*.

"To Serve and to Keep: Toward a Biblical Understanding of Humanity's Responsibility in the Face of the Biodiversity Crisis." Pages 116–40 in *Keeping God's Earth: The Global Environment in Biblical Perspective*. Edited by Noah J. Toly and Daniel I. Block. Downers Grove, IL: InterVarsity, 2010.

"Toward an Evangelical Response to Environmental Challenges." With Noah J. Toly. Pages 11–21 in *Keeping God's Earth: The Global Environment in Biblical Perspective*. Edited by Noah J. Toly and Daniel I. Block. Downers Grove, IL: InterVarsity, 2010.

"Transformation of Royal Ideology in Ezekiel." Pages 208–46 in *Transforming Visions: Transformations of Text, Tradition, and Theology in Ezekiel*. Edited by William A. Tooman and Michael A. Lyons. Princeton Theological Monograph Series 127. Eugene, OR: Pickwick, 2010. Reprinted in pages 10–44 in *Beyond the River Chebar*.

"'You Shall Not Covet Your Neighbor's Wife': A Study in Deuteronomic Domestic Ideology." *Journal of the Evangelical Theological Society* 53 (2010) 449–74. Reprinted in pages 137–73 in *The Gospel according to Moses*.

"The View from the Top: The Holy Spirit in the Prophets." Pages 175–207 in *Presence, Power and Promise: The Role of the Holy Spirit in the Old Testament*. Edited by David G. Firth and Paul D. Wegner. Nottingham: Apollos, 2011.

"Bearing the Name of the Lord with Honor." *Bibliotheca Sacra* 168 (2011) 20–31. Reprinted in pages 61–72 in *How I Love Your Torah, O Lord!*

"Reading the Decalogue Right to Left: The Ten Principles of Covenant Relationship in the Hebrew Bible." Pages 21–60 in *How I Love Your Torah, O Lord!* Reprinted as "The Decalogue in the Hebrew Scriptures." Pages 1–28 in *Reading the Decalogue through the Centuries: From the Hebrew Scriptures to Benedict XVI.* Edited by J. Greenman and Timothy Larsen. Louisville: Westminster John Knox, 2012.

"The Power of Song: Reflections on Ancient Israel's National Anthem, Deuteronomy 32." Pages 163–90 in *How I Love Your Torah, O Lord!*

"Will the Real Moses Please Rise? An Exploration into the Role and Ministry of Moses in the Book of Deuteronomy." Pages 68–103 in *The Gospel according to Moses.*

"No Other Gods: Bearing the Name of YHWH in a Polytheistic World." Pages 237–71 in *The Gospel according to Moses.*

"'In Spirit and in Truth': The Mosaic Vision of Worship." Pages 272–98 in *The Gospel according to Moses.*

"The Tender Cedar Sprig: Ezekiel on Jehoiachin." *Hebrew Bible and Ancient Israel* 1 (2012) 173–202. Reprinted in pages 45–73 in *Beyond the River Chebar.*

"Moses and the Pentateuch: An Investigation into the Biblical Evidence." *Areopagus Journal* 12.2 (Spring 2012): 6–14.

"'That They May Hear': Biblical Foundations for the Oral Reading of Scripture in Worship." *Journal of Spiritual Formation and Soul Care* 5 (2012): 5–34.

"Who Do Commentators Say 'the Lord' Is? The Scandalous Rock of Romans 10:13." Pages 173–92 in *On the Writing of New Testament Commentaries: Festschrift for Grant R. Osborne on the Occasion of his 70th Birthday.* Edited by S. E. Porter and E. J. Schnabel. Texts and Editions of New Testament Study 8. Leiden: Brill, 2012.

"How to Translate the Bible." *Wheaton* 16, no. 1 (2013) 32.

"What Do These Stones Mean? The Riddle of Deuteronomy 27." *Journal of the Evangelical Theological Society* 56 (2013) 17–41.

"In Praise of Moshe: A Tribute to Moshe Greenberg." Pages 253–58 in *By the River Chebar.*

"Zion Theology in the Book of Ezekiel." Pages 1–9 in *Beyond the River Chebar.*

"Envisioning the Good News: Ten Interpretive Keys to Ezekiel's Final Vision." Pages 158–74 in *Beyond the River Chebar.*

"Guarding the Glory of YHWH: Ezekiel's Geography of Sacred Space." Pages 175–96 in Beyond the River Chebar.

"Eden: A Temple? A Reassessment of the Biblical Evidence." In *From Creation to New Creation: Essays on Biblical Theology and Exegesis in Honor of G. K. Beale.* Edited by Daniel M. Gurtner and Benjamim L. Gladd. Peabody, NJ: Hendrickson, forthcoming.

"The Levitical Cities: An Investigation into Their Significance in Ancient Israelite Religious Life." In *Current Issues in Priestly and Related Literature: The Legacy of Jacob Milgrom and Beyond.* Edited by Roy Gane and Ada Taggar-Cohen. Resources for Biblical Study. Atlanta: Society of Biblical Literature, forthcoming.

"The God Ezekiel Wants Us to Meet." In *The God Ezekiel Creates*. Edited by A. Mein. Library of the Hebrew Bible/Old Testament Series. New York: Continuum, forthcoming. Reprinted in pages 44–72 in *By the River Chebar*.

Contributions to Dictionaries, Handbooks, and Encyclopedias

"Nations," "New Year," "People," "People of Eden," "Sojourner, Alien, Stranger," and "Table of Nations" in *International Standard Bible Encyclopedia*. Edited by Geoffrey W. Bromiley. Grand Rapids: Eerdmans, 1979–88.

"Ezekiel: Theology of," "Spirit, Spirit of God" (with M. V. Van Pelt and W. C. Kaiser Jr.), and "Nations, Nationality" in *New International Dictionary of Old Testament Theology and Exegesis*. Edited by Willem A. VanGemeren. Grand Rapids: Zondervan, 1997. "Ezekiel, Theology of, reprinted in pages 25–43 in *By the River Chebar*.

"Deuteronomy," "Ezekiel," "Ezekiel, Book of," "Judges," "Law, Ten Commandments, Torah," "Pentateuch," and "Ruth" in *Holman Illustrated Bible Dictionary*. Edited by Chad Owen Brand, Charles W. Draper, and Archie W. England. Nashville: Broadman and Holman, 2003.

"Deuteronomy, Book of." Pages 165–73 in *Dictionary for Theological Interpretation of the Bible*. Edited by K. J. Vanhoozer. Grand Rapids: Baker, 2005. Reprinted in "Deuteronomy." Pages 67–82 in *Theological Interpretation of the Old Testament: A Book-by-Book Survey*. Edited by K. J. Vanhoozer. Grand Rapids: Zondervan, 2008. Subsequently reprinted in pages 1–20 in *The Gospel according to Moses*.

"God." Pages 336–55 in *Dictionary of the Old Testament: Historical Books*. Edited by B. T. Arnold and H. G. M. Williamson. Downers Grove, IL: InterVarsity, 2005.

"Who Wrote the Pentateuch and When Was It Written?" Pages 158–59 in *The Apologetics Study Bible*. Edited by T. Cabal. Nashville: Broadman and Holman, 2007.

"Leader, Leadership, OT." Pages 3:621–26 in *New Interpreter's Dictionary of the Bible*. Edited by K. D. Sakenfeld. Nashville: Abingdon, 2008.

"Ruth 1: Book of." Pages 672–87 in *Dictionary of the Old Testament: Wisdom, Poetry and Writings*. Edited by Tremper Longman III and Peter Enns. Downers Grove, IL: InterVarsity, 2008.

"Worship." Pages 867–78 in *Dictionary of the Old Testament: Prophets*. Edited by Mark J. Boda and J. Gordon McConville. Downers Grove: InterVarsity, 2012.

"Covenance: A Whole Bible Perspective." *Lexham Logos Dictionary*. 2012.

"Ruth and Work: The Contribution of the Book of Ruth to a Biblical Theology of Work." Theology of Work Project. Edited by William G. Messenger. 2013. http://www.theologyofwork.org/old-testament/ruth-and-work

Book Reviews

Review of E. Martens, *Jeremiah* (1986). *Mennonite Brethren Herald* 25 (August 1989) 24.

Review of Robert L. Hubbard, Jr., *The Book of Ruth* (1988). *Criswell Theological Review* 4 (1989) 177–79.

Review of Ralph W. Klein, *Ezekiel: The Prophet and His Message* (1988). *Critical Review of Books in Religion* (1990) 148–50.

Review of J. Piper and W. Grudem, eds., *Recovering Biblical Manhood and Womanhood: A Response to Evangelical Feminism* (1991). *The Standard* 81 (June 1991) 32–34.

Review of H. F. Fuhs, *Ezechiel II 25-48* (1988). *Religious Studies Review* 17 (1991) 61–63.

Review of Ellen F. Davis, *Swallowing the Scroll: Textuality and the Dynamics of Discourse in Ezekiel's Prophecy* (1989). *Journal of Biblical Literature* 110 (1991) 144–46.

Review of Mark F. Rooker, *Biblical Hebrew in Transition: The Language of the Book of Ezekiel* (1990). *Journal of Biblical Literature* 111 (1992) 521–23.

Review of Steven Shawn Tuell, *The Law of the Temple in Ezekiel 40–48* (1992). *Journal of Biblical Literature* 113 (1994) 131–33.

Review of Iain Duguid, *Ezekiel and the Leaders of Israel* (1994). *Themelios* 21 (1995) 18–19.

Review of Jeffrey A. Fager, *Land Tenure and the Biblical Jubilee: Uncovering Hebrew Ethics through the Sociology of Knowledge* (1993). *Themelios* 20 (1995) 23.

Review of Isaac Rabinowitz, *A Witness Forever: Ancient Israel's Perception of Literature and the Resultant Hebrew Bible* (1993). *Journal of the Evangelical Theological Society* 39 (1996) 646–47.

Review of Leo G. Perdue, *The Collapse of History: Reconstructing Old Testament Theology* (1994). *Review and Expositor* 93 (1996) 436–37.

Review of Leslie C. Allen, *Ezekiel 1–19* (1994). *Critical Review of Books in Religion* 9 (1996) 143–44.

Review of Rainer Albertz, *A History of Israelite Religion in the Old Testament Period: Volumes 1 and 2* (1994). *Journal of the Evangelical Theological Society* 39 (1996) 327–28.

Review of Barnabas Lindars, *Judges 1–5: A New Translation* (1995). *Journal of the Evangelical Theological Society* 40 (1997) 292–93.

Review of W. W. Hallo, ed., *The Context of Scripture, Volume 1: Canonical Compositions from the Biblical World* (1997). *Review and Expositor* 94 (1997) 607–8.

Review of Ronald E. Clements, *Old Testament Prophecy: From Oracles to Canon* (1996). *Review and Expositor* 94 (1997) 299.

Review of Uwe F. W. Bauer, *Warum nur übertretet ihr SEIN Geheiss: eine synchrone Exegese der Anti-Erzählung von Richter 17–18* (1998). *Journal of Biblical Literature* 119 (2000) 550–52.

Review of Edward Lipiński, *Semitic Languages: Outline of a Comparative Grammar* (1997). *Journal of the Evangelical Theological Society* 42 (1999) 485–86.

Review of Gale A. Yee, ed., *Judges and Method: New Approaches in Biblical Studies* (1995). *Journal of the Evangelical Theological Society* 42 (1999) 105–6.

Review of Kelvin G. Friebel's, *Jeremiah's and Ezekiel's Sign-Acts: Rhetorical Nonverbal Communication* (1999). *Journal of the Evangelical Theological Society* 44 (2001) 729–31.

Review of "Noah's Ark," a Film by Hallmark Entertainment for NBC. *Baptist Press* (April 1999).

Review of Richard D. Nelson, *Joshua: A Commentary* (1997). *Ashland Theological Journal* 31 (1999) 114–15.

Review of Robert H. O'Connell, *The Rhetoric of the Book of Judges* (1996). *Journal of the Evangelical Theological Society* 42 (1999) 106–9.

Review of C. Van Dam, *The Urim and Thummim: A Means of Revelation in Ancient Israel* (1997). *The Southern Baptist Theological Journal* 4.4 (2000): 99–101.

Review of David Penchansky and Paul L. Redditt, eds., *Shall Not the Judge of All the Earth Do What Is Right?: Studies on the Nature of God in Tribute to James L. Crenshaw* (2000). *The Southern Baptist Journal of Theology* 5 (2001) 98–100.

Review of Risa Levitt Kohn, *A New Heart and a New Soul: Ezekiel, the Exile and the Torah* (2002). *Themelios* 29 (2004) 50.

Review of James Chukwuma Okoye, *Israel and the Nations: A Mission Theology of the Old Testament* (2006) and Michael Parsons, ed., *Text and Task: Scripture and Mission* (2005). *International Bulletin of Missionary Research* 31.2 (2007) 102.

Review of Ralph K. Hawkins, *The Iron Age I Structure on Mt. Ebal: Excavation and Interpretation* (2012). *Bulletin for Biblical Research* 23 (2013) 94-96.

Dissertations Supervised

Lowery, Jenny Manasco. *The Form and Function of Symbolic Vision Reports in the Hebrew Bible*. Ph.D. diss., The Southern Baptist Theological Seminary, 1999.

Woo, Timothy Wen-Chiu. *The Deuteronomist's Use of Epithets in the Characterization of David*. Ph.D. diss., The Southern Baptist Theological Seminary, 2000.

Betts, Terry J. *Ezekiel the Priest: A Custodian of Tôrâ*. Studies in Biblical Literature 74. New York: Peter Lang, 2005 [Ph.D. diss., The Southern Baptist Theological Seminary, 2002].

Mitchell, Eric Alan. *A Literary Examination of the Function of Satire in the mišpaṭ hammelek of 1 Samuel 8*. Lewiston, NY: Edwin Mellen, 2007 [Ph.D. diss., The Southern Baptist Theological Seminary, 2002].

Holland, Richard Lloyd. *The Exposition of Ecclesiastes 2:1–11 as a Means of Teaching the Collegians of Grace Community church, Sun Valley, California, to Find Their Satisfaction in God*. D.Min. diss., The Southern Baptist Theological Seminary, 2002.

Mooney, D. Jeffrey. *"On This Day Atonement Will Be Made for You": A Theology of Leviticus 16*. Ph.D. diss., The Southern Baptist Theological Seminary, 2003.

DeRouchie, Jason S. *A Call to Covenant Love: Text Grammar and Literary Structure in Deuteronomy 5–11*. Gorgias Dissertations 30. Piscataway, NJ: Gorgias, 2007 [Ph.D. diss., The Southern Baptist Theological Seminary, 2005].

Harriman, James E. *Our Father in Heaven: The Dimensions of Divine Paternity in Deuteronomy*. Ph.D. diss., The Southern Baptist Theological Seminary, 2005.

Smith, Gregory S. *The Testing of Faith: A Pentateuchal Theology of Testing*. Nashville: Broadman & Holman, 2012 [Ph.D. diss., The Southern Baptist Theological Seminary, 2005].

Turner, Kenneth J. *The Death of Deaths in the Death of Israel: Deuteronomy's Theology of Exile*. Eugene, OR: Wipf & Stock, 2011 [Ph.D. diss., The Southern Baptist Theological Seminary, 2005].

Cribb, Bryan H. *Speaking on the Brink of Sheol: Form and Message of Old Testament Death Stories*. Gorgias Dissertations 43. Piscataway, NJ: Gorgias, 2009 [Ph.D. diss., The Southern Baptist Theological Seminary, 2005].

Josberger, Rebekah L. *Between Rule and Responsibility: The Role of the 'ab as Agent of Righteousness in Deuteronomy's Domestic Ideology*. Ph.D. diss., The Southern Baptist Theological Seminary, 2007.

Ansberry, Christopher B. *Be Wise My Son, and Make My Heart Glad: An Exploration of the Courtly Nature of the Book of Proverbs*. BZAW 422. Berlin: De Gruyter, 2010 [Ph.D. diss., Wheaton College Graduate School, 2009].

Hwang, Jerry. *The Rhetoric of Remembrance: An Exegetical and Theological Investigation into the "Fathers" in Deuteronomy*. Siphrut 8. Winona Lake, IN: Eisenbrauns, 2012 [Ph.D. diss., Wheaton College Graduate School, 2009].

Trimm, Charles M. *"YHWH Fights for Them!" The Divine Warrior in the Exodus Narrative*. Piscataway, NJ: Gorgias, forthcoming [Ph.D. diss., Wheaton College Graduate School, 2012].

Owens, Daniel. *Portraits of the Righteous in the Psalms: An Exploration of the Ethics of Book I*. Eugene, OR: Pickwick, 2013 [Ph.D. diss., Wheaton College Graduate School, 2012].

Gile, Jason. *Deuteronomic Influence in the Book of Ezekiel*. Ph.D. diss., Wheaton College Graduate School, 2013.

Newkirk, Matthew. *Just Deceivers: An Investigation into the Motif and Theology of Deception in the Books of Samuel*. Ph.D. diss., Wheaton College Graduate School, 2013.

Patton, Matthew. *Hope for a Tender Sprig: King Jehoiachin in Biblical Theology*. Ph.D. diss., Wheaton College Graduate School, 2013.

Tributes from the Block Family

The title *For Our Good Always* is taken from Deut 6:24, which occurs in one of Deuteronomy's foundational family discipleship passages. Here Moses exhorts parents to clarify for their children the place and importance of heeding God's Word, which the Lord gave "for our good always, that he might preserve us alive, as we are this day" (ESV). The text stresses that walking with God grows out of the garden of gracious past redemption and in the light of gracious future promises (Deut 6:20–25).

The editors of this volume have all enjoyed Daniel Block as a doctoral father, watching him model the resolve of Ezra, who "set his heart to study the Law of the Lord, and to do it and to teach his statutes and rules in Israel" (Ezra 7:10). Yet there are three who have been even closer to Dan. His own family has enjoyed the benefit first-hand of a man who has taken seriously that to be called as a guardian and teacher of God's Word requires that he must first "manage his own household well" (1 Tim 3:4). In light of this truth, we as editors asked Dan's wife Ellen and his children Jason and Jonelle to reflect on living and growing with Daniel Block as husband and father. They offer the following tributes in his honor.

*   *   *   *   *

It is a great honor to submit some reflections on growing up with Professor Daniel I. Block, or as I call him, Dad. As most fathers are to their children, my dad has been many things to me, including my protector, teacher, loan officer, supporter, adversary, bill payer, friend, and role model. Yet when I think of my dad, two images come most to my mind—images that may seem incompatible but that to me are intertwined.

The first is of my dad as a gardener. To varying degrees, we are all products of our environments, and my father's upbringing in rural Saskatchewan gave him a love for nature and an interest in horticulture. If any of you have been to my parent's home, you know their yard is a place of great joy to them. I remember working in the yard with my dad. He loved being out and always seemed happy when he was digging in the dirt, transplanting a hosta or tree. What I caught watching and participating in that yard (sometimes with great reluctance) was that he was and is a great student of the outdoors. He observes carefully in order that he can understand, and then he goes and plants in a manner that best complements the flora and fauna with which he is working. The end result is magnificent and brings great joy to those who come and relish it with him.

The second vision I have of my dad finds him in his study at home. For me it was a place of wonder and fear as a child. Wonder in that I never really grasped what it was that he was doing in there, and fear in what would occur if I knocked over the endless piles of books or papers on the floor! Thankfully, I never caused the latter (or at least that is how I have chosen to remember it), and a real understanding of his work and passion did come, but only later.

During my time in university, I had the opportunity to read Frederick Buechner's memoir *Now and Then*. Buechner talks about how a certain Bible professor made the Old Testament come to life. He not only taught the Old Testament, but also embodied the life-giving nature of the Old Testament itself. He made the students see that the stories of Abraham and Moses were not only accounts of ancient Israel, but also our stories. I was struck by the fact that Buechner could have been talking about my dad. This insight also helped me fully appreciate my father's profession and why he is so passionate about it. Just as he is with his gardening, my dad has always strove to study, practice, and then teach the Old Testament. This is how we fully come to understand God's working in our own lives.

My father's passion and discipline work together in both his gardening and his research. In one evening he can recommend the best manure to use for replanting hostas (horse or chicken?) and then give his thoughts on Deuteronomy and the significant role it plays in all of Scripture. Most of you will know him as a teacher or a colleague. I have the gift of knowing him in all three spheres of Ezra 7:10 and more.

I trust the submissions to this collection will bring you joy and will make you want to hear the Old Testament Scriptures as your story. I also hope that you will then go out and plant some flora and fauna. I recommend perennials, because my dad taught me that they last longer and because there is a chance that Moses encountered one that would not burn.

Thanks Dad!
Jason E. Block

* * * * *

"For Ezra had set his heart to study the Law of the LORD, and to do it and to teach his statutes and rules in Israel." My dad has lived Ezra 7:10. A lot of my memories are of him holed up in his office, sitting on his very old antique wooden chair. It began in the open studded walls in the basement of our Steinbach house, and then later looked out over the garage and the snow drifts in Minnesota. In Louisville and Chicago, his study has overlooked his beautiful yard and garden. Though he spent a lot of time there, he was always available to be interrupted. The door of his office may have been closed, but it was never locked. His studies and preparation for classes never excluded me from asking him questions.

His love for the Bible was contagious, and he delighted in seeing his students share his enthusiasm and love for all Scripture. My dad's students loved him, and I was able to see that even as a six-year-old. There were always students at our house just having fun. And as I became an adult, those students became my friends. It was at this time that I truly began to see that my father's love for God and his Word were like a fire that he hoped would spread to his current students who would in turn eagerly share the good news to the next generation.

Thank you, Dad, for showing love to your students because of your love for God. In doing so, you have blessed me as well!

Jonelle Yates

* * * * *

We have had quite the journey! It is now 50 years since Dan and I first met at Bible College. Neither of us had any idea where this journey would take us. That is the beauty of God's providence. We started out as farm kids on the plains of Canada and began our life together in 1966 with the motto "Lead Us On." God was faithful and gracious to bring us together, and he has never failed us. Four decades of Dan's teaching, research and writing have shaped and formed both of us in remarkable ways. When I first met Dan he was quiet and shy, but there was a depth of character and a desire to walk with God that made an impression. His work has now spanned four decades in four different institutions. Each school has been God's place for us for that particular time. The joys in meeting and loving students, friends, and colleagues in each of these places have been unique and heart warming. Dan's love for teaching and mentoring students has only increased as the years have gone by. On more than one occasion, he has said, "I feel sorry for people who don't enjoy going to work." As to writing and research he has remarked, "I had to go to bed last night because I knew it was good for me, but I was on a roll, and I really wasn't tired." In his mind, God's Word, and in particular the Old Testament, is alive and transforming, and nothing pleases him more than to see his students share the passion. To practice the Word is key to Dan's Christian walk, and our family, friends, and neighbors are all recipients of this grace in his life.

I know Dan will be honored by this Festschrift. He will turn to his students and colleagues and thank them for their kindness, but in the end he will give glory to God for his loving kindness (ḥesed).

May the journey continue—with love,
Ellen

Part 1

The Message of Deuteronomy

Deuteronomy and Ancient Hebrew History Writing in Light of Ancient Chronicles and Treaties

Alan Millard

How did biblical history writing begin? Distinct from ancient royal inscriptions, it shares some features with Neo-Babylonian chronicles. Yet those have ancestors in the second millennium B.C.—notably in Hittite treaties. Although Neo-Assyrian treaties are widely adduced as models for Deuteronomy, the book exhibits elements at home in the second millennium in curses and its Historical Prologue and is perhaps the earliest piece of Israelite history-writing.

1. History Writing in the Ancient Near East

1.1. *Royal Inscriptions*

Kings of Assyria and Babylonia and pharaohs of Egypt have left numerous monuments vaunting their victories, their great construction works, their devotion to their gods, and the goodness of their gods to them. Their inscriptions supply much of the information for modern historians of the ancient Near East from the third to the first millennia B.C. In contrast, very few rulers of West Semitic kingdoms in the Iron Age have left similar inscriptions; the Moabite Stone, the Tel Dan Stele, and the Zakkur Stele are the most important. From the kings

---

Author's Note: The book of Deuteronomy, like many ancient treaty texts, has more curses than blessings, but chapter 30 holds a promise of restoration, inevitably absent from other ancient treaties. For all its shadows, the book is primarily concerned for the welfare of the people of Israel and their understanding of God's word. Like other students, Dan Block came to the University of Liverpool in order to study for his doctorate, but he did that not merely to gain the key that could lead to a teaching position, but with an aim to increase his knowledge of the Bible and so his comprehension of the sacred texts. While gaining that knowledge brought satisfaction, he has always been eager to apply it to the exegesis of Scripture and to life. A scholar respected across the field of OT studies, Dan's concern for the welfare of God's people, on the pattern of Deuteronomy, has not diminished, despite his weighty academic activities. May you be blessed, Dan, in all you do, "when you go out and when you come in" (Deut 28:6).

of Israel and Judah there are none. That absence has several possible explanations.

Expressly regarding the failure of anyone to discover stones engraved for David or Solomon, the opinion is widely canvassed in recent decades that it is a stretch of imagination to suppose that "an empire emerged in Palestine during the early Iron Age ... lasted for almost half a century, and then disappeared without a single epigraphic trace."[1] Yet we should keep in mind both the history of the capital, Jerusalem, which was repeatedly destroyed and rebuilt, and the frequent slighting of old inscriptions in later ages, as in the case of the Tel Dan Stele which was smashed and its pieces reused as building material, large parts of it still unrecovered. As remarked on previous occasions, no inscription of Herod the Great has been found within his kingdom. (Coins do not count in this context, nor the amphorae labeled in Latin with his name in Italian wineries and imported to Masada.)[2] While ancient royal inscriptions from neighboring nations make notable contributions to modern knowledge of the history of Israel and Judah, they do not offer examples of history writing in the manner of Samuel and Kings, running through a succession of reigns.

1.2. Ancient Near Eastern Chronicles

In most royal inscriptions in Mesopotamia and the Levant the king speaks in the first person as author, while in Egypt he speaks in the third person. However, each of these inscriptions belongs, generically, to a single generation; the only elements of continuity lie in genealogies and boasts of how their speakers' deeds eclipse their predecessors.

1.2.1. Babylonian and Seleucid Chronicles

Closer to the third-person biblical narratives, which present generations and reigns in sequence, are the "chronicles." Best known is the *Babylonian Chronicle*, a name given to a single tablet, which tells of events in years spanning 745 to 668 B.C. According to its colophon, it contains the "first section" (*pirsu rēštu*), presumably of a longer text, and it was copied in the twenty-second year of Darius I (500 B.C.). Smaller tablets cover shorter periods of time, often giving more details for each year, as do the tablets reporting the fall of Nineveh or the capture of Jerusalem, while some entries in one tablet overlap or duplicate those in another.

---

1. J. M. Miller, "Separating the Solomon of History from the Solomon of Legend," in *The Age of Solomon: Scholarship at the Turn of the Millennium* (ed. L. K. Handy; Leiden: Brill, 1997) 14.
2. A. Millard, "King Solomon in His Ancient Context," in *The Age of Solomon*, 30–53, esp. p. 49.

Chronicles were still being compiled in similar style under the Seleucid kings. There are chronicle tablets with entries for years prior to 745 B.C., although they are less extensive and some are restricted to a single topic, such as the celebration of the New Year Festival. While all the tablets appear to have been composed and written in the sixth century B.C. or later, they clearly took information from older sources for events of previous centuries,[3] and where entries can be checked against contemporary documents, they prove to be accurate in almost every case. One tablet states its exemplar was a writing board, that is, a wax tablet (*lēʾu*).[4] Whether the exemplars were "chronicles" or other compositions is impossible to determine.

No Babylonian tablet gives a reason for the creation of chronicles. (Esth 6:1 depicts chronicles of Xerxes' reign being read to Xerxes himself to put him to sleep!) Apart from one Seleucid example, which the scribe says he produced "for his education" and prosperity, placing it in a temple,[5] no scribe reveals his intention in writing a chronicle. This leaves modern scholars to speculate. In the *Babylonian Chronicle* itself there is nothing that makes its purpose clear. In some of the other chronicle tablets military campaigns dominate; in others, entirely different events. A singular text, the *Esagila Chronicle* (also known as the *Weidner Chronicle*), illustrates how disasters befell kings who failed to sustain the cult of Marduk in Babylon, whereas reverent kings prospered.[6] Available copies of that text come from the seventh and sixth centuries B.C., but the composition can be dated five or six centuries earlier.

Finding the ideologies underlying ancient historical narratives is essential to understanding them adequately and many studies in recent decades have attempted to do so, aided by more complete editions of the major texts.[7] Royal aggrandizement is obvious, as are national pride and exaltation of patron deities. Yet the purposes of the impersonal Babylonian chronicle texts are obscure. Except in the case of the *Esagila*

---

3. J. Van Seters, *In Search of History* (New Haven, CT: Yale University Press, 1983) 90.

4. The most recent edition is J.-J. Glassner, *Mesopotamian Chronicles* (Writings from the Ancient World 19; Atlanta: SBL, 2004). The "wax tablet" note is on pp. 212–13, line 23. For detailed discussion, see J. A. Brinkman, "The Babylonian Chronicle Revisited," in *Lingering over Words: Studies in Ancient Near Eastern Literature in Honor of William L. Moran* (ed. T. Abusch, J. Huehnergard, and P. Steinkeller; Harvard Semitic Studies 37; Atlanta: Scholars, 1990) 73–104.

5. Glassner, *Mesopotamian Chronicles*, 290–91.

6. Ibid., 263–69.

7. Impetus came from papers in F. M. Fales, ed., *Assyrian Royal Inscriptions: New Horizons in Literary, Ideological, and Historical Analysis* (Oriens Antiqui Collectio 17; Rome: Istituto per l'Oriente, 1981).

Chronicle, there is no indication of interest in explaining or evaluating the events recorded; the entries are simply factual statements.

1.2.2. Middle-Assyrian Chronicles

While the composition of the Babylonian chronicle texts is usually assigned to the Neo-Babylonian period or later, the sixth century B.C. onwards, five fragments exist from one or more tablets found at Ashur, which were written in the twelfth or eleventh centuries B.C., containing chronicles of Assyrian kings ruling between ca. 1325 and 1100 B.C. This shows that scribes were writing chronicles long before the Neo-Babylonian era.[8] Beside them can be considered the lists of Assyrian eponyms, which were drawn up in the eighteenth century B.C. at the merchant colony in Kanesh in Anatolia and at Mari under Assyrian rule. Those at Kanesh are limited to names and surnames; those at Mari include brief notes of events that happened during the years of many of the officials.[9] That custom reappears in the Assyrian *Eponym Chronicle*, extant for the years 858 to 699 B.C.[10] Although they are shorter than normal entries in the Babylonian chronicles, these notes could be the forerunner of chronicle-like compositions. Again, the purpose of the notes in either period is unknown. It is probably the accident of survival and discovery that deprives us of eponym chronicles from the seventeenth to tenth centuries; only disconnected pieces of eponym lists have been found from that time.[11] Copies of the *Sumerian King List* made early in the second millennium B.C. have occasional notes added to the names of kings, but they do not appear in the one earlier copy made during the Third Dynasty of Ur.[12] This could imply they were added later, although there

---

8. Van Seters tried to deny these fragments are chronicles on the grounds that each fragment only deals with one ruler, the dates are vague, third-person narrative also occurs in some royal inscriptions, the dedication of spoils is alien to the Babylonian chronicles, and there is a hint of divine aid (*In Search of History*, 82–83). As it is likely that some fragments come from the same tablet, the first point fails, and the second does, too, once it is observed that no fragment preserves its left side, which would have contained the date (as Glassner has restored [*Mesopotamian Chronicles*, 184–91]). The use of the third person is normal in chronicles, so its appearance elsewhere does not disprove their chronicle nature, and there are several unique entries in other chronicles, so dedication of spoils cannot be excluded. Finally, explanation of some events as the result of divine aid is common across the ancient Near East (see M. Weinfeld, "Divine Intervention and the Ancient Near East," in *History, Historiography and Interpretation: Studies in Biblical and Cuneiform Literature* [ed. H. Tadmor and M. Weinfeld; Jerusalem: Magnes Press, 1983] 121–47).

9. Glassner, *Mesopotamian Chronicles*, 160–65.

10. Ibid., 164–77.

11. C. Saporetti, *Gli eponimi medio-assiri* (Bibliotheca Mesopotamica 9; Malibu, CA: Undena, 1979).

12. P. Steinkeller, "An Ur III Manuscript of the Sumerian King List," in *Literatur, Politik und Recht in Mesopotamien. Festschrift für Claus Wilcke* (ed. W. Sallaberger, K. Volk, and

may have been copies listing the kings and their reigns only beside copies with the added notes, just as the *Eponym Lists* from Assyria have only the men's names, or the names and their titles, beside the *Eponym Chronicles*, which have an event for each year.

1.2.3. Historical Prologues in Hittite Treaties

Documents presenting another chronicle-like composition come from the Hittite realm: the treaties drawn up in the Late Bronze Age and preserved in the citadel at Hattusha. The basic formula of these treaties, now familiar, comprises title, historical prologue, stipulations, deposit or reading, witnesses, curses and blessings. The historical prologue may comprise a simple statement that the Hittite king had placed the vassal on his throne, so he was expected to adhere to the terms of the agreement; or it may give a longer recital of the relations that led up to the making of the treaty.[13] While most of the historical prologues deal with only the present and the previous generation, a few mention earlier times and one reaches further back. Soon after 1300 B.C., the Hittite Muwatalli II renewed a treaty his father, Mursili II, had made with the king of Aleppo, Talmi-sharruma.[14] The copy of the original had been stolen, so a new copy was made in the name of the Hittite successor. After the introductory explanation, the greater part of the preserved text recounts episodically the history of earlier relations between the two kingdoms, friendly and hostile, from about 1630 B.C. It mentions six previous Hittite rulers, from the Hattusili and Mursili who destroyed Aleppo's domain, to Tudhaliya who entered peaceful relations with Aleppo about 1400 B.C., then to his successor Hattusılı against whom Aleppo turned, so losing territory, and to Suppiluliuma I who re-conquered Aleppo, through Mursili II to Muwatalli II. The narrations of past events in the treaties give the reason for their creation; they are, in effect, the etiologies of the treaties. The participants could remember events of the past two or three generations, but for older times records would be needed. These might be earlier treaties, but where there had been rebellion and lengthy intervals without good relations, other sources could be such detailed royal annals as those preserved for the Hittite kings Mursili II (ca. 1321–1295 B.C.).[15] Clearly, the Hittite chancery held various historical records.

A. Zgoll; Orientalia Biblica et Christiana 14; Wiesbaden: Harrassowitz, 2003) 267–92.

13. G. M. Beckman, *Hittite Diplomatic Texts* (2nd ed.; Writings from the Ancient World 7; Atlanta: Scholars, 1999) 65 (for the treaty between Mursili II and Niqmepa of Ugarit), 54–55 (for the treaty between Suppiluliuma and Tette of Nuhashshi).

14. Ibid., 93–95.

15. Translation by R. H. Beal in *The Context of Scripture* II (ed. W. W. Hallo and K. L. Younger; Leiden: Brill, 2000) 82–90.

2. Ancient Hebrew History Writing and Deuteronomy

Similarities of content have led to the conclusion that as exiles in Babylonia the authors of the books of Kings found a model for their composition in the *Babylonian Chronicle*. There are shared elements such as the relationship between two kingdoms (Assyria and Babylonia) recorded in different chronicles and in correlated dates, notices of royal burials, cultic behavior and punishment of impious kings.[16] Those authors "probably brought with them from Judah the basic historical materials and theories."[17] The question arises, "Did the authors of Kings already have chronicle-like records from which they made their extracts, as they repeatedly assert?"

The Middle Assyrian chronicle fragments with the earlier *Eponym Chronicle* both attest the composition of chronicle-like texts in the second millennium B.C., while the historical prologues to Hittite treaties, especially that between Muwattalli and Aleppo with its long time span, show how such information might be used in contexts that offer more narrative.

Since the publication of George Mendenhall's work in 1954 the parallel between the form of the Hittite treaties and the form of the book of Deuteronomy has been generally recognized, giving rise to contrasting views.[18] On the one hand, a minority of scholars maintain this parallel implies a date for Deuteronomy's composition before 1200 B.C.;[19] on the other hand, the majority argue that the book was composed in the eighth or seventh centuries B.C. to promulgate the teachings that led to the reforms of Hezekiah or of Josiah. Some argue for yet later dates, with the completion of the book after the exile.[20]

---

16. M. Liverani, "The Books of Kings and Ancient Near Eastern Historiography," in *The Book of Kings: Sources, Composition, History and Reception* (ed. B. Halpern and A. Lemaire; SVT 129; Leiden: Brill, 2010) 163–84, esp. pp. 172–78, 180, 184.

17. Ibid., 178.

18. G. E. Mendenhall, "Law and Covenant in Israel and the Ancient Near East," *BA* 17 (1954) 26–46, 49–76, reprinted as *Law and Covenant in the Ancient Near East* (Pittsburgh: The Biblical Colloquium, 1955).

19. In favor of the earlier date are M. G. Kline, *The Treaty of the Great King* (Grand Rapids: Eerdmans, 1963); K. A. Kitchen, *Ancient Orient and Old Testament* (London: Tyndale, 1966) 90–102; idem, *On the Reliability of the Old Testament* (Grand Rapids: Eerdmans, 2003) 283–312; idem with P. J. N. Lawrence, *Treaty, Law and Covenant* (Wiesbaden: Harrassowitz, 2012); cf. P. Lawrence, *The Books of Moses Revisited* (Eugene, OR: Wipf & Stock, 2011) 47–94.

20. See, for example, T. Römer, *The So-Called Deuteronomistic History: A Sociological, Historical and Literary Introduction* (London: T. & T. Clark, 2007).

2.1. Deuteronomy's Proposed Dependence on Assyrian Treaties

On the grounds of objective form criticism, looking at Deuteronomy in the light of the forms of Hittite treaties, a late second-millennium date for the shape of the book can hardly be denied; the historical prologue in particular does not occur in extant first-millennium treaties.[21] Apparently militating against that date for the production of the book is the discovery of treaties that Esarhaddon of Assyria imposed on his vassals in 672 B.C. (hereafter VTE, "Vassal Treaties of Esarhaddon"), because they exhibit various close parallels in sequence and wording to Deuteronomy. The primary publication by Donald Wiseman in 1958[22] unleashed a torrent of studies drawing conclusions from those parallels.[23] The curses offer the most striking comparisons, leading many to conclude that Deuteronomy was written in the seventh century, based upon an Assyrian treaty, quite apart from the arguments of earlier commentators arising from literary and theological analyses. Especially close correspondences have been claimed between some curses in Deut 28:27–33 and lines 419 to 430 in VTE.[24] Yet in order to produce this close correspondence, verse 26 of Deuteronomy 28 has to be placed between verses 29 and 30 and line 421 has to be omitted from lines 419–30 in VTE, rendering the similarity slightly less compelling.[25]

The vivid curses of VTE lines 528–32a and Deut 28:23, threatening a brazen sky and iron-hard ground, have been taken as parade examples of Hebrew adoption from Assyrian. However, a distinction between the forms of curses in the Assyrian Vassal Treaties has often been overlooked. There are two types of curses, termed "Standard" and "Ceremonial" by Simo Parpola.[26] The Standard Curses invoke Babylonian gods to inflict harm on apostates. Examples in VTE were part of an ongoing scribal tradition that can be traced back for over one thousand years in "boundary stones" (*kudurrus*) and royal inscriptions, notably in the Law Stele of Hammurabi.[27] Distinctively, the Ceremonial Curses

---

21. Kitchen, *On the Reliability*, 290–91; Lawrence, *The Books of Moses Revisited*, 69.
22. D. J. Wiseman, "The Vassal Treaties of Esarhaddon," *Iraq* 20 (1958).
23. First expounded by R. Frankena, "The Vassal Treaties of Esarhaddon and the Dating of Deuteronomy," *Oudtestamentische Studien* 14 (1965) 122–54. Cf. M. Weinfeld, *Deuteronomy and the Deuteronomic School* (Oxford: Clarendon Press, 1972).
24. See M. Weinfeld, "Deuteronomy, Book of," *ABD* 2:161–70.
25. As noted by Mi-Ja Jang in an unpublished University of Liverpool dissertation and by Kitchen, *On the Reliability*, 293.
26. S. Parpola and K. Watanabe, *Neo-Asssyrian Treaties and Loyalty Oaths* (State Archives of Assyria 2; Helsinki: Helsinki University Press, 1988) xli–xlii.
27. See, for example, curses in A. Livingstone, "A Neglected Kudurru or Boundary Stone of Marduk-nadin-ahhe," *Revue d'Assyriologie* 100 (2006) 74–82.

are simple imprecations with similes: "Just as a stag is pursued and killed, so may your enemy pursue and kill you, your brothers and your sons" (VTE line 576). These curses are written in the Assyrian dialect and have few antecedents in Akkadian. Observing that difference, as well as their nature as simile curses, Kazuko Watanabe, in re-editing VTE, preferred to treat the Ceremonial Curses as West Semitic imports into Assyria, not vice-versa.[28] Some of the Hittite treaties contain simile curses, too: "If you . . . do not observe the words of this treaty, the gods will destroy you . . . they will draw you out like malt from its husks."[29] Now the Ceremonial Curses of VTE include the curse of brazen sky and iron-hard ground. Although this curse is peculiar to Deuteronomy and VTE (with the elements reversed in Lev 26:19), it is noteworthy that the hardness of the metals is not found as a simile in Babylonian, but is known in Egyptian and Hittite in the second millennium B.C. Ramesses II said to his troops before the Battle of Qadesh (ca. 1274 B.C.), "Do you not realize that I am your wall of iron?" Furthermore, bronze was used metaphorically of the pharaoh by Abi-milku, king of Tyre, who wrote in a letter to Akhenaten, "To your servant . . . you are a brazen wall set up for him."[30] In Hittite the phrase "words of iron" was customarily applied to gifts of land the kings made from the seventeenth century B.C. onwards.[31]

2.2. *Deuteronomy's Probable Second-Millennium Origin*

These observations militate against the case for Deuteronomy's dependence upon Assyrian treaties and point to the possibility of an earlier origin, in keeping with the external evidence from the treaty form.[32] The book of Deuteronomy presents itself as the words of Moses, but if it was produced five or six centuries later, or even more, to propagate a particular theological position, the evident formulation on the pattern of the Hittite treaties has to be explained. Billie Collins acknowledges

---

28. K. Watanabe, *Die adê-Vereidigung anlässlich der Thronfolgeregelung Asarhaddons* (Baghdader Mitteilungen Beiheft 3; Berlin: Mann, 1987) 33–34, 44.

29. From Treaty of Suppiluliuma I and Shattiwaza of Mitanni; see Beckman, *Hittite Diplomatic Texts*, 48, 52. More examples of simile curses occur in the Hittite "Soldiers' Oath"; see A. Goetze, "The Soldiers' Oath," *ANET* 353–54. See also M. Zehnder, "Building on Stone? Deuteronomy and Esarhaddon's Loyalty Oaths," *BBR* 19 (2009) 341–74, 511–35.

30. See A. Millard, "King Og's Bed and Other Ancient Ironmongery," in *Ascribe to the Lord: Biblical and Other Studies in Memory of Peter C. Craigie* (ed. L. Eslinger and G. Taylor; JSOTSup 67; Sheffield: Sheffield Academic, 1988) 490–91; W. L. Moran, *The Amarna Letters* (Baltimore, MD: Johns Hopkins University Press, 1992) no. 147, line 53.

31. Millard, "King Og's Bed," 491.

32. For further arguments and comparisons, see Kitchen, *On the Reliability*, 291–93, and Zehnder, "Building on Stone," 341–74, 511–35.

the influence of the Hittite treaties on Israelite literature, but nevertheless maintains a first-millennium date for Deuteronomy: "The Hittite treaties . . . served as a model for shaping the covenant between God and the Israelites. The intervening centuries between the floruit of the treaty form and its emergence in the biblical text as a covenant form sometime at the end of the eighth (or later) are not an insurmountable chronological barrier, given the likelihood of continuity in the oral and even scribal traditions between the Late Bronze and Iron Ages in Israel."[33] However, if Deuteronomy was written in the first-millennium, the difficulty remains of reconciling the use of an obsolete framework with the adoption of current Assyrian elements, as many propose. If Assyrian treaties were known to Hebrew scribes, even imposed on Judah's kings, it would seem incongruous not to apply their distinct first-millennium form to the Hebrew work.

The source of the non-Assyrian form of the Ceremonial Curses can readily be seen to be the Aramaic-speaking peoples. By the seventh century B.C. the Aramaic impact on Assyrian, of which there are traces already in the ninth century,[34] becomes evident in loanwords and in word order, beside notes in Aramaic on cuneiform tablets and legal deeds written wholly in Aramaic on clay tablets.[35] The alien word order is obvious in the commencement of some Assyrian royal inscriptions. In Akkadian a king normally introduces himself as "RN . . . am I" (e.g., ḫammurabi . . . anāku; tukulti-ninurta . . . anāku; sîn-aḫḫē-erība . . . anāku).[36] The Assyrian kings of the ninth and eighth centuries usually opened their inscriptions simply with their names, without any pronoun: "Shalmaneser, king of all peoples . . ." (šulmānu-ašarēdu šar kiššati

---

33. B. J. Collins, *The Hittites and their World* (Archaeology and Biblical Studies 7; Atlanta: SBL, 2007) 110–11, 222.

34. For example, A. Millard, "The Graffiti on the Glazed Bricks from Nimrud," appendix to J. Curtis, D. Collon, and A. Green, "British Museum Excavations at Nimrud and Balawat in 1989," *Iraq* 55 (1993) 35, 36.

35. See W. von Soden, "Aramäische Wörter in neuassyrischen und neu- und spätbabylonischen Texten. Ein Vorbericht. I (agâ-*mūš)" *Orientalia* 35 (1966) 1–20; idem, "II (n-z und Nachträge)," *Orientalia* 37 (1968) 261–71; idem, "III", *Orientalia* 46 (1977) 183–97. For Aramaic notes see D. Schwiderski, *Die alt- und reichsaramäischen Inschriften, 2: Texte und Bibliographie* (Berlin: de Gruyter, 2004) 19–34. For deeds see A. Lemaire, *Nouvelles tablettes araméennes* (Geneva: Droz, 2001).

36. Laws of Hammurabi i 50–53, xlvii 9–10; A. K. Grayson, *Assyrian Rulers of the Third and Second Millennia BC (To 1115 BC)* (The Royal Inscriptions of Mesopotamia Assyrian Periods 1; Toronto: University Press, 1987) 244; D. D. Luckenbill, *The Annals of Sennacherib* (Oriental Institute Publications 2; Chicago: University of Chicago Press, 1924) 150 VIII, 151 XII, XV.

. . .).³⁷ In the seventh century the wording may be altered so that the pronoun stands at the head of the sentence: "I am RN, . . ." (e.g., rarely *anāku sīn-aḫḫē-erība* . . . ; more frequently *anāku aššur-bān-apli* . . .).³⁸ Contrary to Akkadian syntax, this seems to be an imitation of West Semitic practice, as noted by Arno Poebel in 1932.³⁹ It is already present in the western-colored language of the Akkadian inscription honoring the fifteenth-century B.C. King Idri-mi of Alalakh (line 1 *anāku idri-mi*).⁴⁰ Although no other royal inscriptions of the Late Bronze Age have been unearthed in the Levant, personal pronouns stand in first place in some Akkadian documents written there.⁴¹ In the tenth century B.C., Bel-eresh, an Assyrian viceroy stationed on the Habur River, commenced his record in Akkadian, "I am Bel-eresh . . ." (*anāku bēl ereš*) and he held his post in an area populated by Aramaean tribes.⁴² In this light, West Semitic inscriptions opening with "I am . . ." (Mesha of Moab, ʾnk mšʿ . . . ; Zakkur of Hamath [ʾ]nh zkr . . .) need not be understood as an imitation of Assyrian royal monuments, as has recently been suggested,⁴³ since the West Semitic formula was long-established. Its most obvious example is the introductory declaration at Mount Sinai, "I am YHWH" (Exod 20:2, repeated in Deut 5:1). (The same word order obtains in Hittite.)

Common language (vocabulary, phraseology) and theology identify the Deuteronomistic style throughout the books of Joshua, Judges, Samuel, Kings, and Jeremiah. Assuming Deuteronomy is the "Book of

---

37. A. K. Grayson, *Assyrian Rulers of the Early First Millennium BC II (858–645 BC)* (The Royal Inscriptions of Mesopotamia Assyrian Periods 3; Toronto: University of Toronto Press, 1996) 7, 28, 44, etc.

38. Luckenbill, *Sennacherib*, 150 X; R. Borger, *Beiträge zur Inschriftenwerk Assurbanipals* (Wiesbaden: Harrassowitz, 1996) 14, 92, 175, 193; cf. E. Leichty, *The Royal Inscriptions of Esarhaddon, King of Assyria (680–669 BC)* (The Royal Inscriptions of the Neo-Assyrian Period 4; Winona Lake, IN: Eisenbrauns, 2011) nos. 43, 44, 64, 74.

39. A. Poebel, *Das appositionell bestimmte Pronomen der I. Pers. Sing. in den westsemitischen Inschriften und im Alten Testament* (Assyriological Studies 3; Chicago: University Press, 1932) 85–86. For Hebrew, see F. I. Andersen, *The Hebrew Verbless Clause in the Pentateuch* (Nashville: Abingdon, 1970) 42–45.

40. S. Smith, *The Statue of Idri-mi* (Occasional Papers 1; London: British Institute of Archaeology in Ankara, 1949); E. L. Greenstein and D. Marcus, "The Akkadian Inscription of Idrimi," *Journal of the Ancient Near East Society of Columbia University* 8 (1976) 68.

41. J. Huehnergard, "On Verbless Clauses in Akkadian," *Zeitschrift für Assyriologie* 76 (1986) 242–47.

42. A. K. Grayson, *Assyrian Rulers of Early First Millennium BC (1114–859 BC)* (The Royal Inscriptions of Mesopotamia Assyrian Periods 2; Toronto: University of Toronto Press, 1991) 127.

43. S. L. Sanders, *The Invention of Hebrew* (Urbana, IL: University of Illinois Press, 2009) 6, 138.

the Law," which was found in Josiah's reign and had been composed in the previous decades, Deuteronomistic style finds a home in the seventh and sixth centuries B.C. The case is convincing for most biblical scholars. Nevertheless, the possibility of an enduring tradition deserves attention. Continuity is a characteristic of Assyrian royal inscriptions, the so-called Annals, from the twelfth century to the seventh. Titles and epithets are repeated from one king to the next, and the same similes are applied, so one king might "roar like Adad" (the storm god) in the ninth century and another in the seventh.[44] As they marched from place to place, kings from Tiglath-pileser I to Ashurbanipal repeatedly "demolished, tore down and burned with fire" hostile towns they conquered.[45] If the Hebrew law book was many centuries old when it was rediscovered and soon became a new standard for religious leaders in Josiah's time and after, those converted to its tenets would be likely to follow its pattern of thought and imitate its language. Moreover, if the book had its origin in the Late Bronze Age, as it indicates itself, it could have shaped the outlook of subsequent writings, for its ideology and style may not have been forgotten, regardless of whether people were aware of the existence of the book itself.[46]

2.3. *Deuteronomy's Potential Influence on Israel's History Writing*

In this light, the Historical Prologue of Deuteronomy (1:6–3:29) may be seen as a model for later accounts of Israel's career. Her behavior was to be judged in the light of her past loyalty to her suzerain. This hardly differs from the ideology of ancient royal inscriptions in which kings evaluated themselves according to their obedience and devotion to their gods. Inevitably, they were always positive since their reports are autobiographical, intended for present and future generations to admire; also inevitably, their verdicts on their enemies are always negative! The *Epic of Tukulti-Ninurta I,* king of Assyria ca. 1244–1208 B.C., exemplifies this, relating how the Assyrian had the right to campaign against and conquer the Kassite king of Babylon, Kashtiliash, because he had broken the treaty existing between the two kingdoms.[47] The Babylonian *Esagila Chronicle* condemns kings who supposedly slighted

---

44. Said of Ashurnasirpal II and of Sennacherib; see *CAD* 17/1 Š.1 (1989) 64a.
45. *CAD* 11 N.1 (1980) 273b.
46. Compare the "Deuteronomisms" in the book of Amos; for example, see S. M. Paul, *Amos: A Critical and Historical Commentary on the Book of Amos* (Hermeneia; Minneapolis: Fortress, 1991) 21–22, 112–13.
47. See the translation by B. R. Foster, *Before the Muses. An Anthology of Akkadian Literature* (3rd ed.; Bethesda, MD: CDL, 2005) 298–317.

or neglected the cult of Marduk and in doing so this late second-millennium composition echoes verdicts given by works written closer to the times of the kings concerned. The Sumerian poem *The Curse of Agade*, extant in copies made from about 2000 B.C. onwards, condemns Naram-Sin of Akkad for impious actions.[48] It was a natural expectation that disloyalty to the gods, or oath-breaking by an overlord's vassals, would be punished.

The picture of one generation of Hebrew scribes after another, constructing continuing chronicles episode by episode on a similar framework with individual variations, accords with information available from the ancient Near East.[49] Partly by observing variations in phraseology, André Lemaire demonstrated that a similar process of accretion is apparent in Samuel and Kings in 1986.[50] Biblical references to scribes in the courts of David and Solomon hint at the people who could have been responsible for initiating the writing of those texts (Seraiah, 2 Sam 8:17; Elihoreph and Ahijah, 1 Kgs 4:3; note too, David's uncle, Jonathan, a scribe, mentioned in 1 Chr 27:32). Although no contemporary literary manuscripts survive and epigraphic material from the period of the United Monarchy is sparse, limited to a few graffiti and ostraca (including that from Khirbet Qeiyafa[51]), the Gezer Calendar, and the Tel Zayit abcedary, increasing discoveries point to an availability of writing, at that time and before, for a variety of purposes from which recording past events cannot be excluded.[52]

May the Historical Prologue in Deuteronomy not be the seed from which Israel's history writing sprouted? That Prologue looks back to explain and evaluate the circumstances in which it was uttered; the subsequent, on-going "history" would then explain and evaluate a recent or current state of affairs. Thus ancient Israel would give birth

---

48. J. S. Cooper, *The Curse of Agade* (Baltimore: Johns Hopkins University Press, 1983).

49. See the summary by H. M. Barstad, "The Common Theology of the Ancient Near East," in *History and the Hebrew Bible: Studies in Ancient Israelite and Ancient Near Eastern Historiography* (Forschungen zum Alten Testament 61; Tübingen: Mohr-Siebeck, 2008) 54–63.

50. A. Lemaire, "Vers l'Histoire de la Rédaction des Livres des Rois," *ZAW* 98 (1986) 221–36, translated in *Reconsidering Israel and Judah: Recent Studies on the Deuteronomistic History* (ed. G. N. Knoppers and J. G. McConville; Winona Lake, IN: Eisenbrauns, 2000) 446–61.

51. See A. Millard, "The Ostracon from the Days of David found at Khirbet Qeiyafa," *TynBul* 62.1 (2011) 2–13.

52. A. Millard, "Scripts and their uses in the 12th–10th Centuries BCE" in *The Ancient Near East in the 12th–10th Centuries BCE. Culture and History* (ed. G. Galil, A. Gilboa, A. M. Maeir, and D. Kahn; Alter Orient und Altes Testament 392; Münster: Ugarit Verlag, 2012) 405–12.

to a way of recounting her past by taking a current mode from her neighbors and fashioning it independently to produce a continuous account of cause and effect. That would make Hebrew writers the first historians. Having Herodotus as "the father of history" for the classical world gives him no priority over other cultures; the human mind responds in similar ways to similar situations (cf. the invention of writing in Mesopotamia and Egypt, China, and South America). Most narrative texts from the ancient Near Eastern world display clear religious convictions, so the fact that the Hebrew writers' convictions are plain should not be taken as grounds for denying them originality or reliability. Their selectivity surely implies some critical attitude to the sources they name, and, inasmuch as their presentation claims to be true, they denote others as false. They had a definite purpose in writing, to make clear the reaction of their God to the actions of his people.[53]

---

53. See earlier A. R. Millard, "Story, History, and Theology," in *Faith, Tradition, and History* (ed. A. R. Millard, J. K. Hoffmeier, and D. W. Baker; Winona Lake, IN: Eisenbrauns, 1994) 37–64, esp. 39–40.

"Because of the Wickedness of These Nations" (Deut 9:4–5)

The Canaanites—Ethical or Not?

RICHARD S. HESS

From biblical times to the present, many have assumed the Canaanites to be a completely degenerate people whose religious and cultural practices justified Israel's wars against them. Recently, the "new atheists" have represented Canaanites as innocent and good-natured people upon whom Israel and its malevolent deity preyed. This study examines the literary evidence from both the biblical and larger West Semitic sources to suggest a more nuanced alternative to this important question. In fact, in the literary genres preserved from the Bronze Age archives of Mari, Emar, Ugarit, and elsewhere, these peoples appear to have represented a variety of ethical directions. The same is true of some individuals from Canaan as mentioned in the Bible. The implications for the analysis of Canaanite religion caution against drawing "broad strokes" in attempts to justify or condemn perceived Israelite attitudes toward this people.

1. Questions of Definition

The subject of this essay raises some significant methodological questions. First is the question of the type of literature under investigation. In discussions of ethics, wisdom literature is assumed as the most relevant. Even here, however, we may ask what constitutes wisdom literature. Arguably, whether narrative, biographical, religious, divinatory, epistolary, annalistic, poetic, or other, most literary types

---

Author's Note: I am delighted to express my appreciation to Dan Block for his faithful Evangelical witness in the interpretation of the Old Testament in terms of both its theological message and the ancient context in which it was written. Dan's contribution to the study of the biblical text through commentaries, monographs, and articles has consistently provided a reliable guide for the understanding and application of God's Word to the church today. Dan's role as president of the Institute for Biblical Research led that organization into a new era promoting the irenic articulation of Evangelical scholarship in dialogue with the broader professional guild. May the LORD bless you and keep you!

contain wisdom elements. However, there are also those forms of literature traditionally identified as wisdom in the ancient Near East and in Israel. These usually consist of proverbs, dialogues, or didactic narratives. Other wisdom forms include, instruction, debates, and riddles.[1] These are the proper starting point for the study of wisdom literature.

A second area of concern has to do with the focus on Canaanite wisdom. This is a more complex matter. There is the question of whether Canaanite is an appropriate term. There is also the issue of the putative distinctions between Canaanite as understood in the Bible and Canaanite as understood in the ancient Near East.[2] Finally, there is the question of what constitutes distinctive Canaanite wisdom literature. In the relevant Egyptian and biblical sources, Hebrew *kĕna'an* and Akkadian *kinaḫḫi* identify a geographical area that includes regions of modern Israel, Palestine, Lebanon, and southern Syria. However, it would exclude Jordan and northern Syria where sites such as Ugarit and Emar lay. So, technically these important archives are not part of Canaan. Nevertheless, it is clear that matters of language, onomastics, religion, and other areas of culture are shared between the north and Canaan. The broader, modern, linguistic term "West Semitic" reflects this reality and is more accurate for our concerns.

Further, is the term "Canaanite" an appropriate label, given the putative differences between the biblical view of Canaanite or West Semitic culture and that found in the ancient Near Eastern texts? Lemche proposed that the use of Canaan in the Bible was a postexilic reality written back into early texts and had nothing to do with Canaan as known from many Egyptian and West Semitic sources of the second millennium B.C.E., when this term was used.[3] However, his arguments

---

1. K. L. Sparks, *Ancient Texts for the Study of the Hebrew Bible: A Guide to the Background Literature* (Peabody, MA: Hendrickson, 2005) 56–83, surveys these sorts of Egyptian, Mesopotamian, West Semitic, and Hittite literature. For distinct genres of Hittite wisdom, see below.

2. This debate occurred in the 1990s, prompted by N. P. Lemche, *The Canaanites and Their Land: The Tradition of the Canaanites* (JSOTSup 110; Sheffield: JSOT, 1991); idem, "Greater Canaan: The Implications of a Correct Reading of EA 151:49–67," *BASOR* 310 (1998) 19–24. See R. S. Hess, "Occurrences of Canaan in Late Bronze Age Archives of the West Semitic World," in *Israel Oriental Studies 18: Past Links: Studies in the Languages and Cultures of the Ancient Near East* (ed. S. Izre'el, I. Singer, and R. Zadok; Winona Lake, IN: Eisenbrauns, 1998) 365–72; idem, "Canaan and Canaanites at Alalakh," *UF* 31 (1999 vol.; Münster: Ugarit-Verlag, 2000) 225–36; N. Na'aman, "Four Notes on the Size of Late Bronze Age Canaan," *BASOR* 313 (1999) 31–38; A. F. Rainey, "Who Is a Canaanite? A Review of the Textual Evidence," *BASOR* 304 (1996) 1–16; idem in A. F. Rainey and R. S. Notley, *The Sacred Bridge: Carta's Atlas of the Biblical World* (Jerusalem: Carta, 2006) 34–36.

3. Lemche, *The Canaanites and Their Land*.

have not been widely accepted.[4] Instead, it is generally recognized that both the biblical and extrabiblical sets of textual evidence have in mind the same original reality, however differently they may present some specific items.[5] Among other pieces of evidence, the correspondence of the name itself and the generally agreed upon boundaries of Canaan are identical in both the Bible and the ancient Near East.

If the biblical Canaan geographically matches that of the other texts, can we use the Bible as a resource for ethics? Possibly, but experience dictates that those cultures who define themselves in opposition to others are usually not the best source for an objective account of their moral behavior. To the contrary, there is evidence that such observations may be hostile or at least preserve a bias. So the famous stories about sexual excess at Roman Corinth appear to have originated in sources composed by those representing its archrival, Athens. In a similar manner, the barbarity and oppression of the Persians received great press among Greek writers opposed to the Persian power. Perhaps it is only to be expected that the same would be true of those Canaanite or West Semitic peoples whom Israel encountered, or some would say, from whom Israel emerged. The biblical writers needed to distinguish the orthodox Israelite life and faith from their surrounding neighbors. Therefore, the ethical norms that one encounters tend to be negative in their own assessments. The book of Judges portrays the surrounding West Semitic nations as oppressive of weaker Israel. The books of Kings describe human sacrifice of royal sons (2 Kgs 3:36–37). The prophets strongly condemn both the enormity of violence and brutality exacted on defeated enemies (Amos 1–2), and widespread sexual activity and immorality (Hos 4:14–15).

At the same time, the biblical writers do not hesitate to charge their own nation with such wickedness. This can be found in the book of Deuteronomy, where the wickedness ascribed to the Canaanites (Deut 9:4–6) is attached to the history of Israel itself before occupying the Promised Land (9:7–24). It becomes the expectation of what Israel might do in the land (9:27; 28:15–68) and later the judgment for how

---

4. See the bibliography in note 3 and R. S. Hess, review of N. P. Lemche, *The Canaanites and Their Land: The Tradition of the Canaanites*, *Them* 18.2 (January 1993) 25.

5. See, e.g., L. L. Grabbe, "Ugaritic and 'Canaanite': Some Methodological Observations in Relation to Biblical Study," in *Ugarit and the Bible: Proceedings of the International Symposium on Ugarit and the Bible. Manchester, September 1992* (ed. G. J. Brooke, A. H. W. Curtis, and J. F. Healey; Ugaritisch-Biblische Literatur 11; Münster: Ugarit-Verlag, 1994) 113–22.

they did live in the land (2 Kgs 17:7–41; 22:15–20; and many texts in the prophetic books).

However, it is also true that a careful reading of the biblical text appears to balance all these condemnations against Israel's West Semitic neighbors. Unlike some of the nations in Judges, Hiram of Tyre rejoices at Solomon's success and assists in the building of temples and palaces (1 Kings 5–10). As recorded in 2 Kings 3, Edom joins Israel and Judah in their attack against Moab. While the sacrifice of children may be described in some biblical contexts, the Philistine king Achish preserves alive David and his army. Coming from Moab, Ruth will take care of her aging mother-in-law on her own, rather than return to her family home. Violence, always found between nations, does not disappear, but the examples of Hiram and the peaceful relations that Israel often enjoyed with its neighbors suggest that brutality was not the only mode of relating that ancient Israel and Judah knew with the surrounding nations. With respect to sex, in Genesis 20 and again in chap. 26, Abimelech of Gerar recognized immorality in the act of adultery and sought to avoid it with both Abraham and Sarah and with Isaac and Rebekah. Thus a study of the Bible results in an ambiguous evaluation with respect to West Semitic ethics. Some instances lead to condemnation while others exemplify models of character and of community ethics.

If it is true that there is not a clear moral definition of the Canaanites in the Bible, this has not been the assumption of scholars in the past. Among the antiquated dichotomies that Mark Smith describes in the history of the study of Ugaritic religion is the distinction between "the so-called high, moral religion of Israel and the base, depraved religion of the Canaanites."[6] This position was advocated by William F. Albright in the middle of the twentieth century but has now been thoroughly critiqued and largely rejected in serious studies in the field.[7]

---

6. M. S. Smith, "Recent Study of Ugaritic Religion in Light of the Ugaritic Texts," in *Ugarit at Seventy-Five* (ed. K. L. Younger Jr.; Winona Lake, IN: Eisenbrauns, 2007) 3.

7. D. Hillers, "Analyzing the Abominable: Our Understanding of Canaanite Religion," *JQR* 75 (1985) 253–69; M. S. Smith, *The Early History of God: Yahweh and the Other Deities in Ancient Israel* (San Francisco: Harper & Row, 1990); idem, *The Origins of Biblical Monotheism: Israel's Polytheistic Background and the Ugaritic Texts* (Oxford: Oxford University Press, 2001); idem, *The Early History of God: Yahweh and the Other Deities in Ancient Israel* (2nd ed.; Grand Rapids: Eerdmans, 2003); J. Day, *Yahweh and the Gods and Goddesses of Canaan* (JSOTSup 265; Sheffield: Sheffield Academic Press, 2001). For the original comments of Albright, see W. F. Albright, *Yahweh and the Gods of Canaan* (London: Athlone, 1968).

Nevertheless, the wickedness of the Canaanites, especially in areas of sexual perversion and promiscuity, continues to be a theme to which ethicists such as Christopher Wright and Paul Copan appeal in order to justify Israel's aggression against Canaan.[8] Wright has recently written: "The degraded character of Canaanite society and religion is more explicitly described in moral and social terms in Leviticus 18:24–25; 20:22–24 and in Deuteronomy 9:5; 12:29–31. It includes sexual promiscuity and perversion particularly associated with fertility cults as well as the callousness of child sacrifice."[9]

Thus, for example, we may consider Deut 9:4–5 and its clear statement regarding the judgment of God against the sins of those who lived in the Promised Land, before the emergence of Israel there. In so doing we learn that the biblical understanding ascribes an absolute, divine condemnation on those Canaanites in the land.

Over against this interpretation are those who claim either a philosophical or ethnic identification with Canaanite ethics and their oppression by ancient Israel. Thus native American Robert Allen Warrior posits that the treatment of the Canaanites presents fundamental questions about how one constructs a national identity in relation to others.[10] In this he follows both Robert Oden and Randall Bailey who see the question as one of how Israel framed its national identity over against those around them.[11]

Extreme rhetoric is found in the works of the "new atheists" such as Richard Dawkins and Christopher Hitchens who emphasize the innocent Canaanites and the xenophobic and pitiless Israelites.[12] Dawkins writes how Joshua exterminated the Canaanites and uses modern

---

8. C. J. H. Wright, *Old Testament Ethics for the People of God* (2nd ed.; Downers Grove, IVP, 2004) 473–76; P. Copan, "Is Yahweh a Moral Monster? The New Atheists and Old Testament Ethics," *Philosophia Christi* 10 (2008) 24–25.

9. C. J. H. Wright, *The God I Don't Understand: Reflections on Tough Questions of Faith* (Grand Rapids, MI: Zondervan 2008) 93.

10. R. A. Warrior, "A Native American Perspective: Canaanites, Cowboys, and Indians," in *Voices from the Margin: Interpreting the Bible in the Third World* (ed. R. S. Sugirtharajah; 3rd ed.; Maryknoll: Orbis, 2006) 235–41.

11. R. A. Oden Jr., *The Bible without Theology: The Theological Tradition and Alternatives to It* (San Francisco: Harper & Row, 1987) 475; R. C. Bailey, "They're Nothing but Incestuous Bastards," in *Reading from This Place: Social Location and Biblical Interpretation in the United States* (ed. F. S. and M. A. Tolbert; Minneapolis: Fortress, 1995) 124–37; idem, "He Didn't Even Tell Us the Worst of It!" *USQR* 59.1 (2005) 15–24.

12. R. Dawkins, *The God Delusion* (Boston: Houghton Mifflin, 2006) 247; C. Hitchens, *God Is Not Great: How Religion Poisons Everything* (New York: Hachette Book Group, 2007) 101–2.

analogies that all assume impotence and innocence on the part of his victims:

> The ethnic cleansing begun in the time of Moses is brought to bloody fruition in the book of Joshua, a text remarkable for the bloodthirsty massacres it records and the xenophobic relish with which it does so.... And the Bible story of Joshua's destruction of Jericho, and the invasion of the Promised Land in general, is morally indistinguishable from Hitler's invasion of Poland, or Saddam Hussein's massacres of the Kurds and the Marsh Arabs.[13]

More usefully, Cheryl Anderson and Frank Yamada point to the philosophy of Emmanuel Levinas, who emphasized the need to recognize those such as the Canaanites as "the Other," to engage in face-to-face encounters with "the Other," and to use these experiences as a basis for forging ethical decisions for justice among oppressed humans in the world.[14]

It is surprising that, except for the writings of Albright and his later successors and critics, all these discussions regarding the ethics of the Canaanites, whether pro or con, restrict themselves to the testimony of the Bible and ignore the growing collection of evidence in the West Semitic world.[15] The decision to avoid other literary sources, for whatever reason, impoverishes the discussion on all sides and undermines validity to all the arguments and conclusions presented by the ethicists and philosophers. It is essential to examine the West Semitic sources and to draw conclusions, however limited and provisional. This will allow for initial dialogue and understanding, and perhaps move beyond the polemics of the present proponents.

A final question asks what is meant by the terms, "Personal and Social Ethics." In many recent discussions, and especially where we make use of primarily (or solely) textual sources, this expression has been replaced by "Character Formation and Community Ethics." This is not

---

13. Dawkins, *The God Delusion*, 247.

14. C. B. Anderson, "Biblical Laws: Challenging the Principles of Old Testament Ethics," in *Character Ethics and the Old Testament: Moral Dimensions of Scripture* (ed. M. D. Carroll R. and J. E. Lapsley; Louisville: Westminster John Knox, 2007) 37–49; F. M. Yamada, "Ethics," in *Handbook of Postmodern Biblical Interpretation* (ed. A. K. M. Adam; St. Louis: Chalice, 2000) 80–81. See also E. Levinas, *Totality and Infinity: An Essay on Exteriority* (trans. A. Lingis; Pittsburgh; Duquesne University, 1969); idem, *In the Time of the Nations* (trans. M. B. Smith; London: Athlone, 1994).

15. One reviewer of this study disputed, "Just who are the scholars who" do this? To the contrary, Wright, Dawkins, and the others cited above do in fact restrict themselves to the Bible, however scholarly and insightful their works otherwise might be.

an easy collection of terms to summarize. Lisa Sowle Cahill identifies character ethics with the formation of the community and its narrative as emphasized in the moral philosophy of Stanley Hauerwas.[16] Richard Hays observes how the community embodies an alternative moral order.[17] The community and its literary and other sources thus form a set of values or disposition among its individual members; one that shares a collective moral identity.

Walter Brueggemann has noted that character ethics contends with universal principles insofar as it considers guidance for a particular historical community.[18] He would return to Levinas, who rooted his own understanding of the "Other" in Martin Buber's "I-Thou" relationship, which he used to describe the dynamic between God and God's people. Here, however, the emphasis considers the "Other" as defined in human terms; justice toward one's family, one's neighbors, and one's nation. This also includes resisting the temptation of violence in dealing with other peoples. Thus, in asking questions about social justice, we need to examine where the West Semitic literature touches on matters related to dealings with the family, the society, and the surrounding nations.

2. Textual Sources from the West Semitic World: Letters, Myths, Legal, and Economic Texts

When one looks at the textual sources among the West Semitic peoples, there is an abundance of material from the Middle and Late Bronze Age in Syria. It may be worthwhile to survey some other sources for social ethics before turning to the less attested wisdom literature. The archives discussed here have their origin in populations where the dominant presence of West Semitic names among the citizenry strongly suggests a West Semitic culture, however much influenced by other cultures to the east, north, and south. This survey provides glimpses and impressions of these ancient societies.

---

16. S. M. Hauerwas, *A Community of Character: Toward a Constructive Christian Social Ethic* (Notre Dame: University of Notre Dame Press, 1981). See L. S. Cahill, "Christian Character, Biblical Community, and Human Values," in *Character and Scripture: Moral Formation, Community, and Biblical Interpretation* (ed. W. P. Brown; Grand Rapids: Eerdmans, 2000) 3–17.

17. R. B. Hays, "Scripture-Shaped Community: The Problem of Method in New Testament Ethics," *Int* 54 (1990) 46; Cahill, "Christian Character," 9.

18. W. Brueggemann, "Foreword," in *Character Ethics and the Old Testament*, vii–xi.

2.1. Mari

There are thousands of letters from 18th-century Mari, many of which have been published. Wolfgang Heimpel has translated many of these and provided a particularly poignant account of Kirum, the daughter of King Zimri-Lim of Mari, who along with her sister had married someone who was a vassal to Zimri-Lim. His name was Haya-Sumu of the town of Ilan-Tsura.[19] Kirum became unhappy about the marriage arrangements and longed to return to her father Zimri-Lim at Mari. Various envoys were sent to Haya-Sumu. At first he agreed to the separation but then changed his position and refused to allow any official to escort Kirum back to her father. Rather, Haya-Sumu seems to have switched allegiance to Mari's enemies and, along with Kirum's sister, threatened Kirum. She wrote her father about her anxiety and depression, and she threatened suicide if he did not come to her aid. Haya-Sumu again reportedly expressed his intention to kill Kirum with a bronze dagger. This is the last we hear of Kirum. Heimpel comments, "In a world where a wife was called the 'maid' of her husband and treated accordingly, Haya-Sumu might have killed Kirum and remained within the bonds of accepted behavior."[20]

On the other hand, sexual morality allowed for diverse attitudes among women as well as men. Thus, in another text a woman engaged to be married becomes involved with another man in kissing and masturbation without sexual intercourse.[21] She publicly confirms this by undergoing the river ordeal. As is so often the case, the values behind this account remain unclear. Is this a moral statement about premarital sex, even after engagement with other partners? Or is it a concern to establish the paternity of children who might have been born to the woman? Whatever the solution, the additional evidence of a female general in the army of a female "king" attests to some diversity in gender roles.[22]

The Mari letters reveal a time of shifting alliances where one's word mattered little. Human life seems to have followed suit so that a king could recommend that his subjects sell their children into slavery in

---

19. W. Heimpel, *Letters to the King of Mari: A New Translation, with Historical Introduction, Notes, and Commentary* (Mesopotamian Civilizations 12; Winona Lake, IN: Eisenbrauns, 2003) 80–81.
20. Heimpel, *Letters to the King of Mari*, 81; D. Bodi, *The Michal Affair: From Zimri-Lim to the Rabbis* (Sheffield: Sheffield Phoenix, 2005) 64–87.
21. Heimpel, *Letters to the King of Mari*, 386 (ARM 26.488).
22. Heimpel, *Letters to the King of Mari*, 101, 484.

order to buy food. When they refused, he sold four hundred of his own troops.[23] Incarceration in the Mari letters involved hard labor where inmates died of starvation and disease.[24] A servant of Mari's king blinded a group of boys by royal command, perhaps due to the belief that blinded boys made for better musicians.[25] In another letter the father of a slave offers a ransom for his son, but he is refused by the owner who demands more money. While the father is procuring funds, the son dies, either due to natural causes or because he was murdered by someone appointed by the owner. The one accused of the death makes appeals, but they go unheard. He is subject to a vengeance killing of agonizing brutality.[26]

Slaves had no rights of their own.[27] They were usually branded. They could be sold and released by other more powerful figures. Letters contain appeals to the king for the permission of slave women to marry freed men; some are denied despite the presence of children, while others are permitted with the requirement of a substitute slave. The case of a female slave who was beaten to death required a river ordeal to establish the identity of the one who killed the woman; but it is not clear if this was a concern to demonstrate guilt, to identify the abuser of someone else's property, or for some other reason.[28]

2.2. Emar

Well north of Mari lay the city of Emar whose 13th-century archive, though smaller than its southern neighbor, contains more economic and legal documents and fewer letters. Thus the ethical picture to emerge will be different due to the different genres of texts as well as other factors.

---

23. Heimpel, *Letters to the King of Mari*, 142, 390 (ARM 26.494).
24. Heimpel, *Letters to the King of Mari*, 208. For evidence of prison uprisings and escapes, see ARM 10.150 and ARM 26.524.
25. Heimpel, *Letters to the King of Mari*, 287–88 (ARM 26.297).
26. Heimpel, *Letters to the King of Mari*, 366 (ARM 26.434), interprets these letters as describing revenge for a murder. See also J.-M. Durand, "La vengeance à l'époque Amorrite," in *Recueils d'études à la mémoire d'André Parrot* (ed. D. Charpin and J.-M. Durand; Florilegium Marianum VI = Mémoires de N.A.B.U. 7; Paris: Societe pour l'Étude du Proche-Orient Ancien, 2002) 39–50. Durand sees here a vendetta whereas Westbrook argues that this was the reverse of a vendetta, in which the authorities decided the case through trial. See R. Westbrook, "Reflections on the Law of Homicide in the Ancient World," *Maarav* 13 (2006) 160.
27. Heimpel, *Letters to the King of Mari*, 596.
28. Ibid., 275 (ARM 26.254).

Gary Beckman has provided a useful analysis of ethics from the perspective of these texts.[29] The family unit often consisted of the patriarchal head with his wife (rarely wives) and their children. Some of the males among the children may have been old enough to marry and have children, all the while remaining in the house of their parents or in adjacent homes. A few slaves might round out the picture of the family. The patriarch held significant power so that in at least two cases he sold family members as slaves. There are, however, instances in which a woman was the head of the family.

There are also references to non-sibling "brothers" and to a larger clan, but these groupings seem less defined and less involved in legal concerns than the tribal units in the Mari texts of a half millennium earlier. Indeed, certain ceremonies and legal nomenclature appear designed to separate any common property rights among the clans. Even so, other texts recognize traditional responsibilities of a close relative to redeem one who has been sold into debt slavery or who has had their ancestral property sold.

Women could function as primary heirs of land and other property, as well as having involvement in all sorts of business transactions. In inheritance rights, they could legally assume headship of a household, being given a fictional gender as "father and mother" or "male and female."

There are dozens of adoption contracts. In a few cases, abandoned children are adopted. In others, a new spouse adopts the children of the parent who has been married. Adult adoptions are far more frequent, however. There is the adoption of a new son-in-law by the father of the bride who thereby assures that his grandchildren will continue his line, rather than the line of the son's family. In cases of debt, the debtor could adopt the creditor or vice versa.

Marriage contracts reflect the tendency to make arrangements between the families representing the bride and groom. Bride price, as paid to the wife's family, was often stipulated. It could form all or part of the bride's dowry. Married women could also inherit from their original family, even after having received a dowry. Divorce was sometimes made explicit in the marriage contract. Widows far outnumber widowers, suggesting older husbands and younger wives. Widows were

---

29. G. Beckman, "Family Values on the Middle Euphrates in the Thirteenth Century B.C.E.," in *Emar: The History, Religion, and Culture of a Syrian Town in the Late Bronze Age* (ed. M. W. Chavalas; Bethesda: CDL, 1996) 57–79.

discouraged from remarrying. They were to seek any needed financial support from their children.

2.3. Ugarit

A large number of diverse texts have been found and published from the site of ancient Ugarit, close to the Mediterranean. Most of these texts are best dated to the same century as those from Emar.

As at Emar and also at Alalakh, polygamy was accepted, especially among the wealthier families.[30] Here as well marriage included a gift from the groom's family to that of the bride, and then a dowry that the bride brought with her into the marriage. Adoption contracts specify only sons or brothers, but, unlike Emar, all who are adopted are adults. The concerns seem to be financial. The adoptee supported the aging parents and usually received the inheritance of land or money. As at Emar private property could be bequeathed to the next generation, with the oldest son often enjoying a favored status. A son could even receive an inheritance while the parents lived, especially if he was leaving the family.

The queen mother at Ugarit held a special position of influence and could act as a go-between for those who wished access to her son the king. Women in general could inherit from their husbands. There was also the possibility of a widow or divorcee returning to her parent's family. Legally, she could transact her own cases regarding property, adoption, and divorce.

As at Mari, there seems to have been a special case involving difficulties in moving a queen from one city to another. In another case from Ugarit, however, the queen had escaped from the king of Ugarit and fled to her native land of Amurru. The king of Ugarit wished her return due to words or actions involving a "great sin." The Amurru leader was not inclined to agree but did so when pressed by the Hittite overlord and given a substantial sum of money from the Ugarit sovereign. The king of Ugarit exacted his revenge on the hapless queen. We are never told explicitly what this great sin was. However, on the basis of biblical and Egyptian attestations of this term, William Moran has suggested

---

30. See J.-P. Vita, "Chapter Eleven. The Society of Ugarit," in *Handbook of Ugaritic Studies* (ed. W. G. E. Watson and N. Wyatt; Handbook of Oriental Studies, Erste Abteilung, The Near and Middle East 39; Leiden: Brill, 1999) 455–98. See also A. F. Rainey, "Chapter III: Institutions: Family, Civil, and Military," in *RSP: The Texts from Ugarit and the Hebrew Bible Vol. II* (ed. D. E. Smith and S. Rummel; Rome: Pontifical Bible Institute, 1975) 69–107.

that it constituted adultery.[31] If so, it suggests that the views on sexual morality within marriage were similar to those at Mari and Emar. Karel van der Toorn has argued that both in Mesopotamia and in the Bible adultery was viewed as a property infringement against the husband and as a sin or taboo.[32] The West Semitic cultures under consideration seem to have shared this view.

This must all be kept in context with the story sometimes called the Birth of the Gracious Gods (*KTU* 1.23; *COS* 1:274–83). This account of El's sexual exploits remains more graphic than the other myths from Ugarit. Again, it is difficult to know how to fit this into the overall picture of the society. It may describe a patriarchal culture where what is permitted sexually for the males remains forbidden for the females. However, attestations of an equality of legal rights for some females in other genres may suggest that the sexual mores varied according to circumstance as well as, or more than, gender.

As at Emar, there was special concern with observing rites for one's dead parents and ancestors. The dramatic evidence from Ugarit includes family tombs located directly beneath the houses. Groups of families formed villages in the countryside of Ugarit. Elders governed these towns and represented their concerns at the palace. Specialist occupations throughout the kingdom were represented by guilds, each with its own chief.

2.4. *Summary*

These texts from Ugarit, like those at Mari and Emar, allow for some generalizations. It would appear that the Mari evidence suggests ethical ambiguity to a greater extent than what we have seen in the later texts from Emar and Ugarit. Thirteenth-century moral expectations regarding family and aspects of society appear more clearly defined. Does this suggest a shift over the half millennium between these archives? Perhaps, but it may also be reflected in the nature of what is primarily epistolary literature at Mari versus that which is weighted more heavily in favor of legal and economic documents from the later archives. Letters tend to report what is happening on the ground and

---

31. W. L. Moran, "The Scandal of the 'Great Sin' at Ugarit," *JNES* 18 (1959) 80–81. Reprinted in *Amarna Studies: Collected Writings* (ed. J. Huehnergard and S. Izre'el; HSS 54; Winona Lake, IN: Eisenbrauns, 2003) 177–78.

32. K. van der Toorn, *Sin and Sanction in Israel and Mesopotamia: A Comparative Study* (Studia Semitica Neerlandica 22; Assen and Maastricht: Van Gorcum, 1985) 17–18. The biblical evidence is not so strong in this matter, especially in such legal outlines as the Decalogue where the command to avoid adultery is separated from that of prohibiting theft.

also to allow for negative exaggeration in order to persuade the addressee how bad one's problems really are. The contracts, adoptions, wills, and other documents do not exaggerate in this way nor are they concerned as much with describing the authentic actions of real people. Instead, they describe the ideals that one hopes, expects, and endeavors to realize.

3. West Semitic Wisdom Texts Regarding Character Formation and Community Ethics

We now turn to an important collection of texts, the wisdom literature of the West Semitic world. The search for native wisdom texts in this environment has its own difficulties. On the one hand, there are those proverbial sayings that occasionally appear in letters and prophetic texts. Some better known examples include:

- When ants are smitten, they do not just curl up, but they bite the hand of the one who smote them.[33]
- Beneath straw the water runs.[34]
- Chop one finger into two. Vs. The hem shall be knotted among us forever.[35]

These proverbs address justified retribution, the need to see what lies beneath the surface, and the importance of unity. However, these proverbs reflect universal wisdom and reveal little that might be considered distinctive in the West Semitic world. As such, we may be better served by the identification and study of longer literary pieces.

Among all the wisdom literature, we may select several examples according to criteria likely to identify texts that are distinctive to the West Semitic world or at least favored by cultures there. Of course, not all wisdom literature in West Semitic archives can be considered as significant to those peoples in terms of its contents. Many of the texts are scribal practice writings used for refining skills in writing and reading Akkadian and other languages. So it seems best to select those West

---

33. EA 252.16–19; *ANET*, 486. See R. S. Hess, "Smitten Ant Bites Back: Rhetorical Forms in the Amarna Correspondence from Shechem," in *Verse in Ancient Near Eastern Prose* (ed. J. C. de Moor and W. G. E. Watson; AOAT 42; Kevelaer: Butzon & Bercker; Neukirchen-Vluyn: Neukirchener, 1993) 95–111, especially pp. 101–2; A. F. Rainey, *Canaanite in the Amarna Tablets. A Linguistic Analysis of the Mixed Dialect Used by the Scribes from Canaan. Volume II. Morphosyntactic Analysis of the Verbal System* (Handbook of Oriental Studies. Erste Abteilung. The Near and Middle East 25; Leiden: Brill, 1996) 54, 65.

34. ARM 26.197.13–14; ARM 26.199.44; ARM 26.202.10–11. See M. Nissinen, *Prophets and Prophecy in the Ancient Near East* (SBLWAW 12; Atlanta: Society of Biblical Literature, 2003) 28–31, 35.

35. ARM 26.438; ARM 26.449. See Heimpel, *Letters to the King of Mari*, 369, 372–74.

Semitic wisdom texts that may give evidence of greater interest and impact in their world.

Although it remains impossible to be certain regarding the extent of their influence, a good starting point for influential wisdom texts would be with those that recur. At least these suggest a wider usage and popularity, something impossible to deduce from texts that are attested only once. This can include excerpts that appear multiple times in longer accounts, such as the Ugaritic description of filial piety in the *Aqhat Legend* and the reference to multiple peoples in the disputed Ugaritic text *KTU* 1.40. It can also describe those texts for which we have multiple copies preserved in the West Semitic world, such as the *Dialogue of Shupe-ameli* and the *Wisdom of Ahiqar*.

Of course, this criterion does not guarantee that these texts must be distinctive to the West Semitic world or even widely known and used there. However, the fact that the texts do not generally appear elsewhere but that they do occur repeatedly within this cultural milieu is the best criteria I can find to suggest that such texts may represent authentic and widespread wisdom teachings. In an important way this approach parallels the concerns of L. Gregory Jones in the use of Bible reading, knowledge, and immersion in the formation of Christian character and identity.[36] Here as well, character ethics grows out of the repeated and widespread reading of particular texts.

3.1. Filial Piety in the Aqhat Epic

The *Aqhat Legend* from thirteenth-century Ugarit contains an account of the ideal son in relation to his father. This is repeated in four places in the epic.[37] It has been the object of numerous translations and studies.[38] The six poetic couplets describe the duties of the ideal son for

---

36. L. G. Jones, "Formed and Transformed by Scripture: Character, Community, and Authority in Biblical Interpretation," in *Character and Scripture*, 18–33.

37. *KTU* 1.17.I.27–34, I.45–49, II.1–8, and II.16–23 (see *ANET* 150; *COS* 1:343–45).

38. See for example: Y. Avishur, "The 'Duties of the Son' in the 'Story of Aqhat' and Ezekiel's Prophecy on Idolatry (Ch. 8)," *UF* 17 (1985) 49–60; M. J. Boda, "Ideal Sonship in Ugarit," *UF* 25 (1993) 9–24; J. C. de Moor, "The Ancestral Cult in KTU 1.17:I.26–28," *UF* 17 (1985) 407–9; J. F. Healey, "The Pietas of an Ideal Son in Ugarit," *UF* 11 (1979) 353–56; J.-M. Husser, "Culte des ancêtres ou rites funéraires? A propos du 'Catalogue' des devoirs du fils (KTU 1.17:I–II)," *UF* 27 (1995): 115–27; O. Loretz, "Heimführung des betrunkenen Greises/Vaters nach KTU 1.17 I 30–31," *UF* 38 (2006; published 2007) 437–43; D. Pardee, "The 'Aqhatu Legend (1.103)," in *COS* 1:343–58; S. B. Parker, "Aqhat," in *Ugaritic Narrative Poetry* (ed. S. B. Parker; SBLWAW 9; Atlanta: Scholars Press, 1997) 49–80; M. S. Smith, "A Potpourri of Popery," *UF* 30 (1998) 645–64, especially p. 659; N. Wyatt, "The Story of Aqhat," in *Religious Texts from Ugarit: The Words of Ilimilku and His Colleagues* (The Biblical Seminar 53; Sheffield: Sheffield Academic Press, 1998) 246–312.

which the main character Dan'ilu longs. Three of the couplets address filial responsibilities honoring the dead father or the ancestral deity and providing offerings in the temples of Baal and El. The other three do not explicitly mention religious matters. While some see these couplets as also connected with religious or ceremonial matters, such as celebrating at a marzeach[39] or maintaining sanctuary roofs for sacrifices, others find here simply normal duties for respecting and maintaining one's male parent.[40] No matter which approach is accepted, the descriptions characterize values that reflect the society's attitude toward the family.

The first such couplet describes the son who shuts the jaws of those who slander his father and drives away any who try to grumble against him. The theme is defending the father's honor in social contexts where the father may be mocked or derided.

A second couplet describes the son who takes the hand of his drunken father, or even carries him when he has had too much wine. These actions would ensure that the father is not left to fend for himself when he is drunken and liable to make a fool of himself.

The third such couplet is the last one in the collection. It describes the son who makes certain that his father's roof is in good repair against the rain and who keeps his father's garments clean. Like the other two couplets this one can also be understood to promote the honor of the father so that he is not ashamed in public or when entertaining in his home (or even when sacrificing, if that is an implication here). The couplets address a variety of threats to the family honor from enemies, from lack of one's own self control, and from the deterioration of home and clothing through the natural elements. As has been noted by Knut Heim in his study of proverb collections in the Hebrew Bible, one may consider whether these couplets are all related to a common theme.[41] That theme would seem to be the common concern for preserving the respect and honor of the family in the society. Because none of these couplets assume a particular class or level of wealth or influence, they may reach across all social strata. As with other ancient Near Eastern wisdom and

---

39. A widely known cultic "celebration" of the ancient Near East that was associated with elite groups. It included several days of feasting and was sometimes connected with funerary rites (Jer 16:5, Amos 6:7). See R. S. Hess, *Israelite Religions: An Archaeological and Biblical Survey* (Grand Rapids: Baker, 2007) 110–11, 262–63, 292–93.

40. For the former, see O. Eissfeldt, "Sohnespflichten im Alten Orient," *Syria* 43 (1966) 49–67; Boda, "Ideal Sonship in Ugarit"; Wyatt, *Religious Texts from Ugarit*, 258–59. For the latter, see Pardee, "The 'Aqhatu Legend (1.103)," 344.

41. K. M. Heim, *Like Grapes of Gold Set in Silver: An Interpretation of Proverbial Clusters in Proverbs 10:1–22:16* (BZAW 273; Berlin: Walter de Gruyter, 2001).

proverbs, these couplets emphasize action and deeds rather than reflection and philosophy.

3.2. KTU 1.40 and the List of Foreign Peoples

There is much debate about the nature of this liturgical Ugaritic text. Many have seen it as a liturgy for atonement, corresponding to the Day of Atonement in Leviticus 16.[42] However, Dennis Pardee has found here a ritual for national unity.[43] The text occurs in *KTU* 1.84 as well. It also appears in four other fragments widely dispersed among the places where texts have been found at Ugarit.[44]

Pardee rightly questions the nature of the text as an atonement ritual. The customary Hebrew root for atonement, *k-p-r*, does not occur. However, the word for sin *ḫ-ṭ-ʾ*, does appear. Seven people groups are mentioned, along with those who are oppressed and impoverished. Some sort of concern is expressed for these groups, either in terms of excluding them from the rituals, as de Moor and Sanders maintain, or in terms of somehow including them in the societal rites. Given the cosmopolitan nature of the city of Ugarit, it would seem that de Tarragon was correct to identify the rites with some sort of positive appreciation of these people.[45] The ritual is best seen as one expressing a desire for unity among all the peoples in a proper relationship before the divine. Further, sins such as theft, oppression, murder, impatience, and quarreling are listed after each of the multiple appearances of this list of peoples. These suggest the values of a society concerned to incorporate other peoples and to act with a sense of fairness, using the repeated term, *mšr*.

---

42. See for example, J. C. de Moor and P. Sanders, "An Ugaritic Expiation Ritual and Its Old Testament Parallels," *UF* 23 (1991) 283–300; G. del Olmo Lete, *Canaanite Religion: According to the Liturgical Texts of Ugarit* (trans. W. G. E. Watson; Bethesda: CDL, 1999) 144–65.

43. D. Pardee, *Ritual and Cult at Ugarit* (ed. T. J. Lewis; SBLWAW 10; Atlanta: Society of Biblical Literature, 2002) 77–83. See also N. Wyatt, "KTU 1.40: A Liturgy for a Rite of Atonement for the People of Ugarit," in *Religious Texts from Ugarit: The Words of Ilimilku and His Colleagues* (The Biblical Seminar 53; Sheffield: Sheffield Academic Press, 1998) 343. Wyatt finds here a rite where the peoples list their grievances and the whole community seeks forgiveness for these.

44. The fragments are RS 24.270A, RS 24.270B, RS 24.650B, and RS 24.652G+K. See Pardee, *Ritual and Cult at Ugariat*, 77–78.

45. A. Caquot, J.-M. Tarragon, and J.-L. Cunchillos, *Textes Ougaritique. Tome II. Textes religieux et rituels. Correspondance* (LAPO 14; Paris: Cerf, 1989) 143.

3.3. Dialogue of Shupe-Ameli

Of all of these West Semitic examples of wisdom literature, one of the most interesting in terms of its ethical contents is the *Dialogue of Shupe-Ameli*. This text provides a rare example of an entire composition devoted to wisdom and yet distinctive to the West Semitic world. The text of Shupe-Ameli appears in two slightly variant Akkadian forms in tablets found at Emar and Ugarit.[46] However, this text is not attested in Mesopotamia.[47] A Hittite version has also been found at Tell Boghaz-köy, ancient Hattusas.[48] Collated editions of versions have been published since the 1990's and have provided further study of this unique text.[49]

The first and longest of the two parts represents the advice that the father gives to his son. These are standard proverbial instructions found elsewhere in cuneiform wisdom literature. Victor Hurowitz observes that several items lend support to the view that these sections

---

46. The relevant Akkadian texts from Ugarit were published first. See J. Nougayrol, "Sagesse," in *Ugaritica V* (ed. J. Nougayrol et al.; Mission de Ras Shamra 16; Paris: Impremerie Nationale, Librairie Orientaliste Paul Geuthner, 1968) 273–90, 436–37 (number 163; RS 22.439); D. E. Smith, "Wisdom Genres in RS 22.439," in *Ras Shamra Parallels: The Texts from Ugarit and the Hebrew Bible Vol. II* (ed. D. E. Smith and S. Rummel; AnOr 50; Rome: Pontifical Biblical Institute, 1975) 216–47; J. Khanjian, "Wisdom," in *Ras Shamra Parallels*, 372–400. For the Emar fragments, see D. Arnaud, *Emar VI. Tome 1: Textes sumériens et accadiens. Planches* (Rescherches au pays d'Aštata; Synthèse no. 18; Paris: Editions Recherche sur les Civilisations, 1985) 271–72; idem, *Emar VI. Tome 2: sumériens et accadiens. Planches* (Recherches au pays d'Aštata; Synthèse no. 18; Paris: Editions Recherche sur les Civilisations, 1985) 450–52; 583, 543; idem, "778. Sagesse syrienne," in *Emar VI/4: Textes de la bibliothèque: transcriptions et traductions* (Mission archéologique de Meskéné-Emar: Recherches au pays d'Aštata: Synthèse no. 28; Paris: Editions Recherche sur les Civilisations, 1987) 377–82 (Msk 74107aj, Msk 74177a, Msk 74197a = Msk 74177e, Msk 74233p, Msk 74233q, Msk 74233r).

47. Contra Sparks, *Ancient Texts for the Study of the Hebrew Bible*, 61, who suggests the presence of texts in Old Babylonian Nippur and in Neo-Assyrian Assur. It seems as though there has been a confusion with a different text, an originally Sumerian composition recounting early rulers as reported by W. G. Lambert, "Some New Babylonian Wisdom Literature," in *Wisdom in Ancient Israel* (ed. J. Day, R. P. Gordon, and H. G. M. Williamson; Cambridge: Cambridge University Press, 1995) 37–42.

48. G. Keydana, "Die hethitische Version," *UF* 23 (1991) 69–74.

49. M. Dietrich, "Der Dialog zwischen Šūpē-amēli und seinem 'Vater': Die Tradition babylonischer Weisheitssprüche im Westen," *UF* 23 (1991) 33–68; idem, "Babylonian Literary Texts from Western Libraries," in *Verse in Ancient Near Eastern Prose* (ed. J. C. de Moor and W. G. E. Watson; AOAT 42; Kevelaer: Butzon & Bercker; Neukirchen-Vluyn: Neukirchener, 1993) 41–67, especially pp. 52–62; St. Seminara, "Le Istruzioni di Šūpē-amēlī: Vecchio e nuovo a confronto nella 'sapienza' siriana del Tardo Bronzo," *UF* 32 (2000) 487–529; V. Avigdor Hurowitz, "The Wisdom of Šūpē–amēlī: A Deathbed Debate between a Father and Son," in *Wisdom Literature in Mesopotamia and Israel* (ed. R. J. Clifford; SBL Symposium Series 36; Atlanta: Society of Biblical Literature, 2007) 37–51.

describe standard wisdom fare: the repeated address, "my son"; the interest in daily life, economical thriftiness, and good behavior; and several sections that have close parallels with the Sumerian *Instructions of Shuruppak* and the Akkadian *Counsels of Wisdom*.[50] The father's counsel concludes with an exhortation that the son remain with his brother and assist in making the family property prosper.

The son, however, begins with an observation about the need to wander. He examines the nature of life in a manner different from the father. All property and success is subject to theft and the forces of nature in this life. If somehow one succeeds in holding on to what one has, one loses it all at death. Here is a negative critique of traditional wisdom and its attempt to guide others to success. Such an approach is infrequent in the comparative wisdom literature. Hurowitz compares it to the *Dialogue of Pessimism* and the biblical book of Qoheleth.[51]

There is an additional wisdom text containing some measure of pessimism, although the earliest version is Sumerian. It is found in four texts from the Old Babylonian period, at least some of which come from Nippur. There are several fragments of this wisdom material in Akkadian from Ugarit and Emar of the thirteenth century, as well as a related text from the library of Ashurbanipal. Lambert, who believes that all these texts are related to a common literary tradition, first brought them to the attention of biblical scholars in a 1995 article.[52] The textual tradition reviews legendary heroes of old and their great achievements. In the end, however, their achievements are vanity. One day of happiness is better that tens of thousands of years in the grave. The Emar and Ugarit texts locate happiness in the consumption of alcohol and repeat the theme that vanity (literally "wind") has always been present. Like the Old Babylonian *Gilgamesh Epic* and the *Adapa Myth*, which occurs at Amarna, there is a recognition that no mortal lives forever, but that all must die. The text mentioned here, however, carries this matter further by suggesting how transitory all that is associated with human life is and by seeing it as "wind" or vanity.

---

50. Hurowitz, "The Wisdom of Šūpê–amēlī," 42.

51. Ibid., 43–45.

52. This paragraph is a summary of Lambert, "Some New Babylonian Wisdom Literature," 37–42. The Ugarit and Emar texts, including both the fragments mentioned by Lambert and some additional ones (*Ugaritica* 5 numbers 164, 165, and 166; Emar VI.4 767), have been published in a text critical study by M. Dietrich, "'Ein Lebe ohne Freude . . .': Studie über eine Weisheitskomposition aus den Gelehrtenbibliotheken von Emar und Ugarit," *UF* 24 (1992) 9–29.

All this is implicit in the son's response in the Shupe-Ameli text, but it introduces an additional innovation in contrast to other contemporary wisdom texts. It juxtaposes a critical analysis of the traditional understanding of wisdom with an example of that traditional wisdom. The effect is to provide a direct challenge to traditional wisdom side by side with that wisdom. This appears here in the Late Bronze Age. It would not be attested again until the Hebrew Bible's juxtaposition of Proverbs with Qoheleth. Such a contrast of mainstream and reactionary wisdom provides a unique insight into a more sophisticated reflection on the entire wisdom enterprise than has been found elsewhere. In the scribal community at least, the discussion of ethics was not simply a list of proverbs. Instead, it asked questions about the ultimate meaning of life and challenged traditional understandings of observing accepted norms of conduct.

3.4. Wisdom of Ahiqar

The final example of wisdom literature moves us about eight centuries beyond the Bronze Age pieces that have been considered thus far. It departs from the Babylonian culture and language and turns to consider an early Aramaic text. Coming from a different time, culture, and language than the earlier texts, the *Wisdom of Ahiqar* provides an illustration of wisdom literature and its ethical outcomes in its own cultures. Jonas Greenfield's study of this work positions it within the wisdom tradition of the West Semitic world and its environment.[53]

The figure of Ahiqar may appear as a counselor to the Neo-Assyrian king, Esarhaddon, in a Late Babylonian tablet dated ca. 165 B.C.E. Whatever the historical reliability of this late document, Ahiqar was known in the Babylonian scribal tradition of the Hellenistic period. His name was associated with the Arameans. Nevertheless, the proverbs found in the Elephantine text, the book of Tobit, and the later versions have no parallels in the Akkadian wisdom compositions. The character of Ahiqar at Elephantine in the late fifth century has titles that associate him with Esarhaddon's father and predecessor, Sennacherib (705–681 B.C.E.). The narrative sections of the Elephantine material are assumed in the Ahiqar of Tobit and re-emerge with some differences in the later Syriac versions. They describe a wise sage who takes his nephew as an apprentice sage. The nephew turns on him and Ahiqar escapes with his

---

53. J. C. Greenfield, "The Wisdom of Ahiqar," in *Wisdom in Ancient Israel*, 43–52. A convenient edition of the proverbs can be found in J. M. Lindenberger, *The Aramaic Proverbs of Ahiqar* (Johns Hopkins Near Eastern Studies; Baltimore: Johns Hopkins University Press, 1983); cf. *ANET* 427–30.

life through earlier good deeds toward his appointed executioner and by means of his wisdom. The proverbs exemplify some of the wisdom taught by Ahiqar to his nephew.

The Syriac proverbs differ from those in the Aramaic collections. As Greenfield notes, the story of Ahiqar may form one of the few traditions from the pre-Christian heritage of Syriac culture to survive.[54] The Syriac materials form the basis for most of the later echoes of Ahiqar in the many cultures that this story and wisdom literature influenced. On the whole, the proverbs of Ahiqar reflect a traditional view of wisdom. Their distinctive form and content, and the differences between the Aramaic and Syriac versions, suggest the unique development of West Semitic wisdom literature in this period.

The proverbs advocate an ethic of humility, patience, honesty, and caution before a king. They also endorse other traditional virtues that compare with the character of Ahiqar in the narrative. Thus, while the specifics appear to belong to distinctive West Semitic traditions, the overall themes affirm the greater world of proverbial literature as found throughout the ancient Near East and in the Bible.

4. Conclusion

In conclusion, we may observe that West Semitic wisdom makes its own distinctive and special contributions to individual and social ethics, especially in its critique and reflection of the traditional sources of these ethics. However, it also stands within the broader traditions of Mesopotamian and biblical didactic literature. Overall, it suggests an ethic not so far removed from that of the surrounding cultures. If anything, evidence of exceptional brutality seems to appear earlier rather than later. The reflective traditions found in the wisdom literature move forward to incorporate traditional community ethics while developing their own distinctive contributions that include the evaluation and critique of existing forms. In light of this, attempts to generalize regarding "Canaanite ethics," whether positive or negative, are over-simplified and not productive of a more accurate and nuanced understanding of these cultures using the available literary sources native to or at least copied by these peoples.

In terms of the evaluation of the Canaanites in Deut 9:4–5, we find that the "wickedness" of the Canaanites, in terms of the moral failings from the ethical prescriptions of the Bible in general and of Deuteronomy in particular, is attested in the surrounding nations. Israel's avoid-

---

54. Ibid., 51.

ance of the worship of other gods and goddesses was the chief concern of Deuteronomy (6:4–9, 12:2–4, et passim). However, linked to this were acts of injustice in social, sexual, and other areas. The failings of the people associated with the land of Canaan provide the backdrop for the moral legislation found in chapters 12–26 of Deuteronomy.

This paper has sought to demonstrate that, much like other peoples of their own time and not unlike peoples of every age, the Canaanites were not uniformly wicked or righteous by any moral standard. The Bible attests that their wickedness reached a point that called for judgment when Israel appeared on the scene (Gen 15:16, Deut 9:4–5). Throughout their history, however, Canaanites included those with a higher level or morality as well as those similar to the ones described in Deuteronomy.

This provides us with two concluding observations. First, by considering the broader background of the people of Canaan and the morality revealed in their literature, we learn that these people were human, just like Israel and like us today. All people, living where and when they do, must make their own moral decisions. Together, these have an impact on the society in general and on the manner in which the God of the Bible views that nation.

Second, there is a point for Christians to consider. Because our own moral character and practice often appears very comparable to that of the Canaanites, we need to be challenged to see that the standard of covenant faithfulness in life and obedience to which God called his people in Deuteronomy remains in effect today. While all the specifics of the ceremonial and cultic laws may not apply, the moral principles that Jesus and the apostles of the New Testament reiterated call us to a higher standard than the world around us. Yet, like the Canaanites and the Israelites, we cannot live that standard on our own. For this reason, biblical texts such as Ephesians 1, 2, and 6, and Rom 12:1–2 and 13:14 exhort us to find that strength in the one whom God raised from the dead and in the power of the Holy Spirit that he has provided.

Admonitory Examples in Hittite and Biblical Legal Contexts

HARRY A. HOFFNER JR.

1. Introduction

Today's readers of the biblical books of Exodus, Numbers, and Deuteronomy may find it unusual to encounter such a mixture of legal formulation and anecdotal material in the same context. But students of the legal texts of the ancient Hittite kingdom will not find this combination occurring in original legal or judicial texts to be unusual.

As early as the beginning of the Hittite Old Kingdom, during the reign of king Ḫattušili I, several admonitory vignettes occur in the context of a royal edict, the *Political Testament of Ḫattušili I*.[1] In the reign of his successor Muršili I, a composition called the *Palace Chronicle* includes stories of royal officials who either were derelict in their duties toward the king[2] or defrauded him[3] and were suitably

---

Author's Note: It has been my great privilege to know Dan Block for the past twelve years, beginning with meeting him at a conference at Trinity Evangelical Divinity School in August 2001, when he was serving on the faculty of the Southern Baptist Seminary in Louisville, KY. But since he joined the faculty of Wheaton College Graduate School and the local church that I attend, I have come to know him on a much deeper level: not just as a superb biblical scholar, but also as a gifted preacher and a man committed to teaching the Church in many lands, including Europe, Africa, and Southeast Asia. I cannot imagine a person better suited to training young men and women for preaching and teaching the Scriptures than Dan Block. It is a great honor and pleasure for me to contribute to this volume in his honor.`

1. Edited in I. Klock-Fontanille, "Le testament politique de Ḫattušili Ier ou les conditions d'exercise de la royauté dans l'ancien royaume hittite," *Anatolia Antiqua* 4 (1996) 33–66; English translation by G. Beckman, "Bilingual Edict of Ḫattušili I" in *COS* 2.15: 79–81.

2. An unnamed baker (^{LÚ}NINDA.DÙ.DÙ) allowed a pebble (*paššila-*) to be embedded in the king's *tunink*-bread, for which he was burned to death (P. Dardano, *L'aneddoto e il racconto in età antico-hittita: La cosidetta 'cronaca di palazzo'* [Biblioteca di Ricerche Linguistiche e Filologiche 43; Rome: Il Calamo, 1997] 29).

3. A man named Pappa, who held the office of *uriyannis* (quartermaster?), charged with distributing food to the king's troops, siphoned off some of the supplies for his own profit. His offense did not threaten the king's royal person directly, as the baker's did (see

punished.[4] The descriptions of the punishments include graphic details—some humorous, some gory—that cater to the taste of the audience for the sensational. The stories in the *Palace Chronicle* were admonitory as well, since Muršili would certainly not have wished such incidents to be imitated by his guests and perpetrated against himself![5]

Further examples of admonitory stories embedded in legal compositions are found in texts originating in the late Old Kingdom and the early New Kingdom. Offenses against the gods and the king perpetrated by named individuals are described in an edict from the reign of King Telipinu. And a treaty document from the early New Kingdom includes a vivid example of improper conduct by a vassal that affected the king's sister. (For these examples, see below.)

In what follows I propose to present and interpret several of these admonitory examples, to show how they functioned within the judicial and diplomatic spheres of the Hittite state, and to compare them with similar examples from the canonical form of the Exodus–Deuteronomy corpus. By so doing it is my hope to convince readers that the author of the biblical material was following a contemporary procedure in inserting brief accounts of defiance against Yahweh and his designated human leaders.

I shall focus upon examples cited in Hittite legal materials that are negative and admonitory. This is not to deny that other types of an-

---

previous note), so when he was caught, they only made him drink salt water and broke a clay vessel over his head (Dardano, *L'aneddoto*, 31).

4. Some have claimed that the *Palace Chronicle* was composed to describe a royal banquet during which the guests were entertained by contexts. For a detailed defense of this interpretation, citing relevant supporting evidence from earlier authors, see A. Gilan, "Bread, Wine and Partridges—A Note on the Palace Anecdotes (*CTH* 8)," in *Tabularia Hethaeorum: Hethitologische Beiträge Silvin Kosak zum 65. Geburtstag* (ed. D. Groddek and M. Zorman; Dresdener Beiträge zur Hethitologie 25; Wiesbaden: Harrassowitz, 2007). *CTH* = E. Laroche, *Catalogue des textes hittites: Études et Commentaires* (Paris: Klincksieck, 1971).

5. As noted by Gilan, I once thought that this composition, the so-called *Palace Chronicle* (*CTH* 8), contained a loose collection of anecdotes detailing misdemeanors by royal officials, items of which could then be inserted in legal texts as illustrative examples. But if so, in their present state none of these is accompanied by any warning drawn from the event. Perhaps the warning could be added once one of these was actually inserted in a legal text, but to date we have no actual evidence of one of these recurring in another text. And the presence in the *Palace Chronicle* text of other events such as the archery contest and the banquet scene is difficult to reconcile with such a narrow purpose. I would therefore accept Gilan's interpretation with some reservations, leaving open the possibility that even when used for purpose of "entertainment" the stories of malfeasance could also have served as warnings to the audience.

ecdotes are occasionally inserted in Hittite legal documents. A good example is paragraph §55 in the Old Hittite law collection,[6] where a group of individuals called "men owing ILKU (= Hittite *šaḫḫan*) duties" make an appeal to an unnamed king—who is identified as the predecessor ("father") of the currently reigning one—for exemption from these obligations. Their request was that work currently being done in fulfillment of that obligation might instead earn them wages. The appeal was refused, the king making a personal appearance before the assembly (Hittite *tuliya-*) of nobles to announce his ruling. The appealing delegation was given this ruling: "You too must perform (the *šaḫḫan* services) just like your colleagues (that is, others currently under this obligation)." No special exemption was to be given them. The brief account is inserted in the law collection at an appropriate point, in the immediate context of laws dealing with what classes of people were required to render *luzzi-* or *šaḫḫan*-services (see laws §§46–56).

The example of law §55 comes immediately after a paragraph (§54) in which a record is given of eleven groups, some identified by specific regions, who were exempt from rendering either *luzzi-* or *šaḫḫan*-services. It offered a natural point at which to introduce the historical case of another group that the king denied such an exemption. The inclusion of this story makes it clear that the king alone possessed the final power to grant exemptions,[7] and that it was by no means guaranteed that he would do so on insubstantial grounds, such as the claim of the petitioners, "no one pays us a wage." Similar appeals are known from epistolary texts, where the king's officials in outlying provinces acted to arbitrate whether or not individuals belonging to certain social classes were being defrauded by local officials when they held them liable for *šaḫḫan*.[8]

---

6. Edition in H. A. Hoffner Jr., *The Laws of the Hittites: A Critical Edition* (Documenta et Monumenta Orientis Antiqui 23; Leiden: Brill, 1997) 66–68; English translation in COS 2.19: 112.

7. In examples such as the one cited in the next note, provincial magistrates like Ḫimmuili were authorized to make preliminary rulings on the king's behalf, but these were subject to royal review and could be overruled, as we see from Ḫattušili's letter to Ḫimmuili.

8. See the letter from the scribe Tarḫunmiya to Ḫimmuili, who is his superior residing in Tapikka (modern Maşat Höyük), requesting a ruling against local officials there who claim that he owes *šaḫḫan* and *luzzi* on his estate located in the Tapikka province: in H. A. Hoffner Jr., *Letters From the Hittite Kingdom* (SBL Writings From the Ancient World 15; Atlanta: Society of Biblical Literature, 2009) 194–96, esp. 195, lines 19–39. Tarḫunmiya urges Ḫimmuili to investigate the records and see that he has never before been subject to these obligations. In another letter sent to this same Ḫimmuili by Ḫattušili, a royal scribe in the king's own service, Ḫattušili admonishes him for not settling the grievance

Since this example does not serve as admonitory in quite the same way as the other examples to be discussed below, I keep it separate. But it shares one important aspect with both the other Hittite examples, and some of the biblical ones: it is inserted in the midst of a series of laws that might otherwise be considered judicial rhetoric, never actually practiced. By inserting at an appropriate point an example of a historical occasion where appeal from this obligation was requested, the compiler of the laws seeks to show that these laws actually operated in Hittite society. They were not simply a scribal exercise.[9]

Another group of examples that I keep separate are the anonymous ones contained in the Aesopian parables found in the Hurro-Hittite bilingual *The Song of Release*.[10] These consist of stories of animals and inanimate objects that are then interpreted in human counter-types. From §17 it would appear that three Hittite terms described such parables: *uttar* 'tale/story', *ḫatreššar* 'instructions/advice', and *ḫattatar* 'instructive example' (lit., 'wisdom/wise plan'). Here is a typical example taken from §§18–19:

> A dog ran off with a *kugulla*-bread from in front of an oven. He pulled it out of the oven and dropped it in oil.[11] In oil he dropped it and sitting down began to eat it. This is not a dog, but a human being:[12] (he) whom his lord makes the lord of an administrative unit. He took more tribute (than allowed) behind (the back of) that city. He became arrogant. He no longer looks after the city. (The citizens) managed to inform on him to his lord (that is, to the king). Then he began to pour out before his lord those items of tribute which he was continually swallowing.[13]

Since examples of this type do not involve actually named persons, they are unlikely to represent the same type of admonitory examples

---

of Tarḫunmiya, and reminding him that scribes should be exempt from *šaḫḫan* and *luzzi* obligations; see Hoffner, *Letters*, 190–94, esp. lines 10–17.

9. In many discussions that I had in the years 1969–1974 with my late Yale colleague, Professor J. J. Finkelstein, he firmly maintained that all of the Mesopotamian law codes were merely scribal exercises. It is well known that the code of Ḫammurapi is never invoked in Old Babylonian legal documents, and it is doubtful if judges in the local courts endeavored to follow it in their rulings. It is my view, however, that the Hittite laws did represent the traditions that would have been followed in local courts, and the citation here of a particular case of appealing to the king for an exemption seems to support that theory.

10. Translated in H. A. Hoffner Jr., *Hittite Myths* (2nd rev. ed.; Writings from the Ancient World 2; Atlanta: Scholars, 1998) 68–72.

11. To make it more tasty.

12. That is, the dog represents a type of person.

13. The fact that in this and the following parable the person must finally disgorge all his ill-gotten gains suggests that in the two animal stories it is implied that the animals vomited up what they had devoured.

as I discuss in the coming pages. And they do not occur in the context of a legal text, although the tone of the passages is clearly ethical and admonitory. Furthermore, although the contents of *The Song of Release* may have been known by a wide circle of court officials through the accompanying Hittite translation, the text is—after all—translated *foreign* literature, not a native Hittite historical or administrative text.

2. Hittite Examples

2.1. Old Hittite: The Proclamation of King Telipinu

Admonitions typically addressed matters related to the authority and well-being of the king's person. The most obvious aspect of the king's physical well-being is his very life. Therefore, although the Hittite term used in the *Telipinu Proclamation* to describe these crimes (*ešḫar* literally 'blood/bloodshed') can refer more broadly to any murder, in this document the particular incidents so denominated were regicide.[14]

The *Telipinu Proclamation* (*CTH* 19), which for many years was the primary source for reconstructing the history of the Hittite Old Kingdom,[15] was re-edited in 1984 and exists today in several recent translations.[16] The structure of the document is that of a royal edict. But like the much later Apology of Ḫattušili III, the introductory historical prologue is so long as to give the impression that one is dealing with a straightforward historical narrative. In its tone and intent it also partakes of the character of what might be called a political apology—again, resembling the later Apology of Ḫattušili III.[17]

---

14. Regicide is the deliberate killing of a monarch.
15. R. S. Hardy, "The Old Hittite Kingdom," *AJSL* 58 (1941) 177–216.
16. I. Hoffmann, *Der Erlaß Telipinus* (Texte der Hethiter 11; Heidelberg: Carl Winter, 1984). For translations, see H. M. Kümmel, "Der Thronfolgeerlaß des Telipinu," in *Rechtsbücher* (ed. R. Borger; Texte aus der Umwelt des Alten Testaments 1; Gütersloh: Gerd Mohn, 1982) (German); van den Hout in *COS* 1.76: 194–98 (English); Goedegebuure in M. W. Chavalas, ed., *The Ancient Near East: Historical Sources in Translation* (Blackwell Sourcebooks in Ancient History; Malden, MA: Blackwell, 2006) 222–28 (English); and A. Bernabé and J. A. Álvarez-Pedrosa, *Historia y Leyes de los Hititas. Textos del Imperio Antiguo. El Código* (AKAL/Oriente 3; Madrid: Akal, 2000) 154–61 (Spanish). For thorough coverage of secondary literature on the Telipinu Proclamation (*CTH* 19), see the constantly updated database of the Hethitologie Portal at http://www.hethport.uni-wuerzburg.de/hetkonk/hetkonk_abfrage.php. A brief summary is in K. L. Sparks, *Ancient Texts for the Study of the Hebrew Bible: A Guide to the Background Literature* (Peabody, MA: Hendrickson, 2005) 392–93 (who, however, misspells the royal name Ḫuzziya as 'Hazziya').
17. On the relationship of these two texts and their apologetic nature, see H. A. Hoffner Jr., "Propaganda and Political Justification in Hittite Historiography," in *Unity and Diversity: Essays in the History, Literature, and Religion of the Ancient Near East* (ed. H. Goedicke and J. J. M. Roberts; Baltimore: Johns Hopkins University Press, 1975).

In this text—with the exception of the unnamed "princes' servants" of §7 (i 21–23)—the culpable figures are usurpers, men who killed incumbent kings and took their places. In each case—Ḫantili I, Zidanta I, Ammuna, and Ḫuzziya I—they were guilty of murdering either their own royal predecessor or his sons. Since they themselves became reigning kings, and thus could not receive punishment from the king, they received it from the gods in the form of crop failures and defeat on the battlefield (§§13, 20–21).

Regicide should have been tried and punished in the highest court of the land, where the judges were the assembly of nobles called the *pankuš* (translated 'Council' in §30 by van den Hout, 'assembly' by Goedegebuure).[18] But because the members of this assembly failed in their duty to hold the royal culprits accountable to the laws, the gods punished the royal culprits themselves and with them also the entire kingdom. The lesson drawn and warning given in this text is that in the future the assembly of nobles must perform that duty (§§30–33) and thus avoid evil consequences upon the entire kingdom, themselves included.

- §30 (2:46–49) Furthermore, whoever becomes king and seeks evil for (his) brother (or) sister, you too are his council and tell him straight: "This (is) a matter of blood." Look at the tablet (that says): "Formerly, blood(shed) became excessive in Ḫattuša, and the gods took it out on the royal family."
- §31 (2:50–58) If anyone does evil amongst both (his) brothers and sisters and lays eyes on the king's head, summon the assembly and, if h[i]s

---

18. On the meaning of the term noun *panku-* (which is derived from an adjective meaning 'entire'), see *CHD* P: 90–92 sub *panku-* B, mng. 3 "the totality of the king's retinue as an advisory and admonitory body." For its role and functions, see H. G. Güterbock, *Authority and Law in the Hittite Kingdom*, Journal of the American Oriental Society Suppl. 17 (1954) 20; A. Goetze, *Kleinasien* (2nd rev. ed.; Handbuch der Altertumswissenschaft. Kulturgeschichte des Alten Orients; München: C. H. Beck, 1957) 86–87; G. M. Beckman, "The Hittite Assembly," *JAOS* 102 (1982) 435–42; C. Mora, "Il ruolo politico-sociale de *pankus* e *tuliyas*: Revisione di un probleme," in *Studi Orientalistici in ricordo di Franco Pintore* (ed. Onofrio Carruba et al.; Pavia: GJES Edizioni, 1983); M. Marazzi, "Überlegungen zur Bedeutung von *pankuš* in der hethitisch-akkadischen Bilinguis Ḫatušilis I," *WO* 15 (1984) 96–102; P. H. J. Houwink ten Cate, "De Hethitische wettenverzameling," *Phoenix* 33 (1987) 50–59; F. Imparati, "Autorità centrale e istitutioni collegiali nel regno ittita," in *Esercizio del potere e prassi della consultazione* (ed. A. Ciani and G. Diurni; «Utrumque Ius» Collectio Pontificiae Universitatis Lateranensis 21; Rome: Libreria Editrice Lateranense, 1991; reprint, Eothen 12(1) 369–88); T. R. Bryce, *The Kingdom of the Hittites* (Oxford: Clarendon, 1998) 116–18; and idem, *Life and Society in the Hittite World* (Oxford: Oxford University Press, 2002), 23–24. *CHD = The Hittite Dictionary of the Oriental Institute of the University of Chicago* (ed. H. G. Guterbock, H. A. Hoffner, and T. P. J. van den Hout; Chicago: The Oriental Institute of the University of Chicago 1989–).

testimony is dismissed, he shall pay with his head. They shall not kill secretly, however, like Zuruwa, Tanuwa, Taḫurwaili, and Taruḫšu. They shall not commit evil against his house, his wife (and) his children. So, if a prince sins, he shall pay with (his) own head, while they shall not commit evil against his house and his children. For the reason for which princes usually die (does) not (affect) their houses, their fields, their vineyards, their male (and) female servants, their oxen (and) their sheep.

- §32 (2:59–65) So now, if some prince sins, he shall pay with (his) own head while you shall not commit evil against his house and his son. Giving (away) even a princes' blade of straw (or) a chip of wood is not right. Those who commit these evil deeds, the [Chiefs of Staff(?)], (that is,) the Major-Domos, the Chief of the Palace Attendants, the Chief of the Royal Bodyguard, and the Chief-of-the-Wine, [if?] they want to take a prince's houses and say thus: "I wish that city to be mine," then he commits evil against the city lord.
- §33 (2:66–73) But now, from this day onwards in Ḫattuša you, palace attendants, royal bodyguards, golden-chariot fighters, cupbearers, waiters, cooks, staff bearers, grooms, commanders of a [field] bat[talion], remember this word. Let Tanuwa, Taḫurwaili, and Taruḫšu be a warning to you! If someone commits evil again, either the Major Domo, the Chief of the palace attendants or the Chief of the Royal Bodyguard or the Chief of commanders of a field battalion—whether a lower (or) higher ranking one—you too, Council, seize (him) and devour him with your teeth![19]

And because homicide is the dominant crime of the named kings, at the very end of the text, in what would otherwise seem an irrelevant matter, the author rehearses the judicial procedure in cases of the murder of any free citizen (§49 iv 27–29).

In this instance, therefore, we have a literary composition of legal character, which is illustrated by examples of individual usurpers who committed the offense of *ešḫar* (murder, especially regicide) and received punishment at the hands of the gods. Divine punishment would not have resulted from failure to punish the murders of ordinary citizens. Rather, what called forth divine wrath was the failure of the Hittite *pankuš* to punish the killing of the kings whose line the gods had ordained to rule in Hattusa.

The Hittite terminology differs from the ancient Israelite, but the concept of the sanctity of the royal person is inherent in David's refusal to take Saul's life when Saul was seeking to kill him, and on several occasions he could have done so (1 Sam 24:6, 10; 26:9, 11, 16, 23; see 2 Sam 1:14, 16). In particular, Telipinu's action in removing Ḫuzziya from the

---

19. Translation taken from van den Hout in *COS* 1.76: 194–98.

kingship but refusing to execute him[20] is only a variation on David's behavior. David not only refused to take Saul's life, but he also refused to remove him from the kingship by force, leaving the matter in the hands of Yahweh himself.

2.2. New Hittite Instructions Texts [21]

In New Hittite texts regulating the duties of the king's servants, generally the commands are given to groups as a whole ("you kitchen personnel," "you shoemakers who make the king's shoes," "you leatherworkers who make the chariots on which the king rides," "you water-carriers [of the king]"). But one also finds specific named individuals whose offenses are described as warnings.

In the text titled *Instructions for Palace Personnel* (CTH 265[22]), for example, we read of the case of a water-carrier by the name of Zuliya, who did not properly filter the water in the container designated for the king to drink from. When a hair was found in that water, since Zuliya was the supervisor (*parā uwanza*) of that water supply,[23] he was required to undergo an ordeal to determine if the presence of the hair was due to his own negligence.[24] The ordeal yielded one of two possible verdicts: *parkuiš* 'pure' (meaning 'innocent'), and *papranza* 'impure' (meaning 'guilty'). When the ordeal showed him to be *papranza*, he was executed. The record of his execution is immediately followed in the text by an explicit warning: "You water-carriers (for the king) be

---

20. §§22–23: "Now, Ḫuzziya became king, and Telipinu had Ištapariya, his (that is, Ḫuzziya's) eldest sister <as his wife>. When Ḫuzziya wanted to kill them, the matter came to light and Telipinu banished them (that is, Ḫuzziya and his brothers). Five (were) his (that is, Ḫuzziya's) brothers and he assigned houses to them (saying): 'Let them go (and) live! Let them each eat (and) drink! May nobody do harm to them! And I declare: They did evil to me, but I [will not do] evil to them.'" (My translation, which differs only slightly from that in *COS*.) Ḫuzziya's apparent motive was to avoid having Telipinu replace him, using the marriage to his sister as a legal basis.

21. On this class of texts from a biblicist's point of view, see Sparks, *Ancient Texts*, 77–78. For an outline of the content of this particular text, see ibid., 209–10.

22. Edited in J. Friedrich, "Reinheitsvorschriften für den hethitischen König," in *Altorientalische Studien Bruno Meissner zum 60. Geburtstag gewidmet von Freunden, Kollegen und Schülern* (Mitteilungen der Altorientalischen Gesellschaft 4; Leipzig: Harrassowitz, 1928); and translated in *ANET* 207; M. Vieyra, "Les textes hittites," in *Les religions du Proche-Orient asiatique* (ed. R. Labat et al.; Paris: Fayard/Denoel, 1970), 560. The genre and characteristics of this text are explored in F. P. Daddi, "Die mittelhethitischen *išḫiul*-Texte," *AoF* 32 (2004) 280–90; "Palace Servants and Their Obligations," *Or* 73 (2004) 451–68.

23. The *ANET* (207) translation, "then Arnilis (said): 'Zuliyas was careless/negligent'," is incorrect. What Arnili actually said was "Zuliyas was the supervisor (of the water supply)" (*parā uwanza*; see *CHD* P: 142–43). This is why the ordeal became necessary. Guilt was only suspect, not yet established.

24. When told that Zuliya was in charge of the water, the king ordered: *Zuliyaš-wa ḫapā paiddu*, "Zuliya must go to the river (ordeal)!"

careful (lit., 'afraid') about the water! Always strain the water through a filter! [Remove] the impurity of the water!"[25]

The presence of this clear deduction and warning proves that the story was told to keep future recurrences from happening. So even if Gilan's theory about the *Palace Chronicle* should prove correct, that those anecdotes were dramatizations to entertain and to glorify the king and were not admonitory examples, this text shows that admonitions given to groups of royal officials in general were regularly accompanied by specific instances involving known persons and followed by a specific warning. Whether Zuliya's failure was due to carelessness or was deliberate, the penalty would have been the same, since the purity of the king's sacred person had been put at risk.

The parallel with the offense of Nadab and Abihu in Leviticus 10 is striking, since it was the holiness of Yahweh that was violated by the offering of incense on alien coals. Because that holiness was put in jeopardy by their act, it made no difference whether or not the act was deliberate defiance or oversight. The protection of Yahweh's holiness and of the Hittite king's purity were equally serious matters. So both cases of infraction are related in the context of a legal description of the duties of the relevant officials.

But equally relevant are the measures described in Deut 23:10–14 to prevent impurity inside the wilderness encampment, "Because Yahweh your God travels along with your camp, to save you and to hand over your enemies to you, therefore your camp must be holy, so that he may not see anything indecent among you and turn away from you" (Deut 23:14, NRSV adapted). Yahweh is the true King of Israel, and his purity exceeds that of his people, as the purity of the Hittite king exceeded that of his subjects. In both cases the purity of the ruler must not be violated, and those who do will be severely punished.

2.3. New Hittite Treaties

What was true of texts used to instruct and admonish royal officials in the service of the king was also true of state treaties with foreign vassal kings. A parade example is found in the treaty of Šuppiluliuma I with Ḫukkana of Ḫayaša (*CTH* 42).[26] Three quarters of the way through

---

25. *KUB* 13.3 iii 36–39.

26. *CTH* 42, edited in J. Friedrich, *Staatsverträge des Ḫatti-Reiches in hethitischer Sprache. 2. Teil.* (Mitteilungen der Vorderasiatisch-Aegyptischen Gesellschaft 34/1; Leipzig: J. C. Hinrichs'sche Buchhandlung, 1930) 103–63; translated into English in G. M. Beckman, *Hittite Diplomatic Texts* (Writings from the Ancient World 7; Atlanta: Scholars, 1996) 22–30; translated into Spanish in A. Bernabé and J. A. Álvarez-Pedrosa, *Historia y Leyes de los Hititas. Textos del Reino Medio y del Imperio Nuevo* (AKAL/Oriente 8; Madrid: Akal, 2004) 74–80; translated into German in J. Klinger, "Der Vertrag Šuppiluliumas I. von

the treaty, after most of the usual general issues have been dealt with—historical prologue (§1), exclusive allegiance to the Hittite suzerain (§2), divine witnesses to the treaty (§7–8), curse for disobedience (§9–10), blessing for loyalty (§11), military cooperation (§12–14), guarding against revolts (§15–22), confidentiality with the suzerain (§23–24)—the Hittite overlord turns to a sensitive and extremely important issue that one would not expect to be included in a state treaty, namely the sexual conduct of the vassal king (§§25–28). Why was this included? Because the vassal king in question was married to the Hittite king's sister, and because—unlike in more "civilized" vassal kingdoms in Western Anatolia and in North Syria—Ḫukkana's people, the Ḫayaša, had strange sexual mores, which the Hittite king found to be 'barbaric' (*dampupi*, see §25). This meant that Šuppiluliuma's sister might easily be involved in certain sexual behavior, which according to Hittite law was not only repugnant but worthy of the death penalty. (The Hittite laws term such inherently indecent sexual behavior *ḫurkel*.) For these reasons, the treaty had to include strict warnings to Ḫukkana against what the Hittite ruler considered loose sexual morals.

In addition to its use in describing persons 'unskilled' or 'untaught' in crafts,[27] the term *dampupi-* also can mean 'lay' or 'profane', serving as the antonym of 'consecrated, holy' (*šuppi-*) or 'priestly'.[28] Its use to describe Ḫukkana's people might therefore be seen as terming them outsiders, not chosen by the gods of the Hittites, not 'consecrated', and therefore not held to the same high standards of conduct. If so, this parallels the description of practices common among the Canaanites, but proscribed to Israel, a common theme in Deuteronomy (12:2–4, 29–32; 14:1–2; 18:9–14). A passage like Deut 14:1–2 is a noteworthy example of

---

Ḫatti mit Ḫukkana von Ḫayaša," in *Texte der Umwelt des Alten Testaments, Neue Folge 2: Staatsverträge, Herrscherinschriften und andere Dokumente zur politischen Geschichte* (ed. B. Janowski and G. Wilhelm; Gütersloh: Gütersloher Verlagshaus, 2005). Other aspects of the text are treated in H. Otten, "Sororat im Alten Kleinasien?" *Saeculum* 21 (1970) 162–65; A. Altman, "The 'Deliverance Motif' in the 'Historical Prologues' of Suppiluliuma I's Vassal-treaties," in *Confrontation and Co-existence* (ed. P. Artzi; Bar-Ilan Studies in History 2; Ramat-Gan: Bar-Ilan University, 1984); O. Carruba, "Die Hajasa-Verträge Hattis," in *Documentum Asiae Minoris Antiquae: Festschrift für Heinrich Otten zum 75. Geburtstag* (ed. E. Neu and C. Rüster; Documentum Asiae Minoris Antiquae: Festschrift für Heinrich Otten zum 75. Geburtstag; Wiesbaden: Harrassowitz, 1988).

27. Hittite laws §§147, 177; translation in *COS* 2.19: 114–19.

28. In an oracle text inquiring the cause of divine anger, a reason given was that "an unconsecrated person (*dampupiš*) entered the (holy) house of the god" (*KUB* 5.7 obv 46); a cult ritual states: "into the inner sanctum with the god Išḫara and ... no *dampupiš* person shall go" (*KUB* 40.2 obv 17–18), and still another cult text instructs: "The *dampupieš* persons may eat up [the ...], ... but the consecrated meat (*šuppa*) they do not give (to them)" (*KBo* 3.63 ii: 2–6).

prohibiting conduct on the basis of differentiation from other peoples not chosen by God, not "children of Yahweh your God," and not taught by God, as Israel was. The Hittites were not alone in using such terms to describe foreigners who did not enjoy insider status: in the Old Assyrian texts the Assyrian merchants called the native Anatolians *nuwā"ū*, the very same word which in Akkadian-Hittite bilinguals is translated by *dampupi-* (*CAD* N 356–57). What might be acceptable behavior for outsiders is unacceptable among the chosen people. Ḫukkana was born among the Kaška outsiders, but had married into Šuppiluliuma's people, and the royal family to boot. He could not bring the customs of his former life in with him.

After warning Ḫukkana not to have sex with women other than his Hittite wife, Šuppiluliuma decided to cite a known case to warn Ḫukkana. He wrote (§28): "Who was Mariya? And for what reason was he put to death? Didn't a lady's maid walk by and he give her the once-over? But my royal father himself looked out the window and caught him in his offense, saying, 'You—why did you give her the once-over?' And so he lost his life for that reason. The man died just for looking from a distance. So you beware!" We smile at the extreme strictness of this prohibition not even to look. But the point is clear: Šuppiluliuma reinforced a demand for sexual fidelity not only by putting it into a treaty, a document whose content had to be affirmed by oath before the gods, but also by a striking story of a real offender.

2.4. *The Rationale for Selecting the Offenses to Exemplify*

None of the persons cited in the legal texts that were punished for various offenses were guilty of offenses against their fellow subjects: homicide, personal injury, adultery, theft, property damage, etc. It appears that the criterion governing the selection was that the offense had to be against the person of the king or against his authority. This was because the Hittite king was deputized by the chief god of the pantheon, the storm god, to rule in his place. Hittite kings may not have been considered divine during their lifetimes, as were the kings in Egypt, but they exercised some of the same prerogatives as the storm god.[29]

A classic passage from the Hittite archives summarizes this role:[30]

---

29. For the issue of whether or not the Hittite king was considered divine during his lifetime, see H. A. Hoffner Jr., "The Royal Cult in Hatti," *Text, Artifact, and Image: Revealing Ancient Israelite Religion* 346 (2006) 132–51.
30. H. Bozkurt, M. Çığ, and H. G. Güterbock, eds., *Istanbul Arkeoloji Müzelerinde bulunan Boğazköy Tabletlerinden Seçme Metinler* (Istanbul: Maarif Matbaası, 1944) = *IBoT* 1.30: 1–8 (NS); see Goetze, *Kleinasien*, 88, and Güterbock, *Authority and Law in the Hittite Kingdom*, 16.

> When(ever) the king worships the gods, the $GUDU_{12}$-priest recites this: May the *tabarna* king be dear to the gods. The land belongs to the storm god alone. Sky and earth and the people belong to the storm god alone. He (the Stormgod) made the *tabarna* king his governor.[31] He gave him the whole land of Ḫattuša. May the Labarna continue governing the whole land with his hand. May the Stormgod destroy the one who violates[32] the person[33] or the borders of the Labarna, [the king].

According to this text, recited every time the king worshiped, just as the land and its people belonged exclusively to the storm god—that is, not also to the other deities—so the storm god's authority over land and people belonged exclusively to the king, and to no other person in the realm. The king's status was unique in Hittite society. His person (literally, 'body') was sacred. Violations of the royal body included, of course, assassinations such as are described in the *Telipinu Proclamation* (see section 2.1), but also the violation of the king's purity such as were involved in the offense of the baker described in the *Palace Chronicle* (see section 1, n. 2) and that of the water carrier Zuliya (see section 2.2). Violations of the king's "borders" (*irḫa-*) included not only the geographical boundaries of his kingdom but also the areas of his authority, the "limits" that he imposed on the behavior of his subjects.

For that reason Hittite law imposed the ultimate punishment on persons who challenged any decree or command of the king. Hittite law §173 reads as follows: "If anyone rejects a judgment of the king (*DI-IN LUGAL*, that is, his ruling or decree), his house will become a heap of ruins. If anyone rejects a judgment of a magistrate, they shall cut off his head. If a slave declares himself free from his owner, he shall go into a clay jar."[34] All three of the cited offenses express resistance to authority—the king, a magistrate, a slave owner, and all draw the death penalty. The triad is ordered by degree of severity, with the questioning of the king's authority as the most serious, punishable by the extermination of the culprit's entire family.[35] In the above-cited passage the storm god himself is expected to destroy anyone who infringes upon

---

31. Hittite: *maniyaḫḫatalla-* 'administrator, deputy, governor', *CHD* L–N: 169.

32. The Hittite verb *šalik-* means invading a person's private 'space'. It can include a real assault, sexual or otherwise. It can denote mere physical contact, a touch. For examples of its use, see *CHD* Š: 100–104.

33. Literally, 'the body' or 'the members' (NÍ.TE.MEŠ = *tuekkuš*).

34. Hoffner, *Laws of the Hittites*, 138, 217–20 (parallel with the case of Achan in Joshua 7 cited on p. 218 n. 64); see also translation in *COS* 2.19: 106–19.

35. This is the meaning of the phrase É-*SÚ pu-p[u-u]l-li ki-i-ša* "his house (that is, household, family) shall become a heap of rubble (*pupulli*)." On *pupulli* see *CHD* P: 382, where also a bilingual Akkadian–Hittite lexical text is cited in which Akkadian *te-lu* 'tell, mound covering a ruined city' = URU-*aš p[u-pu-ul-li*] 'ruins of a city'.

the king's person or authority. However, the storm god's punishment was usually implemented by the human agents of the king.

2.5. General Characteristics of the Hittite Examples

One could cite a few other examples, but the ones already cited here are representative and illustrate the types of documents in which one is likely to find such cases. From these examples one can extract the characteristics of their use.

2.5.1. Individuals are usually named

The naming of individuals assures that the incidents are historical. In the *Palace Chronicle*, all the examples involve named individuals—twenty-six in all[36]—except for the unnamed baker in whose bread a pebble was found. In the *Telipinu Proclamation*, the offenders were men who became kings by murdering their predecessors, and because those offenses were not properly judged by the *pankuš*, the gods punished the nation (section 2.1). In the New Hittite Instructions text (section 2.2), the offender was Zuliya, the supervisor of the water-carriers. In the Ḫukkana treaty, the potential offender was Ḫukkana, a man from an alien culture who had become a vassal of the Hittite king and married the king's sister (section 2.3). What kind of individuals are these? Certainly disparate in rank: some Hittite kings, one Ḫayašan vassal, and one a royal supervisor of the water-carriers. But all served the king personally in one capacity or another and were directly responsible to him.

2.5.2. The offense is briefly described

What was the nature of the offense? In the *Telipinu Proclamation*, the offense was regicide. In the instructions text, the offense was not protecting the king's body from impurity in what he drank. In the Ḫukkana treaty, if Ḫukkana had imitated Mariya's sexual offense, it would have constituted betrayal and defilement of Ḫukkana's wife, who was the sister of the Hittite king. Šuppiluliuma was regretfully willing to look past the "barbarian" (*dampupi*) sexual behaviors of other men in Ḫayaša. But for Ḫukkana to do it, after taking the king's sister in marriage, by extension would be a violation of the king's own person.

2.5.3. Discovery and punishment are described

In the case of the *Telipinu Proclamation*, the murder of kings from Muršili I on down to Ammuna was generally known among the king's court, but no action was taken by the *pankuš*, bringing upon the whole kingdom the wrath of the gods. In the case of Zuliya, the king himself discovered a hair in his drinking water and instigated an investigation

---

36. See the list of their names in Dardano, *L'aneddoto*, 61–62.

to determine who was at fault. Inquiry yielded a suspect in Zuliya, and an ordeal determined his guilt.

What was the nature of the punishment? In all cases the punishment was death. The first case is peculiar in that the punishers were the gods and those who suffered death were Hittites at large rather than specifically the members of the *pankuš*. In the cases of Zuliya, Mariya, and several persons mentioned in the *Palace Chronicle*, they were executed.

2.5.4. Who was the offense against?

In the *Telipinu Proclamation*, the offense was against the storm god (and by extension his family of subordinate deities), who made those murdered kings his deputies. In the last two cases, the offense was against the king; therefore the punishment is given by the king, not by direct divine retribution.

2.5.5. Is a moral drawn?

In the *Telipinu Proclamation*, the Zuliya case, and the Ḫukkana treaty, there is a specific warning given against committing this offense in the future. In the *Palace Chronicle* anecdotes, it seems only to be implied.

3. Biblical Examples

3.1. Individual versus Corporate Examples

The rebellious behavior of the people of Israel as a whole is adduced repeatedly in the pentateuchal narratives during the wilderness wanderings, is summarized in Deuteronomy 1 and 9, and is utilized as late as the Apostle Paul's letters as models of what believers should *not* do (1 Corinthians 10). Such group behavior can serve a function similar to that of the named individuals. A group can be as large as the entire people of Israel other than Moses, or it can be a very large segment of the people. However, the closest parallels to the Hittite examples cited above are the cases where, after instructions are given to the people as a whole about what they are to do or to avoid doing, a story is told of one or two individuals who violated that command and suffered the death penalty,[37] or only survived because Moses interceded for them.[38]

In Old Testament historical narratives, examples of the unwise behavior of individuals in Israel's past are related in order to warn and instruct. Joab anticipates that, when David hears of the death of Uriah, he may criticize the messenger by recalling how Abimelech, son of Jerub-

---

37. Examples include Korah, Dathan and Abiram (Numbers 16, recalled in Deut 11:6).
38. Aaron's life was spared after the worship of the golden calf because Moses interceded (Deut 9:20–21).

baal, approached too close to the wall of a fortress under siege and was killed by a woman dropping a millstone on his head (2 Sam 11:20–21). Stories like that of Abimelech informed the daily life of soldiers on the battlefield.

In the New Testament, believers are urged to learn from the examples of disobedience of the nation of Israel as a whole (1 Corinthians 10), but also from the examples of obedience and faith of individuals (Hebrews 11). In rebutting the accusations of his Pharisee critics, Jesus had occasion to cite the atypical behavior of individuals like David or the group behavior of priests as examples of how a law was to be construed (Matthew 12).

Although there are numerous examples of disobedience and punishment in the book of Exodus involving the entire people of Israel, or at least large numbers, there are no admonitory examples found there that involve individuals. But one finds several such examples scattered in the books of Leviticus and Numbers, recalled also in Deut 9:20–21 and 11:6, along with one important example from Joshua. All but one that I shall briefly discuss below concern named individuals, several of them occupying positions or roles of great responsibility.

3.2. *Miriam and Aaron (Numbers 12)*

The example involving the two highest authorities below Moses himself is found in Numbers 12. It was an example of rejecting the unique authority of Moses, who in this pre-monarchic period was the closest approximation to a king that Israel had. Like ancient Hittite kings, Moses mediated divine authority. Like the Hittite storm god, Yahweh alone owned heaven, earth, the land, and the people. He had delegated Moses (and in later times, the Davidic line of kings) to exercise his authority. Moses' and the kings' legitimate authority must not be questioned or challenged, so long as they ruled according to Yahweh's directives and embodied Yahweh's righteousness. Moses was both the channel of divine revelation and authority and the one held responsible by God for the disobedience of his people. In ancient Israel only Yahweh himself occupied a position of authority higher than Moses or (later) the king.

The offense of Miriam and Aaron was the questioning of this unique authority that Yahweh had bestowed upon Moses. That this authority was indeed unique is clearly stated in Num 12:6–8. The basis of the challenge is expressed as follows: "Has Yahweh spoken only (*raq*) through Moses? Has he not spoken through us also (*gam bānû*)?" (12:2). Implied is the claim that Moses enjoyed an authority common to all prophets, which Miriam and Aaron considered themselves also to be. In verses

6–8, Yahweh denied this false claim that Moses was only one prophet among many (*lōʾ kēn ʿabdî Mōšeh* 'not so *with* my servant Moses'). The fact that Moses had married a Cushite woman (12:1) forms no part of their charge,[39] and therefore Yahweh does not address this criticism of Moses when he confronts Miriam and Aaron. The pair's claim is not that Moses should not also be obeyed, but that his authority is simply on a par with their own.

Yahweh confronts them in person, coming down in the pillar of cloud that during the daytime indicated his presence and leadership, and came to rest (*wayyaʿămōd*)[40] at the entrance of the Tent of Meeting. Although the usual term *šaʿar* 'gate' is not used here, the entrance (*petaḥ*) of the tabernacle enclosure corresponds structurally to the city gate, where legal cases were heard and adjudicated.[41] And since this entrance was not the entrance to the entire camp, but to the tabernacle enclosure, it corresponded more to the palace gate than to the city gate, thus the king's own court. Since the tabernacle enclosure was situated at the very center of the wilderness encampment scheme, this was also a very public place, where representatives of all the tribal encampments surrounding it would observe the proceedings.

When Yahweh finished refuting the claims of Miriam and Aaron and condemning their action, the cloud of his presence departed, leaving Miriam leprous (*mĕṣōraʿat*, verses 10–16; cf. Deut 24:8–9). Contrary to expectation, only she and not also Aaron suffered physical punishment. Although it was not literal physical death, it was the symbolic equivalent, for leprosy made the surface of the body as white as that of a corpse (*kaššāleg* 'like the snow') and excluded the person from the

---

39. Whether this Cush is an Arabian one or an African one is of no importance to this charge. Apparently, the point was that she was a foreigner, not a native-born Israelite. Perhaps the mention of the marriage was only to give a reason for the antagonism of the two siblings with Moses, rather than being part of their charge.

40. There is word-play here, since the word for the cloudy pillar (*ʿammûd*) is based on the same root ʿ-m-d.

41. H. W. Hertzberg (*I and II Samuel* [OTL 9; Louisville: Westminster/John Knox, 1965] 336) denies that the royal court was held in the city gate, preferring instead that it was at the gate (or door) of the palace. So too, Solomon's palace contained a "porch of judgment" (*ʾūlām ha-mišpāṭ*) where the king administered justice (1 Kgs 7:7), see R. de Vaux, *Ancient Israel: Its Life and Institutions* (New York: McGraw-Hill, 1961) 152. The lower courts, on the other hand, were held in place where nothing could be hid from the public, namely at the gate of the city (C. H. J. de Geus, *Towns in Ancient Israel and in the Southern Levant* [Palästina antiqua 10; Leuven: Peeters, 2003] 34–35; O. Borowski, *Daily Life in Biblical Times* [SBLABS 5; Boston: Brill, 2003] 47–48). This was also true in Mesopotamia (F. Joannès and C. Michel, eds., *Dictionnaire de la civilisation mésopotamienne* [Paris: R. Laffont, 2001] 691 ["process"]; and *ABD* 4:770–71).

worshiping community of the living. That she was eventually restored through the intercession of Aaron and Moses does not detract from the fact that her punishment was tantamount to physical death. Her white shroud was the white coating of flaking skin. Hers was the same death penalty that attended defiance of Hittite royal authority.

3.3. Nadab and Abihu (Leviticus 10, Num 3:4, 26:61; Deut 11:6)

Nadab and Abihu were sons of Aaron and thus stood in line to inherit the high priestly office. Their position was therefore almost as high as that of Miriam and Aaron. Among their duties was offering (*hiqrîb*) incense according to the cult rules laid down by Yahweh through Moses. Incense (*qĕṭōret*, Lev 7:1) was produced by burning aromatic substances on the surface of hot coals, which were referred to under the metonym *ʾēš* 'fire'. What was offered to Yahweh was both the cloud of incense fumes (*qĕṭōret*) and the coals (*ʾēš*) which produced it. The coals had to be taken from the perpetually burning fire on the altar. Coals taken from anywhere else were called *ʾēš zārâ* 'alien (that is, illicit) fire'.[42]

On this occasion the cloud of incense that rose to Yahweh is called "alien," because the incense (*qĕṭōret*) was burned upon coals (*ʾēš*) not taken from the altar but from elsewhere. Possibly the two brothers did this unthinkingly, not as a deliberate act of defying Yahweh's orders and the authority of both Moses and Yahweh himself. But if so, still it was an act of carelessness and neglect, that would be comparable to the culpable carelessness of the baker in the *Palace Chronicle* (see section 1, n. 2) or the water-carrier Zuliya, who allowed a hair in the drinking water of the Hittite king, which would have defiled his sacred person (see section 2.2).[43]

The punishment given to the brothers was similar to that prescribed in Hittite law §173 (see section 2.4): they died leaving no descendants (see *ûbānîm lōʾ hāyû lākem* 'and sons were not to them' in Num 3:4). But the manner of their execution differed from the Hittite one, in that Yahweh himself struck them dead, and the high priestly office bypassed them, devolving upon Aaron's younger sons Eleazar and Ithamar and their descendants (Num 3:4, 1 Chr 6:3–15). The manner of their execution (Lev 10:2) has an element of poetic justice in that, as their offense

---

42. Since both Hebrew *zār* and the Greek term *allotrion* employed by the LXX can elsewhere denote a foreigner (the Greek term is a regular LXX translation of "Philistine"), the translation "alien" is appropriate. NRSV uses the term "unholy" here and "illicit" in Num 3:4 and 26:61.

43. Most likely, Zuliya's offense was indeed negligence, but the phrase *parā uwanza* does not refer to this aspect (see 2.2 and n. 23).

was offering illicit fire (*'ēš zārâ*) to Yahweh, he became a consuming fire (*'ēš 'ōkelet*, Deut 4:24, 9:3; cf. Heb 12:29) to them: "Fire (*'ēš*) came forth from Yahweh and consumed (*wattō'kal*) them" (Lev 10:2) in the same way it had the substitutionary sacrifice in the immediate context (Lev 9:24). In Heb 12:28–29 believers are urged to offer to God an acceptable worship (that is, not *'ēš zārâ*) in gratitude, reverence and awe; otherwise, the worship will be unacceptable ("alien"), and they will face the displeasure of the God who was a consuming fire to Nadab and Abihu.

3.4. Korah and his Followers (Numbers 16)

Korah, the primary transgressor in this case, like Miriam, Nadab and Abihu, was of illustrious lineage, as his genealogy in Num 16:1 indicates: descended from Levi through Kohath and Izhar. Like many of the persons cited in the Hittite texts as examples of transgressing law and suffering for it, the Israelite examples include persons from the highest echelons of leadership. He is depicted as leading a rebellion against the dictates of Sinai, along with three confederates from the tribes of Reuben, and 250 "princes of the community" (*nĕśî'ê 'ēdâ*) and "men of repute" (*'anšê šēm*) from among the Israelite community (16:2; cf. Deut 11:6).

In other words, this was not a matter of private opposition to Moses and Yahweh, but a conspiracy that hoped to topple the existing authority. The complaint—which was really the grievance of Korah rather than of the Reubenites—was that Moses and Aaron were the only descendants of Levi granted the special privileges that were theirs (16:8–11). Yahweh had declared Moses and Aaron "holy" (*qādôš*), but Korah and his friends claimed that every Israelite was equally "holy" (16:3).

Yahweh's answer would be given by a concrete trial: the 250 leaders of Korah's group and Moses and Aaron would all stand before Yahweh to offer incense, a priestly privilege. And if all survived, their claim would be proven. Of course, nothing of the kind happened: the ground beneath the feet of Korah and the three Reubenite leaders opened up and swallowed them all and their households (16:19–35). Then fire issued from Yahweh and burned the 250 confederate princes alive. The text emphasizes that the form of the punishment was to be unprecedented (*'im bĕrî'â yibrā' YHWH* 'if Yahweh creates something new', 16:30), to show that it was no accident but a punishment deliberately sent by Yahweh.

The text indicates not only that this was a challenge to the authority of Moses, the highest level of human leadership in Israel (comparable to the king in Hatti), but that it constituted sacrilege: a rejection of the authority of Yahweh himself ("For truly, it is against Yahweh that you and all your company have banded together," 16:11).

That the incident was intended as a warning to others is clear not only from its inclusion here in a legal context, or by the invitation given by Yahweh to the people at the time to separate themselves from the instigators and thus disassociate themselves from both the offense and its punishment (16:23–27), but by the transformation of the fire pans used by the rebels into hammered sheets of gold to plate the altar (17:3), to be explained to subsequent generations "to serve as a warning (᾽ôt 'sign') to the people of Israel."

3.5. Unnamed Egyptian Blasphemes the Name (Lev 24:10–23)

From the highest echelons of Israelite leadership and "men of repute (lit., 'name')," we come now to an unnamed individual. Not only is the culprit anonymous: he is also only half Israelite, his mother being of the tribe of Dan, while his father was an Egyptian who had married into Israel and left Egypt with the people of Israel. One day he got into a fight with another man who was a full Israelite, during which fight he used the sacred name of Yahweh to curse a member of Yahweh's people. This was blasphemy and a violation of one of the ten fundamental articles of Yahweh's covenant (῾ĕśeret haddĕbārîm 'the Ten Articles') (Exod 20:7). Clearly, this could not be a minor infraction!

Yet one had to consult Yahweh himself to learn how it would be punished (Lev 24:12–16), not only in this man's case, but more significantly—since he had become a precedent case—in all future occurrences of this offense. This codicil to the existing law that emerged (Lev 24:15–22) would make no distinction between full Israelites and half Israelites: the same law (mišpaṭ ᾽eḥad) would apply equally (24:22). Here we have, not just an example to illustrate an existing law, but an example of an infraction that gave birth to a clarifying codicil.

3.6. Unnamed Israelite Violates the Sabbath by Gathering Sticks (Num 15:32–36)

A similar example is that of the unnamed Israelite man who was apprehended gathering sticks on the Sabbath (Num 15:32–36). Here too the culprit is anonymous and the law violated is one of the ten fundamental articles of the Sinai covenant. Here too the culprit was placed in custody until it was clear how he must be punished. In fact, that issue is addressed in Exod 31:14–15 and 35:2—Sabbath-violators must be put to death and cut off from the people. Accordingly, the special word from Yahweh (Num 15:35) indicated the mode of putting to death (stoning) and of cutting off from the people (carrying out the stoning outside the camp).

3.7. Achan (Joshua 7)

I here offer one last example, this time from outside the Pentateuch, but which is linked directly to Deuteronomic instruction (see esp. Deut 7:3–5, 25–26). The account of Achan's violation of the law of *ḥerem* in Joshua 7 follows immediately the record of Joshua's instruction by Yahweh that *ḥerem* was to be imposed upon the city of Jericho (Josh 6:17–18) and the account of the compliance of the Israelites as a whole (6:21), with the exception of Achan. Since the principle of corporate responsibility applied, Achan's violation (7:1) brought judgment from Yahweh upon the nation—in the defeat at Ai (7:2–5)—and was only remedied when the nation took action to judge and punish the offender and his complicit family (7:10–26). Yahweh identifies the offender, communicating through the system of sacred lots. The offender must then confess and describe his actions (7:19–21), and finally he is punished by stoning (7:24–26), a form of execution reserved for the most serious offenses against Yahweh.

That the Achan affair is historical is no less likely than that the offenses described in the above-discussed Hittite texts. But that it was recorded in precisely this context, as an admonitory example, was to show to future generations the certainty of Yahweh's detection and punishment of that offense. Furthermore, it accords with the clear intention of the similar personal examples of named individuals in the Hittite texts.

3.8. General Characteristics of the Biblical Examples

As in the case of the Hittite examples, all but two of the biblical examples cited above involve named individuals. Their offense, its discovery, and its punishment are briefly described. The punishment is decreed by Yahweh, the king whose covenant and law has been breached. All examples are directly related to legislation or instructions given in the immediate context, so that the admonitory function is obvious and direct.

Of course, there are examples in the historical recollections of Deuteronomy, as in Exodus through Numbers, of kings of foreign peoples—Sihon and Og (Num 21 and Deut 1–4), and the unnamed pharaoh of Egypt (Exod 5, 7–12)—who challenged the authority of Yahweh, Israel's

King. The pharaoh put it very bluntly: "Who is Yahweh that I should obey him?" (Exod 5:2). These kings and their peoples were punished for failing to acknowledge Yahweh's royal authority. But these cases would be analogous to a different set of themes from ancient Near Eastern royal literature: the military annals and the diplomatic correspondence.[44] This subject was outside my intended purview for this study.

4. Comparison of Specific Examples and Types

It is significant that neither in the Bible nor in the Hittite texts are there illustrative examples of ordinary offenses such as theft or property damage or sexual crimes that are not directly impinging the king or a deity. The examples of embezzling in the *Palace Chronicle* are actually cases of defrauding the king and violating the instructions for conduct issued by the king.

Since all examples in Israel's legal corpus antedate the Israelite monarchy, the obvious parallel to the offenses against the Hittite king are either those against Yahweh as king or against his vice-regents, Moses and Aaron. The violations of the *ḥerem*-ban (for example, the case of Achan) is a violation of a law already incorporated in the Pentateuch in Deuteronomy 7. It is a direct offense against Yahweh, because the items to be "devoted" (or destroyed utterly) are thought to be "given" to Yahweh. To retain any of those objects or persons is to steal from Yahweh himself. It is true, however, that in the case of Achan the illustrative example is not embedded in the legal text itself, as are the other examples I have cited. In that sense—and only in that sense—it probably belongs in the same category as the offense of Uzzah in 2 Samuel, who stretched out his hand to steady the ark and inadvertently violated Yahweh's holy space, for which he lost his life. Achan's sin was deliberate, while Uzzah's was not. Yet the effect of each was the same: Yahweh's sacredness was violated.

5. Conclusions

The examples of individual and named admonitions drawn from legal, judicial, and covenant contexts of the Pentateuch follow in general the pattern observed in Hittite texts. The offenses are not simple infractions of civil law, but constitute clear defiance of the authority of Yahweh himself in Sabbath legislation (unique to Yahweh and to Israel),

---

44. As preliminary examples, see the following sections of the Annals of Muršili II in translation: *COS* 2.16: 85 (left column), 87–88. Additional examples can be added from other annals texts.

in blaspheming the name of Yahweh, and in disobeying the laws of Yahweh's cult and sacred ban (ḥerem). This pattern corresponds to what we have found in the Hittite examples, which concern rejection of the divine authority of the storm god by the violation of the sacred person and commands of his deputy, the king. No conclusion is drawn here regarding Israelite or Mosaic direct borrowing of this practice from the Hittites.

How does this insight contribute to the Christian reading of these texts? What is the enduring message to the Church provided by these examples and this pattern? I believe it lies in the recognition of the vital importance of honoring God's authority, mediated through his written Word and those whom he has commissioned to lead us. This conviction lies at the very heart of the Book of Deuteronomy, as well. The pharaoh opposed Yahweh's command and perished. Israel as a people in the wilderness opposed Yahweh's commands through Moses and an entire generation perished (Deut 1:19–45). Sihon and Og opposed Yahweh's authority and were destroyed (Deuteronomy 2–3). At Massah, Kibroth-hattaavah, Kadesh-barnea, and at the very foot of Sinai the people rebelled and were judged.

Despite strong feelings to the contrary in the modern world, the Church is not a democracy, and authority is not equal among believers. As in New Testament times God "gave" apostles, prophets, evangelists, pastors, and teachers for the building up of the body of Christ (Eph 4:11), so today he has "given" pastors and teachers for the same ministry. That these persons are fallible no one would deny. But that we owe them respect for the sake of their roles is also clear (Heb 13:17; cf. 1 Cor 16:16). The marks of true spiritual leadership sketched in Deuteronomy in the career of Moses—humility and total submission to the Word of God—serve to identify true leaders in the Church of the Twenty-first Century. The Church today must not be characterized by rebels against the authority of Holy Scripture, for it constitutes the very voice of our God, our King, and our Savior.

"These Are the Words Moses Spoke"

Implied Audience and a Case for a Pre-Monarchic Dating of Deuteronomy

Peter T. Vogt

1. Introduction

The date of Deuteronomy has long been a contested issue in modern scholarship. Although Christians and Jewish scholars accepted the traditional association of Deuteronomy with Moses throughout the medieval, Reformation, and premodern eras, W. M. L. de Wette challenged that understanding in the 18th century. De Wette maintained that the book of Deuteronomy was not simply a blueprint for the Josianic reforms of the 7th century B.C., but was also the product of the period in which it was used.[1] This association of Deuteronomy with the monarchic period became the prevailing critical understanding of the book.[2]

The discovery of ancient Near Eastern (ANE) political treaties in the mid-20th century provided fertile ground for examination.[3] The ANE treaties were heavily scrutinized, with advocates of various dates

---

Author's Note: I am grateful to Dan Block for the immeasurable impact he has had on my life and ministry. He was instrumental in "infecting" me with a passion for the Old Testament and helping me identify my calling to teach Old Testament (and, Lord willing, similarly infect a new generation of students with a passion for the Old Testament). His unique combination of rigorous scholarship and devotion to the Lord and his people continues to serve as a positive example for me in my ministry.

1. De Wette's argument was presented in a lengthy footnote in his doctoral dissertation ("Dissertatio critica qua a prioribus Deuteronomium Pentateuchi libris diversum, allus cuiusdam recentioris auctoris opus esse monstratur', pro venia legendi publice defensa lenae a. 1805," in W. M. L. de Wette, *Opscula Theologica* [Berlin: G. Reimer, 1830] 149–68), which he completed at the University of Jena in 1804. See the helpful presentation of de Wette and his contribution to Deuteronomic studies in Gordon J. Wenham, *The Structure and Date of Deuteronomy* (Ph.D. diss., University of London, 1970) 16–43; and J. W. Rogerson, *W. M. L. de Wette, Founder of Modern Biblical Criticism: An Intellectual Biography* (JSOTSupp 126; Sheffield: Sheffield Academic, 1992).

2. See, for example, J. Wellhausen, *Prolegomena to the History of Ancient Israel* (New York: Meridian, 1957) 34; and S. R. Driver, *A Critical and Exegetical Commentary on Deuteronomy* (3rd ed.; ICC; Edinburgh: T. & T. Clark, 1901) xliv–xlvi.

3. See the seminal work of G. E. Mendenhall, "Covenant Forms in Israelite Tradition," *BA* 17 (1954) 50–76.

seeking and finding evidence to support their views in the various treaty data.[4]

Finally, parallels with ancient law codes were identified in the quest to ascertain a date for Deuteronomy. Similarities to the Code of Hammurabi, both in terms of content and form, were used to argue for a premonarchic date for the book.[5] Others maintained that a continuity of legal traditions in the ANE world could account for such similarities, and, moreover, the number of parallel texts is so small as to be inconclusive in terms of dating the book.[6]

It is fair to say that discussion of the date of Deuteronomy has largely reached a standstill. The evidence is capable of being read in a variety of ways, and all sides are able to support their view on the basis of relevant data.

Missing in most of these analyses is serious consideration of the implied audience of Deuteronomy and how that determination may shed light on the question of the date of the book. In this essay, I will examine how two key texts may have functioned for the implied audience, and I will argue that consideration of the audience "tips the scale" in favor of the view that Deuteronomy is best understood as a product of the premonarchic era.

2. *The Audience of Deuteronomy*

A positive recent turn in hermeneutical theory has been an emphasis on texts as acts of communication, and a concomitant awareness of the complexity of that communicative endeavor.[7] Communication (including textual) is more nuanced and intricate than many recognize. Inte-

---

4. Those who used the ANE treaties to argue for an early date for Deuteronomy include M. G. Kline, *Treaty of the Great King: The Covenant Structure of Deuteronomy: Studies and Commentary* (Grand Rapids: Eerdmans, 1963) 27–44, and K. A. Kitchen, *Ancient Orient and Old Testament* (Chicago: InterVarsity, 1966) 90–102. Others saw the treaties as evidence for a first-millennium date for Deuteronomy. They include A. F. Campbell, "An Historical Prologue in a Seventh-Century Treaty," *Bib* 50 (1969) 534–35. See also D. J. McCarthy, *Treaty and Covenant* (2nd ed.; AnBib 21a; Rome: Biblical Institute, 1981) 27–152.

5. See G. J. Wenham, "The Date of Deuteronomy: Linch-Pin of Old Testament Criticism (Part One)," *Them* 10/3 (1985) 19. Wenham highlights in particular the fact that in the second-millennium law codes there are no god lists, and in the blessings and curses sections, blessings precede curses. This is the same as in Deuteronomy 28, and is different from the treaties.

6. M. Weinfeld, *Deuteronomy and the Deuteronomic School* (Oxford: Oxford University Press, 1972; repr. Winona Lake, IN: Eisenbrauns, 1992) 116–57. Cf. also idem, *Deuteronomy 1–11: A New Translation with Text and Introduction and Commentary* (AB 5; New York: Doubleday, 1991) 6–9.

7. See the helpful introduction to this approach in J. K. Brown, *Scripture as Communication: Introducing Biblical Hermeneutics* (Grand Rapids: Baker, 2007).

grally related to this is speech-act theory, which helpfully recognizes that speech (whether oral or written) does more than simply convey information. Texts *do* things.[8] Rather than always and exclusively simply transferring data or informing an audience, texts persuade, warn, encourage, exhort, rebuke, and edify—to name just a few possible uses.

In interpreting the meaning of a text, primary consideration must be given to the author's communicative intention in writing.[9] But this consideration must also include discerning what is verbally accomplished by the utterance, which Austin calls an "illocution,"[10] and how the author intends the audience to respond, known as "perlocutionary" intention.[11]

Another useful avenue of exploration that has been largely overlooked is the idea of the implied audience. This construct highlights the fact that every text "has a group of readers in mind."[12] Moreover, the author writes a text with this audience in mind. The implied audience (or implied reader) is one that responds as the author intends. Considering the text from the perspective of the implied reader allows the interpreter to be able to better determine what a correct reception of the text would look like.[13] It grounds interpretation and helps the "actual" reader to "associate with the feelings and responses indicated by the text,"[14] rather than the responses that might more naturally arise in light of the interpreter's own context and worldview.[15]

---

8. A useful introduction to speech-act theory may be found in J. L. Austin, *How to Do Things With Words* (2nd ed.; Cambridge, MA: Harvard University Press, 1975). Austin's work advances and clarifies the earlier pioneering work of J. Searle, *Speech Acts: An Essay in the Philosophy of Language* (Cambridge: Cambridge University Press, 1969).

9. I deliberately use the term "communicative intention" to highlight the fact that when interpreting a text, we are seeking to understand what the author intended to communicate. Other facets of the author's intentionality, as well as their thoughts, emotions, and experiences may be unknown to us and, even if known, cannot be a part of our analysis. For more on this, see Brown, *Scripture as Communication*, 47–51.

10. Austin, *How to Do Things*, 98–100.

11. It is debated whether perlocutionary intention should be considered an aspect of meaning. My preference, with Brown (*Scripture as Communication*, 112–13), is to see this as part of the meaning of a text (though not necessarily central to that meaning). See also K. J. Vanhoozer, "From Speech Acts to Scripture Acts: The Covenant of Discourse and the Discourse of the Covenant," in *After Pentecost: Language and Biblical Interpretation* (ed. C. Bartholomew, C. Greene, and K. Möller; SHS 2; Grand Rapids: Zondervan, 2001) 25–30.

12. G. R. Osborne, *The Hermeneutical Spiral: A Comprehensive Introduction to Biblical Interpretation* (2nd ed.; Downers Grove, IL: InterVarsity, 2006) 211.

13. Brown, *Scripture as Communication*, 40. See also W. C. Booth, *The Rhetoric of Fiction* (2nd ed.; Chicago: University of Chicago Press, 1983) 177.

14. Osborne, *Hermeneutical Spiral*, 211.

15. A related construct is the idea of the implied author. This refers to the presentation of the empirical author within the text. The implied author presents the perspective of the empirical author both implicitly and explicitly in the text.

The importance of recognizing the implied reader may be seen when considering one aspect of Bernard Levinson's influential work on Deuteronomy, which argues that the book's legislation reflects the struggle to revolutionize late seventh-century Judean society by reworking earlier texts.[16] One methodological difficulty in his approach (which Levinson himself concedes[17]) has to do with the audiences he sees as being addressed by the various strata in Deuteronomy. Levinson views Deuteronomy 13, for example, as a product of Josiah's reign that appropriates "the literary and political model of the neo-Assyrian state treaties ... and [transfers] that loyalty oath ... to Yahweh."[18] On the other hand, he sees in Deut 17:2–7 a deliberate reinterpretation of the earlier material, using the same language from the other law. But Deuteronomy 17 is *also* seen as part of Josiah's centralizing reform program.[19] It is unlikely that the same audience would on the one hand see Deuteronomy 13, which Levinson sees as mandating summary execution for incitement to apostasy, as authoritative and at the same time accept the strict due process requirements of Deuteronomy 17. This is all the more so when it is recognized that Deuteronomy 13 itself may presuppose a judicial proceeding prior to execution, as Deut 13:10 states: "Your hand must be the first in causing him to die, *and then the hands of all the people*." The audience, whether king, scribes, or people, would surely recognize the differences between the two laws, despite the reuse of language in the later law. One weakness of Levinson's approach is a failure to address the way in which the text would have been received and understood by the implied audience. Consideration of the implied audience thus can help provide an additional means of validating interpretations.

These dimensions of interpretation may also be useful in analyzing the date of Deuteronomy, as consideration of the intended and likely effect on the implied audience may help more clearly ascertain what time period is the most likely provenance for the book. We should note, however, the caution that consideration of the implied audience *alone* cannot be the sole means of dating a book, but can, rather, provide what Kingsbury calls an "approximate index"[20] for the book's date. With that in mind, we will now turn our attention to some key texts and examine the intended effect on the implied audience.

---

16. B. M. Levinson, *Deuteronomy and the Hermeneutics of Legal Innovation* (Oxford: Oxford University Press, 1997).
17. Ibid., 136–37, n. 97.
18. Ibid., 122.
19. Ibid., 9, 109, 116.
20. J. D. Kingsbury, *Matthew as Story* (2nd ed.; Philadelphia: Fortress, 1988) 147.

3. Moab, Edom, and Ammon and the Implied Audience

3.1. The Nations of Moab, Edom, and Ammon in Deut 2:1–23

One often overlooked text when considering the date of Deuteronomy is Deut 2:1–23.[21] Here the author recounts the journey towards the land after the catastrophic rebellion at Kadesh-Barnea. In providing instructions as to how to relate to the nations on the way, the author emphasizes the fact that Yahweh has given land to the nations, just as he is giving land to the Israelites. This may be seen when noting the seven times that the idea of "giving the land" to Israel appears in chapter 1 compared with the six occurrences of "giving the land" to the nations in chapter 2 (through negative and positive statements).

"Giving the Land" to the Israelites	"Giving the Land" to the Nations
"See! I gave to you the land" (1:8a) "[the land] that I, Yahweh, swore to give to your ancestors " (1:8b) "which Yahweh our God is giving to us" (1:20) "See! Yahweh your God has given the land to you" (1:21) [the good land] "which Yahweh our God is giving us" (1:25) [the good land] "that I swore to give to your ancestors" (1:35) "to them I will give [the land]" (1:39)	"Because I am not giving you their land" (2:5a) "For I have given [Mt. Seir] to Esau as an inheritance" (2:5b) "Because I am not giving you their land [of inheritance]" (2:9a) "Because I have given [Ar] to the descendents of Lot" (2:9b) "Because I am not giving you the land of the descendents of Ammon" (2:19b) "Because I have given [the land] to the descendents of Lot as an inheritance" (2:19c)

This juxtaposition serves to provide helpful context for understanding the promise made to the Israelites, insofar as the giving of land is not something Yahweh does only for Israel; rather, he gives land to the nations as well. As Wright notes, Israel's uniqueness was found "not in merely receiving land from Yahweh, but in its covenant relationship with Yahweh."[22] That covenant relationship, moreover, is based on Yahweh's election of Abraham to be a blessing to the nations.

We should also note that in highlighting Yahweh's provision of land even for the nations, the author specifically refers to the Edomites as "brothers" to the Israelites (Deut 2:4, 8). This serves to emphasize not

---

21. A notable exception is C. Vang, "The So-Called 'Ur-Deuteronomium'—Some Reflections on Its Content, Size, and Age," *Hiphil (Scandinavian Evangelical E-Journal)* 6 (2009) 1–22.
22. C. J. H. Wright, *Deuteronomy* (NIBC; Peabody, MA: Hendrickson, 1996) 36.

only the kinship relationship that exists (as the Edomites are descendants of Esau and the Moabites and Ammonites from Lot), but also the obligation Israel has to be a blessing to all nations, including even those who opposed them at points.[23]

We must now consider how this text may have affected the implied audience and draw some conclusions about that audience. Clearly, the author wants the implied reader to see the nations of Moab, Edom, and Ammon as being under Yahweh's sovereignty and care, in that he provides land for them as he does for Israel. Moreover, the fact that the Israelites are not only to avoid war with them but also to refrain from inflicting on them the "psychological anguish"[24] that comes from imminent conflict (note "harass" [צור] in vv. 9 and 19) demonstrates that they are to have compassion on even those who were hostile to them. Finally, the Edomites are specifically referred to as "brothers," which suggests that they are to be seen not as adversaries, but as family, deserving of protection, consideration, assistance, etc. The perlocutionary intention of the author here seems to be to foster a sense of goodwill toward the nations and to help the implied audience appreciate that Yahweh is sovereign over all nations, not just Israel.

3.2. The Nations of Moab, Edom, and Ammon in the Historical Books

When we consider what time period this implied audience may reflect, we must consider whether this charitable attitude toward these nations was constant throughout the biblical depiction of Israel's history, or whether it may be potentially isolated to a particular time period. We will begin with an overview of the relationship between Israel and these nations in the historical books.

The book of Judges highlights conflict between the Israelites and Moabites, as well as the Ammonites. Because of the sin of the Israelites, Eglon king of Moab was given power over the Israelites. In delivering the Israelites, Ehud struck down 10,000 Moabites, and Judg 3:30 notes that "Moab was humbled that day under the hand of Israel." This clearly suggests that an attitude of enmity, not charity, marked the relationship between Moab and Israel, at least during that period. In describing the Israelites as having "humbled" (כנע) the Moabites, they have clearly gone beyond the mere "harassment" prohibited by

---

23. Note that the Moabites and Ammonites were not to be conquered or treated as a foe, despite the fact that they were to be excluded from the assembly in Israel "forever," according to Deut 23:3–6.

24. I. Swart, "צור," *NIDOTTE* 5:791.

Deuteronomy 2, as the term כנע means to humiliate, most commonly though the imposition of political force.[25] Later, Jephthah conquered the Ammonites, and in his message to the Ammonite king (Judg 11:15) he notes that the Israelites did not seize any Ammonite territory, in keeping with the commands of Deuteronomy 2.

Similarly, 1–2 Samuel records a history of hostile relations between Israel and the nations of Edom, Moab, and Ammon. Saul's first military action after his accession was against the Ammonites (1 Sam 11:8–11), and 1 Sam 14:47 notes that Saul fought against the "enemies" of Israel: Moab, the Ammonites, Edom, the kings of Zobah, and the Philistines. The fact that no specific offense is described on the part of the Moabites, Ammonites, and Edomites points to a continuing state of hostility. In the same way, David defeated the Moabites, who were made subject to him (2 Sam 8:2). He also conquered the Edomites (2 Sam 8:14).[26]

David's interactions with the Ammonites are particularly telling. Despite his peaceful overtures to Hanun, king of the Ammonites, the fearful Ammonites attacked the Israelites, and David responded by conquering the Ammonites and their territory (2 Samuel 10–12). It is possible that David's initial attempt to show mercy to the Ammonites was at least partially in response to the command in Deuteronomy 2. This view is more likely in light of another instance in which David appears to adhere to the instructions of Deuteronomy. When David fought Hadadezer, King of Zobah, he captured 1,000 chariots. Despite the obvious military advantage of such spoils, 2 Sam 8:4 notes that David hamstrung all but 100 of the horses. It is possible that David does so in obedience to the law of the King in Deut 17:16, which forbids the Israelite king from multiplying horses for himself. Thus the implied author apparently describes David as obeying the commands of Deuteronomy in these two instances, at least.

Likewise, 1–2 Kings assumes hostility between the kingdoms of Israel and Judah and the nations of Edom and Moab (Ammon does not play any significant role in the book of Kings). Moab is described as rebelling against the king of Israel in 2 Kings 3. This could be a continuation of David's subjugation of Moab described in 2 Sam 8:2, though the Mesha Stele maintains that the subjugation of Moab began during the reign of Omri.[27] In dealing with the rebellion, a coalition led by the

---

25. W. Dumbrell, "כנע," *NIDOTTE* 2:667–68.

26. According to the Septuagint, Syriac, and some Hebrew MSS, David gained fame for striking down 18,000 *Edomites* in the Valley of Salt (2 Sam 8:13). Most Hebrew MSS, including the MT, read Arameans.

27. B. Oded, "Mesha Stele," in *EncJud* (2nd ed.) 14:75–76.

kings of Israel, Judah, and Edom attack the Moabites and invade the land of Moab (2 Kgs 3:24).

In the same way, Edom is described as rebelling against Judah and setting up its own king in the time of Jehoram (2 Kgs 8:20). Jehoram's attempts to re-subjugate Edom failed, and the narrator notes that "Edom has been in rebellion from under the hand of Judah until this day" (2 Kgs 8:22). What is noteworthy for our purposes is the attitude and perspective of the implied author of Kings. He sees Edom's desire for independence and, presumably, territorial integrity as evidence of its rebellion. In this account, Edom is not only "harassed" and attacked by Judah, the domination of Edom by Judah is apparently seen as acceptable and even unremarkable.

Finally, Amaziah defeated 10,000 Edomites in battle and captured the Edomite city of Sela, renaming it Joktheel (2 Kgs 14:7). The implied author regards the territorial integrity of Edom as unimportant and he considers the lack of brotherhood extended to the Edomites unobjectionable.

The portrayal in 1–2 Chronicles is largely consistent with 1–2 Kings in terms of relations with Israel and assumptions regarding the nations of Moab, Edom, and Ammon. 2 Chronicles provides further details about the relationship between Israel and Ammon, noting that both Uzziah and Jotham subjugated the Ammonites (2 Chr 26:8, 27:5). Similarly, 2 Chr 25:12 sets forth additional details about Amaziah's treatment of the Edomites, noting that in addition to killing 10,000 Edomites in battle, the Judahites captured an additional 10,000 men who were marched to the top of a cliff and then thrown down, so that "all were burst open." Here, as in the book of Kings, the implied author apparently regards the hostile treatment of the Ammonites and Edomites as expected.

3.3. *The Nations of Moab, Edom, and Ammon in the Prophetic Books*

The prophetic books adopt a similar stance toward the nations in question. Isaiah envisions judgment on them (Isa 11:14), and there is an extended oracle against Moab in chapters 15 and 16. Jeremiah includes Edom, Ammon, and Moab among the nations who will be judged (Jer 9:26, 25:21, 27:3) and also includes a specific oracle against Moab in chapter 48, and against Ammon and Edom in chapter 49. Jeremiah's depiction of Edom is particularly telling, as it suggests that Edom's offenses are especially egregious. Amos 1–2 includes Edom, Ammon, and Moab in the oracles against the nations, and the Edomites are further accused in other oracles as assisting in the human trafficking of captives (Amos 1:6, 9). Similarly, Edom is judged in Joel 3:19, and Moab and Ammon are singled out in Zeph 2:8–11. Mal 1:4–5 likewise includes a judgment of Edom, saying that the Edomites will be a "people with whom Yahweh is displeased forever" (Mal 1:4).

The most significant prophetic critique of any of these nations comes in the book of Obadiah, which is entirely directed at the nation of Edom. The most serious accusation leveled against the Edomites, which is pervasive throughout the book, is that they participated in, or at least profited richly from, the destruction of Jerusalem and Judah.[28] This accusation is particularly pointed in vv. 11–14, where the author's use of "brother" in vv. 10 and 12 stresses the kinship relationship between Judah and Edom.

3.4. The Implied Audience of the Historical and Prophetic Books

It is, of course, impossible to fully analyze here the audiences of the historical and prophetic books. These books are the products of different authors and time periods, and they address vastly different issues. Based on the presentations described above, however, we can begin to draw some general conclusions about the perspective(s) of the authors and how the audiences were expected to respond.

The historical books consistently envision a sense of hostility between the Israelites and the nations of Moab, Ammon, and Edom. The authors assume that the implied reader will see these states as enemies of Israel and Judah. Moreover, the fact that Israel subjugates them so frequently without any condemnation of Israel on the part of the narrator suggests that the authors expected the audiences to accept (initially, at least) that this was just and right in light of the offenses of these nations.

Similarly, the prophetic discussion of these nations highlights their culpability and their offenses against the people of God. The implied reader is meant to see these nations as deserving God's judgment for their actions. They are portrayed as enemies of God's people, and there is little in the prophetic critique to elicit sympathy for them on the part of the implied reader. Obadiah's use of "brother" neatly parallels Deuteronomy's use of the term, in that special favor is expected to be shown because of the kinship relationship between the two nations. Edom's failure to treat Israel as a brother is thus seen as an especially egregious offense.

---

28. D. Stuart, *Hosea–Jonah* (WBC 31; Waco, TX: Word, 1987) 419.

4. The Implied Audience of Deuteronomy 2:1–23 and the Date of Composition

We may now examine how the portrayal of the nations in the historical and prophetic books points toward a date for Deuteronomy's depiction of the relationship between Israel and these nations.

If the historical books contain accurate depictions of the attitudes and actions of the time, it is hard to conceive of a point in the monarchic period at which Deuteronomy could reasonably have been written. This is all the more so when we consider how the text may have functioned. According to many scholars, Deuteronomy is a product of the monarchic period, written, in part at least, to solidify the claims of the monarchy in Jerusalem.[29] It represents, in this view, a rather substantial upheaval of life in the nation. The fact that these reforms were carried out under the authority of the "Book of the Law of Moses" that was found in the temple presumably made the dramatic changes tolerable to those who were most affected by them.

We must also bear in mind that advocates of a monarchic provenance for Deuteronomy maintain that the book is a product not primarily of an ancient period, but of the time of its discovery. Thus, the authors were free to include those things that would advance their interests and leave out those things that hindered them. However, inclusion of a text like Deut 2:1–23, with its positive attitude toward the nations of Edom, in particular, as well as Moab and Ammon, may well have served to undermine the actual policies being enacted or considered. Given that Deuteronomy, however dated, most likely addresses the nation as a whole,[30] any analysis of Deut 2:1–23 must be reconciled with the priorities, policies, and goals of the monarchy. Given the data of the historical books, this seems difficult, if not impossible, to do.

For example, as we noted, Deut 2:4, 8 explicitly conceives of the Edomites as brothers to the Israelites, and it forbids the Israelites from threatening them in any way. Yet Josiah's early reign markedly

---

29. E.g., Weinfeld, *Deuteronomy*, 55–57, 83–84.

30. The audience of Deuteronomy is a complex subject that, at the same time, has not been adequately considered in most analyses. That the people as a whole are addressed in Deuteronomy may be seen in the fact that entire community, not a king, is tasked with maintaining justice in Deut 16:18–20. See P. T. Vogt, *Deuteronomic Theology and the Significance of Torah: A Reappraisal* (Winona Lake, IN: Eisenbrauns, 2006) 210–12. This is in contrast to R. D. Nelson, who postulates a "process of scribal recopying and restructuring by a limited circle of contributors for a limited circle of readers over a relatively brief period of time" (*Deuteronomy: A Commentary* [OTL; Louisville: Westminster John Knox, 2002] 8). Nelson sees Deuteronomy as emerging out of dissident scribal schools during Manasseh's reign that were later incorporated as policy during the time of Josiah.

resumed the anti-Assyrian policies of Hezekiah. Capitalizing on the death of Ashurbanipal in 629 or 627 B.C., Josiah seized control of the former Northern Kingdom, and also re-asserted control over the southern region of Simeon (2 Chr 34:6–7).[31] This latter thrust would have brought Judah in potential conflict with Edom, which had been a tributary of Assyria. In the chaos of the waning years of the Assyrian Empire and the rise of the Babylonians, with the conflicting and shifting loyalties that were on display, it seems unlikely that a stance of peaceful neutrality toward the Edomites would be politically wise or even feasible. Moreover, the risk of conflict with Edom was real, and inclusion of a text like Deut 2:1–23 would potentially undermine popular support for the campaigns. This becomes all the more clear as the Edomites eventually sided with the Babylonians and participated in the destruction of Jerusalem and Judah (Ps 137:7, Lam 4:21–22, Ezek 25:12–14).

A similar problem exists with other periods as well. If Deuteronomy were written earlier in the monarchic period, the problem of actual, rather than merely potential, conflict with the Edomites, Moabites, and Ammonites makes the inclusion of Deuteronomy's stance toward these nations unlikely. An exilic or postexilic provenance is also rendered unlikely, due to the Edomites' participation in the destruction of Jerusalem. The perspective toward Edom seen in Malachi and Ezekiel are particularly difficult to reconcile with Deuteronomy's peaceful stance.

It is true, of course, that Deuteronomy may have been written precisely to counter the warlike spirit of the times and to foster a desire for peace with the Edomites, Moabites, and Ammonites. Given the history between the nations, however, Deut 2:1–23 seems too weak to foster the kind of change of attitude necessary to transform the popular understanding of these nations as enemies deserving subjugation into neighbors (or even brothers) who are not even to be harassed.

I conclude, then, that Deut 2:1–23 more likely dates to a time prior to the experience of actual conflict with the nations in question. This understanding, in turn, suggests a somewhat different perspective on the material in 1–2 Kings. As we have seen, 1–2 Kings envisions enmity between the nations of Israel/Judah and Moab, Edom, and Ammon. But if, as I have argued, Deut 2:1–23 is best seen as a premonarchic text, then the attitude envisioned in Deuteronomy should be seen as an expectation for Israel in its dealings with the nations. If so, this warrants a different perspective on certain passages. That is, Israel and Judah's failure to treat Edom as a "brother" could be seen not as a justifiable

---

31. W. W. Hallo and W. K. Simpson, *The Ancient Near East: A History* (San Diego: Harcourt Brace Jovanovich, 1971) 143.

response to Edom's provocations but as *their* failure to live as Yahweh commanded in terms of relations with the nations around them. Israel, after all, was called to be a blessing to the nations (Gen 12:1–3), and a spirit of peaceful coexistence could best allow Israel to be the paradigmatic witness to the nations it was called to be.[32] In this light, Israel and Judah's "harassment" and war with Edom, Moab, and Ammon is a failure to properly live the kind of radically counter-cultural existence to which the people of God were called, and the conflict would thus be further evidence to suggest that the reason for the exile was Israel and Judah's failure to live as God commanded. It is, moreover, a call to repent of the nationalistic tendency that was in evidence in the monarchic period and devote themselves to living as the people of Yahweh. This interpretation is in keeping with how the purpose and message of 1–2 Kings is sometimes conceived.[33]

5. "The Place" of Sacrifice and the Implied Audience

5.1. "The Place" of Sacrifice in Deuteronomy

Another overlooked consideration in attempting to date the book of Deuteronomy is the treatment of the place of worship. Scholars have focused on the nature of "the place" and the relationship between it and Yahweh's name,[34] but less attention has been given to the implications of the discussion for the date of the book.

Deuteronomy 12 makes clear that there is to be one place of sacrifice in the land. In contrast to the multiple sites of the Canaanites, Deut 12:5 says, "But you shall seek the place that Yahweh your God shall choose out of all your tribes to establish his name there as its dwelling place, and there you shall come."[35] This is then clearly identified as the place of sacrifice in the following verses:

---

32. On Israel's role as a paradigmatic nation, see P. T. Vogt, *Interpreting the Pentateuch: An Exegetical Handbook* (HOTE; Grand Rapids: Kregel, 2009) 87–90. See also Wright, *Deuteronomy*, 11–14.

33. See, e.g., D. M. Howard Jr., *An Introduction to the Old Testament Historical Books* (Chicago: Moody, 1993) 172–73.

34. S. L. Richter, *The Deuteronomistic History and the Name Theology: lešakkēn šemô šām in the Bible* (BZAW 318; Berlin: De Gruyter, 2002).

35. The translation of Deut 12:5 presents challenges. The MT presupposes an otherwise unattested nominal form שֶׁכֶן. This is often emended to לְשַׁכְּנוּ, and seen as a Piel of שׁכן. This is then seen as a doublet of לָשׂוּם (see, e.g., E. Tov, *Textual Criticism of the Hebrew Bible* [2nd ed.; Minneapolis: Fortress, 2001] 42, n. 19). McConville notes that there is "ambiguity concerning whether the suffix of לְשַׁכְּנוּ refers to 'it', that is, the 'name', or to 'him', that is, Yahweh" (*Deuteronomy*, 211). But he rightly argues (ibid.) that the verb תִדְרְשׁוּ is required to complete the command begun at the beginning of the verse. This suggests

And there you shall bring your burnt offerings, your sacrifices, your tithes, your special offerings, your votive offerings, your freewill offerings, and the firstborn of your herds and flocks. And you shall eat there in the presence of Yahweh your God and rejoice in the output of your work, you and your families, because Yahweh your God has blessed you. (Deut 12:6–7)

The subsequent provision for non-sacrificial slaughter in vv. 15 and 20 further illustrates that sacrifice is limited to the place of Yahweh's choosing.[36]

A striking feature of Deuteronomy 12 is the fact that "the place" is never identified. Perhaps more significantly, the only place named in Deuteronomy as a place of sacrifice is Mount Ebal in Deut 27:4–5. This is surprising in light of the claim that Deuteronomy was written in the monarchic period in order to strengthen the claims of the monarchy centered in Jerusalem.[37] We might expect that Jerusalem would be named if the author were attempting to solidify the claims of Jerusalem and the monarchy. At a minimum, we might expect that no other site would be singled out as a potential competitor to the sanctuary in Jerusalem. We will examine the significance of this below.

5.2. "The Place" in the Historical and Prophetic Books

According to Josh 18:1, the tent of meeting was set up at Shiloh. This is clearly the only authorized place of sacrifice, since the Reubenites, Gadites, and the half tribe of Manasseh who live in the Transjordan region are accused of rebellion when they build an altar for themselves (Josh 22:16). Their defense is that the altar they built was commemorative, not for sacrifice (22:24–27). Tellingly, they refer to the altar simply as a "model" (תבנית) of Yahweh's altar (v. 28), and they disavow any intention to offer sacrifices at any altar other than the "altar of Yahweh

---

that the verse should be read as referring to its dwelling, and refers to the name itself. This is also consistent with v. 11, and is the preferable translation.

36. Whether Deuteronomy 12 envisions a sole sanctuary or a central sanctuary along with other authorized Yahweh-sanctuaries is debatable. G. J. Wenham maintains that Deuteronomy mandates a central sanctuary but allows other sanctuaries as well ("Deuteronomy and the Central Sanctuary," *TB* 22 [1971] 103–18). He is followed in this by E. H. Merrill, *Deuteronomy* (NAC 4; Nashville: Broadman & Holman, 1994) 223–24. On the other hand, McConville argues that Deuteronomy establishes a sole sanctuary that was located in a succession of places (J. G. McConville and J. G. Millar, *Time and Place in Deuteronomy* [JSOTSupp 179; Sheffield: Sheffield Academic, 1994] 117–23; see also McConville, *Deuteronomy*, 230–32). This is the most likely position. See the discussion in Vogt, *Deuteronomic Theology*, 169–79.

37. Representative of this view is Weinfeld, *Deuteronomic School*, 166–71.

our God that is in front of his tabernacle."[38] Shiloh remained the authorized place of sacrifice until the time of Eli and Samuel, though apparently it was moved at times to other locations (such as Bethel [Judg 20:27]).

Judges marks the beginning of a transition from the scrupulous commitment to the sole sanctuary seen in Joshua to the widespread acceptance of other sanctuaries seen in 1–2 Samuel and 1–2 Kings. According to Judg 2:10, the generation after Joshua "did not know Yahweh or the things he had done for Israel." This lack of knowledge led to idolatry and syncretism (v. 11). It also resulted in the establishment of multiple Yahweh sanctuaries, many of which were idiosyncratic in their practice at best, if not explicitly syncretistic (Judg 6:25, 8:33–34, 10:6, 17:1–5). The worship at these local sanctuaries "degenerated into . . . 'poly-Yahwism': local differentiation of the Yahweh cult traditions and forms."[39]

The lack of commitment to a single (or central) sanctuary continues in 1–2 Samuel. Following the separation of the ark of the covenant from the tabernacle in 1 Samuel 4, the people offered sacrifices at Mizpah (1 Sam 7:9), Gilgal (1 Sam 11:15, 13:9–14), and Hebron (2 Sam 15:12).

Jerusalem is the chosen place from the time of David onward, as the ark is brought there from Kiriath Jearim (2 Samuel 6). Nevertheless, the book of Kings shows that the Israelites worshiped at the "high places" (במות) in addition to the sanctuary in Jerusalem.[40] Particularly telling is the appearance of a formulaic use of the term: "But the high places [במות] were not removed. The people continued to offer sacrifices and burn incense on the high places." Its appearance as a summary of the king's actions in five instances[41] highlights that the practice of worship at sites other than Jerusalem was prevalent, but it was nevertheless an indictment of the king and people.[42]

The postexilic historical books adopt a similar stance. 1–2 Chronicles indicates that sacrifices were offered at Gibeon, the location of the tabernacle following its separation from the ark (1 Chr 16:39–40). This is apparently still the case at the beginning of Solomon's reign, as Solomon brings the assembly to Gibeon to offer sacrifices (2 Chr 1:1–3),

---

38. See the discussion of the significance of this altar in D. M. Howard Jr., *Joshua* (NAC 5; Nashville: Broadman & Holman, 1998) 413–14.

39. D. I. Block, *Judges–Ruth* (NAC 6; Nashville: Broadman & Holman, 1999) 41.

40. 1 Kgs 3:2–4; 11:7; 12:31–32; 13:2, 32–33; 14:23; 15:14; 22:43; 2 Kgs 12:3; 14:4; 15:4, 35; 16:4; 17:9, 11, 29, 32; 18:4, 22; 21:3; 23:5, 8–9, 13, 15, 19–20.

41. 1 Kgs 22:43; 2 Kgs 12:3; 14:4; 15:4, 35.

42. The opposite is true as well: Hezekiah and Josiah are commended for their actions in destroying the high places in favor of the central sanctuary, as well as its purification.

despite the fact (noted by the Chronicler) that the ark was established in Jerusalem. Overall, the presentation in 1–2 Chronicles is similar to that in 1–2 Kings, as the presence of alternatives to the central sanctuary is seen as an indictment of king and people. Ezra and Nehemiah strikingly depict Jerusalem as the sole place of sacrifice.

The treatment of the place of worship in the prophetic books is consistent with that seen in the historical books. The prophetic critique addressed to Israel and Judah includes an insistence that sacrifice offered at multiple locations is disloyalty to Yahweh.[43] Isa 65:3, for example, accuses the people of provoking Yahweh to anger by "offering sacrifices in gardens and burning incense on bricks." This is similar to the accusation in Hos 4:13. Jeremiah's call to proper Sabbath observance in Jer 17:26 describes as a consequence of faithfulness the people bringing their sacrifices and offerings to the "house of Yahweh," a reference to the temple (as is clear from the beginning of the call in Jer 17:19). Similarly, Ezekiel 40–46 envisions restoration of sacrifice at the rebuilt temple and altar in Jerusalem.

5.3. *"The Place" of Sacrifice and the Implied Audience of the Historical and Prophetic Books*

Though the preceding discussion of the place of sacrifice in the historical and prophetic books was necessarily brief, we can nevertheless discern how the implied authors intended the readers to respond. They intended the implied audience to understand the importance of a central sanctuary. Moreover, they present sacrifice at a central sanctuary as a means of living out loyalty to Yahweh and, therefore, a crucial part of covenant faithfulness.

This may be seen most clearly in the fact that the books depict multiple altars—even Yahweh-centered ones—as indicative of disloyalty to Yahweh and a breakdown of the expected order. As we noted, Judges

---

43. Much scholarly attention has been focused on the question of the overall stance of the prophets toward sacrifice. In the first half of the 20th century, it was common to see sacrifice and the sacrificial system as antithetical to the worship priorities of the prophets, particularly the preexilic ones. Pfeiffer refers to the sacrificial system of the cult as "the heathen element of the religion of Israel, derived from the religion of Canaan and attacked by the prophets" (*Religion in the Old Testament: The History of a Spiritual Triumph* [ed. C. C. Forman; New York: Harper & Brothers, 1961] 191). This view has largely been rejected, and it is fair to say that the preexilic prophets saw sacrifice as a legitimate part of Yahweh worship, though they rejected sacrifices offered by the people when they were living in disobedience to the covenantal terms of the torah. This important question is obviously beyond the scope of this essay; for a helpful treatment of the issues, see E. C. Lucas, "Sacrifice in the Prophets," in *Sacrifice in the Bible* (ed. R. T. Beckwith and M. J. Selman; Grand Rapids: Baker, 1995) 59–74.

portrays the multiple sanctuaries as a negative development. The implied author sees the proliferation of altars as symptomatic of the increasing Canaanization[44] of Israelite society. Similarly, the prophetic books treat alternative worship sites as indications of lack of loyalty to Yahweh and his covenant.

Most significant, of course, is the way 1–2 Kings singles out the high places and alternative worship sites as evidence of failure on the part of king and people to show fidelity to the covenant. The implied author of 1–2 Kings assesses the individual kings to a large extent on the basis of their actions with respect to the high places (במות).[45] Indeed, Hezekiah and Josiah in particular are singled out precisely for their actions in eliminating the high places and support for the central sanctuary in Jerusalem. The case of Hezekiah illustrates this most clearly. His devotion to Yahweh stands in marked contrast to the idolatry of both his father and his son and successor, Manasseh. One of the key distinctives of Hezekiah's reign is the elimination of the high places (במות), and Manasseh's rebuilding of them highlights his disloyalty. This reinforces for the implied audience the importance of the central sanctuary and the need for worshiping Yahweh in the manner and at the place of his choosing.

Clearly, then, the implied audiences of the historical and prophetic books were meant to see sacrifice at the place of Yahweh's choosing as integral to covenant loyalty. Alternative sites were to be viewed as tolerable prior to Yahweh's revelation of a permanent site (1 Kgs 3:2) but ultimately indicative of disloyalty to Yahweh and dangerous for the spiritual vitality of the people. The perlocutionary intention of the implied authors of these books is that the implied reader will seek Yahweh only at "the place" and offer sacrifices in accordance with his instructions.

6. The Implied Audience of Deuteronomy 12 and 27 and the Date of Composition

Once again we must consider what implications about the date of composition may be drawn from the conclusions reached about the implied audiences of Deuteronomy and the historical and prophetic books. As was the case with Deut 2:1–23, it is hard to conceive of a time in the monarchic period when Deuteronomy 12 and 27 were likely to have been composed. The place of sacrifice was unquestionably Jeru-

---

44. Block, *Judges–Ruth*, 57–59.
45. See I. Provan, *1 and 2 Kings* (NIBC 7; Peabody, MA: Hendrickson, 1995) 48.

salem following the building of the temple and the unification of the ark and the tent of meeting. If the historical and prophetic books are illustrative of the prevailing views of the times they describe, then alternative worship sites were meant to be seen as a threat to the success of the people.

Deuteronomy 12, as we have seen, conspicuously leaves the location of the authorized place of worship unnamed.[46] If Deuteronomy were written in the monarchic era to solidify the monarchy and the priority of Jerusalem, it is strange that Jerusalem is not named or referred to by the authors of the book. Again, advocates of a monarchic date for Deuteronomy maintain that the book was written in the time of its discovery; consequently, the authors were free to include those things that advanced their interests. One might expect that the same authors who, in this reconstruction, placed Deuteronomy on the lips of Moses would use his prophetic voice and authority to support the claims of Jerusalem. Instead, Deuteronomy 12 mandates the destruction of all pagan altars and the establishment of "the place" Yahweh will choose, rather than referring to Jerusalem either directly or even obliquely.

The absence of the use of "high place" (במה) or "high places" (במות) in Deuteronomy further supports the case that Deuteronomy was written in the premonarchic era. The altar law in Deut 12:2 describes pagan worship sites in terms similar to the critique of the high places elsewhere. It commands the people to "destroy all the places where the nations you are dispossessing worship their gods—on the mountains, the hills, and under every green tree." In its depiction of Ahaz, for example, 2 Kgs 16:4 describes him as offering sacrifices and burning incense at the high places and "on the hills, and under every green tree."[47] This is the exact wording of the description of pagan worship sites in Deut 12:2, though the term "high places" (במות) is absent in Deuteronomy.

For Weinfeld and others, this common usage points to a common author and is considered "Deuteronomistic" language.[48] This, further,

---

46. Curiously, I. Cairns maintains that "clearly, the final edition of Deuteronomy identifies the 'one place' with Jerusalem," despite there being no reference to Jerusalem in the book and the reference to Ebal in Deuteronomy 27 (*Word and Presence: A Commentary on the Book of Deuteronomy* [ITC; Grand Rapids: Eerdmans, 1992] 18).

47. Similar language is found in 1 Kgs 14:23 and 2 Kgs 17:10.

48. Weinfeld, *Deuteronomic School*, 322, 366. See, however, the argument of N. F. Lohfink, who maintains that caution should be exercised in determining whether a text should be considered "Deuteronomistic" on the basis of vocabulary alone ("Was There a Deuteronomistic Movement," in *Those Elusive Deuteronomists: The Phenomenon of Pan-Deuteronomism* [ed. L. S. Schearing and S. L. McKenzie; JSOTSupp 26; Sheffield: Sheffield Academic, 1999] 36–66). Though the use of the phrase in 2 Kgs 16:4 would likely

is seen as strengthening the case for dating Deuteronomy in the monarchic period. In this view, the two texts reflect the same perspective and are used to strengthen the claims of the Jerusalem sanctuary.

However, the fact that terms that are so important in developing the themes and theology of 1–2 Kings are absent in Deuteronomy may point to a different provenance for the two compositions. If Deuteronomy were a product of the monarchic period and if the author(s) wanted to polemicize against the high places in support of the Jerusalem sanctuary, we might expect the author to include in the foundational legislation in Deuteronomy 12 references to the places that were actually being used in the monarchic period as alternative worship sites. The similarity of phrases in Deuteronomy and 1–2 Kings (without the use of "high place" [במה] or "high places" [במות]) may simply point to the significant influence of Deuteronomy, rather than a common author or time period.

Another important consideration is the fact that Deuteronomy 27 actually identifies an alternative worship site, on Mount Ebal (Deut 27:4). The command in Deut 27:6–7 to bring burnt offerings and fellowship offerings to the altar erected on Ebal, as well as the call to "rejoice" (שמח) in the presence of Yahweh there, clearly fulfills of the command in Deut 12:11–18, which calls for bringing the offerings to "the place" and rejoicing there.

In terms of dating Deuteronomy, the presence of the reference to Ebal in chapter 27 is significant. If Deuteronomy were in fact a product of Josiah's time, then the scribal school responsible for Deuteronomy included in it a call to worship at a place that had been under Assyrian domination for over 80 years. It is true that Josiah's reclamation of the territories of the Northern Kingdom made the establishment of an altar on Ebal a realistic possibility, but this would serve to undermine, rather than strengthen, the primacy of Jerusalem in the public imagination. After all, only Ebal is named in Deuteronomy as a legitimate worship site. The inclusion of reference to Ebal in a book written in the monarchic period would possibly bring about a "restoration" movement that sought to scrupulously obey the instructions of Moses, thus weakening the claims of Jerusalem and even the monarchy itself as actually practiced (Deut 17:14–20).[49] It is even less likely that Deuteron-

---

qualify as "Deuteronomistic" in Lohfink's proposed approach to the issue ("Was There A Deuteronomistic Movement," 39), the absence of the key terms "high place" (במה) or "high places" (במות) is significant.

49. The law of the king is radical in its presentation of the king as a student of torah and model Israelite (see Vogt, *Deuteronomic Theology*, 216–20). The denial of the very roles

omy could date to Hezekiah's time, when Assyrian dominance of the region (including the former Northern Kingdom and Ebal) was firmly established.

These considerations of the effect of the text on the implied audience suggest that Deuteronomy is best seen as a product of a time when there was no actual monarchy in Jerusalem. This points to either the pre- or post-monarchic periods. Given that Jerusalem was still considered "the place" in the Postexilic Period (cf. Ezra 1:3–4), the reference to Ebal can further help "tip the scales" in favor of a premonarchic date of the book. As was the case with Deuteronomy's treatment of Edom, Ammon, and Moab, this is not determinative in itself, but is, rather, an approximate index that can perhaps move analysis beyond the impasse that marks contemporary study of the date of Deuteronomy.

7. Contemporary Significance

While the arguments for the date of Deuteronomy may seem like something only an academic could love, the issue is an important one for the church. Increasingly, the historical accuracy of Scripture has been questioned, even by those who maintain a "high" view of scriptural authority.[50] This will surely affect the next generation of students, pastors, and scholars, as well as laypeople in the church.

At issue is the authority of Scripture. Deuteronomy presents itself as the words of Moses (Deut 1:1), a perspective assumed on the part of NT writers as well.[51] The book purports to be the final speeches of Moses, given to the people on the verge of entry into the land. These speeches are Moses' "last best chance" to tell the people what they need to be successful at being the people of God in the land. As such, Deuteronomy's vision for life lived in relationship with Yahweh is not entirely theoretical or utopian.[52] Rather, it is presented as something the

---

actually carried out by Israelite (and other ANE) kings further argues against seeing Deuteronomy as the product of a time when the monarchy was extant. In a similar way, the laws of warfare are presented as wars of the people, not the king, thus further reducing the king's influence. This makes it even less likely that Deuteronomy was a product of courtly scribal activity, if not of the monarchic period as a whole. On the view of the laws of warfare as envisioning wars of the people, see Nelson, *Deuteronomy*, 248.

50. See the recent works by K. L. Sparks (*God's Word in Human Words: An Evangelical Appropriation of Critical Biblical Scholarship* [Grand Rapids: Baker, 2008]) and P. Enns (*Inspiration and Incarnation: Evangelicals and the Problem of the Old Testament* [Grand Rapids: Baker, 2005]).

51. See Matt 8:4; 19:7–8; 22:4; Mark 1:44; 7:10; 10:3–5; 12:19, 26; Luke 2:22; 5:14; 20:28, 37; 24:27; John 1:17, 45; 3:14; 5:46; 7:19, 22–23; Acts 3:22; 15:21; 26:22; 28:23; Rom 9:15; 10:5, 19; 1 Cor 9:9.

52. On the nature of Deuteronomy's vision, see Vogt, *Deuteronomic Theology*, 227–31.

people were to actually carry out as part of their mission as the people of Yahweh.

If the book were actually written in the monarchic period, then the association with Moses is diminished at best, if not eliminated. The intentions of the implied author are altered, as are the desired responses on the part of the implied audience. This has significant implications for interpretation, as well as the authority of the text.

I am not suggesting that the case presented here definitively proves Mosaic authorship of Deuteronomy. Rather, I have demonstrated that the book is better seen as a product of the premonarchic era. But if it is premonarchic, then there is greater likelihood of association with Moses, as the text itself claims. In this way, the authority of the text is underscored, and the trust accorded to it by the people of God is upheld.

Laws and Ethical Ideals in Deuteronomy

Gordon J. Wenham

1. Introduction

"You shall love your neighbor as yourself" is an admirable motto, but very difficult to fulfill properly. Can one ever say that one has treated any of one's neighbors with as much care as oneself, let alone treated all of them that way? It is a high ethical ideal to which many aspire, but few reach. But if complete love of neighbor is the goal, which examples of falling short can be tolerated and which failures must be punished or at least criticized? The legal collections of the Old Testament give many examples of unneighborly behavior and prescribe appropriate punishments. For example, "If a man steals an ox or a sheep, and kills it or sells it, he shall repay five oxen for an ox, and four sheep for a sheep" (Exod 21:37[22:1]). Or, "If a man commits adultery with the wife of his neighbor, both the adulterer and the adulteress shall surely be put to death" (Lev 20:10).

There is clearly a large gap between loving one's neighbor as oneself and stealing his ox or his wife. Elsewhere I have argued that in reading the Old Testament it is important to be aware of this gap between biblical ideals and what is enforced by legal sanction.[1] Thieves and adulterers are punished for their deeds, but those who merely covet their neighbors' goods or wives escape sanction but not moral condemnation. I have suggested that the authors of the Old Testament narratives both judge the behavior of their characters not just by whether they adhere to the minimal standard of the penal law but whether they fulfill their ethical ideals.[2] The reader of these stories is expected to do the

---

Author's Note: I first came to know Dan Block when we worked together on the revision of Genesis for the *Living Bible*, which eventually became the *New Living Translation*. They were very congenial times thanks to Dan's learning and gracious leadership. In Britain we would call him a "real gentleman." But he is a gentleman with prodigious energy and application, who has produced some outstanding work across the biblical canon. I count it a real privilege to have worked with him.

1. G. J. Wenham, "The Gap between Law and Ethics in the Bible," *JJS* 48 (1997) 17–29.

2. Idem, *Story as Torah: Reading the Old Testament Ethically* (Edinburgh: T & T Clark, 2000) 73–107.

same. For example, though polygamy was legal in Israel, this does not mean it was regarded as ethically desirable, for God created only one wife for Adam (Gen 2:22–24). So when polygamous situations are described either in narrative (e.g., Genesis 29–31) or in the law (e.g., Deut 21:15–17), we should not suppose that polygamy is being commended. It is much more likely that such texts are illustrating its disadvantages.

This gap between law and ideal is also present in Deuteronomy. Moses demands, "You shall love the LORD your God with all your heart and with all your soul and with all your might" (Deut 6:5). On the other hand, mild indifference to the LORD is not punished; only outright rebellion is, such as the worship of other gods: "If your brother . . . entices you secretly, saying, 'Let us go and serve other gods,'. . . . You shall stone him to death with stones" (Deut 13:7–11[6–10]).[3] But can one say anything more than that the penal law only states the floor of tolerable behavior? That is, if you love the LORD so little that you secede to worship other deities, your behavior is more than morally reprehensible. It cannot be tolerated in a holy nation, so you must be exterminated. The holy nation (Deut 7:6) cannot survive such covenantal infidelity. This article will attempt to explore the nature of this gap between what is the ideal ethic and actions that are so intolerable that they demand punishment. Are there grades of intolerable behavior? Are there different expectations of different people? Is the ethical idealism of Deut 6:5 moderated in practice?

2. Samples of the Tension between Laws and Ethical Ideals

2.1. Care for the Poor

The existence of a gap between what is desirable in theory and what actually can be achieved in practice is explicit in several passages in Deuteronomy. The laws helping the poor cover a variety of topics: no interest on loans or pledges (Deut 23:20[19]; 24:6, 10); prompt payment of wages (24:14–15); leaving grain fields, vineyards, and olive groves partially unharvested (24:19–22)—all are measures designed to ensure that the poor can survive. It is an acknowledgment of the brotherhood of all Israelites. The rich are not to use their power over those indebted to them; rather the affluent are to show them charity by letting them share at least in a limited way in their wealth. But Deuteronomy's ideal is clear: If Israel strictly obeys God's commandments, "there will be no

---

3. On this text see C. A. Reeder, *The Enemy in the Household: Family Violence in Deuteronomy and Beyond* (Grand Rapids: Baker, 2012) 27–37.

poor among you; for the LORD will bless you in the land that the LORD your God is giving you for an inheritance to possess—if only you will strictly obey the voice of the LORD your God, being careful to do all this commandment that I command you today. For the LORD your God will bless you, as he promised you" (15:4–6).[4]

However, hardly has the prediction that there will be no poor in the land been uttered than we have a law dealing with the situation if "one of your brothers should become poor" (Deut 15:7), and then the prediction, "There will never cease to be poor in the land" (15:11). Ideally Israel should keep the law with her whole heart, and then she would enjoy such prosperity that there would be no poor in the land. But Deuteronomy is pervaded by the fear that the nation will repeat its past mistakes.[5] Chapter 1 recalls in detail the episode of the spies, when unwarranted fear led to the abandonment of the conquest. The positive depiction of the defeat of Sihon and Og in chs. 2 and 3 is soon followed by a retelling of the Sinai experience and dire warnings of the dangers of idolatry, which could lead to exile and loss of the land (ch. 4). This same tension between hope and fear is seen at the other end of the book. After chapter 28 has set out the blessings for obedience and the curses for breaking the law, chapters 29 and 30 consider the situation when Israel will be suffering exile in punishment for her sin and assure them that restoration is indeed possible if they repent. More than that, "The LORD your God will make you abundantly prosperous in all the work of your hand, in the fruit of your womb and in the fruit of your cattle and in the fruit of your ground. For the LORD will again take delight in prospering you, as he took delight in your fathers" (30:9), if "you shall again obey the voice of the LORD and keep all his commandments that I command you today" (30:8).

Thus the injunctions to be generous to the Israelite who falls into debt—to lend to him even though the seventh year is approaching, to give a golden handshake of livestock, grain and wine when he leaves (Deut 15:7–14)—are not viewed as endorsing the poor man's poverty, but as a means of ameliorating it. If Israel fulfilled the commandments perfectly, she would enjoy such prosperity that there would be no poor.

2.2. *Warfare*

If the tension between what would be ideal and what is practical is most clearly articulated in Deuteronomy 15, this is by no means the

---

4. On Deuteronomy's ideal, see J. G. McConville, *Deuteronomy* (AOTC 5; Leicester: Apollos, 2002) 259–60.

5. For fuller discussion see P. A. Barker, *The Triumph of Grace in Deuteronomy* (Carlisle: Paternoster, 2004).

only passage where it is felt. The laws on war in chapter 20 also exemplify it. The whole passage falls in the section (chs. 19–21) illustrating the implications of the sixth commandment, "You shall not kill."[6] This begins with a section that restrains the avenger of blood from taking revenge where his relative has been killed by accident (19:1–13). It then deals with a situation where a false accusation on a capital charge could lead to an innocent person being executed. Strict application of the talion principle, it is suggested, will prevent such behaviour in the future: "then you shall do to him as he had meant to do to his brother. So you shall purge the evil from your midst" (19:19). Thus the legislation in chapter 19 is more concerned with preventing further loss of life after a homicide, whether deliberate or accidental, than with prescribing punishment.

The same concern is evident in the laws about war. Deuteronomy looks forward to a time "when he gives you rest from all your enemies around, so that you live in safety" (Deut 12:10; cf. 3:20, 12:9, 25:19). Indeed it envisages all their enemies running away (28:7). It glorifies peace not war. And this vision informs the specific regulations about waging war in chapter 20. Uncompleted tasks at home take priority over conscription into the army. If someone has built a new house and not dedicated it, has planted a vineyard and has not enjoyed its fruit, or betrothed a wife but has not married her, he is excused from serving in the army (20:5–7). These exemptions from military call up show that the law prioritizes civilian pursuits over warfare. The ideal is peace and security, not the obliteration of the enemy. So if Israel has to fight, it must first offer terms of peace: "When you draw near to a city to fight against it, offer terms of peace to it. And if it responds to you peaceably and it opens to you, then all the people who are found in it shall do forced labor for you and shall serve you. But if it makes no peace with you, but makes war against you, then you shall besiege it" (20:10–12) and all the male inhabitants shall be killed and the rest taken as plunder. This is how distant towns are to be treated. But those in the land of Canaan must be put to the ban lest they lead Israel astray to follow their worship practices (20:16–18).

But does banning the Canaanites exclude them from the offer of peace mentioned in Deut 20:10–12? Read in isolation this passage is not clear. With Maimonides and Lohfink,[7] it is possible to read verses 10–19 as follows:

---

6. See S. Kaufman, "The Structure of the Deuteronomic Law," *Maarav* 1.2 (1978–79) 105–58.

7. For Maimonides, see J. H. Tigay, *Deuteronomy* (JPSTC; Philadelphia: Jewish Publication Society, 1996) 472. N. Lohfink, "חָרַם *ḥāram*," *TDOT*, 5:197: "The war law in Dt.

V. 10: Peace offer to any city
V. 11: Offer accepted by distant city
Vv. 12–15: Offer declined by distant city
Vv. 16–18: Offer declined by Canaanite city

On this reading the offer of peace is made to Canaanite cities as well as distant towns. And if they had accepted it, they would be treated like distant cities: they would not have been put to the ban but forced to work for Israel as the Gibeonites were (see Joshua 9).

Though this is an attractive reading of Deuteronomy 20, it does not seem to be the obvious understanding of other passages in Deuteronomy to Judges, which apparently insist that Israel has an obligation to execute the ban on the Canaanites and other inhabitants of the land (Deut 2:34, 3:6, 7:2, Josh 6:21, 8:26, 10:28–40, Judg 1:17). But even if this is the right view, the ban on the Canaanites must be seen as a merely temporary duty. Once Israel is securely established in the land and the Canaanites have been eliminated, the problem of religious cleansing becomes just an internal one, when Israelite individuals or cities apostatize (Deuteronomy 13, 17). If this situation had ever come to pass, only the problem of external distant enemies would have remained. Then just the regulations of Deut 20:10–15 would have applied; they insist on peace being offered to the enemy as a first step.

2.3. Food

Food laws are another area where the tension between ideals and what is legally permissible may be detected. The strain is already evident in Genesis. According to Gen 1:29–30 humans and animals were originally supposed to eat every plant of the field; in other words, they were vegetarian.[8] There was no provision for humans to eat meat. This primitive vegetarianism was part of the violence-free age that preceded the fall. From Gen 3:15 ("I will put enmity between you and the woman") to 6:11 ("the earth was filled with violence"), there is an avalanche of violence that nearly sweeps away all life on earth. The flood returns the earth to its earliest state when waters of the great deep covered its face (1:2–3). The ebbing of the flood waters is equivalent to a new creation: the dry ground, plants, and birds reappear, while Noah

---

20:10–18 must also be understood from this perspective: Israel's obligation to offer peaceful terms of surrender to the enemy before a war (vv. 10f) holds not only for the cities that are 'very far' (v. 15), but also for the cities that Yahweh has designated as Israel's inheritance (v. 16). The other form of war, namely ḥrm (vv. 16f), is to be practiced only upon rejection of terms."

8. C. Westermann, *Genesis 1–11: A Commentary* (trans. J. J. Scullion; Minneapolis: Augsburg, 1984) 161–65.

is viewed as a second Adam, forefather of the whole human race. But how are Noah and his descendants to avoid descending into the maelstrom of violence that destroyed the first pre-flood world?

Part of the solution lies in the institution of the death penalty on a strictly regulated basis. Instead of the seventy-sevenfold revenge threatened by Lamech (Gen 4:24), only one person, the murderer himself, shall be put to death (9:5–6). That hopefully would be a rare event. But eating meat is also to be allowed as long as the blood is not consumed: "Every moving thing that lives shall be food for you. And as I gave you the green plants, I give you everything. But you shall not eat flesh with its life, that is, its blood" (9:3–4). Here in narrative form we have the distinction being made between what would be ideal (vegetarianism) and legal requirement (meat without blood).[9] And the same issue is addressed in Deuteronomy with a further clarification about where meat may be eaten.

Deuteronomy envisages meat eating essentially to be an aspect of sacrifice. Therefore, as in Leviticus 17, it should be done only at the chosen place. In Leviticus this means in the forecourt of the tabernacle (Lev 17:2–5); those who fail to comply are threatened with being cut off (17:8–9).[10] Similarly, Deuteronomy 12 says, "But you shall seek the place that the LORD your God will choose out of all your tribes to put his name and make his habitation there. There you shall go, and there you shall bring your burnt offerings and your sacrifices. And there you shall eat before the LORD your God" (Deut 12:5–7). This is to be the arrangement when they are living in the land and at peace with all their enemies (12:9–14). But the fulfillment of that dream creates a problem: many of the population will be too far from the chosen place to go there whenever they want to eat meat. So Deuteronomy allows for some non-sacrificial slaughter away from the central sanctuary: "However, you may slaughter and eat meat within any of your towns, as much as you desire, according to the blessing of the LORD your God that he has given you. The unclean and the clean may eat of it, as of the gazelle and as of the deer. Only you shall not eat the blood; you shall pour it out on the earth like water" (Deut 12:15–16).

Three points are made here and subsequently reiterated in Deut 12:20–28. First, such non-sacrificial slaughter may be done anywhere "in any of your towns." Second, because the slaughter is non-sacrificial,

---

9. Wenham, *Story as Torah*, 83.
10. For discussion of Leviticus 17, see J. Milgrom, *Leviticus 17–22* (AB 3B; New York: Doubleday, 2000) 1447–1514.

the eater does not have to be in a state of ritual cleanness—"the unclean and the clean may eat it" (Deut 12:15)—as is essential if one is to eat sacrificial meat (Lev 7:19–20). This is the same principle as applies to eating wild game; only domestic animals can be used in sacrifice. Third, the blood must not be consumed, but it must be poured out like water.

This concession, which allows for non-sacrificial slaughter of some animals, is not a substitute for sacrifice itself, which must still be restricted to the chosen place: "You may not eat within your towns the tithe of your grain or of your wine or of your oil, or the firstborn of your herd or of your flock, or any of your vow offerings that you vow, or your freewill offerings or the contribution that you present, but you shall eat them before the LORD your God in the place that the LORD your God will choose" (Deut 12:17–18).

One may see these regulations as a compromise between what the lawgiver would really like—no eating of meat at all and sacrifice only at the chosen place—and practical necessity. Thus, some meat eating of clean animals without the blood may be enjoyed outside the chosen place as a concession to the desires of the dispersed population.

2.4. Synthesis

This brief review of some of the laws on poverty, homicide, and food show that the book of Deuteronomy is quite conscious of the distinction between what is ethically or theologically desirable and what the law can realistically enforce. The book's legislation in these areas shows a consciousness of the gap between the ideal and the requirements of the law. We shall now explore the shape of this gap by reviewing some of the punishments laid out in the penal law.

3. Ethical Ideals and the Punishments of the Penal Law

The Ten Commandments are moral imperatives, but breaking most of them constitute crimes.[11] Worshiping other gods and enticing others to do the same requires the death penalty in the form of a public stoning (Deut 13:11[10]; 17:5; cf. 18:20). If a whole town apostatizes, then its inhabitants are put to the sword (13:15). By thus eliminating the worst sinners in society, the evil is purged from the nation's midst (13:6[5]; 17:7). Unlike Lev 24:10–16, Deuteronomy prescribes no punishment for blasphemy. The same is true of the Sabbath commandment, for whose

---

11. R. Westbrook, "Punishments and Crimes," *ABD* 5:547.

transgression Num 15:32–36 requires the death penalty,[12] but Deuteronomy does not mention any penalty for not observing the Sabbath. On the other hand, flouting parental authority is severely punished: "If a man has a stubborn and rebellious son who will not obey the voice of his father or the voice of his mother, and, though they discipline him, will not listen to them,. . . . Then all the men of the city shall stone him to death with stones. So you shall purge the evil from your midst, and all Israel shall hear, and fear" (Deut 21:18, 21). Similarly premeditated homicide (Deut 19:11–13) requires the murderer to be executed by the avenger of blood, to "purge the guilt of innocent blood from Israel." Adultery by a married or inchoately married woman likewise attracts the death penalty (22:22, 21, 24): in two of these cases involving the inchoately married woman, stoning is the prescribed mode of execution,[13] and in all cases the death penalty is said to purge the evil from your midst.

If taking a slave or selling one can be regarded as a kind of theft, it too is punishable by death (Deut 24:7), but presumably stealing less valuable items would have attracted lesser penalties (cf. Exodus 22). Finally false witness is punished by an exact application of the talion. Someone who makes false accusations against another will be punished in the way the falsely accused would have suffered had the accusation been justified. This too will act to purge the nation and deter others from bringing false charges (Deut 19:19–20).

Running through this penal legislation is the concern to "purge the evil."[14] The death penalty does, in a literal fashion, set a minimum standard of behavior within the nation. Commit murder, adultery, or apostasy within Israel and you yourself will be eliminated. This will ensure the purity of the nation and the land. But to avoid doing these things is not enough. Like the rest of Scripture Deuteronomy does not see merely refraining from criminal behavior as sufficient. It encourages, even commands, much more.

For example, it is not sufficient merely to punish homicide—by death for premeditated killing or banishment to a city of refuge for accidental

---

12. Cf. the Psalter, which makes little of these commandments; see G. J. Wenham, *Psalms as Torah* (Grand Rapids: Baker, 2012) 102–5.

13. Tigay refers to crimes punished by stoning as acts of high treason: "They could cause the punishment of the entire community or undermine its stability, thus they were viewed as threats to national safety. Punishment of these crimes by stoning enabled the entire public to participate and thereby express its outrage against the crime and the threat it posed to society's welfare" (Tigay, *Deuteronomy*, 133).

14. Deut 13:6[5]; 17:7, 12; 19:19; 21:21; 22:21, 22, 24; 24:7.

manslaughter (Deut 19:5; cf. Num 35:25–28)—for Israel is urged to take measures to prevent fatal accidents: "When you build a new house, you shall make a parapet for your roof, that you may not bring the guilt of blood upon your house, if anyone should fall from it" (Deut 22:8). While slave-trading is liable to the death penalty (24:7), banning it by no means exhausts one's duty towards slaves. Those released in the seventh year should be stocked up with sheep and oxen, grain and wine (15:13–14). An escaped slave should not be returned to his owner, but allowed to live in freedom wherever he likes (23:15–16). Women captured in war may be married by their captors, but they cannot be reduced to slavery (21:10–14). All this expresses an attitude that slavery should not exist, but given that it does, it is one manifestation of poverty, necessitating that the well-to-do help slaves as much as they can. Turning a fellow Israelite into a chattel that can be traded is absolutely forbidden (24:7), and escaped slaves must be helped to retain their freedom (23:15–16).

The major difference between the Exodus version and the Deuteronomy text highlights a pervasive concern of the law. Whereas Exodus justifies resting on the seventh day as an imitation of God's rest from creation on that day, Deuteronomy says, "You shall remember that you were a slave in the land of Egypt, and the LORD your God brought you out from there with a mighty hand and an outstretched arm. Therefore the LORD your God commanded you to keep the Sabbath day" (Deut 5:15). Thoughtfulness and generosity is expected to characterize Israel's attitude to its poorest and most vulnerable citizens. At the great festivals of Weeks and Tabernacles, when the nation gathered to recall its past, they are told, "You shall rejoice in your feast, you and your son and your daughter, your male servant and your female servant, the Levite, the sojourner, the fatherless, and the widow who are within your towns" (16:14; cf. 16:11; 12:12, 18).

But there are many other injunctions that aim to safeguard the poor and vulnerable.[15] Judges are not to show partiality or accept bribes, "for a bribe blinds the eyes of the wise, and subverts the cause of the righteous" (Deut 16:19). The poor are those most likely to require loans to tide them over, but these loans are to be interest-free (23:20–21[19–20]). And those who lend to the poor are forbidden to take vital tools such as a millstone as a pledge (24:6) or keep a pledged garment overnight (24:10–13). Day laborers are to be paid each day, not kept waiting for

---

15. See D. L. Baker, *Tight Fists or Open Hands? Wealth and Poverty in Old Testament Law* (Grand Rapids: Eerdmans, 2009).

their pay: "You shall give him his wages on the same day, before the sun sets (for he is poor and counts on it), lest he cry against you to the Lord, and you be guilty of sin" (24:15). These are essentially warnings about taking advantage of the vulnerability of the poor.

Other injunctions are more positive. For example, anyone may pick handfuls of his neighbor's grain or grapes and eat them on the spot, as long as they are not taken home in a bag (Deut 23:25–26[24–25]). But the sojourner, fatherless, and widow are allowed to collect forgotten sheaves and pick whatever is left over after harvesting in the vineyards and olive groves (24:19–22). These regulations seem deliberately designed to help the poor, especially those with no land of their own. But no mechanisms are mentioned to enforce these commands. They rely on the goodwill of the well-to-do to act in a spirit of generosity, imitating the generosity of God (see Deut 10:17–18), who brought them out of Egyptian slavery, a motif that occurs nearly 50 times in the book. From time to time there are warnings of divine displeasure, if these injunctions are ignored; but no effective temporal penalties are invoked. They may be described as making one guilty of sin (15:9, 24:15).

Somewhere between offenses that attract the death penalty and the exhortations just considered come a group of offenses that are said to be an abomination to the Lord and a group of sins that are formally cursed. The term "abomination" (תועבה) denotes something culturally unacceptable, "persons, things or practices that offend one's ritual or moral order."[16] Thus the Egyptians found shepherding or eating with foreigners abominable (Gen 43:32, 46:34), while Leviticus 18 brands the worship and sexual practices of the Canaanites as abominable (Lev 18:26, 27, 29, 30). The latter sense is the most frequent in Deuteronomy. Canaanite worship customs are often described as an abomination to the Lord (תועבת יהוה; Deut 7:25–26; 12:31; 13:15[14]; 18:9, 12; 20:18; 23:19[18]; 27:15). These practices the Lord hates (12:31). To follow Canaanite customs is to be disloyal to the covenant, so it is no wonder that they arouse divine displeasure, and clearly would attract the death penalty if the perpetrators were caught. But in many instances these offenses would be done in private or within the family, whose mutual ties might well mean the offense was not brought to the judges' attention. Describing potentially capital sins as "abominations" warned those who believed they would escape human punishment, that they would not evade divine justice. This element of secrecy would explain why

---

16. M. A. Grisanti, "תעב," *NIDOTTE* 4:314.

eating unclean meat (14:3), abusing a wife for financial gain (24:1–4),[17] and using unfair weights and measures (25:13–16) are also described as abominations.

The list of curses in Deuteronomy 27 seems somewhat heterogeneous, with misleading a blind man, incest, and idolatry all mixed up together. But what seems to unite this list is the secrecy involved.[18] This is explicit in v. 15, where someone makes an idol and *"sets it up in secret,"* and in v. 24, "cursed be anyone who strikes down his neighbor *in secret*." If either of these offenses were known publicly, capital punishment would be expected, but their secrecy rules that out. However the offenders are still cursed, and therefore may expect to suffer at God's hands. The other offenses that are cursed—dishonoring parents, moving landmarks, misleading the blind, treating sojourners, fatherless and widows unjustly, incest, bestiality, and taking bribes—could all be difficult to demonstrate in court. But this does not mean that they will escape God's attention.

4. Conclusion

The distinction between ethical ideals and legally enforceable rules is a helpful one, not just in the books of biblical narrative such as Genesis and Judges, but within the so-called second law called Deuteronomy. One must remember that Hebrew תורה would be better translated "instruction" than "law," so that moral exhortation or instructive story can just as well count as תורה as legal regulations or penalties for misbehavior. Deuteronomy contains both enforceable law and expressions of ethical ideals. We have argued that blatant transgression of most of the Ten Commandments could lead to the execution of the culprits. In this way the penal sanctions define the floor of tolerable behavior in ancient Israel. Transgressors are literally eliminated from the nation. Idolaters and adulterers are just two types of sinners that, if Deuteronomy's law were enforced, would not have existed in Israel.

However, family solidarity on the one hand and attempts to keep sins secret on the other must have meant that the majority of offenses went unpunished by human authority. But Deuteronomy insists that offenders will not escape divine judgment. They may believe no one knows their sin, but sins that deserve death are an abomination in

---

17. R. Westbrook, "The Prohibition on Restoration of Marriage in Deuteronomy 24:1–4," in *Studies in Bible* (ed. S. Japhet; Scripta Hierosolymitana 31; Jerusalem: Hebrew University Magnes Press, 1986) 387–405.

18. Tigay, *Deuteronomy*, 253.

God's sight, that is, they are just incompatible with life under the covenant. We are not told what form divine retribution will take, but it may be like the *karet* penalty in Leviticus, which probably involves premature inexplicable death.[19] Chapter 27 with its list of secret offenses puts it more simply: those who do such things are simply cursed; that is, they will bring on themselves and their fellows the horrendous fate described in 28:15–68.

But for Deuteronomy, like the rest of the Old Testament, godly living is not defined by simply refraining from the serious sins dealt with in the penal law. It involves caring for the vulnerable in society, the fatherless, the widow, the sojourner, and the poor. It involves giving refuge to the fleeing slave and treating the pretty captive honorably. It involves taking precautions so that others do not injure themselves by falling off one's roof. These are obviously merely illustrations of a positive caring attitude to one's fellow man that the book is keen to inculcate. And when it comes to religious duties, it is not just a question of not worshiping other gods or avoiding blasphemy or resting on the Sabbath; it involves joyous celebration of the great festivals that recalled God's saving work on Israel's behalf. In all these ways Deuteronomy advocates love for God and love of one's neighbor.

---

19. For fuller discussion see J. Milgrom, *Leviticus 1–16* (AB 3A; New York: Doubleday, 1991) 457–60.

Counting the Ten

An Investigation into the Numbering of the Decalogue

JASON S. DEROUCHIE

The Bible is explicit that God revealed *ten* Words to his people at Mt. Sinai (Exod 34:28; Deut 4:13, 10:4), and it goes to reason that we should know how to count them, especially in light of the unique status these words bear in Scripture.[1] But in the history of interpretation there has been three principal perspectives on how properly to enumerate these ten, and the distinct forms of the Decalogue in Exod 20:1–17 and Deut 5:5–21 only intensify the challenges.[2]

Author's Note: Perhaps no other individual has had as much influence on my approach to scholarship and academic ministry as Daniel Block. He is a dear mentor, brother, and friend, and I count my five years as his doctoral son some of the most significant in my life with respect to character and skill development. The psalmist's delight in the good instruction of the Lord is reflected in Dan's study, life, and teaching, and I am so grateful for this example. My earliest musings on the present topic took place in his office, and I joyfully offer this completed piece in his honor. May Yahweh bless and keep you and continue to use you as an instrument of his grace for his glory, for your joy, and for the good his people. Parts of the present study grow out of my book, *A Call to Covenant Love: Text Grammar and Literary Structure in Deuteronomy 5–11* (Piscataway, NJ: Gorgias, 2007) 115–17, 127–32. Earlier drafts of this paper were presented under the title "Numbering the Decalogue: A Textlinguistic Reappraisal" at both the annual meeting of the Evangelical Theological Society in November 2006 and the upper Midwest region meeting of the Society of Biblical Literature in April 2007.

1. While often termed the "Ten *Commandments*," the Hebrew label preserved in Exod 34:28, Deut 4:13, and Deut 10:4 is "Ten *Words*" (עשרת הדברים), which is also the etymology of the term Decalogue (from the Greek δέκα 'ten' + λόγοι 'words'). Nevertheless, Moses declares that the Ten Words were "commanded" (Piel צוה, Deut 4:13), and Jesus explicitly calls them "commandments" (ἐντολάς, Matt 19:17–19). Both of these factors may have some bearing on the question of numbering, and they suggest that the traditional title "Ten Commandments" is not misdirected. For a discussion of the role and significance of the Ten Words in Scripture, see my accompanying essay in this volume titled "Making the Ten Count: Reflections on the Lasting Message of the Decalogue."

2. In the history of interpretation, critical scholars have questioned whether it is indeed proper to treat the "ethical Decalogues" of Exod 20:1–17 and Deut 5:6–21 as the truest, most original "Ten Words." Indeed, many attempt to find a "ritual Decalogue" in Exod 34:11–26 and believe this list to be the most ancient "Ten Words." I believe a close reading of the text as it stands removes the proposed tensions and clearly designates that

Most recent studies of the Ten Words accept without discussion the traditional Reformed numbering. Throughout the centuries, however, interpreters have questioned their proper itemization, debating issues of form, style, semantic content, and cantillation, especially with reference to the boundaries of "Words" one, two, and ten.[3]

Contemporary studies in discourse grammar (i.e., textlinguistics or discourse analysis) open new avenues for discerning literary structure and flow-of-thought in Hebrew texts. Utilizing a nuanced understanding of participant reference, connection, and other literary devices like inclusio and repetition, this study reevaluates the numbering of the Decalogue and argues that a modified form of the Catholic-Lutheran enumeration most closely aligns with the formal text-grammatical signals and finds strong support from the perspective of style, semantic content, and cantillation.[4]

---

the phrase עשׂרת הדברים 'the Ten Words' is only properly applied to Exod 20:1–17 and Deut 5:6–21. See Appendix A for my argument.

3. The following contemporary studies have wrestled with the numbering of the Decalogue: L. Hartman, "The Enumeration of the Ten Commandments," *CBQ* 7 (1945) 105–8; W. L. Moran, "The Conclusion of the Decalogue (Ex 20,17 = Dt 5,21)," *CBQ* 29 (1967) 543–54; Bo Reicke, *Die zehn Worte in Geschichte und Gegenwart. Zahlung und Bedeutung der Gebote in den verschiedenen Konfessionen* (Tubingen: Mohr-Siebeck, 1973); M. D. Koster, "The Numbering of the Ten Commandments in Some Peshiṭta Manuscripts," *VT* 30.4 (1980) 468–73; M. Breuer, "Dividing the Decalogue into Verses and Commandments," in *The Ten Commandments in History and Interpretation* (essay trans. G. Levi; ed. B.-Z. Segal and G. Levi; Jerusalem: Magnes, 1985) 291–330, esp. 309–14; P. L. Maier, "Enumerating the Decalogue: Do We Number the Ten Commandments Correctly?" *Concordia Journal* 16.1 (Jan 1990) 18–26; N. Jastram, "Should Lutherans Really Change How They Number the Ten Commandments?" *Concordia Journal* 16.4 (Oct 1990) 363–69; H. D. Hummel, "Numbering the Ten 'Commandments': A Response to Both Jastram and Maier," *Concordia Journal* 16.4 (Oct 1990) 373–83; P. L. Maier, "A Response to Nathan Jastram," *Concordia Journal* 16.4 (Oct 1990) 370–72; L. Smith, "Original Sin as 'Envy': The Structure of the Biblical Decalogue," *Dialog* 30 (1991) 227–30; R. Youngblood, "Counting the Ten Commandments," *BR* 10 (Dec 1994) 30–35, 50, 52; B. Arnett, "Counting to Ten: Enumerating and Interpreting the Decalogue of Exodus 20," *Journal for Biblical Ministries* (spring 2009) 58–74; R. R. Hutton, "A Simply Matter of Numbering? 'Sovereignty' and 'Holiness' in the Decalogue Tradition," in *Raising Up a Faithful Exegete: Essays in Honor of Richard D. Nelson* (ed. K. L. Noll and B. Schramm; Winona Lake, IN: Eisenbrauns, 2010) 211–23; D. I. Block, "How Shall We Number the Ten Commands? The Deuteronomy Version (5:1–21)," in idem, *How I Love Your Torah*, 56–60; and idem, *The Gospel according to Moses: Theological and Ethical Reflections on the Book of Deuteronomy* (Eugene, OR: Cascade, 2012) 169–73.

4. After the bulk of this research was completed, written, and presented, I found N. Jastram's 1990 article, which also employs discourse analysis to establish the numbering of the Decalogue and supports the Catholic-Lutheran numbering ("Should Lutherans Really Change How They Number the Ten Commandments?" *Concordia Journal* 16.4 [Oct 1990] 363–69). His paper is helpful and complements the present essay; his is the second

1. History of Interpretation

Table 1 (p. 96) highlights the primary ways Jews and Christians have enumerated the Decalogue through the centuries. The chart displays the six main grouping of textual witnesses, which are generally arranged chronologically from left to right under each main heading. The various numberings are limited to twelve main statements, and some of the differences between Exodus 20 and Deuteronomy 5 are noted in parentheses.[5] Because the following discussion includes a number of technical details related to the Jewish Masoretic cantillation tradition, some readers may find it useful simply to overview the table and then move on to section 2, where I engage in my own analysis of the Ten Words.

The Jewish Masoretic tradition has retained two distinct and contradictory cantillation systems for arranging the Decalogue—the so-called "upper" and "lower" tropes.[6] For ease of reference, Table 2 (p. 98)

---

study in a four-part series in *Concordia Journal* related to the numbering of the Ten Words (see n. 3).

5. The order of the prohibitions against murder, adultery, and theft vary throughout the witnesses. According to J. W. Wevers, it is simply not clear why the order varies (*Notes on the Greek Text of Exodus* [Septuagint and Cognate Studies 30; Atlanta, GA: Scholars, 1990] 314; idem, *Notes on the Greek Text of Deuteronomy* [Septuagint and Cognate Studies 39; Atlanta, GA: Scholars, 1995] 104). For a full discussion of the witnesses, see D. Flusser, "Do not Commit Adultery, Do Not Murder," *Textus* 4 (1964) 220–24; idem, "The Ten Commandments and the New Testament," trans. Gershon Levi, in *The Ten Commandments in History and Interpretation* (ed. Ben-Zion Segal and Gershon Levi; Jerusalem: Magnes, 1985) 219–46.

Murder > Adultery > Theft	LXX Exod and Deut (A); Sam Exod and Deut; Pesh Exod and Deut; MT Exod and Deut; 4Q41(Deut^n); 4Q129(Phyl B); XQ3(-Phyl 3); 1Q13(Phyl); Josephus, *Ant.* 3:92; Matt 5:21; 19:18; Mark 10:19
Murder > Theft > Adultery	Hos 4:2
Adultery > Theft > Murder	LXX Exod (S/B)
Adultery > Murder > Theft	LXX Deut (S/B); LXX Exod (LC [?]); Philo, *Decal.* 10:36 and *Spec. Laws*, 3:8, Nash Papyrus; Luke 18:20; Rom 13:9; Jas 2:10–11
Theft > Murder > Adultery	Jer 7:8–11

6. Similar upper and lower cantillation tropes are evident in the *BHS* at the episode of Reuben and Bilhah in Gen 35:22–23. As for the occurrence in the Ten Words, Breuer notes: "We are forced to the conclusion that the upper and lower cantillations for the beginning of the Decalogue, from the 'I am the LORD' to 'My commandments', not only do not complement one another, but actually disagree with one another," for the upper tropes separate the statements "I am Yahweh your God" and "There shall never be to you other gods," whereas the lower tropes bring them together ("Dividing the Decalogue

Table 1. The Numbering of the Decalogue throughout History

	Jewish				Christian	
	Philo Josephus Min. of Rabbis	Lower Cant. (Verses)	Maj. of Rabbis Tg. Ps.-Jon. Upper Cant.	Parashiyyot (Paragraphs) Post-Mas. Cant.	Augustine Catholic Lutheran	Origen Augustine Orthodox Reformed
I am Yahweh your God (Exod 20:2 // Deut 5:6)	1	[1]	1	1	Intro	Intro
Never other gods (Exod 20:3 // Deut 5:7)			2		1	1
Never make a carved image (Exod 20:4–6 // Deut 5:8–10)	2	[2–4]				2
Never bear Yahweh's name in vain (Exod 20:7 // Deut 5:11)	3	[5]	3	2	2	3
Remember (/Observe) the Sabbath (Exod 20:8–11 // Deut 5:12–15)	4	[6–9]	4	3	3	4
Honor your father and mother (Exod 20:12 // Deut 5:16)	5	[10]	5	4	4	5
Never murder (Exod 20:13 // Deut 5:17)	6	[11]	6	5	5	6
(And) Never commit adultery (Exod 20:14 // Deut 5:18)	7		7	6	6	7
(And) Never steal (Exod 20:15 // Deut 5:19)	8		8	7	7	8
(And) Never bear false witness (Exod 20:16 // Deut 5:20)	9		9	8	8	9
(And) Never covet your neighbor's house (/wife) (Exod 20:17a // Deut 5:21a)	10	[12]	10	9	9	10
(And) Never covet (/desire) your neighbor's wife, etc. (/house, field, etc.) (Exod 20:17b // Deut 5:21b)				10 (only Deut)	10	

separates the two systems as evidenced in the *BHS* of Exod 20:1–17. The two systems can be easily distinguished by contrasting the placement of the three most common disjunctive accents: *silluq*, which marks the end of a verse ( ); *athnach*, which signals the main pause and semantic middle of a verse ( ); and *zaqeph qaton*, which subdivides the Silluq or Athnach portion of a verse ( ).

The most normative Jewish interpretation, as expressed by the majority of rabbis, *Targum Pseudo-Jonathan*, and the upper Masoretic cantillation signs (tropes) (see column 3 of Table 1 or column 1 of Table 2), holds that the clause "I am Yahweh your God" (Exod 20:2 // Deut 5:6) is the first of the Ten Words and that statements two and three make up Word two: "There shall never be other gods" through "those who love me and keep my commandments" (Exod 20:3–6 // Deut 5:7–10). Both statements on coveting (Exod 20:17 // Deut 5:21) are then read together as the tenth Word.[7]

In contrast, the lower Masoretic cantillation system, which is likely the older tradition, argues for a different numbering (column 2 of Table 1 or Table 2).[8] The system most directly distinguishes not Command-

---

into Verses and Commandments," 305). He also identifies a third alternative system that is post-Masoretic in origin and links all the first-person material from "I am Yahweh your God" through "my commandments" (Exod 20:2–6 // Deut 5:6–10) (293, 299–300, 310, 319–20). However, this third framework fails to separate the "coveting" commands, which is the necessary corollary to secure *ten* Words (319–20). While most Jewish scholars like Nahmanides attempted to fix this problem by arguing that the purpose of joining "I am Yahweh your God" with what follows was not to create one Word instead of two but simply "to ally the two Commandments," Breuer shows the untenable nature of this view (320–21).

7. For the classic Rabbinic interpretation, see the *Mekhilta de Rabbi Ishmael* (2nd ed.; trans. J. Z. Lauterbach; Philadelphia: Jewish Publication Society, 2004, orig. 1933) 313–43 (*Baḥodesh* 5–9); cf. Rabbi Hamnuna in Mak 24a; Rabbi Levit in TJ Ber 1.8, 3c. For a further list, see J. H. Tigay, *Deuteronomy* [JPSTC; Philadelphia: The Jewish Publication Society, 1996] 355 n. 24). In the upper Masoretic cantillation system, a *silluq* (full stop) follows the first statement, thus distinguishing "I am Yahweh your God" and "There shall never be to you other gods" as two Words. This view is generally taken to be the "traditional" Jewish arrangement of the Decalogue because it alone is explicitly expressed in the Masoretic cantillation (Breuer, "Dividing the Decalogue into Verses and Commandments," 302, 314, 329). While a different numbering is implied in the lower cantillation system (see below), the enumeration must be inferred, for the system lays out twelve verses of roughly equal length rather than ten discrete Words. For a full description, overview, and evaluation of the upper and lower Masoretic cantillation systems, see ibid., 291–330.

8. Breuer argues that the lower tropes retain "the *original* scheme of the Masorah" ("Dividing the Decalogue into Verses and Commandments," 327–29, quote from 329) because (1) within the synagogue custom of cantillation the number of verses reported for each biblical book always agrees with the lower system and "these numbers are apparently older than the similar numbers calculated for the weekly pericopes—just as the

Table 2. Exod 20:2–17 with Upper and Lower Cantillations Separated

Upper Tropes (Distinguishing 10 "Words")	**Lower Tropes** (Distinguishing 12 "Verses")	
אָנֹכִי יְהוָה אֱלֹהֶיךָ אֲשֶׁר הוֹצֵאתִיךָ מֵאֶרֶץ מִצְרַיִם מִבֵּית עֲבָדִים:	אָנֹכִי יְהוָה אֱלֹהֶיךָ אֲשֶׁר הוֹצֵאתִיךָ מֵאֶרֶץ מִצְרַיִם מִבֵּית עֲבָדִים:	2
לֹא יִהְיֶה־לְךָ אֱלֹהִים אֲחֵרִים עַל־פָּנָי:	לֹא יִהְיֶה־לְךָ אֱלֹהִים אֲחֵרִים עַל־פָּנָי:	3
לֹא תַעֲשֶׂה־לְךָ פֶסֶל וְכָל־תְּמוּנָה אֲשֶׁר בַּשָּׁמַיִם מִמַּעַל וַאֲשֶׁר בָּאָרֶץ מִתַּחַת וַאֲשֶׁר בַּמַּיִם מִתַּחַת לָאָרֶץ:	לֹא תַעֲשֶׂה־לְךָ פֶסֶל וְכָל־תְּמוּנָה אֲשֶׁר בַּשָּׁמַיִם מִמַּעַל וַאֲשֶׁר בָּאָרֶץ מִתָּחַת וַאֲשֶׁר בַּמַּיִם מִתַּחַת לָאָרֶץ:	4
לֹא־תִשְׁתַּחֲוֶה לָהֶם וְלֹא תָעָבְדֵם כִּי אָנֹכִי יְהוָה אֱלֹהֶיךָ אֵל קַנָּא פֹּקֵד עֲוֹן אָבֹת עַל־בָּנִים עַל־שִׁלֵּשִׁים וְעַל־רִבֵּעִים לְשֹׂנְאָי:	לֹא־תִשְׁתַּחֲוֶה לָהֶם וְלֹא תָעָבְדֵם כִּי אָנֹכִי יְהוָה אֱלֹהֶיךָ אֵל קַנָּא פֹּקֵד עֲוֹן אָבֹת עַל־בָּנִים וְעַל־שִׁלֵּשִׁים וְעַל־רִבֵּעִים לְשֹׂנְאָי:	5
מִצְוֹתָי: ס וְעֹשֶׂה חֶסֶד לַאֲלָפִים לְאֹהֲבַי וּלְשֹׁמְרֵי	מִצְוֹתָי: ס וְעֹשֶׂה חֶסֶד לַאֲלָפִים לְאֹהֲבַי וּלְשֹׁמְרֵי	6
לֹא תִשָּׂא אֶת־שֵׁם־יְהוָה אֱלֹהֶיךָ לַשָּׁוְא כִּי לֹא יְנַקֶּה יְהוָה אֵת אֲשֶׁר־יִשָּׂא אֶת־שְׁמוֹ לַשָּׁוְא: פ	לֹא תִשָּׂא אֶת־שֵׁם־יְהוָה אֱלֹהֶיךָ לַשָּׁוְא כִּי לֹא יְנַקֶּה יְהוָה אֵת אֲשֶׁר־יִשָּׂא אֶת־שְׁמוֹ לַשָּׁוְא: פ	7
זָכוֹר אֶת־יוֹם הַשַּׁבָּת לְקַדְּשׁוֹ:	זָכוֹר אֶת־יוֹם הַשַּׁבָּת לְקַדְּשׁוֹ:	8
שֵׁשֶׁת יָמִים תַּעֲבֹד וְעָשִׂיתָ כָּל־מְלַאכְתֶּךָ:	שֵׁשֶׁת יָמִים תַּעֲבֹד וְעָשִׂיתָ כָּל־מְלַאכְתֶּךָ:	9
וְיוֹם הַשְּׁבִיעִי שַׁבָּת לַיהוָה אֱלֹהֶיךָ לֹא־תַעֲשֶׂה כָל־מְלָאכָה אַתָּה וּבִנְךָ־וּבִתֶּךָ עַבְדְּךָ וַאֲמָתְךָ וּבְהֶמְתֶּךָ וְגֵרְךָ אֲשֶׁר בִּשְׁעָרֶיךָ:	וְיוֹם הַשְּׁבִיעִי שַׁבָּת לַיהוָה אֱלֹהֶיךָ לֹא־תַעֲשֶׂה כָל־מְלָאכָה אַתָּה וּבִנְךָ־וּבִתֶּךָ עַבְדְּךָ וַאֲמָתְךָ וּבְהֶמְתֶּךָ וְגֵרְךָ אֲשֶׁר בִּשְׁעָרֶיךָ:	10
כִּי שֵׁשֶׁת־יָמִים עָשָׂה יְהוָה אֶת־הַשָּׁמַיִם וְאֶת־הָאָרֶץ אֶת־הַיָּם וְאֶת־כָּל־אֲשֶׁר־בָּם וַיָּנַח בַּיּוֹם הַשְּׁבִיעִי עַל־כֵּן בֵּרַךְ יְהוָה אֶת־יוֹם הַשַּׁבָּת וַיְקַדְּשֵׁהוּ: ס	כִּי שֵׁשֶׁת־יָמִים עָשָׂה יְהוָה אֶת־הַשָּׁמַיִם וְאֶת־הָאָרֶץ אֶת־הַיָּם וְאֶת־כָּל־אֲשֶׁר־בָּם וַיָּנַח בַּיּוֹם הַשְּׁבִיעִי עַל־כֵּן בֵּרַךְ יְהוָה אֶת־יוֹם הַשַּׁבָּת וַיְקַדְּשֵׁהוּ: ס	11
כַּבֵּד אֶת־אָבִיךָ וְאֶת־אִמֶּךָ לְמַעַן יַאֲרִכוּן יָמֶיךָ עַל הָאֲדָמָה אֲשֶׁר־יְהוָה אֱלֹהֶיךָ נֹתֵן לָךְ: ס	כַּבֵּד אֶת־אָבִיךָ וְאֶת־אִמֶּךָ לְמַעַן יַאֲרִכוּן יָמֶיךָ עַל הָאֲדָמָה אֲשֶׁר־יְהוָה אֱלֹהֶיךָ נֹתֵן לָךְ: ס	12
לֹא תִּרְצָח: ס	לֹא תִּרְצָח: ס	13
לֹא תִּנְאָף: ס	לֹא תִּנְאָף: ס	14
לֹא תִּגְנֹב: ס	לֹא תִּגְנֹב: ס	15
לֹא־תַעֲנֶה בְרֵעֲךָ עֵד שָׁקֶר: ס	לֹא־תַעֲנֶה בְרֵעֲךָ עֵד שָׁקֶר: ס	16
לֹא תַחְמֹד בֵּית רֵעֶךָ לֹא־תַחְמֹד אֵשֶׁת רֵעֶךָ וְעַבְדּוֹ וַאֲמָתוֹ וְשׁוֹרוֹ וַחֲמֹרוֹ וְכֹל אֲשֶׁר לְרֵעֶךָ: פ	לֹא תַחְמֹד בֵּית רֵעֶךָ לֹא־תַחְמֹד אֵשֶׁת רֵעֶךָ וְעַבְדּוֹ וַאֲמָתוֹ וְשׁוֹרוֹ וַחֲמֹרוֹ וְכֹל אֲשֶׁר לְרֵעֶךָ: פ	17

This comparison is adapted from M. Breuer, "Dividing the Decalogue into Verses and Commandments," 295.

ments or Words but twelve "verses" of roughly equal length (marked in Column 2 of Table 1 by brackets and highlighted in gray in Column 2 of Table 2). However, all the Words are understood to fall along the "verse" breaks. So although one "verse" may include many Words (e.g., the statements "You shall never murder" through "You shall never bear false witness" making up "verse" 11 [Exod 20:13–16 // Deut 5:17–20]) and although one Word may include many verses (e.g., the Sabbath commandment including "verses" 6–9 [Exod 20:8–11 // Deut 5:12–15]), the division into verses never cuts against the division into Words. Stated differently, "Only full Commandments combine to form one verse; and only full verses combine to form one Commandment."[9] The most significant point to observe, however, is that the upper and lower cantillation systems place the statement "There shall never be to you other gods" (Exod 20:3 // Deut 5:7) in *different* Words: the upper tropes approach it as the *introduction* to what follows (beginning a unit that continues with "You shall never make a carved image"), whereas the lower tropes treat it as the *conclusion* to what precedes (closing a unit that begins with "I am Yahweh your God").[10]

One tradition that aligns with the verse divisions of the lower cantillation system is found in Philo, Josephus, and a minority of the rabbinic witnesses (column 1 of Table 1).[11] Here the first Word begins with "I am Yahweh your God" (Exod 20:2 // Deut 5:6) and ends with the negative "There shall never be to you other gods" (Exod 20:3 // Deut 5:7). The ban on image making (Exod 20:4–6 // Deut 5:8–10) is then viewed as the second Word, and again the coveting prohibitions (Exod 20:17 // Deut 5:21) are viewed together as Word ten.

A different Jewish tradition that also aligns with the verse arrangement of the lower accentuation system is retained in the paragraph

---

books themselves are older than the division into weekly scriptural lessons" (327); (2) the lower system alone is "faithful to the plain sense of the text, and the usual biblical style," whereas in the upper cantillation system of the Ten Words "it fashions inordinately long and short verses"; (3) the very name applied to the lower system in the early Masoretic period was *ta'ama qadma* ("the ancient trope") (see Codex Sassoon 507, also known as the Damascus Pentateuch, MS5); and (4) the lower system alone always adheres to the syntactical rules of the tropes.

9. Breuer, "Dividing the Decalogue into Verses and Commandments," 304.

10. Ibid., 305. Breuer argues that this "contradicting" set of tropes in the upper and lower cantillation systems suggests that "the two systems come from two different sources," specifically the upper from the "Easterners" (Babylonia) and the lower from the "Westerners" (Palestine). While the Masorah usually decides in favor of the western tradition, "in this instance it let the two systems stand side by side, and so both of them entered the Tiberian Masorah" (323).

11. See Philo, *Decal.* 12.50–51; Josephus, *Ant.* 3.91 (cf. 3.101). For examples of rabbinic witnesses, see Rabbi Ishmael in *Sifre Numbers*, 112; cf. *Hor.* 12a; *Mak.* 24a.

divisions of the MT (the so-called *parashiyyot* [פרשיות]) (column 4 of Table 1).[12] Here the first Word is made up of the extended section in which God speaks in first person—"I am Yahweh your God" through "those who love *me* and keep *my* commandments" (Exod 20:2–6 // Deut 5:6–10).[13] The second Word then begins with "You shall never take the name of Yahweh in vain" (Exod 20:7 // Deut 5:11), and the final prohibitions "You shall never covet your neighbor's house (/wife)" and "You shall never covet (/desire) your neighbor's wife (/house, field), etc." (Exod 20:17 // Deut 5:21) are distinguished as discrete Words.[14] While some in Jewish circles have concluded that the separation of the coveting commandments as distinct paragraphs was an "error" brought about by the necessity to arrive at *ten* Words after linking all the first-person address into one paragraph,[15] a strong case can be made for the legitimacy of this division.

Indeed, following a Christian tradition that dates at least back to Augustine, most Catholics and Lutherans have enumerated the Words in this way, though commonly marking "I am Yahweh your God" (Exod 20:2 // Deut 5:6) as the preface to the Decalogue and "There shall never be to you other gods" (Exod 20:3 // Deut 5:7) as the actual first Word (column 5 of Table 1).[16] Often in these circles, and especially among

---

12. While these divisions are not present in the Leningrad Codex, the editors of the *BHS* added them in accordance with their placement in other Masoretic manuscripts (W. R. Scott, *A Simplified Guide to BHS* [4th ed.; N. Richland Hills, TX: BIBAL, 2007] 1). They are marked in the MT by a large space and the sigla ס, which is referred to as the *sətûmāʾ*, signaling a "closed" paragraph (see E. Yeivin, *Introduction to the Tiberian Masorah* [trans. E. J. Revell; Masoretic Studies 5; Missoula, MT: Scholars, 1980] 40–42). Intriguingly, the *sətûmāʾ* is absent between the coveting commands in the MT of Exod 20:17, but it is present between the parallel commands in Deut 5:21. The "missing" *sətûmāʾ* results in only nine paragraphs in Exod 20:2–17, whereas Deut 5:6–21 includes the expected ten. Notably, the majority of manuscripts consulted by Kennicott included the *sətûmāʾ* even in Exod 20:17 (see C. F. Keil and F. Delitzsch, *Commentary on the Old Testament* [10 vols.; Peabody, MA: Hendrickson, 2002] 1.2:111 [on Exod 20:1]).

13. This appears to be the same tradition witnessed to in the alternative post-Masoretic set of tropes (Breuer, "Dividing the Decalogue into Verses and Commandments," 310).

14. This was the arrangement of Maimonides, as expressed in the Ben Asher manuscript and the Leningrad Codex.

15. So *Minḥat Shai* on Exod 20:4. Similarly, in his introduction to the Decalogue within his long commentary, Ibn Ezra denounces the separation of the coveting commands (see M. Greenberg, "The Decalogue Tradition Critically Examined," in *The Ten Commandments in History and Interpretation* [essay trans. M. Shorashim], 96 n. 17).

16. See Augustine, "Questions of Exodus," in *Quaestionum in Heptateuchum libri*, 7.2.71 (see J. Zycha, ed., *Sancti Aureli Augustini: Quaestionum in Heptateuchum Libri VII Adnotationum In Iob Liber Unus [1895]* [Kessinger, 2010]); P. Lombard, *The Sentences*, 3.33:1.2 (see idem, *The Sentences Book 3: On the Incarnation of the Word* [trans. G. Silano; Turnhout (Belgium): Brepols, 2008]); P. Melanchthon, "Exposition of the Decalogue," in *Loci communes*

Catholics, the deuteronomic version is used as the base text, for it more clearly distinguishes the two commandments against coveting by using two different verbs (חמד 'covet'; Hith. אוה 'desire') and by explicitly separating the "wife" from the servants, livestock, and material goods (Deut 5:21). This shape is distinguished from the Exodus version where the charge not to "covet" (חמד) your neighbor's house is followed by the order not to "covet" (חמד) your neighbor's wife, servants, livestock, and all other belongings (Exod 20:17).

In distinction to this approach, Calvin aligned with Philo, Josephus, Origen, and alternative comments by Augustine in distinguishing as two Words the charge against having other gods (Exod 20:3 // Deut 5:7) and the ban against shaping a graven image (Exod 20:4–6 // Deut 5:8–10) (column 6 of Table 1). This group also retains the union of the statements about coveting (Exod 20:17 // Deut 5:21), seeing no exegetical basis for separating the final two prohibitions.[17]

2. Learning to Count the Ten

As summarized in Table 3 (p. 102), the history of the Decalogue's interpretation has witnessed no less than three different numbering traditions.[18] The present study attempts to move beyond the interpretive impasse by raising new questions and by positing new significance to past observations.

(see idem, *The Chief Theological Topics: Loci Praecipui Theologici* 1559 [2nd Eng. ed.; trans. J. A. O. Preus; Saint Louis, MO: Concordia, 2011] 91–114). Cf. "Commandments of God," in *The Catholic Encyclopedia: An International Work of Reference on the Constitution, Doctrine, Discipline and History of the Catholic Church* (Appleton, 1907–1912) found at http://www.newadvent.org/cathen and the newly published *Catechism of the Catholic Church* (2nd ed.; New York: Doubleday, 2003), which devotes over 100 of its 756 pages to the Decalogue (see pp. 553–672). Breuer rightly notes that the only view not supported in any way by the Masorah is that which treats the statement "I am Yahweh" as standing outside the Decalogue and "There shall never be to you other gods" as the first Word ("Dividing the Decalogue by Verses and Commandments," 312–13).

17. Origen, *Homilies on Exodus*, 8.3 (see Origen, *Homilies on Genesis and Exodus* [Fathers of the Church Series 71; trans. R. E. Heine; Washington, DC: Catholic University of America Press, 1982] 185–96); Augustine, *Against Two Letters of the Pelagians*, 3.4.10 (see Augustine of Hippo, "A Treatise Against Two Letters of the Pelagians," trans. R. E. Wallis, in *A Select Library of the Nicene and Post-Nicene Fathers of the Christian Church, First Series, Volume V: Saint Augustin: Anti-Pelagian Writings* [ed. P. Schaff; New York: Christian Literature Company, 1887] 406); cf. idem, *Letters* 55.11.20; *Sermons* 33.3; J. Calvin, *Institutes of the Christian Religion*, 2.8.12 (see *Calvin: Institutes of the Christian Religion* [2 vols.; ed. J. T. McNeill; trans. F. L. Battles; Philadelphia: Westminster, 1960] 1:377–79).

18. It is important to note that the complexities related to the numbering of the Decalogue led to many other enumeration proposals in Jewish circles; for an overview, see Breuer, "Dividing the Decalogue into Verses and Commandments," 314–18.

Table 3. Three Primary Ways the Decalogue Has Been Numbered

	Maj. Jew	Cath-Luth	Orth-Ref
I am Yahweh your God	1		
Never other gods	2	1	1
Never make a carved image			2
Never bear Yahweh's name in vain	3	2	3
Remember (/Observe) the Sabbath	4	3	4
Honor your father and mother	5	4	5
Never murder	6	5	6
(And) Never commit adultery	7	6	7
(And) Never steal	8	7	8
(And) Never bear false witness	9	8	9
(And) Never covet your neighbor's house (/wife)	10	9	10
(And) Never covet (/desire) your neighbor's wife, etc. (/house, field, etc.)		10	

Specifically, the rest of this paper will address a number of grammatical and literary features in the Decalogue that, when properly understood, help us count the Ten. Every language is governed by certain rules that determine how and when various lexemes are used in order to guide communication. While the grammar of biblical Hebrew is different from, say, English, it nevertheless is directed by common linguistic constraints. If communication is going to be comprehensible, Hebrew, like English, must have a way to track participants, to signal the logical relationship between clauses, and to highlight dramatic pause, transition, or units of thought. These types of discourse grammatical features along with elements of style will now be used to itemize the Ten Words.

2.1. Preparatory Remarks

For years scholars have wrestled with the historical development of the Decalogue and the diachronic relationship of the differing versions in Exodus and Deuteronomy. A detailed assessment of this issue is beyond the scope of the present study, but I do offer a number of observations in Appendix B that have guided my assessment that follows.

Section 2 focuses on the Decalogue's structure rather than message, though the discussion does set some trajectories for the latter.[19] To assist

---

19. For more on the message of the Ten Words, see my second essay in this volume titled "Making the Ten Count: Reflections on the Lasting Message of the Decalogue."

tracking my textual analysis in this paper, Table 4 (pp. 104–5) uses an amended ESV text to underscore the distinctions between the forms of the Ten Words in Exodus and Deuteronomy. Areas where the texts are different but overlapping are signaled with a <u>double underline;</u> a <u>single underline</u> marks those places where one text includes something that the other does not.

2.2. Numbering Words Five through Ten

I begin this discussion at the end of the Decalogue, because here my analysis is simplified with only two different numbering traditions and because this discussion will bring greater clarity to the comments that follow on Words one and two. The Decalogue ends with a clear grouping (Exod 20:13–17 // Deut 5:17–21) that is signaled by the pithy nature of the six prohibitions and by the lack of any direct reference to "Yahweh your God" or of any expressed grounds or motivations (see Table 5, p. 107). At stake here is whether the final two injunctions against coveting/envy are to be read together as a single Word (so the majority Jewish and Orthodox-Reformed views) or separately as distinct Words (so Catholic-Lutheran view).

As an initial observation, Exod 20:17 bears a level of interpretive ambiguity that makes enumeration difficult. On the one hand, the repetition of the verb חמד 'covet' clearly identifies a topical parallel between the two prohibitions. Furthermore, if בית in 20:17a is understood as 'household', the independent clause that follows in 20:17b is easily read as an expansion or clarification of this household's makeup, which would include the neighbor's wife, servants, livestock, and material goods.[20] Linguists have long recognized that Hebrew clauses lacking a fronted conjunction signal discontinuity in a text, often to mark apposition or explication, as would be the case in 20:17b (= option 1). However, asyndeton can also signal a fresh beginning in discourse (= option 2), which suggests the possibility that Exod 20:17b could be a *distinct* Word that actually is *not* intended to unpack the "house" of 20:17a.[21]

---

20. While the term בית 'house' can refer to the structural dwelling inhabited by but in distinction from its inhabitants (e.g., Gen 33:17; Judg 11:31, 34), it can also point to the inhabitants themselves—namely, one's family (i.e., "household"), whether made up of husband, wife, children, and servants (e.g., Gen 7:1, Josh 24:15, 1 Sam 27:3) or simply the biological offspring on the father's side (e.g., Gen 24:38, Num 17:17, 1 Sam 20:16). See "I בית," *HALOT* 124–25.

21. On the absence of connection (= asyndeton) in Hebrew as a marker of disjunction, whether for apposition/clarification (option 1 above) or for new unit initiation (option 2 above), see F. I. Andersen, *The Hebrew Verbless Clause in the Pentateuch* (JBLMS 14; Nashville: Abingdon, 1970) 28; idem, *The Sentence in Biblical Hebrew* (JLSP 231; New York: Mouton, 1974) 27; S. G. Dempster, "Linguistic Features of Hebrew Narrative: A Discourse Analysis of Narrative from the Classical Period" (Ph.D. diss., University of Toronto,

Table 4. A Comparison of the Decalogue in Exodus and Deuteronomy

J	C/L	O/R	Exod 20:2-17	Deut 5:6-21
1			² I am Yahweh your God, who brought you out of the land of Egypt, out of the house of slavery.	⁶ I am Yahweh your God, who brought you out of the land of Egypt, out of the house of slavery.
2	1	1	³ There shall never be to you other gods before me.	⁷ There shall never be to you other gods before me.
		2	⁴ You shall never make for yourself a carved image or any likeness of *anything* that is in heaven above, or that is in the earth beneath, or that is in the water under the earth. ⁵ You shall never bow down to them or serve them, for I Yahweh your God am a jealous God, visiting the iniquity of the fathers on the children—unto the third and unto the fourth *generation*—to those who hate me, ⁶ but showing steadfast love to thousands *of generations*—to those who love me and keep my commandments. ס	⁸ You shall never make for yourself a carved image, any likeness of *anything* that is in heaven above, or that is in the earth beneath, or that is in the water under the earth. ⁹ You shall never bow down to them or serve them, for I Yahweh your God am a jealous God, visiting the iniquity of the fathers on the children even unto the third and unto the fourth *generation*—to those who hate me, ¹⁰ but showing steadfast love to thousands *of generations*—to those who love me and keep my commandments. ס
3	2	3	⁷ You shall never bear the name of Yahweh your God in vain, for Yahweh will not hold him guiltless who bears his name in vain. פ	¹¹ You shall never bear the name of Yahweh your God in vain, for Yahweh will not hold him guiltless who bears his name in vain. ס
4	3	4	⁸ Remember the Sabbath day, to keep it holy. ⁹ Six days you shall labor and do all your work, ¹⁰ but the seventh day is a Sabbath to Yahweh your God. On it you shall not do any work—you, or your son, or your daughter, your male servant, or your female servant, or your livestock, or the sojourner who is within your gates.	¹² Observe the Sabbath day, to keep it holy, as Yahweh your God commanded you. ¹³ Six days you shall labor and do all your work, ¹⁴ but the seventh day is a Sabbath to Yahweh your God. On it you shall not do any work—you, or your son, or your daughter, or your male servant, or your female servant, or your ox, or your donkey, or any

An Investigation into the Numbering of the Decalogue 105

5	4	¹¹ For in six days Yahweh made the heaven and the earth, the sea, and all that is in them, and rested on the seventh day. Therefore Yahweh blessed the Sabbath day and made it holy. ס		of your livestock, or the sojourner who is within your gates, that your male servant and your female servant may rest as well as you.
	5		¹⁵	And you shall remember that you were a slave in the land of Egypt, and Yahweh your God brought you out from there with a mighty hand and an outstretched arm. Therefore Yahweh your God commanded you to keep the Sabbath day. ס
		¹² Honor your father and your mother, that your days may be long in the land that Yahweh your God is giving you. ס	¹⁶	Honor your father and your mother, as Yahweh your God commanded you, that your days may be long and that it may go well with you in the land that Yahweh your God is giving you. ס
6	5	¹³ You shall never murder. ס	¹⁷	You shall never murder. ס
7	6	¹⁴ You shall never commit adultery. ס	¹⁸	And you shall never commit adultery. ס
8	7	¹⁵ You shall never steal. ס	¹⁹	And you shall never steal. ס
9	8	¹⁶ You shall never testify a deceptive witness against your neighbor. ס	²⁰	And you shall never testify a false witness against your neighbor. ס
10	9	¹⁷ You shall never covet your neighbor's house.	²¹	And you shall never covet your neighbor's wife. ס
	10	You shall never covet your neighbor's wife, or his male servant, or his female servant, or his ox, or his donkey, or anything that is your neighbor's. פ		And you shall never desire your neighbor's house, his field, or his male servant, or his female servant, his ox, or his donkey, or anything that is your neighbor's. ס

In support of this latter possibility, one must ask why the verb חמד 'covet' is repeated at all if indeed 20:17b is intended only to clarify the makeup of the "household." The list of wife, servants, livestock, and material goods could have simply been placed directly after the noun בית 'house' to express apposition. Comparably, if 20:17b merely explicates the initial coveting prohibition, why is the noun-phrase רעך 'of your neighbor' repeated after "wife" and not simply replaced with a 3ms pronominal suffix as is found on the rest of the members of the list: "*his* male servant, or *his* female servant, or *his* ox, or *his* donkey"?[22]

With these observations, what is clearly apparent is that the two prohibitions against coveting are cast as independent clauses, each initiated with the same negative durative construction (לא + *yiqtol*) that is found in the previous four commandments, all of which are treated as separate Words in the various numbering systems (Exod 20:13–16; cf. Deut 5:17–20). Recognizably, the same structure is evident between the independent clauses of Exod 20:4–5 (cf. Deut 5:8–9), and none of the three enumeration systems treat these as separate Words.[23] Nevertheless, the unbroken staccato-like pattern of prohibitions against murder, adultery, theft, false witness, and coveting a house leads naturally into reading the formally identical element in 20:17b as the final note in the succession.

As attention shifts to Deut 5:21, a number of differences are apparent that support viewing the final two prohibitions of the Decalogue as discrete Words. First, while the verb חמד 'covet' is retained in the first prohibition of 5:21a, the Hithpael of אוה 'desire, crave' is used in 5:21b, thus drawing a firmer conceptual distinction (though still overlapping) between the independent clauses.

Second, the isolation of the commandment against coveting a neighbor's wife in Deut 5:21a makes it impossible to read 5:21b as an ex-

---

1985) 42–47; DeRouchie, *A Call to Covenant Love*,120–32, 225; D. A. Garrett and J. S. DeRouchie, *A Modern Grammar for Biblical Hebrew* (Nashville: B&H, 2009) 284–85. From a cross-linguistic perspective, S. H. Levinsohn has observed that in the non-narrative texts of the Greek NT, asyndeton occurs in comparable contexts: (1) "when there is a close connection between the information concerned" (i.e., the information belongs together in the same unit, whether for restatement or association) and (2) "when there is no direct connection between the information concerned" (i.e., the information belongs to different units with the asyndetic clause orienting the reader to a new direction) (*Discourse Features of New Testament Greek: A Coursebook on the Information Structure of New Testament Greek* [2nd ed.; SIL International, 2000] §7.2).

22. Both of these questions are also raised by Jastram, "Should Lutherans Really Change How They Number the Ten Commandments?" 366.

23. However, in the history of Jewish interpretation, this has happened (see Breuer, "Dividing the Decalogue into Verses and Commandments," 314–18).

Table 5. A Textual Comparison of Exod 20:13–17 and Deut 5:17–21

Exod 20:13–17		Deut 5:17–21	
לא תרצח	13	לא תרצח	17
לא תנאף	14	ולא תנאף	18
לא תגנב	15	ולא תגנב	19
לא־תענה ברעך עד שקר	16	ולא־תענה ברעך עד שוא	20
לא תחמד בית רעך	17	ולא תחמד אשת רעך	21
לא־תחמד אשת רעך ועבדו ואמתו ושורו וחמרו וכל אשר לרעך		ולא תתאוה בית רעך שדהו ועבדו ואמתו שורו וחמרו וכל אשר לרעך	
13 You shall never murder. 14 You shall never commit adultery. 15 You shall never steal. 16 You shall never testify a <u>deceptive</u> witness against your neighbor. 17 You shall never covet your neighbor's <u>house</u>. You shall never <u>covet</u> your neighbor's <u>wife</u>, or his male servant, or his female servant, <u>or</u> his ox, or his donkey, or anything that is your neighbor's.		17 You shall never murder. 18 <u>And</u> you shall never commit adultery. 19 <u>And</u> you shall never steal. 20 <u>And</u> you shall never testify a <u>false</u> witness against your neighbor. 21 <u>And</u> you shall never covet your neighbor's <u>wife</u>. <u>And</u> you shall never <u>desire</u> your neighbor's <u>house</u>, <u>his field</u>, or his male servant, or his female servant, his ox or his donkey, or anything that is to your neighbor.	

plication of the preceding clause. While the two prohibitions may still plausibly be read together, the relationship between them must be understood in a way different than the advocates of the Jewish majority and Orthodox-Reformed view have traditionally treated the parallel in Exod 20:17a–b.

Third, the inclusion of שדה 'field' after 'house' in Deut 5:21b suggests that in the Decalogue בית simply means 'physical dwelling place' and not 'household'. Although land can be connected to household inheritance (e.g., Judg 11:2), in Scripture territory still stands distinct from the household itself.[24] So while servants, livestock, and material goods could be considered part of one's household, there is no evidence that suggests a field could be. As such, the list (at least in Deuteronomy) should likely not be seen as explicating "house." Furthermore, William L. Moran observed long ago that in ANE literature "house and field"

---

24. While the *Dictionary of Classical Hebrew* 2:151 (8 vols.; ed. D. J. A. Clines; Sheffield: Sheffield Phoenix, 1993–2011) suggests that a household can include territory, I see no conclusive evidence for this in any of the examples cited.

serve as a formulaic pair for "immovable property," and the evidence above suggests they should be read as such in the Decalogue.[25]

Fourth, Deuteronomy's inclusion of the conjunction *wa* (ו) before each of the commandments in 5:18–21b supports the conclusion that the final prohibition of the Decalogue should be read as its own Word. While most English versions fail to translate the conjunction,[26] *wa* was intended to be heard (and read), and it plays an important structuring role that can only be relayed in another language when the form is represented in translation.[27]

---

25. Moran, "The Conclusion of the Decalogue," 549. In the same context, he further observes, "If other [often movable] properties are specified as parts of or in some way attached to 'the house and the field,' the latter expression always occupies initial position." He summarizes, "The legal documents in question present the following typical scheme: 'house and field' + specifications (buildings, various forms of cultivation, personnel, livestock) + generic formula ('everything [else] belonging to him')" (550). At one place, there is even a list that bears exact correspondence of element and order to the list in Deut 5:21b (551). Throughout the OT, "house and field" appear together in Gen 39:5; Lev 25:31; Jer 6:12, 32:15; Isa 5:8; Mic 2:2; and Neh 5:3, 11. Both the LXX and Nash Papyrus include "field" in Exod 20:17, but this seems most likely due to deuteronomic influence. D. I. Block notes that inclusion of "field" in Deut 5:21b "restores the full complement of seven items, like the list of those who are to benefit from the Sabbath rest in Exod 20:10" ("Reading the Decalogue Right to Left: The Ten Principles of Covenant Relationship in the Hebrew Bible," in idem, *How I Love Your Torah*, 41 n. 76).

26. At Deut 5:18–21, the "and" is present in the ESV but is absent in the ASV, KJV, NASB, NASU, NIV83, NRSV, HCSB, CEB, and NIV, likely due less to text-critical conclusions and more to the tendency of Hebraists to view *wa* as a mere multivalent connector with little clear functional purpose. (For a traditional approach to the use of *wa*, see T. O. Lambdin, *Introduction to Biblical Hebrew* [New York: Charles Scribner's Sons, 1971] §132 [pp. 162–65]; §197 [pp. 279–81]; *IBHS* §39.2; and *The Dictionary of Classical Hebrew* [2:596–98], which gives no less than 15 meanings and sub-meanings to *wa*. I disagree with this approach. For a historical survey of the interpretation of *wa* with a compelling argument that *wa* always serves as a coordinator, see R. C. Steiner, "Does the Biblical Hebrew Conjunction ו- Have Many Meanings, One Meaning, or No Meaning at All?" *JBL* 119 [2000] 249–67.) On another note, the connector *wa* is present before the negative in the MT and 4Q129(Phyl B), and it is represented in the Vulgate in all but the last prohibition (suggesting, ironically, that the Catholic Jerome was reading the commands against envy as a unit). Likely due to an intentional or unintentional attempt to harmonize with Exodus, the *wa* is also not represented in the various Greek versions, Sam Deut, 4Q134(Phyl G), XQ3(Phyl 3), the Peshitta, and *Tg. Ps.-J.* (cf. M. Weinfeld, *Deuteronomy 1–11* [AB 5; New York: Doubleday, 1991] 279).

27. In his commentary on Genesis, Robert Alter chose to render "every 'and' and every element of parataxis" in translation, being convinced that the ubiquitous *wa* was intended to be heard and serves "an important role in creating the rhythm of the story, in phonetically punctuating the forward-driving movement of the prose" (*Genesis: Translation and Commentary* [New York: W. W. Norton & Co., 1996] xx). My view goes further than this, for I believe the Hebrews used *wa* specifically to identify blocks of discourse that were to be read as units.

Specifically, *wa* (with its allomorphs) is a coordinator that links elements of equal syntactic value (phrases to phrases, clauses to clauses, texts to texts). The result is a chain of grammatical units that are to be read together.[28] While at times the connector's semantic value is bleached, Richard C. Steiner has convincingly argued that *wa* always retains a single meaning of logical connection (= "and"), which by default expresses coordination.[29] Unlike asyndeton, *wa* generally does not stand at absolute beginnings in a text because an initial structure by nature is not coordinated with any other structure.[30] Therefore, when *wa* occurs, the interpreter must view the unit it introduces as part of a larger text structure, which in this case begins with the asyndetic commandment against murder in Deut 5:17 that starts the chain. Although examples exist where clauses fronted with *wa* serve to explicate preceding thoughts, there must be other elements in the context that override the default meaning of coordination.[31] And because it is clear that

---

28. See Dempster, "Linguistic Features of Hebrew Narrative," 40–41; DeRouchie, *A Call to Covenant Love*, 107–20, 225; idem, "*Wa* and Asyndeton as Guides to Macrostructure in the Reported Speech of Deuteronomy" (paper presented at the annual meetings of the Evangelical Theological Society and the Society of Biblical Literature, Boston, MA, November 2008); cf. Garrett and DeRouchie, *A Modern Grammar for Biblical Hebrew*, 284–85.

29. Steiner, "Biblical Hebrew Conjunction," 249–67; cf. Andersen, *The Hebrew Verbless Clause in the Pentateuch*, 28; idem, *The Sentence in Biblical Hebrew*, 27. For an expanded summary of Steiner's work, see DeRouchie, *A Call to Covenant Love*, 108–10. On a side note, in personal email correspondence, SIL linguist S. H. Levinsohn stated: "I consider *waw* to be default for texts that are chronologically organized (narratives and procedures) and marked (associative) for those that are not. Conversely, I consider asyndeton to be marked for texts that are chronologically organized, whereas juxtaposition (asyndeton?) is default for those that are not."

30. So, for example, *wa* almost never begins quotations, because quotations mark absolute beginnings. Where we do find speech-initial *wa*, it is best understood to be serving as a "contextual coordinator within dialogue" (C. L. Miller, "The Pragmatics of *waw* as a Discourse Marker in Biblical Hebrew Dialogue," *ZAH* 12 [1999] 165–91; cf. Dempster, "Linguistic Features of Hebrew Narrative," 43–44). On the use of *wa* fronting biblical books, where one would expect an absolute beginning, see DeRouchie, *A Call to Covenant Love*, 351–53.

31. Andersen (*The Sentence in Biblical Hebrew*, 27) writes: "An apposition sentence [i.e., one marked by asyndeton] can be an alternative surface realization of a coordination relationship [as in the complete series of Ten Words in the Exodus version], and a coordination sentence can be an alternative relationship of an apposition relationship. Hence, in classifying such sentences, attention must be paid to the deep relationships as well as to the surface features." By "deep relationships" (also called "deep structure"), Andersen refers to the way texts communicate meaning at levels other than surface form. Contextual clues work with grammar to guide communication. (For more on the view that various deep structure clause-type realities can be expressed in the surface structure in different ways, see ibid., 186–91, and the discussion of Generative-Transformational Grammar in D. Crystal, *A Dictionary of Linguistics & Phonetics* [5th ed.; Malden, MA: Blackwell, 2003]

none of the six prohibitions that end the Decalogue in Deuteronomy (including 5:21b) can be seen as explicating what precedes, the default interpretation is to read 5:21b as a new, final element in the series of commandments that began in 5:17.[32]

What is important to emphasize at this point is that both the formal and stylistic features and the semantic content of the Decalogue call for treating the last two prohibitions as discrete Words (Exod 20:17a–b // Deut 5:21a–b), an enumeration that has ancient support in the Masoretic paragraph divisions. The lack of conjunction at the head of Exod 20:17b created the possibility for the final injunction against coveting to be read either as its own Word (= fresh beginning) or as a description of the previous prohibition against coveting (= explication). The differences in the deuteronomic version, however, render the explication interpretation impossible (at least in Deuteronomy) and thus establish the likelihood that the two statement against coveting are to be read as *distinct* Words. And as we shall now see, the fact that Deuteronomy treats as a single, extended unit Words six through ten (through fronted *wa*) helps disclose an overall structure to the Decalogue that may assist in identifying Words one and two.

2.3. Distinguishing Words One through Four

In contrast to the concluding unit just assessed, the rest of the Decalogue is characterized by the repetition of the phrase יהוה אלהיך 'Yahweh

---

199–200, 471–73.) For a developed discussion of the restating or specifying use of *wa*, see D. W. Baker, "Further Examples of the *WAW Explicativum*," *VT* 30.2 (1980) 129–36. He provides a thorough list of verses in the Hebrew Bible that have been suggested by others to contain this use of *wa*. Those I found that link clauses are Gen 24:16, 38:8; Exod 9:2; Lev 2:13; Deut 23:1; 32:28, 30, 36; 33:23; 2 Sam 14:6; Isa 42:2, 59:9; Ezek 3:15; Job 34:35; Prov 3:12; with infinitive construct constructions: Isa 32:7, Jer 17:10, Neh 8:13.

32. Some of the early Jewish rabbis who wrestled with the significance of this text block believed the conjunctions signaled a chain reaction, so that the breaking of one commandment would lead to the breaking of all the rest (e.g., *Mekhilta de R. Simeon ben Yohai* on Exod 20:14: "If he broke one law he would break the other" (Weinfeld, *Deuteronomony 1–11*, 313). (For a discussion of the translation difficulties and interpretation of Jas 2:10–11 as it relates to this idea, see Flusser, "Do not Commit Adultery, Do Not Murder," 224–25.) More recently, M. Weinfeld has argued that the inclusion of "and" in Deut 5:18–21 "enhances the uniformity of the second pentad by making it, as it were, one sentence" (*Deuteronomy 1–11*, 313; cf. N. Lohfink, "The Decalogue in Deuteronomy 5," in *Theology of the Pentateuch: Themes of the Priestly Narrative and Deuteronomy* [trans. L. M. Maloney; Minneapolis: Fortress, 1994] 257). Similarly, J. G. McConville has observed that the *wa* connectors treat the injunctions against murder, adultery, theft, bearing false witness, and the different forms of coveting as one "coherent block, rather than separate commands" (*Deuteronomy* [AOTC 5; Downers Grove, IL: InterVarsity, 2002] 122). He also adds that the "and" conveys "a sense of coherent consequentiality" thus "building up a total picture of the standards to be observed in the covenant community" (129).

your God' and by the use of ground or motivation clauses throughout. Here there are six asyndetic statements that demand our attention, the first indicative and the rest volitional, and each must either stand as a discrete Word (= fresh beginning) or clarify, expand, or fill out a nearby Word (= apposition/explication):[33]

- "I am Yahweh your God ..." (Exod 20:2 // Deut 5:6);[34]
- "There shall never be to you other gods ..." (Exod 20:3 // Deut 5:7);[35]

---

33. While further justification for this assertion is supplied in the footnotes that follow, two points are noteworthy here. First, the asyndetic commandment in Exod 20:5 // Deut 5:9 against bowing down and serving should be viewed not as a discrete Word but as explanatory, whether to the prohibition against images in Exod 20:4 // Deut 5:8 or to the injunction regarding the exclusivity of Yahweh in Exod 20:3 // Deut 5:7. The dependence on the preceding context is highlighted by the use of the 3mp pronominal suffixes that demand antecedents: "you shall never bow down to *them* or serve *them*." Second, the asyndetic clause in Exod 20:9 // Deut 5:13 ("Six days you shall labor") begins a text block that runs to Exod 20:11 // Deut 5:15; together the unit explains the nature of the Sabbath "command" in Exod 20:8 // Deut 5:12. Within this explicatory unit is inserted another appositional, parenetic statement (Exod 20:10 // Deut 5:14) that further clarifies the character of the Sabbath directive.

34. Scholars question whether the combination אנכי יהוה אלהיך in Exod 20:3 // Deut 5:7 is best translated with "Yahweh" as part of the predicate ("I am Yahweh your God") or as an appositive to the 1cs pronoun ("I, Yahweh, am your God"; see NJPS, NAB, and A. Peobel, *Das appositionell Bestimmte Pronomen der 1. Pers. Sing. in den westsemitischen Inschriften und im Alten Testament* [Assyriological Studies; Chicago: University of Chicago Press, 1932] 53–58). In context, the former option seems more likely for three reasons: (1) of the 308 instances in Deuteronomy where אלהים 'God' + suffix is directly preceded by יהוה 'Yahweh', all but four are clearly appositional (see Deut 5:6, 9; 6:4; 29:5[6]); (2) the phrase appears to be intentionally repeated in the Words against bearing Yahweh's name in vain, remembering/observing the Sabbath, and honoring one's parents, where "your God" must be appositional to the divine name (Exod 20:7, 10, 12 // Deut 5:11, 12, 14–16); (3) the collocation אני יהוה 'I am Yahweh' (without "your God") occurs very frequently in the Torah and cannot be translated in any way other than "I am Yahweh" (see Lev 18:4–5; cf. Exod 6:2, 6, 8, 29; 12:12; Lev 18:5; 19:12, 14, 16, 18, 28, 32, 37; 20:8; 21:12; 22:2, 3, 8, 30–33; 26:2, 45; Num 3:13, 41, 45; and the discussion in Weinfeld, *Deuteronomy 1–11*, 284–86; Tigay, *Deuteronomy*, 355 n. 28). V. H. Hamilton observes that אנכי 'I' is used when "*your* God" is singular (Exod 20:2, 5; Deut 5:6, 9), but אני is used when "*your* God" is plural (Lev 11:44; 18:2, 30; 19:2; 20:7, 24; 25:38, 55; 26:14; 15:41) (*Exodus: An Exegetical Commentary* [Grand Rapids: Baker, 2011] 322, note on 20:2).

35. The Hebrew of Exod 20:3 // Deut 5:7 is in third person, not second person like the rest of the Decalogue: לא יהיה־לך אלהים אחרים על־פני. This fact moved H. G. Reventlow to argue that the clause should be read not as an imperative but as an indicative, with Yahweh declaring the banishment of all rival deities: "There will [*not* shall] not be to you any other gods ..." (*Gebot und Predigt im Dekalogue* [Gütersloh: G. Mohn, 1962] 25–28). In light of both grammatical and form-critical arguments, few scholars have followed this view (see R. Knierim's critique, "Das erste Gebot," *ZAW* 77 [1965] 20–39). Within the OT, there are other examples where a first or third person *yiqtol* with לא expresses a negative prohibition (see 1 Sam 14:36 [1st], Ezek 48:14 [3rd], Prov 16:10 [3rd]; so GKC §107o). In light of the rest of the volitional injunctions that follow in the Decalogue, it seems best to

- "You shall never make for yourself a carved image . . ." (Exod 20:4[–6] // Deut 5:8[–10]);
- "You shall never bear Yahweh's name in vain . . ." (Exod 20:7 // Deut 5:11);
- "Remember/Observe the Sabbath . . ." (Exod 20:8[–11] // Deut 5:12[–15]);[36]
- "Honor your father and your mother . . ." (Exod 20:12 // Deut 5:16).

Throughout history, all interpreters have agreed that the last three of these statements make up discrete Words. What is at stake, therefore, is whether the prohibition against bearing Yahweh's name in vain (Exod 20:7 // Deut 5:11) is Word two or three, and if the latter, how one should demarcate Words one and two. More specifically, one must answer two related questions:

Is the declaration "I am Yahweh your God" (Exod 20:2 // Deut 5:6) its own discrete Word, the first of the Ten (so majority Jewish view), or is it a foundational preface (i.e., historical prologue) either to the whole Decalogue or to the particular charge related to Yahweh's exclusivity (Exod 20:3 // Deut 5:7)?

Is the asyndetic commandment against a sculptured image (Exod 20:4 // Deut 5:8) best read as its own Word (= fresh beginning) or as a clarifying expansion (= apposition, explication) on "There shall never be to you other gods" (Exod 20:3 // Deut 5:7)? We will address each issue in turn.

2.3.1. The Initial Indicative Clause— Neither an Independent Word Nor a Preamble

With reference to the enumeration of the first Word, it is noteworthy that the 1cs pronominal suffix at the end of the prepositional phrase עַל־פָּנָי 'before *me*' in Exod 20:3 // Deut 5:7 grammatically binds the prohibition against other gods to Yahweh's self-presentation ("I am Yahweh your God") in Exod 20:2 // Deut 5:6. The result is that the command to

---

read Exod 20:3 // Deut 5:7 in a volitional way, even though here we clearly have a long *yiqtol*. For a similar use of לֹא יִהְיֶה, see Deut 25:13–14.

36. Both Exodus and Deuteronomy begin the Sabbath commandment using an infinitive absolute for the imperative (Exod 20:8 // Deut 5:12). For comparable uses in the Pentateuch, see Exod 13:3; Lev 2:6, 6:7[14]; Num 15:35, 25:17; Deut 1:16, 15:2. Years ago, J. D. W. Watts argued that the infinitive absolute never stands alone as a substitute for a finite verb but instead is defined by a following verbal construction that carries an imperatival sense; he gives זכר in Exod 20:8 gerundive force: "Remembering the Sabbath to hallow it, six days you shall labor" ("Infinitive Absolute as Imperative and the Interpretation of Exodus 20,8," *ZAW* 74 [1962] 141–45). Regardless, the statement about the Sabbath should be read volitionally.

worship Yahweh alone is only understandable when linked with the identification clause that precedes. Furthermore, because the indicative clause and the first injunction grammatically form a unit, two conclusions naturally follow: (1) they are likely *not* distinct Words, and (2) the presentation statement "I am Yahweh your God" is best understood as an introduction to Word one and *not* as a covenantal historical prologue to the whole Decalogue.[37] The link between these verses also means that, while some of the ten Words include indicative prefatory or supporting material, each of the Ten is volitional at its core, calling the covenant community through two positive orders and eight prohibitions to a life of radical love for God and neighbor.[38]

These conclusions, drawn from discourse grammar, call into question the views of those rabbis that treat Exod 20:2–3 // Deut 5:6–7 as distinct Words, and they also contrast with all other interpretations that fully distinguish the statement of divine supremacy and redemption from the initial order not to have other gods.[39] The conclusions also explain how Moses could assert that the Ten Words were "commanded" (Piel צוה, Deut 4:13) and clarify why Jesus referred to the Ten Words as "commandments" (ἐντολάς, Matt 19:17–19). In the Decalogue, the identity of Yahweh as Israel's redeemer provides the syntactic and theological foundation for the charge to keep Yahweh central in Israel's

---

37. Contrast, for example, the comment by P. J. Gentry: "The fact that the covenant is broadly structured according to a Hittite treaty demonstrates plainly that verse 2 . . . is, in fact, the historical prologue of the treaty, so that the first command is just verse 3" (P. J. Gentry and S. J. Wellum, *Kingdom through Covenant: A Biblical-Theological Understanding of the Covenants* [Wheaton, IL: Crossway, 2012] 330). While I would agree that many elements of the Hittite treaties are present, the text grammar suggests that the Decalogue is employing the general pattern in its own unique way. Furthermore, Breuer notes that while contemporary scholars tend to view the initial indicative statement in Exod 20:2 // Deut 5:6 as separate from the Decalogue proper, this "system is clearly rejected by the Masorah; it does not conform to either the upper or the lower cantillation, nor does it agree with the paragraph divisions" and "it was also not accepted by the later punctators [sic]" ("Dividing the Decalogue into Verses and Commandments," 313).

38. B. S. Childs sees the prohibitions as "charting the outer limits of the covenant" and the positive statements as providing "positive content for life within the circle of the covenant" (*The Book of Exodus* [OTL; Louisville: Westminster, 1974] 398).

39. As highlighted above, the remnants of a third set of cantillation tropes actually unite into a single group the statements "I am Yahweh your God" and "There shall never be to you other gods" (Breuer, "Dividing the Decalogue into Verses and Commandments," 300–301). Because the majority of Jewish interpreters separated the two statements as distinct Words, the linking of the two in some post-Masoretic traditions forced many later scholars to wrestle with how the relationship of the statements should affect numbering, for it was "as though two Commandments were delivered as one Commandment" (301 n. 9).

affections and loyalty—a connection that is explicitly retained in numerous other texts throughout the OT (see Exod 19:4–6, Deut 6:12–15, Judg 6:8–10, Hos 13:4, Ps 81:10–11[9–10]).[40]

2.3.2. Never a Carved Image—
Assessing the Makeup of the First Word

With respect to the relationship between the prohibition against having other gods (Exod 20:3 // Deut 5:7) and the two asyndetic injunctions that begin with the ban against making a sculptured image (Exod 20:4–6] // Deut 5:8–10]), Philo, Josephus, a minority of the rabbis, and the Orthodox-Reformed interpreters have seen in them the first *two* Words of the Decalogue. In contrast, most rabbis and the Masoretes who crafted the upper tropes viewed the latter prohibitions to be explaining or concretizing (= apposition, explication) what it means to have no other gods before Yahweh. Similarly, the Catholic-Lutheran tradition commonly interprets the entire series of initial prohibitions as a single Word, the first of the Ten. A number of textual features, most of which are related to discourse grammar, support this latter view.

First, it is noteworthy that Yahweh speaks in first person in each of the statements that span from "*I* am Yahweh your God" (Exod 20:2 // Deut 5:6) to "showing steadfast love to thousands of those who love *me* and keep *my* commandments" (Exod 20:6 // Deut 5:10) (i.e., the first Word in the Catholic-Lutheran view). In the rest of the Decalogue, however, Yahweh is portrayed in third person.[41] The personal per-

---

40. See Greenberg, "The Decalogue Tradition Critically Examined," 99 with n. 24; Breuer, "Dividing the Decalogue into Verses and Commandments," 308. Recognizably, because all the commands are in some way expressions of loyalty to Yahweh above all else, Yahweh's self-identity can elsewhere provide the ground for calls to widespread, life-encompassing obedience (see Lev 18:2–6, 19:36).

41. B. S. Childs notes that the shift from first to third person is common in other laws of the Pentateuch (e.g., Exod 34:19, 23; 22:26–27; Lev 19:5, 8, 12, 19). However, while recognizing that the final redactor must not have felt tension with the inconsistency in the Decalogue, Childs fails to offer a conclusive historical reason for the phenomenon (*The Book of Exodus*, 394, 399). Along with seeing the change from first to third person in the Decalogue as a tool for uniting material that is to be read together, I propose the shift could be a formal marker signaling when the leaders of Israel ran to Moses and requested that he serve as mediator of Yahweh's voice (Exod 20:19, Deut 5:27). While it is clear that Yahweh spoke all Ten Words to the people (Deut 5:22), the leaders engaged Moses immediately after Yahweh began to speak (5:23; cf. Exod 20:18–19). Furthermore, Deuteronomy 5 introduces the Ten Words with Moses already serving as covenant mediator, and the difficult infinitive construct לאמר 'to say' at the end of Deut 5:5 may as easily modify Moses' "declaring" (להגיד) in 5:5 as Yahweh's "speaking" (Piel דבר) in 5:4. With this, it is at least possible that the record "And [Moses] said to them" (Exod 19:25) that comes just before the Decalogue points to Moses relaying God's Words to the people (so Hamilton, *Exodus*, 316). Significantly, the לאמר 'to say' speech frame that introduces the Decalogue in both

spective in the text, therefore, calls readers to view as a single unit the prohibitions against other gods and the injunctions against crafting an image and worshipping the wrong object.

Second, an inclusio that holds together all the first-person address is suggested by the repeated use of the phrase יהוה אלהיך 'Yahweh your God' in the initial declaration "I am Yahweh your God" (Exod 20:2 // Deut 5:6) and in the ground clause following the charge to guard what one worships and serves ("for I Yahweh your God am a jealous God," Exod 20:5 // Deut 5:9).[42] As already noted, the phrase "Yahweh your God" sets apart the initial Words of the Decalogue from the grouping of concise prohibitions that end it (Exod 20:13–17b // Deut 5:17–21b). In Exodus 20, the prohibition against bearing Yahweh's name in vain and the commands to keep the Sabbath and to honor one's parents each use the phrase one time. This limited appropriation could lead one to see—as in the Orthodox-Reformed view—the self-presentation statement and the first prohibition as the first Word, and the charges against shaping a graven image and against wrong worship as the second, for each would bear one use of "Yahweh your God." However, the inclusio interpretation seems more likely because in the Deuteronomy account, the phrase "Yahweh your God" is used three times in the Sabbath commandment and twice in the charge to honor parents, thus showing that there was no explicit intention to limit the use of the phrase to one occurrence per Word.

Third, the phrase אלהים אחרים 'other gods' (plural) in Exod 20:3 // Deut 5:7 provides the most likely antecedent referent for the 3mp

---

Exod 20:1 and Deut 5:4–5 by nature marks a non-prototypical speech event—namely, one that summarizes several similar speeches or one long speech, presents the statements of many people as one statement, has one character in the story cite a prior statement by another character in the story, comes through an agent or prop rather than a full character or is from someone who is not actually present and participating in the current conversation, or functions as the official record of the principal points made by speakers and is thus less vivid conversation than it is a documentation of the essential points made by the speakers (C. L. Miller, "Discourse Functions of Quotative Frames in Biblical Hebrew," in *Discourse Analysis of Biblical Literature—What It Is and What It offers* [ed. W. R. Bodine, Society of Biblical Literature Semeia Studies; Atlanta: Scholars, 1995] 165; idem, *The Representation of Speech in Biblical Hebrew Narrative: A Linguistic Analysis* [Harvard Semitic Museum Monographs 55; Atlanta: Scholars, 1996] 425–29; for summaries of Miller's work, see DeRouchie, *A Call to Covenant Love*, 205–12; Garrett and DeRouchie, *A Modern Grammar for Biblical Hebrew*, 323–27). One would expect לאמר to introduce Deuteronomy's version of the Decalogue, because Moses the mediator is recalling the Decalogue from an earlier time; however, the use of לאמר in Exodus is less expected and may serve as a signal that even that version of the Decalogue came through the agency of Moses.

42. Jastram, "Should Lutherans Really Change How They Number the Ten Commandments?" 364.

pronominal suffixes in Exod 20:5 // Deut 5:9 ("You shall never bow down to *them* or serve *them*"). Earlier it was noted that discourse grammar bound together Yahweh's self-identification as Israel's savior with the prohibition against perceiving any sovereign other than him (Exod 20:2–3 // Deut 5:6–7). So too now the same grammar signals that the unit of thought marked by the initial prohibition against other gods should be read in conjunction with the prohibitions against making a carved image and against wrong worship and service.

Those holding to the Orthodox-Reformed numbering locate the antecedent referent to the 3mp suffixes of Exod 20:5 // Deut 5:9 in the previous verse (and not Exod 20:3 // Deut 5:7), but they vary in whether the antecedent is the singular פסל 'image', the phrase כל־תמונה 'any likeness',[43] or the three-part relative clause in combination with its singular head (lit., "any likeness that is in heaven . . . or in the earth . . . or in the waters . . .").[44] None of these options are likely, however, for outside the Decalogue the word pair "to bow down and serve" (Exod 20:5 // Deut 5:9) is a stereotyped expression that always has as its object "other gods" or "the host of heaven," never physical images (, at least explicitly).[45] Furthermore, the designation of Yahweh as אל קנא 'a jealous God'

---

43. While the noun phrase כל־תמונה 'any likeness' is fronted with *wa* in Exod 20:4 and therefore joined with פסל 'carved image', the word pair should not be viewed as a compound plural entity. This conclusion is drawn in light of the absence of any conjunction in the parallel Exod 20:4, which suggests that the second phrase describes (= apposition, explication) פסל and that the "and" in Deut 5:8 is best read as "even," much like the combination "man *and* father" can point to one and the same individual with the latter nominal element giving greater clarity to the former in a given context. Thus, "You shall never make for yourself a carve image—even any likeness. . . ."

44. With respect to the first option, the noun פסל is used 31 times in the OT, always in the singular, and in two of these instances, parallelism or apposition within a clause suggests that the singular פסל can bear a plural referent. Isa 42:17 reads, "They shall be turned back; they shall be utterly put to shame—those who trust *in the image* (בפסל); those who say to a molten image (למסכה), 'You (pl) are our gods.'" Similarly, Ps 97:7 asserts, "All the servants of *an image* (פסל) are put to shame, those who boast in the idols (באלילים)." While not conclusive, these texts do suggest the possibility that פסל is the antecedent of the 3mp suffixes and that the prohibition against images is distinct from the prohibition of other gods. As for כל, when appearing in construct with an undetermined noun in the singular, the term is usually best rendered "every" rather than "all" (*HALOT*, 474; Ringgren, "כֹּל *kōl*," *TDOT* 7:136). However, the basic meaning of כל as 'totality' may make it possible that the plural suffixes could refer back to this form. Finally, while no grammatical parallels are easily apparent, it is obvious that the relative clause following כל־תמונה 'any likeness' includes three distinct prepositional phrases, and it is possible that when viewed together they could provide the necessary plural referent for the pronominal suffixes.

45. W. Zimmerli, "Das Zweite Gebot," in idem, *Gottes Offenbarung: gesammelte Aufsätze zum Alten Testament* (TB 19; Munich: Kaiser, 1963) 235 n. 3, 236–38. See Exod 20:5, 23:24; Deut 4:19, 5:9, 30:17; 1 Kgs 9:9; 2 Kgs 17:35, 21:3; Jer 22:9; 2 Chr 7:22, 33:3.

in Exod 20:5 // Deut 5:9 elsewhere refers directly to the threat of evil influences or rival deities competing for Israel's allegiance with no explicit reference to manufactured idols (see Exod 34:14; Deut 4:24, 6:15, 32:16, 21; cf. Josh 24:19; Ezek 39:25; Joel 2:18; Zech 1:14, 8:2).[46] Consequently, the proper referent for the 3mp suffixes in Exod 20:5 // Deut 5:9 seems to be the אלהים אחרים 'other gods' of Exod 20:3 // Deut 5:7, the result of which is the grouping of all three of the initial prohibitions.[47]

Fourth, each of the Words in the beginning of the Decalogue appear to be guided by an intentional commandment + ground or motive clause. Along with the ground clause related to Yahweh's jealousy in Exod 20:5 // Deut 5:9, causal reasons (usually signaled by כי 'because') are supplied for the commandments related to not bearing Yahweh's name in vain (Exod 20:7 // Deut 5:11) and for remembering/observing the Sabbath (Exod 20:8–11 // Deut 5:12–15),[48] and a purpose clause (למען 'so that') is used to motivate listeners to honor their parents (Exod 20:12 // Deut 5:16). In each of these three Words, only *one* ground or motivation statement is given for each unified commandment, and this suggests the likelihood that all three of the initial prohibitions should be read as a unit bearing a single ground clause—namely, never have other gods, craft an image, or worship and follow other gods "*for* I Yahweh your God am a jealous God" (Exod 20:5 // Deut 5:9).[49]

---

46. Block, "How Shall We Number the Ten Commandments?" in idem, *How I Love Your Torah*, 60; and idem, *The Gospel according to Moses*, 172. The only potential text I find that may suggest otherwise is Ezek 8:3, which uses the ambiguous phrase סמל הקנאה המקנה 'the image of jealousy, which provokes jealousy'.

47. On this point, I am in agreement with E. Nielsen, who asserted with reference to Exodus 20: "Vv. 5–6 are syntactically linked with v. 3 in such a way that together with it they form a frame round the prohibition of images in v. 4, making it a subdivision of the commandment not to have other gods. In other words on these grounds it is not so arbitrary to take vv. 3–6 as a single commandment" (*The Ten Commandments in New Perspective* [trans. D. J. Bourke, SBT, Series 2.7; Naperville, FL: SCM, 1968] 11–12).

48. While the Sabbath command is worded differently in Deuteronomy, the ground clause in Deut 5:15 is signaled by the inference marker על־כן 'therefore' that directly follows.

49. Zimmerli, "Das Zweite Gebot," 237–38; Jastram, "Should Lutherans Really Change How They Number the Ten Commandments?" 364. After recognizing the role of the ground clauses in each of the initial words of Exodus 20, Childs, who himself follows the Orthodox-Reformed numbering, notes that "this interpretation means that in its present redaction the second commandment of v. 4 has been incorporated within the framework of the first commandment" (*The Book of the Exodus*, 405). Gentry and Wellum (*Kingdom through Covenant*, 329) suggest that the reason ground clauses are given for the Commandments related to Yahweh's exclusivity, the bearing of his name, and keeping the Sabbath—but not for any of the others—is that these three alone were unparalleled in the law codes of other ANE materials, an assertion they claim is supported by J. J. Stamm

Table 6. The Alternating Arrangement of the Decalogue

I	Worship of Yahweh	Exod 20:2–6 // Deut 5:6–10	long
II	Yahweh's name	Exod 20:7 // Deut 5:11	short
III	Sabbath	Exod 20:8–11 // Deut 5:12–15	long
IV	Parents	Exod 20:12 // Deut 5:16	short
V	Moral commandments	Exod 20:13–17 // Deut 5:17–21	long

Fifth, when the initial declaration and three prohibitions are read together as the first of the Ten Words, the whole is seen to express an alternating arrangement with respect to length (= long + short + long + short + long). The following structure is adapted from a comparable one by Norbert Lohfink, and it shows that elements of style buttress a modified Catholic-Lutheran numbering (see Table 6).[50]

Sixth, a number of parallel texts support linking the injunction against other gods with the prohibitions against shaping a graven image and misguided worship. In Lev 19:4, for example, the declaration "I am Yahweh" provides the foundation for a prohibition against idolatry: "Do not turn to other gods or make any gods of cast metal. I am Yahweh your God." Similarly, the statement, "for I Yahweh your God am a jealous God," which grounds the prohibition against bowing down to and serving entities other than Yahweh in Exod 20:5 // Deut 5:9, is the identical reason given in Deut 6:14–15 for heeding the commandment, "You shall never pursue after other gods."[51] Finally, in Ps 81:10–11[9–10], the call to align with and bow down to Yahweh alone is linked with the recollection of Yahweh's deliverance of Israel from Egypt: "There shall be no strange god among you, and you shall not bow down to a foreign god. I am Yahweh your God, who brought you up out of the land of Egypt."

3. A Fourth Option for Numbering?

Before synthesizing my argument for a modified Catholic-Lutheran view, I want to summarize and reject an alternative option to the Decalogue's numbering that heretofore has gone unexplored. Keeping in mind the role of asyndeton to mark both new beginnings and explica-

---

and M. E. Andrew, *The Ten Commandments in Recent Research* (SBT, Second Series 2; Naperville, IL: Alec R. Allenson, 1967).

50. Lohfink, "The Decalogue in Deuteronomy 5," 257.
51. Cf. Breuer, "Dividing the Decalogue into Verses and Commandments," 308.

tion, it is possible that the first of the Ten Words may actually be "You shall never make a carved image" and that the combination "I am Yahweh your God" + the prohibition against having other gods could stand *the thesis commandment* over the whole Decalogue, providing a summation of all the other Ten Words. Using the less ambiguous version in Deuteronomy 5, Table 7 (p. 120) summarizes the different approaches to the Decalogue's structure, including this fresh proposal. Clauses fronted with *wa* use an upward pointing arrow (↑) to mark connection, whereas those lacking a conjunction (= asyndeton) are signaled by the sign for a null-set (∅). Indentation signals the asyndetic clause is understood to explicate a preceding clause.

In this newly proposed reading, the charge against shaping a graven image along with all the other nine Words explicates what it means to give Yahweh sole allegiance. As many have recognized, the Supreme Commandment to love Yahweh with all in Deut 6:4–5 (cf. Matt 22:37–38; Mark 12:29–30; Luke 10:27) is easily seen as the positive restatement of the injunction against having other gods. As such, full-orbed love for God in a way that counters all rivals would mean to refrain from worshipping idols and using God's name in vain, to keep the Sabbath holy and to honor one's parents, and to resist murdering, committing adultery, stealing, bearing false witness, coveting a neighbor's wife, and desiring a neighbor's house and moveable property. A positive benefit of this interpretation is that it may give greater clarity to the distinction elsewhere in Deuteronomy between the singular המצוה 'the Commandment' and the plural החקים והמשפטים 'the statutes and the judgments' (see Deut 5:31, 6:1, 7:11). The reason "the Commandment" appears to describe all of Moses' teaching is that it captures in its heart the entire message of the Ten Words and, by extension, the book.[52]

---

52. I find intriguing the arguments of S. Kaufman, G. Braulik, and J. H. Walton that the structure of the Decalogue provided an organizing principle for the final form of Deuteronomy 12–26 (see S. Kaufman, "The Structure of the Deuteronomic Law," *Maarav* 1 [1979] 105–58; G. Braulik, "The Sequence of the Laws in Deuteronomy 12–26," trans. L. M. Maloney, in *A Song of Power and the Power of Song: Essays on the Book of Deuteronomy* [ed. Duane L. Christensen; SBTS 3; Winona Lake, IN: Eisenbrauns, 1993] 313–35 [trans. of "Die Abfolge der Gesetze in Deuteronomium 12–26 und der Dekalog," in *Das Deuteronomium: Entstehung, Gestalt und Botschaft* (ed. N. Lohfink; BETL 68; Leuven: Leuven University Press) 252–72]; J. H. Walton, "Deuteronomy: An Exposition of the Spirit of the Law," *Grace Theological Journal* 8/2 [1987] 213–25; idem, "The Decalogue Structure of the Deuteronomic Law," in *Interpreting Deuteronomy: Issues and Approaches* (ed. D. G. Firth and P. S. Johnston; Downers Grove, IL: InterVarsity, 2012) 93–117; cf. J. D. Currid, *Deuteronomy* [Darlington, UK: Evangelical Press, 2006]). R. D. Nelson, D. I. Block, and others propose that a key difficulty with such reconstructions is the reapplication of the order to honor one's parents to the topic of public authorities, whether officers, judges, kings, priests,

Table 7. Different Approaches to the Decalogue's Structure
Based on the Role of wa and Asyndeton

		1. Majority Jewish View		2. Orthodox-Reformed View
∅	1	I am Yahweh your God		I am Yahweh your God
∅	2	Never other gods	1	Never other gods
∅		Never make a carved image	2	Never make a carved image
∅	3	Never bear God's name in vain	3	Never bear God's name in vain
∅	4	Observe the Sabbath	4	Observe the Sabbath
∅	5	Honor your father and mother	5	Honor your father and mother
∅	6	Never murder	6	Never murder
↑	7	And never commit adultery	7	And never commit adultery
↑	8	And never steal	8	And never steal
↑	9	And never bear false witness	9	And never bear false witness
↑	10	And never covet your neighbor's wife	10	And never covet your neighbor's wife
↑		And never desire your neighbor's house, etc.		And never desire your neighbor's house, etc.

		3. Catholic-Lutheran View		4. Another Possible View
∅		I am Yahweh your God		I am Yahweh your God
∅	1	Never other gods		Never other gods
∅		Never make a carved image	1	Never make a carved image
∅	2	Never bear God's name in vain	2	Never bear God's name in vain
∅	3	Observe the Sabbath	3	Observe the Sabbath
∅	4	Honor your father and mother	4	Honor your father and mother
∅	5	Never murder	5	Never murder
↑	6	And never commit adultery	6	And never commit adultery
↑	7	And never steal	7	And never steal
↑	8	And never bear false witness	8	And never bear false witness
↑	9	And never covet your neighbor's wife	9	And never covet your neighbor's wife
↑	10	And never desire your neighbor's house, etc.	10	And never desire your neighbor's house, etc.

To follow this view or any other view that distinguishes the first two prohibitions requires that the second prohibition ("You shall never make a carved image") bear no semantic or syntactic dependence on the first ("There shall never be to you other gods"). However, I have already shown the unlikelihood of this thesis and have offered a number of arguments in favor of reading Exod 20:2–6 // Deut 5:6–10 as a complete unit that must be read together. In the end, therefore, this fourth numbering option is suspect.

4. Synthesis: How to Count the Ten Words

Throughout the history of interpretation, scholars have proposed at least three different itemizations of the Decalogue. This study has attempted to move beyond the interpretive impasse by approaching the Ten Words using textlinguistic and stylistic analysis and incorporating these findings with observations from semantic content and cantillation. The conclusions have supported a modified Catholic-Lutheran view of numbering, with the only change being that Yahweh's initial declaration to be Israel's redeemer must be read as the foundational prelude to the first Word and not as a covenantal prologue to the whole Decalogue.

In the analysis, the distinctions in Deuteronomy 5 were shown to bring greater clarity to the more ambiguous account in Exodus 20, most directly with the numbering of Words five through ten. Deuteronomy shapes the final six negative injunctions into a single unit by use of the *wa* conjunction, which suggests that each prohibition, including the two injunctions against coveting, be read not only alongside of but also in distinction from the others. Deut 5:21 also uses two different verbs in the prohibitions against evil desire, includes "field" before the list of household members, and transposes "house" and "wife," thus separating the latter from the list and placing the charge against lust (i.e., coveting a neighbor's wife) on its own line. All these elements were used

---

or prophet (Deut 16:18–18:22) (R. D. Nelson, *Deuteronomy* [OTL; Louisville: Westminster John Knox, 2002] 79; D. I. Block, "Preaching Old Testament Law to New Testament Christians," in *The Gospel according to Moses*, 117 n. 31; idem, *Deuteronomy* [NIVAC; Grand Rapids: Zondervan, 2012], 301–2; cf. Tigay, *Deuteronomy*, 534 n. 19). However, as is highlighted in §2.3 of my accompanying essay "Making the Ten Count," Paul himself in 1 Tim 5:3 appears to see a broader application of the commandment to honor one's parents that includes the treatment of the elderly within the household of God (see P. H. Towner, *The Letters to Timothy and Titus* [NICNT; Accordance electronic ed.; Grand Rapids: Eerdmans, 2006] 338). Nevertheless, regardless of one's view regarding this thesis, most will affirm that the Decalogue significantly captures the core volitional thrust of the OT in general and of Deuteronomy in particular.

in support of treating the final two commandments against coveting as discrete Words.[53]

As for Words one through four, the shift from first- to third-person orientation, the tracking of pronominal referent, the distinct use of ground and motivation clauses, and features of style were all employed to argue that the initial indicative statement and the three asyndetic commandments that follow were to be read together as the first Word of the Ten. In light of this numbering, the whole Decalogue is legitimately regarded as ten *commandments* (contrary to the majority Jewish view), and the indicative self-identification clause at the head is rightly viewed as a foundational prelude to the first Word, which focuses on the worship of Yahweh alone. The prohibition against ever considering Yahweh as anything but the absolute Sovereign (Exod 20:3 // Deut 5:7) flows from the reality of his redeeming work on Israel's behalf (Exod 20:2 // Deut 5:6). Furthermore, it is clarified by the two explicative asyndetic charges not to replace or misrepresent God by a manufactured image or with misdirected worship (Exod 20:4–6 // Deut 5:8–10). All three of these prohibitions are then grounded in Yahweh's just jealousy.

In the end, features of discourse grammar, style, and semantic content are shown to give greatest support to a modified Catholic-Lutheran numbering of the Decalogue. This view is also buttressed by the Masoretic paragraph divisions (the *parashiyyot*) and is likely preserved in the oldest of the Masoretic witnesses, the verse division signaled through the lower cantillation system. God gave us ten Words, and they can now be counted correctly.

---

53. Many scholars immediately discount the Catholic-Lutheran numbering because it requires that the Exodus and Deuteronomy version of the Decalogue actually have different elements for the ten. Specifically, they assert that the separation of "wife" from the list in Deut 5:17 requires that the commands against coveting/envy be read as one Word, lest the deuteronomic version say something different than the Exodus version. However, even with all the changes made to the commands to keep the Sabbath and to honor one's parents, Moses asserted that his thrust was no different than Yahweh's original charge at the mountain, for in Deuteronomy everything was "just as Yahweh your God commanded you" (Deut 5:12, 16). In the words of Lohfink, this formulaic back-reference ensures that "in spite of the changes and additions that have been made [in the deuteronomic version], at bottom nothing is commanded that is not also in the older version" ("The Decalogue in Deuteronomy 5," 262). Furthermore, because the developments in Deuteronomy appear to be linked intentionally to the book's domestic ideology, there is just grounds for the preacher to adapt the text without altering its essence (see D. I. Block, "'You Shall Not Covet Your Neighbor's Wife': A Study in Deuteronomic Domestic Ideology," *JETS* 53 [2010] 449–74; repr. in idem, *The Gospel according to Moses*, 137–68).

Now, knowing how to count the Ten Words means nothing if we fail to make them count. As a step toward this end, I have written a parallel essay in this volume titled "Making the Ten Count: Reflections on the Lasting Message of the Decalogue."

Appendix A. The Real Decalogue: Exodus 20 // Deuteronomy 5, not Exodus 34

It seems necessary to justify the identification of Exod 20:1–17 and Deut 5:6–21 as the "Ten Words" (עשׂרת הדברים) referred to in Exod 34:28, Deut 4:13, and 10:4. In the history of interpretation, critical scholars have often identified a number of "Decalogues" in Scripture, most notably the "ethical Decalogues" of Exod 20:1–17 and Deut 5:6–21 and the "ritual or cultic Decalogue" of Exod 34:11–26, the latter often being considered most original.[54] However, a close reading of the text as it stands removes the proposed tensions and clearly designates which lists are to be regarded as the covenantal "Ten Words."

It is true that Exod 34:11–26 includes a series of apodictic principles and that directly after them in verse 28 the phrase "Ten Words" shows up for the first time in Scripture. However, only if one begins with verse 17 are *ten* directives evident, and as will be shown, Exodus 34 itself calls the reader to look elsewhere for the actual Ten Words of the covenant (34:1, 28). The prescriptions in Exodus 34 are best seen as sample laws from the Covenant Code of Exodus 20–23 (esp. ch. 23), perhaps even a festival calendar, and should not be confused with the actual Decalogue.[55]

With respect to Exod 34:11–26, the misunderstanding has arisen because the prescriptions themselves are directly followed first by Yahweh's charge to Moses to write down "these words" in accordance with which God made a covenant with his people (a clear reference to 34:11–26) and then by the narrator's record that the "the words of the covenant, the Ten Words," were written on the tablets (34:27–28). Do we have here a command–fulfillment sequence, wherein Moses obeys by writing the ten covenantal words on the tablets?

---

54. This view is espoused most recently by D. H. Aaron, *Etched in Stone: The Emergence of the Decalogue* (New York: T & T Clark, 2006). Other scholars have posited a "curse Decalogue" in Deut 27:15–26, but the curses number twelve, not ten, and they are never associated with the Decalogue. Still others have pointed to the commands in Leviticus 19 as a new Decalogue, but while some of the instructions are clear echoes (e.g., revering one's parents, keeping the Sabbath, and resisting idolatry in 19:3–4), the total number of commands is well beyond ten.

55. So too W. J. Harrelson, "Ten Commandments," *IDB* 4:570.

This is unlikely, for with a back-reference to the divine activity promised and fulfilled in Exod 24:12, 31:18, and 32:15–16, Yahweh announced in 34:1 that *he*, not Moses, would write *the same Words* on the new tablets that *he* had written before with his own finger: "Yahweh said to Moses, 'Cut for yourself two tablets of stone like the first, and I will write on the tablets the words that were on the first tablets, which you broke.'" Yahweh, not Moses, is the antecedent to the 3ms verb ויכתב 'and he wrote' in verse 28, which means that "these words" that Moses is charged to write in verse 27 (i.e., 34:11–26) are *not* the actual Ten Words of the covenant.

Later in Deuteronomy, Moses highlights that the Words of Exod 20:1–17 were indeed the very same Decalogue of 34:28. First, in Deut 4:12–13, the prophet states specifically that Yahweh declared his covenant, the Ten Words, out of the fire and wrote them on two tablets of stone (cf. Exod 31:18). In echo of Exod 34:1 and 28, he then stresses in Deut 10:4 that Yahweh "wrote on the tablets, in the same writing as before, the Ten Words that Yahweh had spoken to you on the mountain out of the midst of the first on the day of the assembly."

These passages leave no question regarding the makeup of the Decalogue. The biblical author connected the phrase "Ten Words" only to the lists in Exod 20:1–17 and Deut 5:6–21.

Appendix B. Observations on the Relationship of Exodus and Deuteronomy's Versions of the Decalogue

There has been a long history of discussion regarding the historical development of the Decalogue, and a number of scholars disagree about the diachronic relationship of the differing versions in Exodus and Deuteronomy.[56] A detailed assessment of this issue is beyond the scope of the present study, but a few observations are still in order here. First, the narrative that governs the final form of the whole Pentateuch presents the Exodus Decalogue as preceding Deuteronomy's version by some forty years, for Exod 20:1–17 is part of the initial record of the Sinai theophany, whereas Moses speaks Deut 5:6–21 as a back-reference

---

56. For an overview of this issue, see the surveys of scholarly discussion in Childs, *The Book of Exodus*, 388–401; and Weinfeld, *Deuteronomy 1–11*, 262–67; cf. Harrelson, "Ten Commandments," *IDB* 4:570, 572; C. J. H. Wright, "Ten Commandments," *ISBE* 4:786–89; R. F. Collins, "Ten Commandments," *ABD* 6:383–84; J. W. Marshall, "Decalogue," in *Dictionary of the Old Testament: Pentateuch* (ed. T. D. Alexander and D. W. Baker; Downers Grove, IL: InterVarsity, 2003) 171–72; P. D. Miller, "The Ten Commandments," *The New Interpreter's Dictionary of the Bible* (5 vols.; ed. K. D. Sakenfeld; Nashville: Abingdon, 2009) 5:517–19.

to this event after Israel's defeat of the Amorite kings, some four decades later (Deut 1:3–4, 4:45–46). Second, while Deut 5:6–21 evidences a number of distinctions from the Exodus version, Deuteronomy itself treats its Decalogue as a reiteration of the very "Ten Words" spoken by God out of the midst of the fire at the mountain of God—namely, as an echo of Exod 20:1–17 (cf. Deut 5:4–5, 22 with 4:12–13 and 10:4). Regardless of how one attempts to clarify the diachronic relationship of the texts, the shape of the final form suggests that any proposed tensions were not felt by the Pentateuch's final redactor. Third, unlike the Exodus version, the text of Deuteronomy itself suggests that it is a secondary account that rests on a law that Yahweh previously proclaimed at Sinai. This is most evident in the twice stated subordinate clause כאשר צוה יהוה אלהיך 'just as Yahweh your God commanded you', which stands as a plus in Deuteronomy's Words on the Sabbath and honoring one's parents (Deut 5:12, 16). As Lohfink concluded, this formulaic back-reference ensures that "in spite of the changes and additions that have been made [in the deuteronomic version], at bottom nothing is commanded that is not also in the older version."[57] As highlighted above, this observation is significant as we considered the theological implications of the Decalogue's numbering and the variations evident between Exodus and Deuteronomy.

---

57. Lohfink, "The Decalogue in Deuteronomy 5," 262. While I agree with Lohfink on this point, I do not agree with his historical conclusions or with his assertion that the Sabbath is "the principal commandment" of the deuteronomic Decalogue.

"Keep These Words in Your Heart" (Deut 6:6)
A Spirituality of Torah in the Context of the Shema

J. Gordon McConville

In this essay I wish to explore what is meant by the command of Moses to Israel in Deut 6:6: "Keep these words that I am commanding you today in your heart" (NRSV). I find something intriguing, even paradoxical, in this conjunction of "words" and "heart." The "words" in Deuteronomy take several concrete forms: the words spoken by Moses in his speeches on the plains of Moab; the words written on plaster on the stones set up on Mount Ebal (Deut 27:2–3); and the words of Moses as written in "the book of this law" (28:61), which was to be kept beside the ark of the covenant (31:9, 25–26) and to be read by the Levites every seven years at the Feast of Booths (31:10–11). We might extend this catalogue to include the words spoken directly by God, as in the Decalogue. All these instances have a certain outward, visible or audible, existence. So the idea of having "words in your heart" raises the question how that relates to these external forms. The text touches on one of the great paradoxes of Deuteronomy, namely, the givenness of its "words" ("Do not add . . ."; "no prophet like Moses," 34:10), yet its sense that there may yet be more to be disclosed ("a prophet like me," 18:15), and its understanding that a work of interpretation will always need to be done (17:8–13).

The command in question lies close to the heart of Deuteronomy itself. It follows immediately on the so-called Shema ("Hear O Israel: the LORD our God, the LORD is One," Deut 6:4), and the ensuing love

---

Author's Note: I am delighted to dedicate the following study to Dan Block, whose scholarship and friendship I have valued enormously over many years. It is a pleasure to share with him especially in the study of torah in Deuteronomy, to which he has contributed so much (see most recently Daniel I. Block, *How I Love Your Torah, O LORD! Studies in the Book of Deuteronomy* [Eugene, OR: Cascade Books, 2011] and idem, *The Gospel According to Moses: Theological and Ethical Reflections on the Book of Deuteronomy* [Eugene, OR: Cascade Books, 2012]). I particularly endorse his view emphasized in the first volume (esp. pp. 19–20) that the torah should be seen as a gift of grace for Israel's life, and not subjected in principle to the Pauline arguments about grace and law in a very specific context.

commandment ("You shall love the LORD your God with all your heart, and with all your soul, and with all your strength," 6:5 NRSV). The elements that make up Deut 6:4–6 belong closely together, as I will try to show. That is, there is a connection between the name of God and the commands that follow. And there is a further connection between the love commandment and the profiling of the person addressed in terms of "heart, soul, and might" (as usually translated). All of this requires elucidation.

1. The Name of Yahweh

The Shema begins by naming God. It is not a new naming of God,[1] but rather a predication of the known name Yahweh. In the double utterance of it, it carries an echo of Exod 34:5–7, in which Yahweh appears to Moses in a cloud, and "proclaims" his name "Yahweh" (v. 5), then does so again in a double utterance of it (v. 6aβ; "Yahweh, Yahweh"). The LORD proceeds to declarations about the divine nature (vv. 6b–7), leading in turn to a renewal of the covenant, including a form of the Decalogue (vv. 10–28). Behind this text, furthermore, lies the imparting of the name to Moses at the burning bush, in which the name Yahweh is given, ultimately, in answer to the question: "What is his name?" The giving of the name is in fact hedged around in remarkable ways. It is prepared for by the uncanny sign of the bush that is burning but not consumed and by the warning to Moses that he stands on holy ground (3:2–5). It is then adumbrated in the dialogue with Moses, with the paronomastic phrase 'But I will be with you' (כי אהיה עמך), situating the disclosure of the name in a promise. The build up continues in the mysterious אהיה אשר אהיה 'I am/will be who I am/will be', which recurs in part in "I am (אהיה) has sent me to you" (3:14). Only at length does the disclosed name settle into the familiar "Yahweh," to which is added: "This is my name for ever, and this is my title (זכרי) for all generations" (3:15).

These preliminary observations testify to a certain tension in the disclosure of the name of Yahweh. Most importantly, it comes with tremendous solemnity and mystery, closely attached to the very person of God. The prohibition of its wrongful use is part of the Decalogue's insistence on the worship of Yahweh alone (Exod 20:7, Deut 5:11).[2] Yahweh's

---

1. *Pace* C. H. Gordon, "His Name is 'One,'" *JNES* 29 (1970) 198–99, who argued that אחד 'one' was indeed a name of God.

2. See D. I. Block, "Bearing the Name of the LORD with Honor," *BSac* 168 (2011): 20–31, repr. in idem, *How I Love Your Torah*, 61–72.

own portentous double utterance of it in Exod 34:6 accompanies an appearance to Moses at the crucial moment of the covenant renewal after the apostasy at Sinai (Exod 34:5–8). And it his name 'for ever' (לעלם), his 'title' (זכרי) "for all generations." As Seitz argues, the name Yahweh bears unchanging testimony to the call upon Israel to know and worship this God and not another.[3]

Yet there is also something about the name that cannot be fully apprehended, not surprisingly in view of its close association with the person of God. If the name Yahweh must not "be used wrongfully" (lit., "be lifted up to vanity") (Exod 20:7, Deut 5:11), it is because it may not and cannot become an instrument of manipulation. So the question, "What is his name?" amounts to an enquiry not only about identity but about meaning.[4] And this is why its first disclosure comes thoroughly wrapped in declarations of intent ("I will be with you"; "I will be what I will be"). The latter of these, the *idem per idem*, strangely combines the notion of promised action with that of being itself. The formulation seems to turn back the question: "What is his name?" At the same time it draws attention to the divine purpose, as in "I will be with you." The location of the disclosure at Horeb points forward to the covenant that will in due course be concluded there, so that Yahweh's naming of himself is at the same time a promise of his faithfulness to Israel. In a sense the entire story from Exodus to Deuteronomy, and beyond, is a kind of unfolding of the answer given first in Exod 3:14–15. The disclosure is at the same time a non-disclosure, inasmuch as Israel waits to see what God "will be." For Seitz, the unique "I am has sent me to you" (v. 14) means that "the potentially circular 'I am as I am' is not a rebuttal (cf. *'ănî 'ăšer 'ănî*) but a clue to the meaning of the proper name YHWH." He continues, "God's name involves something that he will be or become."[5] However, Israel does not simply wait and see what Yah-

---

3. This aspect of the divine name has been elaborated by C. Seitz, "The Divine Name in Christian Scripture," in idem, *Word Without End: the Old Testament as Abiding Theological Witness* (Grand Rapids: Eerdmans, 1998) 251–62.

4. Seitz makes the point that the question is put by Israel to Moses, perhaps to verify that he, as an incomer, actually knows the name of their God (which they already know). The phrase "I will be with you" in Exod 3:12 is addressed in the singular, that is, to Moses. However, Seitz goes on, if Moses is learning the name Yahweh here for the first time, he is also learning something of what it means, which might as yet be unknown to Israel (C. Seitz, "The Call of Moses and the 'Revelation' of the Divine Name," in idem, *Word Without End*, 229–47 [237–38]).

5. Seitz, "Call of Moses," 239. In the context of the "revelations" of the name Yahweh in Exod 3:14–15 and 6:3, the point is that Yahweh has not hitherto been known in terms of the significance of the name, because that remains to be disclosed at the exodus (pp. 242–43). Seitz is arguing against the view of R. W. L. Moberly that the name Yahweh

weh will become. Rather, the history that is still to unfold involves the participation of Israel as covenant partner. This is an implication of the covenantal context in which the divine name now becomes an issue in the narrative.

2. Yahweh as "One"

The Shema echoes the already known naming of Yahweh, but now brings its own addition: "Yahweh is One." What is meant here by אחד 'one'? The two possibilities proposed in the scholarly literature are that it means (a) Yahweh is "one" in a way that says something about him in himself, or (b) Yahweh *alone* is our God. I have elsewhere adopted the former interpretation, and suggested that אחד here connotes a unity in Yahweh, which corresponds to his integrative rule over all things. Yahweh's "oneness " is "in terms of his power to deliver Israel, his entitlement to their obedience, and his capacity to bless them in the land he will give." The predication "one" of Yahweh in Zech 14:9 does this on a universal scale.[6]

Our starting point for such an investigation is in the observations already made, that the meaning of the name of Yahweh as given in Exodus anticipates further exposition, and that such exposition will involve an elaboration of the relationship between Yahweh and Israel. The immediate context of the Shema confirms these observations, since it is immediately followed by the command to love Yahweh with heart, soul, and might, and to "keep these words that I am commanding you today in your heart." The Shema is itself a command ("Hear!"), and this imperative is bound syntactically by waw-consecutives with *qatal* forms to the series of commands down to Deut 6:9. Hearing the predication of the name is inseparable from hearing and doing the commands.

---

is in fact revealed for the first time in Exod 3:14–15 (Moberly, *The Old Testament of the Old Testament: Patriarchal Narratives and Mosaic Yahwism* [OBT; Minneapolis: Fortress, 1992] 24). Moberly, however, also believes that the manner of the revelation of the name conveys "implications related to what God will be or do" (p. 22).

6. J. G. McConville, *Deuteronomy* (AOTC; Leicester: Apollos, 2002) 141. In adopting this rendering, I accept that the phrase presents considerable difficulties. I am not sure that one can distinguish finally between the two options of "One" and "alone." D. I. Block has made a strong case for the latter (Block, "How Many Is God? An Investigation into the Meaning of Deuteronomy 6:4–5," *JETS* 47 [2004] 193–212; repr. in idem, *How I Love Your Torah*, 73–97 [80–82]). There are in my view a few cases where אחד is best taken as "alone" (1 Chr 29:1 is probably the best example). Yet I still think the natural term for "alone" in the present text would be לבדו. I think too that to render אחד as "One" does not in any case rule out "alone": a unitary interpretation of "One" is bound to include the idea that Yahweh *alone* is Israel's God. In the end, it will be a matter of interpretation in context (with J. G. Janzen, "On The Most Important Word in the Shema [Deuteronomy VI 4–5]," *VT* 37 [1987] 280).

Gerald Janzen, pursuing a "unitary" understanding of Yahweh's "oneness," thought that אחד connoted the consistency of God's character, demonstrated in his power and commitment to save Israel. He found theological analogy in texts in Job and Jeremiah. For example, in Job 31:15, Job's point is that the integrity that he asserts for himself corresponds to an integrity that he also claims of God. Job 23:13, on the other hand, subverts this attribution of the divine integrity. Both texts, however, make the connection between "oneness" and the divine integrity.[7]

Janzen pursues his argument by demonstrating a connection between the Shema and the words of Yahweh in Jer 32:38–41. The passage expounds the covenantal relationship between Yahweh and Israel expressed in the formula: "They shall be my people and I will be their God" (Jer 32:38). And in its poetic structure, Jer 32:38–41 elaborates the reciprocity of Yahweh's loyalty to Israel and Israel's to Yahweh. In this discourse, echoes of the Shema may be heard. Most striking is the immediate sequel to the covenant formula, namely: "I will give them one heart and one way (לב אחד ודרך אחד)" (v. 39), with its twice repeated אחד, closely linked to the noun לב. This is reinforced in v. 40, with Yahweh's assertion: "I will put the fear of me in their hearts (בלבבם)." And finally, Yahweh expresses his own intention to restore Israel in the phrase: "I will plant them in this land in faithfulness (אמת) with all my heart and all my soul (בכל לבי ובכל נפשי)," a declaration of his own entire commitment that corresponds closely to the demand for entire commitment made of Israel in the Shema.[8]

Janzen argues that this echo of the Shema demonstrates Yahweh's integrity and faithfulness in ever-changing situations, including, as in the exile, where these attributes may be doubted. At stake in both Deuteronomy and Jeremiah is faithfulness and integrity on both sides of the covenantal relationship. The name and naming of God are inseparable from the realization of the covenant purpose in Israel, both as regards his determination to maintain this, and as regards the command laid upon Israel to do the same. For this reason, the name of God is inextricably bound up with ongoing disclosure of the divine character alongside exhortation to Israel to be faithful, as in, for example, Deut 10:12–22, an exposition of the Shema within Deuteronomy.[9]

---

7. Janzen, "The Most Important Word," 286–87.
8. Ibid., 288–91.
9. See ibid., 294. In the same place he cites P. Miller's view that the phrase "The LORD is one" indicates his consistency, that he is "not divided within 'self' in any way" (Miller, "The Most Important Word: The Yoke of the Kingdom," *Iliff Review* [1984] 17–29 [22]).

3. "Love, Heart, Soul, and Might"

It follows from the argument so far, that the exhortations to Israel, beginning with the love commandment in Deut 6:5, serve the aim to bring about a correspondence between the integrity of Yahweh and that of Israel in the context of the covenantal relationship. Our investigation of what is entailed in this now falls into two parts, first, a consideration of the meaning of the terms ואהבת . . . בכל לבבך ובכל נפשך ובכל מאדך 'You shall love . . . with all your heart, and with all your soul, and with all your strength' (6:5 NRSV), and second, an enquiry into what is meant by the words על לבבך 'on your heart'.

The words ואהבת . . . בכל לבבך ובכל נפשך ובכל מאדך have usually been translated: "You shall love [the LORD your God] with all your heart, with all your soul and with all your might" (which I have hitherto followed here in citing standard translations). However, the meaning of three of the key terms here is contested. Does "loving Yahweh" have an affective aspect? Does לבב really connote "heart," or might it better be translated as "mind"? Is it right to translate נפש as "soul"?

3.1. Loving with One's "Heart"

The terms לבב and לב are a headache for translators. Despite the strong tradition of rendering it as "heart," it is widely considered to be the seat of thought, and so translators opt for "mind" in some contexts. An initial illustration in Deuteronomy is found in 29:3[4], in which the Hebrew לב is closely associated with "knowing" (לב לדעת). The RSV, therefore, followed by the NIV, translates: "to this day the LORD has not given you a mind to understand, or eyes to see or ears to hear." In contrast, the ESV chooses "heart," perhaps to maintain an echo of the command in Deut 6:5. The dilemma felt by modern translators was known also to their predecessors in the LXX and the NT.[10] These different choices suggest that in translation we can only approximate the term's range of meaning, and that in choosing one or the other English term, we are forced into a distinction that may not have been recognized by the Hebrew writers and hearers. A proper sense of its meaning can arise only from a study of its use.

Michael Carasik finds in Deuteronomy a theology of the mind. He looks for evidence of the ways in which knowledge and information

---

10. Deut 6:5 LXX [A] has ἐξ ὅλης τῆς καρδίας σου, but LXX [B] employs διανοιας 'mind' instead of καρδίας 'heart' (see M. Weinfeld, *Deuteronomy 1–11* (AB; New York: Doubleday, 1991) 338, who apparently overlooks the A reading. Both Matt 22:37 and Mark 12:29–30 have forms of καρδία, but also διάνοια instead of "might." Luke 10:27 adds διάνοια after "strength."

were processed by the Israelites, or what he calls their "psychology of knowledge." In pursuing this argument, Carasik maintains that there is such a thing as a state of awareness, or inner attitude, distinct in principle from intention and action, though related to these.[11] He does so in studies of 'learning' (למד), 'knowledge' (דעת), and 'memory' (זכר), always pursuing the idea of inner awareness. In relation to memory in Psalm 78, he writes that the authors "were consciously aware of the *psychological* effect of what they were doing, deliberately intent on evoking memory in the minds of their readers."[12] His aim is to show that the "heart" represents an inner life that displays a particular character. The "heart" could be, on the one hand, "crooked" (Ps 101:4) or proud ("high," Ezek 31:10), or, on the other hand, "upright" (Deut 9:5).

For Carasik, the biblical conception of the mind was inescapably theological, "intricately tied up with an understanding of the relationship between God and humanity."[13] Left to itself, the mind tends to be a locus of opposition to God.[14] The biblical writers, therefore, believe the mind has to be constrained by God's action upon it. Jeremiah's metaphor of God "writing on the heart" aims to unite the permanence associated with writing to the "constant awareness of God's teaching" in the person's experience.[15] In his account, therefore, Carasik is precisely addressing the question we raised at the outset, the relationship between the tangible and external and that which goes to the center of the person's being.

In his extended account of Deuteronomy ("The Mind that Plans"), he pursues the relationship between Israel's original experience of God at Horeb and the writing that cultivates its memory. His analysis is based on his view that, in human awareness, generally the sense of sight precedes that of hearing.[16] He points to the use of the imperative of האר 'see' to introduce propositions offered to the understanding (as in Exod 7:1, 2 Sam 7:2, Josh 6:2, etc.), and concludes, "it is important that the

---

11. M. Carasik, *Theologies of the Mind in Biblical Israel* (SBL 85; New York: Peter Lang, 2006) 75–80, cf. p. 47.
12. Ibid., 85.
13. Ibid., 10–11.
14. Ibid., 113–24.
15. Ibid., 110. He contrasts Ezekiel's metaphor of a "heart of flesh." Where Jeremiah looks for a kind of rigidity in the heart, Ezekiel wants to replace the heart that is rigid with stubbornness with one that is malleable.
16. Ibid., 32–43. He says, for example, "*All* human cultures are primarily visual," and he believes this to be grounded in biology (33). This is in the service of his contention that ancient Hebrew thinking processes were essentially the same as other peoples', ancient and modern.

Israelite metaphor for thought was a *visual* image."[17] In Deuteronomy, it is seeing, not hearing, that conveys immediate experience, as in, for example, Deut 3:21: "It is your own eyes that have seen what the LORD your God did to those two kings [Sihon and Og]."[18] The key event, of course, is Horeb, which is also essentially visual, because even though the people "saw no form" (4:12, 15), they did see a great fire (4:36). With this premise he then accounts for the preponderance of word and hearing in the book by arguing that the words, while secondary to vision, function to impress on the mind the content of the vision. Visual and verbal are related, necessarily, because only the verbal is repeatable.[19] The purpose of the repeated commands to "remember" is that Israel should recreate an image of the determinative experience in the mind.[20] What is required by these "psychological commands" is a state of mind or attitude.[21]

In his pursuit of a strictly intellectual reading of Deuteronomy's appeal to the לב or לבב, he acknowledges at this point that the intellectual and the emotional cannot be kept apart in the book's thought. There is an integration of these in what he calls "psychological commands."[22] He questions W. L. Moran's interpretation of the command to "love Yahweh" in terms of the loyalty required of vassals in international treaties,[23] believing that it has an emotional dimension, and that both the emotions of love and joy are commanded in the context of the laws. Yet his treatment suggests that its purpose is to ensure willing obedience to the commands. This is the key theological issue for him. The human mind poses a problem to the writers of Deuteronomy, because it is ultimately "untameable": ". . . the perfect society of Deuteronomy cannot tolerate independent thought."[24] This explains its rhetorical devices, to constrain the human mind into obedience. The study that began as an enquiry into the processes of the mind, on the premise that these are essentially the same across all cultures, turns out to have this theological dilemma at its root. If the human heart is a locus of opposition to God, and must be acted upon by God in order to bring it into obedience, can

---

17. Ibid., 41. This view is called into question in the review by D. Lambert (review of *Theologies of the Mind in Biblical Israel*, RBL 08/2007).
18. Ibid., 185.
19. Ibid., 186–87.
20. Ibid., 193.
21. Ibid., 196–97.
22. Ibid., 199–201.
23. W. L. Moran, "The Ancient Near Eastern Background of the Love of God in Deuteronomy," *CBQ* 25 (1963) 77–87.
24. Carasik, *Theologies of the Mind*, 212–13.

human beings be said to be independent moral agents? His answer is as follows: "The overall impression is not a world of robotic slaves, but of men and women whose observance of God's commandments is a live and integral thing, coming to each from the natural promptings of the heart."[25] This is right. But it seems we are in different territory from a study of the processes of the mind.

Carasik's study raises important questions. His belief in the priority of the visual in human experience is questionable. There are, first, exegetical difficulties with it. His idea that the role of words in Deuteronomy serves to bring to mind an essentially visual experience that the audience had shared is difficult to sustain, not least because even the putative original audience in Moab was a generation removed from the Horeb experience. This perspective comes to expression in Deut 1:35–36, 2:16, and is maintained throughout chapters 1–3. When Moses addresses the Moab audience as if they were actually present at Horeb (as in 4:9–14 and 5:3) this is a device to establish continuity and solidarity between all the generations of Israel.[26] For the Moab audience, the Horeb generation is in principle in no different a relationship to them than to the patriarchs.[27] Carasik recognizes that for future generations, understanding can only come by hearing, and he deals with this by making a separation between the normative "holistic" understanding of "immediate experience" and the deuteronomic provision for transmitting the laws to future generations.[28] But such a separation is not convincing, for the reasons just given. The deuteronomic discourse concerning moral and intellectual agency is couched consistently in terms of the transmission and reception of words, and this must be central to its contribution to an understanding of the human person. His argument about the priority of the visual in cognition therefore becomes at best redundant.

A second issue arising from Carasik's study is the relationship between the strictly intellectual and other aspects of the human experience. Carasik has aimed to discover Israelite processes of thought, and finds in Deuteronomy, on the broad canvas of history, "the first

---

25. Ibid., 213.
26. On this subject, see J. Hwang, *The Rhetoric of Remembrance: An Investigation of the "Fathers" in Deuteronomy* (Siphrut 8; Winona Lake, IN: Eisenbrauns, 2012); idem, "The Rhetoric of Theophany: The Imaginative Depiction of Horeb in Deuteronomy 9–10," in this volume.
27. Carasik postulates precisely such a distinction, because he believes the Moab generation did actually experience the event at Horeb (Carasik, *Theologies of the Mind*, 193).
28. Ibid., 193.

coherent attempt to understand the mind."[29] There is a tension, however, between this focus on the intellect and the inescapability of both the emotional aspects of human experience and the theological issues associated with the conflicted relationship between humans and God. Is it true that the appeal to the emotions in deuteronomic discourse is subordinate to the aim of producing intellectual assent to the commandments?[30]

One important context for this question is the study of emotion in modern cognitive psychology. K. A. Kuhn has called for a reappraisal of the place of emotions in the understanding of biblical narrative, on the premise of a close relationship between emotion and intellectual judgment. Many emotions, he argues, derive from conscious appraisals related to our values and are therefore a gauge of what matters most to us. While there is a certain universality to human emotions, they are also culturally conditioned, and therefore are subject to alteration, as are our beliefs.[31] He cites Deuteronomy in its entirety as an example of the rhetorical appeal to the emotions.[32]

This belief underlies Jacqueline Lapsley's study of the command to love Yahweh in Deuteronomy. She challenges Moran's thesis that this command is essentially the language of treaty, intended to maintain loyalty by obedience to command, and thus lacking an emotional element.[33] With Jeffrey Tigay and others, she argues that loving God "with all your heart and with all your soul" involves passion and desire as well as obedience.[34]

---

29. Ibid., 215.

30. A similar question is raised by D. Lambert (review of Carasik, *RBL* 08/2007). On thought and speech, he cites Gen 27:41, Ps 49:4, and Eccl 5:1. Incidentally, he thinks that Moran was on the right track when he understood "love" in Deuteronomy "in behavioural rather than internal, emotional terms."

31. K. A. Kuhn, *The Heart of Biblical Narrative: Rediscovering Biblical Appeal to the Emotions* (Minneapolis: Fortress, 2009) 23–27.

32. Kuhn, *The Heart of Biblical Narrative*, 8, citing for example Deut 4:4–7, 20. He recognizes a debate among cognitive philosophers about whether all emotional responses are related to conscious judgments and values, or whether emotions are essentially preor non-cognitive. He concludes, however, that both of these views can be held in some measure, and he finds support for his view in the work of M. C. Nussbaum, *Upheavals of Thought: The Intelligence of Emotions* (New York: Cambridge University Press, 2001).

33. Moran, "Ancient Near Eastern Background," 77–87.

34. J. E. Lapsley, "Feeling Our Way: Love for God in Deuteronomy," *CBQ* 65 (2003) 350–69 (350–51); J. Tigay, *Deuteronomy* (JPS Torah Commentary; Philadelphia: Jewish Publication Society, 1996) 77. Lapsley cites in addition, Walter Brueggemann, *Theology of the Old Testament: Testimony, Dispute, Advocacy* (Minneapolis: Fortress, 1997) 420; D. T. Olson, *Deuteronomy and the Death of Moses* (OBT; Minneapolis: Fortress, 1994) 51.

In pursuing her argument, she first acknowledges cultural variation in the ways in which the relationship between intellect and emotion are apprehended, and especially a modern tendency to "privatize" emotions.[35] Second, she argues that an understanding of "love of God" in Deut 6:5 should be situated within the usage of "love" in Deuteronomy, and indeed its narrative framework, and that of the Pentateuch.[36] In this connection she finds a reciprocity between Israel's love for God and God's love for Israel, which she explores in Deut 10:12–11:1. Here she discovers an emotive aspect in Yahweh's setting his love upon Israel (10:15), and in his "love" for the stranger (10:18), and concludes that the love of the stranger required of Israel must have an emotive aspect too.[37] She further resists the division between obedience and emotive response by arguing that the use of external forms and rituals can produce a religious or emotional response. It is even possible to "command a feeling."[38]

Lapsley is right, in my view, to insist that the love command in Deut 6:5 is addressed to the whole person in her full capacities.[39] There is no clear distinction, in biblical thought, between spheres of intellect and emotion, nor therefore a notion of torah-obedience that consists merely in intellectual assent. Psalm 119 could be called in as further evidence for this, with its language of "delight" in the torah.[40] She is right too to set the Shema in the context of wider deuteronomic (and other) usage, and on the reciprocity of the divine love and the love of Israel in response. This reciprocity fits well, as we have seen, with the structure of the Shema and the following commands.

It follows from the preceding that the "heart" in Deuteronomy is a place of both intellectual conviction and emotional assent, and that these two aspects of human response belong closely together. In this

---

35. Lapsley, "Feeling Our Way," 354, who cites Nussbaum, *Upheavals of Thought*, 236.
36. Lapsley, "Feeling Our Way," 355–56.
37. Ibid., 361–62.
38. Ibid., 356–57, 365 (here citing Tigay, *Deuteronomy*, 76–77). On the relationship between external forms and emotional response, she refers to G. A. Anderson, *A Time to Mourn, A Time to Dance: The Expression of Grief and Joy in Israelite Religion* (University Park, PA: Pennsylvania State University Press, 1991), and Y. Muffs, *Love and Joy: Law, Language and Religion in Ancient Israel* (New York/Jerusalem: Jewish Theological Seminary, 1992). Note also work on memory that suggests that it has a constructive, imaginative aspect, e.g., D. Schacter, *Searching for Memory: The Brain, The Mind and The Past* (New York: Basic Books, 1996).
39. She cites in support S. D. McBride, "Yoke of the Kingdom: an Exposition of Deuteronomy 6:4–5," *Int* 27 (1973) 273–306 (304).
40. E.g., Ps 119:20, 35, 97, 131, and passim; see further J. G. McConville, "Happiness in the Psalms," in *Acta Theologica Supplementum* 15 (2011) 81–100 (87).

portrayal of the human person there is continuity between intellect and passion. There is more yet to say about this portrayal of unified response. David Lambert, in a review of Carasik, pointed out that it is difficult to confine the activity of the לב 'heart' to interior mental processes, since the work of the לב is often indistinguishable from speech, and even the purpose to act.[41]

Mark K. George has pursued this unity of the inward and the verbally expressed and enacted. George puts the search for an understanding of "heart" in the broad narrative context of Deuteronomy (though he does not set it up in that way), and he asks what it means to say that King David was 'a man after [Yahweh's] heart' (איש כלבבו) (1 Sam 13:14).[42] The phrase implies some correspondence between the "heart" of Yahweh and that of David.[43] It serves in the narrative to distinguish David from Saul, yet as George shows, the two characters, as presented in 1 Samuel 16–31, are remarkably similar. What finally distinguishes David from Saul is never explicitly stated,[44] but George argues that David constructs his "religious identity" by his habit of enquiring of Yahweh and of declaring his trust and confidence in him: "David and Yhwh have a dialogue, something Saul and Yhwh do not have."[45] Having a heart "after Yhwh's heart" meant in effect, not only right worship practices, but "continual inquiry of Yhwh's counsel and guidance before one acted, as well as faith and confidence that Yhwh would act on one's behalf."[46] George's study places the "heart" in the sphere of counsel and action. In the case of David, it is woven into the life and character of the man in his relationship with God. It is clear from this why attempts to understand לב according to any template that distinguishes between the inner and outer life meet difficulty. Rather, the life of David offers a narrativized study of the building of a character in terms of a right disposition of the "heart" in relation to God.

Our analysis of the "heart" (לבב) in Deuteronomy has demonstrated a unity of the person that embraces both the intellectual and the emo-

---

41. Lambert, review of Carasik, *RBL* 08/2007.
42. M. K. George, "Yhwh's Own Heart," *CBQ* 64 (2002) 442–59.
43. Some have taken this to mean "a man of Yahweh's choice," e.g., P. K. McCarter, *I Samuel* (New York: Doubleday, 1985) 229, citing 1 Sam 14:7 and Ps 20:5[4]. The phrase can no doubt be taken in this way in some contexts. Jonathan's usage in 1 Sam 14:7 is a case in point, yet in context it carries an ironic echo of 1 Sam 13:14, and the fuller meaning there. Since Saul too was chosen by God (1 Sam 9:16), it seems unlikely that the phrase in question distinguishes David and Saul in this sense.
44. George, "Yhwh's Own Heart," 451.
45. Ibid., 453–54.
46. Ibid., 458.

tional and the inward processes of decision together with their expressions in speech and action. In the triad of "heart, soul, and strength," we turn next, more briefly, to the term frequently translated "soul," the Hebrew נפש. What, if anything, is added to the portrayal above by this addition of the "soul"?

3.2. Loving with One's "Soul"

As is well known, נפש is capable of bearing various meanings, including physical ones, such as "throat," and the person simply as an individual (as one among a number), as well as denoting the person's innermost or essential being. The range of meanings is interesting in itself, suggesting that the idea of the person in her essential being is not separable from herself in her physical being, so that it can be hard to decide in some contexts whether to translate with a physical term or with the familiar "soul."[47]

The point has echoes of the unity of inward and external that we have just observed in relation to לבב. However, the נפש corresponds in some sense to the person as such: the psalmist can address himself as נפשי (Ps 103:1–5). Yet in this kind of instance, נפש is not a mere cipher for a pronoun but reaches to express something of the human being in all his or her dimensions. The point may be illustrated by the parallel between נפשי 'my soul' and כל קרבי 'all that is within me' in v. 1. What is denoted by this phrase remains open and indefinite; נפש does not connote some inner spiritual essence here. Rather it suggests the complexity of the human person.

Modern readers will respond immediately to this, because of what modern psychology knows of human complexity. The psalmist has no access to such avenues of knowledge. But he knows that the "real" person cannot be conceived as some inner essence: the נפש is one who sins and is forgiven, who becomes ill and is healed, who receives the love of Yahweh, enjoys the good that he gives, and has his youth "renewed like the eagle's." The person, therefore, is one who goes on being formed by the vicissitudes of life in relationship with Yahweh, and who plays an active and moral part in that life by "blessing" Yahweh and "not forgetting all his benefits."

No single term in English catches all this. "Personality" comes close, if it depicts the person in the complexity of what makes their distinctive and characteristic features. But the נפש has depths ("all that is within

---

47. A case in point is Ps 63:6[5], where נפש is taken by *HALOT* as "throat" (p. 712), but NRSV has, "My *soul* is satisfied as with a rich feast."

me"), so that full knowledge of it seems unattainable. The psalmist's call to his very being, in its full dimensions, chimes with the modern sense that the self may not be fully knowable, or even coherent. In principle, a full account of the human being is beyond reach—it is contingent in some sense on all attempts, including psychological, to plumb and understand it. The present text responds to this, I think, by seeing the person as an unfinished project, one that is being made in the context of a living relationship with Yahweh, its unity apprehended, perhaps, by faith.

In the context of the Shema, which evidently aims to express the wholeness of the person, if לבב indicates something like a settled purpose and characteristic behaviour, נפש adds a sense of the person in her full being, with the rider that the person continues to be made in the vicissitudes of life in relationship to Yahweh. Together, the terms form a strong evocation of the person in her totality. This totality is not a static essence, however, but is precisely an agent who is called upon to hear and obey.

3.3. Loving with One's "Might"

The final term of the love command, "with all your might," calls on the person to love with all her available resources. This may be taken to embrace personal resources as well as contingent ones such as wealth. It recognizes, incidentally, the limitations of any person's resources, and that these will vary from one person to another.[48]

3.4. The Communal Nature of the Call to Love

It should be noted at this stage, that the Shema is addressed to the collectivity of Israel. The use in Deuteronomy of the singular form of address, alongside the plural, for the corporate entity of Israel is well known. Such use does not preclude a capacity for individuation within the same rhetorical context.[49] The Shema and its immediate co-text are a case in point, since the corporate "Israel" shades over into individuals and families with children, hands, foreheads, and doorposts (Deut 6:6–9). This multiple aspect of the addressee means that all that has been said above about the call to "love" Yahweh and the semantic reach of לבב and נפש applies not only to individuals but to Israel as a totality. The devotion to Yahweh demanded here is to be true of individuals, of

---

48. See Weinfeld, *Deuteronomy 1–11*, 339, on the nature of these resources.
49. I have shown this elsewhere, with reference, for example, to Deut 15:1–18 (see McConville, "Singular Address in the Deuteronomic Law and the Politics of Legal Administration," *JSOT* 97 [2002] 19–36).

individuals in their capacity as members of Israel, and of the community of Israel as a whole.

4. What "Words"?

We come now to the command: "Keep these words that I am commanding you today in your heart" (Deut 6:6). This is a corollary both of the premise of the Shema, "Yahweh your God, Yahweh is One" (as argued above), and of the love command, to which it is particularly connected by the repetition of לבבך 'your heart'. At the outset, we raised the question of how the idea of "words in the heart" might relate to the various external forms of "words" in Deuteronomy. As we begin to answer this question, we must first ask what particular words are in view here.

One possible answer is that they are simply the words of Deut 6:4–5, or even as little as the words יהוה אלהינו יהוה אחד. This could fit with the continuation in vv. 7–9, where writing them on hand, forehead, and doorposts appears to entail a small amount of text.[50] However, there are reasons to think a broader referent may be in view.

In the closely parallel passage in Deut 11:18–21, Moses' predication of "these (my) words" (דברי אלה) is under no such restriction and apparently refers to "the general paraenetic discourse of Deuteronomy."[51] Of other parallels to the phrase in Deuteronomy, that in 31:1, 28 comes closest to this, referring to the full range of the Mosaic instruction.[52] There are other possibilities too, however. In Deut 5:22, 'these words' (את הדברים האלה) refer to the Decalogue that immediately follows (cf. Deut 4:10, Exod 20:1).[53] In Deut 12:28, כל הדברים האלה 'all these words' could refer to the commands about worship contained in chapter 12. In Deut 6:6, the term "today" probably aligns the instruction with those that denote the full extent of Moses' preaching on that long day in Moab when he delivered his several deuteronomic addresses. However, it seems that Moses' various references to the words he is speaking can fluctuate between certain specifics and the full range of his speech

---

50. R. W. L. Moberly inclines to take it this way, though conceding that it is impossible to be sure ("Toward an Interpretation of the Shema," in *Theological Exegesis: Essays in Honor of Brevard S. Childs* [ed. C. Seitz and K. Greene-McCreight; Grand Rapids: Eerdmans, 1999] 124–44 [127 n. 10]).

51. Weinfeld, *Deuteronomy 1–11*, 340. Cf. E. Merrill: "[The term] encompasses the full corpus of the covenant text as communicated by Moses, but which is encapsulated especially in the Shema of vv. 4–5" (*Deuteronomy* [NAC; Broadman and Holman, 1994] 167).

52. See also Deut 30:1, 32:45.

53. Weinfeld, *Deuteronomy 1–11*, 340.

in Deuteronomy. The issue is more complex even than this, moreover, because of the difficult question of the relationship between the "book" in which Moses writes down his words to be read in the assembly, and the book of Deuteronomy as such, which records that he did so (Deut 31:9–11).

Having observed this, what precisely is required to be kept "in your heart"? It is clear from the foregoing that the relation between "keeping words in the heart" and the external forms taken by Moses' words is not a simple one, such as learning by rote, since the "words" are not a specified set, equivalent to any single external form. Rather, I suggest that the relation is understood according to the meaning of the terms in the love command, discussed above. There we saw that a command to love Yahweh with all one's לבב aimed at a life lived in its entirety, according to the person's full capacities, in the worship of Yahweh and in dependence on him for counsel. The point was pursued in relation to the life of David, "the man after God's own heart." The focus on לב/לבב was narrativized there in the building of a life. The condition of the לבב is known as the person is tested through the vicissitudes of life, experiences both triumph and disaster, and finds a settled purpose that conveys true character. The deuteronomic command also contemplates obedience in the context of length of days. The regularities of life, as in Deut 6:7–9, imply temporal depth, as does the aspect of teaching to children so that they too might have long life in the land. Length of life in individual terms overlaps here with length of life in terms of the people as a whole.

Deuteronomy differs from the story of David in the sense that it foregrounds "words," where "words" may be taken to stand for Deuteronomy's full linguistic panoply of torah. Since the relation between "keeping words on the heart" and the various external forms of Moses' words in the book is not straightforward, we are bound to ask how the Mosaic torah is held to impinge upon the life of the person and community. There are two factors to note here.

First, the analogy with King David and the depth dimension in the deuteronomic vision suggest that the command will be successfully kept, not by a single decision in advance, or a decisive effort of heart and mind, but in the context of the life as it is lived over time. The keeping of torah is a thing to be practiced. The idea of the application of the full capacities of the person makes room for the concept of human maturing, the development of full powers within a life-cycle, consistent with the notion of torah as guidance and instruction. Such maturing is in the context of the moral landscape of the human life, with its profound temptations, a factor well known to Deuteronomy and undergirding its strongly hortatory style. Human maturing within covenant faithfulness cannot be taken for granted, but must be cultivated through proper attention to torah and discipline of the self.

Second, the fact that the "words" cannot be precisely identified with any specific external form of them confirms the need for growth in understanding what keeping torah means in practice. I have argued elsewhere that Deuteronomy has precisely this hermeneutical function, when one compares its specific forms with other pentateuchal forms—such as the deuteronomic Decalogue compared with that in Exodus 20, and particular laws as compared with analogous laws in the Book of the Covenant.[54] That is, the "keeping of laws on your heart" is a mandate to Israel and Israelites to give their full attention to understanding what torah means within life's processes of growth and change and in ever new circumstances.

5. Conclusions

I set out to consider the meaning of the exhortation to Israel that they should have "these words on their heart" (Deut 6:6). As the command comes in the context of the predication of Yahweh's name in the Shema (6:4), I began by considering the meaning of that predication in relation to the commands that followed, and we saw that it carried with it an entailment that Israel should respond to Yahweh's self-giving by keeping covenant with him. The particular development of this vision of reciprocal self-giving is in the command to Israel to "love Yahweh with all your heart, all your soul, and all your strength" (v. 5), then in the call to have these "words on your heart" (v. 6).

We then explored the meaning of the term "heart" as used in this and related contexts, concluding that it both embraces the intellectual and emotional aspects of human being and unites the inward processes of planning with its outward expressions in speech and action. The portrayal of the human being, therefore, is a holistic one. When the meaning of נפשׁ 'soul' is brought to bear on this, it too expresses a unity of the

---

54. McConville, "Metaphor, Symbol and the Interpretation of Deuteronomy," in *After Pentecost: Language and Biblical Interpretation* (ed. C. Bartholomew, C. Greene, and K. Möller; SHS 2; Grand Rapids: Zondervan, 2002) 329–51 (esp. pp. 346–47). I think my point here is close to Dan Block's recognition that the Decalogue did not have exceptional authority in Israel, above the other laws. Rather, as he goes on, "If any single document incorporated into the Pentateuch was elevated above the rest in the thinking of Israel's spiritual leaders or the authors of Scripture, it had to be the deuteronomic Torah of Moses" ("Reading the Decalogue Right to Left: The Ten Principles of Covenant Relationship in the Hebrew Bible," in idem, *How I Love Your Torah*, 53–54).

person, now from the aspect of personality, and with the recognition of human complexity, which allows an opening for biblical and modern explorations of the person to be brought to bear on each other.

Finally, we asked which words in particular were in view in Deut 6:6, and found that the reference could not be limited to one identifiable set. Rather, the force of the exhortation as a whole, from the Shema through to the portrayals of right response to Yahweh in the ensuing verses, is to urge the human person to grow and develop in her full capacities, taking the torah as a whole as guide, and in the context of a covenantal relationship with Yahweh.

This was the ideal held out both to Israelites as a whole, as they corporately sustained and renewed their relationship with Yahweh in regular worship, and to individuals who identified themselves as and with "Israel." The text envisages a fully developed covenantal life, in which people are invited to engage in a lifelong deepening of their understanding of what it means to be human in God's world, and embody it in speech and practice.

The Rhetoric of Theophany
The Imaginative Depiction of Horeb in Deuteronomy 9–10

JERRY HWANG

1. Introduction

It is impossible to overstate the significance of Mount Sinai in forging the identity of God's people through the ages. The theophany's immediacy for all generations is captured by Moses' assertion that the covenant at Sinai was made "not with our fathers, but with us, with all of us who are alive here today" (Deut 5:3). This declaration collapses the distinctions between the first and second generations of Israel, for the first generation's disobedience at Kadesh (1:26–33; cf. Num 14:1–4) led to their destruction during the wilderness wanderings (Deut 1:34–35, 2:14–16; cf. Num 14:26–35). Only their children, the second generation, actually survived to hear "the words that Moses spoke to all Israel across the Jordan in the wilderness" (Deut 1:1). The anachronism of transporting a new generation back to Sinai is a crucial feature of Deuteronomy's rhetoric of covenant renewal.[1]

The reimagining of Sinai (also known as Horeb)[2] for new generations resonates beyond the plains of Moab, however. As a document to be publicly recited every seven years at the Feast of Tabernacles (31:9–13), Deuteronomy invites both the immediate "you" of the book's narrative world as well as future generations of "you" to renew their covenant with YHWH.[3] The paradigmatic quality of Sinai is well-described by

---

Author's Note: It is a pleasure and privilege to dedicate this essay to Daniel Block, my *Doktorvater*. His patient mentoring has shaped me beyond measure as a minister, teacher, and scholar.

1. See my discussion of Deuteronomy's use of anachronism as a rhetorical device in J. Hwang, *The Rhetoric of Remembrance: An Investigation of the "Fathers" in Deuteronomy* (Siphrut 8; Winona Lake, IN: Eisenbrauns, 2012).

2. "Horeb" is Deuteronomy's preferred name for Sinai (Deut 1:2, 6, 19; 4:10, 15; 5:2; 9:8; 18:16; 28:69[29:1]); the term "Sinai" only occurs in poetry (33:2).

3. J. G. McConville, "Metaphor, Symbol, and the Interpretation of Deuteronomy," in *After Pentecost: Language and Biblical Interpretation* (ed. C. Bartholomew; Grand Rapids: Zondervan, 2001) 342–46.

Michael Fishbane: "Sinai is . . . not a one-time event, but for all times; it is not only grounded in the historical past, but hovers in the living present. Sinai stands at the mythic core of religious memory, and the explication of its teachings is a sacred ritual for Judaism."[4]

The urgency of actualizing the theophany at Sinai/Horeb finds intriguing reinforcement in Deuteronomy's repeated narration of the events at the mountain. Moses opens his first address (1:6–4:40) by briefly mentioning Horeb (1:6–18) as the starting point for Israel's departure to Kadesh (1:19). Kadesh represents the climax of Israel's apostasy (1:19–46), which gives rise to the ensuing punishment in the wilderness (2:1–15). Deut 4:10–15 then moves the narrative timeline backwards by recalling the theophanic elements of God's speech at Horeb. Unlike Deuteronomy 5, here the content of the divine words at Horeb is subordinate to the fact that "YHWH spoke to you from the midst of the fire; you heard the sound of words, but you saw no form— only a voice" (4:12). Moses subsequently expands his cataphoric allusion to the "Ten Words" (4:13) by enumerating the terms of the Decalogue (5:6–21) as well as recounting Israel's request for a mediator (5:22–33). The theme of Moses as mediator is developed further in the recollection of his intercession after Israel's idolatry with the molten calf (9:7–10:11). Lastly, the glorious God of Sinai is depicted in mythopoetic terms as the divine warrior who descends from the mountain where he resides amidst his holy ones (33:2). By highlighting different aspects of Israel's experiences at the mountain, these complementary depictions of Horeb indicate that Deuteronomy presents the rhetorical recasting of Israel's foundational stories, especially the Horeb narratives in Exodus 19–34. As Gerhard von Rad eloquently noted,[5] the dynamic homiletical character of Deuteronomy stands at odds with caricatures of the book as a static recapitulation of legal material.[6]

Recounting the past always entails interpretation rather than mere recitation of facts.[7] The transformative quality of memory raises two questions for the relationship between Deuteronomy and its associated

---

4. M. Fishbane, *Sacred Attunement: A Jewish Theology* (Chicago: University of Chicago Press, 2008) 49.

5. G. von Rad, "Ancient Word and Living Word—Deuteronomy" in *From Genesis to Chronicles* (ed. K. C. Hanson; trans. E. W. T. Dicken; Minneapolis: Fortress, 2005) 89–98.

6. The LXX translators titled the Book of Deuteronomy using their problematic rendering of the Hebrew phrase משנה התורה הזאת 'the copy of this Torah' (Deut 17:18) as the Greek phrase τὸ δευτερονόμιον τοῦτο 'this second law'.

7. R. S. Hendel, *Remembering Abraham: Culture, Memory, and History in the Hebrew Bible* (Oxford: Oxford University Press, 2005); J. Blenkinsopp, "Memory, Tradition, and the Construction of the Past in Ancient Israel," in *Treasures Old and New: Essays in the*

narrative traditions: How does Moses transform and apply the events at Horeb for a new generation? And what might such reinterpretation suggest about the literary relationship between Deuteronomy and the narratives in Exodus? The study that follows will compare the golden calf narrative (Exodus 32–34) and Deuteronomy's fourth retelling of Horeb (Deut 9:7–10:11) using synchronic and diachronic methods.[8] I will argue that the differences between these accounts of Horeb are better explained as an intentional rhetorical strategy than as the work of multiple redactors or editors. The differences between the genres of the Exodus and Deuteronomy accounts also challenge the redactional links usually traced between the various golden calf episodes of Exodus 32–34 and Deuteronomy 9–10 on the one hand, and Jeroboam's calves in 1 Kings 12 on the other.[9]

2. History of Research and Methodology

Interpreters have long observed discrepancies between the golden calf stories in Exodus 32–34 and Deuteronomy 9–10.[10] Earlier attempts to reconcile these accounts tended to use a diachronic approach, with synchronic approaches arriving later in the discussion. While a full survey of interpretation is unnecessary here, three trends are particularly relevant for the sake of my comparison of Exodus with Deuteronomy.

First, the older source-critical view that Exodus 32–34 and Deuteronomy 9–10 are disjointed compositions has yielded much ground to the judgment that each of these passages bears its own literary integrity. The narrative doublets in Exodus 32–34 may be explained as part of the storyteller's craft or compiler's theological agenda rather than as

---

Theology of the Pentateuch (Grand Rapids: Eerdmans, 2004) 1–17; M. S. Smith, "Remembering God: Collective Memory in Israelite Religion," *CBQ* 64 (2002) 631–51.

8. I use the term "diachronic" to denote attempts to trace the transmission history of the text, and the term "synchronic" to refer to literary study of the final form. However, Jean-Pierre Sonnet notes that the terms "genetic" and "poetic" are more precise for emphasizing that final-form analysis still analyzes "diachronic" aspects within texts, such as the progressive unfolding of themes and plots within stories (*The Book within the Book: Writing in Deuteronomy* [Leiden: Brill, 1997] 7 n. 11). Since the terminology of diachrony and synchrony has become a *de facto* standard, I continue using this terminology despite the ambiguities observed by Sonnet.

9. The pivotal place of Deuteronomy between Pentateuch and Deuteronomistic History has been noted by many, including J. Van Seters, "Deuteronomy between Pentateuch and the Deuteronomistic History," *HvTSt* 59 (2003) 947–56.

10. The best list of such differences is still found in S. R. Driver, *A Critical and Exegetical Commentary on Deuteronomy* (ICC; Edinburgh: T. & T. Clark, 1901) 112–17. See also Y. Ho Chung, *The Sin of the Calf: The Rise of the Bible's Negative Attitude Toward the Golden Calf* (LHBOTS 523; New York: T. & T. Clark, 2010) 71–87.

a haphazard combination of older sources.[11] Similarly for Deuteronomy 9–10, momentum for detailed source and redaction criticism has largely dissipated in the wake of literary studies that take these chapters as a coherent whole.[12]

It should be noted, however, that the growing consensus for literary unity has not resulted in any systematic attempt to account for the synoptic differences between Exodus 32–34 and Deuteronomy 9–10. Most treatments of these two texts remain either purely diachronic in comparing Exodus with Deuteronomy while neglecting to examine their respective literary contexts,[13] or purely synchronic in analyzing the final form of one book or the other without attempting to explain their literary relationship.[14] Eep Talstra has provided the only substantive study in English that attempts a combination of diachrony and synchrony, but his work focuses on Deuteronomy 9–10. Furthermore, his analysis is also marred by an archaic return to denoting sources and redactors through changes in grammatical number (the so-called *Numeruswechsel*).[15] Thus it is necessary to examine the final forms of both

---

11. E.g., M. Widmer, *Moses, God, and the Dynamics of Intercessory Prayer* (FAT 2/8; Tübingen: Mohr Siebeck, 2004) 135–41; J. Van Seters, *The Life of Moses: The Yahwist as Historian in Exodus-Numbers* (Louisville: Westminster John Knox, 1994) 319; J. I. Durham, *Exodus* (WBC 3; Waco, TX: Word Books, 1987) 418; H. C. Brichto, "The Worship of the Golden Calf: A Literary Analysis of a Fable on Idolatry," *HUCA* 54 (1983) 1–44; R. W. L. Moberly, *At the Mountain of God: Story and Theology in Exodus 32–34* (JSOTSup 22; Sheffield: Sheffield Academic Press, 1983). For a review of source-critical views on Exodus 19–34, see E. W. Nicholson, *God and His People: Covenant and Theology in the Old Testament* (Oxford: Clarendon, 1986) 121–50.

12. E.g., N. Lohfink, "Deuteronomium 9,1–10,11 und Exodus 32–34: Zu Endstruktur, Intertextualität, Schichtung und Abhängigkeiten," in *Gottes Volk am Sinai: Untersuchungen zu Ex 32–34 und Dtn 9–10* (ed. M. Köckert and E. Blum; Veröffentlichungen der Wissenschaftlichen Gesellschaft für Theologie 18; Taschenbuch: Gütersloher Verlagshaus, 2001) 42–87; H.-C. Schmitt, "Die Erzählung vom Goldenen Kalb Ex. 32 und das Deuteronomistische Geschichtswerk," in *Rethinking the Foundations: Historiography in the Ancient World and in the Bible: Essays in Honour of John Van Seters* (ed. S. L. McKenzie and T. Römer in collaboration with H. H. Schmid; BZAW 294; New York: de Gruyter, 2000) 240–42. For a recent dissenting voice arguing for literary disunity in Deuteronomy 9–10, see E. Otto, "Deuteronomiumstudien II—Deuteronomistische und postdeuteronomistische Perspektiven in der Literarturgeschichte von Deuteronomium 5–11," *ZABR* 15 (2009) 65–215, here pp. 122–49.

13. E.g., K. Schmid, "Israel am Sinai: Etappen der Forschungsgeschichte zu Ex 32–34 in seinen Kontexten," in *Gottes Volk am Sinai*, 9–40; Schmitt, "Erzählung," 235–50.

14. E.g., P. A. Barker, *The Triumph of Grace in Deuteronomy* (Paternoster Biblical Monographs; Paternoster: Waynesboro, GA, 2004) 78–106; R. H. O'Connell, "Deuteronomy IX 7–X 7, 10–11: Panelled Structure, Double Rehearsal and the Rhetoric of Covenant Rebuke," *VT* 42 (1992) 492–509.

15. E. Talstra, "Deuteronomy 9 and 10: Synchronic and Diachronic Observations," in *Synchronic or Diachronic? A Debate on Method in Old Testament Exegesis* (ed. J. C. de Moor; OTS 34; Leiden: Brill, 1995) 187–210.

Exodus and Deuteronomy using synchronic methods before assessing their diachronic relationship.

Second, the direction of literary borrowing between Exodus 32–34 and Deuteronomy 9–10 is now undergoing reevaluation in light of the apparent unity of both passages. While the canonical shape of the Pentateuch as well as the JEDP sequence of the documentary hypothesis both point to the dependence of Deuteronomy 9–10 on Exodus 32–34,[16] a vocal minority of scholars has proposed that some form of the Deuteronomy passage antedated Exodus in the development of Israel's literary traditions. Among others, John Van Seters and Joseph Blenkinsopp regard Deuteronomy's first-person account of the golden calf as the catalyst for either a post-exilic Yahwist (Van Seters) or unknown tradents of the Pentateuch working in the Neo-Babylonian period (Blenkinsopp) to compile the third-person narrative of Exodus 32–34.[17] Since Exodus language is found in Deuteronomy and vice versa, any attempt to delineate the literary relationship between the books must wrestle with the dilemma of why their canonical forms contain each other's characteristic terminology.

Third, scholars who hold that Deuteronomy postdates Exodus have observed that Deuteronomy would be reusing the traditions of Exodus in a creative rather than rigid way. As Walter Brueggemann notes, the generic differences between third-person narrative (e.g., Exodus 32–34) and first-person preaching (e.g., Deuteronomy 9–10) mean that Deuteronomy is "surely no copy in any stenographic sense of anything we know from Moses, the Book of Exodus, the Covenant Code or anything else."[18] Studies of inner-biblical interpretation between these books have similarly noted that Deuteronomy displays a tension between claiming to follow its antecedent traditions while reformulating them for a new audience.[19]

This combination of new and old terminology in Deuteronomy suggests that many diachronic studies have been misguided in using lexical similarities and differences between Deuteronomy and Exodus as their

---

16. Driver is typical for regarding Deut 9:7–10:11 as "based . . . upon the narrative of JE, of which it is a free reproduction" (*Deuteronomy*, 112).

17. J. Blenkinsopp, "Deuteronomic Contribution to the Narrative in Genesis–Numbers: A Test Case," in *Those Elusive Deuteronomists: The Phenomenon of Pan-Deuteronomism* (ed. L. S. Schearing and S. L. McKenzie; JSOTSup 268; Sheffield: Sheffield Academic Press, 1999) 84–115; Van Seters, *Life of Moses*, 290–318.

18. W. Brueggemann, "Imagination as a Mode of Fidelity," in *Understanding the Word: Essays in Honor of Bernhard W. Anderson* (ed. J. T. Butler, E. W. Conrad, and B. C. Ollenburger; JSOTSup 37; Sheffield: JSOT Press, 1985) 22.

19. Brueggemann, "Imagination," 23; B. M. Levinson, "The Hermeneutics of Tradition in Deuteronomy: A Reply to J. G. McConville," *JBL* 119 (2000) 269–86.

primary criteria to distinguish redactional layers. Shared terminology between Exodus and Deuteronomy does not establish a common origin or authorship any more than divergent terminology proves that the texts arose independently.[20] From the perspective of methodology, the decisive factor in moving between synchrony and diachrony should be a literary analysis of the contexts in which terminology is reused, not the sheer fact of its reuse.

These developments in Deuteronomy scholarship point to the following procedure in comparing golden calf stories in Exodus and Deuteronomy. In section 3, I will begin by arguing for the traditional view that Deuteronomy 9–10 is based upon Exodus 32–34 rather than the reverse.[21] Then the final form of Deuteronomy 9–10 will be examined to discern its rhetorical logic as well as its imaginative transformation of the Exodus traditions. After summarizing Deuteronomy's theology of covenant making and renewal at Horeb, section 4 will move from synchrony to diachrony by examining the redactional links among Exodus 32–34, Deuteronomy 9–10, and 1 Kings 12. The imaginative role

---

20. On the presence of Deuteronom(ist)ic language in Exodus, Christine E. Hayes notes that "linguistic resonances with material in Deuteronomy are not determinative of Deuteronomistic provenance" ("Golden Calf Stories: The Relationship of Exodus 32 and Deuteronomy 9–10, in *The Idea of Biblical Interpretation: Essays in Honor of James L. Kugel* [ed. H. Najman and J. H. Newman; Atlanta: Society of Biblical Literature, 2008] 65). Likewise regarding Deuteronom(ist)ic language in Genesis–Numbers, Suzanne Boorer observes that "it cannot be concluded, without further evidence, that similar formulations are due to the same hand. Similarity in expression is just as likely to be due to a later hand copying an earlier formulation" (*The Promise of the Land as Oath: A Key to the Formation of the Pentateuch* [BZAW 205; Berlin: Walter de Gruyter, 1993] viii).

The observations of Hayes and Boorer underscore the methodological problems of linking "Deuteronomic" language to a "Deuteronomistic" school of tradents. Since scholars are rather inconsistent in their use of the descriptors "Deuteronomic" and "Deuteronomistic," my study will use "Deuteronomic" to refer to the canonical book and its characteristic terminology, and "Deuteronomistic" to refer to the Deuteronomistic History (i.e., Joshua–Kings) and the school of tradents that compiled this literary work. For further discussion see R. Coggins, "What Does 'Deuteronomistic' Mean?" in *Those Elusive Deuteronomists*, 22–35.

21. This is not to say, however, that the JEDP documentary hypothesis has gone unchallenged. The disintegration of the Wellhausenian schema has been chronicled by G. J. Wenham, "Pondering the Pentateuch: The Search for a New Paradigm," in *The Face of Old Testament Studies* (ed. D. W. Baker and B. T. Arnold; Grand Rapids: Baker, 1999) 116–44. In reality, the relative dating of Deuteronomy after Exodus is compatible with a variety of positions: (1) the documentary hypothesis in its classic JEDP form, since Exodus 32 is typically considered JE (cf. n. 16 above); (2) literary approaches and/or canonical criticism, which read the final form of Deuteronomy in light of the preceding books; and (3) the ancient Jewish and Christian tradition of Mosaic authorship, which posits that Moses wrote most, if not all, of the Pentateuch.

played by Deuteronomy 9–10 in bridging Exodus 32 and 1 Kings 12 undermines redactional proposals arguing that Exodus 32 is one of the latest texts in the Old Testament, as held by John Van Seters and others.

3. Literary Borrowing and Imaginative Reuse in Golden Calf Stories

The growing consensus on the literary unity of both Exodus 32–34 and Deuteronomy 9–10, while granting the possibility of minor glosses in each passage,[22] means that a synoptic comparison may proceed with the final form of both texts. Which direction of literary borrowing is more likely to exist between Exodus 32–34 and Deuteronomy 9–10? Since the Deuteronomy account begins with the summons of Moses to "Remember, do not forget ... [the events of Horeb]" (Deut 9:7), it seems better to test the working hypothesis that Moses builds upon elements from the Exodus narrative that are known to his audience, instead of John Van Seters's view that the compiler of Exodus has "created narrative scenes out of hortatory passages [in Deuteronomy]."[23] If it could be shown that Deuteronomy refers to events in passing because they are well-known to the audience, then it becomes unlikely that parenesis precedes narrative in the development of the Pentateuch. Numerous narrative elements recounted in Deut 9:7–10:11 possess just such an axiomatic quality.

Before examining Deuteronomy's account of Horeb in detail, it is suggestive to begin in a somewhat peripheral place. Deut 9:22–24 compares Israel's apostasy at Horeb to three other episodes at Taberah, Massah, and Kibroth-hattaavah (see Num 11:1–3; Exod 17:1–7; and Num 11:4–35, respectively). The rhetorical effectiveness of the comparison between these episodes and Horeb depends on all of them having already become a byword for the hearers. Since Moses mentions Taberah, Massah, and Kibroth-hattaavah without further explanation, his hearers were evidently familiar with these traditions of murmuring in the wilderness. Even if it were correct to excise these verses as secondary, as redaction critics have often done,[24] there remains the question of how

---

22. E.g., T. B. Dozeman attributes the references to Aaron (Deut 9:20) and Eleazar (10:6–7) to a Priestly editor, but otherwise holds to the literary unity of both Exodus 32–34 and Deuteronomy 9–10 ("The Composition of Ex 32 within the Context of the Enneateuch, in *Auf dem Weg zur Endgestalt von Genesis bis II Regum. Festschrift Hans-Christoph Schmitt zum 65. Geburtstag am 11.11.2006* [ed. M. Beck and U. Schorn; BZAW 370; Berlin: Walter de Gruyter, 2006] 182).

23. Van Seters, *Life of Moses*, 285.

24. E.g., Boorer, *Land as Oath*, 276; Van Seters, *Life of Moses*, 302.

the audience of Deuteronomy could understand these terse references without access to prior traditions. Whichever direction of literary borrowing between Exodus and Deuteronomy is proposed, some form of the murmuring narratives in Exodus–Numbers must still undergird the Deuteronomy account in order for the comparison with Horeb to be meaningful. The common hypothesis that a redactor added Deut 9:22–24 hardly resolves the problem.

The "given" nature of Deuteronomy's background material is also evident in Moses' extended review of Horeb in Deut 9:7–21, 25–29; 10:1–5, 10–11. Here the audience's familiarity with Horeb is indicated not through brief statements, as in the passing mention of Taberah, Massah, and Kibroth-hattavah (9:22–24), but with formulaic language in which Moses refers to known narrative traditions. Without any elaboration, the covenant ratification ceremony at Horeb is described in skeletal fashion as "the covenant that YHWH made with you" (9:9). Similarly, the words spoken at the mountain are cited as "the words that YHWH spoke with you" (9:10), and the people are said to have transgressed commands that they should have remembered as "the way that I [YHWH] commanded them" (9:12; cf. v. 16). Deuteronomy's repeated use of the relative clauses "that YHWH commanded/spoke/promised" indicates that the covenant regulations promulgated by Moses are familiar in both the narrative world of the book as well as the real world of its readers.[25] These relative clause formulae are designed to evoke the audience's memory of God's direct speech at Horeb, most notably, but not confined to, the Decalogue.

A comparison of the golden calf's destruction in Exod 32:20 and Deut 9:21 further supports the conclusion that "without having the story in Exod 32 in the background, certain details in the episode of the Calf in Deuteronomy would be meaningless."[26] The lexical links between Exod 32:20 and Deut 9:21, coupled with a few significant discrepancies, have made these verses something of a crux in Pentateuchal criticism (see table, top of p. 153).

Though the differences between the verses remain controversial,[27] it is striking that Exod 32:20 and Deut 9:21 share the use of five terms in

---

[25]. D. E. Skweres, *Die Rückverweise im Buch Deuteronomium* (AnBib 79; Rome: Pontifical Institute, 1979); J. Milgrom, "Profane Slaughter and a Formulaic Key to the Composition of Deuteronomy," *HUCA* 47 (1976) 1–17.

[26]. M. A. Zipor, "The Deuteronomic Account of the Golden Calf," *ZAW* 108 (1996) 20–33, quote from 22 n. 6.

[27]. E.g., D. Frankel, "The Destruction of the Golden Calf: A New Solution," *VT* 44 (1994) 330–39.

The Rhetoric of Theophany

Exod 32:20 (ET)	Exod 32:20 (MT)	Deut 9:21 (MT)	Deut 9:21 (ET)
He took the calf that they had made and burned (it) with fire and ground it until it was crushed and he scattered (it) on the face of the waters and made the sons of Israel drink.	ויקח את־העגל אשר עשו וישרף באש ויטחן עד אשר־ דק ויזר על־פני המים וישק את־ בני ישראל	ואת־חטאתכם אשר־עשיתם את־העגל לקחתי ואשרף אתו באש ואכת אתו טחון היטב עד אשר־דק לעפר ואשלך את־עפרו אל־ הנחל הירד מן־ההר	Now the sin that you had made, the calf, I took it and burned it with fire and ground it completely until it was crushed as dust, and I threw its dust into the brook that comes down from the mountain.

nearly identical order: עשה 'to make', לקח 'to take', שרף 'to burn', טחן 'to grind', and דקק 'to crush'. The collocation of these five verbs, several of them rare in the OT,[28] points to a direct literary relationship between the verses. But which passage gave rise to the other? Several features of the more expansive language in Deut 9:21 suggest that this verse derived from Exod 32:20 rather than the other way around. First, Deuteronomy's use of the term "sin" to identify the calf picks up the *Leitwort* "sin" from the broader context in Exodus in which Israel's idolatry is repeatedly described as "sin" (Exod 32:21, 30, 31, 32, 34; 34:7, 9).[29] Since Exodus 32–34 uses two terms for "sin" (חטאת, חטאה),[30] whereas Deuteronomy 9 uses only one (חטאת),[31] it is more probable that the author of the Deuteronomy account possessed some form of Exodus 32–34 which was then summarized in Deuteronomy 9. Conversely, it would be unlikely for an ostensive post-Deuteronomistic compiler of Exodus to turn a freestanding and otherwise cryptic reference to "sin" in Deuteronomy 9 into a *Leitwort* which was then woven throughout the narrative in Exodus 32–34, all while adding another nominal form (i.e., חטאה).

The view of Blenkinsopp and Van Seters, that the canonical form of Exodus 32–34 postdates Deuteronomy 9–10 and the Deuteronomistic

---

28. C. T. Begg, "The Destruction of the Calf (Exod 32,20/Deut 9,21)," in *Das Deuteronomium: Entstehung, Gestalt und Botschaft* (ed. N. Lohfink; BETL 68; Leuven: Leuven University Press, 1985) 234 nn. 111–12.

29. C. T. Begg, "The Destruction of the Golden Calf Revisited (Exod 32,20/Deut 9,21)," in *Deuteronomy and Deuteronomic Literature: Festschrift C. H. W. Brekelmans* (ed. M. Vervenne and J. Lust; BETL 133; Leuven: Leuven University Press, 1997) 475.

30. חטאה is found in Exod 32:21, 30, 31; 34:7; whereas חטאת is found in Exod 32:30, 32, 34; 34:9. It is notable that Exod 32:20 uses both terms for "sin" in close proximity.

31. חטאת is found in Deut 9:18, 21, 27.

reforms, is inadequate to explain the relative lack of Deuteronomic terminology in Exodus 32–34. If Exodus really drew from Deuteronomy, it is surprising that more terminology from Deuteronomy 9–10 is not found in Exodus 32–34, especially considering the ubiquity of Deuteronomic language in Joshua–Kings, whose final redaction is usually attributed to the same Deuteronomistic school.[32] Similarly, any redactional proposal to date Exodus 32–34 after Deuteronomy 9–10 provides no explanation for eyewitness statements such as Moses' reminder that the smashing of the golden calf happened "before your very eyes" (Deut 9:17).[33] It remains necessary to explain why Exodus 32–34 contains a sprinkling of Deuteronom(ist)ic terminology,[34] but the balance of evidence indicates that the Exodus account came first.

The Deuteronomy account also adds several terms that foreshadow incidents in the rest of the Deuteronomistic History. First, the verb כתת 'to destroy' is later used to describe Hezekiah's "destruction" of the bronze serpent called Nehushtan (2 Kgs 18:4). Second, the use of the adverbial form 'completely' (Hiphil infinitive absolute of יטב) to describe the calf's destruction anticipates how the people "completely" destroy Baal altars following the overthrow of Queen Athaliah (2 Kgs 11:18). Third, the reduction of the golden calf to "dust" (עפר) evokes Josiah's identical actions against the "dust" of the Asherim (2 Kgs 23:6).[35]

---

32. See the groundbreaking discussion of Deuteronomy's literary style and theological influence in Joshua–Kings by M. Noth, *The Deuteronomistic History* (JSOTSup 15; Sheffield: JSOT Press, 1981).

33. Similar expressions of Israel's eyewitness experiences are found in Deut 1:30; 4:34; 6:22; 29:1[2]. In reversing the chronological priority of Exodus over Deuteronomy, redaction critics typically bring Jeroboam's golden calves in 1 Kings 12 into the discussion. It is argued that the supposedly plural אלהים 'gods' of Exod 32:4 derive from 1 Kgs 12:28, which, as a key text of the Deuteronomistic History, must in turn postdate Deuteronomy 9. However, it is doubtful that the אלהים in Exod 32:4 must be plural and therefore dependent on Jeroboam's calves. While noting the similarities between Exodus 32 and 1 Kings 12, Gary N. Knoppers demonstrates that the dissimilarities between them point to the latter passage being a polemical reworking of the former to attack Jeroboam's cultic innovations ("Aaron's Calf and Jeroboam's Calves," in *Fortunate the Eyes that See: Essays in Honor of David Noel Freedman* [ed. A. B. Beck et al.; Grand Rapids: Eerdmans, 1995] 92–104).

34. E.g., J.-L. Ska uses the "Deuteronomistic theological language" in Moses' intercession in Exod 32:7–14 to argue that Deuteronomy 9 came first (*Introduction to Reading the Pentateuch* [trans. Sr. P. Dominique; Winona Lake, IN: Eisenbrauns, 2006] 93). However, rather than settling the issue, his observations that the Exodus 32 and Deuteronomy 9 both contain an oath to the patriarchs (Exod 32:13; Deut 9:27; cf. 9:5), the verb "to remember" (Exod 32:13; Deut 7:18; 8:18; 9:7, 27), and the expression "stiff-necked" (Exod 32:9; Deut 9:6, 13) merely raise the question of whether Exod 32:7–14 or Deut 9:7–10:11 arose first.

35. G. M. de Tillesse, "Sections 'Tu' et Sections 'Vous' dans le Deutéronome," *VT* 12 (1982) 29–87, citation from p. 60.

The Narrator in Exodus	Moses in Deuteronomy
Sin of the golden calf (Exod 32:1–6)	(no parallel)
YHWH desires to destroy the people (32:7–10)	YHWH desires to destroy the people (9:12–14)
Moses' <u>first prayer</u> and YHWH's relenting from wrath (32:11–14)	Moses descends the mountain and smashes the tablets (9:15–17)
Moses descends the mountain and smashes the tablets (32:15–19)	Moses' <u>prayer</u>, but no words recorded (9:18–19)
(no parallel)	Moses <u>prays</u> for Aaron (9:20)
Moses destroys the golden calf (32:20)	Moses destroys the golden calf (9:21)
Moses rebukes Aaron (32:21–24)	(no parallel)
(no exact parallel; cf. 32:11–13)	Words of Moses' <u>prayer</u> (9:25–29)
The Levites slay the offenders (32:25–29)	(no parallel)
(out of order; cf. 34:1–4)	New tablets of the covenant (10:1–5)
Moses' <u>second prayer</u> (32:30–32)	YHWH answers Moses' <u>prayer</u> (10:10–11)
YHWH punishes the people (32:33–35)	(no parallel)

Given such "pluses" in Deuteronomy and their resonances with the Deuteronomistic History, it is more likely that Deuteronomy 9–10 represents a theological reinterpretation of Exodus 32–34 which also takes a proleptic glance at the later history of Israel, rather than the opposite contention that the Exodus account came after its counterpart in Deuteronomy but was then stripped of all but a few Deuteronom(ist)ic elements by a post-exilic Yahwist. As Christopher Begg notes, the likelihood of literary dependence of Deut 9:21 on Exod 32:20 has broader implications for the relationship between the two passages: "The author of Deut 9,7b–10,11 presumes throughout his version reader's familiarity with the story of Exodus 32–34 *to which he then gives his own emphases.*"[36]

4. Rhetoric and Imagination in Deuteronomy 9–10

Given that Deut 9:7–10:11 is a literary unity which has been adapted from Exodus 32–34, the problem of resolving the synoptic differences between the two passages remains. What are the "emphases," to borrow Begg's term, highlighted by Deuteronomy in retelling the story of

---

36. Begg, "Revisited," 478, emphasis added. A broader examination along the same lines by Hayes ("Golden Calf Stories") yields the same conclusion.

the golden calf? Taking the Exodus narrative as a baseline, it quickly becomes apparent that the storyline of the Deuteronomy account diverges in notable ways from that of Exodus (see table, p. 155).[37]

The literary differences between golden calf stories have typically received a redactional explanation,[38] with chronological irregularities taking center stage: Why in Deuteronomy does Moses make multiple references to periods of "forty days and nights" (Deut 9:9, 11, 18, 25; 10:10) whereas Exodus refers only once to such a period after the golden calf incident (Exod 34:28; cf. 24:18)? When Moses compares his subsequent trips up the mountain with "the first time" (Deut 10:10; cf. 9:18), which of his earlier ascents provides the basis for the comparison? Are Deuteronomy's dual references to YHWH "hearing" (שׁמע) the prayers of Moses (Deut 9:19, 10:10) to be reckoned as different occasions? Norbert Lohfink has argued that the five occurrences of the phrase "forty days" divide the passage into five successive scenes: (1) the ratification of the covenant (9:9–10); (2) the disruption of the covenant (9:11–17); (3) Moses' actions to resolve this disruption (9:18–21); (4) God's renewal of the covenant due to Moses' intercession (9:25–10:9); and (5) a new beginning in YHWH's command to resume the journey (10:10–11).[39] Lohfink recognizes some overlapping narrative elements in these scenes but generally regards these episodes as occurring in chronological succession.

However, a reexamination of this passage's rhetorical logic reveals that the Moses of Deuteronomy undertakes a decidedly nonlinear approach in retelling the golden calf story. Most significantly among the changes in Deuteronomy, Moses rearranges the chronology of Exodus to highlight his role as intercessor. YHWH's threat to destroy the people (Exod 32:7–10; Deut 9:12–14) is not followed in Deuteronomy by Moses' intercession and YHWH's gracious answer, as in Exod 32:11–14, but by Moses' descent from the mountain and smashing of the tablets (Deut 9:15–17). Deuteronomy omits YHWH's relenting from wrath and accentuates the destruction of the tablets, thereby heightening the sense of peril experienced by the audience as they listened to Moses.[40] If the

---

37. Chart adapted and expanded from J. Taschner, *Die Mosereden im Deuteronomium: Eine kanonorientierte Untersuchung* (FAT 59; Tübingen: Mohr Siebeck, 2008) 228. This chart excludes Deut 9:22–24 and 10:6–9, two passages that are generally regarded as parenthetical.

38. E.g., E. Aurelius, *Der Fürbitter Israels: Eine Studie zum Mosebild im Alten Testament* (ConBOT 27; Stockholm: Almqvist & Wiksell, 1988) 8–56; G. Seitz, *Redaktionsgeschichtliche Studien zum Deuteronomium* (BWANT 13; Stuttgart: Kohlhammer, 1971) 51–69.

39. Lohfink, "Endtextstructur," 50–53, 56–61.

40. Hayes, "Golden Calf Stories," 75.

sacred tablets, which symbolized God's covenantal relationship with his people, could be "smashed" (שׁבר Piel) so abruptly (9:17), and Moses could describe the burning, crushing, grinding, and disposal of the golden calf in such categorical terms, could the total destruction of the people themselves be far behind?

Israel fully deserved annihilation for its idolatry. This fact lends weight to Moses' earlier statement that "you provoked YHWH to anger and YHWH was so angry with you that he would have destroyed you" (9:8).[41] Moses at this moment speaks with unassailable authority, for here is found a rare instance in which his voice merges with YHWH as they assert together that Israel has "turned aside quickly from the way that I/YHWH commanded them/you" (9:12, 16).[42] But just as his audience is led to believe that no hope remains, Moses introduces the pivotal theme of his intercession and fasting for "forty days and nights" (9:18) as well as YHWH's willingness to hear his prayers (9:18–19). The threat of destruction thus stands at its height before the possibility of deliverance is ever broached.

The nonlinear narration of Moses' intercession only adds to the tension. His speech draws out the intercession over three scenes: (1) his physical act of prostration (9:18–19); (2) the actual words of his prayer (9:25–29); and (3) YHWH's gracious answer (10:10–11). The first narrative frame begins ominously when Moses says, "I threw myself down [נפל Hithpael] before YHWH" (9:18), an unusual and vivid construction which does not use פלל, the Old Testament's most common verb for prayer.[43] Moses' self-abasement is not explained as an act of intercession until he indicates later that he "prayed" (פלל) for Aaron "at that

---

41. The shift from grammatical singular (i.e., collective emphasis) to plural (i.e., individual emphasis) in Deut 9:7b prepares the way for Moses to emphasize the guilt of the individual members of his audience in 9:8. See the discussion of the *Numeruswechsel* as rhetorical device by T. A. Lenchak, *Choose Life! A Rhetorical-Critical Investigation of Deuteronomy 28,69–30,20* (AnBib 129; Rome: Pontifical Institute, 1993) 12–16; cf. J. J. Niehaus, *The Deuteronomic Style: An Examination of the Deuteronomic Style in the Light of Ancient Near Eastern Literature* (Ph.D. diss., University of Liverpool, 1985) esp. 403–4; J. G. McConville, "Singular Address in the Deuteronomic Law and the Politics of Legal Administration," *JSOT* 97 (2002) 19–36.

42. Robert Polzin notes that this is one of only nine instances of YHWH's direct speech in Moses' second address in Deuteronomy 5–26 (see 5:6–21, 28–31; 9:12, 13–14, 23; 10:1–2, 11; 17:16; 18:17–20) (*Moses and the Deuteronomist* [New York: Seabury, 1980] 48). Among these cases of divine direct speech, Deut 9:12 is the only instance followed by Moses' immediate and verbatim repetition of YHWH's words (Deut 9:16).

43. G. J. Venema, *Reading Scripture in the Old Testament: Deuteronomy 9–10, 31, 2 Kings 22–23, Jeremiah 36, Nehemiah 8* (OtSt 48; Leiden: Brill, 2004) 18. While פלל forms occur 84× in the OT, נפל Hithpael only occurs in Gen 43:18; Deut 9:18, 25[2×]; Ezra 10:1.

Content of Moses' Prayer	Antecedent Passages in Exodus–Numbers	Parallel Verses in Deuteronomy
Soothing of YHWH's anger	Exod 32:11	Deut 9:26
Appeal to the patriarchal promises	Exod 32:13	Deut 9:27a
Confession of Israel's guilt and sinfulness	Exod 32:30–33	Deut 9:27b
Appeal to YHWH's reputation among the nations	Exod 32:12; Num 14:16	Deut 9:28
Request for forgiveness and covenant renewal	Exod 34:9	Deut 9:29

time also" (9:20). Such ambiguity in Moses' prayers heightens the suspense, for even when Moses asserts that his prayers for Israel had been heard (9:19), a sense of foreboding remains through the lack of any explicit answer to his prayers for Aaron (9:20). Until the following two scenes of intercession unfold, the audience remains in the dark about the words that Moses prayed and how God responded to him.[44]

The second scene of intercession (9:25–29) draws the tension even tighter by telescoping several episodes from Exodus into a single event. Moses' language summarizes and combines elements of three different prayers from Exodus 32–34 while also borrowing some terminology from Numbers 14 (see table above).[45]

One notable difference exists between the accounts in Exodus and Deuteronomy of YHWH's actions after Moses' prayers for Israel. Unlike Exod 32:11–14, Deut 9:25–29 does not mention that YHWH "relented" (נחם [Niphal]) from punishing Israel (cf. Exod 32:14). In both Exodus and Deuteronomy, Moses pleads with YHWH, "Remember Abraham, Isaac, and Jacob" (Exod 32:13 // Deut 9:27),[46] but whether YHWH will honor the promises to the patriarchs remains unstated in the Deuteronomy account until the third scene of intercession (Deut 10:10–11). This lacuna again leaves the audience in limbo, a tension that is prolonged by YHWH's subsequent command to remake the tablets (10:1–5) as well as a narrative excursus on the Levites (10:6–9).

---

44. Dozeman is likely correct that Deut 9:18 and 9:25–29 refer to the same event but are narrated separately in order to draw out the suspense ("Exodus 32," 181).
45. Table adapted from Lohfink, "Endstrucktur," 57.
46. Hayes notes that the patriarchs are transformed from being recipients of an immutable promise (Exod 32:13) into role models as "servants" (Deut 9:27a), who contrast with a sinful people ("Golden Calf Stories," 77).

After heaping up the guilt of Israel and thereby increasing the stakes of Moses' prayers, the third scene (10:10–11) arrives at a resolution by presenting his intercession as an unqualified success. A positive answer to the prayers of Moses represents a complete reversal of YHWH's original desire to "destroy" (שמד Hiphil; 9:8, 18–19) his people: "YHWH listened to me.... YHWH was not willing to destroy [שמד Hiphil] you" (10:12). In contrast to Exod 32:33–35, in which YHWH still punished the people for their sin despite Moses' prayers, Deuteronomy's third scene of intercession (10:10–11) omits any reference to the punishment of Israel. The epoch-making intercession of Moses means that the only things to be destroyed remain the stone tablets (9:17) and the golden calf (9:21), but not the people. With the covenant now restored, Moses can once again lead the people on the journey to fulfill the ancestral promises: "Arise, proceed on your journey and possess the land that I swore to their fathers to give them" (10:11). With this command to depart from Horeb to Canaan, the hearer of Deuteronomy is transported back in the narrative world to Deut 1:7, the juncture in the book at which Israel was first commanded to depart from Horeb to Kadesh, the final stop before entering the land.[47]

An examination of the broader literary context of Deut 9:7–10:11 confirms that Moses is undertaking an imaginative rather than chronological approach to retelling Israel's history. The hortatory section of Deut 9:1–10:11 opens with an imaginary speaker's mocking statement that Israel is doomed to fail in conquering the land: "Who can stand before the sons of Anak?" (9:2).[48] Moses contests such an act of "disobedient imagination"[49] with the rejoinder that YHWH has already begun the conquest of Canaan before Israel has even crossed the Jordan: "YHWH your God *is crossing over* [עבר Qal participle] before you as a consuming fire" (9:3).[50] Israel needs to trust the God who fulfills his promises, "just as YHWH has spoken to you" (9:3).

---

47. N. Lohfink, "Reading Deuteronomy 5 as Narrative," in *A God So Near: Essays on Old Testament Theology in Honor of Patrick D. Miller* (ed. B. A. Strawn and N. R. Bowen; Winona Lake, IN: Eisenbrauns, 2003) 264–65.

48. See Hwang, *Rhetoric of Remembrance*, 174–76, for discussion of other acts of imagination.

49. Brueggemann, "Imagination," 23.

50. It is striking that Deut 9:3 provides one of only two references in Deuteronomy to YHWH's own "crossing" of the Jordan (cf. 31:3), and even represents the only occurrence where YHWH is said to go "before you." Every other instance of the עבר Qal participle refers to Israel's own crossing (Deut 2:4, 18; 3:21; 4:14, 22, 26; 6:1; 9:1; 11:8, 11, 13; 30:18). Similarly, every other reference to someone who will "go before" the people refers either

Since the certainty of conquest might lead to smugness, Moses continues his discourse by preempting another act of "disobedient imagination," but this time on Israel's part: "Do not say in your heart when YHWH your God has driven them out before you, '*Because of my righteousness* YHWH has brought me in to possess this land'" (9:4).[51] In rebutting Israel's pride, Moses twice asserts that conquest of the land will occur because of the unrighteousness of the Canaanite nations rather than Israel's own righteousness (9:4, 6). To reinforce this damning point, Moses then undertakes his imaginative recital of the golden calf story in Deut 9:7–10:11. Every aspect of the imaginative retelling of Horeb is thus calculated to maximize the audience's sense of complicity in those events while also emphasizing Moses' role as intercessor. Such a rhetorical agenda indicates that the first-person imagination of Deuteronomy 9–10 should not be expected to conform to the literary conventions of the third-person narrative in Exodus 32–34.

5. *The Diachronic Relationship among Exodus 32, Deuteronomy 9–10, and 1 Kings 12*

Deuteronomy's imaginative reuse of Exodus has significant implications for the relationship between the Pentateuch and the Deuteronomistic History. Golden calf stories provide a thread that links Exodus 32 and Deuteronomy 9–10 with 1 Kings 12, the seminal narrative of Jeroboam's installation of golden calves at Bethel and Dan. But in contrast to the canonical progression from Exodus and Deuteronomy to 1 Kings, John Van Seters has influentially argued that Exodus 32 represents a post-exilic and post-Deuteronom(ist)ic composition which combines elements from the golden calf stories in Deut 9:7–10:11 and 1 Kgs 12:26–32.[52] My discussion above has already shown the unlikelihood of Van Seters's view that Exodus 32 depends on Deuteronomy 9–10. The following section argues that Deuteronomy's creative recasting of Horeb provides the bridge between Exodus 32 and the depiction of Jeroboam's golden calves at Dan and Bethel (1 Kgs 12:26–32), something of an "original sin" that ultimately leads to the fall of the Northern Kingdom (2 Kgs 17:7–23).

---

to Moses (e.g., 10:11) or Joshua (e.g., 3:28). Thus Deut 9:3 stands apart in imaginatively describing YHWH as the personal vanguard of Israel.

51. Within the Mosaic speeches, F. García López identifies monologues of timidity (Deut 7:17–19, 21) and arrogance (8:17–18, 9:4–7; cf. 15:9) ("Analyse littéraire de Deutéronome V–XI," *RB* 84 [1977] 481–522, here pp. 483–86). They follow a standard form: (1) introduction; (2) the monologue proper; (3) and Moses' rebuttal of the monologue's concerns, whether timidity or arrogance.

52. Van Seters, *Life of Moses*, 290–318.

Van Seters's case for the late date of Exodus 32 hinges largely upon his contention that the golden calf tradition underlying this chapter stands much closer to 1 Kings 12 than to Deuteronomy 9–10. Van Seters notes three similarities in the golden calf stories of Exodus and 1 Kings: (1) Both Aaron and Jeroboam proclaim, "These are/Behold your gods, O Israel, who brought you up from the land of Egypt" (Exod 32:4; 1 Kgs 12:28b); (2) both calves are made of gold (Exod 32:3; 1 Kgs 12:28a); and (3) both calves are the object of festal sacrifices (Exod 32:6; 1 Kgs 12:32–33).[53] The numerous similarities between these texts had already been observed by others,[54] though Van Seters departs from the dominant view by asserting that Exodus 32 derives from 1 Kings 12 rather than vice versa.

Van Seters asserts that the brevity of Deuteronomy 9–10 vis-à-vis the longer account in Exodus 32 points to the relative priority of Deuteronomy over Exodus. He opines that Deuteronomy 9–10 could not postdate Exodus 32 because it becomes difficult to explain how the Deuteronom(ist)ic school, with its near-obsession with idolatry, would have omitted the detailed description of the people's sin in Exod 32:1–6.[55] Likewise it is surprising that a Deuteronom(ist)ic editor would bypass an opportunity to uphold Joshua in Deuteronomy 9–10 as a paragon of obedience, since Joshua is one of the most prominent characters in the Deuteronom(ist)ic tradition (see Deut 1:38; 3:21).[56] Since Van Seters regards 1 Kings 12 as a post-exilic text,[57] and Exodus 32 putatively contains a superset of elements found in Deuteronomy 9–10 and 1 Kings 12,[58] he concludes that Exodus 32 was composed by a post-exilic Yahwist.

Given the vast scope of Van Seters's writings on the tradition history of the Pentateuch,[59] my study must limit itself to critiquing his proposal that Exodus 32 postdates both Deuteronomy 9–10 and 1 Kings 12. Most significantly, Van Seters has overlooked several Deuteronom(ist)ic features in 1 Kings 12 which suggest that this account of Jeroboam's disobedience represents an adaptation of Deuteronomy 9–10 with some supplements from Exodus 32.

---

53. Ibid., 295.
54. Most notably by M. Aberbach and L. Smolar, "Aaron, Jeroboam, and the Golden Calves," *JBL* 86 (1967) 129–40.
55. Van Seters, *Life of Moses*, 307.
56. Ibid., 310.
57. Ibid., 296–99.
58. Ibid., 310–18.
59. Besides his book *Life of Moses*, see J. Van Seters, *Abraham in History and Tradition* (New Haven: Yale University Press, 1975); idem, *Prologue to History: The Yahwist as Historian in Genesis* (Philadelphia: Westminster John Knox, 1992); idem, *The Pentateuch: A Social-Science Commentary* (Sheffield: Sheffield Academic Press, 1999).

First, the narrative of Jeroboam's manufacture of the golden calves repeatedly emphasizes the rebellious imagination of his "heart" (1 Kgs 12:26, 33). Jeroboam's monologue "in his heart" about constructing cultic places at Dan and Bethel echoes Deuteronomy's frequent warnings against waywardness "in your heart" (Deut 7:17, 8:17, 9:4). In this regard, it is striking that 1 Kings 12, a third-person narrative, stands closer to the first-person account in Deuteronomy rather than the third-person narrative in Exodus 32. The complete absence of the Deuteronomic language of "heart" in Exodus 32 makes it unlikely that this chapter originated after Deuteronomy 9–10 and 1 Kings 12. If these Deuteronom(ist)ic texts were really available for a post-exilic Yahwist to use in writing Exodus 32, it becomes difficult to explain why this writer would pass up a perfect opportunity to reinforce the guilt of Aaron and the people by adding a glimpse into their sinister "heart."

Second, the description of Jeroboam in 1 Kings 12 is patterned after the figure of Aaron in Exodus 32 as refracted through the theological lenses of Deuteronomy 9–10. As Christine Hayes points out, Jeroboam strongly resembles Aaron in the Deuteronom(ist)ic tradition for becoming the object of divine wrath, facing the threat of annihilation, but finally dying a natural death (Deut 9:20; 1 Kgs 13:34; 14:20).[60] Exodus 32 does implicate Aaron for making the golden calf (Exod 32:4, 21, 35), but only condemns the people for their sin (32:9–10, 30–31). Thus it is likely that 1 Kings 12 depicts Jeroboam as a new Aaron who provokes Israel to commit a "sin" (1 Kgs 12:30; cf. Deut 9:18, 21) in keeping with the theological trajectory of Deuteronomy 9–10, while also adding narrative details from Exodus 32 about the construction of the calf in order to highlight the extent of Jeroboam's personal involvement in idolatry.

Third and most importantly, Van Seters has misinterpreted the lack of narrative detail in Deuteronomy 9–10. As already noted, Van Seters understands the omission of the people's sinful behavior in Deuteronomy 9–10 to mean that 1 Kings 12 more closely resembles Exodus 32. But this fixation on the unique features of Deuteronomy 9–10 overlooks how this passage represents only one of several Deuteronomic portrayals of Horeb that are intertextually linked and therefore inseparable.[61]

---

60. Hayes, "Golden Calf Stories," 89.
61. The discussion below is greatly indebted to G. Braulik, "Deuteronomium 4 und das gegossene Kalb: Zum Geschichtsgehalt paränetischer Rede," in *Houses Full of Good Things: Essays in Memory of Timo Veijola* (ed. J. Pakkala and M. J. Nissinen; Publications of the Finnish Exegetical Society 95; Göttingen: Vandenhoeck & Ruprecht, 2008) 11–26. This is not to say, however, that Braulik considers the Deuteronomic portrayals of Horeb to derive from the same historical period. He considers Deuteronomy 4 post-exilic but Deuteronomy 9–10 pre-exilic (ibid., 14 n. 7).

1 Kings 12 not only confirms the latter passage's dependence on the former, but also reinforces the Deuteronomistic History's emphasis on the inability of Israel's leaders to avert the exile. The imaginative rhetoric of theophany in Deuteronomy 9–10 thus provides a bridge that links Israel's past apostasy (Exodus 32) with its future apostasy (1 Kings 12).

6. Conclusion

Repetition in biblical literature furnishes an important datum for both diachronic and synchronic methods.[66] My analysis has attempted to show that the repeated accounts of Sinai/Horeb in Deuteronomy are best explained as a rhetorical recasting of Israel's foundational stories at the mountain (Exod 19:1–Num 10:10) rather than a redactor's disjointed work. Numerous synoptic issues remain in harmonizing the Pentateuch's varying descriptions of Sinai/Horeb,[67] but the complementary nature of these accounts invites a combination of synchronic and diachronic methodologies that explores their rhetorical shape before attempting to trace their redactional links. The intertwined nature of story and parenesis in Deuteronomy tends to problematize any redactional proposal that begins with the presupposition that law and narrative must belong to different tradition layers.[68] The importance of Sinai/Horeb in Israel's self-understanding demands rhetorically charged rehearsals of these events to highlight old truths and to create new experiences of God's presence. Such imagination in conjuring up the past furnishes a prime example of how, in Søren Kierkegaard's words, "'Repetition' is and remains a religious category."[69]

mission to bring lasting revival (*The Moses Tradition* [JSOTSup 161; Sheffield: JSOT Press, 1993] 142).

66. B. M. Levinson, *"The Right Chorale": Studies in Biblical Law and Interpretation* (FAT; Tübingen: Mohr Siebeck, 2008) 16–17.

67. Wellhausen regarded Horeb as the Elohist's term for the mountain, whereas Sinai is characteristic of the Priestly source. A redactional approach to the same problem has been attempted more recently by L. Perlitt, "Sinai und Horeb," in *Beiträge zur alttestamentlichen Theologie: Festschrift für Walther Zimmerli zum 70. Geburtstag* (ed. H. Donner, R. Hanhart, and R. Smend; Göttingen: Vandenhoeck, 1977) 302–22.

68. E.g., R. G. Kratz, *The Composition of the Narrative Books of the Old Testament* (trans. John Bowden; London: T. & T. Clark, 2005) 116: "The distinction between the [narrative] framework and the law is fundamental to the analysis of Deuteronomy."

69. S. Kierkegaard, *Fear and Trembling; Repetition* (trans. and ed. H. V. Hong and E. H. Hong; Kierkegaard's Writings 6; Princeton, NJ: Princeton University Press, 1983) 326; cited in B. A. Strawn, "Keep/Observe/Do — Carefully — Today! The Rhetoric of Repetition in Deuteronomy," in *A God So Near: Essays on Old Testament Theology in Honor of Patrick D. Miller* (ed. B. A. Strawn and N. R. Bowen; Winona Lake, IN: Eisenbrauns, 2003) 215.

The description of apostasy in Deuteronomy 9–10 bui[lds on] Deuteronomy 4 through their shared use of the key verbs שחת ['to be/become corrupt' and עשה 'to make', two terms use[d] to describe the golden calf incident. While Deuteron[omy 4 uses] this collocation of verbs to describe idolatry in gen[eral (Deut] 4:16, 25), Deuteronomy 9 makes this collocation's link [to the golden] calf explicit: "Arise, go down from here quickly, for yo[ur people] you brought out of Egypt have become corrupt [שחת]... [they have] quickly turned aside from the way that I commanded [them;] made [עשה] a molten image for themselves" (9:12; cf [...]. Trans]forming the warnings of Deuteronomy 4 into a para[digm] of idolatry, Deuteronomy 9–10 concretizes the conseq[uences] using the historical realities of Israel's past. The gol[den calf] as described in Exodus 32–34, furnishes the narrativ[e key to] understanding the prohibition on other gods and im[ages in the] Decalogue (Deut 5:6–9) as well as foreshadowing ap[ostasy in the] future (31:29). Thus Deuteronomy 9–10 cannot be sep[arated from] Deuteronomic accounts of Horeb since they each cont[ribute to a multi-]faceted theological argument against idolatry.

Contrary to Van Seters's view, the microcosmic cha[racter of Deuter]onomy 9–10 points to an alternative explanation for th[e extensive] detail about the people's sinful behavior. Since the au[thor of Deuter]onomy 9–10 knows that the sins of the first exodus [generation were] already dealt with in the wilderness (see 1:19–46),[62] [Deuteronomy's] Horeb develops the *Leitmotif* of theophany in a diffe[rent way,] highlighting Moses' intercession to save the people.[63] [The future] history of Israel lacks Moses-like intercessors since th[e Northern King-]dom is led by Aaron-like figures that repeat the parad[igm of "Je-]roboam, son of Nebat."[64] The absence of a Moses typo[logy,] coupled with the dominance of an Aaron typology, p[recludes the pos-]sibility of forgiveness for idolatry and seals the fate [of the Northern] Kingdom.[65] The omission of certain features from D[...]

---

62. Van Seters, *Life of Moses*, 370–77, acknowledges that Deut 1 [came] from the hand of the Deuteronomistic Historian. By Van Seters's o[wn logic, it] seems that the audience of Deuteronomy 9–10 (also a Deuteronom[ist) has] been aware of the spy narrative and the first exodus generation's d[eath] since these texts reside in identical or adjacent tradition layers.

63. V. Sénéchal, *Rétribution et intercession dans le Deutéronome* (B[erlin: Wal-]ter de Gruyter, 2009) 431–32.

64. This formulaic phrase and its variations are found in 1 Kg[s 15:34; 16:2,] 19, 26, 31; 21:22; 22:52; 2 Kgs 3:3; 10:29, 31; 13:2, 6, 11; 14:24; 15:9, 18, [24, 28].

65. Though Josiah might seem a counterexample to this trend, [note] that Josiah is portrayed as a "new David" and "new Moses" who

For Your Good Always
Restraining the Rights of the Victor for the Well-Being of the Vulnerable (Deut 21:10–14)

REBEKAH JOSBERGER

My interest in the role of the father in ancient Israel was first sparked by a discussion of the topic in Daniel Block's essay, "Marriage and Family in Ancient Israel."[1] Consistent with his understanding that the Old Testament "views leadership in general to be a privilege granted to an individual in order to serve the interests of those who are led,"[2] Block emphasizes "responsibility" over the concept of "right" or "privilege" usually associated with patriarchal authority.[3] Block's focus on the responsibility of the head of household (HOH) for those under his care offers a corrective to the pejorative connotations associated with the prevalent notion of Israel as a patriarchal society. Furthermore, his emphasis on responsibility commensurate with rights envisions a paradigm whereby abuses of authority within the text can be concretely labeled as such rather than glossed over or ignored.[4]

Author's Note: This article is written as a tribute to Dr. Daniel Block, my academic אָב, who by his own righteous example embodies the principles of servant leadership that seem to undergird so many of the texts of Deuteronomy. Among countless other ways that he has influenced my life, he stood steadily as my advocate so that I could enjoy the learning process unencumbered by the current cultural debate that surrounds a woman in ministry. If every person in a position of leadership exercised his or her authority with the care and grace that Daniel Block consistently exemplifies, there would be no room in this world for bitterness.

    1. D. I. Block, "Marriage and Family in Ancient Israel," in *Marriage and Family in the Biblical World* (ed. K. M. Campbell; Downers Grove, IL: InterVarsity, 2003) 33–102.

    2. Ibid., 44.

    3. Ibid. Block's ideas regarding the role and responsibilities of the father in ancient Israel are also reflected in various other treatments of Deuteronomy, in particular, C. J. H. Wright, *Deuteronomy* (NIBC; Peabody, MA: Hendrickson, 1996); and J. H. Tigay, *Deuteronomy* (JPSTC; Philadelphia: Jewish Publication Society, 1996).

    4. Where the issue of the relationship of a HOH to the members of his family is addressed within scholarship (typically within commentaries and studies on women's issues), treatments tend toward either a defense of the text (and thus an avoidance of evidence of the abuse of authority within the OT), or such extreme offense at male authority that the OT comes to be blamed for many of the problems faced by women throughout

The following study of Deut 21:10–14 is an outgrowth of a doctoral dissertation written to test Block's hypothesis that the biblical presentation of the ideal role of the Israelite אב 'father' is not that of privileged rule but of profound responsibility.[5] The dissertation examines the function, role, and responsibilities of the Israelite HOH specifically in relationship to the primary members of his household, his wife/wives and children, as prescribed in the book of Deuteronomy. The picture that emerges from this study is not that of a patriarchal dictator ruling over his household with unquestioned authority for the primary purpose of promoting his own well-being. Rather, the seven texts studied[6] suggest that Deuteronomy's ideal vision for Israel's domestic life includes a HOH who exercises his authority for the well-being of his family and the community.[7]

More surprising than Deuteronomy's call to responsibility is the emphasis on the restriction of a HOH's authority. Deut 21:10–14 provides an excellent example of a text that has as an underlying theme an attempt to curb the potential abuse of power within the patricentric society to which and within which God chose to reveal himself.[8] Although scholars are justified in condemning the abuse of authority by HOHs in OT narratives, the concern of certain family texts in Deuteronomy is precisely to protect family members from such abuse. While the HOH's basic societal rights are not challenged (the HOH still retains the primary social, legal, and perhaps religious authority within Israel), the

---

history. See the summary of scholarly discussion in R. Josberger, *Between Rule and Responsibility: The Role of the 'āb as Agent of Righteousness in Deuteronomy's Domestic Ideology* (Ph.D. diss., The Southern Baptist Theological Seminary, 2007) 7–33.

5. The family, or בית אב 'father's house', typically consisted of a father (HOH) and his wife, along with adult sons or grandsons and their wives and children. (Adult daughters and granddaughters would join the households of their husbands upon marriage.) Members of the household also included some who were not related by blood, namely servants, maidservants, and possibly even foreigners and resident Levites. Even livestock seem to have been considered part of the household. Within the בית אב, the functional role of the אב 'father' extended to each member of his household.

6. Deut 21:10–14, 21:15–17, 21:18–21, 22:13–21, 24:1–4, 24:5, and 25:5–10. The study was limited to the passages in the Deuteronomic Code (Deut 12–26) that specifically address the relationship between the אב and the primary members of his household.

7. Western culture increasingly (if also incorrectly) equates well-being with happiness. However, Deuteronomy understands well-being as devotion to Yhwh demonstrated through a life characterized by covenant faithfulness—namely, worship of Yhwh alone and adherence to covenant stipulations that would result in divine blessing. It is to this end that a father was expected to act when relating to or on behalf of members of his household.

8. Here I adopt Block's use of the term "patricentric" (father-centered) rather than "patriarchal" as a more fitting descriptor of ancient Israelite culture (see his "Marriage and Family in Ancient Israel," 41–44).

Table 1. Text and Translation of Deut 21:10–14

Text	Verse	Translation
כִּי־תֵצֵא לַמִּלְחָמָה עַל־אֹיְבֶיךָ	10a	When you go forth to battle against your enemies, and[a]
וּנְתָנוֹ יְהוָה אֱלֹהֶיךָ בְּיָדֶךָ	10b	YHWH your God gives them into your hand, and
וְשָׁבִיתָ שִׁבְיוֹ:	10c	you take captives, and
וְרָאִיתָ בַּשִּׁבְיָה אֵשֶׁת יְפַת־תֹּאַר	11a	you see among the captives a beautiful woman, and
וְחָשַׁקְתָּ בָהּ	11b	you desire her, and
וְלָקַחְתָּ לְךָ לְאִשָּׁה:	11c	you take her to be a wife, and
וַהֲבֵאתָהּ אֶל־תּוֹךְ בֵּיתֶךָ	12a	you bring her into your house;
וְגִלְּחָה אֶת־רֹאשָׁהּ	12b	then she shall shave her head, and
וְעָשְׂתָה אֶת־צִפָּרְנֶיהָ:	12c	she shall do her nails, and
וְהֵסִירָה אֶת־שִׂמְלַת שִׁבְיָהּ מֵעָלֶיהָ	13a	she shall cast aside the garments of her captivity from upon her, and
וְיָשְׁבָה בְּבֵיתֶךָ	13b	she shall dwell in your house, and
וּבָכְתָה אֶת־אָבִיהָ וְאֶת־אִמָּהּ יֶרַח יָמִים	13c	she shall mourn for her father and her mother for thirty days, and
וְאַחַר כֵּן	13d	after this
תָּבוֹא אֵלֶיהָ	13e	you may go to her, and
וּבְעַלְתָּהּ		you may become her husband, and
וְהָיְתָה לְךָ לְאִשָּׁה:	13f	she will be your wife.
וְהָיָה	14a	Now,
אִם־לֹא חָפַצְתָּ בָּהּ		if you do not delight in her,
וְשִׁלַּחְתָּהּ לְנַפְשָׁהּ	14b	then you shall send her freely, and
וּמָכֹר לֹא־תִמְכְּרֶנָּה בַּכָּסֶף	14c	you may not sell her for silver, and
לֹא־תִתְעַמֵּר בָּהּ	14d	you may not treat her as a commodity
תַּחַת אֲשֶׁר עִנִּיתָהּ:	14e	because you have degraded her.

a. The initial *waw* of each phrase is placed at the end of the preceding line to allow the reader to follow the flow of ideas more readily.

exercise of those rights is restricted in order to safeguard the weaker, or hierarchically inferior, members of society. The text of Deuteronomy works both positively (promoting welfare) and negatively (preventing abuse) for the purpose of protecting and preserving righteousness in Israel[9]—even in the midst of a fallen world.[10]

The subject matter of Deut 21:10–14 makes the text particularly difficult to handle. With the harsh reality of war as its backdrop, the subjugation of women as its focus, and the mysterious symbolic rituals in its midst one can only wonder what, if anything, this text has to say about righteousness. Yet perhaps herein lies the beauty of this text. The torah addresses the most difficult human situations and calls for righteous behavior, nonetheless.

1. The Setting

Two settings deserve consideration within these short verses. First, there is the context of the woman's war-ravished homeland.[11] As unpleasant as war may be, it is a very real part of Israel's existence, and God is actively involved in Israel's warfare.[12] The reality of war is nei-

---

9. Although Deuteronomy in some ways resembles other ancient Near Eastern law codes, it is driven more by a concern for righteous living than for justice. Thus laws in Deuteronomy tend to be theologically motivated based on a concern for the peoples' right relationship with Yhwh, rather than fairness or financial compensation (Deut 16:20). See D. I. Block, *Deuteronomy* (NIVAC; Grand Rapids: Zondervan, 2012), 399–447. See also P. T. Vogt, *Deuteronomic Theology and the Significance of Torah: A Reappraisal* (Winona Lake, IN: Eisenbrauns, 2006) 212–13.

10. Some may suggest that these assertions reflect a very optimistic view of the text—one that would defend this patricentric society as idyllic, even prescriptive. However, to acknowledge these two underlying themes in the torah of Deuteronomy is to acknowledge that these correctives likely were needed. Apart from their instructions, conditions were anything but idyllic. Indeed, the picture that emerges from the narratives of the OT includes both abuse and neglect.

11. Presumably this text is referring to a non-Canaanite nation based on the injunction to kill every living thing among the Canaanite nations (Deut 7:1–6, 20:16–18).

12. God commands Israelites to wage war (Deut 2:24, 20:10–18), sets limits on their warfare (2:5, 20:19), gives instructions for their behavior during wartime (ch. 20), arranges circumstances so that they will be forced to wage war (2:30), goes with them (20:1, 4), fights for them (20:4), and controls their victory and defeat (20:4; 21:10).

On the complex issue of war in the OT, see G. von Rad, *Der Heilige Krieg im Alten Israel* (Göttingen: Vandenhoeck & Ruprecht, 1958), translated into English by M. J. Dawn, *Holy War in Ancient Israel* (Grand Rapids: Eerdmans, 1991); Y. Yadin, *The Art of Warfare in Biblical Lands in the Light of Archaeological Study* (2 vols.; New York: McGraw-Hill, 1963); P. Craigie, *The Problem of War in the Old Testament* (Grand Rapids: Eerdmans, 1978); T. R. Hobbes, *A Time for War: A Study of Warfare in the Old Testament* (OTS 3; Wilmington, DE: Michael Glazier, 1989); and S. Niditch, *War in the Hebrew Bible: A Study in the Ethics of Violence* (New York: Oxford University Press, 1993).

ther condemned nor glorified—it is presupposed. War is gruesome and inhumane, but according to Deuteronomy, it is one of the ways that God has chosen to act in history.

War provides both the historical and literary setting for the passage. The literary flashback to chapter 20 reminds the reader of the extreme vulnerability of this beautiful captive woman.[13] According to Deut 20:14 the women, children, livestock, and spoils of a conquered city outside the Promised Land belong to Israel. As abrasive as it may sound to modern ears, according to the conventions of ancient warfare, the belongings of the vanquished foe were transferred to the victor. These women and children were destined to lives of slavery in service to Israel, and the livestock and spoils were to be added to Israel's national wealth.

What little has been written on the treatment of women as prisoners of war in the ancient Near East reveals a gruesome picture. The extra-biblical evidence is primarily iconographic and portrays women as captive and enslaved.[14] Evidence from the biblical text suggests that foreign treatment of captured Israelite women and children ranged from servitude, as in the case of Naaman's servant girl who seems to have been well-treated,[15] to the heinous abuse depicted in Amos 1:13 in which the Ammonite warriors ripped open the wombs of pregnant women in Gilead. In Judg 5:30 Canaanite war practices are celebrated in song: "Are they not finding and dividing their spoil? To every man

---

13. The lexical and thematic links between Deut 21:10–14 and Deuteronomy 20 are noted by commentator and casual reader alike. Due to these similarities, it is sometimes suggested that 21:10–14 originally belonged as part of the material on warfare in chapter 20. See A. Rofé, "The Laws of Warfare in the Book of Deuteronomy: Their Origins, Intent and Positivity," *JSOT* 32 (1985) 26–27; and S. R. Driver, *A Critical and Exegetical Commentary on Deuteronomy* (3rd ed.; ICC; Edinburgh: T. & T. Clark, 1978) 236. Rofé's explanation ("Laws of Warfare," 27) for the insertion of 21:1–9 between chapter 20 and 21:10 as an "editorial mishap" is unsatisfactory. Although there is an obvious relationship between chapter 20 and 21:10–14, the emphasis on household concerns (marriage and subsequent divorce) in 21:10–14 is at home in chapter 21. See also D. L. Christensen, *Deuteronomy 21:10–34:12* (WBC 6B; Nashville: Thomas Nelson, 2002) 472–73.

14. See for example Yadin, *Art of Warfare*, 2:338, 2:396–97, and 2:432–35; Z. Bahrani, *Women of Babylon: Gender and Representation in Mesopotamia* (London: Routledge, 2001) 124–30; and M. Cifarelli, "Gesture and Alterity in the Art of Ashurnasirpal II of Assyria," *ArtB* 80 (1998) 220–23. The practice of taking the captives and spoils of war was standard and widespread in ancient Near Eastern cultures (temporally and geographically). For a developed discussion of the extra-biblical evidence on the treatment of woman in wartime in the ancient Near Eastern world, see Josberger, *Between Rule and Responsibility*, 41 n. 7.

15. This suggestion is inferred from her expression of interest in her master's healing (2 Kgs 5:2–3).

a girl or two!" (lit., "a womb, a pair of wombs"). Regarding the use of womb(s) as a metonymy for women, Block writes, "Preference for this overtly sexual expression reflects the realities of war: to victorious soldiers the women of vanquished foes represent primarily objects for their sexual gratification, another realm to conquer."[16] Here Canaanite treatment of women in wartime extends far beyond servitude.

From the homeland of the conquered woman, the text shifts to the second setting—namely, that of the warrior's home. Although she has been taken under the protective wing of an Israelite household, she is now completely at the mercy of the HOH. In a time when national and religious identities were intricately bound with social identity, this woman is an outsider. Within this setting she is a heathen foreigner, a defeated foe, and a woman who has been completely cut off from her father's house. She has no social standing, few rights, and no direct advocate.[17]

2. The Characters

Deut 21:10–14 is addressed to the victorious Israelite warrior—a conquering hero caught in the rush of adrenaline that accompanies victory.[18] It is to this man that the text speaks—to one who already enjoys a certain measure of authority in this patricentric (and thus, to a degree, androcentric) culture, and who now has the plunder of a defeated nation at his disposal.

However, the primary concern of this law is not for the warrior himself but for guiding his behavior toward the beautiful captive woman. Thus the captive woman is the *raison d'être* of this text. She is in a vulnerable situation, the urgency of which cannot be overstated. In the war-torn city the beautiful woman is in her homeland, but her homeland is no longer able to offer her any security. Perhaps her best hope would have been to be sold into slavery, while her worst fears may have made the fate of her slain countrymen seem preferable.

In terms of her immediate status, she is in every way inferior to this soldier. Socially, he is a man in a patricentric society, and he thus holds

---

16. D. I. Block, *Judges, Ruth* (NAC 6; Nashville: Broadman & Holman, 1999) 243.

17. What advocate a bride would normally have would come from the household of her father. In this case, however, this woman has been cut off from her family (see Deut 21:13—"she shall [*perhaps* may] mourn for her father and mother for thirty days"). Whether her parents were killed in the war, were separated from her by distance, or were severed from her by her integration into Israelite society, they are as good as dead to her.

18. The jubilation of dividing the spoils is evident in biblical poetry; see Gen 49:27, Exod 15:9, Isa 9:2[3], Isa 33:23; cf. 1 Sam 30:16.

the authority.[19] Physically, the warrior is almost definitely stronger than she. Politically, he is the valiant conqueror and she the defeated foe. Religiously, she is a pagan, which to an Israelite should have been considered repugnant. This religious stigma would only have increased when she was taken back to Israel. Here her religious inferiorities would have been two-sided: Not only would her Israelite captors have seen her as one who did not know or serve YHWH, she would also have seen herself as one who served a god who had just been defeated and who was thus impotent.[20] Even her one asset, her beauty, has turned into a liability. Thus Deut 21:10–14 addresses a situation in which the strongest member of Israelite society (made even stronger by virtue of his recent success) is free to prey on the weakest member, the most vulnerable and most likely to be abused.

3. *The Issues*

There are actually two issues addressed in this short text. The first issue is the warrior's desire to take this beautiful woman as a wife. The second is his desire to divorce her. In each, the man affects a significant change to the woman's social status (from defeated foe to wife and from wife to non-wife). Matters are complicated by the fact that she is first a stranger and then a stranger in a strange land.

3.1. *From Defeated Foe to Wife (Deut 21:10–13)*

Deut 21:10–13 addresses the case of a man wishing to take a captive woman as his bride, causing the sphere of war to collide with the sphere of family law. These verses set forth guidelines to govern the exercising of his right to take a beautiful, captive woman in marriage in order to ensure that he does so in a manner that considers the well-being of this

---

19. Even if women were considered valuable members of society (as they were in Israel, see C. Meyers, *Discovering Eve: Ancient Israelite Women in Context* [New York: Oxford University Press, 1988] 24–46), this woman would have been dependent on men for her protection. Whether she had been married, widowed, or still living at home (the text does not say), the men who should offer this woman protection were rendered powerless by their defeat. This helplessness is probably why the text is not concerned with the woman's marital status (that, along with the fact that according to Deut 20:13 all the men were to have been slain).

20. In surrounding polytheistic cultures of the ancient Near East, gods were often seen as rulers of territories or domains. Simply put, if the beautiful woman's nation was defeated by Israel, then her nation's gods were defeated by Israel's God. Not only has her god been defeated, but she is also then brought to a land that, to her way of thinking, may have been beyond the territory of her god(s)' domain. See D. I. Block, *The Gods of the Nations: Studies in Ancient Near Eastern National Theology* (2nd ed., ETS Studies; Grand Rapids: Baker, 2000) 75–91.

Table 2. Three Options for the Beginning of the Apodosis in Deut 21:11–12

Option 1 (21:11c)	Option 2 (21:12a)	Option 3 (21:12b)
When you go to war ... And YHWH ... gives ... And you take them captive And you see ... a woman ... And you desire her Then take her And bring her to your home And she must shave her head ...	When you go to war ... And YHWH ... gives ... And you take them captive And you see ... a woman ... And you desire her And you (want to) take her Then bring her to your home And she must shave her head ...	When you go to war ... And YHWH ... gives ... And you take them captive And you see ... a woman ... And you desire her And you take her And bring her to your home Then she must shave her head ...

a. These translations are intended merely to serve as a visual presentation of the different options. Translational values were chosen based on space restriction.

vulnerable woman. The purpose of this law is to call the Israelite man to treat his new wife with at least a minimum level of respect—all the while caring for her welfare by offering her the protection and provision of his household.

Alternative views, arguably influenced by the KJV and NIV, typically see the focus of this law as directed toward establishing the man's right to marry the captive woman (i.e., "you may take her," or "if ... you want to take her, you may bring her into your home").[21] The translational ambiguity arises from the fact that the Hebrew of these verses contains no clear grammatical marker to delineate the protasis ("if") and the apodosis ("then").[22] The apodosis helps to mark the shift from the setting of the law (that which is assumed to be the case) to the focus of the law (that which is being instructed). As shown in Table 2, there are three possible locations for the beginning of the apodosis: the beginning of 21:11c, the beginning of 21:12a, or at the beginning of 21:12b.

By placing the apodosis in 21:11c, option 1 results in a translation that establishes the man's right to marry one of war's living casualties.[23]

---

21. The NIV begins the apodosis at v. 11c: "if you notice among the captives a beautiful woman and you are attracted to her, you may take her as your wife" (similarly, NIV11). The KJV begins the apodosis at v. 12a: "Then thou shalt bring her home to thine house...."

22. In Hebrew conditional clauses, the apodosis is often marked by a *weqatal* form (*IBHS* 38.2). This can generate confusion when the protasis also consists of a series of *weqatal* forms.

23. The JB, NEB, and NIV all translate this passage with the apodosis beginning in v. 11c.

This translation blends nicely with the ethical bent of Deuteronomy by presenting the text as anti-rape legislation in which the only acceptable way for a man to act on his desire is to marry the captive woman. If he desires a captive woman, he may take her as his wife, but he is prohibited from the typical ravages of war. One might argue, then, that this text (as translated in option 1) is necessary because it establishes an exception to the Deuteronomic prohibition against intermarriage and thereby acts both positively (allowing the warrior to benefit from the plunder of war) and negatively (implicitly prohibiting rape on the battlefield).

The difficulty with this argument is that there is no blanket statement forbidding intermarriage in the Israelite constitutional texts such as would necessitate that an exception to the rule be clearly stated.[24] The rationale for the prohibition against intermarriage was based not on race but on faith. The potential religious seduction of an Israelite by a non-Yahwistic spouse would have been minimized by the woman's status as a captive. This woman's self-perceived spiritual impotence may explain why her integration into an Israelite household is not a major concern. Whether she views her god as having been defeated or as requiring appeasement she is unable to offer, she seems to pose very little spiritual threat. As nice as it might be to label this text as anti-rape legislation, it seems to superimpose a desired ethical softening of a harsh cultural reality.[25]

---

24. The OT's stance on intermarriage is consistent in this regard: marriage between an Israelite and a non-Israelite was considered toxic to the faith of the Israelite spouse (Exod 34:15, 16; Deut 7:3, 4; Judg 3:5, 6; 1 Kgs 11:1, 2, 8; Ezra 9, 10; Neh 13:23–27). The law codes of the OT only record one direct prohibition against intermarriage, and this prohibition is limited to seven distinct people groups (Deut 7:1, 3), presumably referring to Canaanites in their entirety. Later prophets and narrators of Israelite history clearly assume that the people should know of the dangers of intermarriage and abstain (1 Kgs 11:2; Ezra 9, 10). To complicate matters, narrative texts record numerous examples of intermarriage, and some are recorded with no discernable pejorative appraisal (Moses and Zipporah, Rahab and Salmon, Ruth and Boaz).

25. Anti-rape legislation specific to the battlefield would not have been necessary within Israel. The law codes of the biblical text were not considered exhaustive, nor were they meant to be. They represented underlying principles for governing behavior. For example, while some contend that Deuteronomy evidences inconsistent sexual expectations between men and women (see J. Ridderbos, *Deuteronomy* [trans. Ed M. van der Maas; Bible Student's Commentary; Grand Rapids: Zondervan, 1984] 224–25), it can also be argued that a righteous Yahwist would have understood that sexual relationships were to be reserved for the marriage relationship alone. If a man may not sleep with a woman who is married or betrothed to someone else, and a father is to protect his daughter from sleeping with anyone before she is married, a man in Israelite culture was restricted to his wife—making sexual relations within marriage the righteous standard. See also R. M.

The placement of the apodosis at the beginning of verse 12 (option 2) is unlikely because it is not sensitive to the nuances of the text. This translation may be influenced by the *soph pasuq* (major accent signaling a verse division) and finds support in the LXX.²⁶ However, the shift in setting from foreign soil to the Israelite household that occurs at this point in the text is just as likely an explanation for the major accent. Those who place the apodosis here follow two different translation options. The first is to simply translate, "if . . . you take her, then bring her home." Rendered this way, the placement of the apodosis here makes little sense. If he is marrying the woman, of course he will take her home, if only to protect his interest in her. To counter this difficulty, some translate the Hebrew verb לקח 'to take' in a modal sense: "if . . . you *want* to take her, then bring her home. . . ." While a modal sense is grammatically possible for a *yiqtol* verb, its insertion in a string of indicative verbs is forced and atypical of Hebrew. Moreover, the main impetus for this translation seems to be an improper conflation of the prior verb חשק 'to desire' and לקח 'to take'.²⁷

The third option ("you bring her to your household, *then* she shall shave her head") is perhaps the least familiar, although it is still well supported.²⁸ Understood this way, Deut 21:10–14 is not addressing the issue of a man's right to marry a foreign woman from among the captives; this right is presupposed. Rather, this legislation sets the parameters for how this marriage is to be carried out. Placing the apodosis here in the middle of verse 12 coincides with the first grammatical shift

---

Davidson, *Flame of Yahweh: Sexuality in the Old Testament* (Peabody, MA: Hendrickson, 2007) 361.

Some argue the opposite extreme that this text is not anti-rape, but legalized rape (see, e.g., H. C. Washington, "Violence and the Construction of Gender in the Hebrew Bible: A New Historicist Approach," *BI* 5 [1997] 344). While this terminology is extreme and fails to take into account the significant social distinctions between rape and marriage in the ancient Near Eastern culture, it does serve to call attention back to the harsh realities faced by this woman.

26. The future indicative verb at the beginning of verse twelve clearly marks the apodosis. Deut 21:10–12a: Ἐὰν . . . λάβῃς αὐτὴν σαυτῷ γυναῖκα, καὶ εἰσάξεις αὐτὴν ἔνδον εἰς τὴν οἰκίαν σου 'If . . . you take her for yourself as a wife, then you will bring her into your house'.

27. In context, וחשקת בה 'you desire her' refers to desire for the woman, but in this translation the idea of desiring is carried onto the next verb, לקח 'to take', in the sense of "desiring to marry." The conflation of the two verbs is improper.

28. This translation is attested by the ESV and NRSV and is supported in scholarly works as well (see, e.g., C. Pressler, *The View of Women Found in the Deuteronomic Family Law* [BZAW 216; New York: Walter de Gruyter, 1993] 10–11; and J. G. McConville, *Deuteronomy* [AOTC 5; Downers Grove, IL: InterVarsity, 2002] 329).

present in the text, that from 2ms pronoun (you) to 3fs pronoun (she).²⁹ It also has the advantage of not breaking up the natural succession of 3ms verbs, and a break here nicely aligns with what has already been noted concerning the cultural backdrop of war in Israel. It was taken for granted that, following victory, a warrior would be entitled to the plunder. The issue at hand is not the man's rights, but rather his responsibilities to and for the woman.

This translation, as the others, has its difficulties. One of the problems it raises is that the man's role in Deut 21:12b–13b is somewhat vague. This legislation is addressed to the man, yet at the focal point of the text his involvement is undefined. Moreover, this translation places the emphasis of the passage on rituals whose symbolism is foreign and whose significance is lost to us.³⁰ To be fair, these issues are difficult no matter where one chooses to see the beginning of the apodosis. The difficulty is more pronounced in this reading because the ritual stipulations are understood to form the heart of this legislation by virtue of their position at the beginning of the apodosis.

Problems raised in translation often serve as a benefit by drawing attention to a difficulty and forcing the reader to investigate more closely. In this way, the weaknesses of this proposed translation may be re-cast as strengths. Regarding the issue of the man's undefined role, it is precisely this ironic twist that also would have caught the attention of the ancient audience. Just when the warrior expects to hear what the law requires of him, the focus of the text shifts to the woman. Whether she is forced, coerced, compliant, or willing, the woman is the principal actor—not the man.

On one level, the meaning of the text is the same regardless of the subject used: certain requirements must be met before the warrior may marry the woman. But language is a powerful tool that functions on

---

29. In the LXX and the Temple Scroll (11QT) the shift in subject from 2ms to 3fs does not occur until "she will dwell" and "she will mourn." According to these witnesses, the instructions to shave her head, do her nails, and cast off her captive garments are directed to the warrior. See 11QT Col. 63:12, 13, as presented by Y. Yadin, *Megillat ham-Miqdas, The Temple Scroll* (Jerusalem: The Israel Exploration Society, 1983) 3.1 plate 78. The text critical principle of choosing as original the reading that explains the others suggests that the witnesses with the subject shift to 3fs are more reliable at this point. Whether a copy error or intentional change, it is easy to see how a scribe might have made the shift from 3fs to 2ms—either by analogy with the preceding string of five consecutive 2ms verbal forms in the text or because male-directed speech is common and expected in this genre.

30. These rituals include shaving (גלח, Piel) the head, doing (עשה) the nails, and casting off (סור, Hiphil) the clothes of her captivity. For a discussion of their interpretation, see below.

many levels. While it could be said that the meaning is not affected by the subject shift, the tone is. There is a subtle but significant difference between the warrior being given the right to act against the woman (*you* shave her head), and his being given the responsibility to see that certain conditions are met (*she* shall shave her head). How remarkable given the culture, the woman's deplorable situation, and the male-oriented disposition of these instructions that the text speaks of her as her own person and not as an object to be acted against.

This series of rituals directed toward the woman creates a further difficulty in understanding this text, one that arises not from problems in the text itself, but from our own inability to recapture the significance of the string of rituals this woman is to perform. She is to shave her head, do her nails, and remove the clothing of her captivity. She is also to dwell in the warrior's home and to mourn for her father and mother for thirty days. Scholars have searched the Hebrew Scriptures and the archives of the ancient world for any parallel word or idea to help us understand the symbolism intended by these activities.[31] Unfortunately, the precise meaning of some of these phrases, especially the shaving of the head and the doing of the nails, continues to elude even the most diligent scholarly investigation.[32] The most likely suggestions are that these activities are associated with mourning rites or that they signify a disassociation with her past and a corresponding association with the land and people of Israel.[33]

---

31. Suggestions concerning the significance of these rituals include (1) to set the woman apart from other Israelites, (2) to make her less attractive, thus discouraging the man from marrying a foreigner, (3) to symbolize the casting off of her slavery, (4) to visually display the severing of ties with her old life and her attachment to Israel, (5) to facilitate her mourning process, or (6) any combination of the above. Such suggestions usually follow detailed study of lexical usage and of ancient Near Eastern customs (although some are clearly driven by a theological agenda). For a developed discussion of these options and their support in the ancient world, see Josberger, *Between Rule and Responsibility*, 51–54.

32. The problem is not that the significance of these actions is unknown, but rather that they are each symbolic of so many things. For example, even if the study of shaving is restricted to the term גלח, in the OT the symbolism of the action includes shame (2 Sam 10:4), purification (Lev 14:8), and mourning or contrition (Jer 41:5). In other contexts the symbolism is more subtle (2 Sam 14:26—perhaps strength) or mysterious (Judg 16:17, 19, 22). The more common verb for the shaving associated with mourning is קרח (Lev 21:5, Jer 16:6, Ezek 27:31, Mic 1:16; cf. Isa 3:24).

33. See G. von Rad, *Deuteronomy: A Commentary* (OTL; Philadelphia: Westminster, 1966) 137; R. Clifford, *Deuteronomy with an Excursus on Covenant and Law* (OTM 4; Wilmington, DE: Michael Glazier, 1982) 113; and M. E. Biddle, *Deuteronomy* (SHBC 4; Macon, GA: Smyth & Helwys, 2003) 323. For a more extensive discussion of the significance of these rituals, see Josberger, *Between Rule and Responsibility*, 53 n. 32–33.

The symbolism of the removal or casting aside (Hiphil of סור) of the garments of her captivity is more familiar. In the OT the setting aside or taking off of a specific type of clothing signifies a disassociation with whatever status the removed clothing represents.[34] When this woman casts aside the clothes of her captivity, she is laying with them the extreme social stigma that comes from being a captive foreigner among Israelites. Remarkably, when the warrior takes this woman in marriage, he does not simply change her social status from non-wife to wife, but also from plunder to person.

The injunction, "she shall live in your house," is not qualified with explanation, but its significance is easily inferred. Negatively stated, she will *not* live among the captives; positively stated, she *will* benefit from the provision and protection of the warrior's household. The text has already stated that she has been taken to his house. This second mention of his house is not redundant, but emphatic—he must care for her while he waits to marry her.

Especially interesting is the inclusion of a one-month period of mourning during which the captive woman is given the chance to weep for her parents.[35] This phrase does more than alert the reader to the tragic loss the woman has endured and the precarious circumstance in which she now finds herself. It also demonstrates the very heart of this

---

34. In the OT, as perhaps in any culture, clothing is strongly symbolic. Although clothing occasionally figures in mourning rituals (i.e., tearing of garments or putting on sackcloth), the removal of garments is commonly used to denote the disassociation with the cultural stigma attached to that item of clothing. This phenomenon is most clearly evidenced in highly stylized language like poetry or prophetic oracle, although the idea also appears in narrative. See Ezek 21:31 [21:26], 26:16, Job 19:9, Zech 3:4, and Gen 38:14–15. Likewise, the donning of garments signifies an association with the social status symbolized by the clothing (Gen 41:42). It is interesting here that the symbolism is that of disassociation (with her captive status) rather than of association. For a brief but helpful overview of the role of clothing in Scripture, see C. E. Palmer, "Clothes," in *New Dictionary of Biblical Theology* (ed. T. D. Alexander et al.; Downers Grove, IL: InterVarsity, 2000) 416–18.

35. The literature is full of speculation as to the purpose of this one-month mourning period. Those uncomfortable with the idea of this international marriage propose that the month allowed the man time to cool off and change his mind. See R. Hammer, trans., *Sifre: A Tannaitic Commentary on the Book of Deuteronomy* (YJS 24; New Haven, CT: Yale, 1986) 224–25. More recent suggestions, influenced by sociological models, suggest that waiting a full month provided assurance that the woman was not pregnant and that any future offspring would belong to the new husband. See Washington, "Violence and the Construction of Gender," 350–51. Both suggestions are reasonable, but neither finds support in the text. The passage plainly states that she is to mourn the loss of her father and mother. A thirty-day mourning period is also mentioned in Num 20:29 and Deut 34:8. Elsewhere an appropriate mourning period is listed as seven days (Gen 50:10, 1 Sam 31:13, 1 Chr 10:12).

piece of legislation. This valiant (strong and powerful) man is to treat this heathen, captive (powerless and vulnerable) woman as a human being. Regardless of their initial difference in social status, or perhaps precisely because of this difference, he is required to respect her human need to grieve, and he must give her a period of time, however brief, to begin to adjust and to cope with her new surroundings. Even before he formally marries her, he is to demonstrate at least the minimum level of respect insofar as he is not to treat her as a war trophy, but as a person. Only *after* these conditions are met is this man allowed to exercise his right to this woman.[36]

The main issue of the text is the change in social status of the woman from that of foreign captive to the wife of an Israelite. The text is addressed to the warrior, for it is he who initiates this change (with no apparent regard for the thoughts or wishes of the woman). In today's society of political correctness, it is all too tempting to approach the text with the question, "Why or how should he have that right?" But the question driving the text is, "*How should he exercise that right?*" This text does not call the warrior's right into question, but it demands that he exercise that right in a manner that demonstrates at least some level of patience, protection, provision, compassion, and respect. Even more remarkable, the foreign woman in this text is elevated socially to a position similar or equal to that of an Israelite woman simply based on her marriage to an Israelite man.[37]

3.2 *From Wife to Non-Wife (Deut 21:14)*

Deut 21:14 furthers the instruction of the preceding verses while moving on to address a new issue, namely the change in the woman's social status from wife to non-wife.[38] Here again, the rights of the man are assumed (this time his right to divorce), and the text focuses on how he must act, or not act, in his exercising of that right.[39] Like 21:10–13,

---

36. The rhythmic repetition of the *weqatal* verbs is abruptly interrupted by an emphatic ואחר כן 'after this' in verse 13. The text is very clear on the proper sequence of events. He is not to touch her until after he has taken her into his home, seen that she is cared for, and given her a month to grieve.

37. See McConville, *Deuteronomy*, 330; and Tigay, *Deuteronomy*, 194. Ridderbos claims that the woman is free after the divorce (Deut 21:14) but not during the marriage (*Deuteronomy*, 219). Whether this woman is of the status of a free woman or not is unclear from the text. What is clear from 21:10–14 is that, upon divorce, this woman was to be granted her freedom, and until that point she was to be treated as a wife, not as a captive.

38. The term "sent" (שׁלח, Piel) is clear divorce language (see Deut 22:19, 29; 24:1–4; Isa 50:1; Jer 3:1, 8; and Mal 2:16).

39. In v. 14 there is some confusion as to where the protasis (if . . .) ends and the apodosis (then . . .) begins. The options are as follows: (1) "If you do not delight in her, *then*

this text is addressed to the man, but the focus of the text is his treatment of the woman. Whereas verses 10–13 spell out the responsibilities of a warrior who takes a captive woman, verse 14 explicitly restricts his actions against this woman, should he later choose to divorce her.

The restrictions in verse 14 are directed toward the man's authority. The types of restrictions suggest that the potential for abuse in this situation stems from the woman's former status as a captive, and not his position as her husband.[40] This former warrior had at one time assumed a great deal of authority over this woman, and he may have presumed that his authority ought to continue even after he tired of her. The potential for abuse in this situation is magnified by the fact that, likely, this woman had no one protecting her outside of her husband's household. Yet upon divorce, this man's power to influence the social status of his former wife is terminated.

Furthermore, the restrictions suggest that the woman's status after divorce might be in question. The behavior forbidden in Deut 21:14 (influencing her decisions and selling or profiting from her in some way) might have been considered acceptable treatment of a foreign, captive woman. But 21:14 is clear: upon divorce, this woman is free.[41] Rights this man may have presumed are curtailed. His authority is terminated and the potential for further abuse is restrained. Once again this vulnerable woman finds an advocate in the text.

The specific restrictions are straightforward and stated both positively (she is free) and negatively (he is not to treat her as a commodity). Regarding her freedom from his authority, the phrase לנפשה 'according

---

send her freely, you must not sell her . . ." and (2) "If you do not delight in her and you send her freely, *then you must not sell her.* . . ." The confusion in 21:14 is more easily solved than in 21:10–13. According to the rules of Hebrew grammar, the second option is not grammatically valid because an infinitive absolute cannot take a *waw* of apodosis (Joüon, §176m). Although grammatically significant, this observation does little to affect the interpretation. Either way, the emphasis is on the manner of sending (freely, according to the will of the woman).

40. From the discussion of divorce in Deut 24:1–4, we learn that a husband of a free woman would not presume to tell her what to do once he divorced her (and selling her for profit would be unthinkable).

41. It is tempting to argue that she is free only in regard to this man's treatment of her, but presumably someone else could still treat her according to the prescriptions for war set forth in Deuteronomy 20. However, the text specifically states that she is to be sent "according to her wish/desire." This phrase is powerful in demonstrating that she alone may decide her next move. She is under no one's authority but her own. Nevertheless, although free, a woman in this situation still would have been extremely vulnerable. In an ideal situation a divorced Israelite woman would have been able to count on a certain level of support from her father's household (e.g., Lev 22:13), but this woman appears to have no one and nothing.

to her wish/desire' is unusual, but it simply means that after he divorces her she is free to make her own decisions. This construction also appears in Jer 34:16 to describe slaves who are freed from their servitude.[42] The comparison to the text in Jeremiah does not permit one to compare marriage to slavery, but confirms that the construction ל 'to' + נפש 'a soul' signifies a freedom to act according to one's own plan or desire without being forced to submit to the influence or authority of another.[43] In case there is any doubt, the phrase ושלחתה לנפשה 'according to her wish/desire' is strengthened and clarified by the following prohibition in which the man is emphatically commanded not to sell her or profit from her in any way.[44]

The final clause of Deut 21:14 explains why he may not take advantage of this woman for his own profit: תחת אשר עניתה 'because you degraded her'. The precise meaning of ענה 'to lower, debase' in contexts involving women deserves comment.[45] Traditionally scholars equate this term with rape or other illicit sexual behavior.[46] However, as van Wolde has demonstrated, ענה is an evaluative term denoting the social or juridical movement downward. The term ענה is not equated with

---

42. But in Jeremiah they later are subjected unjustly to slavery once again.

43. See A. D. H. Mayes, *Deuteronomy* (NCBC; Grand Rapids: Eerdmans, 1979) 303.

44. The instruction not to sell her is emphatic, as marked by the infinitive absolute: ומכר לא־תמכרנה 'you must not sell her'. The following verb (Hithpael of עמר) occurs only here and in Deut 24:7. Particularly noteworthy is the fact that in both contexts, this word is linked with מכר 'to sell'. Whether this is a reference to how a slave would be treated or is to be understood as having commercial significance, there appears to be economic significance involved. (For the first view, see G. Brin, *Studies in Biblical Law: From the Hebrew Bible to the Dead Sea Scrolls* [JSOTSup 176; Sheffield: JSOT 1994] 28 n. 17; for the second view, see M. David, "Hit'amēr (Deut. XXI 14; XXIV 7)," *VT* 1 [1951] 219–21; and A. Alt, "ZU HIT'AMMĒR," *VT* 2 [1952] 153.) This man is not to benefit from this woman in any way after their divorce. To do so would be an abuse of his authority.

45. The verb ענה occurs about eighty times in the Hebrew Bible. An exact count is difficult to determine because it is not always clear which root, 'to answer' or 'to be made low', is intended (e.g., Ps 55:20[19]). From these uses, it appears that the term has to do with exercising power or authority (properly or improperly) over something or someone else so as to lower it. Different means are used to inflict this "lowering" (e.g., fasting to humble the soul, loud noises in attempt to subdue a lion, sexual assault to degrade a woman), but the term ענה is evaluative and focuses on the results of that action rather than the action itself. The results are almost always painful or difficult to bear, even if the final outcome is positive (as in Ps 119:71).

46. See Pressler, *View of Women*, 15–16. Pressler understands ענה 'to degrade' in this passage as referring to legalizing what would otherwise be illicit behavior. Frymer-Kensky is alone in suggesting anything to the contrary. Ironically, she argues that the humiliation or mistreatment is the result of the warrior *not* having intercourse with her, but sending her away before the marriage is consummated (T. Frymer-Kensky, "Law and Philosophy: The Case of Sex in the Bible," *Semeia* 45 [1989] 100 n. 7).

rape or other sexual (mis-)conduct, but it is used to describe or evaluate the *outcome* of those actions,[47] actions that debase the woman, lowering her status such that it affects her social standing and/or her legal rights.[48] Furthermore, the general assumption that ענה in 21:14 must reflect sexual misconduct is somewhat surprising since this verb is used elsewhere in the OT to express the lowering or debasing of a woman in a manner that does not involve sexual activity.

In the OT, the Piel of ענה occurs nineteen times with a female object.[49] Of these, seven appear within a context that is clearly non-sexual.[50] Four of these occurrences, spanning two contexts, are particularly significant in that the subject is male and the object is female. In Exod 22:21–22[22–23] (2×) the subject of the Piel 2ms verb of ענה 'you degraded her' is the addressee—the adult Israelite male. He is not to degrade any widow or fatherless individual. This text refers to taking advantage of those who are most vulnerable in Israelite society and is not intended as a prohibition against sexual exploitation. Consequently, ענה can be used to depict a man degrading a woman (or child) apart from any sexual

---

47. When rape or other illicit sexual conduct is involved, these actions are signified by other words in context (see Gen 34:2 and 2 Sam 13:14 with שכב). See E. van Wolde, "Does ʿINNÂ Denote Rape?" *VT* 52 (2002) 541, where van Wolde analyses the word order in the usages of ענה with a female object, noting a pattern in the verbal sequence. Interestingly, Deut 21:10–14 is not included in this analysis.

48. Van Wolde, "Does ʿINNÂ Denote Rape?" 543–544. One element of van Wolde's study requires comment. After recognizing the spatial character of ענה (denoting movement downward), she observes that many of her thirteen selected texts appear in context with spatial language. As her first point of evidence she notes that "the verb ʿinnâ is often linked to the preposition *tahat*, 'under,'" and cites Gen 16:9, Deut 21:14, and 22:29 (p. 531). However, the presence of תחת, which she translates as "under," in Deut 21:14 does not support van Wolde's claim. In this verse, תחת is a preposition meaning 'in place of' or 'instead of' and denotes a logical, not spatial, relationship between the preceding prohibition and the subsequent imbedded clause (עניתה 'you degraded her'). Here תחת is followed by אשר (relative particle), which functions as a nominalizer, indicating that the following phrase (עניתה 'you degraded her') be understood as the object of the preposition תחת. Idiomatically, this construction may be translated "because" (logical), but not "under" (spatial) (contra van Wolde's treatment of Deut 21:14 at pp. 534–35). See *HALOT*, "תחת," 1721–23. This same grammatical construction appears in Deut 22:29, disqualifying the second of three texts upon which van Wolde builds this particular argument. However, van Wolde's conclusion that ענה is an evaluative term indicating a social movement downward is well supported without this linguistically unfounded claim. It finds support within the fundamental root of ענה and from context.

49. Gen 16:6, 9; 31:50; 34:2; Exod 22:21–22[22–23] (2×); Num 30:14[13]; Deut 21:14; 22:24, 29; Judg 19:24; 20:5; 2 Sam 13:12, 14, 22, 32; Ezek 22:10; Lam 5:11. Interestingly, van Wolde handles only thirteen of these, omitting Exod 22:21–22[22–23] (2×), Num 30:14, Ezek 22:10, and Lam 5:11.

50. Gen 16:6, 9; 31:50; Num 30:14[13]); cf. Exod 22:21–22[22–23] (2×). These seven occurrences span four contexts.

deed. Perhaps even more significant is the use of ענה in the narrative setting of Gen 31:50 in which Laban makes Jacob swear an oath that he will not degrade (ענה) Rachel and Leah. It is unlikely that Laban is worried about Jacob sleeping with his own wives. Laban is concerned that Jacob not act in a way that lowers the social or juridical standing of his daughters, Rachel and Leah, perhaps by taking other wives or possibly even through divorce.[51] Here we have a specific male, Jacob, with the ability to degrade his wives without acting out sexually against them.[52]

The fact that ענה can refer to the humbling or degrading of a woman without requiring that she be approached sexually is particularly helpful in Deut 21:14 where the assumption that the term must reflect sexual misconduct is not supported by the immediate context. Although an argument from silence, it ought to be noted that while one might assume that rape on the battlefield was a common occurrence, there is no mention of such activity in this text. The only reference to sexual conduct occurs within the context of a marriage situation and is a facet, not a focus, of the text.[53] Any discussion of sexual activity in the text and its social/juridical ramifications for the woman must be approached from the perspective of the marital context.

Having established that (1) ענה is an evaluative term denoting social or juridical lowering, (2) in the Hebrew Bible the use of ענה with a male subject and a female object is not constrained to the evaluation of sexual conduct, and (3) sexual conduct is not a viable referent for this term in this context, the question then becomes, to what activity is ענה referring in Deut 21:14? The passage as a whole focuses on four activities in which this woman has been involved: captivity, the so-called stipulations, marriage, and divorce. According to the text, by what means did this man degrade or socially lower this woman?

The first possible referent is captivity. The move from free woman to Israelite captive obviously involves a downward move in this woman's social status. However, according to the perspective of this text, the

---

51. The possibility that domestic or physical abuse is in view here is unlikely due to the parallel between ענה and the prohibition against taking other wives (Gen 31:50).

52. Van Wolde writes, "Laban is not referring to any physical abuse of his daughters, but is referring to very practical, legal-economic matters" ("Does 'INNÂ Denote Rape?" 534).

53. That sexual intercourse takes place is clear from the text, but the only explicit reference to sexual activity in this passage occurs within the context of marriage (for a list of references where בוא 'to go in' + אל 'to' signifies a sexual encounter, see *DCH*, 2:113). The social ramifications would relate to her becoming a wife, and the social change for this woman focuses on the marriage not the intercourse. Thus, neither sexual degradation nor loss of virginity is at issue here.

man's first direct involvement with this woman is when he "sees" her. She is already a captive at this point. Although he undoubtedly plays a role in her becoming a captive, his is an indirect role. In fact, it is God who is credited with handing the foreign nation over to the Israelites. Therefore, the text is not likely referring to captivity as the manner in which this man has degraded her.

The second possible cause of degradation is the enactment of the rituals. As discussed, there are four stipulations this woman was expected to carry out: shave her head, do her nails, discard her captive garments, and mourn for thirty days. It is easy to imagine that these activities would be degrading to this woman. The matter is complicated by our own difficulty in understanding the significance of two of the rituals, namely shaving the head and doing the nails. However, of the two whose significance is clear, one denotes a social movement away from captivity (removal of garments associated with captivity), and the second evidences a rare and culturally unexpected level of patience and respect (thirty-day mourning period).[54] The more elusive stipulations (shaving her head and doing her nails) probably also refer to either a mourning ritual or are symbolic of a cultural transfer. If these interpretations are correct, it is unlikely that the rituals signify the man's social degradation of this woman.

The third possible act of degradation based on the actions performed in this text is marriage. This option should be the easiest to dismiss. However, perceived offense and cultural differences between ancient and modern times sometimes cloud the obvious, namely that marriage would have been an advancement over captivity in terms of social status and juridical rights.[55] The assertion that marriage involved a social escalation should not be understood as implying that this woman was "one of the lucky ones" who should have been grateful or flattered by her new station. She may well have felt personally degraded. Yet, if she began as a captive, and the warrior brought her into his home as a wife, his actions did not lower but rather lifted her social standing within the Israelite community.

---

54. It is "unexpected" given her status as a captive. It is hard to imagine that any ancient Near Eastern culture placed a high priority on meeting the emotional needs of its captives.

55. Today's reader is offended at the man's presumed right to this beautiful, vulnerable woman. His taking her for marriage with no apparent thought to her wishes is easily interpreted as an obvious disregard for her personhood. This offense is only escalated when it finds its base in a culture that holds to the ideals of the Geneva Convention and further values the freedom of an individual to choose his or her own mate.

The final possible referent for the humiliation of this woman is the act of divorce. As indicated by the Hebrew term used to express the concept, divorce in Israel involved a sending forth of the wife from the household and a severing of the marital relationship. It is hard to imagine that divorce would have been any less painful or difficult at that time than now. The public humiliation implicit the term "unclean" in Deut 24:4 or a husband's slandering his bride and giving her a bad name in 22:14 both suggest that there may have been a strong stigma attached to divorce. More significant, however, are the concrete social ramifications of a woman's change in marital status from wife to divorcée. A divorced woman lost whatever protection and provision she gained through marriage.[56] She also lost whatever position of authority she would have held within her household. Hints in the OT suggest that, as a wife, she would have ruled alongside her husband in certain matters pertaining to running the household.[57] For example, many of the instructions concerning children in the book of Deuteronomy list the mother alongside the father, indicating that she was equally responsible (and accountable) for them.[58] Finally, she lost whatever influence her husband's social status might have afforded her as a member of his household. Divorce degraded an Israelite woman, lowering her social status and leaving her without the protection or position that would have been hers as a member of her husband's household.[59]

Divorce provides the most likely referent for ענה in Deut 21:14.[60] It is contextually relevant, provides a close antecedent, and involves an

---

56. A woman who lost the protection of a household either through divorce or the death of her husband was in a vulnerable situation. On the roles of a woman in ancient Israel, especially in relation to men, see P. A. Bird, *Missing Persons and Mistaken Identities: Women and Gender in Ancient Israel* (OBT; Minneapolis: Fortress Press, 1997), and Meyers, *Discovering Eve*. Akkadian texts from Emar in the Late Bronze Age explain how a divorced woman was to leave her husband's home without a stitch of clothing (naked). This gesture communicated not just shame but also a total lack of economic security. See J. Huehnergard, "Five Tablets from the Vicinity of Emar," *RA* 77 (1983) 17–24, 30; idem, "Biblical Notes on Some Akkadian Texts from Emar (Syria)," *CBQ* 47 (1985) 431–34.

57. Bird, *Missing Persons and Mistaken Identities*, 30, 57.

58. Deut 5:16; 21:10–14, 18–21; 22:13–19. The extent of a woman's authority may have varied greatly depending on a number of factors such as her position among other wives (e.g., Sarai and Hagar, Leah, Rachel, Bilhah, and Zilpah), her husband's affections, and the number of children she bore.

59. The social and legal vulnerability of an unmarried woman is well represented by the repeated reference to the plight of widows in the book of Deuteronomy (Deut 10:18, 14:29, 24:17–22, 27:19).

60. The implications of Deut 21:10–14 for our understanding of marriage and divorce are profound. Regarding marriage, it is remarkable that this union not only marked a shift in the captive woman's marital status (non-wife to wife), but that the marriage also

obvious example of an instance in which this man has exercised his authority against this woman in a way that degrades her socially. Other behavior enacted by the warrior was humiliating and perhaps even abusive according to modern standards. Yet the one behavior that negatively affected her social and legal standing within the community was divorce. So great is its offense that she is protected from further social degradation—especially that which the man might selfishly enact against her for his own benefit. Deut 24:14 protects the vulnerable woman by limiting the rights of the one who would presume to exercise authority over her once he has displayed a blatant disregard for her well-being.

4. Conclusion

Although wrought with challenging issues, Deut 21:10–14 reflects the beauty displayed when righteousness collides with a fallen world. The setting is raw and the characters real. The "stuff" of these verses mirrors the complexity of humanity and not an unattainable, idealized image. Extremes are merged—victory and defeat, celebration and suffering, power and vulnerability—such that they no longer can be clearly distinguished. The resulting complexity resembles real life. Therein lies the beauty of Deuteronomy. It is a divine word addressed to fallen people without fear of their brokenness.

The underlying concern of this text is how a man ought to exercise his right to marry and, should he so choose, later divorce a captive woman. Of the obvious offenses in Deuteronomy 21 and the text's response to such offenses, Christopher Wright comments,

> We might like to live in a world without wars and thus without prisoners of war. However, OT law recognizes such realities and seeks to mitigate their worst effects by protecting the victims as far as possible. If we ask whose power is being restricted, the answer, equally clearly, is the victorious soldier. The law is thus a paradigm case of the OT's concern to defend the weak against the strong, war being one of the most tragic human expressions of that situation.[61]

---

affected her disassociation with her captive status. As for divorce, its offense and detrimental social effects are evidenced by the fact that the same term ענה is used to evaluate it as is used elsewhere to evaluate rape.

61. Wright, *Deuteronomy*, 234. Wright does a commendable job of recognizing the driving focus of this text. His is not an in-depth study of the passage, but an evaluation of the passage in light of the rest of his work on Deuteronomy. This may explain why he concentrates heavily on the elements of war at the expense of the familial matters, which, although they are not initial, do appear to be primary in importance.

Wright recognizes that the driving theme of this text is the desire to protect the victim of war and that this goal is reached by curtailing the rights of the soldier.[62] His focus on the defense of the weak against the strong demonstrates recognition of the lopsided distribution of rights represented in this passage. However, it is not only in the context of war that this woman faces abuse, but also in the context of family, especially in the case of divorce.

Into this complex situation, Deuteronomy speaks words of regulation and restriction. Although addressed to the male, this text has as its primary focus the well-being of the woman. This study does not wish to deny the presence of male dominance or the captive woman's subservience, nor to imply that the text solves every problem this woman faces. It is precisely because of these issues that this text exists. What is amazing about this passage is that the text of Deuteronomy dares to encroach on the assumed rights of the HOH, holding back his authority and forcing him to consider the well-being of the one over whom he holds that authority. It does so by assigning rights to one who had no rights, and in doing so, curtailing the rights of the one whose authority theoretically would have had no bound. In short, Deuteronomy tackles a situation fully reflective of the fallen world and in which potential for abuse looms heavily.

Regarding the righteous response of a man who finds himself in this situation, Deut 21:10–13 emphasizes the warrior's responsibility to exercise his authority in a manner that promotes the well-being of this vulnerable woman. He is to consider the needs of the woman even as he acts out of his desires for her. He is to treat his vanquished bride not as a captive but as a wife. He is to acknowledge her humanity in her time of transition, to offer provision and protection in his own household, and to place her need to mourn above his own desires for her. As HOH he is to exercise his authority in a manner that demonstrates restraint, respect, and dignity (rather than humiliation)—even in a cultural situation in which he might feel entitled to added authority.[63]

---

62. In a similar vein, Pressler speaks of Deut 21:14 as defining the woman's legal status by limiting the man's actions (*View of Women*, 15): "The law clearly expresses a male dominated situation. It addresses the male. It assumes that the male is the primary actor: he desires and takes, he no longer desires and sends out. While it defines the woman's legal status (she may not be sold), it does so by limiting the man's actions. The captive bride is clearly subordinate, but she is nonetheless viewed as a person with clearly defined rights ... rather than as chattel."

63. If these principles are carried to their logical conclusion, this man, who has the potential to cause this woman unmentionable harm, has the capacity to be a tremendous

Furthermore, Deut 21:14 speaks restraint to his authority should he demonstrate an abuse of his power by degrading her socially. The text does not protect the woman from the social degradation of divorce, but it curtails the rights of her husband in that process by freeing her from his control. According to the rationale given in the text ("because you degraded her"), when he fails to consider her well-being above his own and demonstrates an abuse of his power by acting in a way that socially degrades her, his authority over her is terminated.[64]

According to Deut 21:10–14, the HOH is to reflect righteousness in Israel by embodying servant leadership. When he fails to do so and acts in a way that degrades her, the text steps in to protect her from further abuse.[65]

---

blessing to this woman. He can offer her provision, protection, position, relationship, and a religion with lasting ramifications.

64. Further study suggests that the same principle applies in the case of the slandered bride (Deut 22:13–21) and the woman who is not allowed to remarry her former husband (24:1–4). See Josberger, *Between Right and Responsibility*, 112–36, 136–72.

65. Implicit in this text is a charge to the community to support the family (by ensuring the stipulations are carried out) and to safeguard the vulnerable should the HOH act against her.

Deuteronomy's Theology of Exile

KENNETH J. TURNER

The Babylonian exile of the sixth century B.C.E. was a watershed in the life and faith of Israel. Its historical, political, and theological realities demanded a reconsideration of what it meant to be the "people of God." Scholars generally agree that the experience and aftermath of this crisis provided a context for the production of "fresh theological literature."[1] For all successive Jewish faith, exile would become a major paradigm for self-understanding, and a theological construct for interpreting life and anticipating the future. Even in a "postexilic" setting, exile can be considered as an ongoing, unresolved experience.[2]

When read in a canonical context, the notion of exile arises long before the historical experience of the nation in the sixth century.[3] Exile underlies many other biblical accounts: Adam and Eve's banishment from the garden of Eden; Cain's wandering through the land of Nod; Abraham's journey to the land of Canaan; Jacob's flight from his homeland; Joseph's

---

Author's Note: Dan Block and I spent the same ten years at Southern Seminary. His impact on my life is inestimable. His teaching and scholarship are only outmatched by his commitment to the gospel, the church, his family, and his students. No one models better what it means to be a Christian scholar. Though I am extremely thankful for his academic training and supervision, he has meant far more to me as a mentor, pastor, and brother in Christ.

1. See W. Brueggemann, "A Shattered Transcendence? Exile and Restoration," in *Biblical Theology: Problems and Perspectives: In Honor of J. Christiaan Beker* (ed. S. J. Kraftchick et al.; Nashville: Abingdon, 1995) 169–82.

2. See Ezra 9:6–15, Neh 9:36–37, Daniel 9. This irony of a "postexilic exile" continues beyond the Hebrew canon; see the relevant essays in J. M. Scott, ed., *Exile: Old Testament, Jewish and Christian Conceptions* (JSJSup 56; Leiden: Brill, 1997); and idem, *Restoration: Old Testament, Jewish and Christian Conceptions* (JSJSup 72; Leiden: Brill, 2001). N. T. Wright has created a lively debate in NT studies with his claim that part of Jesus' mission was to bring about the end of Israel's "exile" (see section 3.5 and references [esp. in n. 86] at the end of this essay.

3. On exile as the theme of the "metanarrative" of the Hebrew Bible, see T. R. Hatina, "Exile," in *Dictionary of New Testament Background* (ed. C. A. Evans and S. E. Porter; Downers Grove, IL: InterVarsity, 2000) 348; R. P. Carroll, "Exile! What Exile? Deportation and the Discourse of Diaspora," in *Leading Captivity Captive: 'The Exile' as History and Ideology* (ed. L. L. Grabbe; JSOTSup 278; Sheffield: Sheffield Academic, 1998) 63; idem, "Deportation and Diasporic Discourses in the Prophetic Literature," in *Exile: Old Testament, Jewish, and Christian Conceptions*, 64.

deportation to Egypt; Moses' wandering in the wilderness; David's escape from Saul; and Assyria's deportation of the Northern Kingdom. The major theological contours of the nation's exile and restoration are first developed, however, in Deuteronomy. The notion of exile arises in covenantal contexts as a threat to Israel if she persists in idolatrous worship (Deut 4:25–28), and serves as the climax of the covenant curses (28:15–68). Both of these texts are followed by the possibility of restoration (4:29–31, 30:1–10). Thus, even before the Israelites enter the land of promise, Moses predicts its loss and repossession.

This essay explores Deuteronomy's understanding of exile, which is a prominent though often under-appreciated theme in the book and which, when overlooked, impedes a proper grasp of both Deuteronomic theology and the theology of exile through the Bible.[4] Though exile is explicit in a few texts, it casts a shadow over the whole book.[5] While the book speaks of a potential historical experience in the nation's future, "exile" is also a dynamic theological concept. In short, exile represents the death of Israel. In losing her land, Israel apparently also loses her identity, history, and covenant relationship with Yahweh. Restoration from exile, then, is a resurrection from death to life. Since exile is a recurring theme in Deuteronomy, the theology of the book must be considered in light of its vision of exile and restoration. These themes will be traced through a study of the book's vocabulary for exile, including connections between exile and earlier stages in Israel's journey, and the relationship of exile to broader topics in the theology of Deuteronomy.

1. Death Language:
The Vocabulary of Exile in Deuteronomy

The theological connection between exile and death is not new.[6] In Deuteronomy, this connection begins with its distinctive choice of vocabulary for exile.[7] Surprisingly, Deuteronomy employs a rather lim-

---

4. This essay is a synthesis of my book, *The Death of Deaths in the Death of Israel: Deuteronomy's Theology of Exile* (Eugene, OR: Wipf & Stock, 2011). Some parts are direct extracts from the previous work; others are revisions or additions—all used by permission of Wipf and Stock Publishers (www.wipfandstock.com).

5. McConville makes this point for both Deuteronomy and the Deuteronomistic History in "Restoration in Deuteronomy and the Deuteronomic Literature," in *Restoration: Old Testament, Jewish, and Christian Conceptions*, 12–15.

6. Note, for example, the reference to exile and restoration in the subtitle of D. E. Gowan, *Theology of the Prophetic Books: The Death and Resurrection of Israel* (Louisville: Westminster John Knox, 1998).

7. For the full discussion and references, see Turner, "The Vocabulary of Exile," *Death of Deaths*, ch. 2 (pp. 33–76).

ited use of the normal OT vocabulary. The primary roots, גלה 'go into exile' and שבה 'take captive', are all but absent. The sense of גלה as 'exile' is never employed, and only one of six references to שבה refers to the captivity of Israelites (Deut 28:41). Secondary or parallel terms for exile appear occasionally (27 times),[8] but their application to exile is selective; the clearest examples are נדח 'go through, flee' (Deut 30:1; cf. v. 4), נהג 'drive' (4:27, 28:37), and פוץ 'be dispersed, scattered' (4:27, 28:64, 30:3). Thus, with the exception of a substantive use of שבה and a few secondary terms, whatever Deuteronomy has to say about exile it does so without reference to the normal terminology for the topic.

How else does Deuteronomy speak of exile? The most obvious statements of exile are revealing—namely, the programmatic statement in chapter 4 and part of the curse list in chapter 28:

- Deut 4:25–28. When you father children and children's children, and have grown old in the land, if you act corruptly by making a carved image in the form of anything, and by doing what is evil in the sight of Yahweh your God, so as to provoke him to anger, I call heaven and earth to witness against you today, that you will soon utterly perish (תאבדון אבד) from the land that you are going over the Jordan to possess. You will not live long in it, but will be utterly destroyed (תשמדון השמד). And Yahweh will scatter (פוץ) you among the peoples, and you will be left few in number among the nations where Yahweh will drive (נהג) you. And there you will serve gods of wood and stone, the work of human hands, that neither see, nor hear, nor eat, nor smell.
- Deut 28:61–64. Every sickness also and every affliction that is not recorded in the book of this law, Yahweh will bring upon you, until you are destroyed (השמדך). Whereas you were as numerous as the stars of heaven, you shall be left few in number, because you did not obey the voice of Yahweh your God. And as Yahweh took delight in doing you good and multiplying you, so Yahweh will take delight in bringing ruin (להאביד) upon you and destroying (ולשמיד) you. And you shall be plucked off the land that you are entering to take possession of it. And Yahweh will

---

8. According to lexicons, there are eleven secondary terms: ברח 'go through, flee', דבר 'turn, drive away, subjugate', זרה 'scatter, fan, winnow', טול 'hurl, cast', נדד 'retreat, flee, depart, wander', נדח 'impel, thrust, banish', נהג 'drive', נתץ 'pull down, break down', פוץ 'be dispersed, scattered', רדף 'pursue, chase, persecute', and רחק 'be far'. For full discussion and references, see Turner, *The Death of Deaths in the Death of Israel*, 38–46. Six of these eleven appear in Deuteronomy: נדח (4:19; 13:6, 11, 14; 19:5; 20:19; 22:1; 30:1, 4, 17); נהג (4:27, 28:37); נתץ (7:5, 12:3); פוץ (4:27, 28:64, 30:3); רדף (1:44; 11:4; 16:20; 19:6; 28:22, 45; 32:30); and רחק (12:21, 14:24, 30:11).

scatter (פוץ) you among all peoples, from one end of the earth to the other, and there you shall serve other gods of wood and stone, which neither you nor your fathers have known.

Other than the uses of פוץ and נהג, noted above, the concept of exile is driven here by two nearly synonymous terms of destruction and annihilation: אבד and שמד.⁹ An examination of their usage in the OT shows some variety, especially with אבד, but a strong focus is on the destruction or annihilation of groups of persons. This presents a clear tension, requiring careful reflection on what Deuteronomy is doing by equating exile with "destruction."

The overall Deuteronomic usage of אבד and שמד is not restricted to exile.¹⁰ These terms arise in contexts reflecting on covenant relationship in general and various stages of Israel's "journey" in particular.¹¹ Many of these references clearly exhibit the typical connotation of absolute destruction—especially in contexts describing the exodus, Horeb, and the wilderness experience.¹² For example, due to the golden calf incident,

---

9. The long list of covenant curses in Deut 28:15–68 employs אבד and שמד a total of eleven times. Besides vv. 61–64, note two other clusters: "Yahweh will send on you curses, confusion, and frustration in all that you undertake to do, until you are destroyed and perish (עד השמדך ועד־אבדך) quickly on account of the evil of your deeds, because you have forsaken me.... They [diseases, etc.] shall pursue you until you perish (עד אבדך).... From heaven dust shall come down on you until you are destroyed (עד השמדך)" (vv. 20–24); "All these curses shall come upon you and pursue you and overtake you till you are destroyed (עד השמדך), because you did not obey the voice of Yahweh your God.... They shall be a sign and a wonder against you and your offspring forever.... And he will put a yoke of iron on your neck until he has destroyed (עד השמידו) you. Yahweh will bring a nation against you from far away.... It shall eat the offspring of your cattle and the fruit of your ground, until you are destroyed (עד השמדך); it also shall not leave you grain, wine, or oil, the increase of your herds or the young of your flock, until they have caused you to perish (עד האבידו אתך)" (vv. 45–51). Exile is mentioned for the first time explicitly in the curse list in vv. 36–44, using more conventional language: "Yahweh will bring you (יולך) and your king whom you set over you to a nation that neither you nor your fathers have known. And there you shall serve other gods of wood and stone. And you shall become a horror, a proverb, and a byword among all the peoples where Yahweh will lead you (ינהגך) away" (vv. 36–37); "You shall father sons and daughters, but they shall not be yours, for they shall go into captivity (בשבי ילכו)" (v. 41).

10. In Deuteronomy, there are 15 occurrences of אבד and 28 occurrences of שמד. See Turner, *The Death of Deaths in the Death of Israel*, 47–61 (especially Tables 2 and 3 on pp. 48–50).

11. Ibid., 52–61, provides the full discussion of the use of אבד and שמד in each of the stages in Israel's journey (the focus on Israel's "journey" is drawn from J. G. McConville and J. G. Millar, *Time and Place in Deuteronomy* (JSOTSup 179; Sheffield: Sheffield Academic, 1994).

12. The exodus is depicted as Yahweh's destruction of the Egyptians (ויאבדם, Deut 11:4). The verb שמד occurs multiple times in Moses' recalling of the golden calf incident at Horeb (9:6–21) and in passages describing the wilderness period overall (chs. 1–3;

Yahweh exclaims to Moses, "Let me alone, that I may destroy them (ואשמידם) and blot out their name from under heaven. And I will make of you a nation mightier and greater than they" (Deut 9:14). Also, due to Israel's relentless recalcitrance at various wilderness sites (9:22–23), Moses boldly intercedes, "because Yahweh had said he would destroy (להשמיד) you" (9:25)—using the synonym שחת 'corrupt, ruin, destroy' (9:26) and describing the result of the action as "putting to death" (9:28).

Descriptions of the conquest and future life in the land, however, are less consistent concerning the "destruction" connoted by אבד and שמד. On the one hand, parallel language suggests annihilation. The call to conquest involves "devoting them to the ban (חרם)" and "showing no mercy" (Deut 7:2), "making their name perish (והאבדת)" from under heaven" (7:24), and "making them perish (והאבדתם) quickly" (9:3). Once in the land, Israel is warned that covenant infidelity would result in receiving the same fate as the nations (e.g., 6:14–15; 7:4, 26; 8:19–20; 11:16–17; 30:17–18).

On the other hand, at times the language of absoluteness is tempered. For example, the "destruction" of the nations will not be punctiliar; rather, God will clear them away "little by little," and Israel "may not make an end of them at once" (Deut 7:22). Moreover, Israel's threatened "destruction" comes with certain qualifying phrases: Israel will perish "off the good land" (11:17); she will not live long "in the land" (30:18). The emphasis here on the covenantal relationship between the people and the land opens up interpretive possibilities. Specifically, Israel is said to "perish/be destroyed" when there is a rupture in the people–land bond, which is central to the concept of exile. Since the terms אבד and שמד are used with respect to exile elsewhere, it is possible that exile is suggested in early stages of Israel's journey.

Given the shared vocabulary (אבד and שמד) between Israel's exile and other important historical moments and periods, exile cannot be viewed in isolation from the past, but as the end of the nation's journey. This yields a sense of continuity, which must balance the sense of discontinuity discussed above. Exile involves a reversal—a reversal of history, a reversal of promise. These points demand that we pay

---

9:22–24). In each case Yahweh is the agent of the (potential) destruction of his people (לה שמיד in 1:27; 9:18, 19, 20, 25; ואשמידם in 9:14; cf. Yahweh's "destroying" [Hiphil שמד] idolaters of the second wilderness generation in 4:3). The worship of the golden calf is viewed as the paradigmatic sin for Israel through the wilderness: "Remember and do not forget how you provoked Yahweh your God to wrath *in the wilderness*. From the day you came out of the land of Egypt until you came to this place, you have been rebellious against Yahweh. *Even at Horeb* . . ." (Deut 9:7–8a).

close attention to the details of, and connections among, various texts. Though space does not allow this full investigation here, it is important to set the primary and secondary references within their broader, shared literary and theological contexts.[13]

Still, we ought to sense a fundamental tension between the basic meaning of אבד and שמד and the notion of exile, and then consider the theological implications. These terms are words of extermination—"perish," "destroy," "annihilate," and the like. This "no-survivor" thought world is clearly different from that of exile, which, by definition, necessitates survival (however unpleasant it might be). On the one hand, it is no surprise to find devastation and loss associated with the experience of exile; corporate land loss and deportation inevitably involves the destruction of homes and businesses, the breakdown of political and religious institutions, and even the death of individuals. On the other hand, more seems to be going on in the text; the presence of אבד and שמד in the contexts of exile cannot be explained simply as colorful commentary on the processes of invasion and deportation. The people will continue to exist physically in exile; yet, as a single entity, Israel is said to "perish" and "be destroyed." So, it is not Israel as an historical or socio-religious people, but Israel as Yahweh's elect son and servant (Deut 1:31, 7:6, 14:1) that is put to death. Exile constitutes the death of Israel as a nation in covenant—a covenant comprised of a dynamic relationship between Yahweh, the nation, and the land. Whatever existence continues, it is discontinuous with the past.

2. Exile as a Theological Concept

2.1. What is Exile?

Simply defined, exile involves removal of a population from its homeland. On the brink of Israel entering the land promised to her, Moses repeatedly raises the topic of exile in the midst of exhorting her to fidelity in her unique covenant relationship with Yahweh. As we have seen, however, exile in Deuteronomy is more than an historical event; it is a theological concept that signifies Israel's death. However, lest one draw the wrong inference, it is crucial to realize that the equation of exile with death is theological rhetoric and hyperbole. I am *not* suggesting that exile constitutes complete dissolution of the covenantal relationship between Yahweh and Israel as an *historical actuality*. Such a lit-

---

13. For this more detailed treatment, see Turner, *The Death of Deaths in the Death of Israel*, 77–223 (chs. 3–4), which examine the themes of exile and restoration in the specific texts themselves and the location of these texts within the structure of the book.

eral reading would contradict the patriarchal promises, which ground the promise of restoration beyond exile (e.g., Deut 4:29–31). Rather, the *rhetoric* of death allows for a proper theological understanding of the *reality* of exile and, especially, of restoration.

Three general observations are in order. First, exile is threatened as a consequence of infidelity (e.g., Deut 4:25–28, 28:58–68). If Israel proves unfaithful, she will incur the curses of the covenant. The fact that exile is the final or ultimate curse (ch. 28) suggests that it is a consequence of prolonged and wholesale disobedience. In Deuteronomy, sin can be judged and dealt with in ways that fall short of exile. Specific laws prescribe the administration of justice for crimes performed by individuals or groups. Even the nation as a whole may go wayward at times, but it can be restored through repentance and a return to following the covenant. Therefore, exile assumes that Israel would have continually rejected many opportunities to repent and continue her relationship with Yahweh. Thus, exile is the result, not of a violation here or there, but of complete abandonment of the covenant itself (29:24[25]) and total rejection of Yahweh's commands (e.g., 28:15, 58). Specifically, exile is the result of idolatry (4:25), a violation of the First and Second Commandments, because idolatry is the symbol of wholesale rejection of Yahweh (28:20).

Exile thus constitutes a rupture of the covenant triangle involving Yahweh, Israel, and the land. A rift in the Yahweh–Israel connection (via idolatry) results in a breach of the Israel–Land connection (via exile).[14] Certain aspects of the portrayal of exile in Deuteronomy might *suggest* (note the rhetoric) that this brokenness is permanent. Israel will "surely perish" and be "utterly destroyed" (Deut 4:26; cf. 28:63). Her exile entails the reversal of covenant history—an anti-exodus return to Egypt (28:68). In exile, Israel will be forced to perpetuate her crime of worshiping other gods (4:28, 28:64). Thus, the catalyst becomes the consequence; what got them there will keep them there.

Without understanding this rhetoric of the finality of Israel's broken relationship with Yahweh—that Israel is dead to Yahweh—we will not fully grasp the force and meaning of restoration from exile. If restoration is to come, it must involve more than a healing of wounds and

---

14. Cf. the statement by S. Talmon, "'Exile' and 'Restoration' in the Conceptual World of Ancient Judaism," in *Restoration: Old Testament, Jewish, and Christian Conceptions*, 111: "Exilation not only disrupts the unity of family and community, and tears apart the bond of the deported with their land, it also dissolves the solidarity of Yhwh and his people." It must be emphasized, however, that the dissolution is the cause of the exile rather than a mere result of it.

settling of grievances; it must involve some kind of "new" covenant relationship. Also, the restoration can in no way be something that is due Israel.

A second basic conclusion concerning exile in Deuteronomy is that exile is predicted as an eventual fact in Israel's future. The major texts on exile strongly suggest this inevitability, such as with the כי clause in 4:25 and the overall tone of 28:45–68.[15] By the end of the book, however, the inevitability of exile is beyond doubt. It is impossible to read the assumption of Israel's demise in a purely conditional sense in the promise of restoration (30:1–10) and the Song of Moses (ch. 32). How do we account for the juxtaposition of the "conditionality" (*if*) and "unconditionality" (*when*) of exile? A simple answer would be that the threat of exile serves as a negative motivation for obedience for each generation still in the land, but that some future generation will indeed fail and go into exile. Given the sense of corporate solidarity, however, this bifurcation is not completely satisfactory. The failure of a future generation indicates the failure of "all Israel." We will return to this tension in the next section.

For the present discussion, the more pressing question is, why the certainty of exile? The primary basis of this certainty is knowledge of Israel's corrupt nature and heart (e.g., Deut 9:6, 12:8, 29:3, 31:18–21; cf. 5:29). Israel *will* not because she *can*not (i.e., be faithful). Therefore, exile—Israel's death—is the exposure and inevitable result of a deadness that already exists internally. Israel is untrustworthy (5:29), stubborn (9:6, 13; 31:27), rebellious (9:7, 24; 31:27), corrupt (9:12, 31:29), untamed (12:8), prone to idolatry (31:16–21), and her heart is uncircumcised (10:16) and without understanding (29:3[4]). These descriptions make clear that Israel's restoration, if it is to come, must begin with a new disposition and ability to heed Yahweh.

A third basic conclusion about exile in Deuteronomy is that Yahweh himself will send Israel into exile. This is a logical consequence of the covenant-focused reasons for exile given above. Given the treaty parallels, Yahweh as the suzerain exacts punishment on the rebel vassal.[16] Yahweh's direct role is also explicit in the text. Repeatedly, his personal involvement is heightened by descriptions of his anger being provoked prior to the actual punishment of exile (e.g., Deut 4:25,

---

15. See the discussion of the כי clauses in Deut 4:25 and 30:1 in Turner, *The Death of Deaths in the Death of Israel*, 113–16, 171–72.

16. In the ANE treaties, the suzerain often appealed to the gods to exact this punishment. But, of course, there is no higher authority to which can be appealed in the case of Yahweh.

29:22–26[23–27]; cf. 28:63). The description of exile in 4:26–27 does not even mention mediate agents; the only explicit agent is Yahweh himself. Even in chapter 28, which mentions the destruction brought on by foreign peoples (vv. 25, 33, 48–53), these are expressly brought to Israel by Yahweh (vv. 48, 49). In the main paragraph on exile (28:58–68), Yahweh again is the sole agent of Israel's affliction (vv. 59–61), destruction (vv. 62–63a), removal from the land to other places (vv. 63b–64), psychological trauma (vv. 65–67), and return to Egypt (v. 68). Far from the expected implication that Israel fell because of the impotence of her god (cf. 9:28), the foreigner will interpret the actions of Yahweh rightly (29:21–27[22–28]). Exile displays Israel's death, but Yahweh is very much alive.

The combination of the last two observations—the inevitability of exile and Yahweh's sovereign superintendence—implies that exile is part of a larger divine plan (cf. Deut 29:28[29]).[17] This is not the place to venture into the theological and philosophical conundrum of reconciling divine sovereignty with human freedom, but in Deuteronomy, what Yahweh wants of Israel is something only Yahweh can give, even as he chooses not to—at least not (on a national scale) before exile. In light of this, Yahweh's longing for Israel to have a heart of fear and obedience (5:29) is set against the reality that Yahweh has not given her "a heart to understand or eyes to see or ears to hear" (29:3[4]). Also, while the circumcision of Israel's heart is commanded (10:16), it will only happen by a work of (postexilic) grace (30:6). The latter point can be extended to all the commandments, summed up in the call to love Yahweh with complete heart and soul (6:5; cf. 30:6). Developing this larger divine plan would necessitate placing Deuteronomy within the larger story (for the Christian, this would include the NT), but the Deuteronomic vision of exile and restoration helps set the stage. It begins with the declaration, "See now that I, I am he, / And there is no god besides me; / I kill and I make alive" (32:39).

2.2. Exile as a Framework for Restoration

A major rationale for Deuteronomy's focus on exile as death is to provide the theological framework in which to interpret restoration from exile. The observations above have already advanced the discussion on the topic of restoration, but it is worth summarizing the Deuteronomic vision in a more straightforward manner. In Deuteronomy, restoration from exile is both possible and predicted (Deut 4:29–31,

---

17. Cf. McConville, "Restoration in Deuteronomy," 14.

30:1–10). This restoration will involve both a return to Yahweh and a return to the land. The order of events in the process is sharply debated[18] but is extremely important theologically. It appears to me, at least, that the process involves the following succession of events, which reflect various uses of שׁוב: (1) a preliminary "turn" of the heart in exile (i.e., conviction) due to Yahweh's foundational mercy (4:30–31, 30:1a); (2) a spiritual "return" to Yahweh with a desire to obey his voice (i.e., repentance) (4:29–30, 30:1b–2); (3) a return to the land by the power of Yahweh (30:3–5); and (4) a "return" to obeying all the commandments, enabled by the divine circumcision of the heart (4:30; 30:6, 8).

The identification of conviction as the initial step in the process of restoration is most telling for my understanding. I take the temporal phrases in Deut 4:30 ("[when] all these words [or 'things'] find you") and 30:1 ("When all these words [or 'things'] come upon you") to indicate an initial work of divine grace upon Israel's heart that allows her to recognize her desperate condition and desire to seek Yahweh and be obedient. When this occurs, Yahweh will bring Israel back to the land and circumcise her heart, allowing for unending covenant faithfulness. In this reading, Israel's repentance is prompted by divine revelation and activity; the first action is not something that Israel does, but one that is done to her.[19]

When considering Moses' preaching solely from the angle of motivation for obedience, in which exile is a threat for persistent disobedience, the announcement of future restoration appears illogical and unwarranted.[20] But the other conclusions of exile above must be kept in mind.

---

18. See the discussion on Deut 30:1–10 in Turner, *The Death of Deaths in the Death of Israel*, 165–77.

19. In 30:1, Israel's first action is not an "action" at all, but a "taking to heart" the things that have been revealed. My ordering of these events allows a more satisfactory explanation than either of the two competing options that are more popular on "the relationship between Yahweh's decision to restore Israel and Israel's willingness to repent and be redeemed" (J. G. McConville, *Deuteronomy* [Apollos Old Testament Commentary 5; Downers Grove, IL: InterVaristy, 2002] 423–24). The first option takes repentance as the initial step in restoration; thus, Yahweh's return to Israel in relationship and Israel's circumcision of heart and return to the land are predicated upon her return to Yahweh. While I agree that Israel's repentance precedes the circumcision of her heart, the view that Israel's repentance is the initial step in restoration runs counter to at least three other conclusions: the condition of Israel's heart prior to any divine work of grace; the inevitability of restoration; and the fact that restoration is explicitly based on Yahweh's promise to the patriarchs (Deut 4:31). The second alternative considers the divine circumcision of the heart to precede Israel's repentance and return to the land. While this view is correct in that it maintains divine priority, it forces an improbable interpretation of the structure of 30:1–10.

20. Thus, the common assumption that the predictions of restoration (Deut 4:29–31, 30:1–10) are later interpolations; e.g., J. H. Tigay, "Excursus 5: The Promises of

The inevitability of exile is predicated upon a problem with Israel's heart. This is why the centerpiece of restoration is the circumcision of the heart (Deut 30:6). Thus, in being restored, Israel is also changed, ensuring that her future life in the land will be one of continual obedience and fidelity to Yahweh and the covenant. The sovereign work of Yahweh in restoring Israel answers to his direct and ultimate agency in Israel's exile. Since the restoration is based on Yahweh's promise to the patriarchs (e.g., 4:31), in the end, Israel's entire history is viewed as under the complete control of Yahweh.

If exile is death, then restoration is resurrection—a return to life from death. This new life is altogether *new*. In other words, the hope is not simply for a *restitutio in integrum*—a return to how things were.[21] Were this the case, Israel would be doomed to fail again. Rather, the resurrected life involves an anthropological transformation (i.e., heart circumcision) that will guarantee obedience for every generation henceforth (note "and the heart of your offspring" in 30:6). Therefore, the newness of the "new covenant" relationship is not so much in the demands of the covenant (see the discussion on covenant below) as much as the ability and willingness of Israel to keep them.

3. Exile and the Theology of Deuteronomy

Since exile is such a pervasive theme in Deuteronomy, it naturally interacts with other themes in the book. As McConville notes, "Deuteronomy's exilic vision is in line with its primary theology."[22] Deuteronomic

---

Reinstatement (4:29–31 and 30:1–10)," in *Deuteronomy* (Jewish Publication Society Torah Commentary 5; Philadelphia: The Jewish Publication Society, 1996) 432. For a similar view with respect to the promise of restoration in Amos see R. P. Carroll, "Deportation and Diasporic Discourses in the Prophetic Literature," in *Exile: Old Testament, Jewish, and Christian Conceptions*, 69: "Thus the ending of the book of Amos (9:13–15) effectively reverses the force of most of the contents of the scroll. . . ."

21. McConville ("Restoration in Deuteronomy," 39–40) calls this restoration "eschatological" because "it refuses to be bound to any one realization of its vision, and lives with an unresolved tension between the real and ideal." Carroll ("Deportation and Diasporic Discourses," 68) assumes that the idiom שוב שבות 'restore the fortunes' is a conventional phrase in the prophetic scrolls that "tends to indicate a notion of the restoration of things to how they were in the past." While this may be the case elsewhere, the conventional sense does not fit the use of the idiom in Deut 30:3. This misunderstanding of the Deuteronomic vision is apparent, for example, in M. C. Pate et al., *The Story of Israel: A Biblical Theology* (Downers Grove, IL: InterVarsity, 2004) 96: "The prophets, however, do not proclaim a restoration after the destructive exile that simply returns to the old Deuteronomic status quo." Surely, Deuteronomy 30 envisions something greater than the "status quo"!

22. McConville, "Restoration in Deuteronomy," 31. McConville's statement comes in the midst of an argument against the view that the exile theme in Deuteronomy is "merely a reflex based on the defeat of its first hopes" (ibid.).

theological themes—even apart from their relationship to exile—often involve complexities and dialectics well known in Deuteronomic (and OT) studies. Therefore, as we focus on five specific themes, the subheadings below are labeled "problems." The purpose of this section is to highlight the tensions and see how the theme of exile interacts with them. In some instances, appreciation of exile may aid in resolving certain debates. In other instances, an understanding of exile will intensify the perceived tensions.

3.1. The "Problem" of History

Despite the future orientation of Moses' speeches in Deuteronomy, he draws heavily on the past experiences of the nation. The issues of history interrelate with the other theological concerns in this section, but the primary tension that concerns us here involves the continuities and discontinuities between various Israelite generations. As such, it is an issue of the identity of "Israel." Though generations are sharply distinguished at times,[23] Deuteronomy usually considers Israel to be a singular identity that transcends the generations. She is on a journey that began with the patriarchs and, following a long stint in Egypt, has continued over several rough and windy roads in the desert. On the brink of the land, Moses calls Israel to continue her journey into the land.[24] In two senses, however, entry into the land does not mark the final stopping point. First, in a metaphorical sense, true rest in the land involves an ongoing "journey" of faith in and dependence upon Yahweh. A faithful Israel is a nation that is always "on the move." Second, in a more literal sense, Moses predicts that Israel's initial possession of the land is not the final stage in her journey. In the future, Israel will be exiled into a foreign land—an anti-exodus trek that constitutes a reversal of Israel's history. In the end, however, Israel will return to the land and remain there forever.

The conflation of generations is most notable in Moses' use of anachronistic address. He identifies the present generation at Moab with the people who experienced events in the past, including election (Deut 7:7;

---

23. E.g., Deut 2:16, 11:2; cf. 5:3, though the rhetoric of the text actually emphasizes solidarity rather than distinction (see below).

24. The journey motif is expounded most fully in McConville and Millar, *Time and Place*. Concerning corporate solidarity and the promise of land, P. D. Miller ("The Gift of God: The Deuteronomic Theology of the Land," *Int* 23 [1969] 454) states, "The land is given 'to them' or 'to you' or 'to us.' Deuteronomy can say that Yahweh swore to give it to our fathers or Yahweh swore to our fathers to give it to *us*. There is no real distinction. The promise to the fathers was a promise to us. The gift to the fathers was a gift to us. The recipients coalesce."

cf. 32:6), suffering in Egypt (6:21, 26:6–7, 29:16; cf. 10:19), the exodus,[25] Horeb,[26] and various stages in the wilderness.[27] The rhetoric is most pronounced in Moses' claim that it was "with us" and "not with our fathers" that Yahweh made a covenant at Horeb (5:2–3).[28] Also, Moses description of events in Israel's distant future takes the same form. The "you" that Moses addresses is the "you" that will go into exile (4:25–28, 28:58–68; cf. 31:16–21, 29) as well as be restored (4:29–31, 30:1–10).[29]

Several reasons may account for this stance. Positively, the oneness of Israel allows Yahweh to be faithful to his promise to the patriarchs, in which he swore to give them the land.[30] The "fathers" did not see the fulfillment in their own day, but they would receive it, in effect, when their descendants finally possessed the land. Conversely, each succeeding generation can find hope in Yahweh's past pledge (see Deut 6:20–23). Ideally, Israel would see her possession of the land as an unmerited gift based on an ancient promise (see 9:4–5). However, the possibility exists that a given generation would claim an unwarranted, absolute entitlement to the land based on its solidarity with the patriarchs (see Ezek 33:24). This danger is offset by the emphasis on the conditionality of the patriarchal covenant (see below on the "problem" of covenant).

Another positive purpose of stressing continuity is to show that the covenant renewal at Moab is a sign of Yahweh's continued allegiance to Israel. Yahweh has effectively forgiven the sins of the wilderness generation, so the present (and each succeeding) generation's relationship with Yahweh is on the same basis as the past. This provides hope for continual renewals in the land.[31] This is the point of the never-ending "today" of faithful response to the covenant.

---

25. Throughout Deuteronomy, the present generation is assumed to be part of the group Yahweh brought out of Egypt. See 4:20; 6:22–23; 7:8, 19; 8:14; 9:7; 11:3–4; 13:4[5], 9[10]; 15:15; 16:1, 3, 6, 12; 17:16; 20:1; 23:4; 24:9, 18, 22; 25:17; 26:8; 29:1[2]. Cf. 34:12.

26. Cf. 1:6, 9–18; 4:10–14, 23, 34–36; 5:2–33; 9:8–19; 10:10; 33:2.

27. The wilderness period that "you" or "we" experienced (anachronistically) includes more general overviews (2:15; 8:2–4, 15–16; 9:7; 29:4–5[5–6]) as well as specific incidents: the initial refusal to enter the land at Kadesh-barnea (1:19–46); idolatry at Beth-peor (4:3); and testing Yahweh at Massah, Taberah, and Kibroth-hattaavah (6:16, 9:22).

28. See J. Hwang, *The Rhetoric of Remembrance: An Investigation of the "Fathers" in Deuteronomy* (Siphrut 8; Winona Lake, IN: Eisenbrauns, 2012).

29. Moses does speak of descendants in 4:25 and 30:6, but the present generation is included in both the exile and the restoration. Cf. 6:20–25.

30. For variations of the land-grant formula with respect to the patriarchs, see, e.g., 1:8; 6:10, 18, 23; 7:8; 8:18; 9:5; 11:9; 30:20.

31. Cf. McConville, "Restoration in Deuteronomy," 39: "The fusing of the generations is of the essence of the deuteronomic paranesis. And its effect is to generate the possibility of constant renewals."

Negatively, corporate solidarity explains the pessimism of Yahweh and Moses about Israel's ability to obey the commandments. A major function of the accounts of Israel's stubbornness and faithlessness at Horeb (Deuteronomy 9) and in the desert (chs. 1–2; 9:7, 22–24) is to demonstrate the corrupt nature of Israel's heart and will. Moses' thesis statement in 9:6b states it succinctly: "You are a stiff-necked people." Thus, the lesson of these past experiences for the present generation is not simply an imperative, "Don't be like your predecessors," but an indicative, "You are like your predecessors!" This raises the question of the function of the laws and commands in the book that we will discuss later (see below on the "problem" of Israel's ability).

It appears, then, that the emphasis concerns historical continuity and corporate solidarity. Therefore, the theme of exile complicates the matter. Exile does manifest aspects of continuity. Since all the curses are directed toward Israel as a whole (to "you"), exile, as the ultimate curse, is also threatened to the present generation (note "you/your" throughout Deut 4:25–28, 28:58–68). Moreover, the corrupt nature of Israel's heart explains why exile is presented as ultimately inevitable. The continuities, however, are overshadowed by the discontinuities ushered in by the exile. The death of the nation means the end (and failure) of the journey and the covenant relationship. Along this horizon, exile is unlike the wilderness period in which God halted Israel's anti-exodus journey (see 2:2–4) after waiting for one generation to die (see 2:14), therefore renewing the covenant (see 5:2–3). Instead, exile is the culmination of a thorough anti-exodus (see 28:68) with no termination point (see 29:27) and *apparently* signifies a completely broken covenant (29:24; 31:16, 20).[32] Also, unlike the positive functions of the wilderness as a time of divine providential care and instruction (2:7, 8:2–5), the exile is consistently portrayed as the display of divine retribution and abandonment (28:65–68).

Israel's restoration must be understood first from the sense of discontinuity due to exile. The finality of exile makes restoration something much more than another stage in an ongoing journey. In essence, it is the start of a new journey[33] that will involve a new covenant that seems to go beyond the covenant renewals of the past (see below). Israel

---

32. Note the emphasis on the word "apparently." I am not saying that exile *actually* shattered the covenant relationship; this would contradict the fact that restoration is based on the patriarchal covenant. Rather, the imagery of death is part of the theological rhetoric so that the full force of the newness of restoration can be emphasized.

33. Cf. Yahweh's intent, following Israel's idolatry of the golden calf, to "start over" and transfer the promise to the descendants of Moses: "Let me alone, that I may destroy them (וְאַשְׁמִידֵם) and blot out their name from under heaven. And I will make of you a

herself will be new; she will have a new heart that will enable an obedience she never knew before, and she will have the prospect of a future life with God that will never end.

The "newness" of Israel's restoration has its limits. What is not new is Israel's covenant partner. The exile had not changed Yahweh. He needed no correction, growth, or transformation of heart. The constancy of Yahweh is the basis for the elements of continuity that are found in restoration. The basic demand to heed his voice and love him wholeheartedly (Deut 30:2, 6) is unaffected in the new order of things. The basis of restoration—the promise to the patriarchs—also remains the same. Continuity of the divine plan, in the end, is the fundamental issue in solving the "problem" of Israel's history.

3.2. The "Problem" of Covenant

The term ברית 'covenant' refers to three different covenants in Deuteronomy: the patriarchal covenant, the covenant at Horeb, and the Moab covenant.[34] The main issue at hand is the relationship among these covenants. It is strategic to begin with the relationship between Horeb and Moab. Moab is not a replacement of Horeb; better expressions (emphasizing continuity) include "repetition," "augmentation," "extension," "identification," "recapitulation," and "renewal." Support for this understanding of the relationship is found, especially, in the identification of the Moab generation with those at Horeb (4:9–24, 5:2–31), and in the juxtaposition of Moab and Horeb (28:69[29:1]; cf. 29:24[25]; 31:9, 16, 20, 25, 26).

The connection between Horeb and Moab allows us to make a couple of significant observations. First, as covenant renewal, Moab signals Yahweh's forgiveness of Israel's sins in the wilderness and his readiness to continue his covenant relationship (from Horeb) with her. The notion of renewal is intrinsic to the nature of Moab. Within the narrative of Deuteronomy 1–3, Moab functions as a second Kadesh-barnea.[35]

---

nation mightier and greater than they" (9:14). The use of שמד, which is connected to exile in Deuteronomy, implies a radical disjunction.

34. The references include the patriarchal (4:31, 7:12, 8:18), Horeb (4:13, 23; 5:2, 3; 7:9; 9:9, 11, 15; 10:8; 28:69[29:1]), and Moab (17:2; 28:69[29:1]; 29:8[9], 11[12], 13[14], 18[19], 20[21], 24[25]; 31:9?, 16, 20, 25?, 26?; 33:9). It is not clear which covenant is in view in the phrase, "the ark of the covenant of Yahweh" (31:9, 25, 26). In 10:8, Horeb is clearly in view. But 31:9 states that Moses wrote down "this law," which refers to the Torah in Deuteronomy (and so is connected more directly to Moab). Because Moab is an extension of Horeb, however, the exact identification in 31:9 is insignificant. A fourth use of ברית is used in the prohibition of making a "covenant" with the nations of the land (7:2).

35. On Moab as a second Kadesh-barnea, see McConville and Millar, *Time and Place*, 41, 61.

Kadesh-barnea was supposed to be the point of entry into the land (1:2), but instead it became the place of rebellion (1:26–46). Israel turned eleven days into forty years, much of which was spent at Kadesh (1:46). Thus, Kadesh-barnea became the launching point of a reversal of Israel's journey to the land—an anti-exodus back toward Egypt (2:1). Moab, then, is a symbol of Yahweh's reversal of the reversal. Therefore, Moab is more than a place of entry into the land—it is a symbol of divine grace and commitment to the people. This fundamental stance of grace must be kept in mind.

Second, the Moab covenant is an application of the Horeb covenant to life in the land. By this, I mean much more than the fact that the laws in Deuteronomy are geared specifically for landed existence.[36] The recounting of Horeb in chapter 5 contains three aspects that are paralleled in Moab: Yahweh's giving of commandments (5:6–21); Israel's right response of fear and intent to obey (5:23–29); and Yahweh's declaration that a heart of reverence and submission yields long life (5:29). The accent on grace—not only in the declaration of redemption that prefaces the "law" (5:6), but also in God's unconditional forgiveness of Israel's infidelity in the wilderness, should prevent a legalistic reading of the passages that speak of fidelity to the words given at Moab as resulting in possession and continued occupation of the land (e.g., 4:1; 5:32–33; 6:1–3, 18, 24; 11:8–9). The call to decision at Moab is first and foremost a call to remember what Yahweh has done—in the exodus (e.g., 4:20), at Horeb (e.g., 4:9–10), and in the wilderness (e.g., 8:2–5). Israel's posture of dependence upon Yahweh at Moab, which had just been demonstrated in Israel's following Yahweh's lead in the defeat of Sihon and Og (2:26–3:11), is the key to a successful future. As Millar states, "Life for Israel is to be life at Moab, even when firmly rooted in Canaan."[37] As we shall see, however, Israel's positive posture at Moab was temporary and fleeting, just as it was at Horeb (cf. 5:29, 9:6ff.).

---

36. Cf. the contention by N. Lohfink ("Die 'ḥuqqîm umišpaṭim' im Buch Deuteronomium und ihre Neubegrenzung durch Dtn 12,1," *Bib* 70 [1989] 1–27) that the final redaction of the law code of Deuteronomy was valid only for the time when Israel occupied the land. He argues that "in the land" and "all the days that you live upon the earth" (12:1) should be taken in a restrictive sense, in contrast to the view in 5:29 and 31 that considers the law valid for all time.

37. McConville and Millar, *Time and Place*, 61. Cf. W. Brueggemann, *The Land: Place as Gift, Promise and Challenge in Biblical Faith* (2nd ed.; Overtures to Biblical Theology; Minneapolis: Fortress, 2002) 44–45: "That moment [at Moab] stands as a paradigm for what is under way at the boundary of the new land, fraught with problems and loaded with promise." On the importance of "remembering," see McConville and Millar, *Time and Place*, 61 n. 87: "Forgetting Yahweh is tantamount to forgetting the decisions faced and

The emphasis on continuity between Horeb and Moab raises the question whether or not Moab offers anything "new." The additional laws of Moab can hardly be said to be "new," since these laws tend to be extensions and applications of similar laws in the Book of the Covenant (cf. Exodus 21–24).[38] In anticipation of the following comparison between the patriarchal and Horeb covenants, it is significant that Moab embeds the Horeb covenant within Israel's story, which runs from the patriarchs to future restoration from exile.[39] The inevitability of the storyline of Moab means that, in a sense, Israel cannot break the Moab covenant, for it incorporates the unfolding plan of a sovereign God. When Moses speaks of Israel abandoning or breaking the covenant (Deut 29:24; 31:16, 20), he only means that Israel will renege on her commitment to keep the terms of the covenant presented to her and will be unfaithful to Yahweh.[40] But Israel cannot keep Yahweh from doing what he has purposed to do.[41] Therefore, the Moab covenant is both conditional and unconditional, depending on the perspective from which it is approached.

Moab's juxtaposition of the patriarchal and Horeb covenants within a unified storyline calls for care in considering the relationship between the latter two covenants. A common view is to see a complete contrast between an unconditional covenant (patriarchal) and a conditional covenant (Horeb).[42] The fundamental problem is that both covenants

---

made at Moab, and turning from the life of decision (which by definition must be a life of uncertainty and dependence) to a life of complacency, betraying an underlying pride of achievement."

38. The connections between the laws in Deuteronomy 12–26 and the Decalogue strengthen this point (see Turner, *The Death of Deaths in the Death of Israel*, ch. 4).

39. This juxtaposition itself is not new, for Leviticus 26 ends its list of blessings and curses (cf. Deuteronomy 28) with a paragraph about the possibility of restoration beyond exile that appears to exhibit a sensitive juxtaposition of the two covenants (see Lev 26:40–45; for a helpful discussion of the difficulties and debates of this text, see J. Milgrom, *Leviticus 23–27* [AB 3B; New York: Doubleday, 2000] 2329–42). For a brief comparison between Lev 26:40–45 and the restoration texts in Deuteronomy (4:29–31, 30:1–10), see Turner, *The Death of Deaths in the Death of Israel*, 236–37.

40. This is clear by the parallel phrases of "forsaking me" (31:16) and "despising me" (31:20). The emphasis on idolatry as the foundational sin generally makes the same point.

41. I have suggested (Turner, *The Death of Deaths in the Death of Israel*, 156–57) that the wisdom maxim in 29:28 may actually have to do with this distinction. Thus, while the facts of exile and return are now being revealed to Israel, how and when they occur are still a mystery known only to Yahweh. Israel's occupation in the present is to obey and teach those things of which they have full knowledge and possession.

42. This view is witnessed, for example, in Pate et al., *Story of Israel*, 96: "Based on the conditional Mosaic covenant of Deuteronomy, the prophets proclaim judgment for sin committed. However, the prophets also reach back to the unconditional Abrahamic and

are "conditional" and "unconditional" (albeit in different senses), especially in light of Moab.

First, the Horeb covenant is "conditional" in that different conditions of the covenant (fidelity or infidelity) will yield different outcomes for the people (blessing or curse). Since both possibilities are written into the covenant, however, the covenant itself will be fulfilled one way or the other. The certainty of fulfillment makes Horeb "unconditional." The new aspect of the covenant of Moab of Israel's certain failure and exile, followed by restoration and blessing, increases the confusion.

Second, the patriarchal covenant is clearly "conditional" in Deuteronomy.[43] Two of the three explicit references to the patriarchal covenant occur in conditional blessings (Deut 7:12, 8:18; cf. 6:18, 7:13). The "unconditional" character of this covenant is retained in the focus on land as something Yahweh "swore" to the fathers,[44] or more generally as the land that Yahweh is "giving" to Israel based on the promise to the fathers.[45] Still, some of these references also emphasize that Israel must go and take possession of the land,[46] or that obedience is a condition to possessing the land.[47]

It seems, then, that the language of "conditional" and "unconditional" proves unhelpful in understanding the relationship between the covenants. We have yet to establish the nature of the connection. Since both the patriarchal and Horeb covenants exhibit "conditional" and "unconditional" elements, one could argue for continuity between the two. Indeed, there exists some confusion in the commentaries identifying the "fathers" as either the patriarchs or the Horeb generation in several texts (Deut 4:31, 5:3, 7:12, 8:18).[48] The juxtaposition of election and the blessings of obedience in 7:6–16, especially, blurs the distinction

---

Davidic covenants as the basis for their hope of a future restoration." Cf. E. H. Merrill, *Deuteronomy* (NAC 4; Nashville: Broadman & Holman, 1994) 129, on 4:31: "Once more the conditional nature of the Sinai covenant is oriented to the unconditional nature of the so-called Abrahamic."

43. See the discussion and references to a scholarly debate on this in J. G. Millar, *Now Choose Life: Theology and Ethics in Deuteronomy* (Grand Rapids: Eerdmans, 1998) 56–60; cf. Turner, *The Death of Deaths in the Death of Israel*, 238–39 n. 36.

44. Deut 1:8, 35; 4:31; 6:10, 18, 23; 7:8, 13; 8:1; 10:11; 11:9, 21; 26:3, 15; 28:11; 30:20; 31:20, 21, 23; 34:4. Other verses speak of aspects of the patriarchal covenant other than the land that Yahweh "swore" to the fathers: covenant (7:12; 8:18); word (9:5); multiplication (13:18[17]); and covenant relationship (29:12[13]).

45. Deut 1:20, 25; 2:29; 4:1, 21, 40; 5:16, 31; 9:6; 11:17, 31; 12:9, 10; 15:4, 7; 16:20; 17:14; 18:9; 19:1, 2, 10, 14; 21:1, 23; 24:4; 25:15, 19; 26:1; 27:2, 3; 28:8; 32:49, 52.

46. Deut 1:8; 6:18; 8:1; 10:11; 11:9, 31; 30:20.

47. Deut 4:1, 40; 5:16, 31; 16:20.

48. For extended discussion see Hwang, *The Rhetoric of Remembrance*.

between the covenants. Though I would argue that "the covenant . . . that he swore to your fathers" (7:12) refers to the patriarchal covenant, the material blessings of 7:13–16 are more easily associated with the covenant at Horeb. From this perspective, the Horeb covenant (now re-applied in the Moab covenant) is a particular, national expression and application of the patriarchal covenant. The conditions of the Horeb covenant are conditions of the patriarchal covenant appropriately specified for and applied to the nation. Exile and restoration show this continuity most clearly: exile results from the breaking of the Horeb/Moab covenant and results in the loss of the land sworn to the fathers; restoration results from Yahweh's commitment to the patriarchs and results in Israel receiving the blessings of the Moab covenant.

On the other hand, Deuteronomy maintains a distinction between the patriarchal and Horeb covenants that suggests another perspective. More generally, there is a difference in some of the terminology used with respect to each covenant. Horeb/Moab has no parallel to the promissory language (i.e., "sworn," "oath," "giving") of the patriarchal covenant. Instead, Moab speaks of "blessing" for obedience (Deut 11:26–27, 27:12, 28:1–14). Without reverting to the common view contested above, the different emphases between gift and reward must not be overlooked. While the elements of the patriarchal promise may or may not come with conditions, depending on the context, the blessings of Horeb/Moab are always contingent.

More specifically, the greatest note of discontinuity between the patriarchal covenant and the Horeb covenant arises in the context of restoration beyond exile. This is clearest in Deuteronomy 4, where the basis of restoration is distinctly Yahweh's remembrance of "the covenant of your fathers which he swore to them" (4:31).[49] A contrast with Horeb seems intentional, for "covenant" refers to Horeb in 4:13 and 23, and exile is specifically the result of violating the Horeb covenant (4:23–28). A distinction also occurs in 30:1–10, but in a different fashion. The sequence of blessing–curse (30:1), symbolizing the Moab covenant, takes place before the restoration occurs (based on the patriarchal

---

49. Interestingly, such discontinuity is lacking in Lev 26:40–45, which grounds the restoration in both the patriarchal covenant (v. 42) and the covenant made at Sinai (v. 45). I would suggest, preliminarily, that the difference might lie in Deuteronomy's more overtly pessimistic view of Israel's ability to change her ways (and, thus, a greater sense of the inevitability of exile). Also, Lev 26:40 makes human repentance the clear first step, and the need for the uncircumcised heart to be merely "humbled (Lev 26:41) is much weaker than the divine circumcision in Deut 30:6. Finally, the vision of restoration in Leviticus 26 seems no more than a return to how things were before exile.

covenant⁵⁰). Though the object of obedience in the land will be the same commands of Moab (cf. 30:2, 6, 8, 10), there is no apparent threat of curse since it will be unnecessary.

This last point raises a question: what type of covenant relationship will exist in the future? Though Deuteronomy does not give an answer directly, the discontinuities of restoration suggest against a simple return to the covenant of Horeb/Moab. But neither is it simply to be a return to the situation of the patriarchs, since restored Israel is still constituted as a nation and committed to obeying the commands of Moab. It must be some kind of "new covenant." What is new in this relationship is the ability and certainty of Israel to reciprocate fidelity to the covenant. In this setting, all the tensions between the previous covenants disappear, for the command becomes the promise (cf. 10:16, 30:6) and the conditions become realized.[51]

3.3. The "Problem" of Land

As one of the three major components of the covenant triangle (Yahweh, Israel, land), and as the centerpiece of the patriarchal promise, land is directly connected with the above discussion of covenant. The focus on land in Deuteronomy, however, justifies a separate section on the theme.[52] Allusions to other components of the promise to the patriarchs pale in comparison to the focus on the gift of land.[53] Also, the Moab covenant is an extension of the Horeb covenant with stipulations suited specifically for a landed people. Since the loss of this land hangs over the people as a constant threat, it is important to see how the theme of exile relates to the larger theology of land in Deuteronomy.

The tension concerning land in Deuteronomy is that its status as gift and its elevated importance are challenged by other themes in the book.

---

50. There is no explicit reference to the patriarchal covenant in 30:1–10, but I have argued (Turner, *The Death of Deaths in the Death of Israel*, 176–77) that numerous allusions to the covenant imply that it serves as the basis of restoration.

51. Likewise, A. D. H. Mayes (*Deuteronomy* [NCB; Grand Rapids: Eerdmans, 1981] 78–79) states that the possibility of repentance and forgiveness in the final chapters of Deuteronomy helps resolve "the tension between the idea that Israel's status as the people of Yahweh precedes and is independent of the covenant, and the idea that disobedience to the covenant demands bring punishment and destruction."

52. Israel's story in the Pentateuch begins (Genesis 12) and ends (Deuteronomy) with Yahweh's promise of land. The function of Deuteronomy in the Pentateuch, then, is to bring this theme to a climax. See McConville, "Restoration in Deuteronomy," 11.

53. These other components include special relationship with Yahweh (e.g., Deut 4:6–8, 19–20, 32–38; 7:6–11; 8:5; 9:29; 10:15; 26:16–19; 28:9–10; 29:12[13]; 30:9; 32:6–14; 33:29); exalted status in the world (4:6–8; 7:14; 26:19; 28:1, 10, 13); multiplication (1:10–11; 7:13; 8:1; 10:22; 11:21; 13:18; 26:5; 30:5); and curse upon enemies (7:15–16; 28:11; 30:7; 32:43; 33:27; cf. 2:26–3:11; 7:1ff.; 9:1ff.; 11:23, 25; 31:3–5).

A Deuteronomic theology of land begins with the land as a divine gift.[54] It is described as a "good land" (1:25, 8:7), already nourished by Edenic resources (8:7–10, 11:9–12) and endowed with the props for civilization (6:10–11) that Israel would need to be satisfied as a landed people. Indeed, it is a land given *sola gratia*, "in which you will lack nothing" (8:9) from the outset.

But the land is also recognized as a place of testing and a catalyst for temptation.[55] The existence of Canaanites in the land poses a dual temptation: fear and unbelief for those seeking to enter the land (Deut 1:26–33, 7:17–23, 20:1–4; cf. 1:38; 3:2, 28; 31:6–8, 23); and the seduction of idolatry for Israel once in the land (7:1–5, 20:16–18).[56] The blessings of the land also become a test. It is significant that descriptions of the land are followed by warnings of forgetting Yahweh and the graciousness of his gift (6:12, 8:11–17, 11:16). The loss of memory described in these warnings is again manifested by the potential seduction of idolatry (6:14, 8:19, 11:16). These temptations are the reason why the notion of gifted land is balanced by the conditionality of land possession.[57] Obedience to the lawgiver—both to the commands to enter the land and to the detailed laws controlling life in the land—is the demonstration of faith in, and the path to remembering, the land-giver.[58] This dialectic of promise and command is at the heart of the tension concerning the nature of the patriarchal covenant discussed above.

Land, then, is important because it is a symbol of life with Yahweh. It is an arena in which Israel can have fellowship with her God and experience his blessings and care. The heightening of this symbolic value, however, tends to mitigate the significance of land as turf and of the blessings of the land as primarily material. Millar states:

> The land is also the locus of Israel's relationship with Yahweh.... While physical abundance in the land does not lie outside his concerns, the primary matter is Israel's relationship with God as signified by the land. In

---

54. See discussion and references in previous section of the "problem" of covenant. For a helpful analysis of "gift" language in Deuteronomy see J. G. Plöger, *Literarkritische, forgeschichtliche und stilkritische Untersuchungen zum Deuteronomium* (BBB 26; Bonn: Peter Hanstein, 1967) 121–29.

55. Brueggemann, *Land*, 50–65.

56. My position that the *herem* policy in chs. 7 and 20 is hyperbolic makes this threat a constant one for Israel; see Turner, *The Death of Deaths in the Death of Israel*, 192–94.

57. See Brueggemann, *Land*, 49; P. Diepold, *Israels Land* (BWANT 15; Stuttgart: Kohlhammer, 1972) 100.

58. Cf. Brueggemann (*Land*, 56, 57): "Israel's Torah is markedly uninterested in a religion of obedience as such. It is rather interested in care for land, so that it is never forgotten from whence came the land and to whom it is entrusted and by whom.... Torah exists so that Israel will not forget whose land it is and how it was given to us."

the wilderness, the survival or physical comfort of the nation was not the ultimate purpose of Yahweh's intervention (see e.g., 8:3). In Yahweh's land, material blessing should sharpen the focus on the potential intimacy occupation of this land provides. The ultimate indicative is not the land which Yahweh gives, but the relationship which that land affords.[59]

It must be remembered that the setting of Deuteronomy is outside the land even as Yahweh is already in covenant relationship with Israel. This is consistent with the whitewashed assessments of Israel's experience in the wilderness: "You lacked nothing" (2:7); "Your clothing did not wear out on you and your foot did not swell these forty years" (8:4). The statement that Israel "lacked nothing" (2:7) in the wilderness is stark, for it is the same reality promised for existence in the land (8:9). Though the blessings of the land make "no lack" a believable prospect from the start (not just retrospectively, like the wilderness), the point is that Israel had a vital relationship with Yahweh outside the land—despite Israel's consistent unfaithfulness. The land affords the opportunity for Yahweh to fulfill his promises and to work out his plan for Israel in the sight of the world (e.g., 26:19, 28:10), but it is not an indispensable component to establishing or maintaining a covenant relationship with his people. Unlike the other gods, Yahweh is not limited to a local territory, for the whole earth is his.[60]

The themes of exile and restoration relate to these tensions of the land directly. Exile shatters the covenant triangle by dismantling the connection between two of its components, Israel and the land. Still, the Israelite perspective understands the fundamental covenant relationship to be between Yahweh and Israel in direct contrast to the usual ANE perspective that considered deity–land as primary.[61] Therefore, exile is the result, rather than the cause, of the rupture between Yahweh and Israel. In fact, Deuteronomy is virtually silent about a "relationship" between Yahweh and the land, except that he owns it along with the rest of the earth. The closest we get is in the *foreign* response to Yahweh's judgment in Deut 29:21–27. The foreigners are preoccupied with the land—its devastation (29:21–22), Yahweh's judgment upon it (29:23, 26), and the people's removal from it to another land (29:27). Even if "land" is a metonym for "the people of the land" in some of the references, the perspective is unique in Deuteronomy. This text is "the

---

59. Millar, *Now Choose Life*, 56.

60. On Yahweh's control over the whole earth, see Deut 4:26, 32, 39; 10:14; 14:2; 28:49, 64; 30:19; 31:28; 32:1.

61. See D. I. Block, *The Gods of the Nations* (2nd ed; ETS Studies: Studies in Ancient Near Eastern National Theology; Grand Rapids: Baker, 2000) especially 21–33.

exception that proves the rule"—the rule that land is secondary to the covenant.

On the other hand, this passage in Deuteronomy 29 is an indication that land, while secondary, is not irrelevant. It might be a stretch to say that Deuteronomy is missiological,[62] but the book offers glimpses of God's larger concern for the world (see 2:4–23).[63] The acknowledgment that the world is watching (4:6–8, 26:19), and that Yahweh is concerned about foreign evaluation (9:28; 28:9–10, 25, 37; 29:21–23), at least suggests that the covenant relationship between Yahweh and Israel serves as a type of witness to others about the character and power of Yahweh. Because land is central in the minds of others, Yahweh's covenant with Israel must take place with reference to a specific land in order for this witness to have an effect.

The theme of restoration both lessens and emphasizes the significance of the land. On the one hand, the restoration envisioned in Deut 4:29–31 downplays the land. Though the reference to the patriarchal covenant (4:31) implies that return to land is involved, the text only explicitly states that Israel returns to Yahweh in repentance and obedience (4:29–30). The emphasis is consistent with the points made above concerning the unique Israelite perspective and the ability of Israel to have a relationship with Yahweh outside the land. On the other hand, the restoration envisioned in 30:1–10 highlights the importance of land in at least three ways. First, restoration involves return to the land (30:5). Second, the circumcision of the heart, the needed surgery to repair Israel's root problem of rebellion, is held off in the restoration process until Israel is in the land (30:6). In my reading, this order of events is necessary because the outcome of the circumcision of the heart is a constant, perpetually operating covenant relationship. Given the notion of witness, the land is the proper context for Israel's display of complete obedience to Yahweh and for Yahweh's display of commitment to his people. Third, only in the land can there be resolution to the tensions of the patriarchal covenant itself, and to the uncertain relationship between the patriarchal and Horeb covenants.

---

62. On the missiological significance of Deuteronomy, see C. J. H. Wright, *Deuteronomy* (NIBC; Peabody, MA: Hendrickson, 1996) 8–17. Cf. D. I. Block, "The Privilege of Calling: The Mosaic Paradigm for Missions (Deut. 26:16–19)," *BSac* 162 (2005) 387–405; repr. in idem, *How I Love Your Torah, O LORD! Studies in the Book of Deuteronomy* (Eugene, OR: Cascade, 2011) 140–61; Millar, *Now Choose Life*, 147–60.

63. See the discussion on Deuteronomy 2 in the essay in this volume by P. T. Vogt, "'These Are the Words Moses Spoke': Implied Audience and a Case For Pre-Monarchic Dating of Deuteronomy" (pp. 61–80).

Therefore, we must be careful how we speak of the importance of land in the Deuteronomic vision of Israel's future. Israel's possession of the land is significant in its function as the ideal context in which the covenant relationship can be enjoyed by Israel and witnessed by the world, but it is not indispensable to the existence of the covenant relationship itself. This latter point is hinted at by the fact that the covenant is renewed in *Moab*, a place outside the land. The land becomes an indispensable piece, however, in the ultimate (eschatological) fulfillment of Yahweh's plan, as pictured in Israel's restoration.[64]

3.4. The "Problem" of Israel's Ability

Deuteronomy is focused on the concept of decision. One of the most striking features of the book is its preoccupation with exhortation.[65] At Moab, Israel is reminded of her past experiences in order to make the right choice in the present—to be faithful to Yahweh by obeying his commands to enter the land and keep the laws of the covenant while in the land. Will Israel obey in the long run? More importantly, will Israel be able to obey? Scholars debate whether Deuteronomy is optimistic or pessimistic on the matter.[66] The optimistic view is based on two lines of thought. First, the giving of commands and exhortations implies ability to keep them (e.g., 30:11–14). Otherwise, why offer a choice (e.g., 30:20) in the first place?[67] Second, Deuteronomy recounts several positive ex-

---

64. Cf. the statement in McConville ("Restoration in Deuteronomy," 38): "Possession of the ancient land remains the deuteronomic ideal, but the significant qualification entered by the story of the end of Judah is that the life of the covenant people could continue without it." I agree that there is this qualification, but it already exists in Deuteronomy before it is demonstrated in Israel's history. I do not agree, however, with an earlier statement: "The framing of the story [from Deuteronomy to Kings] in non-landedness is, paradoxically, a ground of hope. It is not necessary to suppose that the origin of the story in the promise to the patriarchs entails that the land is an indispensable part of the restored life of the people" (ibid., 37–38). While the covenant relationship can be maintained apart from land, the Deuteronomic vision of restoration cannot be fulfilled without it.

65. S. Amsler, "La motivation de l'éthique dans la par én èse due Deutéronome," in *Beiträge zur alttestamentlichen Theologie: Festschrift für Walther Zimmerli* (ed. H. Donner, R. Hanhart, and R. Smend; Göttingen: Vandenhoeck & Ruprecht, 1977) 11–22. Millar (*Now Choose Life*, 49–51) outlines at least fifteen ways the language of Deuteronomy refers to the action to be taken in response to the divine command. Millar concludes, "The unmatched concentration of paranetic vocabulary confirms that the prevailing atmosphere of the book is the ethical decision facing Israel" (ibid., 51).

66. For a discussion and summary of positions, see Millar, *Now Choose Life*, 161–80. Millar thinks a good case can be made for both sides, but his presentation seems to favor the pessimistic view.

67. On philosophical grounds, one could also argue that it would be unjust for God to punish a lawbreaker if he is ultimately unable to comply. This is beyond the scope of our study, but points to the need to be aware of presuppositions that we all bring to the table.

amples of Israel's past fidelity, which implies that Israel can do likewise in the future. Individuals who proved faithful include the patriarchs (9:27), Caleb (1:36), Joshua (1:38), and Moses himself (34:10–12). The nation as a whole was faithful at Horeb (5:24–28) and in the conquest of Sihon and Og (2:26–3:11). At Moab, Israel appears to be in good position to follow Yahweh into the land (see 4:4; 31:1–13). Since the present study supports the pessimistic view, we need to explain how such a position deals with the positive elements in the text.

I begin by rehearsing the negative portrait of Israel's nature and heart in Deuteronomy. The positive portrayal of Israel's response at Horeb (Deut 5:24–28) is tempered by a hint of doubt by Yahweh concerning Israel's chances of sustaining a posture of fear and obedience (5:29). Israel's right response indeed proved fleeting, as she quickly turned to idolatrous worship of the golden calf (9:8–21). This experience proved paradigmatic for Israel's continual rebellion in the wilderness (9:7, 22–24; cf. 1:26–43), with the added indictment that Israel, at her core, is stiff-necked (9:6, 13; cf. 9:24; 12:8). This inner corruption is never overcome; the positive scenes in the wilderness (e.g., 2:26–3:11; 6:22; 10:22; 11:2–7; cf. conquest in 7:18–23) are overshadowed by the reality that Israel's heart is still uncircumcised at Moab (10:16). Yahweh tells Moses that the people will be unfaithful in the land (31:16, 20; cf. 32:15ff.) because he knows "what they are inclined to do" (31:21). The larger theological reality is that Yahweh has not given Israel the heart she needs to be faithful (29:3[4]). Therefore she will fail, with the inevitable result of suffering the ultimate curse of exile (4:25–28, 28:58–68).

The positive elements need to be understood within this larger negative perspective. First, the sustained exhortation to obey does not engender optimism in the end. As Millar states, "These repeated appeals seem to imply that Israel has the ability to comply. On the surface, this is the case. There may be a sub-text, however. The forceful repetition of the demand of obedience may in fact reveal a certain amount of desperation, presupposing the waywardness of Israel. Within the rhetoric of Deuteronomy, even calls to obedience become ambiguous."[68]

One of the most prominent exhortations is the call to "remember" (or not "forget") Yahweh and his acts. The memory motif is a subtle indictment of Israel's tendency to forget, and so serves as support of the pessimistic view.[69] Second, accounts of the nation's past fidelity are always followed by negative elements. The description of the defeat of Sihon

---

68. Millar, *Now Choose Life*, 166.
69. Brueggemann, *Land*, 50–55.

and Og (Deut 2:26–3:11) is followed by Moses' exclusion from the land (3:25–26). The submission at Horeb (5:24–28) is followed by Yahweh's doubt (5:29), not to mention the sin that followed (9:8–21). The hope in the leadership of Joshua (31:1–13) is followed by knowledge of future failure (31:14–29). Thus, the text never lets Israel's display of fidelity go unchallenged.[70] Third, when things did go well in the wilderness, the emphasis was always on Yahweh's initiative and grace rather than Israel's obedience (e.g., 2:26–3:11, 6:22, 10:22, 11:2–7).

Fourth, the examples of faithful individuals seem to be the exceptions that prove the rule. These references to individual fidelity are overshadowed by the prominent theme of the death of Moses in the book (Deut 1:37; 3:25–26; 4:21–22; 31:1, 14, 16, 29; 32:48–52; 34:1–12).[71] What chance will Israel have in the land if her great leader was excluded? As a caveat, however, the individual Israelite who seeks to be faithful to Yahweh amidst a sinful generation can be assured that Yahweh has not forgotten him or her (see the fuller discussion below on the "problem" of the individual).

The theme of exile and the question of Israel's ability are intimately related. The inevitability of exile is grounded in the pessimistic portrayal of Israel's heart and nature. It is only in restoration that Israel's heart will be circumcised, enabling her to be fully and continually obedient (30:6). From this ultimate horizon, then, the pessimism is reversed into a resounding optimism. Millar concludes:

> Chapter 30 ensures that Deuteronomy is ultimately an optimistic book. Its doctrine of the sinfulness of human nature may mean that Israel is bound to fail, but the promise of God's radical intervention, setting up a new covenant which does change the hearts of his people, means that the book is transformed by a theology of hope. That is why Moses can preach on (30:15–20), calling Israel to persevere in obedience, walking with Yahweh, facing a lifetime of decisions. God's people may be bound to fail today, but they are not trapped in failure forever, for God's solution is coming.[72]

Millar's comment helps us understand the function of the laws and exhortations in Deuteronomy. Exile in Deuteronomy 4 and 28, in line with the dual nature of the Moab covenant (see discussion above), serves

---

70. Pate et al. (*Story of Israel*, 44) further note that chs. 1–11 begin and end with negative events (failure at Kadesh-barnea and the golden calf incident).

71. On the prominence of this theme, see D. T. Olson, *Deuteronomy and the Death of Moses: A Theological Reading* (Overtures to Biblical Theology; Minneapolis: Augsburg, 1994). Note also the death of Aaron in 10:6.

72. Millar, *Now Choose Life*, 180.

both as a potential threat (conditional *if*) and an inevitable future reality (unconditional *when*). The function of the commands must be viewed from both angles. The choice before Israel is a real choice that each generation must make. Israel should be encouraged by Yahweh's proven faithfulness to lead Israel in her journey of faith and to reward those who put their confidence in him.[73] The hope of Yahweh's continued faithfulness beyond exile should motivate Israel in the present ("today") to turn to him whenever she sins. However, from the perspective of the storyline that finds Israel (pen)ultimately in exile, the law also functions as a catalyst and conduit for the manifestation of Israel's stubbornness and unbelief. The law is holy, but Israel is not. Her ultimate refusal to be obedient to what Yahweh commands reveals her deep-seated rejection of Yahweh himself.

The future restoration of Israel causes the law to transcend both these functions. Israel's obedience will still serve as a mirror to her heart, but since the heart will have been transformed, the reflection will be one of trust and confidence in Yahweh. Also, Israel will still be responsible to choose the right path, but she will no longer need the promise of blessing or the threat of curse to motivate her to obedience. Paradoxically, her choice will be inevitable.

3.5. The "Problem" of the Individual

The "problem" of the individual is comparable to the "problems" of history and Israel's ability discussed above. The notion of corporate solidarity conflates the generations so as to speak of one "Israel." Israel's inability to be faithful in the past is evidence that "all Israel" will be unfaithful and ultimately receive the death penalty of exile because her heart remains uncircumcised throughout her history. What does all this have to do with the individual Israelite? Also, what is the position of the individual with respect to the themes of exile and restoration, both of which are national concerns?

Before looking at Deuteronomy, it is worth noting that this issue is part of the debate taking place in NT studies. Many NT scholars now believe that the normative belief of first-century Jews was that they were still in exile, awaiting the full restoration Yahweh had promised.[74] N. T. Wright, a leading proponent of this view, summarizes the position:

---

73. Millar states that the primary function of the laws is to keep Israel on the move, avoiding stagnation (ibid., 204).

74. E.g., Wright, *New Testament and the People of God*, 152–66, 268–72, 299–301; idem, *Jesus and the Victory of God*, xvii–xviii, 126–27, 203–6, 268; Pate et al., *Story of Israel*, 20–22,

Most Jews of this period, it seems, would have answered the question 'where are we?' in language which, reduced to its simplest form, meant: we are still in exile. They believed that, in all the senses which mattered, Israel's exile was still in progress. Although she had come back from Babylon, the glorious message of the prophets remained unfulfilled. Israel still remained in thrall to foreigners; worse, Israel's god had not returned to Zion.[75]

It is significant that a systematic approach, such as Wright's, that focuses on exile also tends to de-emphasize the individual. Wright states, for instance:

> Exile will be undone when sin is forgiven. . . . If [Israel's] sin has caused her exile, her forgiveness will mean her national re-establishment. This needs to be emphasized in the strongest possible terms: the most natural meaning of the phrase "the forgiveness of sins" to a first-century Jew is not in the first instance the remission of *individual* sins, but the putting away of the whole nation's sins. And, since the exile was the punishment for those sins, the only sure sign that the sins had been forgiven would be the clear and certain liberation from exile. This is the major, national, context within which all individual dealing-with-sin must be understood.[76]

While it is beyond the scope of this study to evaluate the merits of these positions,[77] Wright's construct illustrates the "problem" of the individual with which we are concerned.

For all of its national focus, however, Deuteronomy does recognize the existence and significance of the individual.[78] The frequent change

---

105–18; and various essays in Scott, *Exile: Old Testament, Jewish, and Christian Conceptions*; idem, *Restoration: Old Testament, Jewish, and Christian Conceptions*.

75. Wright, *New Testament and the People of God*, 268–69.

76. Ibid., 273 (emphasis original). Cf. ibid., 334: "Individual Jews would find their own 'salvation' through their membership within Israel, that is, within the covenant." See also Wright, *Jesus and the Victory of God*, 271: "From the point of view of a first-century Jew, 'forgiveness of sins' could never simply be a private blessing, though to be sure it was that as well, as Qumran amply testifies. Overarching the situation of the individual was the state of the nation as a whole. . . ." Cf. Schmid and Steck ("Restoration Expectations in the Prophetic Tradition," 59), who argue that within the framework of prophetic salvific statements "[t]he fate of the individual . . . is scarcely included."

77. Wright's de-emphasis of the individual in the NT understanding of repentance and forgiveness has been sharply criticized by, for example, R. H. Stein, "N. T. Wright's *Jesus and the Victory of God*: A Review Article," *JETS* 44 (2001) 211–14.

78. Some scholars find an emphasis on the individual arising in the deuteronomic movement in the time of Hezekiah or later with the pre-exilic prophets, Jeremiah and Ezekiel. See, for example, B. Halpern, "Jerusalem and the Lineages in the seventh century BCE: Kinship and the Rise of Individual Moral Liability," in *Law and Ideology in Monarchic Israel* (ed. Baruch Halpern and D. W. Hobson; JSOTSup 124; Sheffield: Sheffield Academic, 1991) 1–107. Because these scholars also date Deuteronomy relatively late, speaking of

between singular and plural "you" as Moses addresses the people is well known. While the focus is usually on the nation as a whole, the presence of this stylistic feature assumes that the nation is made up of individuals, each responsible to heed Moses' words and pass them on to his or her children (e.g., Deut 4:9, 6:20–25).[79] Individuals are also singled out amidst a generation for behaving in contrast to the bent of the nation. Caleb and Joshua alone are faithful at Kadesh-barnea (1:36, 38). Yahweh differentiates between those who followed the Baal of Peor and those who clung to Yahweh (4:3–4). Moses seems to escape the indictment of the nation at Horeb and in the wilderness (9:6–10:11). Finally, the individual who breaks the covenant by committing idolatry is sifted out from the community by Yahweh, who himself exacts judgment on the person (29:17–20[18–21]).

These examples raise a series of tensions and questions about the role of the individual. The first issue concerns the relationship between individual and national disobedience. Individual lawbreakers, of course, can be dealt with in a way that prevents the community from suffering. This is done through punishment of the individual either by humans (e.g., much of the legislation in Deuteronomy 12–26) or by Yahweh himself (27:15–26, 29:19–20[20–21]).[80] The curses in chapter 28, however, concentrate on national disobedience and judgment. The inference is that the corporate judgment, climaxing in exile, will come when a majority, if not all, of the people prove unfaithful. But how does this square with the sense of inevitability we have established for the curses in chapter 28? The answer must be that the indictment against the nation of being stubborn (קשה ערף] 'stiff [of neck]'; 9:6, 13; 31:27; cf. verb form in 10:16) and rebellious (מרה; 9:7, 24; 31:27[2×]) applies to each

---

some sort of "individualism" in Deuteronomy is not a problem typically. Conservative scholars, however, would argue for a much earlier recognition of the individual, not only from Deuteronomy but also from the Davidic psalms.

79. See J. G. McConville, "Singular Address in the Deuteronomic Law and the Politics of Legal Administration," *JSOT* 97 (2002) 19–36.

80. Deut 29:19–20[20–21] explicitly states Yahweh will single the individual out. The list of curses against individuals in 27:15–26 ("Cursed be anyone who . . .") does not specify concrete (human-enacted) punishment for offence since the sins in view are those that are committed in secret. The assumption is that Yahweh, who alone knows the sin, exacts the punishment. See E. Bellefontaine, "The Curses of Deuteronomy 27: Their Relationship to the Prohibitives," in *A Song of Power and the Power of Song: Essays on the Book of Deuteronomy* (ed. D. L. Christensen; Sources for Biblical and Theological Study 3; Winona Lake, IN: Eisenbrauns, 1993) 58; M. Weinfeld, *Deuteronomy and the Deuteronomic School* (Oxford: Clarendon, 1972) 276–78. The formal connection between chs. 27–28 suggests that the curses in view in ch. 27 are somehow related to the curses in ch. 28, which involve punishments meted out by Yahweh himself.

individual within the nation. Similar terminology is used in 29:18[19], where the individual thinks to himself, "I shall be safe, though I walk in the stubbornness of my heart."[81] In the latter case, the individual transgressor is a picture of the nation, evidenced by Moses' abrupt shift in 29:21[22] to the consequences of covenant breach for the nation (29:21–27[22–28]). Millar seems to have it right: "National catastrophe results from national breach of covenant. The likelihood of each individual falling into apostasy translates into the nation as a whole spurning the grace of Yahweh."[82]

This leads into a second issue: how does the position of universal corruption account for the presence of righteous individuals? In the case of Israel displaying corporate fidelity, the answer was that such displays were temporary and/or external.[83] This same logic might explain many individual acts of righteousness as well (e.g., Deut 4:4), but cannot explain every instance. The assessment of Caleb is especially noteworthy: "he has wholly followed Yahweh" (1:36). Caleb's obedience seems to be an outworking of an internal disposition of fidelity.[84] Did Caleb (and Joshua) somehow escape the Israelite (and human) plight of heart rebellion? It is difficult to answer this question within the bounds of Deuteronomy, but I will attempt a conjecture. Certain individuals like Caleb (I would include, at least, Joshua and Moses) appear already to possess what the nation as a whole lacks: a circumcised heart. We know that, within the divine plan, the nation will only receive this after the exile (30:6), but since Yahweh is the one who must give such a heart (see 29:3[4]), perhaps he chooses to dispense it to certain individuals beforehand. These positive examples of faithfulness, then, would serve both to condemn the nation for its lack and to offer hope by pointing to the reality that awaits all Israel in the future. All this reasoning (and,

---

81. The word for "stubbornness" here is שרר, a synonym of קשה. Note also the "stubborn" (סרר) and "rebellious" (מרה) son in 21:18, 20.

82. Millar, *Now Choose Life*, 174. Cf. S. R. Driver, *A Critical and Exegetical Commentary on Deuteronomy* (2nd ed; ICC; Edinburgh: T. & T. Clark, 1902) 326.

83. The difference between external and internal participation in the covenant is noted in Turner, *The Death of Deaths in the Death of Israel*, 149–57. The renewal of the covenant in Deut 29:9–14[10–15], which shows the nation's outward willingness to abide by the covenant, comes between the darker realities of the absence of the right heart (v. 3[4]) and future judgment (vv. 21–27[22–28]).

84. Cf. the description of Caleb in Num 14:24 as a man who "has a different spirit and has followed me fully. . . ." Though Joshua is not described the same way explicitly, his constant connection with Caleb as faithful spies and as exceptions to Yahweh's judgment on the people implies that Joshua also should be viewed in the same way as Caleb.

admittedly, theological bias), however, takes us too far afield from the text. The tension must be allowed to stand.

The presence of righteous individuals in the nation brings us to the third issue: what about the individual and the exile? It is possible that when Israel is exiled there are no righteous individuals among the people. In this case there would be no problem, for every person would receive his or her just deserts. If we assume that there are righteous individuals, what will become of them? It appears that they will be exiled along with the others, receiving the indictment and judgment that befalls the nation as a whole. This is prefigured already in the person of Moses. Though Moses was not perfect (see Deut 32:51), he would certainly be classified as one of the righteous. His death—his loss of the land—is due, in large part, to the sins of the people (1:37, 3:26, 4:21). Like all other Israelites—righteous and unrighteous—Moses' "restoration" rests in the future restoration of the nation.

Deuteronomy does not add much to a development of the "remnant" motif.[85] The few who remain through the experience of exile are "left ... among the nations" (Deut 4:27)—not to be spared because of their righteousness, but to suffer the concomitant curses of forced idolatry (4:28, 28:64), psychological trauma (28:65–67), and slavery (28:68). Recalling the sinful individual within the community in 29:17–20[18–21], there is no contrasting parallel that pictures Yahweh singling out a righteous individual to avoid judgment. Otherwise, exile would be amputation, not death. Moreover, 30:1–10 envisions the restoration of *all* Israel. It entails resurrection from the dead, not mere survival through devastation.

Deuteronomy has plenty to say about the individual, but only enough to frustrate the reader asking the sort of questions I have posed here. The theme of exile does subsume the concerns of the individual into a larger, corporate sphere. Thus, righteous individuals, in the day of judgment, would not escape exile (e.g., Daniel and his friends). Nevertheless, the individual is not lost altogether. The restoration of Israel includes the restoration of each individual within the nation. Thus, what may be prefigured in individuals like Joshua and Caleb is the hope for all of God's people. Therefore, those who draw on Deuteronomy for its themes of exile and restoration—such as N. T. Wright and other NT

---

85. This is supported by the near absence of references to Deuteronomy in the classic work on the development of remnant theology: G. F. Hasel, *The Remnant: The History and Theology of the Remnant Idea from Genesis to Isaiah* (Berrien Springs, MI: Andrews University Press, 1972).

scholars—would do well to pay attention to what it offers concerning the individual.[86]

4. Conclusion

The theme of exile in Deuteronomy is intricately linked with the overall theology of the book. Particularly, the tensions of the exile theme correspond and interact with broader theological "problems" concerning Israel and her covenant relationship with Yahweh. The paradox of exile as the death but not end of the nation functions to exacerbate these "problems." While restoration brings about the resolution to these problems, many of the details are absent. In some sense, more questions are raised than answered. Of course, this is what we should expect with a transitional and programmatic book like Deuteronomy. It establishes a vision and outlines a plan to reach that vision, but it leaves the future open enough to anticipate surprises and qualifications down the road. The reader must await later revelation to see how God will unfold his plan.

---

86. N. T. Wright was noted in n. 2. See N. T. Wright, *The New Testament and the People of God* (*Christian Origins and the Question of God*, vol. 1; Minneapolis: Fortress, 1992) 152–66, 268–79, 299–301; idem, *Jesus and the Victory of God* (*Christian Origins and the Question of God*, vol. 2; Minneapolis: Fortress, 1996) 126–27, 203–4. For a helpful summary of Wright's thesis, see C. Blomberg, "The Wright Stuff: A Critical Overview of *Jesus and the Victory of God*," in *Jesus and the Restoration of Israel: A Critical Assessment of N. T. Wright's Jesus and the Victory of God* (ed. C. C. Newman; Downers Grove, IL: InterVarsity, 1999) 20. For further discussion of Wright's thesis, including a summary of his understanding of Deuteronomy within the larger discussion, see Turner, *The Death of Deaths in the Death of Israel*, 28–30. For other interactions between Deuteronomy and the NT see R. Bauckham ("The Restoration of Israel in Luke-Acts," in *Restoration: Old Testament, Jewish, and Christian Conceptions*, 435), who locates the primary sources of hope in Deuteronomy 30–33 and Isaiah 40–66. See also D. J. Harrington, "Interpreting Israel's History: The *Testament of Moses* as a Rewriting of Deut. 31–34," in *Studies on the Testament of Moses* (ed. G. W. E. Nickelsburg; SBLSCS 4; Missoula, MT: Scholars Press, 1973) 59–68. S. J. Hafemann ("Paul and the Exile of Israel in Galatians 3–4," in *Exile: Old Testament, Jewish, and Christian Conceptions*, 344) argues that "curse of the Law" in Gal 3:10 is taken from Deuteronomy 27–32 "read as a conceptual whole." C. A. Evans ("Aspects of Exile and Restoration in the Proclamation of Jesus and the Gospels," in *Exile: Old Testament, Jewish, and Christian Conceptions*, 327), however, thinks Jesus drew on the traditions of Daniel, Zechariah, and Second Isaiah, but Evans makes no mention of Deuteronomy.

Part 2

The Influence of Deuteronomy

The Impact of Deuteronomy on the Books of the Deuteronomistic History

Michael A. Grisanti

For several decades, OT scholars have debated the relationship of Deuteronomy to the books customarily called the Deuteronomistic History (DH). Most of that discussion has focused on the layers of traditions that resulted from the work of the Deuteronomist (Dtr), whether one or several individuals. This essay will not focus on the customary areas of debate with regard to the DH, but will seek to identify substantive ways the book of Deuteronomy has left its imprint on the books of Joshua, Judges, Samuel, and Kings (expressions, theological themes, etc.). This brief examination of these issues gives evidence of the fundamental role that the book of Deuteronomy played throughout the OT, but particularly in the Historical Books. This study also manifests the verbal and thematic interconnectedness of the Pentateuch and Historical Books.[1]

I am totally aware of the daunting nature of the task before me, namely, presenting the impact of 34 chapters of Deuteronomy on 147 chapters of the OT (Joshua–Kings). What I seek to accomplish in this essay is very selective and painfully brief in places. After giving a succinct overview of the concept of the DH, I will survey some of the problems that plague those who conduct a quest for Deuteronomisms throughout the OT. The bulk of the paper will attend to some potential Deuteronomic connections between Deuteronomy and the DH. The paper

---

Author's Note: I am excited to have this opportunity to contribute an essay to a volume honoring a man I genuinely love and respect. Even though God has not given me the privilege of serving at the same institution as Dan, he has enriched my life in many ways as a friend and OT scholar. He was one of the men who lit the fire in my heart for the study of Deuteronomy. He is on the short list of men concerning whom I tell my students the following: "Read or buy whatever he writes!" Thank you, Dan, for being a clay vessel in the Master's hands through whom he has accomplished much.

1. S. R. Driver is an example of many scholars who see a strong connection between the book of Deuteronomy and the books of the DH when he writes concerning 1–2 Kings: "Deuteronomy is the standard by which the compiler judges both men and actions" (*An Introduction to the Literature of the Old Testament* [New York: C. Scribner's, 1950] 199).

will conclude with some basic observations concerning the interpretive benefits of this kind of study.

1. The Deuteronomistic History (DH): A Brief Overview[2]

1.1. Martin Noth's Key Affirmations

In the mid-twentieth century, Martin Noth crystallized the thinking of a growing number of OT scholars and regarded Deuteronomy–Kings as "Deuteronomistic Histories." According to this perspective, their authors or editors had interpreted the history of Israel in light of religious concepts based in the book of Deuteronomy.[3] He argued that these five biblical books were not separate works but were five parts of what had been one important historical work, "the Deuteronomistic History (DH)."[4] Based on Noth's conclusions, historical texts of the OT fell into three categories: the Pentateuch, the DH, and the Chronicler's history. Of course, the underlying assumption by Noth and almost all other DH scholars is that the material in the book of Deuteronomy did not coalesce until the seventh century B.C., during the reign of King Josiah (ca. 622 B.C.). An exilic Judean historian, called the Deuteronomist (Dtr), produced this history by drawing on older sources (e.g., Urdt—proto-Deuteronomy).[5] He sought to explain the downfall of the northern (722 B.C.) and southern kingdoms (586 B.C.) *in terms of divine judgment on their covenant treachery.* Later, Dtr added the Deuteronomic law code (Deut 4:44–30:20) as a paradigmatic prologue to his history, affixing Deuteronomy 1–3 as an introduction to the DH.[6]

---

2. In light of the numerous volumes, essays, and articles written on the history and various aspects of the DH, this section provides only a sketchy overview of the way DH studies have developed. For two clear and accessible summaries of the history of DH studies, see S. L. McKenzie, "Deuteronomistic History," *ABD* 2:160–68; S. L. Richter, "Deuteronomistic History," in *Dictionary of the Old Testament: Historical Books* (ed. B. T. Arnold and H. G. M. Williamson; Downers Grove, IL: InterVarsity, 2005) 219–30. Three collections of essays that provide a helpful overview of important issues in DH studies are L. S. Schearing and S. L. McKenzie, eds., *Those Elusive Deuteronomists: The Phenomenon of Pan-Deuteronomism* (JSOTSup 268; Sheffield: Sheffield Academic Press, 1999); G. N. Knoppers and J. G. McConville, *Reconsidering Israel and Judah: Recent Studies on the Deuteronomistic History* (Winona Lake, IN: Eisenbrauns, 2000); T. Römer, *The Future of the Deuteronomistic History* (Leuven: Leuven University Press, 2000).

3. M. Noth, *Überlieferungsgeschichtliche Studien: Die Sammelnden und Bearbeiten Geschichtswerke im Alten Testament* (2nd ed.; Tübingen: M. Niemeyer, 1957) 3–4.

4. Ibid., 10–11.

5. Unlike many later proponents of the DH, Noth contended that an editor or writer did most of the work that produced the DH (M. Noth, *The Deuteronomistic History* [JSOTSup 15; Sheffield: JSOT, 1981] 10).

6. Ibid., 6–10.

For Noth, the terms "deuteronomic" referred to something that was drawn from Urdt (i.e., Deuteronomy), while "Deuteronomistic" signified something deriving from an exilic revision, namely, material influenced by Deuteronomy. According to this understanding, a key task of any interpreter of the DH is to ascertain the content and character of Urdt.

1.2. Key Variations since Noth

In light of numerous passages that introduced a hope for the future, not all scholars were satisfied with the notion that the DH's purpose was limited to explaining the downfall of the kingdoms of Israel and Judah. Drawing on various scholarly discussions of Noth's theory, scholars offered two important adjustments to his proposal.[7] First, Frank Cross ("the Harvard school") proposed preexilic and postexilic redactions of the DH (the Double Redaction View).[8] Various students of Cross perpetuated and developed this notion. Dtr[1] completed the first edition/redaction of this history in the time of Josiah. Dtr[2] modified and updated the DH in the Exilic Period. Second, Rudolf Smend ("the Göttingen school") proposed an exilic core followed by two postexilic redactions of the DH.[9] Each of these redactions introduced a unique perspective to the DH. Unlike Noth and Cross, Smend proposed that the bulk of the DH was composed in the Postexilic Period and then was modified two subsequent times.[10] Although the details vary widely, sub-varieties of these and other similar approaches seek to resolve the tension between the good news and bad news of the historical accounts by postulating different editors and layers of tradition.

1.3. Challenges Facing DH Studies

Steven McKenzie wrote in 1992 that "the existence of the DH has achieved almost canonical status."[11] Only eight years later, however,

---

7. Many of these adjustments revolve around the juxtaposition of the promise of grace and mercy alongside of judgment and divine wrath throughout the DH.

8. F. M. Cross, *Canaanite Myth and Hebrew Epic* (Cambridge, MA: Harvard University Press, 1973) 274–89; cf. R. D. Nelson, *The Double Redaction of the Deuteronomistic History* (Sheffield: JSOT Press, 1981) 13–22.

9. R. Smend, "Das Gesetz und die Volker ein Beitrag zur deuteronomistischen Redaktionsgeschichte," in *Probleme biblischer Theologie G von Rad zum 70* (ed. H. W. Wolff; Munich: C. Kaiser, 1971) 494–509. Cf. J. G. McConville, *Grace in the End: A Study in Deuteronomic Theology* (Grand Rapids: Zondervan, 1993) 83–85. S. Richter suggests that all three of Smend's layers were post-exilic (Deuteronomistic History" 224–25).

10. Smend designates the original composition and then two redactions as follows: DtrG as primary compiler; DtrN as first redaction; DtrP as second redaction (prophetic).

11. McKenzie, "Deuteronomistic History," 161.

Gary Knoppers asserted: "One can no longer assume a widespread scholarly consensus on the existence of a Deuteronomistic History. In the last five years an increasing number of commentators have expressed grave doubts about fundamental tenets of Noth's classic study."[12] One of the main problems that plagues DH studies is the assumed ability to distinguish one Deuteronomistic redactor from another. This assumption leads scholars to repeatedly present one concept as incompatible with another theme, divvying up biblical books or sections of books into many divergent layers. A very low view of the ancient historians' ability to hold different concepts in tension worsens this atomizing of the biblical text.[13] Another major issue to be treated next is "pan-Deuteronomism," that is, connecting "virtually every significant development within ancient Israel's religious practices to a given Deuteronomic redactor or source."[14]

2. Problems with the Quest for Deuteronomisms

2.1. Confusion of Terms

One of the issues that challenges any scholar pursuing studies in the DH involves the varied definitions given to key terms: Deuteronomic, Deuteronomistic, and Deuteronomistic History. Richard Coggins suggests three implications for the terms Deuteronomic or Deuteronomistic. First, they relate to the book of Deuteronomy itself. Second, they can refer to the distinctively Deuteronomic language and style, often used to describe supposed Deuteronomistic redaction of other parts of the OT. Third, these terms can signify the reflection of ideology that is characteristically Deuteronomistic.[15] Coggins contends that part of the confusion is caused by numerous scholars who apply the term Deuteronomistic to examples of all three of the above usages without clear distinctions. At the very least, the ideological parallels are less clear and objective than vocabulary that is actually found in the book of Deuteronomy. It would be helpful for all scholars to use the key terms with consistent and clear definitions.

2.2. The Challenge of "Pan-Deuteronomism"

As suggested above, the concept of Deuteronomism has become so "amorphous that it no longer has any analytical precision and so ought

---

12. G. N. Knoppers, "Is There a Future for the Deuteronomistic History?," in *The Future of the Deuteronomistic History* (ed. T. Römer; Leuven: University Press, 2000) 120.
13. Richter, "Deuteronomistic History," 227.
14. R. Coggins, "What Does 'Deuteronomistic' Mean?" in *Those Elusive Deuteronomists*, 22.
15. Ibid., 34.

to be abandoned."[16] Proponents of the quest for Deuteronomisms seem to assume that a Deuteronomic approach provides an entirely distinct outlook within Hebrew religion (as compared with priestly and prophetic outlooks).[17] Here are a few concerns that must be carefully considered as one identifies potential Deuteronomisms.

First, a number of concepts typically identified as Deuteronomic could just as easily be considered "covenantal" or "mainstream OT theology."[18] Other aspects of God's expectations of his chosen nation occur in the other books of the Pentateuch as well. Those biblical books also make significant contributions to the revelation of God's character.

Second, many allegedly Deuteronomic concepts appear in ANE writings, including Egyptian, Assyrian, and Hittite literature.[19] David Tsumura, for example, rejects the use of allegedly Deuteronomistic phrases to argue for a late dating of 1–2 Samuel,[20] because the presence of these Deuteronomic terms and concepts in the broader ANE literary corpus diminishes their value as clear chronological indicators.

Finally, scholars must clarify the nature of connections between Deuteronomy and other OT books. Do the proposed connections represent verbal parallels, conceptual parallels, or broad allusions? To clarify the nature of the "connection," it might be helpful to identify a decline in specificity from *tight parallels* to *clear conceptual associations* to *more broad allusions*. Also, in light of such complicating factors, simple association of two concepts may be only coincidental and not necessarily indicative of intentional Deuteronomic influence.

An overview of the history, development, and challenges of the DH could easily demand much more time and space than this essay allows. Since my primary interests here are more synthetic and theological, we will move on to a few significant connections between Deuteronomy and the books of the DH.

---

16. R. R. Wilson, "Who Was the Deuteronomist? (Who Was Not the Deuteronomist?): Reflections on Pan-Deuteronomism," in *Those Elusive Deuteronomists*, 82.

17. M. Weinfeld's list of "Deuteronomic Phraseology" offers scores of potential examples of Deuteronomisms. A careful evaluation of his examples must precede any conclusions about direct Deuteronomic influence on other books. See Weinfeld, "Appendix A: Deuteronomic Phraseology," in *Deuteronomy and the Deuteronomic School* (Winona Lake, IN: Eisenbrauns, 1992) 320–65.

18. K. Kitchen, "Ancient Orient, 'Deuteronomism,' and the Old Testament," in *New Perspectives on the Old Testament* (ed. J. B. Payne; Waco, TX: Word, 1970) 17–19.

19. Ibid.

20. D. T. Tsumura, *The First Book of Samuel* (NICOT; Grand Rapids: Eerdmans, 2007) 17–19, 29.

3. Potential Deuteronomic Connections between Deuteronomy and Joshua–Kings

The books commonly assigned to the DH, Joshua–Kings, provide a summary of the nation of Israel's history, beginning with her conquest of the land of Canaan and ending in her eviction from it at the hands of the Assyrians and Babylonians (ca. 1406–586 B.C.).[21]

Although many readers view OT books as just that—books that are very distinct from one another, a careful reading presents a different picture. There are threads or themes that connect the message of each volume together. In addition to this mutual interconnectedness, the biblical historians seem to present their histories from the perspective of the book of Deuteronomy, evaluating the ups and downs of Israel's history by means of a Deuteronomic measuring stick.

After discussing some basic lines of interconnectedness within the books of the DH and between the books of the DH and the book of Deuteronomy, I will give brief attention to some of the key thematic connections that tie these books to each other and to the book of Deuteronomy. Some of these connections reaffirm concepts found in Deuteronomy while others represent a sad twist on what God desired as revealed in Deuteronomy.

In Appendix A (p. 246), I have attempted to offer this overview in chart form, providing a column for each biblical book or set of books to track the themes that course through those books. The four themes I have identified are as follows:

1. The promise and possession of the land of promise;
2. The institution of leadership: besides priests and prophets, there is a progression from non-dynastic mediatorial figures (Moses, Joshua, and judges) to kings in the line of David;
3. The importance of Yahweh's covenant relationship with Israel, including its demand for wholehearted obedience—for the people and their rulers;
4. A place of worship that God chooses and where God has placed his name.[22]

---

21. More precisely, the last action of 2 Kings involves the release of King Jehoiachin from his Babylonian confinement in 562 B.C. (2 Kgs 25:27–30). Evangelical scholars are not agreed on the date for the Exodus (ca. 1446 or 1250 B.C.). For an overview of this debate, see M. Grisanti, "The Book of Exodus," in *The World and the Word: An Introduction to the Old Testament* (eds. E. H. Merrill, M. F. Rooker, M. A. Grisanti; Nashville: Broadman & Holman, 2012) 194–207.

22. In his overview of Deuteronomic theology in Joshua, J. G. McConville also points to three of the four themes I highlight here (*Grace in the End*, 98). He does not refer to the theme of a place of worship in that section.

3.1. The Promise and Possession of the Land of Promise

Throughout the OT, the land of promise receives abundant attention. For example, the basic expression "the land" occurs 86 times in the book of Deuteronomy and 54 times in Joshua. Of course, "the land" is an important concept in other pentateuchal books. It receives unique attention, however, in Deuteronomy. Although God made various promises in the Abrahamic and Mosaic Covenants, "nothing looms larger in Deuteronomy than land."[23] The prominence of "land" in Deuteronomy does not simply derive from word frequency, but the fundamental role it plays in the theology of the book. Throughout Deuteronomy the chosen nation stands at the brink of the long-anticipated initial fulfillment of what Yahweh had promised to Abraham.

At the time depicted by Deuteronomy, the covenant nation is camped across the Jordan River from the land of promise. Besides their geographic proximity to this long anticipated covenant provision, many of the laws that Moses restates in the book directly deal with the conduct of life on this land, which God set apart as a divine stewardship for his chosen people.

The covenant curses and blessings (Deuteronomy 27–28) that are so essential to the theology of Deuteronomy (as they are in Leviticus 26 as well) delineate the concrete implications of Israel's obedience or disobedience to the covenant stipulations for the people's enjoyment or non-enjoyment of that land of promise. As many have suggested, there is a clear connection between the covenant community's relationship with Yahweh and their relationship with this land of promise. The triangle below depicts the relationship between Israel's relationship with Yahweh and their enjoyment of the divinely allotted land.[24]

If the nation becomes characterized by covenant treachery, disrupting their relationship with Yahweh, Yahweh will disrupt their enjoyment of the Promised Land as well. He will evict them from that land

---

23. E. H. Merrill, "A Theology of the Pentateuch," in *A Biblical Theology of the Old Testament* (ed. R. B. Zuck; Chicago: Moody, 1991) 68; cf. W. J. Dumbrell, *Covenant and Creation: A Theology of Old Testament Covenants* (Nashville: Thomas Nelson, 1984) 116–23; P. D. Miller, "The Gift of God: The Deuteronomic Theology of the Land," *Interpretation* 23 (1969) 451–65.

24. D. I. Block provides a similar but more generic triangle with Deity-People-Land at the corners, showing that this was a common ANE conception of relationships. In his explanation, he points out that while the nations viewed the deity-land relationship as primary, for Israel the deity-people relationship was most important. See D. I. Block, *The Gods of the Nations: Studies in Ancient Near Eastern National Theology* (2nd ed.; ETS Studies; Grand Rapids: Baker, 2000) 20. Cf. C. J. H. Wright, *Old Testament Ethics for the People of God* (Downers Grove, IL: InterVarsity, 2004) 19; idem, *God's People in God's Land: Family, Land, and Property in the Old Testament* (Grand Rapids: Eerdmans, 1990) 3–43.

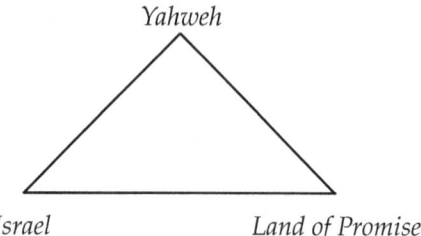

Fig. 1. Land Promise as a Divine Stewardship

by means of foreign invaders, after having visited drought and famine on the land (Deut 28:20–68).

The moral hysteria of the time of the judges demonstrates the partial experience of those drastic covenant consequences. During that period, the nation of Israel had control of various parts of the land of promise *intermittently*, depending on their covenant obedience or disobedience. Eventually, in 2 Kings, both Israel and Judah (the northern and southern kingdoms) experienced the loss of the land of promise. In their explanation of the theological rationale for Israel's defeat by and exile to Assyria in 722 B.C. (2 Kgs 17:7–20), the biblical historians draw heavily on Deuteronomic language and theology. God is doing exactly what he had told them he would do. Deuteronomy 27–30 make it abundantly clear that Yahweh will allow his chosen nation to remain in the land of promise if they obey his demands, but he will evict them if they pursue covenant treachery (esp. Deut 28:36, 63; 30:19–20). Broadly speaking, Israel rejected Yahweh's statutes and demands (2 Kgs 17:12, 15) rather than gladly obeying them (Deut 11:31–32). They worshipped other gods (2 Kgs 17:7–12, 15) rather than worshipping Yahweh alone (Deut 5:7, 6:4–5, 12:1–4). They embraced pagan customs (2 Kgs 17:8) rather than avoiding them (Deut 18:9). They practiced child sacrifice to pagan gods as well as divination and sorcery, in direct violation of Yahweh's prohibition (Deut 18:10–12). Their acts of covenant treachery provoked Yahweh's anger (2 Kgs 17:17), just as Yahweh said it would (Deut 7:4). Because of their devotion to empty, heartless religious ritualism, social injustice, and the abomination of idolatry, God removed them from his gracious provision of the land (2 Kgs 17:7–20; cf. Deut 7:1–5, 13:6–18, 1 Kgs 11:1–10).

An episode in the book of Judges that epitomizes the moral chaos of the period uses classic language of conquest and holy war in relation to the Danites' unwillingness to occupy their divinely allotted tribal inheritance. This carryover of key Deuteronomic expressions used to describe Israel's conquest of the land of Canaan provides the backdrop for the offensive use of these terms by the Danites with regard to their covenant treachery—leaving their divinely allotted land for the area around Laish to the far north. The men who had scouted this region reported to their fellow Danites: "Don't hesitate to go and invade (בוא) and take possession of (ירש) the land! When you get there, you will come to an unsuspecting people and a spacious land, for God has handed it over to you (כי־נתנה אלהים בידכם)." As if these verbs were not enough "to recall the original entry into Canaan, the scouts add a note of piety with the committal formula, assuring their audience that God has given the land into their hands."[25]

The promise of land plays a central role in the book of Deuteronomy as well as the entire Pentateuch. Life in the Promised Land is a central part of the hope of God's covenant nation. Loss of that land is also a major part of Israel's experience of covenant curse.

3.2. The Installation of Covenant Leadership

A second theme that connects the book of Deuteronomy with the DH involves the establishment of covenant leadership over Israel. In addition to the appointment of elders and judges (Deut 1:9–18, 17:8–13) and the establishment of the Levitical priesthood, Deuteronomy and the books of Joshua–Kings provide a glimpse of the process by which Yahweh introduced kingship to Israel.[26] The charter for Israelite kingship occurs in Deut 17:14–20 (cf. Gen 17:6, 16).[27] High standards were laid down for any Israelite monarch. There were kings throughout the ANE, but Yahweh placed three categories of limitations on kings who would rule over his servant nation. Specifically, he had to be a king of God's choosing (17:15), needed to live and rule within some key restrictions (not multiply horses, chariots, wives, silver, or gold, 17:16–17),[28] and must adhere to the Mosaic Law—Yahweh's requirements (17:18–

---

25. D. I. Block, *Judges, Ruth* (NAC 6; Nashville: Broadman & Holman, 1999) 502.

26. Here are some helpful resources for this theme: D. M. Howard Jr., "The Case For Kingship in the Old Testament Narrative Books and the Psalms," *TJ* 9 (1988) 19–35; idem, "The Case for Kingship in Deuteronomy and the Former Prophets," *WTJ* 52/1 (Spring 1990) 101–15.

27. See D. I. Block, "The Burden of Leadership: The Mosaic Paradigm of Kingship," *BSac* 162 (2005) 259–78; repr. in idem, *How I Love Your Torah, O LORD! Studies in the Book of Deuteronomy* (Eugene, OR: Cascade, 2011) 119–40. Numerous passages clearly demonstrate that the Israelite king was to function under God as Israel's king (Deut 33:5).

28. These represent things or people in which he could boast or that could distract him from absolute reliance on Yahweh as his ultimate suzerain.

Table 1. The Evaluation of Some of Israel and Judah's Kings

	God's choosing[a]	Yahweh's restrictions	Adherence to Law
Saul	**No**: 1 Sam 8:5, 19–20; cf. 10:19		1 Sam 13:9–14; 15:10–11, 17–35
David	1 Sam 16:1–13	**No**: wives – 1 Sam 25:43	1 Kgs 11:34
Solomon	1 Kgs 3:7–14	**No**: wives – 1 Kgs 11:1–5	1 Kgs 2:2–4, 9:6–9 **No**: 1 Kgs 11:4–11
Jeroboam	1 Kgs 11:29–39		**No**: 1 Kgs 12:25–33, 13:33–34, 14:1–16
Hezekiah[b]	2 Kgs 18:7		2 Kgs 18:3–6, 19:14–19
Manasseh			**No**: 2 Kgs 21:2–16
Josiah			2 Kgs 22:2, 11–13, 19–20; 23:3, 4–27

a. Not all of the kings of Judah have a clear statement that God chose them. All of them are part of the Davidic/Messianic line.

b. After the sobering indictment of Israel to the north in 2 Kings 17, the biblical historian devotes the next three chapters to Hezekiah who provides a clear example of a king who rules in accordance to the Mosaic Covenant, which is what Israel should have done. In accordance with Deuteronomy 28, 2 Kings 17 illustrates judgment for covenant treachery, while 2 Kings 18–20 demonstrate blessing for obedience and restoration in the wake or repentance.

20). The warning that Samuel gives in 1 Sam 8:11–18 objectifies the dangers of installing a king over Israel. It describes monarchy at its worst.

The accession of Saul as king over Israel does not necessarily represent Israel's rejection of Yahweh's rule. However, it does raise the important question of whether Saul would accept the limits placed upon kingship within Yahwistic theocracy.[29] As Gordon McConville explains, Israel's demand for a king in 1 Samuel 8 "does not reject kingship as such; rather it focuses on both the people's illegitimate request for a king and on Saul's inability to grasp the nature of the role that Yahweh permits him to take. This inability is exposed by his refusal, admittedly under pressure, to comply with the requirements of Samuel in 1 Samuel 8:7–8 (cf. 13:8–15)."[30] The inability of Saul to reign within Yahweh's parameters paves the way for the king of Yahweh's choice, David.

---

29. V. P. Long, *The Reign and Rejection of King Saul* (Atlanta: Scholars, 1989) 236–39.
30. McConville, *Grace in the End*, 115.

These three categories of divine expectations for an Israelite king (Deut 17:14–20) reappear repeatedly as part of the biblical historians' evaluation or description of various Israelite kings. Out of the 40 monarchs of Israel and Judah, Table 1 only considers seven key kings: Saul, David, Solomon, Jeroboam, Hezekiah, Manasseh, and Josiah.

It must also be mentioned that kingship in Israel was vastly important for far-reaching theological reasons. Even in the book of Genesis (17:6, 16; 49:10) Yahweh intended to have a king rule over his covenant nation. Having a king rule over Israel was not simply a matter of pragmatic wisdom, for the very role paved the way for the people's understanding of a coming messiah. Having a king, like David, readied the way for God's establishment of the Davidic covenant (2 Samuel 7). Along with the royal psalms, various passages describe a Davidic king who would rule the nation with unparalleled righteousness, compassion, and justice, leading the nation in heartfelt covenant obedience. Israel's experience of human king after human king, even the best of them, led to a growing preparedness for the promised Messiah-King of Israel, Jesus Christ.

The refrain that "there was no king in Israel" during the period of the Judges occurs three times in the book (17:7, 18:1, 21:25). On the one hand, this expression most likely refers to the absence of human monarchs and provides insight into the monarchic time of composition of the book of Judges. It also serves as a sad comment on the moral anarchy of that day. Besides this, "no king" may highlight Israel's repudiation of Yahweh as covenant lord/suzerain, a major emphasis in Deuteronomy (4:1–32, 5:6–27, 10:12–22, 11:1–32, 26:16–19, 30:15–20).

3.3. The Centrality of Yahweh's Relationship with His Covenant People (and Their Kings)

Although the Mosaic covenant involves numerous rules and regulations, it is much more than that. The foundational core of the Mosaic covenant is relationship: "I will be your God and you will be my people" (Lev 26:12). God calls his servant nation to heartfelt loyalty. This faithfulness to the covenant demands was to enable the nation of Israel to demonstrate God's character to the surrounding world (Exod 19:5–6, Deut 26:16–19). Joshua picks up the Deuteronomic "torch" by continuing the demand for faithfulness to the covenant (Josh 8:30–35, 24:14–28). The book of Joshua illustrates the fortunate consequences of obedience to the covenant—in order to encourage the Israelites to maintain such loyalty.

Much could be said about this relationship with Yahweh that God sets before his people in Deuteronomy and the following historical books. For the sake of space, I will only pursue one thread that relates to God's demand for world-impacting living.

Conduct "in the eyes of" someone occurs throughout the OT with positive and negative connotations. There are four varieties of this descriptive statement, the most common of which are the bipolar expressions used to describe a person's conduct entailed in doing "right" in Yahweh's sight (עשה הישר בעיני יהוה) or doing "evil" in my or his sight (עשה הרע בעיני or בעיניו).[31]

First, besides the five instances in the Pentateuch (Exod 15:26; Deut 6:18; 12:25, 28; 13:19; 21:9), the positive statement ("do right in the eyes of Yahweh") occurs once in a command to Jeroboam I (1 Kgs 11:38), 11 times in a description of Israelite or Judean kings,[32] and once as a description of God's people (Jer 34:5). It is important to point out that the application of this commendation to an Israelite or Judean king never represented *carte blanche* approval of their reign. Only David, Hezekiah, and Josiah receive unqualified commendation.

Second, a spinoff of the above statement, "he has *not* done right in Yahweh's sight," occurs in two instances. The historian indicts Solomon and God's people for embracing idolatry so wholeheartedly (1 Kgs 11:33)[33] as well as King Ahaz for covenant treachery (2 Kgs 16:2).

Third, another spinoff of the first statement refers to doing what is "right" in one's own eyes. This occurs once in the Pentateuch (Deut 12:8) as part of Moses' exhortation that sacrifices must be offered to Yahweh only at a place where he has put his name, in contrast to everyone doing what is right in his own eyes. It also occurs twice in that sad refrain that describes the time of the Judges when "everyone did what was right in his own eyes" (Judg 17:6, 21:25).[34]

Fourth, the other major expression, "do evil in Yahweh's sight," occurs almost three times as frequently as the positive expression. Six occurrences in the Pentateuch refer to individual evil conduct (Gen 38:7; Num 32:13; Deut 4:25, 9:18, 17:2, 31:29). The phrase also serves as the

---

31. Both expressions are Mosaic and occur most frequently in Deuteronomy.

32. Jeroboam (not like David—1 Kgs 14:8), David (1 Kgs 15:5), Asa (1 Kgs 15:11), Jehoshaphat (1 Kgs 22:43), Jehu (2 Kgs 10:30), Jehoash (2 Kgs 12:3[2]), Amaziah (2 Kgs 14:3), Uzziah (2 Kgs 15:3), Jotham (2 Kgs 15:34), Hezekiah (2 Kgs 18:3), Josiah (2 Kgs 22:2).

33. The MT has a 3mp verb while LXX, Syriac, and Vulgate suggest a 3ms verb. Depending on the reading one prefers, this description refers to Solomon and Israelites (most English translations) or just Solomon (NRSV).

34. Just for the sake of completeness, this expression also occurs four times without negative moral connotations, referring to something that pleases a person (Josh 9:25, 2 Sam 19:7[6], Jer 26:14, 40:4–5). In Jer 40:4–5, something "good" or "evil" has no moral significance.

common indictment of God's people during the period of the Judges (Judg 2:11; 3:7, 12 [2×]; 4:1; 10:6; 13:1). The historian applies this Deuteronomic measuring rod to 26 Israelite and Judean kings 30 different times.[35] Three occurrences pronounce the guilt of God's covenant nation (2 Kgs 14:22, 17:17, 21:15).

The first half of the OT exhibits a sad progression in the application of this painful indictment. The pentateuchal passages describe individuals who were characterized by evil. In the book of Judges, this phrase depicts the nation's penchant to sin. In Samuel and Kings, this expression not only describes the covenant treachery pursued by individual kings but also condemns them for leading the nation in their devotion to widespread disobedience. As Daniel Block points out: "The difference between the period of the governors and the monarchy/ies is not the presence or absence of idolatry or evil. Rather, it is the source from which the evil springs. During the monarchy kings led the way in abominable acts; in premonarchic times the people did it on their own."[36]

3.4. A Place of Worship, Which God Chooses and Has Placed His Name

3.4.1. Is Centralization or Purification the Point of Josiah's Reforms?

One of the recurring arguments we encounter in modern scholarship on Deuteronomy and the DH is the primary agenda that Deuteronomy 12 and Josiah's reforms (2 Kgs 22:8–23:27) focused on centralizing worship in Jerusalem. Is that really the best way to understand those passages?

Along with many others, I would argue that Josiah's reforms are much more about cult-purification than cult-centralization.[37] The primary issue that Josiah pursues appears to be the threat of pagan worship places and pagan worship practices rather than an attempt to create a

---

35. United Kingdom—Saul (1 Sam 15:19), David (2 Sam 12:9), Solomon (2 Kgs 11:6); Judah (SK)—Jehoram (2 Kgs 8:18), Ahaziah (2 Kgs 8:27), Manasseh (2 Kgs 21:2, 6, 16), Amon (2 Kgs 21:20), Jehoahaz (2 Kgs 23:32), Jehoiakim (2 Kgs 23:37), Jehoiachin (2 Kgs 24:9), Zedekiah (2 Kgs 24:19); Israel (NK)—Nadab (1 Kgs 15:26), Baasha (1 Kgs 15:34), Zimri (1 Kgs 16:19), Omri (1 Kgs 16:25), Ahab (1 Kgs 16:30; 21:20, 25), Ahaziah (1 Kgs 22:53), Jehoram (2 Kgs 3:2), Jehoahaz (2 Kgs 13:2), Jehoash (2 Kgs 13:11), Jeroboam II (2 Kgs 14:24), Zechariah (2 Kgs 15:9), Menahem (2 Kgs 15:18), Pekahiah (2 Kgs 15:24), Pekah (2 Kgs 15:28), Hoshea (2 Kgs 17:2). Although this indictment is never applied to Jeroboam I, he becomes the epitome of wickedness and covenant treachery for most of the kings of the Northern Kingdom.
36. Block, *Judges, Ruth*, 483–84.
37. Kitchen, "Ancient Orient," 18.

monopoly on worship in Jerusalem. Furthermore, the "centralization" of proper Yahweh worship had taken place long before Josiah with Solomon's construction of the temple in Jerusalem (966 B.C.).[38] In addition to this, the Tabernacle that travelled with Israel throughout their wanderings and then was installed at Shiloh demonstrated Yahweh's desire that most worship of him take place at the central sanctuary. This was practiced hundreds of years before Josiah's reign.

Deut 12:5 employs two important expressions that relate to Israel's place of worship: "the place which Yahweh your God will choose" and "to put his name." In the immediate context, "the place" provides a clear antithesis to "the places" where the Canaanites worshiped their gods (12:2). This "place" is where Israel was commanded and allowed to worship their powerful and incomparable God, Yahweh. Unlike most discussions in DH studies, the passage is not primarily addressing the theoretical issue of the number of sanctuaries or the centralization of the sanctuary. Instead, as M. H. Segal points out, the law found here and at Exod 20:24 permits a plurality of sanctuaries, provided that they were properly located and consecrated. Thus "the place" signifies a single class of sanctuaries, rather than a single place (other singulars of class are noted in Deut 12:18 and 16:14).[39]

3.4.2. The Place Which Yahweh Your God Will Choose

In the first place, the fundamental point made by Deuteronomy 12 is that Israel can only worship God at a place of his choosing. The expression, "the place where Yahweh your God will choose," occurs 21 times in Deuteronomy[40] and twice in the DH (Josh 9:27; 2 Kgs 21:7). On the one hand, the place of Yahweh's choice and name would be where the tabernacle (and later the temple) is located. On the other hand, Moses highlights the kind of place where Israel can worship, namely, one that Yahweh chooses (especially in contrast with Canaanite worship practices).[41] Until God has given Israel rest from all its enemies (Deut 12:10–11), that is, the time of David, the Israelites could follow the pattern

---

38. Noth rejects this notion when he argues that Solomon's prayer (1 Kings 8) contains no reference to the temple's role as a place of offering (Noth, *Überlieferungsgeschichtliche Studien*, 104–5). Even if Solomon does not explicitly refer to the offering of sacrifices in his dedicatory prayer, it is obvious that he regarded the temple as a place for sacrifices by his conduct—offering thousands of sacrifices at the temple when he dedicated the temple to the worship of Yahweh (1 Kgs 8:62–64).

39. M. H. Segal, *The Pentateuch: Its Composition and Its Authorship* (Jerusalem: Magnes, 1967) 87–88.

40. Deut 12:5, 11, 14, 18, 21, 26; 14:23, 24, 25; 15:20; 16:2, 6, 7, 11, 15, 16; 17:8; 18:6; 26:2; 31:11.

41. P. D. Miller, *Deuteronomy* (Int; Louisville: John Knox, 1990) 131.

established in Exod 20:24 (allowing God's people to offer their sacrifices at more than one place). But what kind of place must that location be? Just as he chose Israel (Deut 4:37, 7:6–7, 10:15, 14:2) and the priests (18:5, 21:5), he alone would chose any place where he will receive worship (12:5, 11, 14, 18, 21, 26; 14:23–25; 16:2, 6, 7; 17:8, 10; etc.). Yahweh will "cause his name to dwell" in that place of his choosing. Establishing Yahweh's "name" at the acceptable place of worship demonstrates that he has the ability to mark out a place for himself in light of his sovereignty over and ownership of the land of promise.[42]

3.4.3. The Place Where God Will Put His Name

Second, the covenant nation must worship Yahweh at a place where he "puts his name."[43] Various scholars have debated the exact meaning of this expression. Gordon Wenham suggests that the clearest meaning is that Yahweh dwells in the sanctuary.[44] The name of a deity in the ANE defined in an essential way the character, nature, and function of a deity.[45] Hence, when a god's name was "placed" somewhere (e.g., Baal Peor), the god was there. The names of pagan gods were attached to the places where they appeared or were connected to a given location, especially a cultic site or shrine.[46] In a similar way, Yahweh instructs Israel that he will put his name at those places where he chooses to be recognized and worshiped. Throughout the OT, God's name signifies all that he is. Moses demands that God's chosen people must appear and rejoice before Yahweh (Deut 16:11, 16). Whenever they worship at the sanctuary, it is "before Yahweh," and whatever they present as an offering there is done "before Yahweh" (Deut 26:10, 13). In addition to God's presence being at the sanctuary, Israelite worshippers ask Yahweh, "Look down from your holy dwelling, from heaven" (Deut 26:15). Yahweh's presence is not limited to the sanctuary, for he is present in heaven as well.

---

42. P. T. Vogt, *Deuteronomic Theology and the Significance of Torah: A Reappraisal* (Winona Lake, IN: Eisenbrauns, 2006), 183; cf. C. J. H. Wright, *Deuteronomy* (NIBC; Peabody, MA: Hendrickson, 1996) 159.

43. This expression appears in two forms: "to put his name there" (לשום את שמו שם— Deut 12:5, 21; 14:24) and "to make his name dwell there" (לשכן שמו שם—Deut 12:11; 14:23; 16:2, 6, 11; 26:2). S. L. Richter suggests that this Hebrew expression should be associated with the Akkadian *šakānu* 'to cause to be dwelling' (*The Deuteronomistic History and the Name Theology: leš̌akkēn šemô šām in the Bible and the Ancient Near East* [BZAW 318; Berlin: de Gruyter, 2002] 118–19).

44. G. J. Wenham, "Deuteronomy and the Central Sanctuary," *TB* 22 (1971) 112–13.

45. E. E. Carpenter, "Deuteronomy," in *Zondervan Illustrated Bible Backgrounds Commentary (Old Testament)* (ed. J. H. Walton; Grand Rapids: Zondervan, 2009) 1:471.

46. Richter, *The Deuteronomic History and the Name Theology* 41–42.

In Deuteronomy 12, Yahweh's name is described as dwelling in his sanctuary, similar to the names of the Canaanite gods. In 12:3 Moses commands the Israelites to destroy all their places of worship and to *"wipe out their names* from every place." Then in 12:5 they are told to turn "to the place Yahweh your God chooses from all your tribes *to put his name* for his dwelling and go there."

Other scholars connect the expression "to put his name" with the Akkadian idiom *šuma šakânu*, which indicates a claim to sovereignty.⁴⁷ Rather than being confined to the sanctuary on earth, as God of the whole earth he might make himself known and accept the sacrifices and worship of his people wherever he chose to assert his sovereignty.⁴⁸ Both Gordon Wenham and Sandra Richter suggest that the Hebrew and Akkadian expressions signify overtones of conquest.⁴⁹

Regardless, Israel was to worship Yahweh at a place God chose and at a place where he put his name. A parallel passage helps explain the significance of the expression "to put his name." Exod 20:24 affirms that the Israelites were to erect an earthen altar "wherever I cause my name to be honored/remembered." The essential element in a location for sacrifice is a place where Yahweh reveals himself or brings himself glory by intervening on behalf of the Israelites. It signifies a place where God has distinguished himself. Also, in subsequent biblical narratives sacrifices were occasionally offered (without divine condemnation) at locations other than the primary location for that period of time (Josh 8:30–35; Judg 2:5; 6:26; 13:16–23; 20:26–27; 21:4; 1 Sam 6:14–15; 7:9–10, 17; 10:8; 11:15; 2 Sam 6:13; 24:22, 24–25; 1 Kgs 3:4 [cf. 2 Chr 1:3–6]; 1 Kgs 18:33–38). In addition to being used for God's choice of the city of Jerusalem to put his name there (1 Kgs 14:21; 2 Kgs 21:4, 7; 2 Chr 12:13), this expression "to put his name" or "to cause his name to dwell" occurs in Kings and Chronicles to refer to the temple at Jerusalem (1 Kgs 9:3, 14:21, 2 Kgs 21:7, 2 Chr 6:20).

The way Israelite kings dealt with illegitimate places of worship (i.e., "high places") demonstrates the use of the measuring rod of Deuteron-

---

47. J. A. Thompson, *Deuteronomy: An Introduction and Commentary* (TOTC; Downers Grove, IL: InterVarsity, 1974) 185. Thompson points to a kindred expression that occurs in the OT. In a number of passages where God claims ownership, possession, or sovereignty in respect to a place, people, or nations, the phrase *called by my* (thy) *name* is used (2 Sam 12:28; 1 Kgs 8:43; 2 Chr 7:14; Jer 7:10, 11, 14, 30; 34:15; Dan 9:18, 19). The expression is used for Yahweh's sovereignty over his people (Deut 28:10, 2 Chr 7:14, Isa 63:19, Jer 14:9, Amos 9:12).

48. Richter, *The Deuteronomic History and the Name Theology*, 1–39, 207–17.

49. Wenham, "Deuteronomy and the Central Sanctuary," 113–15; Richter, *The Deuteronomic History and the Name Theology*, 209–11.

omy to evaluate their reigns.[50] The reluctance of an Israelite king and several Judean kings to tear down the high places or their willingness to offer sacrifices and incense on these pagan altars demonstrates their failure to keep the Mosaic Covenant in the area worshipping at the place God chooses (Deut 12:2–5).[51] The lengthy presentation of the theological reason for Israel's defeat by and exile to Assyria includes several references to worship at a high place (2 Kgs 17:9, 11, 29, 32). The biblical historians refer to three Judean kings as those who honored Yahweh and tore down the high places in the land: Asa (1 Kgs 15:14), Hezekiah (2 Kgs 18:14, 22), and Josiah (23:5, 8–9, 13, 15, 19–20). But when a king of God's choosing failed to reject those places that God did not choose, their actions clearly represented their rejection of this Deuteronomic requirement as well as their participation in covenant treachery.

Finally, Israel's covenant disloyalty occasions the divine destruction of this sanctuary that God chose and where he put his name (Jer 7:12–14):

> "But return to my place that was at Shiloh, *where I made my name dwell at first*. See what I did to it because of the evil of my people Israel. Now, because you have done all these things," declares Yahweh, "and because I have spoken to you time and time again but you wouldn't listen, and I have called to you, but you wouldn't answer, what I did to Shiloh I will do to the house that is *called by my name*—the house in which you trust—the place that I gave you and your ancestors."

3.5. Conclusion

At least four important themes receive significant development in the book of Deuteronomy and also play a prominent role in the DH. These involve the promise and possession of the land, the institution of leadership, the importance of Yahweh's covenant relationship with Israel (including its demand for wholehearted obedience), and a place of worship. The remainder of this essay considers a specific passage, 1 Kgs 8:46–53, and the way Deuteronomic theology impacts the biblical historians and the points they make in that passage.

---

50. The phrase "high places" does occur in certain passages in a non-pejorative sense, referring to an important meeting place or legitimate place of worship (1 Sam 9:12–14, 19, 25; 10:5, 13; 22:6; 1 Kgs 3:2–4).

51. For Israel, see Jeroboam (1 Kgs 12:31–32); for Judah, see Solomon (11:7), Rehoboam (14:22–24), Jehoshaphat (22:43), Joash (2 Kgs 12:3), Amaziah (14:4), Azariah/Uzziah (15:4), Jotham (15:35), Ahaz (16:4), and Manasseh (21:3).

4. The Juxtaposition of Covenant Curse and Hope in Solomon's Prayer (1 Kgs 8:46–53)

Although Solomon's dedicatory prayer (after the completion of the temple) occupies a large section of text (1 Kgs 8:22–53), verses 46–53 of his prayer has occasioned numerous discussions concerning the relationship of Deut 4:25–31, 29:17–27, and 30:1–10 to the outlook of the historian.

4.1. The Standard Explanation

As stated above, various DH scholars have proposed two or more redactions of the DH in light of the presence of hope as well as curse in 1 Kgs 8:46–53. In fact, most of these scholars make no attempt to deal with both ideas as a coherent part of the work of the historian(s) behind the narratives of Kings.[52]

4.2. McConville's Helpful Proposal

McConville attempts to reconcile these differing emphases without resorting to redactional layers or editorial activity. In order to establish his point, he provides helpful tables that compare the language of Deuteronomy 29 and 30 with 1 Kings 8. He demonstrates significant points of overlap and emphasis. However, he sets forth a fundamental difference between Deuteronomy 30 and 1 Kings 8 in particular. He posits that these two passages *differ in their expression of hope for the future.*[53] He writes,

> Deuteronomy 30:1–10 looks forward to a return of the people to the land to which they would in due course be exiled. The books of 1, 2 Kings, though conversant with the passage in Deuteronomy, ask only in the prayer of Solomon at the dedication of the temple (1Ki 8:46–53) that when the people repented, their captors might show them compassion. Nowhere do 1, 2 Kings express any other hope than this for the end of the captivity. This difference seems to me to be best explained by the setting of 1, 2 Kings precisely in that period when the full sense of loss was being experienced. These two books, then, are "Deuteronomic" in the sense that they dialogue between the Deuteronomic tradition and the contemporary situation.[54]

He contends that the significant similarities between these passages (Deuteronomy 29, Deuteronomy 30, and 1 Kings 8) do not preclude dif-

---

52. McConville offers a helpful summary of the attempts by DH scholars to explain away this tension ("1 Kings VIII 46–53 and the Deuteronomic Hope," *VT* 42 [1992] 70–71).
53. Ibid., 75–78.
54. Idem, *Grace in the End*, 91.

Table 2. "Events" Related to Israel's Rebellion,
Reprimand, Repentance, and Restoration

Event	Deut 4	Deut 29–30	1 Kgs 8
1. Israel commits covenant treachery.	25ab	29:15–18, 24–25[16–19, 25–26]	46a
2. Israel's sin provokes God to anger.	25c	29:19ab, 23, 26–27 [20ab, 24, 27–28]	46b
3. God evicts his chosen nation from the land of promise and brings covenant curse on Israel.	26–28	29:19c–20, 21–22 [20c–21, 22–23]	46c
4. Scattered among nations, in exile, many Israelites repent and seek Yahweh.	29–30	30:1–2	47–48
5. Yahweh will be faithful to his covenant commitments.	31	30:3a	49–53
6. Yahweh will re-gather his covenant nation from their exile and return them to the land of promise.	—	30:3b–5	—
7. Yahweh will circumcise their hearts and Israel will obey Yahweh.	—	30:6, 8	—
8. God will bring curses on Israel's enemies.	—	30:7	—
9. God will abundantly bless his covenant people, predicated on their obedience.	—	30:9–10	—

ferent perspectives. In other words, a Deuteronomic connection does not require absolute replication of ideas.

4.3. A Modification of McConville's Proposal

Although I agree that Solomon's prayer in 1 Kgs 8:46–53 does not match exactly the view of Israel's future found in Deut 30:1–10, I would suggest that a comparison between 1 Kings 8 and Deuteronomy 29 and 30 *along with* Deut 4:25–31 would help clarify the issue even further.

4.3.1. Comparison of the Key Passages

Examining the various passages involved (Deut 4:25–31, 29:16–30:10, and 1 Kgs 8:46–53), I found that together they address nine discrete "events" (see Table 2, p. 241).[55] First, Deuteronomy 4 and 1 Kings 8 are quite similar, addressing five of the nine "events." Second, Deuteronomy 4 and 1 Kings 8 both do not address the details presented by Deuteronomy 30 concerning Israel's future restoration to the land of promise ("events" six through nine). Third, Deut 29:16–30:10 should be regarded as a unit. Precisely where Deuteronomy 29 leaves off, Deuteronomy 30 picks up. Fourth, related to this last point, Deuteronomy 29 offers no hope at all. Notice the following nine "events" and how the passages delineate them.

Let me summarize the above chart. First, Deuteronomy 4, Deuteronomy 29, and 1 Kings 8 all delineate the first three "events," which are absent from Deuteronomy 30. Second, Deuteronomy 4, Deuteronomy 30, and 1 Kings 8 all delineate "events" four and five. Deuteronomy 4 and 1 Kings 8 climax with the assurance that Yahweh will be faithful to his covenant commitments. Third, Deuteronomy 29 ended with "event" three, and Deuteronomy 30 picks up with "event" four. Finally, Deuteronomy 30 alone delineates "events" six through nine.

4.3.2. The Flow of Deuteronomy 29 and 30

After pointing out the nation's imperceptiveness to the significance of God's intervention on their behalf (through the ten plagues and his faithful care of them during their travels between Egypt and the Plains of Moab) (Deut 29:1–9[2–10]), Moses calls the covenant nation to renew their commitment to the covenant relationship with Yahweh (29:10–14[11–15]). Moses then relates three sets of circumstances to his audience that should motivate them to wholeheartedly commit themselves to this marvelous relationship with Yahweh. First, from Moses' present perspective, he looks to the near future (29:15–20[16–21]). He warns any Israelites against thinking that they can be anonymous covenant rebels. Yahweh will severely judge all those who commit treachery against this covenant. Second, from a distant future perspective, Moses describes a horrific set of circumstances (29:21–27[22–28]). Looking to a hypothetical future scenario where the nation of Israel has disobeyed the stipulations of the covenant and has been judged with devastating impact, later generations of Israelites and Gentiles will be amazed at the destruction that has fallen on Israel.[56] They will learn that the cause

---

55. "Events" refers to nine steps in what the biblical writers describe concerning Israel's disobedience, God's reaction, their eventual repentance, and their restoration to the land of promise.

56. P. Craigie points out that this material is not "primarily prophetic." He goes on to affirm that Moses "employs both the experience of the past and his notion of the potential future to force home upon the Israelites the need for obedience in the present. Before

of all this sorrow was Israel's violation of their covenant with Yahweh by worshiping other gods. Third, Moses describes a day sometime after the horrific destruction caused by covenant curse just described (30:1–10). In order to emphasize the need for Israel to obey Yahweh in the present, Moses looks forward to a future day when the children of Israel will return to Yahweh, will be brought back to the promised land, and will enjoy the abundant blessings of a proper relationship with Yahweh.

The above overview of Deut 29:1–30:10 suggests that the anticipated circumstances of Deut 29:15–20[16–21] must be understood along with 30:1–10 when seeking to understand 1 Kgs 8:46–53. Comparing 1 Kings 8 with Deuteronomy 29 and 30 separately only tells part of the story.

4.3.3. An Important, Overlooked Point

In summary, McConville's point that 1 Kings 8 does not speak *explicitly* of Yahweh's restoration of Israel to the land is absolutely correct. However, that is exactly what Deuteronomy 4 does as well. Beyond that, it is essential to see that both passages end with the affirmation that God will be absolutely faithful to his covenant promises to the chosen nation, Israel. In Deut 4:31, Moses declares that "he will not abandon or destroy you or forget the covenant with your forefathers, which he confirmed to them by oath." The writer of Kings celebrates Israel's status as God's servant nation when he inscribes the following:

> For they are your people and your inheritance, whom you brought out of Egypt, out of that iron-smelting furnace. May your eyes be open to your servant's plea and to the plea of your people Israel, and may you listen to them whenever they cry out to you. For you singled them out from all the nations of the world to be your own inheritance, just as you declared through your servant Moses when you, O Sovereign LORD, brought our fathers out of Egypt (1 Kgs 8:51–53).

Both passages likely refer back to the Abrahamic and Mosaic covenants. At the very least, both passages promise that God will not withdraw from pursuing his intentions for the chosen nation. This seems to allude to the primary function of the Mosaic covenant, i.e., to have the nation of Israel function as a banner nation before the world (Exod 19:5–6; Deut 4:6–8, 7:6, 26:16–19). In terms of the covenant, this was integrally connected to Israel's presence in the land of promise. Consequently, even though Deuteronomy 4 and 1 Kings 8 make no explicit reference to Yahweh reinstalling the servant nation in the land of promise, that

---

they have even entered the land, he warns of their being driven out again and scattered, and then brought back in" (*Deuteronomy*, [NICOT; Grand Rapids: Eerdmans, 1976] 364).

reality appears to be assumed in both passages in light of Yahweh's faithfulness to his covenant promises. If so, the language of 1 Kgs 8:46–53 does not represent a *significant* change from the Deuteronomic hope of Deut 30:1–10. Instead, it tells just part of what God will accomplish on behalf of his people (in agreement with Deuteronomy 4).

5. The Value of This Study

In light of the abundant studies on the DH and the impact of the book of Deuteronomy on those historical books, there are several things about this essay that are not new or profound. The primary purpose of this essay, however, was not to introduce an innovative conclusion to the discipline. Instead, let me suggest at least three reasons why this study has merit and is worth pursuing for each of us. First, the interconnectedness of Deuteronomy and Joshua–Kings is essential to a proper understanding of OT theology. Without recognizing these connections, we will end up with a disjointed view of the message of these historical books in particular. Second, the books of biblical history are not disjointed and distinct presentations of various phases of Israel's history. Instead, important theological threads that derive their source from the message of the book of Deuteronomy tie together the biblical presentation of history. Recognizing that connection helps us better appreciate more clearly the kind of conduct Yahweh wanted from his people as well as the just basis for his severe judgment of his beloved servant nation. Third, we must be very careful to avoid the danger of an undue focus on "Deuteronomisms." Let us avoid the extreme of finding them under every rock and behind every bush!

6. Conclusion

Various scholars have observed the strong connection between the message and theology of Deuteronomy and Joshua–Kings, the books commonly included in DH. For example, the esteemed honoree of this volume has written, "The connections that exist between Judges, the preceding Book of Joshua, and the following Samuel–Kings derive not from a single hand but from the common Mosaic theological and literary tradition in which the Yahwistic authors of all of these books were schooled."[57]

Although this essay has expressed numerous hermeneutical and methodological points of tension with the varied suggestions made by other DH scholars, all readers need to pay attention to the obvious in-

---

57. Block, *Judges, Ruth*, 50.

terconnectedness of Deuteronomy and Joshua–Kings, which studies of the DH have made clear. Our understanding of the message of the OT can greatly benefit through a growing awareness of the impact of Deuteronomy on the subsequent historical books.

While looking for key points of connection between Deuteronomy and the DH, we must hear the cautions offered by various scholars. We should not overplay the evidence and thereby dilute or corrupt the interpretive benefit of recognizing the connections put there by the biblical authors. I know that I have only scratched the surface in this essay. I fully realize that my conclusions at this point are still somewhat preliminary and incomplete. There is much more work to do.

In the end, let us invest ourselves in recognizing the beautiful coherence of the message of the OT, in particular that found in the books that delineate God's dealings with his chosen nation. I am not referring to dry, dusty facts of history, but to theologically driven history writing. The good news as well as the bad news of Israel's history helps us understand more clearly the majestic character of the God we serve and helps us grasp more fully his intentions for the world in which he has placed us.

Appendix A:
Basic Interconnectedness of Deuteronomy and Joshua–Kings

	Deuteronomy	Joshua	Judges	Samuel	Kings
(1)	Moses provides restatement of Yahweh's covenant requirements.	Joshua acknowledges the "book of the Law" (Josh 1:8)			
(2)	Introduces Joshua a a new leader (Deut 31:1–8, ch. 34)	Joshua recalls this transition (Josh 1:1–9)			
(1)	Ceremonies to be performed at Shechem (Deut 27) *(Point of ceremony: To demonstrate that God's covenant requirements serve as the guiding authority of life in the land of promise.)*	Ceremonies carried out at Shechem (Josh 8:30–35, esp. 33b)			
(3)	Promise of possession of the land of promise	Initial possession of the land of promise	Intermittent possession of the land of promise	Solidified possession of the land of promise	Eviction from the land of promise
(2)		Records Joshua's death (Josh 24:29)	Records Joshua's death (Judg 1:1, 2:8)		
(2)			Refrain: "In those days, Israel had no king" (Judg 17:6, 18:1, 19:1, 21:25)	Origin of kingship; Davidic Covenant (2 Sam 7)	Solomon securely on the throne (1 Kgs 1–2); land king of Judah removed from the throne (2 Kgs 25)
(1)			Refrain: "Everyone did what was right in his own eyes" (Judg 17:6, 21:25)	Did right/evil in Yahweh's sight	Did right/evil in Yahweh's sight
(2)			Prepares for the establishment of kingship	Transition from judgeship to kingship	Messianic line still alive
(4)	The place that Yahweh will choose and put his name (Deut 12:5, 11)	The place Yahweh should choose (Josh 9:27)			The place Yahweh has chosen to put his name (1 Kgs 9:3; 2 Kgs 21:7)

Key Threads:
1. Central role of Yahweh's covenant relationship with Israel
2. Covenant leadership—narrowing from a mediatorial figure (Moses) to kings of David's line
3. Land of promise
4. Place of worship ("where Yahweh chooses" and "where he places his name")

Appendix B:
Comparison of Deut 4:25–31 and 30:1–10

Deut 4:25–31	Deut 30:1–10
[25] After you have had children and grandchildren and have lived in the land a long time—if you then become corrupt and make any kind of idol, doing evil in the eyes of the LORD your God and provoking him to anger, [26] I call heaven and earth as witnesses against you this day that you will quickly perish from the land that you are crossing the Jordan to possess. You will not live there long but will certainly be destroyed. [27] The LORD will scatter you among the peoples, and only a few of you will survive among the nations to which the LORD will drive you. [28] There you will worship man-made gods of wood and stone, which cannot see or hear or eat or smell.	
[29] But if from there you seek the LORD your God, you will find him if you look for him with all your heart and with all your soul. [30] When you are in distress and all these things have happened to you, then in later days you will return to the LORD your God and obey him.	[1] When all these blessings and curses I have set before you come upon you and you take them to heart wherever the LORD your God disperses you among the nations, [2] and when you and your children return to the LORD your God and obey him with all your heart and with all your soul according to everything I command you today,
[31] For the LORD your God is a merciful God; he will not abandon or destroy you or forget the covenant with your forefathers, which he confirmed to them by oath.	[3] then the LORD your God will restore your fortunes and have compassion on you
	and gather you again from all the nations where he scattered you. [4] Even if you have been banished to the most distant land under the heavens, from there the LORD your God will gather you and bring you back. [5] He will bring you to the land that belonged to your fathers, and you will take possession of it. He will make you more prosperous and numerous than your fathers. [6] The LORD your God will circumcise your hearts and the hearts of your descendants, so that you may love him with all your heart and with all your soul, and live. [7] The LORD your God will put all these curses on your enemies who hate and persecute you. [8] You will again obey the LORD and follow all his commands I am giving you today. [9] Then the LORD your God will make you most prosperous in all the work of your hands and in the fruit of your womb, the young of your livestock and the crops of your land. The LORD will again delight in you and make you prosperous, just as he delighted in your fathers, [10] if you obey the LORD your God and keep his commands and decrees that are written in this Book of the Law and turn to the LORD your God with all your heart and with all your soul.

Appendix C:
Comparison of Deut 4:25–31 and 1 Kgs 8:46–53

Deut 4:25–31	1 Kgs 8:46–53
25 After you have had children and grandchildren and have lived in the land a long time—if you then become corrupt and make any kind of idol, doing evil in the eyes of the LORD your God	46 When they sin against you—for there is no one who does not sin—
and provoking him to anger,	and you become angry with them
26 I call heaven and earth as witnesses against you this day that you will quickly perish from the land that you are crossing the Jordan to possess. You will not live there long but will certainly be destroyed. 27 The LORD will scatter you among the peoples, and only a few of you will survive among the nations to which the LORD will drive you. 28 There you will worship man-made gods of wood and stone, which cannot see or hear or eat or smell.	and give them over to the enemy, who takes them captive to his own land, far away or near;
29 But if from there you seek the LORD your God, you will find him if you look for him with all your heart and with all your soul. 30 When you are in distress and all these things have happened to you, then in later days you will return to the LORD your God and obey him.	47 and if they have a change of heart in the land where they are held captive, and repent and plead with you in the land of their conquerors and say, "We have sinned, we have done wrong, we have acted wickedly"; 48 and if they turn back to you with all their heart and soul in the land of their enemies who took them captive, and pray to you toward the land you gave their fathers, toward the city you have chosen and the temple I have built for your Name;
31 For the LORD your God is a merciful God; he will not abandon or destroy you or forget the covenant with your forefathers, which he confirmed to them by oath.	49 then from heaven, your dwelling place, hear their prayer and their plea, and uphold their cause. 50 And forgive your people, who have sinned against you; forgive all the offenses they have committed against you, and cause their conquerors to show them mercy; 51 for they are your people and your inheritance, whom you brought out of Egypt, out of that iron-smelting furnace. 52 May your eyes be open to your servant's plea and to the plea of your people Israel, and may you listen to them whenever they cry out to you. 53 For you singled them out from all the nations of the world to be your own inheritance, just as you declared through your servant Moses when you, O Sovereign LORD, brought our fathers out of Egypt.

Appendix D:
Comparison of Deut 4:25–31 and 29:16–28

Deut 4:25–31	Deut 29:16–28
[25] After you have had children and grandchildren and have lived in the land a long time—if you then become corrupt and make any kind of idol, doing evil in the eyes of the LORD your God	[16] Indeed, you know how we lived in the land of Egypt and passed through the nations where you traveled. [17] You saw their detestable images and idols made of wood, stone, silver, and gold, which were among them. [18] Be sure there is no man, woman, clan, or tribe among you today whose heart turns away from the LORD our God to go and worship the gods of those nations. Be sure there is no root among you bearing poisonous and bitter fruit. [19] When someone hears the words of this oath, he may consider himself exempt, thinking, "I will have peace even though I follow my ⸢own⸣ stubborn heart." This will lead to the destruction of the well-watered ⸢land⸣ as well as the dry ⸢land⸣.
and provoking him to anger,	[20] The LORD will not be willing to forgive him. Instead, His anger and jealousy will burn against that person, and every curse written in this scroll will descend on him.
[26] I call heaven and earth as witnesses against you this day that you will quickly perish from the land that you are crossing the Jordan to possess. You will not live there long but will certainly be destroyed. [27] The LORD will scatter you among the peoples, and only a few of you will survive among the nations to which the LORD will drive you. [28] There you will worship man-made gods of wood and stone, which cannot see or hear or eat or smell.	The LORD will blot out his name under heaven, [21] and single him out for harm from all the tribes of Israel, according to all the curses of the covenant written in this book of the law. [22] Future generations of your children who follow you and the foreigner who comes from a distant country will see the plagues of the land and the sicknesses the LORD has inflicted on it. [23] All its soil will be a burning waste of sulfur and salt, unsown, producing nothing, with no plant growing on it, just like the fall of Sodom and Gomorrah, Admah and Zeboiim, which the LORD demolished in His fierce anger. [24] All the nations will ask, "Why has the LORD done this to this land? Why this great outburst of anger?" [25] Then people will answer, "It is because they abandoned the covenant of Yahweh, the God of their fathers, which He had made with them when He brought them out of the land of Egypt. [26] They began to worship other gods, bowing down to gods they had not known—gods that the LORD had not permitted them ⸢to worship⸣. [27] Therefore the LORD's anger burned against this land, and He brought every curse written in this book on it. [28] The LORD uprooted them from their land in ⸢His⸣ anger, rage, and great wrath, and threw them into another land where they are today."
[29] But if from there you seek the LORD your God, you will find him if you look for him with all your heart and with all your soul. [30] When you are in distress and all these things have happened to you, then in later days you will return to the LORD your God and obey him. [31] For the LORD your God is a merciful God; he will not abandon or destroy you or forget the covenant with your forefathers, which he confirmed to them by oath.	

Deuteronomy and Isaiah

H. G. M. WILLIAMSON

1. Introduction

Investigation of the influence of Deuteronomy on Isaiah is hampered by a number of critical issues in relation to both biblical books. Since space precludes extended consideration of them, let me simply set out at the start the presuppositions from which I write in what follows. Readers with different starting points should be able to make any necessary adjustments to suit their preferences. In the present instance this should not, I believe, require any major adjustments to most of the principal conclusions reached.

Concerning Isaiah, I assume the standard critical views about the history of the book's composition. That is to say, any record of the words of the eighth-century prophet Isaiah himself will be included in the first half of the book, down as far as chapter 39. These chapters also include, however, three sections of narratives about the prophet (chs. 7, 20, and 36–39) that he presumably did not write himself, since he appears in the third person. In addition, there are significant portions of these chapters that come from a variety of later dates. The precise contours of this later material are disputed, however. For instance, few would doubt that chapters 24–27 and 34–35 should be included, and an overwhelming majority would also include 4:2–6, 12, some parts of the oracles against the nations in chapters 13–23, and 33. In particular, it should be noted that there seem to be a number of passages of modest length that reflect the outlook of later parts of the book and that may have been added in the process of bringing the whole together into the unity that we now have.[1] The middle section of the book, Isaiah 40–55, mostly reflects the situation of the exilic period, whether in Babylon

---

Author's Note: I am delighted to have this opportunity of paying tribute to Dan Block's scholarship, friendship, and example over many years.

1. For detailed suggestions, see H. G. M. Williamson, *The Book Called Isaiah: Deutero-Isaiah's Role in Composition and Redaction* (Oxford: Clarendon, 1994); J. Stromberg, *Isaiah After Exile: The Author of Third Isaiah as Reader and Redactor of the Book* (OTM; Oxford: Oxford University Press, 2011).

itself or in Judah, while the final eleven chapters seem to be placed and dated in the restored Judean community of the relatively early post-exilic Persian period. Given the extensive time frame covered by the book, it would not be surprising if the influence of Deuteronomy varied from one section to another.

In the case of Deuteronomy our problems are slightly different. Although it is likely that it too developed over a period of time, for the purpose of this essay it can certainly be treated as a unity. However much it may include earlier material, it is unlikely to have reached its present form and been "published," so to speak, before the late monarchical period. It is clear, however, as many chapters in the present volume attest, that its influence may be traced in two ways, both exegetically important. On the one hand, a later author may have known of the book and been influenced by it in any number of ways. On the other hand, it is evident that its outlook and style of writing are not confined to the book of Deuteronomy alone. These features are very clearly apparent in other passages, such as 2 Kings 17 and Jeremiah 7. How and why this should be is not a subject on which all scholars agree but it looks as though in the decades following the publication of Deuteronomy many different passages in the Hebrew Bible were either penned or edited in such a manner as to give them something of a family resemblance as "Deuteronomic." Perhaps we could talk of second-hand influence.

This has been such an important part of biblical research in recent decades that it would be foolish to ignore it also in our investigation. At the same time it raises serious questions of method so that, after this wider sort of influence was postulated over ever more extensive swathes of literature, a reaction has set in more recently with calls for greater methodological rigor.[2] Most recently Nihan has neatly summarized the position by tabulating three different scholarly uses of "Deuteronom(ist)ic": (1) it may refer narrowly to linguistic style; (2) it may refer to a distinct ideology; or (3) it may refer to a group of scribes or a school responsible for writing or editing in a Deuteronomic manner.[3]

---

2. I have space here to mention only two or three relatively comprehensive surveys of this debate; see L. S. Schearing and S. L. McKenzie, eds., *Those Elusive Deuteronomists: The Phenomenon of Pan-Deuteronomism* (JSOTSup 268; Sheffield: Sheffield, 1999); A. de Pury, T. Römer, and J.-D. Macchi, eds., *Israel Constructs Its History: Deuteronomistic Historiography in Recent Research* (JSOTSup 306; Sheffield: Sheffield, 2000); several essays in M. Nissinen, ed., *Congress Volume Helsinki 2010* (VTSup 148; Leiden: Brill, 2012) 307–471.

3. C. Nihan, "'Deutéronomiste' et 'Deutéronomisme': quelques remarques de méthode en lien avec le débat actuel," in Nissinen, ed., *Congress Volume*, 409–41.

Given the lack of any direct evidence for the existence of such a school or otherwise socially determined group, I shall not refer to the last of these three in what follows. It is sufficient to trace the influence of Deuteronomy at the linguistic and ideological levels and leave the precise mechanism by which this came about undecided.

2. Deuteronomy and Isaiah of Jerusalem

Given the dates mentioned above and presupposed here it is clear that we should not expect to find that Isaiah himself was in any way influenced by Deuteronomy. This negative position is further confirmed by the fact that the early poetic material in the book does not directly deal with any of the major concerns of Deuteronomy. In terms of salvation history, for instance, there is no clear reference to the exodus or wilderness period, despite occasional claims to the contrary,[4] and where the allusion is certain, as at 11:16, Isaianic authorship is usually (and rightly) disputed on other grounds. Equally, the election of Israel, the covenant with her, the "statutes and ordinances" as well as the law (*torah*) do not appear in these chapters.[5] Furthermore, the temple paraphernalia as best we can reconstruct them from Isa 6:1–5 do not coincide with the Deuteronomic formulae,[6] and some of the honored religious functionaries, such as the diviner, the one skilled in magic practices, and the expert in charms (3:2–3), seem to be included among those who were later condemned by Deuteronomy (see Deut 18:9–14).[7] By contrast, Isaiah bases his understanding of the relationship between God

---

4. See, for instance, S. Deck, "Kein Exodus bei Jesaja?" in *Ich bewirke das Heil und erschaffe das Unheil (Jesaja 45,7): Studien zur Botschaft der Propheten. Festschrift für Lothar Ruppert zum 65. Geburtstag* (ed. F. Diedrich and B. Willmes; FzB 88; Würzburg: Echter Verlag, 1998) 31–47. Her suggestion that the cry of Isa 5:7 shows awareness of Exod 3:7 is farfetched.

5. The verb for "elect" occurs at 1:29 and 7:15–16, but not with God as subject or Israel as object, and at 14:1, where it is clearly part of the prose redactional join between the two poems in ch. 13 and 14:4b–21. Within the early material the term for "covenant" occurs only in Isaiah 28, where its application is far from that in Deuteronomy. Of course the words תורה and משפט occur, but again not with their specific Deuteronomic sense. For the former, see J. Jensen, *The Use of tôrâ by Isaiah: His Debate with the Wisdom Tradition* (CBQMS 3; Washington, DC: The Catholic Biblical Association of America, 1973), though I cannot agree with all his conclusions, and for the latter see my commentary, *A Critical and Exegetical Commentary on Isaiah 1–27*, i: Commentary on Isaiah 1–5 (ICC; London: T. & T. Clark International) 100–101.

6. Despite suffering from some over-simplification, the study of T. N. D. Mettinger nevertheless highlights some of the major distinctions: *The Dethronement of Sabaoth: Studies in the Shem and Kabod Theologies* (ConBOT 18; Lund: Gleerup, 1982).

7. I have discussed this last example at greater length in my essay, "In Search of the Pre-Exilic Isaiah," in *In Search of Pre-exilic Israel: Proceedings of the Oxford Old Testament*

and his people both historically and, ideally, in the present on what is generally known as the Zion tradition, with its focus on the temple and God's rule through the Davidic monarchy.

3. Deuteronomic Redaction of the Isaianic Collection

If this first point is widely agreed, the same cannot be said of the next and somewhat related topic, namely whether the early collection of Isaianic sayings ever passed through a process of Deuteronomic editing or redaction.

That some of the prophetic books did so became widely accepted following some pioneering work in the 1960s.[8] This approach was first applied to Isaiah in a systematic manner by Vermeylen in a major and influential analysis, in which he both traced what he maintained were two layers of Deuteronomic redaction and also on this basis ascribed to these same circles some more substantial elements in the book that had previously always been regarded uncontroversially as Isaianic.[9] The most striking example of the latter is the Song of the Vineyard in Isa 5:1–7.

Responses to Vermeylen's proposals have come from a variety of directions,[10] which at least have the merit of prompting us to reflect

Seminar (ed. J. Day; JSOTSup 406; London: T. & T. Clark International, 2004) 181–206 (188–89).

8. It is sufficient merely to mention here the ground-breaking article of W. H. Schmidt, "Die deuteronomistische Redaktion des Amosbuches," *ZAW* 77 (1965) 168–93.

9. J. Vermeylen, *Du prophète Isaïe à l'apocalyptique: Isaïe, I – XXXV, miroir d'un demi-millénaire d'expérience religieuse en Israël* (EBib, 2 vols.; Paris: Gabalda, 1977–1978). One may see something of the difference in exegetical terms by comparing the first (1960) and fifth (1981) editions of the commentary of O. Kaiser: the first edition is *Isaiah 1–12: A Commentary* (OTL; London: SCM, 1972); trans. of *Der Prophet Jesaja, Kapitel 1–12* (ATD 17; Göttingen: Vandenhoeck & Ruprecht, 1960); the fifth edition is *Isaiah 1–12: A Commentary* (OTL; London: SCM, 1983); trans. of *Das Buch des Propheten Jesaja, Kapitel 1–12* (ATD 17; 5th ed.; Göttingen: Vandenhoeck & Ruprecht, 1981). Some others who have adopted a similar view are listed by A. Labahn, *Wort Gottes und Schuld Israels: Untersuchungen zu Motiven deuteronomistischer Theologie im Deuterojesajabuch mit einem Ausblick auf das Verhältnis von Jes 40–55 zum Deuteronomismus* (BWANT 143; Stuttgart: Kohlhammer, 1999), 26–30; Z. Kustár, *"Durch seine Wunden sind wir geheilt": Eine Untersuchung zur Metaphorik von Israels Krankheit und Heilung im Jesajabuch* (BWANT 154; Stuttgart: Kohlhammer, 2002) 63–64.

10. Prominent examples include C. Hardmeier, "Jesajaforschung im Umbruch," *VF* 31 (1986) 3–31; A. J. Bjørndalen, *Untersuchungen zur allegorischen Rede der Propheten Amos und Jesaja* (BZAW 165; Berlin: de Gruyter, 1986); C. Brekelmans, "Deuteronomistic Influence in Isaiah 1–12," in *The Book of Isaiah* (ed. J. Vermeylen; BETL 81; Leuven: University Press and Peeters, 1989) 167–76; L. Perlitt, "Jesaja und die Deuteronomisten," in *Prophet und Prophetenbuch: Festschrift für Otto Kaiser zum 65. Geburtstag* (ed. V. Fritz et al.; BZAW 185; Berlin and New York: de Gruyter, 1989) 133–49.

on appropriate method. This becomes all the more urgent if we compare the first part of Isaiah with Jeremiah, where some close links with Deuteronomy are self-evident. Does it make sense to use the same descriptive terminology in academic discourse when two such dissimilar works are apparently being brought under the same umbrella?

For the sake of clarity, it may help if I here summarize detailed conclusions on this topic for the first chapter of Isaiah, all of which are set out more fully elsewhere.[11] I choose this chapter because, on most commentators' view, it combines material from Isaiah himself with some sort of editorial shaping in order to bring together oracles from different periods in his ministry in a form of introduction to the following book. It therefore serves well as a test case for our question at more than one diachronic level.

If we take first the narrower criterion of Deuteronomic language, attention focuses on Isa 1:18–20 as the most probable fruitful source of evidence. Indeed, Vermeylen has listed no less than thirteen words or phrases that, he claims, are not Isaianic but that have significant contact with Deuteronomic literature.[12] In working through each example in turn, however, I have demonstrated first that about half his examples are of no significance for this purpose whatsoever. Of the remainder, while there are some superficial points of comparison with Deuteronomy, they transpire on further analysis to be distinctive even within that category.[13] To give a single example, the clause at the end of the passage, כי פי יהוה דבר 'for the mouth of the LORD has spoken', seems clearly to be of redactional significance as it occurs in identical form elsewhere at 40:5 and 58:14 while the closely similar clause (lacking פי) occurs at 1:2, 21:17, 22:25, and 25:8 (and three times outside the book of Isaiah). Now, as Vermeylen rightly says, the phrase "mouth of the LORD" occurs 48 times in the Hebrew Bible, of which he estimates that there are 21 appearances in priestly literature and 15 in Deuteronomic literature. That in itself hardly makes this diagnostic of Deuteronomic style, but in addition it should be stressed that the fuller form in Isaiah (with the verb of speech) does not occur anywhere else at all except once in Mic 4:4, where the context indicates some close association with the Isaianic tradition (see Isa 2:2–4). The upshot of a full analysis of the wording of Isa 1:18–20 is that there is nothing about v. 18 to indicate that it could not be from Isaiah. Verses 19–20, however, do include a

---

11. See my *Isaiah 1–5*, 7–162.
12. Vermeylen, *Du prophète Isaïe à l'apocalyptique*, 57–63.
13. See my *Isaiah 1–5*, 106–11, in which I draw into the discussion the insights of other scholars who have worked on this material as well.

concentration of unusual features (to that extent, Vermeylen's analysis retains its value), but they do not align it closely with Deuteronomy, even if there are some points of general, though by no means exclusive, connection (e.g., the use of מרה and מאן).

Let us build upon that first conclusion with a glance at Isa 1:10. This verse too seems almost certainly to have been provided by the chapter's editor in order to join the Isaianic verses 11–18 with 5–9. It clearly introduces what follows with its call to listen, while the next verse already has its own divine speech formula; what is more, that speech formula, which takes the extremely rare *yiqtol* form (יאמר יהוה), is repeated in v. 18, suggesting the likelihood that vv. 11–18 were the original unit. In addition, v. 10's metaphorical references to Sodom and Gomorrah evidently pick up the use of the same names from v. 9, while its two imperatives echo the same two in v. 2. Much of the verse's phraseology may therefore be shown to serve as an integrating element within the wider chapter.

The same conclusion may be drawn from the very general nature of the object of what should be listened to: "the word of the LORD" and "the *torah* of our God." This sort of language is relatively stereotypical, and its use elsewhere in comparable redactional additions, such as Isa 5:24b, has again been labeled in both language and theology as typical of the Deuteronomic school.[14]

In my opinion this is again jumping to too restrictive a conclusion. Given the widespread occurrence of this terminology in later biblical literature, as well as the content of these verses that may have parallels in Deuteronomy but that do not share any of its distinctive theological features, it seems wisest to conclude as follows: First, these sorts of editorial additions were relatively late in the composition history of the book.[15] Second, the embellishments served the purpose of shaping and

---

14. Vermeylen, *Du prophète Isaïe à l'apocalyptique*, 174–75; R. E. Clements, *Isaiah 1–39* (NCB; Grand Rapids: Eerdmans; London: Marshall, Morgan & Scott, 1980) 66; Kustár, "Durch seine Wunden sind wir geheilt" 65–67. On this verse it should be noted that alongside some elements that are shared by Deuteronomy others are decidedly not, such as "the Holy One of Israel" and the use of אמרה 'word'; see correctly J. Blenkinsopp, *Isaiah 1–39: A New Translation with Introduction and Commentary* (AB 19; New York: Doubleday, 2000) 215.

15. If space permitted, the same conclusion could be drawn for the redactional line 1:2a. It is worth adding at this point that many of the closest connections between Isaiah 1 and Deuteronomy that have been previously collected in fact relate specifically to what we should now regard as the redactional stitching in the chapter; see, for instance, R. Bergey, "The Song of Moses (Deuteronomy 32.1–43) and Isaianic Prophecies: A Case of Early Intertextuality?" *JSOT* 28.1 (2003) 33–54, and much earlier L. G. Rignell, "Isaiah

presenting the materials of Isaiah for later readers, no doubt drawing on the experience of the nation that showed how his prophetic word had been vindicated and should thus be heeded.[16] Third, in writing, the editor(s) may certainly, therefore, have been influenced by their knowledge of Deuteronomy and the other literature that was directly dependent upon it, but not in any exclusive or scholastic sense. The links with Deuteronomy thus remain indirect at best.

4. Deuteronomy and the Historical Narratives in Isaiah 1–39

There are three passages of varying length in Isaiah 1–39 where the prophet is presented in the third person and where there are close associations with the history of Judah in the eighth century B.C.E. as known from other sources. First, Isa 7:1–17 is a narrative about Isaiah and Ahaz during the so-called Syro-Ephraimite crisis, and of course it includes the Immanuel saying. Most of its first verse is almost identical with 2 Kgs 16:5 from the Deuteronomistic History, and there are some striking echoes of Deuteronomy in what follows; for instance, the encouragement in Isa 7:4, "Take heed, be quiet, do not fear, and do not let your heart be faint," includes phraseology that seems distinctively to echo the priestly war oracle in Deut 20:3 (אל־תירא ולבבך אל־ירך; see otherwise only Jer 51:46), and Ahaz's refusal to "put the LORD to the test" by asking for a sign (Isa 7:12) is reminiscent of Deut 6:16 together with 13:1–3.

The second passage is the short narrative in Isaiah 20 where Isaiah walks naked for three years "as a sign and a portent" against Egypt and Ethiopia at the time of the Ashdod revolt in 711 B.C.E. There is certainly sound historical memory here, but, as Blenkinsopp and Cook have carefully and convincingly demonstrated in great detail, "the language of the narrative is distinctive of the Deuteronomistic History."[17] To give

---

Chapter 1: Some Exegetical Remarks with Special Reference to the Relationship between the Text and the Book of Deuteronomy," *StTh* 11 (1957) 140–58.

16. Towards the close of the first chapter there are, in my opinion, further redactional materials, and these have their closest parallels in the last part of the book; see especially Stromberg, *Isaiah After Exile*, 145–60. If the editing of chapter 1 is thus to be aligned on internal grounds with the major work which brought the bulk of the book to its present form, the suggestions advanced above about the time and nature of the passages discussed in the middle of the chapter can be seen to be very much on target.

17. See P. M. Cook, *A Sign and a Wonder: The Redactional Formation of Isaiah 18–20* (VTSup 147; Leiden: Brill, 2011) 125–45 (the citation is from p. 126), and the previous important study of J. Blenkinsopp, "The Prophetic Biography of Isaiah," in *Mincha: Festgabe für Rolf Rendtorff zum 75. Geburtstag* (ed. E. Blum; Neukirchen-Vluyn: Neukirchener Verlag, 2000) 13–26 (also idem, *Isaiah 1–39*, 321–22).

just a single example out of a number that might be mentioned, the formulaic introduction to a military campaign that occurs in the first verse is closely comparable with more than half a dozen passages elsewhere in 1–2 Kings, but it occurs otherwise only at Isa 36:1, which is itself parallel with 2 Kgs 18:13.

Third, as is well known, Isaiah 36–39 includes extensive narratives about Hezekiah relating to the time of Sennacherib's invasion in 701 B.C.E. with associated incidents, and it has a close parallel in 2 Kings 18–20. Its close association with the Deuteronomistic History is thus beyond question, though quite how the two versions relate to one another is a matter of dispute.

The first and third of these narratives seem certainly to have been written in association with one another, even though Isaiah 7 has no corresponding text in the Historical Books. As Ackroyd first pointed out and as several others have repeated since in greater detail, there are many striking points of correspondence and contrast between them that serve to underline what is presented as the faithless attitude of Ahaz in chapter 7 and the faithful attitude of Hezekiah in chapters 36–39. Conrad, for instance, listed six particular points that enabled him to conclude that "each narrative reflects the same type-scene and contains the same sequence of motifs."[18] Both narratives begin with an invading army that threatens the city of Jerusalem; both include a narrower geographical focus that refers to "the conduit of the upper pool on the highway to the Fuller's Field" (Isa 7:3, 36:2, and nowhere else); both indicate the great distress of the king; both kings then receive a "fear not" oracle of assurance (7:4–9, 37:6–7); both kings are offered a "sign" to confirm God's word (7:11, 37:30); and both narratives record the sparing of the city followed by a prediction of a worse disaster to follow (7:15–17, 39:6–7). On the other hand, there are some clear distinctions between the narratives, such as Ahaz's refusal but Hezekiah's acceptance of a sign and the similarly contrasting relationship of the kings to the prophet Isaiah.

---

18. E. W. Conrad, *Reading Isaiah* (OBT; Minneapolis: Fortress, 1991) 38–40; see previously P. R. Ackroyd, "Isaiah 36–39: Structure and Function," in *Von Kanaan bis Kerala: Festschrift für Prof. Mag. Dr. Dr. J. P. M. van der Ploeg O.P. zur Vollendung des siebzigsten Lebensjahres am 4. Juli 1979* (ed. W. C. Delsman et al.; AOAT 211; Kevelaer: Butzon & Bercker; Neukirchen-Vluyn: Neukirchener Verlag, 1982) 3–21; repr. in *Studies in the Religious Tradition of the Old Testament* (London: SCM, 1987) 105–20; more recently U. Becker, *Jesaja — von der Botschaft zum Buch* (FRLANT 178; Göttingen: Vandenhoeck & Ruprecht, 1997) 28–30 (who includes references to much earlier scholars who had briefly made similar claims) and now most standard commentaries.

Given that these two passages are closely related, it seems plausible to assume that Isaiah 20 was also related in terms of original composition. Though it is much shorter, it shares some of the same characteristic stylistic features with the Deuteronomistic History that the other two texts do, and it is interesting to note also the focus on Isaiah as a "sign and a portent."[19] Although the prophet himself is not a sign in the other two passages, we have already noted that a sign is a focal motif in them both.

Looking at the three passages as a group, it is evident that they all deal with the person of Isaiah the prophet and his role in major national affairs. It is striking, however, that the portrayal of Hezekiah, at least, is in tension with what one might have supposed on the basis of the verse oracles alone. There, although there is no direct reference to Hezekiah by name, Isaiah appears to be sharply critical of many of the policies that were evidently undertaken during his reign and for which he was therefore ultimately responsible. To give just two obvious examples, the overtures to form an alliance with Egypt in preparation for the revolt against Assyria at the start of Sennacherib's reign are strongly condemned in, for instance, Isa 30:1–5 and 31:1–3, while the local preparations in Jerusalem are regarded as unjust human devices in 22:8–11. In Isaiah 36–39, on the other hand, Hezekiah is portrayed in a much more positive light. By contrast with the depiction of Ahaz in Isaiah 7 he becomes a model of trust who seeks out the prophet's prayer and support, which he receives.[20]

While harmonistic strategies have sometimes been devised for holding these apparently conflicting presentations together, it remains the case that the text itself does not overtly present them to us, so that faithfulness to its present form suggests that we should take their differing emphases seriously. Given that only one of these three passages is included in the books of Kings, and that even that one has some literary features that are unparalleled elsewhere in the history,[21] the most plausible hypothesis is to conclude that the three started out as (part of?) a composition later than the lifetime of Isaiah that showed particular

---

19. This feature is one of several elements that suggest that Isa 8:18 may also have been added redactionally when chapters 7 and 20 were included in the developing book of Isaiah; see my article, "A Sign and a Portent in Isaiah 8.18," in *Studies on the Text and Versions of the Hebrew Bible in Honour of Robert Gordon* (ed. G. Khan and D. Lipton; VTSup 149; Leiden: Brill, 2012) 77–86.

20. See in greater detail U. Berges, *Das Buch Jesaja: Komposition und Endgestalt* (HBS 16; Freiburg: Herder, 1998) 266–321; Blenkinsopp, "The Prophetic Biography of Isaiah."

21. See most forcefully K. A. D. Smelik, "Distortion of Old Testament Prophecy: The Purpose of Isaiah xxxvi and xxxvii," *OTS* 24 (1986) 70–93.

interest in the person of the prophet and his remarkable words and deeds. This collection was also evidently interested in the differing responses to his ministry by those in authority and the lessons to be drawn from them. Although we can only guess about the authorial circles within which this work was created, we have already noted several elements that draw it close to the Deuteronomic sphere more widely (including both the book of Deuteronomy itself and the historical writings that were closely associated with it). To these may be added the final of form of 1–2 Kings, which shows interest in the ultimate fall of the nation being due to the failure to heed "my servants the prophets" (2 Kgs 17:13, 23; 21:8–10; 24:2),[22] and to individual prophets elsewhere as God's "servant" (1 Kgs 15:29, 2 Kgs 9:36, 10:10, 14:25), a designation that is reflected also in Isaiah as "my servant" in Isa 20:3 but that does not occur anywhere else in the first half of the book with reference to a prophet.

Part of this hypothesized composition will have been included in the book of Kings for that work's own reasons, and it was from there, apparently, that Isaiah 36–39 was adopted and adapted.[23] The other two passages (both much shorter) will have come directly from the postulated "life of Isaiah" source. It is beyond the scope of the present article to inquire into the precise circumstances and consequences of their inclusion in Isaiah, because these will not be directly connected with Deuteronomy.[24]

With regard to the inclusion of Isa 7:1–17, however, one observation may be pertinent. In this case it is rather clear that this third-person narrative has been inserted between the two first-person narratives in chapters 6 and 8. Furthermore, these latter two chapters are clearly to be taken in closest association with one another as a number of connecting features suggest, perhaps the most prominent of these being that in

---

22. See more fully M. Weinfeld, *Deuteronomy and the Deuteronomic School* (Oxford: Oxford University Press, 1972) 351, and E. Ben Zvi, "'The Prophets'—References to Generic Prophets and their Role in the Construction of the Image of the 'Prophets of Old' within the Postmonarchic Readership/s of the Book of Kings," *ZAW* 116 (2004) 555–67.

23. I have defended this standard view against some who have challenged it in *The Book Called Isaiah*, 189–211. My arguments were criticized by J. Vermeylen, "Hypothèses sur l'origine d'Isaïe 36–39," in *Studies in the Book of Isaiah: Festschrift Willem A. M. Beuken* (ed. J. van Ruiten and M. Vervenne; BETL 132; Leuven: University Press and Peeters, 1997) 95–118, but Vermeylen's position was then itself examined and rejected by F. J. Gonçalves, "2 Rois 18,13–20,19 par. Isaïe 36–39: Encore une fois, lequel des deux livres fut le premier?," in *Lectures et relectures de la Bible: Festschrift P.-M. Bogaert* (ed. J.-M. Auwers and A. Wénin; BETL 144; Leuven: University Press and Peeters) 27–55.

24. For recent well-informed discussions, with much attention to alternative views, see, for Isaiah 20, Cook, *A Sign and a Wonder*, and for Isaiah 36–39, Stromberg, *Isaiah After Exile*, 205–22.

each case the main audience in mind is "this people" (6:9, 10; 8:5, 11, 12), a distinctive designation not found at all in chapter 7. If it is therefore reasonable to assume that part, at least, of the purpose of chapter 8 is to relate the "hardening saying" of 6:9–10 to the response of the people at the time in 8:1–15, then one might go on to suggest that the editor responsible for the present positioning of chapter 7 equally had partly in mind the similarly negative response of the king. In line with the theology that underpins much of the historical writing, the fate of the nation is closely aligned with the faithfulness or lack of faithfulness of the king to the Deuteronomic law, and we have already noted how significant elements in 7:1–17 are dependent on Deuteronomy. It follows, therefore, that in the combined version of Isaiah 6 + 7 that same principle in Ahaz's case is regarded as an illustrative outworking of the hardening saying that in the first-person material applies primarily to "this people" as a whole.[25]

The shape of this part of Isaiah, we may therefore suggest, is not at all unlike that of Amos 7–8 where again a first person narrative of prophetic vision is interrupted by a third-person narrative concerning an encounter between the prophet and the high priest as spokesman for the king (Amos 7:9–17). There too the anticipated judgment of the people as a whole in 7:7–8 and 8:1–2 is referred personally to "the house of Jeroboam" and its leading officials. I have argued elsewhere that this too reflects Deuteronomic concerns so that the present arrangement of the material may most plausibly be attributed to Deuteronomic redaction.[26]

I conclude this section of the discussion, therefore, by suggesting that of the whole book of Isaiah these particular chapters come closest to composition within Deuteronomic circles, however that should be defined, and that in one case, at least, the redactional placement within the book may be taken to reflect similar theological concerns.

---

25. The connections between these two chapters have recently been explored (though with somewhat different interests) by M. de Jong, "From Legitimate King to Protected City: The Development of Isaiah 7:1–17," in *'Enlarge the Site of Your Tent': The City as Unifying Theme in Isaiah* (ed. A. L. H. M. van Wieringen and A. van der Woude; OTS 58; Leiden: Brill, 2011) 21–48. The older series of studies by O. H. Steck also retains its value in this regard: "Bemerkungen zu Jesaja 6," *BZ* N.F. 16 (1972) 188–206; idem, "Rettung und Verstockung: Exegetische Bemerkungen zu Jesaja 7, 3–9," *EvT* 33 (1973) 77–90; idem, "Beiträge zum Verständnis von Jesaja 7,10–17 und 8,1–4," *TZ* 29 (1973) 161–78.

26. See H. G. M. Williamson, "The Prophet and the Plumb-Line: A Redaction-Critical Study of Amos vii," *OTS* 26 (1990) 101–21; repr. in *"The Place Is Too Small for Us": The Israelite Prophets in Recent Scholarship* (ed. R. P. Gordon; Sources for Biblical and Theological Study 5; Winona Lake, IN: Eisenbrauns, 1995) 453–77.

5. Deuteronomy and Isaiah 40–66

Granted the approximate correctness of the standard views on the dating of Deuteronomy and the second half of the book of Isaiah, we should expect to find that the nature of any possible relationship between them would be quite different from the situation that prevailed with regard to Isaiah 1–39. And so indeed it proves to be. As a consequence, we may note that there are studies by respected commentators on the second half of the book that aim precisely to identify the points of greatest similarity between them. They assume a rough contemporaneity between Deutero-Isaiah and the *floruit* of the Deuteronomists and so find no difficulty in speaking of their influence upon the prophetic author. For the purpose of the present discussion, this whole section of the book of Isaiah may be treated together. That does not mean that I regard it as the work of a single author. In addition to the standard division between so-called Deutero- and Trito-Isaiah (chs. 40–55 and 56–66, respectively), it seems unlikely that these sections derive in their entirety from a single hand. However, a decision on this need not affect a discussion of the influence of Deuteronomy on Isaiah except to say that, if this influence relates to more than one compositional layer, we may conclude that it was peculiarly widespread.[27]

Before proceeding, particular mention should be made of the full and detailed study by Antje Labahn.[28] With careful attention to previous scholarship, she analyzes a number of passages in Isaiah 40–55 in order to demonstrate that it is in later additions and redactions that the closest affinity with Deuteronomic theology is to be found (e.g., Isa 51:1–8; ch. 55). By contrast, she finds that there are significant differences between the primary layer in Deutero-Isaiah and Deuteronomy. Her suggestion is that the prophet in the exile in Babylon was largely unaware of the Deuteronomic movement but that mutual influence developed in the early postexilic period once the Isaianic text was being transmitted back in Judah.

---

27. It would clearly exceed the reasonable bounds of this article to discuss all the studies that have dealt with apparent Deuteronomic influence on Isaiah 40–66, either in whole or in part; for a full survey, see Labahn, *Wort Gottes und Schuld Israels*, 30–37. In some of these instances it is again difficult to be sure (as already stressed above) how far one is speaking of the influence of the book of Deuteronomy and how much of more broadly (and vaguely) defined Deuteronomists; for instance, studies of Deuteronomic influence on Isaiah 55 with particular attention to the Davidic covenant clearly draw on the history rather than the law book itself.

28. Labahn, *Wort Gottes und Schuld Israels*; see too her article, "The Delay of Salvation within Deutero-Isaiah," *JSOT* 85 (1999) 71–84.

There is a great deal in Labahn's work from which one may learn and with which some agreement may be found. In the present context, however, we need to note that she is working with the Deuteronomic corpus as a whole, not just the book of Deuteronomy, so that it is not possible to make a simple move from her research to our more narrowly focused concern here. Furthermore, concerning the topics where she finds the primary contrast between Deuteronomy and Deutero-Isaiah, she makes a partial exception for the election of Israel as the people of God, sufficient, I believe, to allow my point on this further down to stand. On the other main points that I discuss, she comes at the first from a different angle from me and so is more inclined to see difference where I find elements of overlap, while to the third she makes little reference.

5.1. Lexical Parallels between Deuteronomy and Isaiah 40–66

A full catalogue of possible links with Deuteronomy can hardly be itemized here, but I shall present a brief representative sample of both points of detail and broader themes. As to detail, we may take note in particular of the helpful listing of many examples by Shalom Paul.[29] Here too, however, we should note that Paul explicitly states that for the purposes of his article he will not draw any distinction between Deuteronomy and the Deuteronomistic school. Most of his analysis, however, is based on particular words and phrases, and in many cases these occur frequently in the Historical Books (and sometimes elsewhere as well) in addition to Deuteronomy itself. Nobody supposes, however, that the Historical Books were wholly written by the Deuteronomists; they may have been responsible for editing and for some parts of the composition, but equally clearly they often drew on other sources and annals. Thus, where particular phraseology is attested in both Deuteronomy and the Deuteronomistic History we cannot appeal to that for specific influence from Deuteronomy. For our present purposes, therefore, a great deal of the material that Paul has assembled cannot be admitted. It is necessary in what follows, as a matter of basic

---

29. S. M. Paul, "Deuteronom(ist)ic influences on Deutero-Isaiah," in *Mishneh Todah: Studies in Deuteronomy and its Cultural Environment in Honor of Jeffrey H. Tigay* (ed. N. S. Fox, D. A. Glatt-Gilad, and M. J. Williams; Winona Lake, IN: Eisenbrauns, 2009) 219–27. It may be noted that for Paul "the unity of Isaiah 40–66 is presupposed" (n. 1). We may note here too the discussion of "Deutero-Isaiah's use of Deuteronomy" by B. D. Sommer, *A Prophet Reads Scripture: Allusion in Isaiah 40–66* (Stanford, CA: Stanford University Press, 1998) 134–40, but the parallels he cites are frequently of separated individual lexemes, so that his method does not allow for any confidence in the results.

sound procedure, to limit examples to those that occur exclusively in Deuteronomy and in Isaiah.

With this caveat in mind, the following seem to be among the more impressive examples.

1. In one of the major climaxes of the book, Isa 52:11–12, there is an urgent command to "depart, depart, go out from there," a command whose substantiation is clearly based on the command to leave Egypt at the time of the Exodus. One way in which this new Exodus will surpass the original one is that "you shall not go out in haste" (יצא + בחפזון), and this is a clear contrast with Deut 16:3, "you came out of the land of Egypt in great haste," where the same two words occur in the same order. The only other place where בחפזון occurs is at Exod 12:11, undoubtedly a related passage in overall terms but distinguished from the other two in that there it qualifies the eating of the Passover rather than the departure itself.
2. A direct citation of Deut 32:39 seems clear at Isa 43:13: the former has "I, even I, am he . . . and no one can deliver from my hand," while the latter has "I am He; there is no one who can deliver from my hand." Despite the slightly different translation of the two main clauses in the NRSV, the Hebrew wording in each case is identical.
3. The name Jeshurun for Israel (not fully explained), which occurs at Isa 44:2, is found elsewhere only at Deut 32:15; 33:5, 26.
4. The description of God as "faithful" (נאמן) at Isa 49:7 finds its only parallel at Deut 7:9.
5. The description of Israel as a "holy people" is common in Deuteronomy (7:6; 14:2, 21; 26:19; 28:9). There may be a link with Exod 19:6, but it is distinguished by the use of "people" (עם) over against "nation" (גוי).[30] Curiously, the Deuteronomic combination occurs elsewhere only at Isa 62:12 and 63:18 (at least until later times; cf. Dan 12:7). Even though it occurs there in a grammatically slightly different form, the lack of a parallel in other literature suggests that this is probably a case of direct influence.
6. The expression that "Israel is saved by the LORD" (נושע ביהוה) (Isa 45:17) may well derive from its only other occurrence in the OT, Deut 33:29. The immediate subject there is "people," but "Israel" occurs in the first half of the parallel line.

---

30. For an emphatic assertion of the significance of this distinction and a comment on the peculiarity of the Deuteronomic diction in this regard, see Weinfeld, *Deuteronomy and the Deuteronomic School*, 227–28.

7. Not mentioned by Paul, I add a further possible example. Although the translation of the first line of Isa 40:31 is disputed (NRSV: "but those who wait for the LORD shall renew their strength, they shall mount up with wings like eagles"), it is difficult not to suppose that there is an echo of Deut 32:11–12: "as an eagle . . . spreads its wings, takes them up, and bears them aloft on its pinions, the LORD alone guided him . . ." (though see too Exod 19:4).
8. Also unmentioned by Paul, Labahn draws attention to the combination of רדף 'to pursue' and צדק 'righteousness', which occurs distinctively only at Isa 51:1 and Deut 16:20.[31]

Although this list does not claim to be exhaustive, it suggests cumulatively that the authors of Isaiah 40–66 were influenced sometimes by their knowledge of Deuteronomic diction. However, it would be difficult to claim, on the basis of distribution, that this was a more significant influence than any other, such as the first part of the book of Isaiah, Lamentations, and Jeremiah, just to give a few obvious examples.[32] To gain a more secure result, therefore, we need also to consider wider themes, whether or not the language in which they are couched is distinctively Deuteronomic.

5.2. Thematic Parallels between Deuteronomy and Isaiah 40–66

Turning now, therefore, to broader themes, I single out three in order to illustrate the general conclusion towards which I wish eventually to move. Needless to say, this does not imply any suggestion that others could not equally well have been chosen.

As Blenkinsopp has written in the course of his brief survey of our topic, "the most striking feature common to Isaiah 40–55 and the Deuteronomistic corpus is the insistence on the incomparability of the God of Israel."[33] This topic has its controversial dimension, as it naturally borders on the much-discussed question of the development of monotheism within ancient Israel. Without getting drawn into that, it is clear

---

31. Labahn, *Wort Gottes und Schuld Israels*, 120–23, 258; her appeal to torah in the heart in Isa 51:7–8 is less certain, however, as this also occurs prominently in Jer 31:33.

32. For discussion, see, for instance, R. Nurmela, *The Mouth of the Lord has Spoken: Inner-Biblical Allusions in Second and Third Isaiah* (Studies in Judaism; Lanham: University Press of America, 2006); Sommer, *A Prophet Reads Scripture*; P. T. Willey, *Remember the Former Things: The Recollection of Previous Texts in Second Isaiah* (SBLDS 161; Atlanta: Scholars, 1997); Williamson, *The Book Called Isaiah*.

33. J. Blenkinsopp, *Isaiah 40–55*: A New Translation with Introduction and Commentary (AB 19A; New York: Doubleday, 2002) 52.

to most readers that these two bodies of literature are those within the Hebrew Bible that are foremost in asserting both positively and negatively that, certainly so far as Israel is concerned, and arguably even in absolute terms, there can be no God other than Yahweh (hereafter "the LORD"). Furthermore this similarity is underlined by the use of some relatively fixed formulae, and, while these also occur elsewhere from time to time, the density of their appearance in our two particular corpora is suggestive of influence and dependence.[34]

For instance we find the use of "I am He" or "I am the LORD" (sometimes with repetition of the pronoun "I") in Deut 32:39; Isa 41:4; 43:10, 11, 13; 45:5, 6, 18, 21; 46:4; 48:12; 52:6. Variations on the phrase "there is none beside him/you/no other" (admittedly with use of slightly different prepositions) occur in Deut 4:35, 39; 32:39; Isa 43:11; 44:6; 45:5, 6, 14, 18, 21, 22; 46:9. Beyond that, in some of the anti-idol polemical passages in Isaiah 40–48 there are some overlaps in wording such as the very frequent use of פסל 'idol' in both corpora (five times in Deuteronomy; nine times in Isaiah 40–48), which contrasts with Isaiah 1–39, where it never occurs even once. We should also note the use of תועבה 'abomination' at Deut 7:25, 26; 27:15; 32:16; Isa 41:24; 44:19, and "the handiwork of an artisan" (or close equivalents) at Deut 27:15; Isa 40:19–20; 41:7; 44:12–13; 45:16; 46:6.

It is noteworthy that nearly all the evidence listed so far is confined to Isaiah 40–48, a section in the book that has a number of distinctive features not shared even with chapters 49–55.[35] Although the incomparability of the God of Israel may be presupposed in the following chapters, occasionally even with Deuteronomic-like language, such as idolatry practiced "under every leafy/green tree" (Deut 12:2; Isa 57:5, as well as relatively frequently elsewhere, of course), it is clearly a topic of more lively, even polemical, concern in Isaiah 40–48. The importance of Deuteronomy in this context and within this geographical and temporal framework is certainly worth reflection. It is normally thought that Deuteronomy looks primarily to internal reform within Israel (or better, Judah). This early evidence of its reception, however, points in an opposite direction; it was taken more as a vigorous assertion of national identity against strong external threats (in this case, in my opinion, from Neo-Babylonian religion as apparently vindicated in military and political supremacy).

The second major theme that warrants mention here is the "election" of Israel with the use of the verb בחר. This is by no means confined to

---

34. See Paul, "Deuteronom(ist)ic influences," 219–22, for fuller details.

35. For details, see, for instance, P. Wilcox and D. Paton-Williams, "The Servant Songs in Deutero-Isaiah," *JSOT* 42 (1988) 79–102; Blenkinsopp, *Isaiah 40–55*, 59–61.

our two bodies of literature, of course, but it is certainly prominent in both. As far as Deuteronomy is concerned, I share the common view of commentators that before the seventh century particular individuals or other institutions could be "chosen" by God but that it was only with the publication of Deuteronomy more or less as we know it that Israel as a corporate whole first became the object of this verb (Deut 4:37, 7:6–7, 10:15, 14:2).[36] This theme is also prominent in the second half of Isaiah (41:8, 9; 43:10, 20; 44:1, 2; 45:4; 49:7); it is also used of the servant in Isa 42:1, and in my opinion that too refers in a specialized sense to Israel.

It is possible, of course, to regard the divine election of Israel as the converse of the stress, already noted, on the uniqueness of the LORD as Israel's God. To that extent, we may not be surprised to note once again that there is a particular concentration of this usage in Isaiah 40–48.[37]

A third topic to which Blenkinsopp draws attention concerns the call to "remember" (זכר) aspects of God's past salvific work. Of course, this is a common enough lexeme, but the concentration in Deuteronomy with this particular emphasis is striking (Deut 5:15; 7:18; 8:2; 9:7; 15:15; 16:3, 12; 24:9, 18, 22; 25:17). The first of these is sufficient to indicate the centrality of this theme to Deuteronomic theology, for it relates to the Sabbath commandment, where, of course, Deuteronomy differs from the parallel in Exod 20:8–11. There, the Israelite is to "remember" the Sabbath and the Sabbath day is linked to the days of creation. Here in Deuteronomy the Israelite is to "observe" (שמר) the Sabbath day (5:12), and in doing so to "remember" that once they were slaves in Egypt from which God had delivered them (5:15). Several of the verses listed above also enjoin remembrance of the slavery in Egypt while the others relate to a number of the incidents recorded on the journey through the wilderness, which followed the exodus.

In the second half of the book of Isaiah this subject is also of importance: Isa 43:18 (negatively, "do not remember the former things," which in the context of the preceding verses clearly refers precisely to the deliverance at the Red Sea after the exodus), 44:21 (a general injunction which may refer back particularly to the deliverance as adumbrated in vv. 6–8), and 46:8–9, where they should remember the "former things of

---

36. This subject has been frequently discussed, of course, and full documentation seems unnecessary. For a simple statement of the case, see, for instance, R. E. Clements, *God's Chosen People: A Theological Interpretation of the Book of Deuteronomy* (London: SCM, 1968) 45–49; Horst Seebass, "בָּחַר *bāchar*," *TDOT* 2:73–87.

37. In my opinion, the use at Isa 14:1 reflects the same provenance (see *The Book Called Isaiah*, 165–66). The uses in 1:29 and 7:15–16 have quite different subjects and objects, of course. It seems likely that the uses in 65:9 and 15, which are also cited by Paul, refer to a narrower circle than the nation as a whole, as the use of the plural form, to go no further, indicates.

old" that only God was able to accomplish. As with the first two points mentioned above, therefore, so here too it is especially in Isaiah 40–48 that we find this close link with Deuteronomy.

5.3. Concluding Reflections on Deuteronomy's Relationship to Isaiah 40–48

Now in all this it is scarcely necessary to point out that there is no suggestion here of any form of exclusive influence of Deuteronomy on Isaiah 40–48. I have already mentioned above a number of other obvious sources of influence, and even with regard to the Pentateuch it is clear that other parts besides Deuteronomy, such as especially the priestly account of the creation, or the traditions that lie behind them, were clearly known to the authors of Isaiah 40–55 (though whether positively or in polemical debate is disputed[38]). What I should wish to emphasize in closing, however, is that in a manner that is certainly quite unlike the situation in the first part of the book and that equally is not closely paralleled in the last parts, there is found within Isaiah 40–48 a use of themes and terminology that have their closest parallels in Deuteronomy and that seem to have been influenced by that book. The themes in question focus on issues relating in particular to the special relationship that exists between God and his chosen people, both in the past and in the present.

In the liberal years in the middle decades of the last century, the focus of study of Isaiah 40–55 was very much on its universalistic dimension, and this is something that certainly very few of us would wish to deny or underestimate. At the same time, however, in the first half of this section of the book (chs. 40–48) there is included a strongly polemical dimension as the prophet struggled to help his readers recover and maintain their religious and hence cultural identity.[39] This shared element with Deuteronomy may thus be regarded as adding a further item to the list of features that is being gradually accumulated in recent research to underline the distinction between Isaiah 40–48 and 49–55. How that distinction should be explained remains finally to be decided, but it is a feature of the work that should certainly play a greater part in our theological reading of the book as a whole.

---

38. See M. Weinfeld, "God the Creator in Gen. 1 and the Prophecy of Second Isaiah," *Tarbiz* 37 (1968) 105–32 (Hebrew).

39. I have tried to suggest how these apparently conflicting points of view may be held together in my book, *Variations on a Theme: King, Messiah and Servant in the Book of Isaiah* (Carlisle: Paternoster, 1998) 113–66.

The Enduring Word of the Lord in Deuteronomy and Jeremiah 36

MICHAEL GRAVES

It has become clear in the past century of biblical scholarship that Deuteronomy and Jeremiah share much in common in terms of phraseology and ideas.[1] Yet, the inter-relationship between the two books is highly complex. Both books have firm anchors in the Preexilic Period: Deuteronomy is closely tied to Josiah's reforms in the seventh century (2 Kgs 22–23) and may have received substantial literary shaping during the eighth century in connection with the development of literacy during the reign of Hezekiah[2]; and the book of Jeremiah is anchored in the life of the prophet Jeremiah, who prophesied in the late Preexilic Period. Both books also seem to have reached their final forms in the Postexilic Period: Deuteronomy was likely brought into its present form

---

Author's Note: I am delighted to take this opportunity to express my respect and gratitude for Prof. Daniel I. Block. Since 2005 I have had the pleasure of serving with him in the department of Biblical and Theological Studies at Wheaton College. Prof. Block uniquely combines faithfulness to Scripture with creativity in scholarship. His energy in teaching and mentoring students is inspiring. Prof. Block is also authentically gracious with his colleagues. I am pleased to contribute an essay to this volume, which gives honor and thanks to Prof. Block for his distinguished career of Christian ministry.

1. For lists of common phraseology and key terms, see W. L. Holladay, *Jeremiah 2* (Hermeneia; Minneapolis: Fortress, 1989) 53–63, 85–86; M. Weinfeld, *Deuteronomy and the Deuteronomic School* (Oxford: Oxford University Press, 1972) 27–32, 138–46, 359–61; J. P. Hyatt, "The Deuteronomic Edition of Jeremiah," in *A Prophet to the Nations* (ed. L. G. Perdue and B. W. Kovacs; Winona Lake, IN: Eisenbrauns, 1984) 252–53; and S. R. Driver, *Deuteronomy* (ICC; New York: Charles Scribner's Sons, 1906) xciii.

2. On the development of literary culture during the time of Hezekiah, see B. Halpern, "Jerusalem and the Lineages in the Seventh Century BCE: Kinship and the Rise of Individual Moral Liability," in *Law and Ideology in Monarchic Israel* (ed. B. Halpern and D. W. Hobson; Sheffield: JSOT, 1991) 79–91. According to C. A. Rollston, epigraphic materials from the early eighth century through the sixth century B.C.E., although developing diachronically throughout the whole period, demonstrate such consistent scribal practices within given time periods (i.e., synchronically) as to suggest formal training of scribes already in the early eighth century B.C.E. (*Writing and Literacy in the World of Ancient Israel* [Atlanta: Society of Biblical Literature, 2010] 95–113). On the style of Deuteronomy, see M. Weinfeld, *Deuteronomy 1–11* (AB; New York: Doubleday, 1991) 82; and Driver, *Deuteronomy*, lxxxviii.

in conjunction with the compilation of the "Deuteronomistic History,"[3] and the text of Jeremiah was still being assembled in the Postexilic Period, as is made clear from the relationship between the Masoretic Text and the Septuagint of Jeremiah.[4] If one accepts that the book of Deuteronomy existed in some form prior to the life of the prophet Jeremiah,[5] then it is natural to assume that many elements shared between the two books represent Jeremiah's dependence on the traditions of Deuteronomy. Nevertheless, because the books of Deuteronomy and Jeremiah were most likely both being worked on during the time period stretching from Hezekiah to after the exile, it is not always possible to know in every case the direction of influence.

But whatever the relationship between any particular set of parallels within the two books, it is evident that Jeremiah and Deuteronomy address many of the same themes. One particular theme, which is strikingly prominent in both Deuteronomy and Jeremiah but rarely featured so prominently elsewhere in the Hebrew Bible, is the theme of writing (including scribes and texts).[6] This focus in both books is not surprising, since Deuteronomy and Jeremiah seem to have passed

---

3. On the Deuteronomistic History, see S. L. Richter, "Deuteronomistic History," in *Dictionary of the Old Testament Historical Books* (ed. B. T. Arnold and H. G. M. Williamson; Downers Grove, IL: InterVarsity, 2005) 219–30; and I. W. Provan, *Hezekiah and the Books of Kings: A Contribution to the Debate about the Composition of the Deuteronomistic History* (Berlin/New York: Walter de Gruyter, 1988). An example of a text in Deuteronomy that may reflect exilic or postexilic editorial explanation dependent on Jeremiah is the phrase in Deut 28:48, "and he will put an iron yoke on your neck," which appears to make use of Jeremiah 28 to expound on the situation envisioned by Deuteronomy (cf. Holladay, *Jeremiah 2*, 62–63).

4. For example, Jer 29:16–20, present in the MT but absent from the LXX, almost certainly was added to the proto-MT version of Jeremiah after the exile. On the implications of the two texts of Jeremiah for the question of the development of the Jeremiah corpus, see E. Tov, *Textual Criticism of the Hebrew Bible* (3rd ed.; Minneapolis: Fortress, 2012) 286–94; and W. McKane, *A Critical and Exegetical Commentary on Jeremiah* (2 vols.; ICC; Edinburgh: T. & T. Clark, 1986), 1:l–li.

5. J. G. McConville plausibly envisions Deuteronomy's origins in a "pre-monarchical constitution" (*Deuteronomy* [AOTC; Downers Grove: InterVarsity, 2002] 38–39). As an example of the kind of supplementation that this original pre-monarchical document may have received, McConville states, "It is a fair question whether the document of the pre-monarchical constitution contained the vision of Israel's future beyond exile (4:29–31; 30:1–10)."

6. Another book that highlights the role of writing, scribes, and texts is Ezra–Nehemiah. It is my view that the core materials of Deuteronomy and Jeremiah are earlier than Ezra–Nehemiah, which is a purely postexilic composition. This accounts for the difference in style between Deuteronomy's prose and the prose sermons of Jeremiah on the one hand, and the prose of Ezra–Nehemiah and Chronicles on the other hand.

through the hands of the same scribal tradition, which started before the exile and continued afterwards.[7]

This essay will explore the relationship between Deuteronomy's conception of writing and the well-known narrative in Jeremiah 36 about the burning of Jeremiah's scroll by king Jehoiakim. It will be argued that Deuteronomy invests great authority in the written word, which it envisions as an instrument for the internalization of the word of YHWH within the hearts of the people of Israel. Against this backdrop, and within the context of the book of Jeremiah, Jeremiah 36 serves not as witness to the increasing authority of texts (as is often supposed), but as a caveat to Deuteronomy's theology of writing: Without the internalization that is supposed to accompany the written word, the physical scroll is of no account. Even if the scroll is burned, the word of YHWH contained in the scroll will endure.

1. Deuteronomy and Jeremiah on the Written Word

1.1. Deuteronomy's Theology of the Written Word

The book of Deuteronomy presents a consistent picture of writing as a means by which Israel is to learn to love and obey YHWH and his commands.[8] YHWH himself is the first individual identified in the book as writing. Near the end of Moses' first speech as presented in

---

7. On Deuteronomy and the scribal tradition, see J.-P. Sonnet, *The Book within the Book* (Leiden: Brill, 1997) 265–66; and Weinfeld, *Deuteronomy*, 177–78. On Jeremiah and this tradition, see M. Leuchter, *Josiah's Reform and Jeremiah's Scroll* (Sheffield: Phoenix, 2006) 13–15, 169–70; and J. A. Dearman, "My Servants the Scribes: Composition and Context in Jeremiah 36," *JBL* 109 (1990) 403–21. D. M. Carr suggests the possibility that the family of Josiah's scribes (and their descendants) used Deuteronomic and Deuteronomistic texts as school texts for the training of scribes, which would explain why those responsible for compiling Jeremiah (and perhaps even Jeremiah himself) would be familiar with this phraseology (*Writing on the Tablet of the Heart* [Oxford: Oxford University Press, 2005] 148–49). See also J. Schaper, who argues that Jeremiah 36 depicts a genuine scribal procedure attested also in cuneiform literature ("On Writing and Reciting in Jeremiah 36," in *Prophecy in the Book of Jeremiah* [ed. H. M. Barstad and R. G. Kratz; Berlin and New York: Walter de Gruyter, 2009] 137–47).

8. See J. Schaper, "A Theology of Writing: The Oral and the Written, God as Scribe, and the Book of Deuteronomy," in *Anthropology and Biblical Studies* (ed. L. J. Lawrence and M. I. Aguilar; Leiden: Deo, 2004) 97–119; and Sonnet, *The Book within the Book*. Both Schaper and Sonnet describe the theology of the book of Deuteronomy as whole, without regard for redactional layers. Whether this approach can successfully uncover a theology of Deuteronomy that can be placed into conversation with the historical Jeremiah's pre-exilic context is open to debate, depending on how much new material one thinks was added to Deuteronomy after the exile. I am operating from the position that the general contours of the book of Deuteronomy existed in Jeremiah's time, and that if any elements of Deuteronomy's theology of writing belong to a redactional layer of the book, they

Deuteronomy, he states that Yhwh wrote his covenant, the "ten words," on two tablets of stone (4:13). After the start of Moses' second speech (beginning at 5:1), he reminds the Israelites of God's act of writing the "ten words" (5:22), and proceeds to command the Israelites to write Yhwh's commands on their doorframes and gates (6:9), so that they will recite them and speak of them always, and thus love Yhwh with all their heart, soul, and strength (6:6–9).[9] After the sin of the golden calf is described, Yhwh writes a second set of tablets to replace the ones that Moses broke (10:4), and Israel is again told to write God's words on their doorframes and houses (11:20), again with the goal of keeping them always in mind (11:18–21), so that they will not turn away to other gods and incite Yhwh's anger (11:16–17). In each case, Yhwh's action of writing leads to Israel's action of writing as a faithful response.[10] Later on, it is prescribed that Israel's king must write for himself a copy of התורה הזאת 'this torah',[11] received from the priests and Levites (17:18). The scroll thus produced is to be read always by the king, so that he will learn to fear Yhwh and observe all its words (17:19–20).

The concluding sections of Deuteronomy include a number of important references to writing.[12] Near the end of Moses' second speech, Moses orders that the words of "this torah" be written on large stones after Israel has crossed over into the land (27:1–8); it is expressly stated that the words be written "very clearly" (v. 8, באר היטב).[13] Although

would have already been part of the Deuteronomic theology in Jeremiah's time, since scribes, texts, and writing played such a significant role in Judah during this period.

9. As Sonnet notes, "The stipulations in 6:6–9 are meant to catalyze the interiorization of the Mosaic teaching and to foster its pervasiveness throughout time (both personal and generational) and space (both private and public)" (*The Book within the Book*, 58).

10. On Yhwh's writing, see also 9:10, "Yhwh gave to me two tablets of stone written with the finger of God."

11. In context, "this torah" refers to Moses' discourse, but for readers of Deuteronomy it probably calls to mind the entirety of the book itself (see G. J. Venema, *Reading Scripture in the Old Testament* [Leiden: Brill, 2004] 215).

12. Another example of writing in Deuteronomy is 24:1–4, which describes the writing of a "certificate of divorce" (ספר כריתת) when a husband sends away his wife. This reflects the power and significance of writing at the level of human relationships, but it is not directly related to Deuteronomy's theology of writing as it relates to the divine-human relationship.

13. The word היטב is used here to mean 'very' or 'thoroughly' (cf. Deut 9:21, 13:5, 17:4, 19:18, and 2 Kgs 11:18). The Piel infinitive absolute of באר used here adverbially has the sense 'clearly' (*HALOT* 106, "to explain, to elucidate"), as in Middle Hebrew: "a disciple of a sage is one who is able to clarify/explain (לבאר) his teaching" (*y. Mo'ed Qat.* 3:7, 83b; see J. Levy, *Wörterbuch über die Talmudim und Midraschim* [4 vols.; Darmstadt: Wissenschaftliche Buchgesellschaft, 1963] 1:188). Thus, in Deut 1:5, "Moses began to explain (באר) this torah, saying, . . ."; and Hab 2:2, "Write the vision clearly (ובאר) on tablets. . . ." The expression באר היטב in Deut 27:8 helps to underscore the fact that the writing is not intended to be a mere monument, but is meant to be understood and taken seriously.

Moses will not be entering the land, the words of "this torah" will.[14] In his third speech (starting at MT 28:69), Moses makes clear that Israel must obey Y{HWH} and keep his commands and statues written in the book of "this torah," and concurrently they will turn to Y{HWH} with their whole heart and soul (30:10; cf. 29:20). Deut 31:9–13 narrates that Moses established the custom of reading "this torah" before all Israel every seven years during Sukkot. This ritual is meant to insure that in future generations everyone—men, women, children, and sojourners—will learn to fear Y{HWH} and observe all the words of "this torah."[15] Finally, writing will serve as witness against Israel when Israel fails to live up to the requirements of "this torah": Moses commands that a song be written for this purpose (31:19–22), and he also instructs Israel to keep the book in which Moses wrote the words of "this torah" next to the ark, to witness against Israel when calamity falls upon them for their rebellion (31:24–29).

Many have noted the consistent use of writing for didactic purposes in Deuteronomy.[16] As J. Schaper points out, writing in Deuteronomy is the medium not only for preserving the divine word, but also for its publication and recitation, and thus internalization and individualization.[17] Thus, Deuteronomy promotes the authority of the written word, but not for the sake of the written word itself; rather, writing is meant to be an instrument to lead Israel to love Y{HWH} and keep his commands.[18]

1.2. *Jeremiah's Critique of the Instruments of Deuteronomic Theology*

If this internalizing spirit of Deuteronomy animated Josiah's reforms, it is easy to understand why scholars have suggested that Jeremiah

---

14. According to Deut 28:58, 61, Israel in the land will be held accountable to follow the words of "this torah" by threat of punishments, such as are written in the book of "this torah."

15. The injunction to read "this torah" every seven years has sometimes been explained on the analogy of ancient Near Eastern vassal treaties that required the regular public reading of the treaty documents (see P. C. Craigie, *The Book of Deuteronomy* [NICOT; Grand Rapids: Eerdmans, 1976] 370–71). Holladay assumes that the regular proclamation of "this torah" every seven years was observed in Judah throughout Jeremiah's lifetime, and he makes these public readings the basis for his reconstruction of Jeremiah's career (*Jeremiah 1*, 1–10).

16. E.g., Carr, *Writing on the Tablet of the Heart*, 135–39; and Weinfeld, *Deuteronomy*, 164.

17. Schaper, "Theology of Writing," 107.

18. As Driver states, "The love of God, an all-absorbing sense of personal devotion to him, is propounded in Dt. as the primary spring of human action (6:5); it is the duty which is the direct corollary of the character of God, and of Israel's relation to him" (*Deuteronomy*, xxi).

initially supported the reform movement, but eventually became disillusioned.[19] The book of Jeremiah occasionally reflects positively on such key Deuteronomic institutions as kingship and the temple sacrificial system, but only when they are considered as ideals, either in the past or in the future.[20] One can imagine that Jeremiah would have been pleased with a king and a temple that actually promoted the kind of love for YHWH and obedience to the "torah" that Deuteronomy enjoins. In any case, it appears that the genuine Deuteronomic theology did not gain much traction in the late Preexilic Period. Perhaps there were leaders who taught that prosperity would flow automatically from the instruments of the reform (such as temple and torah scroll), even apart from the internalization called for by Deuteronomy. Perhaps there were some who focused on the physical instruments because they genuinely misunderstood the ideals of the Deuteronomic theology.[21] But whatever the reason, it appears that there were many in late preexilic Judea

---

19. E.g., H. Cazelles, "Jeremiah and Deuteronomy," transl. by L. G. Perdue, in *A Prophet to the Nations*, 106–11; Weinfeld, *Deuteronomy*, 161; and J. R. Lundbom, *Jeremiah 1–20* (AB; New York: Doubleday, 1999) 109–15. J. Scharbert argues that Jeremiah began his public career before Josiah's reform and that he prepared the way for the reform by calling Judah to moral and religious standards identical with those of Josiah's "Book of the Law," which matched the basic core of our present book of Deuteronomy. Later, according to Scharbert, Jeremiah came to disapprove of the political and nationalistic turn that the reform eventually took ("Jeremia und die Reform des Joschija," in *La livre de Jérémie* [ed. P.-M. Bogaert; Leuven: Leuven University Press, 1997] 40–57).

20. For positive appraisals of kingship in the book of Jeremiah in connection with ideal figures, see Jer 22:15–16 (Josiah), 26:17–19 (Hezekiah), 23:5–6 and 33:15–16 (idealized future king). Jer 33:14–26 is absent from the LXX, and 33:15–16 is probably dependent on 23:5–6, but the first three passages listed above suggest that the historical Jeremiah and his supporters held Davidic kingship in high regard when combined with justice and righteousness. The book of Jeremiah reflects positively on temple and priestly sacrifice at Jer 17:19–27 (see v. 26), 31:14, and 33:17–22. As has already been noted, 33:17–22 is lacking in the LXX and may be part of the redactional development of the book. The idealized futuristic setting of 31:14 envisions priests who are satiated with דשן (cf. Lev 1:16, 4:12, 6:3–4; Num 4:13). (I am reading the MT and 4QJer^c; the LXX has "sons of Levi," which does not work in the poetic line either in sense or in syllable length.) Jer 17:19–27 is often disallowed to the historical Jeremiah on the grounds of its prose style and concern for the Sabbath (cf. Neh 13:15–22). But there is nothing about either the "Deuteronomistic" prose style or Sabbath observance that is incongruent with the historical Jeremiah. Furthermore, Sabbath observance does not represent disingenuous temple sacrifice (as Jeremiah rejects in Jeremiah 7), but obedience to the values of the "torah." Sabbath observance had economic implications and was a justice issue, and so it fits well with the concerns of Jeremiah 7.

21. On this theology, see also Solomon's prayer in 1 Kgs 8:23–61: the temple is meant to be a place for condemning the guilty and acquitting the innocent (vv. 31–32), and for expressing genuine repentance after Israel has sinned (vv. 33–51). On the Deuteronomistic perspective of this text, see Weinfeld, *Deuteronomy*, 35–36. Neither in Deuteronomy

who combined confidence in the symbols of the reform with disregard for the internal values of the reform, to such a degree that Jeremiah became a harsh critic of the instruments of the Deuteronomic theology.[22]

This paradigm for understanding Jeremiah can be applied to the apparent diversity of perspectives found in the book of Jeremiah regarding scribes. On the one hand, Jeremiah is closely associated with scribes and is occasionally portrayed as writing.[23] On the other hand, Jeremiah criticizes the scribes of the "torah." Jer 8:8 says, "How can you say, 'We are wise, and the torah of YHWH is with us'? Indeed, look! The false pen of the scribes has wrought falsely!"[24] This text has been interpreted as evidence that some voices within the Jeremiah tradition were opposed to the Deuteronomic Torah.[25] Similarly, Jer 2:8a–b says, "The

---

nor in the "Deuteronomistic History" is the temple portrayed as a guarantee of security apart from sincere allegiance to YHWH.

22. For example, Jeremiah often criticizes kingship (Jer 1:18, 2:26, 4:9, 8:1–3, 13:12–14, 18–20, 19:1–6, chaps. 21–22, etc.) and the temple-sacrificial system (e.g., Jer 6:19–20, 7:1–15, 7:21–23, 11:15). According to Hyatt, Jeremiah's prediction that the temple would be destroyed unless the people showed true moral reform "must have been wholly incomprehensible and utterly abhorrent to anyone imbued with the spirit of Deuteronomy, with its emphasis on the Jerusalem temple and its cult" ("Deuteronomic Edition of Jeremiah," 118). Yet, Hyatt here misrepresents the spirit of Deuteronomy. It is true that Deuteronomy emphasizes sacrificial worship, but central to the ethos of Deuteronomy is sincere devotion to YHWH and to "this torah," the goal of which is to establish a righteous community (see McConville, *Deuteronomy*, 43). Jeremiah was critical of the instruments of the Deuteronomic theology only because these instruments were being detached from the ideals of the Deuteronomic theology.

23. Jeremiah is said to have written some of his own prophecies (Jer 30:1, 51:59–64; cf. 25:13). He also used scribal metaphors (Jer 3:8, 15:15 [cf. Ezek 3:1–3], 17:1, 17:13, 22:30, 31:33; see also the deed written in 32:9–16), and he worked closely with Baruch the scribe (Jer 32:12–16, chap. 36, 43:3–6, chap. 45). Finally, Jeremiah was supported by the scribal family of Shaphan that had been instrumental in Josiah's reforms (Jer 26:24, 29:3, 36:10–12, 39:14; cf. 2 Kgs 22:3–20). On the Shaphan family, see Lundbom, *Jeremiah 21–36* (AB; New York: Doubleday, 2004) 298–99.

24. The phrase לשקר here seems to mean 'falsely' (e.g., Jer 5:2, 7:9, 27:15) rather than 'in vain' (e.g., Jer 3:23). The phrase עט שקר ספרים may be a construct chain ('the pen of falsehood of the scribes'), or else שקר may be in apposition to עט (i.e., 'the false pen'; see GCK 131.2.b), in which case ספרים 'scribes' appears to be in "genitive relationship" primarily with עט 'pen' (cf. Joüon-Muraoka 129.a.N). It has been suggested that שקר ספרים is the subject of the verb, with עט as the object: "the lie of the scribes has made the pen into a lie" (Holladay, *Jeremiah 1*, 281–82), although the word order (with שקר ספרים coming directly after עט, which follows the verb) does not suggest this. The sense of v. 8 may be clarified with reference to the similar idiom at the end of v. 10, כלה עשה שקר 'everyone does falsehood' (see G. Fischer, *Jeremia 1–25* [HTKAT; Freiberg: Herder, 2005] 335).

25. E.g., Carr, Writing on the Tablet of the Heart, 141. R. P. Carroll sees 8:8 as opposed to Torah scribes and in conflict with the pro-scribe chap. 36 ("Manuscripts Don't Burn—Inscribing the Prophetic Tradition. Reflections on Jeremiah 36," in *"Dort ziehen Schiffe dahin": Collected Communications to the XIVth Congress of the International Organization for the*

priests do not say, 'Where is YHWH?' And the handlers of the torah have not known me." Again, this has been read as Jeremiah opposing the Deuteronomic Torah.[26]

But this would be to miss the point of Jeremiah's critique. Indeed, Jer 2:8c–d continues, "The shepherds rebel against me, the prophets prophesy by Baal, and they go after what does not profit." Jeremiah does not reject the category of "prophet," but only those who prophesy by Baal. Likewise, he does not reject all who handle the "torah," but simply those who do not know YHWH.[27] As for Jer 8:8, the scribes in question were probably court scribes (cf. 2 Kgs 22:3) or at least scribes involved in conducting business transactions (cf. Jer 32:12), and if Jeremiah's temple sermon (7:1–15) was at all accurate in describing legal and business practices of the time, these scribes were in fact violating the religious and ethical mandates of the Deuteronomic "torah."[28] What is more, they apparently continued to insist that they possessed wisdom (cf. Deut 4:6) simply because they were in possession of the physical torah scroll.[29] But Jeremiah insisted that the instrument itself was not enough. In keeping with the Deuteronomic theology, Jeremiah opposed those who put confidence in their possession of the torah scroll as a physical object (the "handlers of torah"), but who did not internalize the message of YHWH as taught in the "torah."

2. A Destroyed Scroll and the Enduring Word in Jeremiah 36

2.1 Israel's Rejection of God's Word

This conclusion regarding Jeremiah's perspective on scribes and torah scrolls has direct bearing on the significance of Jeremiah 36. Within its literary context in the book, the primary function of Jeremiah 36 is to illustrate how thoroughly Israel rejected the word of YHWH, so as to justify why it was necessary that Jerusalem be destroyed and the Da-

---

Study of the Old Testament, Paris 1992 [ed. M. Augustin and K.-D. Schunck; Frankfurt am Main: Peter Lang, 1996] 38).

26. E.g., Leuchter, *Josiah's Reform and Jeremiah's Scroll*, 89.

27. On the importance of knowing YHWH, see Jer 4:22, 5:4–5, 9:3, 6, 24, 24:7, 31:34.

28. In other words, Jeremiah did not oppose the "torah"; rather, he charged these scribes with falsifying the "torah" through their wrong instruction and failure to comply with the "torah" (see C. Maier, *Jeremia als Lehrer der Tora* [Göttingen: Vandenhoeck & Ruprecht, 2002] 302–5). Similarly, Jer 18:18 shows the false confidence of those who thought they were wise in the torah. On Jeremiah's positive association of "torah" with YHWH's word, see Jer 6:19: "They have not heeded my word, and my torah they have rejected." Jer 31:33 exemplifies the ideal of internalization of the torah. See also the following prose passages that are positive towards the torah: 9:13, 16:11, 26:4, 32:23, 44:10, 23.

29. See M. Gilbert, "Jérémie en conflit avec les sages," in *Le livre de Jérémie*, 110–13.

vidic dynasty brought to an end.[30] The story of Jehoiakim burning the scroll exemplifies the kind of stubborn rebellion against YHWH that led to Jerusalem's destruction; and so, although narrating events chronologically prior to the city's destruction, Jeremiah 36 (LXX 43) was placed just before the narrative of the fall of Jerusalem in chapters 37–39 (LXX 44–46).[31]

In fact, since Jehoiakim was seen as embodying Judah's rejection of YHWH, Jeremiah 36 presents Jehoiakim as the antithesis of King Josiah, who symbolized the proper response to YHWH's torah.[32] For example, in the Josiah narrative, the scribe Shaphan reads the book of the torah to Hilkiah in the temple (2 Kgs 22:8) and later to King Josiah in the palace (v. 10). King Josiah then responds by tearing (קרע) his clothes in grief (v. 11) because the people have not obeyed YHWH (vv. 13). As a result, Josiah is praised by Huldah the prophetess (vv. 19–20) for having read and heeded the book (vv. 16, 19), and the king proceeds to the temple to read the scroll before all the people (2 Kgs 23:2; cf. Deut 17:18–20).

On the contrary, in Jeremiah 36, the scribe Baruch reads Jeremiah's words in the temple (Jer 36:10), and after Baruch reads the scroll to the king's officials (vv. 13–15), Jehudi is eventually selected to read the scroll to King Jehoiakim in the palace (v. 21). King Jehoiakim responds by tearing (קרע) the scroll as it was being read and burning it piece by piece (v. 23). Jer 36:24 states explicitly, "The king and all his servants who heard all these words did not fear and did not tear their clothes," which is a clear allusion to the account of Josiah in 2 Kgs 22:11. Thus, Jehoiakim is portrayed as an antitype for King Josiah: where Josiah heeded the words of the torah and tore his clothes in repentance, Jehoiakim tore the scroll, expressing utter rejection of YHWH's torah, and bringing judgment upon the nation of Judah as a result. This is the primary significance of the story in context.

---

30. See E. W. Nicholson, *Preaching to the Exiles* (Oxford: Blackwell, 1970) 45, 50–51; and K. Schmid, *Buchgestalten des Jeremiabuches* (Neukirchen-Vluyn: Neukirchener Verlag, 1996) 245–49.

31. Jeremiah 36 takes place in the fourth year of Jehoiakim (605 B.C.E.), which was also the first year of the rule of Nebuchadnezzar (see Jer 25:1). Jeremiah 37 moves forward to the beginning of Zedekiah's reign (597 B.C.E.), and the narrative continues to the fall of Jerusalem in Zedekiah's eleventh year (586 B.C.E.) and the turmoil that follows. On Jeremiah 36 as the beginning of this unit, see L. Stulman, *Jeremiah* (AOTC; Nashville: Abingdon, 2005) 295–96; and G. Fischer, *Jeremia 26–52* (Freiburg: Herder, 2005) 285

32. See C. D. Isbell, "2 Kgs 22:3–23:24 and Jeremiah 36: A Stylistic Comparison," *JSOT* 8 (1978) 33–45; Dearman, "My Servants the Scribes," 404–8; Schmid, *Buchgestalten des Jeremiabuches*, 246–47; and Venema, *Reading Scripture in the Old Testament*, 127–30.

2.2. The Significance of the Scroll

Yet, what role does the scroll play in this crucial story? Many readers of Jeremiah 36 have noted the relative absence of Jeremiah from the narrative and the prominence given to the scroll.[33] Jeremiah dictates the scroll to Baruch in vv. 1–7, and then moves off center stage, since he is barred from the temple.[34] Baruch reads the scroll in the temple and to the king's officials, and then he also moves off stage (vv. 8–19), as he is told that he and Jeremiah should go into hiding. After this, the scroll is read to the king, who burns it and orders the arrest of Baruch and Jeremiah, whom God has hidden (vv. 20–26). The final section, which brings Jeremiah and Baruch back into the story, recounts the dictation of a new scroll to replace the one that was destroyed (vv. 27–32). The scroll (or its replacement) is the only protagonist to appear in each scene. Reflecting on the scroll's central role in this chapter, many commentators rightly identify the "word of YHWH" (or the like) as a key theological motif of this narrative.[35]

At the same time, it must be kept clear that the word of YHWH, and not the scroll itself, is the true theological center of Jeremiah 36. It would not be accurate to equate the theological role of the scroll in Jeremiah 36 with the kind of scribal culture often associated with Ezra and the Postexilic Period.[36] Jeremiah 36 is not about the power of the scroll. Just as prophets can be killed, scrolls can be destroyed. Indeed, the scroll in Jeremiah 36 does not survive its encounter with Jehoiakim, but the word of YHWH persists because YHWH is committed to fulfilling his word and continuing to reveal it.[37] Accordingly, God hides his prophet

---

33. E.g., Venema, *Reading Scripture in the Old Testament*, 134–36; W. Brueggemann, *A Commentary on Jeremiah* (Grand Rapids: Eerdmans, 1998) 345–46; and Carroll, "Manuscripts Don't Burn," 33.

34. Still, in Jer 36:17–19, the officials ask Baruch if Jeremiah dictated the words of the scroll, and they also mention Jeremiah's name when they tell Baruch and Jeremiah to go into hiding. So the narrator has not removed Jeremiah entirely from the picture. While the scroll does occupy center stage in the chapter, it is doubtful that the writer was making a conscious attempt to marginalize the prophet.

35. See the insightful comments in Stulman, *Jeremiah*, 301–2.

36. These lines are connected perhaps too readily by R. Carroll, *Jeremiah* (OTL; Philadelphia: Westminster, 1986) 668; and W. Brueggemann, *The Theology of the Book of Jeremiah* (Cambridge: Cambridge University Press, 2007) 182. On the "growing prominence of authoritative written texts" in the Postexilic Period, see W. M. Schniedewind, *How the Bible Became a Book* (Cambridge: Cambridge University Press, 2004) 186–87.

37. Fischer, *Jeremia 26–52*, 305, rightly points to the indestructible divine will in the word of God as the key theological motif of Jeremiah 36, but he does so by placing primary emphasis on the advantages of the written word, namely, that it can be read by various people on many occasions and apart from the presence of the original writer. Yet,

in safety (v. 26) so that he can create a new scroll. The narrative declares that, although Jehoiakim could destroy the physical scroll, he could not destroy the reality behind the message of the scroll.

In view of Jehoiakim's boldness and wickedness (from the biblical point of view), one can imagine that he held to some form of the misguided Deuteronomic theology described above, whereby power is ascribed to the physical instrument of the covenant without regard for the values of the covenant. If so, then Jehoiakim may have decided to burn the scroll because he believed that whatever power the scroll had could be nullified by destroying it.[38] But after the scroll is burned, the word of YHWH comes again to Jeremiah and tells him to re-write the words of the scroll, and also to add an oracle of judgment against Jehoiakim for his impertinence (36:27–32). Furthermore, v. 32 concludes, "And still more words similar to these were added to them." In other words, Jehoiakim has not rid himself of judgment by burning the scroll, but has only amplified the judgment, since the same words and even more are now prophesied against him.

Jeremiah generally had a positive view of Deuteronomy's institutions, such as sacrifice and kingship, when these were considered in idealistic terms; but he sharply criticized these institutions when they were not combined with genuine devotion to YHWH and his word. Jeremiah's relationship to the scribes of his day fits this pattern. Jeremiah acted as a scribe and accepted help from scribes who shared his Deuteronomic ideals, but he also criticized scribes who thought they were wise simply because they possessed the torah (i.e., the physical scroll), even though they did not truly know YHWH (see Jer 2:8, 8:8). Jeremiah 36, which sets up the narrative of the fall of Jerusalem, depicts Jehoiakim's ultimate rejection of YHWH's word. Jehoiakim burns the scroll, but the word of YHWH survives and increases in strength.[39]

Jehoiakim shows himself capable of silencing both prophet (Jer 36:5; see also 26:20–23) and scroll (Jer 36:23). One could say that the persistence of the divine will itself (more abstractly considered) as revealed in the word of YHWH is the key theological motif of Jeremiah 36.

38. McKane describes Jehoiakim's behavior here as "religious superstition" (*Jeremiah*, 2:919).

39. The word of YHWH is itself a key motif in Jeremiah: YHWH watches over his word to ensure its fulfillment (Jer 1:12). Jeremiah cannot refrain from speaking YHWH's word, even if he tries (Jer 20:9). Jeremiah cannot control YHWH's word; on one occasion, he has to wait for ten days before it comes (Jer 42:7). YHWH's word is forceful: "Is not my word like fire, declares YHWH, and a like a hammer that shatters a rock?" (Jer 23:29). For Jeremiah, the word of YHWH that came to him was of the same nature as YHWH's "torah" (Jer 6:19).

In Jeremiah, scrolls can be burned (36:23) but the word of YHWH will come again (36:27–32); indeed, one prophet can be killed (Jer 26:20–23) but YHWH will speak through another (26:24). The goal of Jeremiah 36 is not to exalt the status of the physical scroll, but to demonstrate that power does not reside in the scroll, but in the word of YHWH.

3. Historical Reflections on the Theology of the Word in Jeremiah 36

It will be worthwhile to observe how this theological idea of the enduring word of the LORD in Jeremiah 36 was identified and re-applied in both ancient Judaism and the early church. Both groups were rooted in sacred Scriptures and could be described as "religions of the book." At the same time, both groups expressed theologies of the divine word that encompassed more than their sacred books.

3.1. Jeremiah 36 in Early Judaism

If Jeremiah 36 is ultimately about YHWH's word that endures, then we may ask how this word of YHWH was received by readers of Jeremiah in the Judaism that has endured, namely, the Judaism of the rabbis. Rabbinic texts derive several important principles from Jeremiah 36. At the most basic level, Torah scrolls are to be written in ink, in imitation of the scroll in Jer 36:18 ("I wrote them with ink on the scroll").[40] This verse was also used to show that even someone who is an expert in reading Torah should always read from the scroll and not recite from memory ("He dictated all these words to me, while I wrote them with ink on the scroll").[41] Furthermore, the reputation of Jeremiah's scribe Baruch increased greatly in the Judaism of the Second Temple period as well as in rabbinic tradition.[42] But perhaps the most profound implication drawn from Jeremiah 36 was the rule that, in contrast with Jehoiakim (36:24), one is obligated to rend one's clothes when a Torah scroll has been burned.[43] This shows the deep respect the rabbis had for the Torah scroll as a physical object.

---

40. *b. Menah.* 34a; *b. Meg.* 19a; *Sop.* 1; *Sep. Torah* 1.
41. *y. Meg.* 4:1, 74d.
42. On Baruch in early Judaism generally, see J. E. Wright, "Baruch: His Evolution from Scribe to Apocalyptic Seer," in *Biblical Figures Outside the Bible* (ed. M. E. Stone and T. A. Bergen; Harrisburg, PA: Trinity Press International, 1998) 264–89. In rabbinic literature, Baruch was distinguished above all others by his good deeds (*Sipre Num* 99; *Pirqe R. El.* 53); he was considered both the teacher of Ezra (*b. Meg.* 16b; *Song Rab.* 5.5.1) and a prophet (*b. Meg.* 14b; *y. Sotah* 9:13, 24b; *Sipre Num* 78; *Sipre Zuta* to Num 10:29; but cf. *Mek. R. Ish., Pisha*, 1, end, where Baruch does not possess prophetic inspiration).
43. *b. Mo'ed Qat.* 26a; y. *Mo'ed Qat.* 3:7, 83c. Arguing from Jer 36:27 ("after the king had burned the scroll and the words"), one view expressed requires that two rents be made

However, the word of YHWH exemplified by the scroll was even more significantly embodied in the sages who learned, lived, and taught Torah. The body of the rabbinic sage is said to be a receptacle for Torah (*b. Sanh.* 99b). Just as fire leaves a mark on the body, so also words of Torah leave a mark on the body of the sage (*Sipre Deut* 343, on Deut 33:2). The sage is also likened to a flask of sweet-smelling ointment, which releases its pleasing fragrance when it is opened, that is, when the sage teaches Torah (*b. 'Abod. Zar.* 35b).[44] The embodiment of Torah in the sage is symbolized in one particular ruling given by *Talmud Yerushalmi*: Within the context of the obligation to rend one's garments when a Torah scroll has been burned, the text cites Jer 36:27 and then asserts: "Anyone who sees a disciple of a sage who has died is like one who sees a scroll of the Torah that has been burned" (*y. Mo'ed Qat.* 3:7, 83c). The death of a Torah sage is like the destruction of a Torah scroll because both are vessels of the divine word, the Torah of YHWH. But neither the death of any given sage nor the burning of any given scroll is the end of Torah.

In rabbinic thought, the Torah and the people of Israel endure together. The killing of Jews and the burning of Torah scrolls took place during the persecution under Antiochus IV (e.g., 1 Macc. 1:54–61). In the Hellenistic Jewish author Eupolemus, Jeremiah is himself almost burned alive by the wicked Judean king (39.3),[45] a retelling that might reflect the reality of persecution that Jews suffered during the Hellenistic period. As is well known, Jews suffered greatly during the Roman period, especially in connection with the two "Jewish Revolts," as a result of which the temple was destroyed (70 C.E.), and Jews were expelled from Jerusalem (135 C.E.). But the Judaism of Torah continued; the persistence of the Jewish people and the Torah is often illustrated in rabbinic texts through the life and martyrdom of Rabbi Akiba, who continued to practice and teach Torah in the face of persecution and ultimately death.[46]

---

upon seeing a burned Torah scroll, one for the damaging of the parchment ("the scroll"), and one for the damage done to the writing ("the words").

44. A capable student of the sages could be likened to a sponge that absorbs everything (*Sipre Deut* 48). On the preservation of Torah through diligent study, see M. Hirshman, *The Stabilization of Rabbinic Culture 100 C.E.–350 C.E.* (Oxford: Oxford University Press, 2009) 39–47.

45. J. H. Charlesworth, ed., *The Old Testament Pseudepigrapha* (2 vols.; New York: Doubleday, 1985) 2:871.

46. See A. J. Heschel, *Heavenly Torah* (ed. and transl. G. Tucker and L. Levin; New York and London: Continuum, 2005) 140–48.

Indeed, throughout rabbinic literature the Torah and its benefits outlast this earthly existence. Torah study is the supreme activity whose interest can be enjoyed in this world and whose capital will be enjoyed in the world to come (*m. Pe'ah* 1:1). Torah gives life to those who practice it both in this world and in the world to come (e.g., *m. 'Abot* 6:7). Torah is the greatest possession because, whereas worldly goods can be stolen or destroyed, knowledge of Torah endures all these calamities (*Tanḥ, Terumah*, 2). Torah is likewise of greatest value and use in the world to come (*Sipre Deut* 343), as the afterlife is envisioned as a *bet midrash* 'house of study' devoted to the study of Torah (e.g., *Eccl. Rab.* 5.11.5).[47]

God dwells in the midst of those who are engaged in Torah (*m. 'Abot* 3:6). Just as Torah will endure forever, so also Israel, for whose sake Torah was created, will endure forever (*Eccl. Rab.* 1.4.4).[48] In theological terms, the divine word of Torah lives in the sages and the people of Israel who are guided by Torah, and the divine word endures through Israel and its sages.[49] In this line of rabbinic thought, it is in the Jewish community where Torah endures despite incredible opposition.

3.2. Jeremiah 36 in Early Christianity

As with the Jewish sages of antiquity, early Christians read Jeremiah 36 both in relation to their sacred Scripture and also in view of their broader beliefs about the word of the Lord. In terms of Scripture, John Chrysostom preached a sermon *On the Obscurity of Prophecies*,[50] in

---

47. See also *b. B. Meṣi'a* 85a: "Anyone who teaches Torah to the son of his neighbor merits to sit in the academy on high, for it is written: 'If you will cause (Israel) to repent [reading the verb as Hiphil], then I will restore you and you will stand before me.' (Jer 15:19)."

48. As part of this midrash, Prov 3:18 is cited to show that "tree" can stand for Torah, and Isa 65:22 is used to demonstrate that Israel will endure as long as the "tree," that is, Torah. On the necessity of Israel for the existence of Torah, see also *Lev. Rab.* 11.7: "Without sages, there is no Torah." Cf. also *S. Eli. Zut.*, chap. 2, in which the parable is told of a human king who gave wheat and flax to two servants, one of whom did nothing with these materials (to his discredit), and the other of whom made the wheat into bread and the flax into a tablecloth (to his praise). This is seen to illustrate how the Torah as worked out and practiced by Israel (*mishnah*) is the intended completion of what Torah is meant to be. For a thoughtful modern perspective on how the divine will in Torah is discerned continuously in history through the practices of the Jewish people, see L. Jacobs, *A Jewish Theology* (London: Darton, Longman & Todd, 1973) 206–30.

49. The sages of antiquity affirmed the sacredness of all Israel but also rebuked their fellow Jews if they did not pay heed to Torah. On the relationship between the people of Israel and its sages, see J. L. Rubenstein, *The Culture of the Babylonian Talmud* (Baltimore: Johns Hopkins University Press, 2003) 123–42; and E. E. Urbach, *The Sages: their Concepts and Beliefs* (trans. I. Abrahams; Jerusalem: Magnes, 1979) 630–48.

50. *De prophetiarum obscuritate* 1 (PG 56. 163–75). This is the first of a series of two homilies on this topic. The homily has been translated into English by R. C. Hill, *St. John*

which Jeremiah 36 serves to illustrate what Chrysostom believes to be an important reality about the Old Testament and its interpretation. The goal of the sermon is to explain why the Old Testament appears to speak in riddles (αἰνίγματα) and is difficult to grasp. The reason, according to Chrysostom, is that Old Testament authors announced many things about the future that were unfavorable towards their hearers, such as the rejection of the Jews and the destruction of the temple, and if Old Testament writers had not concealed their prophesies in obscurity, their hearers would have put them to death.[51]

Of course, Chrysostom believed that Old Testament prophets did speak some things clearly, namely, things related to their present situations—otherwise, there would have been no point in the prophets speaking to their contemporaries at all.[52] But prophecies about the future, many of which had negative implications for the original audiences, were spoken enigmatically in order to protect the prophets from harm. In Chrysostom's account of Jeremiah 36, Jehoiakim's burning the scroll illustrates the people's rejection of the divine word and their desire to destroy the bearer of the message.[53] In this case, the prophetic message survives because God hid the prophet (36:26); but in most cases, the divine message survived because God "hid" the prophets by the obscurity of what they said.[54] Thus, for Chrysostom, the divine word of judgment that endures in Jeremiah 36 represents the enigmatic nature of the Old Testament, the obscurities of which must be unpacked with patience and care and in light of the coming of Christ.

A different and more theologically interesting Christian treatment of Jeremiah 36 can be found in the commentary on Jeremiah by Theodoret of Cyrus, who likens the enduring word of the Lord in Jeremiah to the divine Word, Jesus. On the topic of God's command to Jeremiah to write another scroll (Jer 36:28), Theodoret says, "But the God of all bade Jeremiah to write the former oracles (λόγους) in a different book: whereas the writing matter was consumed by fire, the divine Law

---

Chrysostom: Old Testament Homilies (3 vols.; Brookline, MA: Holy Cross Orthodox Press, 2003) 3:8–25.

51. Hill, *St. John Chrysostom: Old Testament Homilies*, 13–16. In the midst of his hermeneutical observations about the Old Testament, Chrysostom expresses animosity towards Jews that is not fitting for Christian charity. This homily remains interesting as a reflection on Christian hermeneutics but not for its attitude towards Jews. On Chrysostom's context, see R. Wilken, *John Chrysostom and the Jews* (Berkeley: University of California Press, 1983).

52. Hill, *St. John Chrysostom: Old Testament Homilies*, 21–22.

53. Ibid., 17–21.

54. Ibid., 20–21.

(νόμος) remained intact (ἀβλαβής); likewise also the Word (λόγος), when the body that was assumed (ληφθέντος σώματος) suffered, remained immune to suffering (ἀπαθής)."[55]

Theodoret's association of the scroll's message with the divine Word is grounded in traditional Christian theological language pertaining to Christ.[56] The word (λόγος) of the Lord that came to Jeremiah starting from the beginning of his ministry (Jer 1:2, 1:4, 1:11, 1:13, etc.) was the same Word that became flesh in the incarnation (John 1:1).[57] This word (λόγος) of the Lord came to Jeremiah in order to direct him to dictate the scroll (36:1; LXX 43:1) and to re-write it (43:27), and the content of the scroll is described as the words (λόγους) of the Lord (LXX 43:4, 8, 11; new scroll: 43:28, 32), as well as the words of Jeremiah (43:10). God is made known in the λόγος, which makes prophetic revelation to humanity a natural (albeit lesser) parallel to the divine λόγος, the revealer and mediator.

Theodoret's manner of expression, especially his phrase "the body that was assumed" and his focus on impassibility (ἀπαθής), reflect his adherence to the "Antiochene Christology."[58] In essence, Theodoret wanted to emphasize a crucial role for the full human experience of Jesus and also to maintain the complete impassibility of God in the midst of the incarnation.[59] Both of these theological ideas intersect with Theodoret's reading of Jeremiah 36.

---

55. PG 81. 681–84; English translation by R. C. Hill, *Theodoret of Cyrus: Commentaries on the Prophets* (3 vols.; Brookline, MA: Holy Cross Orthodox Press, 2006) 1:127.

56. Compare the insightful observation of this connection in M. Brummitt and Y. Sherwood, "The Fear of Loss Inherent in Writing: Jeremiah 36 as the Story of a Self-Conscious Scroll," in *Jeremiah Displaced* (ed. A. R. P. Diamond and L. Stulman; New York/London: T. & T. Clark, 2011) 64–65.

57. Christ as the λόγος was a fundamental concept for Christian theology in the second century and continued to be a key term used in fourth- and fifth-century Christology (see A. Grillmeier, *Christ in Christian Tradition*, vol. 1 [transl. J. Bowden; Atlanta: John Knox, 1975] 90–94, 108–17, 134–48, and all throughout parts two and three).

58. For a brief and fair assessment of this theological perspective, see J. N. D. Kelly, *Early Christian Doctrines* (rev. ed.; New York: HarperCollins, 1978) 301–43.

59. Against Apollinarianism, Theodoret (and the Antiochenes before him) argued that Jesus did in fact have a human soul, and was not simply the divine Word within flesh. At the same time, in contrast to the "Alexandrian Christology" (Athanasius-Cyril), Theodoret described Christ as the joining of the divine λόγος and the human person into a single πρόσωπον, such that human experiences of Jesus (such as growing in wisdom [Luke 2:52]) could be said to pertain specifically to the "human person that was assumed" rather than to the "Word that assumes." This manner of talking about two subjects with regard to Christ was the "Antiochene" way to preserve the impassibility of God while at the same time reckoning with the real experiences of Jesus (e.g., Luke 8:23, 22:42–43), statements of Jesus (e.g., John 14:28, 20:17), and statements about Jesus (e.g., Phil 2:9;

First, Theodoret seems to recognize the central role of the scroll in Jeremiah 36. He explains for his readers that this "roll of a book" refers to the scrolls that Jews continued to use in his own day.[60] Theodoret describes how Jeremiah delivered the oracles by inspiration and Baruch wrote them down, with the goal of turning the people to repentance and salvation by making them aware of the threatened troubles. Theodoret continues to narrate the story of the scroll, how Baruch read the scroll, and then the scroll was read to the king, who subsequently burned it. Theodoret observes that the text condemns the king (citing v. 24), but he also notes that the text commends Elnathan, Delaiah, and Gemariah for attempting to stop the king (cf. v. 25). Furthermore, Theodoret is at pains to show that, after the king burns the scroll, the judgment stated against Jehoiakim in vv. 29–30 came true, arguing that even if Jehoiakim's son did follow him on the throne, he was nevertheless taken into captivity after only three months.[61] In short, in contrast with much patristic exegesis (but not unusual for Antiochene exegesis), Theodoret takes the literal subject matter of the text seriously. The historical experiences of Jeremiah, Baruch, and the scroll are seen by Theodoret as conveying meaningful truth. Theodoret's focus on the human dimension of the biblical text runs parallel to his focus on the human person of Jesus. The activity of the scroll in the text receives its due attention hermeneutically, even as the human activity of Jesus receives attention Christologically.

Second, the fact that the divine law remains "unharmed" (ἀβλαβής) by Jehoiakim's attack represents for Theodoret the impassability of God the Word.[62] The picture of the enduring word in Jeremiah 36, which results in the production of a new scroll, is perhaps similar in Theodoret's mind to the statement of Jesus in John 2:19, "Destroy this temple, and

---

1 Tim 2:5) described in the New Testament. Cyril of Alexandria was equally committed to divine impassibility (see J. Pelikan, *The Christian Tradition: A History of the Development of Doctrine, vol. 1: The Emergence of the Catholic Tradition (100–600)* [Chicago: University of Chicago Press, 1971] 230), but he placed greater emphasis on the unity of the two natures of Christ. A passage that captures the "Alexandrian Christology" well is John 1:14 ("the Word became flesh"), which suggests that the divine λόγος (i.e., the second person of the Trinity) is the single subject of the activity of Christ. A passage that captures the "Antiochene Christology" well is Col 2:9, which suggests indwelling, yielding unity but allowing for differences in predication. For a recent and well-researched treatment of Theodoret's Christology, see P. B. Clayton, *The Christology of Theodoret of Cyrus* (Oxford: Oxford University Press, 2007).

60. The LXX at 43:2 has χαρτίον βιβλίου 'leaflet of a book', but in his paraphrase Theodoret refers to it as a κεφαλὶς βιβλίου 'chapter/roll of a book'.

61. Hill, *Theodoret of Cyrus: Commentaries on the Prophets*, 126–27.

62. Cf. ibid., 42.

in three days I will raise it up."[63] Jesus' body was destroyed and raised again because the divine Word remained unharmed by the power of death; in similar fashion, the divine law written on the scroll was unharmed by the burning of the physical scroll. The physical resurrection of Jesus finds its match in Jeremiah 36 not only in the production of a new scroll, but in the fact that Theodoret bases his Christian application of the passage at the end of the chapter on the same basic message that was delivered to Judah in the first scroll:

For our part, I beseech you, let us be in dread of the divine threats, believe the good promises and walk in a manner worthy of the calling in which we are called so as to avoid the experience of the threats and enjoy the promised good things, thanks to the grace and lovingkindness of our Lord Jesus Christ, to whom with the father and the all-holy Spirit belongs the glory, now and forever, for ages of ages. Amen.[64]

The immutability of the Word plays out in Jeremiah 36 as a divine law that persists despite an attempt to destroy it, and this Old Testament message continues in force for Theodoret even to his own day, since it now serves as an admonition given in the name of Christ to his fellow Christians. Theodoret's resolute belief in the immutability of God certainly caused him difficulties when it came to conceptualizing Christ's incarnation theologically, but it also gave him a rich sense of God's eternal and unchanging persistence.

4. Conclusion

Jeremiah 36 is not ultimately about the scroll that is burned, but the word of the LORD that will surely find its fulfillment. Even if Jehoiakim in the narrative believes that he can avert punishment by destroying the scroll, Jeremiah 36 makes clear that the LORD stands behind his pronouncements and will only strengthen them if opposed. Neither in Deuteronomy nor in Jeremiah is writing seen as efficacious apart from the proper response to the word of the LORD contained in the writing. In Jewish and Christian traditions, Jeremiah 36 continues to be read as a narrative about God speaking his enduring word.

---

63. Theodoret, *Epist. 151* (see P. Schaff and H. Wace, ed., *A Select Library of Nicene and Post-Nicene Fathers of the Christian Church*, 2nd series [14 vols.; New York: Christian Literature, 1892] 3:326). For Theodore of Mopsuestia's similar use of John 2:19 in his discussion of Phil 2:5–11, see R. A. Greer, transl., *Theodore of Mopsuestia: The Commentaries on the Minor Epistles of Paul* (Atlanta: SBL, 2010) 316–18.

64. Hill, *Theodoret of Cyrus: Commentaries on the Prophets*, 127.

Deuteronomy and Ezekiel's Theology of Exile

Jason Gile

Exile and return occupy a fundamental place in Ezekiel's theology of judgment and restoration. For Ezekiel, Yahweh's expulsion of his people from their land represents divine punishment for their religious and social transgressions (36:19), which he saw as a failure to keep Yahweh's statutes and ordinances (5:6–7; 11:12; 20:13, 16, 21, 24). Accordingly, the prophet cites specific injunctions in the Holiness Code and Deuteronomy in order to accuse and condemn his fellow Israelites.[1] However, as a prophet whose ministry straddles the periods both before and after the judgment of 587 B.C.E., Ezekiel foresaw a renewed era when Yahweh would bring his people back to their land and display his gracious resolve to maintain his covenant with Israel by causing them to walk in his statutes (11:19–20, 36:27, 37:24).

One particular motif stands out as a dominant image for the prophet's warnings of exile and promises of return: the scattering and gathering of Israel among the nations. This essay will examine the first of these two related images—scattering as a motif for exile—and argue for Deuteronomy's influence on Ezekiel. In what follows I will first demonstrate the correspondences between Ezekiel's language and that of Deuteronomy and then explicitly treat the direction of dependence by arguing for the priority of Deuteronomy's scattering passages and Ezekiel's purposeful allusion to them. Then I will describe the influence of Deuteronomy on Ezekiel's theology more broadly. At the end of the essay, I will address the rhetorical function of Ezekiel's allusions to the pentateuchal language.

Author's Note: It is an honor to dedicate this essay to Daniel Block, a mentor and friend, whose exceptional work on the book of Ezekiel has paved the way for me and many others. An earlier version was presented in the Exile (Forced Migrations) in Biblical Literature Section at the annual meeting of the Society of Biblical Literature, Chicago, 2012.

1. See M. A. Lyons, *From Law to Prophecy: Ezekiel's Use of the Holiness Code* (LHBOTS 507; New York: T. & T. Clark, 2009); J. Gile, *Deuteronomic Influence in the Book of Ezekiel* (Ph.D. diss., Wheaton College Graduate School, 2013).

1. The Motif

Ezekiel warns of exile or promises return more than 20 times using this distinctive motif.[2] The image of scattering or gathering Israel is present to a lesser degree elsewhere in the Hebrew Bible, but nowhere is it more pronounced than in Ezekiel, where it occurs more often than any other book. In addition, as other scholars have noted, although the texts in Ezekiel display minor variations, they exhibit a remarkable consistency of expression not found in other books and thus warrant being called stereotyped formulae.[3]

The Holiness Code and Deuteronomy also contain the motif in variant forms, and the question naturally arises whether Ezekiel's language might derive from earlier traditions about exile. Indeed, there is reason within the book itself to suspect that Ezekiel may have known and drawn from traditional material for the scattering metaphor. In his depiction of the history of the wilderness period in chapter 20, the prophet cites Yahweh's threat to Israel: "I swore to them in the wilderness that I would scatter them among the nations and disperse them through the lands" (v. 23). Although Ezekiel's historiography in chapter 20 is highly stylized,[4] this text suggests that the prophet knew of a prior tradition that Yahweh threatened or committed to exile Israel in the wilderness period. Thus, we find in this passage a warrant to examine Ezekiel's relationship to the pentateuchal texts that speak of exile.[5] The following investigation will consider whether Ezekiel knows and draws from any of these texts, and if so, which one(s).

2. Ezekiel's Scattering Language and the Holiness Code

Before treating the affinities of Ezekiel's language to that of Deuteronomy, here I briefly note that Ezekiel draws from the one passage in

---

2. Ezek 5:2, 10, 12; 6:8; 11:16–17; 12:14–15; 20:23, 34, 41; 22:15; 28:25; 34:13; 36:19, 24; 37:21; 39:27–28; in metaphorical contexts: 22:19; 34:5, 6, 12; of Egypt: 29:12–13; 30:23; 30:26; of Babylon: 22:19.

3. On the gathering formula see, e.g., G. Widengreen, "Yahweh's Gathering of the Dispersed," in *In the Shelter of Elyon: Essays on Ancient Palestinian Life and Literature in Honor of G. W. Ahlström* (ed. W. B. Barrick and J. R. Spencer; JSOTSup 31; Sheffield: JSOT Press, 1984) 227–45; J. Lust, " 'Gathering and Return' in Jeremiah and Ezekiel," in *Le Livre de Jérémie* (ed. P.-M. Bogaert; BETL 54; Leuven: Peeters, 1997) 120–21.

4. See D. I. Block, *The Book of Ezekiel: Chapters 1–24* (NICOT; Grand Rapids: Eerdmans, 1997) 613–15.

5. I use the adjective "pentateuchal" to describe the literary traditions underlying the Pentateuch. I do not assume that the Pentateuch was extant in its final form in Ezekiel's time.

the Holiness Code that speaks of exile.⁶ In the covenant curses of Leviticus 26 Yahweh threatens to remove Israel from the land if they fail to keep his commandments: "I will scatter you among the nations and draw the sword after you (ואתכם אזרה בגוים והריקתי אחריכם חרב)" (v. 33). In three separate instances the prophet cites the language of Lev 26:33, which uses two phrases: אזרה בגוים 'to scatter among the nations' and והריקתי אחריכם חרב 'to draw the sword after you'.

Lev 26:33	ואתכם אזרה בגוים והריקתי אחריכם חרב	**I will scatter** you among the nations, and **I will draw the sword after you.**
Ezek 5:2	והשלשית תזרה לרוח וחרב אריק אחריהם	A third part **you shall scatter** to the wind, and **I will draw the sword after them.**
Ezek 5:12	והשלישית לכל־רוח אזרה וחרב אריק אחריהם	A third part **I will scatter** to all the winds and **I will draw the sword after them.**
Ezek 12:14	אזרה לכל־רוח וחרב אריק אחריהם	**I will scatter** (them) toward every wind, and **I will draw the sword after them.**

The signs of literary dependence in this case are unmistakable due to the verbal and syntactic correspondence between these texts.⁷

3. Ezekiel's Scattering Language and Deuteronomy

However, appealing to the Holiness Code as a basis for Ezekiel's language for exile does not fully account for the majority of instances of scattering in the book where we find a fixed formula for Yahweh's deportation of Israel: הפיץ בגוים וזרה בארצות 'to scatter among the nations and disperse among the lands'.⁸

---

6. Lyons, *From Law to Prophecy*, 118, 183.

7. Although Ezekiel does not use the full phrase אזרה בגוים, the verb זרה and the distinctive phrase חרב אריק אחריהם occur in parallel in both Lev 26:33 and the three instances in Ezekiel. Furthermore, the criterion of recurrence is especially significant here. In addition to Ezekiel's widespread use of the Holiness Code, Lev 26:33 in particular, which also mentions the desolation of the land and its cities, is one of the three most frequently cited verses from the Holiness Code in Ezekiel (Lyons, *From Law to Prophecy*, 78). Finally, similar language of drawing the sword occurs in threats against the prince of Tyre and Egypt in Ezek 28:7 (והריקו חרבותם) and 30:11 (והריקו חרבותם על־מצרים) as well. In chapter 21 Ezekiel makes special use of the sword as an agent of Yahweh's judgment. There, however, the three occurrences of yielding the sword in vv. 8–10[3–5] use different wording (והוצאתי חרבי מתערה) and instead derive from Deuteronomy 32, as I argue elsewhere (J. Gile, "Ezekiel 16 and the Song of Moses: A Prophetic Transformation?" *JBL* 130 [2011] 104–5).

8. We may add a similar phrase that appears to be a modification of the fixed formula. In Ezek 11:16, Yahweh states, "I removed them far off among the nations and scattered them among the lands" (הרחקתים בגוים וכי הפיצותים בארצות). In this instance, the verb הרחיק appears in the first position, and הפיץ drops to the second position. The variation

Ezek 12:15	בהפיצי אותם בגוים וזריתי אותם בארצות
Ezek 20:23	להפיץ אתם בגוים ולזרות אותם בארצות
Ezek 22:15	והפיצותי אותך בגוים וזריתיך בארצות
Ezek 29:12	והפצתי את־מצרים בגוים וזריתים בארצות
Ezek 30:23	והפצותי את־מצרים בגוים וזרתם בארצות
Ezek 30:26	והפצותי את־מצרים בגוים וזריתי אותם בארצות
Ezek 36:19	ואפיץ אתם בגוים ויזרו בארצות

In this formula the verb זרה always occurs in combination with הפיץ, the term that is characteristic of the deuteronomic exile passages and never occurs in the Holiness Code.

The threat of deportation is more prominent in Deuteronomy than the Holiness Code, occurring in Deut 4:27–28; 28:36–37, 41, 64; 29:24–27[25–28] (cf. 30:1, 18). The scattering motif occurs in two of the three chapters. Deut 4:27 and 28:64 warn that "Yahweh will scatter you among [all] the peoples" (והפיץ יהוה אתכם בעמים and והפיצך יהוה בכל־העמים, respectively). Deut 30:3, which promises restoration, also uses the verb הפיץ to describe the places where Yahweh has sent his people. Thus, scattering is an important exile motif for Deuteronomy, occurring in all the passages that mention deportation except chapter 29. Furthermore, in all cases Deuteronomy consistently uses the verb הפיץ, in contrast to Lev 26:33, which uses זרה. Thus, הפיץ is thoroughly deuteronomic, even if it cannot be proven to be exclusively so in common parlance.

Therefore, we may conclude minimally that Ezekiel uses a typical deuteronomic term for his pronouncement of exile. Any further dependence on Deuteronomy is not immediately obvious, since Ezekiel never uses the full deuteronomic phrase הפיץ בעמים 'to scatter among the peoples'. Instead, he uses הפיץ בגוים, 'to scatter among the nations', coupled with זרה בארצות, 'to scatter among the lands'. However, I propose that Ezekiel's formula הפיץ בגוים וזרה בארצות is best explained as a combination of the deuteronomic and priestly locutions, הפיץ בעמים (Deut 4:27, 28:64) and זרה בגוים (Lev 26:33).

In what follows, I will offer several lines of argumentation. First, this hypothesis accords with Ezekiel's fusion of priestly and deuteronomic language and traditions elsewhere, as Risa Levitt Kohn has shown.

---

derives from the influence of the immediately preceding occurrence of the verbal root רחק in v. 15, where the inhabitants of Jerusalem declare, "Go far from Yahweh" (רחקו מעל יהוה). Other references to scattering appear in 6:8 (בגוים בהזרותיכם בארצות) and the numerous restoration passages where the Israelites are described as being gathered from the lands "where they have been scattered" (11:17; 20:34, 41; 28:25; 29:13).

Second, the way the prophet combines these phrases is consistent with Ezekiel's techniques of literary appropriation as outlined by Michael Lyons in his study of Ezekiel's use of the Holiness Code. Third, Ezekiel's awareness of the broader context of at least one of these deuteronomic passages corroborates his dependence on Deuteronomy's exile language. Finally, I will argue that internal evidence in the book of Ezekiel strongly points to one passage in particular known by the prophet. In what follows we will treat each point in turn.

3.1. The Fusion of Traditions in Ezekiel

First, Levitt Kohn has shown that Ezekiel regularly fuses priestly and deuteronomic traditions to create a unique synthesis. In her monograph, *A New Heart and a New Soul: Ezekiel, Exile and the Torah*, she catalogued Ezekiel's use of the language from these two traditions and found examples where he juxtaposes the priestly and deuteronomic material in the same passages.[9] Her premier example is the prophet's account of Israel's history in chapter 20, where he intersperses priestly and deuteronomic language throughout.[10] Other examples of combining locutions from the priestly and deuteronomic writings include his use of Leviticus 26 and Deuteronomy 32 for the agents of death in Ezek 5:16–17,[11] and the combination of the priestly duties presented in Lev 10:10–11 and Deut 17:8, 9; 21:5 in Ezek 44:23–25.

3.2. Ezekiel's Technique of Literary Appropriation

Second, we find a precedent for the specific way that Ezekiel combines the terms. In his study of Ezekiel's use of the Holiness Code, Lyons argues that Ezekiel has a penchant for changing the exact form of expressions found in the Holiness Code and altering his source texts "in regular ways that allow us to speak of *techniques* of modification."[12] Based on an analysis of these techniques, Lyons offers a typology of modifications. Here we will deal with the two techniques relevant to the present discussion.

Lyons interprets Ezekiel's scattering formula as an example of splitting a locution and recombining its parts into parallel lines, a technique

---

9. R. Levitt Kohn, *A New Heart and a New Soul: Ezekiel, the Exile and the Torah* (JSOTSup 358; Sheffield: Sheffield Academic, 2002) 96–104.

10. Ibid., 98–103; idem, "With a Mighty Hand and an Outstretched Arm: The Prophet and the Torah in Ezekiel 20," in *Ezekiel's Hierarchical World: Wrestling with a Tiered Reality* (ed. C. Patton and S. Cooke; SBLSymS 31; Atlanta: Society of Biblical Literature, 2004) 159–68.

11. Gile, "Ezekiel 16," 103–4.

12. Lyons, *From Law to Prophecy*, 88 (italics original).

of literary borrowing found widely in Ezekiel and, according to Benjamin Sommer, in Isaiah 40–66.[13] He writes, "When Ezekiel uses H's locution ואתכם אזרה בגוים ('And you I will scatter among the nations,' Lev 26:33), he splits the clause and redistributes the elements to create a new two-line parallel expression והפיצותי אותך בגוים וזריתיך בארצות ('I will disperse you among the nations and scatter you among the lands')."[14] Thus, Lyons sees Lev 26:33 as the sole influence on the Ezekielian scattering formula, and the introduction of הפיץ is simply the product of Ezekiel's creative recombination. He does not consider the possibility that Ezekiel might have drawn the term from another source.

The scattering formula more likely belongs to another of Lyons' categories of literary appropriation: combination and conflation.[15] In this technique the author does not split and reorder one clause but rather combines and conflates two separate clauses. The postulation of dependence on the deuteronomic phrase הפיץ בעמים carries much more explanatory power for understanding Ezekiel's scattering formula when one observes that the combination of the deuteronomic and priestly locutions resembles Ezekiel's use of other texts. For example, in Ezek 44:20 the prophet draws upon the priestly regulations found in Leviticus 21 and combines elements from verses 5 and 10.[16] We may also cite the recombination of locutions from Leviticus 26 in Ezek 25:7, which exhibits a striking formal similarity with Ezekiel's use of the priestly and deuteronomic phrases in the scattering formula. Like the scattering formula it involves parallel prepositional phrases with "peoples/lands/nations" in adjacent lines.[17]

Lev 26:22	A1 B1	והכריתה את־בהמתכם	It will cut off your livestock
Lev 26:38	A2 B2	ואבדתם בגוים	You will perish among the nations
Ezek 25:7	A1 (B2) A2 X	והכרתיך מן־העמים והאבדתיך מן־הארצות	I will cut you off from the peoples, and make you perish among the lands

Like the first category mentioned, splitting and recombination, it is typical that "Ezekiel does not simply juxtapose independent clauses from

---

13. Ibid., 92–93; B. D. Sommer, *A Prophet Reads Scripture: Allusion in Isaiah 40–66* (Stanford, CA: Stanford University Press, 1998) 68–69.
14. Lyons, *From Law to Prophecy*, 92.
15. Ibid., 95–97.
16. Ibid., 176.
17. Lyons lists this case as an example of splitting and recombining (ibid., 92).

[his sources], but merges them together to create a new statement."[18] Here the prophet combines and conflates two phrases, dropping one element from his sources ("B1") and introducing a new element (designated "X" above).

Ezekiel's use of Lev 26:33 and Deut 4:27 and/or 28:64 exhibits the identical pattern of recombination.

Deut 4:27, 28:64	A1 B1	הפיץ בעמים	He will scatter (you) among the peoples
Lev 26:33	A2 B2	אזרה בגוים	I will disperse (you) among the nations
Ezekiel's formula	A1 B2 A2 X	הפיץ בגוים וזרה בארצות	to scatter (you) among the nations and disperse (you) among the lands

Here Ezekiel combines the priestly and deuteronomic phrases for scattering, אזרה בגוים and הפיץ בעמים,[19] dropping one element (בעמים) and adding another (בארצות).

If this account of the scattering formula's literary background is correct, Ezekiel's source included not only the deuteronomic keyword הפיץ, but the entire deuteronomic phrase הפיץ בעמים. As Lyons observes, "literary borrowing involves a process of selection in which some words from the source text are not used."[20] The absence of Deuteronomy's בעמים in Ezekiel's formula is a result of the literary modification, which discards one element of its source. In summary, Ezekiel's introduction of הפיץ from Deuteronomy accords with his techniques of literary modification, and Ezek 25:7 in particular provides an impressive parallel for the exact modification found in the scattering formula. This observation reinforces the conclusion that Ezekiel's formula combines the priestly and deuteronomic language.

3.3. Ezekiel's Awareness of the Deuteronomic Exile Passages?

But does the prophet simply adopt a deuteronomic phrase that is well-known in contemporary religious parlance, or does he borrow from a particular text? This question is particularly significant given some scholars' tendency to regard the scattering passages in Deuteronomy as exilic additions (to which I will return below). First, based on the criterion of contextual awareness, I will argue that Ezekiel knows at least one of the exile passages in Deuteronomy. Specifically, his allusion

---

18. Ibid., 96.
19. So also S. W. Hahn and J. S. Bergsma, "What Laws Were 'Not Good'? A Canonical Approach to the Theological Problem of Ezekiel 20:25–26," *JBL* 123 (2004) 206.
20. Lyons, *From Law to Prophecy*, 90.

to another distinctive idea in Deuteronomy's exile passages increases the probability that he is drawing from one of these texts. Among Deuteronomy's many references to idolatry, one stands out as especially relevant to Ezekiel and his audience in Babylonian exile. Deuteronomy threatens destruction and eventual exile for disloyalty to the covenant and identifies one particular image of idolatry with Israel's state after the punishment of deportation. In three of the four texts that threaten expulsion from the land, Deuteronomy declares that in exile the Israelites will worship עץ ואבן 'wood and stone'. This statement occurs in chapter 4 after Moses predicts that Israel will fall into idolatry and be scattered among the peoples (vv. 25–28) and twice in the warnings of exile in the covenant curses of Deuteronomy 28 (vv. 36, 64).[21]

Deut 4:27–28	
והפיץ יהוה אתכם בעמים ונשארתם מתי מספר בגוים אשר ינהג יהוה אתכם שמה	And Yahweh will scatter you among the peoples, and you will be left few in number among the nations where Yahweh will drive you.
ועבדתם־שם אלהים מעשה ידי אדם עץ ואבן אשר לא־יראון ולא ישמעון ולא יאכלון ולא יריחן	There you will serve gods, the work of human hands—**wood and stone**—that neither see, nor hear, not eat, nor smell.
Deut 28:36	
יולך יהוה אתך ואת־מלכך אשר תקים עליך אל־גוי אשר לא־ידעת אתה ואבתיך ועבדת שם אלהים אחרים עץ ואבן	Yahweh will bring you and your king whom you set over you to a nation that neither you nor your fathers have known. And there you shall serve other gods—**wood and stone**.
Deut 28:64	
והפיצך יהוה בכל־העמים מקצה הארץ ועד־קצה הארץ ועבדת שם אלהים אחרים אשר לא־ידעת אתה ואבתיך עץ ואבן	Yahweh will scatter you among all peoples, from one end of the earth to the other, and there you shall serve other gods that neither you nor your fathers have known—**wood and stone**.

In these texts עץ ואבן functions as a fixed word pair. This is confirmed by its syntactical position in all three texts, namely, apposition: "the works of human hands—wood and stone" (4:28); "other gods—wood

---

21. Deut 29:16[17] also mentions "wood and stone," along with "silver and gold," in the context of the idols of Egypt (ותראו את־שקוציהם ואת גלליהם עץ ואבן).

and stone" (28:36); "other gods which neither you nor your fathers have known—wood and stone" (28:64). In the context of exile, serving wood and stone amounts to worshiping the local gods.

The locution עץ ואבן appears at a key point in Ezekiel 20. The presence of this rare word pair[22] in the context of the prophet and the elders discussing their situation in exile indicates that its use in Ezekiel alludes to the deuteronomic association of worshiping wood and stone with being in exile. In the beginning of the chapter the elders of Israel approach Ezekiel to inquire of Yahweh. After an extended account of Israel's history of idolatry, Ezekiel says,

Ezek 20:32	
והעלה על־רוחכם היו לא תהיה אשר אתם אמרים נהיה כגוים כמשפחות הארצות לשרת עץ ואבן	What comes into your mind will not come about, when you say: "We will be like the nations, like the tribes of the lands, serving **wood and stone**."

Based on its rarity and distinctiveness, Ezekiel appears to borrow this word pair.[23] But the deuteronomic concept of worshiping עץ ואבן in exile functions more fundamentally in the dialogue between Ezekiel and the elders. Significantly, Ezekiel is the one who mentions עץ ואבן to describe the alleged thought of the elders in exile rather than the elders themselves.[24] The prophet appears to be familiar with Deuteronomy's association of worshipping the local gods in exile and interprets the elders' thought in these deuteronomic terms. Its mention in the present exilic context suggests the prophet is alluding to Deuteronomy's prediction that the people would serve idols in exile. Now in exile, Ezekiel and the elders consider whether it will come to pass in the current generation in Babylon. Ezekiel's apparent knowledge of and allusion to Deuteronomy's distinctive ideas about exile increase the likelihood that he did in fact know at least one of Deuteronomy's exile passages.

---

22. Elsewhere in the Hebrew Bible it only occurs in 2 Kgs 19:18 (= Isa 37:19). Cf. Jer 3:9 (ותנאף את־האבן ואת־העץ).

23. So also T. Ganzel, "The Transformation of Pentateuchal Descriptions of Idolatry in Ezekiel," in *Transforming Visions: Transformations of Text, Tradition, and Theology in Ezekiel* (ed. M. A. Lyons and W. A. Tooman; Princeton Theological Monographs; Eugene, OR.: Pickwick, 2010), 41; Levitt Kohn, *A New Heart*, 92.

24. Contra D. Rom-Shiloni, who argues that v. 32 constitutes a quotation of the elders' inquiry ("Facing Destruction and Exile: Inner-Biblical Exegesis in Jeremiah and Ezekiel," *ZAW* 117 [2005] 194). See Walther Eichrodt, *Ezekiel: A Commentary* (trans. C. Quin; OTL; Philadelphia: Westminster, 1970) 277; Block, *Ezekiel: Chapters 1–24*, 648.

3.4. Ezekiel's Knowledge of an Exile Tradition Reflected in Ezek 20:23?

As noted earlier, internal evidence in the book of Ezekiel suggests the prophet alludes to an earlier tradition. He does not simply speak of the current exile in terms similar to those of the Holiness Code and Deuteronomy, but in one instance actually refers explicitly to an earlier threat from Yahweh to expel his people from the land. Long ago in the wilderness period Yahweh "raised his hand to scatter them among the nations and disperse them among the countries" (Ezek 20:23). In recent years, two scholars have claimed that the phrase "to lift one's hand" does not signify an oath, and therefore Ezek 20:23 does not express a threat or decision by Yahweh to exile Israel in the wilderness.[25] However, as I show elsewhere, their arguments are unconvincing.[26] So, it would seem that Ezekiel knows and is influenced by a tradition that Yahweh swore long ago to expel Israel from the land.

The idea that Yahweh took an oath in the wilderness to scatter Israel among the nations is stated explicitly in the Hebrew Bible only here and in Ps 106:26–27, a postexilic psalm that was clearly influenced by Ezekiel's account of history.[27] Thus, scholars often assert that Yahweh's oath to scatter Israel in the wilderness finds no parallel in biblical tradition that could serve as a basis for Ezekiel's statement. For example, Moshe Greenberg stated that the extant pentateuchal texts are silent about such an oath.[28] It is possible that this element of chapter 20 is simply the product of Ezekiel's theological (re-)interpretation of Israel's history and not a reference to anything we might find in the biblical texts. However, despite the prophet's tendency to shape history to serve his rhetorical purposes,[29] he appears to have a conceptual basis for most elements of his history. Some have pointed to Ezekiel's claim that the Israelites worshiped idols in Egypt as an example of creative historiography that has no basis in traditional materials (Ezek 20:7–8).[30] Yet,

---

25. J. Lust, "Ez., XX, 4–26: une parodie de l'histoire religieuse d'Israël," *ETL* 43 (1967) 488–527, esp. 517–24; C. A. Strine, "The Divine Oath and the Book of Ezekiel: An Analysis of How Ezekiel 20 Uses the 'As I Live' and 'Lifted Hand' Formulae" (paper presented at the annual meeting of the SBL, New Orleans, 2009).

26. See Gile, *Deuteronomic Influence*, ch. 5.

27. G. W. Coats, *Rebellion in the Wilderness: The Murmuring Motif in the Wilderness Traditions of the Old Testament* (Nashville: Abingdon, 1968) 224–31.

28. Greenberg, *Ezekiel 1–20*, 368.

29. Ibid., 383.

30. E.g., M. Fishbane, *Biblical Interpretation in Ancient Israel* (Oxford: Clarendon, 1985) 385; C. Patton, "'I Myself Gave Them Laws That Were Not Good': Ezekiel 20 and the Exodus Traditions," *JSOT* 21 (1996) 76–77.

these verses find more of a basis in Israelite tradition than is generally acknowledged—in particular, Josh 24:14, which represents an earlier tradition that previous generations did in fact worship idols in Egypt.[31]

Rather than a new literary creation, the idea that Yahweh swore to scatter Israel in the wilderness may be based on some tradition, even if the prophet adjusts the details. Indeed, one particular text from Deuteronomy seems to be in view. First, Scott Hahn and John Bergsma have shown persuasively that when related to the pentateuchal account of Israel's exodus, sojourn at Sinai, and wilderness wandering, the narrative flow and literary structure of Ezekiel 20 point to a setting for Ezek 20:23 that coincides with Moses' exposition of the law across the Jordan—namely, Deuteronomy.[32] After Ezekiel says that Yahweh did not make a full end of the first generation, in verse 18 the narrative turns to "their children in the wilderness," that is, the second generation. The rebellion of the second generation in verse 21 would then appear to refer to the idolatry associated with Baal of Peor (Numbers 25).

Accordingly, in Ezekiel's history the time-frame for Yahweh's oath to scatter Israel in 20:23 is the second wilderness generation. If this statement alludes to any pentateuchal threat of exile, the narrative flow of the chapter aligns it with the second-generation legal material, namely, Deuteronomy. Indeed, the narrative context of the deuteronomic instruction names the second generation as Moses' audience (cf. Deut 2:14–16).[33] What then of Ezekiel's characterization of the oath as "in the wilderness"? There is good reason to believe that for Ezekiel the setting of Deuteronomy is outside the promised land, and therefore in the "wilderness." Indeed, the biblical text itself draws a close connection between Israel's sojourn in the wilderness and the setting of Deuteronomy. According to Deut 3:29 and 4:44–49, when Moses expounded the Sinai revelation the Israelites were camped near Beth-Peor, the site of the second generation's wilderness tryst with Baal of Peor (Hos 9:10, Num 25:1–9), to which Ezekiel likely alludes and just beforehand describes as "in the wilderness" (Ezek 20:21–22).[34]

---

31. Lust, "Ez., XX, 4–6: une parodie," 516. Deut 29:15–16[16–17] states that the Israelites saw Egypt's idols.

32. Hahn and Bergsma, "What Laws?" 203–6.

33. Ibid., 206: "The relation of Deuteronomy to the second generation and particularly to the apostasy at Beth-Peor is underscored by the fact that, according to the narrative of Deuteronomy, Israel has not moved from Beth-Peor when Moses imposes on them the Deuteronomic laws."

34. Ibid., 206; M. Weinfeld, *Deuteronomy 1–11*: A New Translation with Introduction and Commentary (AB 5; New York: Doubleday, 1991) 192.

Thus, the close correspondence between the structure of Ezekiel 20 and the pentateuchal narrative suggests that Yahweh's oath to scatter Israel in verse 23 refers to a threat of exile in the period of the second wilderness generation, that is, Deuteronomy. This thesis is reinforced by Ezekiel's constant use of the deuteronomic term הפיץ and, as we will argue below, the similarity between Ezekiel's theology of exile and that of Deuteronomy.

Which text(s) in Deuteronomy might Ezekiel be alluding to in Ezek 20:23? Hahn and Bergsma have hypothesized that the oath to scatter Israel refers to Yahweh's oath in Deut 32:40–41: "For I lift up my hand to heaven and swear, 'As I live forever, if I sharpen my flashing sword and my hand takes hold on judgment, I will take vengeance on my adversaries and will repay those who hate me.'"[35] However, a connection between Ezek 20:23 and Deut 32:40 is unconvincing, primarily because exile is not mentioned or implied anywhere in Deuteronomy 32.[36]

We must therefore look to the two passages in Deuteronomy that in fact describe the scattering of Israel as candidates for Ezekiel's source text: Deut 4:27 and 28:64. The first of these in particular uses language associated with an oath and therefore provides the more likely basis for the prophet's claim in Ezek 20:23.[37] In Deut 4:25–28 Moses says to the Israelites: "If (when) you act corruptly by making a carved image in the form of anything . . . today I call heaven and earth to testify against you, that you will soon utterly perish from the land . . . and Yahweh will scatter you among the peoples." Though this passage lacks an explicit oath saying (חי־יהוה, נשבע, etc.), the act of calling witnesses to testify against the violating party is closely associated with covenant/treaty oaths. In the present case, the call for witnesses is found in the context of a covenant. Verses 25–28 present curses for not keeping "the covenant of Yahweh your God that he made with [Israel]" mentioned in the preceding verse 23. Thus, Moses calls witnesses that they may testify against Israel in the future if they violate the covenant.

The summons for witnesses is a common feature of ANE treaty oaths. Though Deut 4:25–28 does not mention "swearing," it is well known that an oath was an essential conclusion to a treaty or covenant to ensure that the terms agreed upon would be respected and observed. The connection between an oath and calling witnesses is explicit in Moses'

---

35. Hahn and Bergsma, "What Laws?" 205.
36. Ibid., 205 n. 16.
37. Suggested in passing by Levitt Kohn (*A New Heart*, 100 n. 32). Hahn and Bergsma mention it as another possibility ("What Laws?" 205 n. 18).

third address, which displays marked treaty features.³⁸ There his call for heaven and earth to witness against Israel (Deut 30:19) culminates what was earlier described as Israel entering into (עבר ב) a covenant and an oath (את־הברית הזאת ואת־האלה הזאת) (Deut 29:11[12], 13[14]).

In the process of making a covenant, an oath ratified the agreement and made it binding.³⁹ According to Yigael Ziegler, "The oath's power emanates from the fact that every oath contains a conditional curse, even if it is not explicitly delineated in the oath's formula."⁴⁰ When an oath to a treaty or covenant is taken, the speaker declares his intent to keep its terms with the full understanding that failure to do so will incur severe consequences.⁴¹ What role did witnesses play? Usually the gods were called as witnesses. According to Donald Magnetti, an appeal to divine beings was the only effective means to guarantee observance of the treaty, since the gods were called to bear witness to the terms of the agreement and punish those who transgressed it.⁴²

In Deut 4:25–28 Moses does not call on deities to guarantee the covenant between Yahweh and Israel, but rather heaven and earth, as in Deut 30:19 and 31:28 (העידתי בכם היום את־השמים ואת־הארץ). In contrast to summoning heaven and earth to hear (Deut 32:1, Isa 1:2; cf. Mic 1:2, Jer 6:19), Deut 4:26 calls on the heavens and the earth explicitly to bear witness to the covenant and testify against Israel if she violates it by worshiping idols. What will the witnesses testify to?—that Yahweh will scatter them among the peoples as he warned (Deut 4:26–28).

Thus, despite no explicit "swearing" statement in this passage, the mention of calling witnesses in the context of a covenant would have naturally been understood as an oath. Since Ezek 20:23 appears to align with an exile text from Deuteronomy, it seems likely that the prophet found in Deut 4:25–28 a basis for the idea of an oath that Yahweh would scatter Israel among the peoples if they transgressed the covenant.

---

38. On the treaty features of Deuteronomy 29–30, see, for example, A. Rofé, "The Covenant in the Land of Moab (Deuteronomy 28:69–30:20): Historico-Literary, Comparative, and Formcritical Considerations," in *Das Deuteronomium: Entstehung, Gestalt und Botschaft* (ed. N. Lohfink; BETL 68; Leuven: Leuven University Press, 1985) 317.

39. R. Westbrook, "The Character of Ancient Near Eastern Law," in *A History of Ancient Near Eastern Law* (ed. R. Westbrook; HdO 72; 2 vols.; Leiden: Brill, 2003) 1:84.

40. Y. Ziegler, *Promises to Keep: The Oath in Biblical Narrative* (VTSup 120; Leiden: Brill, 2008) 4.

41. Ibid., 3. Cf. G. E. Mendenhall, "Covenant Forms in Israelite Tradition," *BA* 17 (1954) 52: "The oath . . . is a conditional self-cursing, an appeal to the gods to punish the promiser if he defaults."

42. D. L. Magnetti, "The Function of the Oath in the Ancient Near Eastern International Treaty," *American Journal of International Law* 72 (1978) 815.

3.5. Ezekiel's Theology of Exile

The hypothesis of deuteronomic influence on Ezekiel's exile language is corroborated by the distinctive theology of exile that Deuteronomy and Ezekiel share. Unlike Lev 26:33, which only threatens exile after persistent rebellion,[43] the exile passages in Deuteronomy speak of future disobedience and subsequent dispossession of the land as inevitable. In chapters 4 and 29–31 the future apostasy of the people is described as a foregone conclusion. This idea is most explicit in Deut 31:16–20:

> The LORD said to Moses, "Soon you will lie down with your ancestors. Then this people will begin to prostitute themselves to the foreign gods in their midst, the gods of the land into which they are going; they will forsake me, breaking my covenant that I have made with them. My anger will be kindled against them in that day. I will forsake them and hide my face from them; they will become easy prey, and many terrible troubles will come upon them. . . . For when I have brought them into the land flowing with milk and honey, which I promised on oath to their ancestors, and they have eaten their fill and grown fat, they will turn to other gods and serve them, despising me and breaking my covenant." (Deut 31:16–20 NRSV)

Later in the same chapter Moses expresses the same attitude directly to the people and makes a dire prediction:

> I know well how rebellious and stubborn you are. If you already have been so rebellious toward the LORD while I am still alive among you, how much more after my death! . . . For I know that after my death you will surely act corruptly, turning aside from the way that I have commanded you. In time to come trouble will befall you, because you will do what is evil in the sight of the LORD, provoking him to anger through the work of your hands. (Deut 31:27, 29 NRSV)

While this passage does not mention exile explicitly, Deut 29:21–27[22–28] describes a coming turn to idolatry that will result in exile:

> The next generation, your children who rise up after you . . . will see the devastation of that land and the afflictions with which the LORD has afflicted it . . . they and indeed all the nations will wonder, "Why has the

---

43. As Lyons explains, "the judgments in Lev 26 are presented as God's instruments to induce repentance. The author accomplishes this by listing the punishments in order of increasing intensity, and by separating them into groups with refrains that clearly state their restorative purpose," e.g., "if despite this you will not obey" in vv. 18, 21, 23, 27 (*From Law to Prophecy*, 117–18; cf. J. Krašovec, *Reward, Punishment, and Forgiveness: The Thinking and Beliefs of Ancient Israel in the Light of Greek and Modern Views* [VTSup 78; Leiden: Brill, 1999] 164–65). Exile is listed in the last group of curses.

Lord done thus to this land? What caused this great display of anger?" They will conclude, "It is because they abandoned the covenant of the LORD, the God of their ancestors, which he made with them when he brought them out of the land of Egypt. They turned and served other gods . . . so the anger of the LORD was kindled against that land, bringing on it every curse written in this book. The LORD uprooted them from their land in anger, fury, and great wrath, and cast them into another land, as is now the case." (Deut 29:21–27[22–28] NRSV)

According to Gordon McConville, the end of the book "takes for granted that the people will indeed fail to be the true people of the covenant and that this will result in the full force of the curses of ch. 28 falling on them."[44]

Finally, Deut 4:25–28, to which the prophet alludes in Ezek 20:23, may reflect a similar outlook.[45] The interpretive crux is the initial particle כי in 4:25, which may be understood conditionally or temporally. If כי is translated as "when," as many commentators understand it,[46] then this passage also speaks of Israel's future disobedience and exile as inevitable: "when . . . you have grown old in the land and you act corruptly by making a carved image. . . ." Thus, the theology of exile reflected in these chapters describes an unavoidable loss of the land due to Israel's idolatry.[47]

Ezekiel concurs with this sentiment concerning Israel's prospects for obedience. Greenberg hypothesized that the deuteronomic theology of exile alone may have been the impetus for Ezekiel's oath in 20:23, observing that "it is but a step from Moses' prediction of apostasy and exile [in Deuteronomy] to Ezekiel's portrayal of God's oath to exile Israel . . . already taken in the wilderness."[48] Although we have identified a more concrete basis for Ezekiel's oath in Deut 4:25–28, like Deuteronomy, Ezekiel presents an exceedingly bleak picture of Israel's prospects for faithful devotion to Yahweh. Chapter 20 in particular describes Israel's history as one of perpetual rebellion, reaching all the way back to their residence in Egypt (20:8). The apostasy of Israel's first generations

---

44. J. G. McConville, *Grace in the End: A Study in Deuteronomic Theology* (Grand Rapids: Zondervan, 1993) 135.

45. Hahn and Bergsma, "What Laws?" 205 and n. 19.

46. K. J. Turner, *The Death of Deaths in the Death of Israel: Deuteronomy's Theology of Exile* (Eugene, OR: Wipf & Stock, 2011) 113–16; see also idem, "Deuteronomy's Theology of Exile," in this volume; J. G. Millar, *Now Choose Life: Theology and Ethics in Deuteronomy* (New Studies in Biblical Theology; Downers Grove: InterVarsity, 1998) 164.

47. Turner observes that in Deuteronomy "the inevitability of exile is grounded in the pessimistic portrayal of Israel's heart and nature" (*Death of Deaths*, 248).

48. Greenberg, *Ezekiel 1–20*, 385.

after the exodus (20:13, 16, 21) and in more recent times (e.g., 8:1–18) suggests that in Ezekiel's mind the nation was predisposed to rebellion. Ezekiel casts Israel's history expressing a negative view of Israel's capacity to obey. In Jacqueline Lapsley's words, "Because no generation ever did choose to obey Yahweh, the people simply were predisposed to wickedness, and did not possess the capacity to choose otherwise."[49] In order to rectify the situation, like Deuteronomy, Ezekiel spoke of the need for a divine intervention to change Israel's heart (Deut 30:6; Ezek 11:19–20; 36:26–27).[50]

The oath to scatter Israel in Ezek 20:23 suggests that for Ezekiel exile was a certain consequence of Israel's idolatry. Yahweh did not simply threaten or warn that he would exile his people, but he swore to do so.[51] By alluding to Deut 4:25–28 and emphasizing Israel's religious failures from its earliest days, Ezekiel agrees not simply with Deuteronomy's view of Israel's religious aptitude, but also with Deuteronomy's view that the seeds of Israel's loss of the land were present from the very beginning.

4. The Direction of Influence

Having argued on literary grounds that Ezekiel's scattering formula is best explained as a confluence of priestly and deuteronomic language, we may now address more directly questions about the direction of influence. The scattering motif is normally uncontested as an authentic part of the prophet's message in Ezekielian *Literarkritik*, likely because—unlike the gathering motif—it occurs in judgment rather than restoration passages. In order for Ezekiel to draw from Deuteronomy's exile passages, these threats of exile must have been available to the prophet in the early sixth century. In the history of scholarship the threat of exile has sometimes been seen as de facto evidence that a passage derives from the period of the Babylonian exile.[52] According to Gerhard von Rad, "The explanation that Israel was condemned to

---

49. J. E. Lapsley, *Can These Bones Live? The Problem of the Moral Self in the Book of Ezekiel* (BZAW 301; New York: de Gruyter, 2000) 93.

50. See P. Joyce, *Divine Initiative and Human Response in Ezekiel* (JSOTSup 51; Sheffield: Sheffield Academic, 1989) 120–21.

51. E.g., Zimmerli, *Ezekiel 1*, 411; Greenberg, *Ezekiel 1–20*, 368: "Since the people proved to be confirmed rebels, God sealed their fate even before they entered the promised land; it was only a question of time till that fate was realized."

52. See, for example, N. Lohfink, "Auslegung deuteronomischer Texte, IV," *Bibel und Leben* [*BibLeb*] 5 (1964) 250–53; G. von Rad, *Das fünfte Buch Mose: Deuteronomium* (Göttingen: Vandenhoeck & Ruprecht, 1968) 131; H.-D. Preuss, *Deuteronomium* (EdF 164; Darmstadt: Wissenschaftliche Buchgesellschaft, 1982) 72–73, 156–57; T. Römer, "Book of Deuteronomy," in *The History of Israel's Traditions: The Heritage of Martin Noth* (ed. S. L.

be scattered . . . gives a clue for dating the whole, since this preacher knows already of the exile of 587."[53] Similarly, Martin Noth asserted that in the threat of exile in Deut 4:25–28 "Dtr. puts into Moses' mouth the lessons learned from subsequent history with which he himself is familiar."[54]

However, scholars such as Delbert Hillers and Dennis McCarthy have compared the biblical curses with those of ANE treaty texts and argue that the biblical curses need not derive from the experiences of the Babylonian exile or any other period of disaster. Instead, a comparison with the treaty curses of the Near East reveals that the author(s) of the biblical covenant curses drew upon a long and extensive tradition.[55] The quantity and distinctiveness of parallels between the biblical and non-biblical texts led Hillers to conclude that "the existence of a tradition of curses over a thousand years old renders any attempt to relate individual curses [in the Hebrew Bible] to particular historical periods highly suspect."[56] This observation applies to references to exile as well. In ANE treaty documents, the threat of exile for failure to keep the terms of a treaty is well attested.[57] Regarding the implications of these data for the dating of biblical texts, McCarthy writes the following:

> The element of military disaster and its consequences, hunger, slavery, exile . . . is common in the [ANE] curse literature. Hence we cannot reject out of hand any reference to exile as a secondary addition. Why must Deuteronomy be denied the right to use it as a threat as did the composer of Esarhaddon's treaty and of the Sefire text, cases where there is no question of *vaticinium ex eventu*, but only knowledge of the probable result

---

McKenzie and M. P. Graham; JSOTS 182; Sheffield: Sheffield Academic, 1994) 178–212 (186, 200); E. Nielsen, *Deuteronomium* (HAT 1/6; Tübingen: Mohr, 1995) 11.

53. G. von Rad, *Deuteronomy: A Commentary* (OTL; Philadelphia: Westminster John Knox, 1966) 50.

54. M. Noth, *Deuteronomistic History* (JSOTSup 15; Sheffield: JSOT Press, 1981) 34.

55. D. J. McCarthy, *Treaty and Covenant: A Study in Form in the Ancient Oriental Documents and in the Old Testament* (2nd rewritten ed.; AnBib 21a; Rome: Pontifical Biblical Institute, 1978) 172–87; D. R. Hillers, *Treaty-Curses and the Old Testament Prophets* (BibOr 16; Rome: Pontifical Biblical Institute, 1965) 35; M. Weinfeld, *Deuteronomy and the Deuteronomic School* (Oxford: Clarendon, 1972) 116–29.

56. Hillers, *Treaty-Curses*, 35; also cited in D. L. Smith-Christopher, *A Biblical Theology of Exile* (Overtures to Biblical Theology; Minneapolis: Augsburg, 2002) 99; cf. D. I. Block, *The Gods of the Nations: Studies in Ancient Near Eastern National Theology* (2nd ed.; Grand Rapids: Baker, 2000) 104–6.

57. See especially B. Oded, *Mass Deportations and Deportees in the Neo-Assyrian Empire* (Wiesbaden: Reichert, 1979) 41–42. Cf. also the lists of texts in McCarthy, *Treaty and Covenant* (2nd ed.) 173–74; K. A. Kitchen, *On the Reliability of the Old Testament* (Grand Rapids: Eerdmans, 2003) 292–93; Kenneth A. Kitchen and Paul J. N. Lawrence, *Treaty, Law and Covenant in the Ancient Near East* (Wiesbaden: Harrassowitz, 2012) 3:194–95.

of ancient warfare? Hence a simple reference to exile like that of [Deut] 28:36–37 is hardly a sign that the passage is a later addition.[58]

In conjunction with Deuteronomy 28's dependence on a broader curse tradition, we may reasonably conclude that in the period before 587 the biblical authors could have threatened Israel with exile for religious transgressions.[59]

In addition to the tradition of curses that threatened exile, the biblical authors would have been aware that exile was a very real possibility in light of the actual practice of deportation carried out by suzerain states against disloyal vassals. Bustenay Oded has collected extensive evidence for deportations by Assyrian kings, from Ashur-dan II in the tenth century to Ashurbanipal in the seventh century. In particular, Tiglath-pileser III, Sargon II, and Sennacherib practiced the most deportations, with the extant records attributing to them thirty-seven, thirty-eight, and twenty deportations, respectively.[60] The practice of deportation was by no means exclusive to the Assyrians, but was common to all ANE peoples, spanning different periods in history.[61] Kenneth A. Kitchen has compiled numerous examples from the broader Near East.[62]

Thus, in addition to the fact that the biblical authors drew from a curse tradition that included the threat of exile, the ancient historical records indicate that "the concept and practice of exile was a potential threat to the Hebrews and other politically 'small' groups for most of the second and first millennium B.C."[63] Nelson similarly observed that

---

58. D. J. McCarthy, *Treaty and Covenant: A Study in Form in the Ancient Oriental Documents and in the Old Testament* (1st ed.; AnBib 21; Rome: Pontifical Biblical Institute, 1963), 124, quoted in Smith-Christopher, *Biblical Theology*, 99–100 (Cf. the reworked 1978 edition of McCarthy, *Treaty and Covenant*, 180).

59. Also F. M. Cross, *Canaanite Myth and Hebrew Epic: Essays in the History of the Religion of Israel* (Cambridge, MA: Harvard University Press, 1973), 287; D. L. Christensen, *Deuteronomy 1–11* (WBC 6A; Waco, TX: Word, 1991) 93; cf. J. D. Levenson, "Who Inserted the Book of the Torah?" *HTR* 68 (1975) 208 n. 18: "The mere threat and description of exile cannot be taken as a sure reflection of the events of 587. Exile was a threat before it was an historical reality [for Israel]"; R. D. Nelson, *The Double Redaction of the Deuteronomistic History* (JSOTSup 18; Sheffield: JSOT Press, 1981) 23. Nelson regards Deut 4:25–28 and its threat of deportation as preexilic (ibid., 93–94).

60. Oded, *Mass Deportations*, 19–20.

61. Ibid., 41.

62. K. A. Kitchen, "Ancient Orient, 'Deuteronism' [sic], and the Old Testament," in *New Perspectives on the Old Testament* (ed. J. Barton Payne; ETS Supplement Symposium Series 3; Waco, TX: Word, 1970) 5–7.

63. Ibid., 5. Despite taking some texts as exilic, Cross makes the same point, acknowledging that in principle the threat of exile "need not necessarily stem from an exilic editor.

Deuteronomy's threats of exile "do not necessarily presuppose an exilic date, but only an audience familiar with deportation as a feature of Assyrian imperial policy."[64] The ancient Israelites did not need an exile of their own before they could speak of such a phenomenon. Exile would naturally have been mentioned with other catastrophes simply because it was well known from ANE warfare.

Nevertheless, if one still seeks a historical event in ancient Israel to provide an impetus for such threats in the biblical literature, one need not look to the Babylonian exile of 587. The eighth-century Assyrian dispersion of the Northern Kingdom at the hand of Shalmaneser V (followed by Sargon II) provided a precedent for deportation and thus an impetus to warn Judah of a possible exile of its own,[65] especially given the theological interpretation of the fall of Samaria as divine judgment reflected in 2 Kgs 17:7–18.[66] 2 Kgs 17:6 describes Israelites carried away to Assyria and placed "in Halah, and on the river Habor, the river of Gozan, and in the cities of the Medes."[67] Records from Mesopotamia mention the capture of Samaria as well (Babylonian Chronicle 1:28).[68] Thus, it is valid to locate the scattering motif at least as early as the late eighth century in Israel.[69]

Captivity and exile were all too familiar fates in the Neo-Assyrian age. More important, the threat of exile or captivity was common in the curses of the Ancient Near Eastern treaties and came naturally into the curses attached to Israel's covenant" (*Canaanite Myth*, 287).

64. R. D. Nelson, *Deuteronomy: A Commentary* (OTL; Louisville: Westminster John Knox, 2002) 68.

65. So also Hillers, *Treaty-Curses*, 33–34; G. A. Smith, *The Book of Deuteronomy* (Cambridge Bible for Schools and Colleges; Cambridge: Cambridge University Press, 1918) 69, 307; H. Wildberger, *Isaiah 1–12* (Continental Commentary; Minneapolis: Augsburg Fortress, 1991) 274. Cf. A. R. Welch, *Deuteronomy: The Framework to the Code* (London: Oxford University Press, 1932) 136, who cites the siege of Samaria in relation to the curses in Deuteronomy 28 generally.

66. Even if the Deuteronomistic interpretation of the fall of the Northern Kingdom in 2 Kgs 17:7–18 was recorded and incorporated into the Deuteronomistic History after 587, we may expect the sentiment to have earlier precedents.

67. For a synthesis of the biblical and Assyrian sources, see B. Becking, *The Fall of Samaria: An Historical & Archaeological Study* (Studies in the History of the Ancient Near East 2; Leiden: Brill, 1992); B. Oded, "II Kings 17: Between History and Polemic," *Jewish History* 2 (1987) 37–50.

68. A. K. Grayson, *Assyrian and Babylonian Chronicles* (Texts from Cuneiform Sources 5; Locust Valley, NY: Augustin, 1975) 73.

69. Cf. Nelson, *Deuteronomy*, 68: "What Moses foresees as a possible future (idolatry, national destruction, exile into pagan lands) would have been a concrete reality for even the earliest of Deuteronomy's readers, in the shape of the calamity suffered by the northern kingdom."

5. Conclusion

The rhetoric of Ezekiel's allusion to the pentateuchal threats of exile rests in the status of Deuteronomy and the Holiness Code as authoritative instruction for Israel. For Ezekiel they are Yahweh's statutes and ordinances given to Israel in the wilderness (Ezek 20:10–11). Just as Ezekiel viewed his people's sins as transgressions against the statutes contained in these documents and judged Israel according to their standard, he also interpreted the current situation in light of the pentateuchal threats that Yahweh would remove his people from their land if they failed to keep his statutes and ordinances. For Ezekiel the Babylonian exile was the fulfillment of what Yahweh had sworn long ago in the wilderness (20:23). His literary appropriation of these threats reveals that his interpretation of the exile as Yahweh's punishment on his unfaithful people derives in part from the influence of Deuteronomy.

The "Revealed Things"
Deuteronomy and the Epistemology of Job

CHRISTOPHER B. ANSBERRY

The epistemological limits of human knowledge and the transcendence of divine wisdom represent conventional topoi that pervade the literary corpora of the ancient Near Eastern world as well as the Old Testament.[1] The prevalence of these motifs within the formal canons of the ancient world, coupled with the common images and terms employed to conceptualize the relationship between human and divine faculties, indicate the topoi played a formative role in biblical and ancient Near Eastern noetics. Together, they identified the basic contours of the ancient *Weltanschauung* and provided a conceptual framework within which to understand the boundaries of human investigation. While these boundaries vary within individual texts, it appears the extent of human wisdom delineated in Deut 29:28[29] serves as a window into the multifaceted nature of Joban epistemology.

In effect, Deut 29:28[29] illuminates the epistemological gulf that separated Israel from YHWH: "The secret things belong to YHWH our God, but the revealed things belong to us and to our descendants forever, to observe all the words of this torah." The maxim captures the inscrutable nature of divine wisdom, but gives particular attention to

---

Author's note: It is an honor to dedicate this essay to my esteemed teacher, mentor, colleague, and friend, Professor Daniel Block, who embodies the "revealed things" and lives in humble submission to the "secret things."

1. See *Ludlul Bēl Nēmeqi* (W. G. Lambert, *Babylonian Wisdom Literature* [Oxford: Clarendon, 1960; repr., Winona Lake, IN: Eisenbrauns, 1996] 41); "The Dialogue of Pessimism" (B. R. Foster, *Before the Muses: An Anthology of Akkadian Literature* [3d ed.; Bethesda: CDL, 2005] 925–26); Deut 29:28[29], 30:11–14; Ps 145:3; Job 11:7–8, 28:20–21; Prov 25:2–3, 30:4; Sir 1:3, 8; Wis 9:16–18; Bar 3:29–4:1. For a discussion of the topoi, see Lambert, *Babylonian Wisdom Literature*, 327; F. E. Greenspahn, "A Mesopotamian Proverb and Its Biblical Reverberations," *JAOS* 114 (1994) 33–38; R. C. Van Leeuwen, "The Background to Proverbs 30:4aα," in *Wisdom, You Are My Sister: Studies in Honor of Roland E. Murphy, O. Carm., on the Occasion of His Eightieth Birthday* (CBQMS 29; Washington, DC: The Catholic Biblical Association of America, 1997) 102–21; E. L. Greenstein, "The Poem on Wisdom in Job 28 in Its Conceptual and Literary Contexts," in *Job 28: Cognition in Context* (ed. E. van Wolde; Leiden: Brill, 2003) 253–80.

that which is known. Though YHWH has concealed his enigmatic ways from the people,[2] he has revealed the torah so that they might maintain covenant relationship with him in perpetuity (cf. 30:11–14). Here the torah represents the principal source of human knowledge—a clear expression of the divine will that functions as the blueprint for human conduct as well as the vade mecum of divine–human relations.

This notion is given unique expression in the book of Job. In fact, it appears that the dictates of the deuteronomic torah serve as the touchstone of Job's moral vision as well as the locus of his cognitive dissonance. While the wisdom literature in general and the book of Job in particular exhibit a distinct interest in the created order as a source of human knowledge, this methodological approach to reality does not marginalize the epistemological value of the torah. This is apparent in Job's moral vision, which combines the epistemological tenets of the sapiential tradition with language and specific principles from the deuteronomic torah.

In order to identify the place of the deuteronomic torah within Job's ethical vision, it is necessary to explore two basic issues: (1) the distinctive sources of knowledge within the Joban dialogue (Job 3–31); and (2) the role of the deuteronomic torah in Job's epistemology. This essay shall deal with each in turn.

1. The Sources of Knowledge in the Joban Dialogue

In light of the discrete nature of the ancient Near Eastern worldview, it is not surprising that the Joban discourse defies strict classification into modern systems of philosophical thought.[3] Nonetheless, modern concepts may serve as a useful heuristic guide for investigating the epistemological sources that the constituent parties within the debate appeal to in order to justify their positions. In the main, the individual

---

2. While the 'secret things' (נסתרת) have been interpreted in several different ways, the proverbial nature of the maxim, the context of the saying, as well as the correspondence between the expression and Job 28:21 suggest that it refers to the transcendence of divine wisdom in general and the mystery of divine providence in particular. See G. von Rad, *Deuteronomy: A Commentary* (OTL; Philadelphia: Westminster Press, 1966) 180–81; A. D. H. Mayes, *Deuteronomy* (NCB; Grand Rapids: Eerdmans, 1987) 367–68; G. Braulik, *Deuteronomium II 16,18–34,12* (NEchtB; Würzburg: Echter Verlag, 1992) 216; J. G. McConville, *Deuteronomy* (Downers Grove, IL: InterVarsity, 2002) 419; D. I. Block, *Deuteronomy* (NIVAC; Grand Rapids: Zondervan, 2012) 693.

3. For the distinctive, multi-sensorial nature of ancient Near Eastern epistemology and *Weltanschauung*, see M. Malul, *Knowledge, Control and Sex: Studies in Biblical Thought, Culture and Worldview* (Tel Aviv: Archaeological Center Publications, 2002) 125–51, et passim.

voices within the dialogue adduce epistemological support for their respective arguments through the fundamental tenets of the sapiential worldview: tradition and empiricism. Each deserves a brief comment.

Tradition plays a formative role in the dialogue proper, for it shapes the presuppositions, rhetorical strategy, and distinctive moral vision of each party within the debate. In fact, this impregnable edifice serves as the principal source of the friends' knowledge as well as the social–ideational–symbolic structure they seek to defend against the anarchistic harangues of the protagonist.[4] Tradition pervades the individual discourses of the friends and forms the foundation for their claims to knowledge. On the one hand, their knowledge of ancestral tradition accounts for their assumptions concerning retribution (Job 4:7, 8:8–22, 15:18–35, 20:4–29), theological anthropology (15:7–8, 14–16; 25:4–6),[5] and the socio-moral order of the cosmos.[6] On the other hand, their use of traditional religious advice (5:8–16, 8:5–7, 11:13–20, 22:21–30)—as well as idioms, motifs, and literary forms characteristic of the sapiential movement—situates their discourses within the stream of conventional lore and enhances the authority of their rhetoric (4:10–11; 5:6–7, 17–18, 19–22; 11:12, 20; 20:19; 22:3). In view of the substance of their speeches, it appears tradition represents the epistemological root of the friends' argument and the blueprint of their moral vision; it provided a window into the fundamental structure of reality as well as a lens through which to determine what the world order *should* be, or better, what it *must* be.

Together with the friends, Job incorporates tradition in order to authorize his claims to knowledge. However, in contrast to the a priori use

---

4. For this structure and its power over the behavior, customs, beliefs, and thought of people within the ancient oriental world, see ibid., 460–75. As archetypal proponents of tradition, Job's friends give particular expression to its social–ideational–symbolic structure through their "iconic narratives" concerning the fate of the righteous and the wicked. See C. A. Newsom, *The Book of Job: A Contest of Moral Imaginations* (Oxford: Oxford University Press, 2003) 115–25.

5. For the ancient traditions that shaped the theological anthropology of the friends, see "Man and his God" (trans. S. N. Kramer, *ANET* 590–91); "Who Has Not Sinned?" (Foster, *Before the Muses*, 724–25), "The Babylonian Theodicy" (*ANET* 601–4; Foster, *Before the Muses*, 914–22; *COS* 1.154: 492–95). Also see N. C. Habel, "'Naked I Came': Humanness in the Book of Job," in *Die Botschaft und die Boten: Festschrift für Hans Walter Wolff zum 70. Geburtstag* (ed. J. Jeremias and L. Perlitt; Neukirchen–Vluyn: Neukirchener Verlag, 1981) 373–92; M. Remus, *Menschenbild–vorstellungen im Ijob–Buch: Ein Beitrag zur alttestamentliche Anthropologie* (BEATAJ 21; Berlin: Peter Lang, 1993) 20–25.

6. In addition to ancestral tradition, Eliphaz appeals to the collective age of the friends to strengthen their claims to knowledge and accentuate the superiority of their wisdom (15:9–10; cf. 12:11–12).

of tradition by his interlocutors, Job assumes a critical stance toward conventional lore. In general, Job employs tradition in two distinctive ways. First, he integrates tradition into his speeches to level the rhetorical field and enhance the authority of his case. Similar to the friends, Job seasons his discourses with traditional doxologies (9:2–12, 26:5–14), parables from nature (12:7–10), proverbs (6:5–6, 14:1–2), and wisdom sayings (7:1–2, 17:5). In addition, he claims to know the dictates of the tradition as well as the conventional arguments propagated by the friends (12:3, 13:2, 16:2). In so doing, Job demonstrates his knowledge of tradition and counters accusations of ignorance or naïveté.[7]

This knowledge of tradition forms the foundation for the second use of ancient lore in Job's speeches, namely, as the subject of critique and reformulation. Whereas the friends appeal to tradition to justify their arguments and construct a tidy vision of life, Job cites tradition to question its value and expose its incongruous relationship with the real world.[8] Whereas the friends assume an uncritical, submissive stance toward tradition, Job challenges the fundamental tenets of this hegemonic structure through his mental capacity and the lens of experience (6:30, 12:11, 13:1–2).

In essence, personal experience represents the principal source of Job's knowledge as well as the fundamental difference between Job's epistemological vantage point and the perspective of the friends. While the friends refer to certain faculties within the human sensorium to validate their traditional arguments (4:8–9; 5:3, 27; 15:17), these claims do not necessitate actual eyewitness accounts concerning the operation of the act–consequence nexus (*Tat–Ergehen Zusammenhang*). Rather, as von Rad observed, they represent pseudo-observations, employed for rhetorical or pedagogical effect to strengthen an axiomatic belief.[9] This interpretation is reinforced by the fact that the friends do not participate in the events they recount; they cast conventional anecdotes

---

7. E. L. Greenstein, "'On My Skin and in My Flesh': Personal Experience as a Source of Knowledge in the Book of Job," in *Bringing the Hidden to Light: Studies in Honor of Stephen A. Geller* (ed. K. F. Kravitz and D. M. Sharon; Winona Lake, IN: Eisenbrauns, 2007) 69–70.

8. Here it is important to note that Job never cites tradition to substantiate his claims. For a discussion of the logical structure of the distinctive arguments within the dialogue and the epistemological support adduced for each, see Greenstein, "'On My Skin and in My Flesh'," 63–77.

9. G. von Rad, *Weisheit in Israel* (Neukirchen–Vluyn: Neukirchener Verlag, 1970) 56–58; M. V. Fox, "Qohelet's Epistemology," *HUCA* 58 (1987) 145–47; idem, "The Epistemology of the Book of Proverbs," *JBL* 126 (2007) 672–74; Greenstein, "'On My Skin and in My Flesh'," 72–75.

within the context of personal experience to accentuate a known principle and substantiate the tenets of the tradition. Tradition serves as the epistemological quarry from which the friends extract conventional truths to construct poetic accounts concerning the nature of the world. Their accounts are mimetic, rather than experiential. In view of their epistemological dependence upon tradition and its social–ideational–symbolic structure, the friends have no need for empiricism, for tradition supplies the necessary expectations for the various circumstances of life. They wield the power of conventional lore, which no factual or experiential evidence could threaten.

The exception to the friends' stringent dependence upon tradition may be Eliphaz's mystical encounter with a supernatural interlocutor (4:12–21).[10] The experiential nature of this enigmatic visitation is confirmed by the prominent use of the first person singular pronominal suffix as well as physical and psychological terms that illuminate the multifaceted, sensory effect of the specter's veiled appearance (4:12–16).[11] These features, coupled with the prophetic cast of the account, suggest Eliphaz was the recipient of this strange, revelatory message (4:17–21).

However, despite his encounter with the numinous, Eliphaz's experience is quite different from the empiricism of Job. Whereas Job views the world from a human, worm's-eye vantage point and through the spectacles of personal suffering, Eliphaz receives a divine, bird's-eye view of the human condition and understands the world as a detached

---

10. While the majority of commentators assume Eliphaz was the recipient of this nocturnal vision, others attribute the vision to Job (N. H. Tur-Sinai, *The Book of Job: A New Commentary* [Jerusalem: Kiryath-Sepher, 1957] 88–89; H. L. Ginsberg, "Job the patient and Job the impatient," in *Congress Volume: Rome 1968* [VTSup 17; Leiden: Brill, 1969] 95–107; G. V. Smith, "Job IV 12–21: Is it Eliphaz's Vision?," *VT* 40 [1990] 453–63; Greenstein, "'On My Skin and in My Flesh'," 66–68). In the main, this interpretation is based on subsequent references to dreams and visions within the dialogue, the theological perspective of the individual parties in the debate, the way in which the substance of the vision is reiterated elsewhere in the speeches of the friends (15:14–16, 25:4–6), as well as the phenomenon of unmarked quotations in wisdom literature. While aspects of this argument are persuasive, the experience should be attributed to Eliphaz in light of the graphic description of the nocturnal scene (4:12–16), the sharp distinction between the function of Eliphaz's vision and the nature of Job's dreams (see E. L. Ehrlich, *Der Traum im Alten Testament* [BZAW 73; Berlin: A. Töpelmann, 1953] 145–46), as well as the genuine use of the vision by Eliphaz and Bildad elsewhere in the dialogue. See Y. Hoffman, *A Blemished Perfection: The Book of Job in Context* (JSOTSup 213; Sheffield: Sheffield Academic, 1996) 122–31, 146.

11. The polysemous language employed to describe the scene heightens the transcendental nature of the experience: Piel גנב 'came secretly'; שמץ 'a whisper'; שעפים 'disquieting thoughts'; חזינות לילה 'visions of the night'; תרדמה 'deep sleep'; פחד 'dread'; רוח 'spirit, wind'; חלף 'passed by'; Piel סמר 'bristle'; מראה 'appearance'; תמונה 'form'; דממה 'silence'.

observer.[12] The peculiar role of experience in Eliphaz's epistemology is enhanced by the substance of the vision as well as the conclusion to his initial speech. The vision expresses a common ancient Near Eastern topos concerning humanity's congenital sinfulness (4:18–21),[13] while the conclusion of the speech attributes the crux of the argument to tradition (5:27). Though the account in general and the message in particular raise several questions pertaining to Eliphaz's credibility,[14] the substance of the vision and the conclusion of the speech situate the argument within the tidy confines of conventional lore. Whether or not Eliphaz experienced this nocturnal visitation, the message passed his epistemological litmus test. For Eliphaz, experience is a valid source of knowledge, but only when it is substantiated by tradition.

In contrast to the friends, empiricism serves as the epistemological framework through which Job interprets his situation. In fact, personal experience forces Job to construct an alternative vision of life, since his condition does not fit within the context of a traditional understanding of self, world, and God.[15] This alternative worldview is an inversion of the traditional, the epitome of the anti-structure. It is marked by a God whose wisdom and power is manifested in depriving leaders of the skills necessary to establish order within society (12:13–25).[16] It is a

---

12. For the significance of these discrete vantage points for the individual speaker's view of reality, see S. Lasine, "Bird's-Eye and Worm's-Eye Views of Justice in the Book of Job," *JSOT* 42 (1988) 29–53.

13. For the topos, see n. 5 above.

14. In general, three features cast doubt on the reliability of Eliphaz's revelatory experience: (1) Eliphaz moves beyond the epistemological boundaries of the wisdom tradition and grounds his "newfound" revelation in prophetic inspiration; (2) the banality of the message stands in sharp contrast with the elaborate portrayal of the nocturnal experience; and (3) if the rhetorical questions demand a negative response (4:17), then the message is inappropriate to Job's case, for both YHWH and the narrator contend that he is righteous (1:1, 8; 2:3, 10). These features have led many to conclude that the account represents a "claimed experience," a "parodied religious experience," or an ironic portrait shaped for comic effect. See R. Gordis, "Quotations in Wisdom Literature," *JQR* 30 (1939/40) 123–47; repr. in *Studies in Ancient Israelite Wisdom* (ed. J. L. Crenshaw; New York: Ktav, 1976) 221; S. Terrien, *Job* (2nd ed.; CAT 13; Genève: Labor et Fides, 2005) 118; E. Sellin and G. Fohrer, *Introduction to the Old Testament* (trans. D. E. Green; Nashville: Abingdon, 1968) 142; W. Whedbee, "The Comedy of Job," *Semeia* 7 (1977) 11; N. Habel, "The Narrative Art of Job: Applying the Principles of Robert Alter," *JSOT* 27 (1983) 104; L. O. Caesar, "Job: Another New Thesis," *VT* 49 (1999) 439–42. Cf. J. E. Harding, "A Spirit of Deception in Job 4:15? Interpretive Indeterminacy and Eliphaz's Vision," *BibInt* 13 (2005) 154–66.

15. For a discussion of the relationship between experience and knowledge, see von Rad, *Weisheit in Israel*, 13; Fox, "The Epistemology of the Book of Proverbs," 670–71.

16. Habel argues that this piece functions as a satirical poem, which seeks to reverse the tradition delineated in Prov 8:14–16 (*The Book of Job* [OTL; Philadelphia: Westminster, 1985] 216–17).

world in which humanity dwells under the penetrating gaze of a malicious deity, who prevents them from fulfilling their royal charter and subjects them to abject slavery (7:1–2, 17–21). Moreover, it is a world in which the weak are exploited, the wicked are rewarded, and the righteous suffer at the hands of a deity who exercises his sovereignty over the cosmos in an arbitrary fashion (9:13–35, 21:7–34, 24:1–25). Contrary to the friends, personal experience represents the fundamental source of Job's knowledge as well as the author of his rival *Weltanschauung*; it drives him outside the boundaries of tradition and its vision of what the world *should* be to a place in which he is forced to construct a vision of the world as it *appears* to be according to his circumstances.

In view of the epistemological canons of the sapiential tradition, it appears the constituent parties in the dialogue appeal to different sources of knowledge in order to validate their arguments. On the one hand, the friends adduce epistemological support for their positions through the dictates of tradition. Tradition provides the friends with the prescription for Job's malady, the lexicon for their discourses, and the structure for their worldview. That is, tradition produces a vision of the world as it *must* be and offers an intelligible system within which Job may understand his condition. On the other hand, Job appeals to personal experience in order to legitimize his knowledge and justify his claims. Experience serves as the filter through which Job sifts the tenets of tradition and views the world; it provides the basis for his vision of life as well as the blueprint of his alternative *Lebenswelt*.

2. *The Role of the Deuteronomic Torah in Job's Epistemology*

2.1. *Introduction*

These distinctive sources of knowledge provide a backdrop against which to explore the role of the deuteronomic torah in Job's epistemology. While several studies have examined the covenantal cast of the Joban drama through its critique of the deuteronomic covenant in general and the deuteronomic doctrine of retribution in particular,[17] few have investigated the place of the deuteronomic torah in Job's moral vision.[18] This is not surprising, since Job is a foreigner and the wisdom

---

17. See R. Gordis, *The Book of God and Man: A Study of Job* (Chicago: University of Chicago Press, 1965) 135–51; H. H. Rowley, *Job* (2nd ed.; NCB; Grand Rapids: Eerdmans, 1980) 18; W. Brueggemann, *Theology of the Old Testament: Testimony, Dispute, Advocacy* (Minneapolis: Fortress, 1997) 385–90; S. Ticciati, *Job and the Disruption of Identity: Reading Beyond Barth* (London: T. & T. Clark, 2005) 60–61, et passim. Cf. M. Weinfeld, *Deuteronomy and the Deuteronomistic School* (Oxford: Clarendon, 1972) 307–19.

18. See D. Cox, *The Triumph of Impotence: Job and the Tradition of the Absurd* (Analecta Gregoriana 212; Rome: Universita Gregoriana Editrice, 1978) 52, 106–8; W. Janzen, *Old*

tradition operated within the epistemological confines of creation theology.[19] However, the theological perspective of the Joban poet and the "shared approach to reality"[20] among the distinctive traditions within the Old Testament provide a foundation from which to assess the deuteronomic flavor of Job's ethic.[21] This form of analysis may illuminate the multifaceted nature of Job's moral knowledge, the distinctive standard of Job's conduct, and the source of his confidence.

Many have contended that Job possesses a genuine knowledge of morality.[22] In light of the testimony of the prologue and the fact that the divine speeches do not address the issue of Job's righteousness/innocence (צדיק), this seems to be the case. Nonetheless, Job's moral confidence and ethical knowledge raise several questions: What is the source(s) of Job's ethical knowledge? What is the standard by which Job evaluates his moral status? In a world in which people do not know the will of the gods or their requirements, how can Job know that he is righteous/innocent (צדיק)?[23] In order to answer these questions, it is

---

Testament Ethics: A Paradigmatic Approach (Louisville: Westminster John Knox, 1994) 127–28. Also see Ryan O'Dowd's treatment of deuteronomic and sapiential epistemology (*The Wisdom of Torah: Epistemology in Deuteronomy and the Wisdom Literature* [FRLANT 225; Göttingen: Vandenhoeck & Ruprecht, 2009] 162–74), as well as Manfred Oeming's exploration of the relationship between Job 31 and the Decalogue ("Hiob und der Dekalog," in *The Book of Job* [ed. W. A. M. Beuken; BETL 114; Leuven: Leuven University Press, 1994] 362–68).

19. For discussion of creation theology as the framework of Israelite wisdom, see W. Zimmerli, "The Place and Limit of the Wisdom in the Framework of the Old Testament Theology," *SJT* 17 (1964): 146–58; repr. in *Studies in Ancient Israelite Wisdom*, 314–26; idem, *Old Testament Theology in Outline* (Atlanta: John Knox, 1978), 155–66; von Rad, *Weisheit in Israel*, 87–109, et passim; P. Doll, *Menschenschöpfung und Weltschöpfung in der alttestamentlichen Weisheit* (SBS 117; Stuttgart: Verlag Katholisches Bibelwerk, 1985); L. G. Perdue, *Wisdom and Creation: The Theology of Wisdom Literature* (Nashville: Abingdon, 1994); idem, *Wisdom Literature: A Theological History* (Louisville: Westminster John Knox, 2007); K. J. Dell, *The Book of Proverbs in Social and Theological Context* (Cambridge: Cambridge University Press, 2006), 125–54.

20. R. E. Murphy, "Wisdom—Theses and Hypotheses," in *Israelite Wisdom: Theological and Literary Essays in Honor of Samuel Terrien* (ed. W. A. Brueggemann et al.; Missoula: Scholars, 1978) 39.

21. For the distinctly Israelite perspective of the Joban poet, see R. H. Pfeiffer, *Introduction to the Old Testament* (New York: Harper & Row, 1941) 670; Sellin and Fohrer, *Introduction to the Old Testament*, 330; E. L. Greenstein, "The Problem of Evil in the Book of Job," in *Mishneh Todah: Studies in Deuteronomy and Its Cultural Environment in Honor of Jeffrey H. Tigay* (ed. N. S. Fox, D. A. Glatt-Gilad, and M. J. Williams; Winona Lake, IN: Eisenbrauns, 2009) 336–37.

22. See J. T. Wilcox, *The Bitterness of Job: A Philosophical Reading* (Ann Arbor, MI: The University of Michigan Press, 1989) 182–86; M. V. Fox, "Job the Pious," *ZAW* 117 (2005) 354–55.

23. See "Dialogue Between a Man and His God" (Foster, *Before the Muses*, 148; *COS* 1.151: 485); "The Poem of the Righteous Sufferer" (*ANET* 597; Foster, *Before the Muses*,

necessary to explore the nature of Job's ethic and the role of the deuteronomic torah in his epistemology through the clearest expression of his moral vision: the asseveration of innocence (31:1–40).

Job's asseveration of innocence marks the culmination of his final discourse as well as an inclusive articulation of his moral integrity.[24] Here Job paints a graphic portrait of his character within a socio-moral world marked by the fundamental values and formative attitudes of the righteous. While this portrait includes moral profiles that are comparable to the ethical inventories within the various literary corpora of the Old Testament and the ancient Near East,[25] the oath is quite distinct within the ancient world. The moral purview of the confession transcends its ethical counterparts in form and scope. The extended declaration of innocence, complete with explicit self-imprecations, finds no parallel in the ancient world,[26] and Job's attention to the internal dimensions of character introduces a profound development in the moral thought of the Near East.[27]

In effect, the asseveration of innocence represents an elevated ethical vision that combines inner purity with external piety in a comprehensive catalog. This internal–external dialectic is illustrated through the somatic and visceral images that pervade the piece. Together, these

---

399; COS 1.153: 488); "Furious God" (Foster, Before the Muses, 722), "To Any God" (ANET 391–92; Foster, Before the Muses, 763–65); "The Babylonian Theodicy" (ANET 601–4; Foster, Before the Muses, 914–22; COS 1.154: 492–95).

24. In view of the texture of Job's final speech, it appears the protagonist imitates the rhetorical pattern of Eliphaz's opening address (4:2–6). Similar to Eliphaz's introductory exordium, Job moves from his past condition (29:2–25) to his present situation (30:1–31) to an oath of innocence (31:1–40). This suggests that Job's final discourse forms a diptych with Eliphaz's initial speech, marking the conclusion of the dialogue.

25. See B. Alster, The Instructions of Suruppak: A Sumerian Proverb Collection (Mesopotamia: Copenhagen Studies in Assyriology 2; Copenhagen: Akademisk Forlag, 1974); (BWL, 92–95; ANET 594–95; COS 1.176: 569–70); "Counsels of Wisdom" (BWL, 96–107; ANET 426–27; 595–96); J. M. Lindenberger, The Aramaic Proverbs of Ahiqar (JHNES; Baltimore: Johns Hopkins University Press, 1983; ANET 427–30); "The Instruction of Prince Hardjedef" (AEL 1:58–59; ANET 419–20); "The Instruction Addressed to Kagemni" (AEL 1:59–61); "The Instruction of Ptahhotep" (AEL 1:61–80; ANET 412–14); "The Instruction Addressed to King Merikare" (AEL 1:97–109; ANET 414–18; COS 1.35: 61–66); "The Instruction of King Amenhemet I for His Son Sesostris I" (AEL 1:135–39; ANET 418–19; COS 1.36: 66–68); "The Instruction of Any" (AEL 2:135–46; ANET 420–21); "Book of the Dead 125" (trans. R. K. Ritner; COS 2.12: 60–63); "The Instruction of Amenemope" (AEL 2:146–63; ANET 421–24); M. Lichtheim, Moral Values in Ancient Egypt (OBO 155; Göttingen: Vandenhoeck & Ruprecht, 1997); 1 Sam 12:2–5, Isa 1:16–17, 33:15, 58:6–12, Jer 7:1–11, 22:3–7, Amos 5:14–15, Mic 6:8, Ps 24:4, Ps 15, Ps 72.

26. See S. H. Blank, "The Curse, Blasphemy, the Spell, and the Oath," HUCA 23 (1950–51) 90–92; M. B. Dick, "The Legal Metaphor in Job 31," CBQ 41 (1979) 37–50, repr. in Sitting with Job: Selected Studies on the Book of Job (ed. R. B. Zuck; Grand Rapids: Baker, 1992) 331.

27. D. J. A. Clines, Job 21–37 (WBC 18A; Nashville: Thomas Nelson, 2006) 1038.

images serve as a rhetorical device that illuminates Job's firm control over his inner impulses as well as his external actions.[28] This intimate relationship between internal motives and external actions allows the protagonist to redefine the fundamental features of the righteous.

The conventional virtues and formative attitudes of the righteous delineated in the Old Testament as well as the ancient Near East are refracted through the protagonist's internal disposition to produce a moral consciousness that is unparalleled in the ancient world. While the external actions of the righteous are given categorical preeminence in the moral catalogs of the Old Testament and the ancient Near East, the formative attitudes and fundamental dispositions of the righteous are given particular expression in Job's declaration of innocence. In view of Job's virtuous character and conception of the righteous, it is not surprising that he holds fast to his integrity and declares that he is right/innocent (9:21, 13:18, 27:5–6).

However, this moral–forensic conviction raises questions concerning the source(s) of Job's moral vision as well as the standard by which Job measures his integrity. The dialogue includes several texts that indicate a common ethical code between Job and the friends (22:6–9, 24:2–25, 29:11–17). These texts focus on various matters pertaining to socio-economic justice, care for the marginalized, and the illegitimate use of power in social relations, that is, conventional values promoted in the literary traditions of the ancient world. Together with these conventional standards, the dialogues contain a variety of references to Eloah's words, ways, and commands (6:10, 21:14, 22:22, 23:11–12).

Nonetheless, the ethical content of these expressions and the nature of the requirements remain ambiguous. The ambiguity inherent in the book's ethical standard appears to be a deliberate ploy incorporated by the Joban poet to undermine ancient Near Eastern conceptions of human righteousness. The ancient oriental theodicean tradition illuminated the epistemological gulf that separated humans from the gods through the fundamental problem of ignorance: the sufferers fall short because they have no conception of the will of the gods or their requirements.[29] The Joban poet creates a similar conceptual world, but modifies the convention. The poet does not refer to the regulations of the torah or some external code of conduct, for this would be anachronistic within the setting of the piece. Instead, the poet reflects on a way of life devoted to God. The principal contours of this "way" (31:4) are delineated in Job's asseveration of innocence, which includes ethical

---

28. Habel, *The Book of Job*, 433.
29. For the texts, see note 23 above.

values inherent in various streams of Israelite and ancient Near Eastern literary tradition.

2.2. The Source of Job's Moral Vision

The source of Job's moral vision has been traced primarily to two traditions: (1) Israel's psalmic and sapiential literature and (2) Israel's constitutional materials. Each will be addressed in turn.

In light of the ethical values and rhetorical texture of Job's declaration of innocence, many contend that the protagonist's moral vision is derived from Israel's psalmic and sapiential traditions.[30] The formal and thematic features of the piece confirm this notion. On the one hand, the asseveration is comparable to ancient Near Eastern legal declarations in general and the entrance liturgies of the Psalter in particular (Pss 15; 24; cf. 7:3–5).[31] On the other hand, the moral catalog contains motifs and language characteristic of the sapiential tradition. The path metaphor (Job 31:4, 7),[32] the image of divine surveillance (31:4; cf. Prov 5:21), and the pervasive use of body parts are distinctive topoi of the wisdom movement.[33] In addition, the protagonist's concern with sexual ethics (Job 31:1, 9–12; cf. Prov 5:1–23, 6:20–35, 7:1–27), trust in wealth (Job 31:24–25; cf. Prov 30:7–9), and social humaneness expressed through kindness toward an enemy (Job 31:29–30; cf. Prov 25:21–22) enhance the sapiential flavor of the piece. These features, coupled with the focus on motivation and interiority, suggest that Job's moral knowledge is derived from the psalmic and sapiential traditions of ancient Israel.[34]

Nonetheless, the ethical values delineated in Job's asseveration of innocence are not restricted to the sapiential movement or the psalmic tradition. On the contrary, these values are also presented in many ancient oriental literary works as well as the constitutional materials

---

30. G. Fohrer, "The Righteous Man in Job 31," in *Studien zum Buche Hiob (1956–1979)* (Berlin: Walter de Gruyter, 1983) 78–93; M. B. Dick, "Job 31, the Oath of Innocence, and the Sage," *ZAW* 95 (1983) 31–53; Clines, *Job 21–37*, 979. Cf. R. Sutherland, *Putting God on Trial: The Biblical Book of Job* (Trafford, 2004) 21, 143–44. Sutherland contends that Job's moral knowledge is dependent upon natural law.

31. See Dick, "Job 31, the Oath of Innocence, and the Sage," 36–43.

32. For the motif of the "path/way" (דרך, ארח, נתיבה) as a root metaphor in the book of Proverbs, see N. C. Habel, "The Symbolism of Wisdom in Proverbs 1–9," *Int* 26 (1972) 131–57; C. V. Camp, "Woman Wisdom as Root Metaphor: A Theological Consideration," in *The Listening Heart: Essays in Wisdom and the Psalms in Honor of Roland E. Murphy, O. Carm.* (ed. K. G. Hoglund et al.; Sheffield: Sheffield Academic, 1987) 45–76; R. C. Van Leeuwen, "Liminality and Worldview in Proverbs 1–9," *Semeia* 50 (1990) 111–44.

33. Dick, "Job 31, the Oath of Innocence, and the Sage," 47–48.

34. Cf. Dick, "Job 31, the Oath of Innocence, and the Sage," 47–53. Dick contends that the ethical principles delineated in Job 31 are derived from the sapiential tradition as well as the *paideia* of Israel.

of ancient Israel. The former give particular attention to care for the disenfranchised, judicial impartiality, and kindness toward an enemy.³⁵ The latter elaborate on these traditional values and address various matters pertaining to slave rights (Exod 21:18–21, 26–27; Lev 25:6–7; Deut 5:12–15, 15:12–17, 16:9–15; Job 31:13–15), sexual offenses (Exod 20:14, 22:16–17; Lev 18:17, 20:10; Job 31:9–12), enmity (Lev 19:17–18; Job 31:29–30), idolatry (Exod 20:3–6, 23; Lev 19:4; Deut 4:15–19; Job 31:26–28), integrity in interpersonal relationships (Exod 23:2–8; Lev 19:11–18; Job 31:16–23, 38–40), and covetousness (Exod 20:17; Deut 5:21; Job 31:1). Though the asseveration of innocence contains many formal and thematic similarities with Israel's psalmic and sapiential traditions, the oath also includes elements that fall outside the purview of these corpora. These elements serve as a window into the role of the deuteronomic torah in Job's epistemology in general and his moral knowledge in particular. Each feature deserves specific comment.

In the main, the deuteronomic ethos of Job's moral knowledge is conveyed through topics and expressions that are characteristic of the deuteronomic torah. The asseveration proper opens with a general declaration concerning Job's unblemished character (31:5–8). This declaration combines traditional images from Israel's psalmic and sapiential corpora with language redolent of Deut 13:17 (Heb. 18):

Deut 13:18a[17a]	Job 31:7c
ולא־ידבק בידך מאומה "None of the things devoted to destruction shall stick to your hand."	ובכפי דבק מאום "and if any stain has stuck to my hands."

The shared terminology and common sentiment expressed within these texts intimate a general, verbal relationship.³⁶ While these features do

---

35. See "Laws of Ur–Namma" (A 3:104–A 4:170, C I 1–51) (*ANET* 523–25; M. T. Roth, *Law Collections from Mesopotamia and Asia Minor* [2nd ed.; ed. P. Michalowski; SBLWAW 6; Atlanta: Scholars, 1997] 15–17; *COS* 2.153: 409–10); "Laws of Lipit–Ishtar" (1:20–2:40) (*ANET* 159–61; Roth, *Law Collections*, 25–26; *COS* 2.154: 410–14); "Laws of Hammurabi" (1:27–49; 47:59–78) (*ANET* 163–80; Roth, *Law Collections*, 76–77, 133–34; *COS* 2.131: 335–53); "Statue B," §7:38–43 (D. O. Edzard, *Gudea and His Dynasty* [RIME 3/1; Toronto: University of Toronto Press, 1997] 36); "Counsels of Wisdom" (*BWL* 101); "The Instruction of Ptahhotep" (*AEL* 1:72); "The Instruction of Amenemope" (*ANET* 421–24 [excerpts]; *AEL* 2:150; *COS* 1.47: 115–22); "The Instruction of Papyrus Insinger" (*AEL* 3:203); Exod 23:4–5; Lev 19:17–18.

36. See Habel, *The Book of Job*, 433; Clines, *Job 21–37*, 1017. The link between Deut 13:18a[17a] and Job 31:7c is strengthened by the Masoretic *Ketib* of the latter, which reads מאומה 'anything' rather than מאום 'blemish, stain, defect'. This reading produces a virtual

not provide adequate evidence for a genetic relationship between Job's declaration and the deuteronomic prohibition, the comparable language suggests that deuteronomic rhetoric played a formative role in Job's moral consciousness.

This conclusion is reinforced by Job's conception of adultery (31:9–12) and idolatry (31:26–27). Among the topics within the asseveration proper, these oaths exhibit a distinct deuteronomic stamp. Both incorporate the expression לבי נפתה 'my heart was deceived'—an idiom that occurs elsewhere only in Deut 11:16 (cf. 31:9, 27). In addition, both include deuteronomic terms, motifs, and images to describe the reprehensible nature of these acts. The former presents the malediction and the evaluation of the crime from a deuteronomic perspective. The malediction conveys an understanding of retributive punishment that is comparable to the futility curse in Deut 28:30a (cf. 31:10),[37] while the metaphorical evaluation of the crime incorporates terms and a sequence of spheres reminiscent of Deut 32:22 (cf. 31:12):[38]

Deut 32:22	Job 31:12
כי־אש קדחה באפי ותיקד עד־שאול תחתית ותאכל ארץ ויבלה ותלהט מוסדי הרים:	כי אש היא עד־אבדון תאכל ובכל־תבואתי תשרש:
"For a fire is kindled by my anger, which burns to the depths of Sheol; it will devour the earth and its produce, and ignite the foundations of the mountains."	"Indeed that is a fire that consumes as far as Abaddon, and it would burn to the root all my produce."

The use of אש 'fire' and אכל 'to consume', coupled with expressions associated with the netherworld (שאול, אבדון) and the destruction of the produce of the land (תבואה, יבול), suggests Job 31:12 is intimately related to Deut 32:22. Though these texts function in distinct ways, the deuteronomic flavor of Job's conception of adultery is clear. In general,

---

equivalent to the expression in Deut 13:18a. For the reading, see S. R. Driver and G. B. Gray, *A Critical and Exegetical Commentary on the Book of Job together with a New Translation* (ICC; New York: Charles Scribner's Sons, 1921) 222–23; L. Alonso Schökel and J. L. Sicre Díaz, *Job, comentario teológico y literario* (Madrid: Cristiandad, 1983) 544.

37. See D. R. Hillers, *Treaty-Curses and the Old Testament Prophets* (BibOr 16; Rome: Pontifical Biblical Institute, 1964) 28–29, 63; J. E. Hartley, *The Book of Job* (NICOT; Grand Rapids: Eerdmans, 1988) 413 n. 7.

38. See B. Duhm, *Das Buch Hiob* (KHC 16; Tübingen: Mohr, 1897) 147; E. Dhorme, *A Commentary on the Book of Job* (trans. H. Knight; London: Thomas Nelson, 1967) 455; A. de Wilde, *Das Buch Hiob: Eingeleitet, Übersetzt und Erläutert* (OtSt 22; Leiden: Brill, 1981) 299; Clines, *Job 21–37*, 1019.

it appears Job adapts a deuteronomic description of YHWH's anger as well as a sequence of spheres in which this anger burns to describe the catastrophic effects of undisciplined sexual expression (cf. Prov 6:27–29; Sir 9:8). That is, the protagonist shapes the rationale for abstaining from adultery through language and imagery reminiscent of Deuteronomy 32, better known as the Song of Moses.

In addition to the oath concerning adultery, Job employs deuteronomic language and theology to characterize the illicit, seductive nature of idolatry (31:26–27):

Deut 4:19	Job 31:26–27
ופן־תשא עיניך השמימה וראית את־השמש ואת־הירח ואת־הכוכבים כל צבא השמים ונדחת והשתחוית להם ועבדתם אשר חלק יהוה אלהיך אתם לכל העמים תחת כל־השמים	אם־אראה אור כי יהל וירח יקר הלך ויפת בסתר לבי ותשק ידי לפי
"And guard yourselves lest you lift up your eyes to heaven, and when you see the sun and the moon and the stars, all the host of heaven, you be drawn away and bow down to them and serve them, things that YHWH your God has allotted to all the peoples under the whole heaven."	"If I have gazed at the sun when it shone, or the moon moving in splendor, ²⁷and my heart has been secretly enticed, and my mouth has kissed my hand,"

Similar to Deut 4:19 (see also Deut 17:3, 2 Kgs 23:5, Jer 8:1–2), the celestial bodies represent the instrument of seduction as well as the object of devotion.[39] While this form of worship was prevalent in ancient Near Eastern religions,[40] it was expressly forbidden in Yahwistic reli-

---

39. While Job 31:26 uses the term אור 'light' rather than שמש 'sun', these designations are equivalent in several texts (Isa 60:19, 20, Qoh 11:7, 12:2; cf. Job 37:21, Isa 18:4, Hab 3:4).

40. In both Mesopotamian and Egyptian religion, the heavenly bodies were considered the media through which particular deities manifested their presence and exercised their power. These deities operated under the dictates of the cosmic order (ME, Maât) and supervised the activities of people on their celestial journeys. Among these astral deities, the sun god Shamash (Shemesh in Canaan), the moon god Nanna/Sin (Yarikh/YRḤ in Canaan), and the morning star Astarte/Athtar were the most significant in Mesopotamia, while the sun gods Re, Atum, and Amun, the moon god Thoth, as well as the sky goddess Hathor were the most prominent in Egypt. For discussions of the Mesopotamian deities, see E. Lipiński, "Shemesh," *DDD* 764–68; B. B. Schmidt, "Moon," *DDD* 585–93; N. Wyatt, "Astarte," *DDD* 109–14. For the Egyptian divinities, see M. Müller, "Re and Re-Horakhty," in *The Oxford Encyclopedia of Ancient Egypt* (ed. D. B. Redford; 3 vols.; Oxford: Oxford University Press, 2001) 3:123–25; V. A. Tobin, "Amun and Amun-Re," in ibid., 1:82–85; K. Mysliwiec, "Atum," in ibid., 1:158–60; D. M. Doxey, "Thoth," in ibid.,

gion. When the declaration is read against the backdrop of ancient Near Eastern perceptions of the heavenly bodies, the correlation between Job's conviction and the theological perspective of the deuteronomic program is striking. Despite his foreign provenance, Job expresses a view of astral worship consistent with the monotheistic vision and cultic regulations of Deuteronomy. This theological perspective—coupled with the lexical links to Deut 4:19 and 11:16 as well as the surreptitious depiction of idolatry and its unique, clandestine expression in the deuteronomic discourse (13:6; 27:15)—strengthens the deuteronomic flavor of the crime and illuminate the constitutional roots of Job's moral knowledge.[41]

Together with the deuteronomic cast of the oaths concerning adultery and idolatry, Job's ethics of power in various relationships of inequality capture the tenor of the deuteronomic vision.[42] Job's promotion of slave rights embodies the ethos of the deuteronomic program (Job 31:13–15), according to which male and female slaves were regarded as much the image of God as their free counterparts and afforded the same rights extended to free citizens.[43] This magnanimous ethical

---

3:398–400; D. Vischak, "Hathor," in ibid., 2:82–85; J. Assmann, *The Search for God in Ancient Egypt* (trans. D. Lorton; Ithaca: Cornell University Press, 2001) 80–82.

41. In addition to the lexical and theological links between Deut 4:19 and Job 31:26–27, many suggest that Job's conception of the punishment for the crime may allude to the sentence prescribed for worship of the celestial bodies in Deut 17:2–7 (Job 31:28). See Dhorme, *A Commentary on the Book of Job*, 463; Hartley, *The Book of Job*, 419 n. 6; Clines, *Job 21–37*, 1026.

42. For Job's ethics of power and their sociological significance in the declaration of innocence, see M. Hamilton, "Elite Lives: Job 29–31 and Traditional Authority," *JSOT* 32 (2007) 85–87. For an alternative reading of Job's ethics of power, see D. J. A. Clines, "Those Golden Days: Job and the Perils of Nostalgia," in *On the Way to the Postmodern: Old Testament Essays, 1967–1998* (JSOTSup 293; Sheffield: Sheffield Academic, 1998) 2:792–800. Clines contends that Job's nostalgic reminiscences cloud his perception of economics, honor, power, gender, and slavery to such an extent that they give rise to self-deception. In this reading, Job is a flawed character who supports a patriarchal system with his social power.

43. See R. W. Neville, "A Reassessment of the Radical Nature of Job's Ethic in Job XXXI 13–15," *VT* 53 (2003) 181–200. Neville argues that the ethical principle delineated in the declaration focuses on God as the common creator of individuals and, by implication, their source of protection. In view of Mesopotamian family religion, this common maker/deity imposes traditional obligations on the protagonist that would not be exceptional in the ancient world. This conclusion is reasonable, but fails to account for the theological traditions of ancient Israel. The protagonist's/poet's focus on a common creator not only establishes a standard of conduct/accountability, but it also illuminates the status of humans as the *imago Dei*. This status, coupled with the torah's regulations concerning the rights of slaves, suggests that Job's behavior is rooted in human equality and equal rights as well as the creation of the same God.

vision is exceptional within the ancient world. Whereas ancient Near Eastern legal collections protected the interests of the master at the expense of the rights of slaves,[44] the deuteronomic torah protected the rights of slaves at the expense of the interests of their masters.[45] In addition, whereas the Book of the Covenant limited the manumission of indentured servants to male slaves (Exod 21:2–11), the deuteronomic prescriptions extended these rights to both male and female slaves (Deut 15:12–17). The deuteronomic emphasis on the equal and humane treatment of male, female, and runaway slaves created a vision of a life, a world of responsibility in which the rights of the disenfranchised took precedence over the interests of those in positions of power. This ethics of power in master–slave relations is consonant with Job's moral vision, which permitted both male and female slaves to pursue a legal grievance against their master.

The same is true with regard to Job's treatment of the destitute (Job 31:16–23) and the day laborer (31:38–40b). As noted above, Job's treatment of the destitute integrates the ethical sentiment of the torah with images and motifs that pervade the literary corpora of the ancient world as well as the prophetic literature of the Old Testament (Isa 58:7; Ezek 18:7, 16; Tob 4:16–17).[46] While his tender, evocative description of care for marginalized contains traditional virtues associated with the provision and protection of the economically vulnerable, Job's activities are reminiscent of the deuteronomic depiction of YHWH. Similar to YHWH, Job executes justice for the disenfranchised and demonstrates

---

44. See "Laws of Hammurabi" (8:30–9:13; 35:37–36:5; 46:97–102) (Roth, *Law Collections from Mesopotamia and Asia Minor*, 84–85, 113–14, 132). For a discussion of the status and rights of slaves within ancient Near Eastern legal collections and the constitutional corpora of the Old Testament, see G. C. Chirichigno, *Debt–Slavery in Israel and the Ancient Near East* (JSOTSup 141; Sheffield: JSOT, 1993); H. A. Hoffner, "Slavery and Slave Laws in Ancient Hatti and Israel," in *Israel: Ancient Kingdom or Late Invention* (ed. Daniel I. Block; Nashville: Broadman & Holman, 2008) 130–55.

45. This notion is given particular expression in the deuteronomic interpretation of the Sabbath command (Deut 5:14–15), the lavish economic provision for the indentured servant at the time of release (15:12–15), the invitations for marginalized members of the community to participate in the cultic life of the nation (12:12, 18; 16:11, 14; 31:12), as well as the asylum granted to runaway slaves (23:15). For the distinctive nature of Israel's treatment of runaway slaves, see C. H. Gordon, "The Background of Some Distinctive Values in the Hebrew Bible," in *"Go to the Land I Will Show You": Studies in Honor of Dwight S. Young* (ed. J. E. Coleson and V. H. Matthews; Winona Lake, IN: Eisenbrauns, 1996) 57–59.

46. See note 35 above. For the common images and descriptions incorporated in Job's care of the disenfranchised in the ancient world, see the Egyptian tomb autobiographies in Lichtheim, *Moral Values*, 12, 19–20; as well as M. Weinfeld, *Social Justice in Ancient Israel and in the Ancient Near East* (Minneapolis: Fortress, 1995) 223–30.

his love for the destitute by providing them with food and clothing (Deut 10:17–18; cf. Pss 68:5; 146:9). The poetic vignette provides an impressionistic account of the divine ideal; it concretizes the deuteronomic description of Yhwh and epitomizes the deuteronomic vision of compassion toward the destitute (Deut 14:29; 16:11, 14; 24:17, 19–21; 26:12–13; 27:19).

This concrete expression of the deuteronomic ethos not only governs Job's relationship to the poor, but also shapes his economic dealings with employees (Job 31:38–40b).[47] The concluding oath reflects on the debilitating effects of economic exploitation on the land in general and day laborers in particular. Here Job appears to operate under the regulations delineated in Deut 24:14–15 (cf. Lev 19:13, Mal 3:5);[48] he elaborates on the despair of day laborers defrauded of their wages and denies withholding payment for their work or produce. In so doing, he presents an economic ethic as well as a standard of moral conduct that seems to be inspired by the deuteronomic torah.

These literary, thematic, and conceptual links with the deuteronomic torah suggest that Job's moral knowledge extended beyond Israel's psalmic and sapiential traditions to include distinctive elements from Israel's constitutional materials. The asseveration of innocence contains topics and expressions that are unique to the deuteronomic torah. In addition, the extended oath employs specific regulations reminiscent of the deuteronomic program as well as an ethics of power characteristic of the deuteronomic vision of leadership.[49] While the virtues and vices

---

47. While Job 31:39b employs the term בעל 'owner' to refer to the inhabitants of the land, Job's claim on the territory (אדמתי 'my land') suggests בעל should be interpreted as a by-form of פעל 'to do, work'. In this case, Job is referring to workers or day laborers rather than owners of the land. See M. Dahood, "Ugaritic Studies and the Bible," *Greg* 43 (1962) 75; A. van Selms, "Job 31:38–40 in Ugaritic Light," *Semitics* 8 (1982) 30–42; Clines, *Job 21–37*, 973 n. 39.c., 1032; *HALOT* 1:142b; *DCH* 2:237b.

48. See L. G. Perdue, *Wisdom in Revolt: Metaphorical Theology in the Book of Job* (JSOTSup 112; Sheffield: Sheffield Academic, 1991) 187; Clines, *Job 21–37*, 1032.

49. For a discussion of the deuteronomic vision of leadership, see D. I. Block, "The Burden of Leadership: The Mosaic Paradigm of Kingship (Deut. 17:14–20)," *BSac* 162 (2005) 259–78, reproduced in idem, *How I Love Your Torah, O Lord! Studies in the Book of Deuteronomy* (Eugene, OR: Cascade, 2011) 118–39; idem, "Leader, Leadership, OT," in *New Interpreter's Dictionary of the Bible* (ed. K. D. Sakenfeld; 5 vols.; Nashville: Abingdon, 2008) 3:621–26. In the main, Block contends that the deuteronomic torah seeks to rein in the potential exploitation of power for personal privilege and create a vision of leadership governed by righteousness as well as a concern for the interests of those who are led. In view of Job's treatment of the marginalized, it appears he embodies the deuteronomic ideal; he perceives leadership as a call to responsibility, rather than an invitation to power. For more on this vision of leadership in Deuteronomy, see the following essays in the present volume: M. D. Carroll R., "Welcoming the Stranger: Toward a Theology

delineated in the asseveration of innocence correspond with moral concepts documented elsewhere in the Old Testament and the ancient world, the deuteronomic flavor of certain principles indicate the torah served as a vital source of Job's moral knowledge.

In this respect, it seems the Joban poet formulated an ethical vision through terms, motifs, and literary forms characteristic of Israel's psalmic and sapiential traditions, but shaped specific principles in accordance with the rhetoric and ethos of the deuteronomic torah. This moral *bricolage* not only produced an implicit standard against which Job measured his integrity, but it also identified the distinctive sources of the protagonist's ethical knowledge. In view of the rhetorical texture and ethos of the catalogue, it appears this knowledge was rooted in the revealed things, that is, the socio-moral principles revealed in the cosmic order as well as specific regulations revealed in the deuteronomic torah.

3. Conclusion

On the whole, the asseveration of innocence illuminates the multifaceted nature of Job's moral knowledge. The discrete virtues woven into this rich, moral tapestry accentuate the deuteronomic ethos of Job's ethical vision and signal the confluence of Israel's psalmic, sapiential, and constitutional traditions in Job's epistemology. In addition, the extended declaration identifies the basis of the protagonist's confidence as well as the source of his cognitive dissonance. The tension between Job's ethical knowledge and personal experience creates an epistemological crisis that drives the poetic drama. This crisis reaches its climax in Job's declaration of innocence in Job 31 and finds its resolution in the divine speeches. The former demonstrates that Job possesses a genuine knowledge of morality; the latter indicate that Job does not possess the intellectual capacity to determine YHWH's enigmatic providence within the cosmos. The divine speeches do not challenge Job's knowledge of morality; rather they undermine his empiricism and its creation of a chaotic world governed by a capricious deity. While Job knows and lives in accordance with the revealed things of Deut 29:29, his restricted faculties prevent him from understanding the secret things. The divine speeches provided Job with a vision of YHWH's providence that broadened his understanding of the cosmic order and situated human investigation

---

of Immigration in Deuteronomy"; R. Josberger, "For *Your* Good Always: Restraining the Rights of the Victor for the Well-being of the Vulnerable (Deut 21:10–14)"; M. Theocharous, "Stealing Souls: Human Trafficking and Deuteronomy 24:7."

within its proper boundaries. That is, they affirmed his knowledge of the revealed things and produced an understanding of the world that allowed him to live in humble submission to the secret things.

The significance of this epistemological posture can hardly be underestimated. While the limitations of human knowledge preclude an understanding of the secret things, the revelation of YHWH's will within the created order as well as the torah provide his people with a sufficient guide for life. The conflation of Israel's psalmic, sapiential, and constitutional traditions within Job's moral vision indicate that YHWH's will is both knowable and doable (see Deut 30:11–14). However, obedience to the revealed things entails more than intellectual apprehension or external performance. The Joban portrait demonstrates that the hidden, volitional dimensions of character are fundamental to moral righteousness. For Job, it is not enough that a person does what is right; a person must do what is right from the right motive, intention, or disposition. This is Job's conception of the righteous. In light of this moral consciousness, it is not surprising that the asseveration of innocence has been designated as "the purest moral theory in the Bible,"[50] "the crown of ethical development in the Old Testament,"[51] and the highest standard of ethics known prior to the Sermon on the Mount.[52] Nor is it surprising that YHWH affirms Job's moral character as well as his knowledge of the revealed things.

---

50. M. Tsevat, "The Meaning of the Book of Job," *HUCA* 37 (1966) 73–106; repr. in *Studies in Ancient Israelite Religion* (ed. J. L. Crenshaw; New York: Ktav, 1976) 372.
51. Duhm, *Das Buch Hiob*, 149.
52. A. Weiser, *Das Buch Hiob* (ATD; Göttingen: Vandenhoeck & Ruprecht, 1974) 214.

"Fear God and Keep His Commandments" (Eccl 12:13)

An Examination of Some Intertextual Relationships between Deuteronomy and Ecclesiastes

RICHARD SCHULTZ

1. Introduction

Ever since Gerhard von Rad in his final work, *Wisdom in Israel*, presented wisdom as a third theological tradition alongside historical and prophetic traditions, it has been common to speak of the independence of the wisdom corpus within the Hebrew canon.[1] Theologically, according to Ronald Clements, "wisdom is forced to appear at the periphery," being described as an "errant child" (Roland Murphy) or "an orphan in the biblical household" (James Crenshaw).[2] Wisdom literature's apparent lack of reference to Israel's salvation history and to the characteristic elements of Yahwism has resulted in the much-rehearsed neglect of wisdom in twentieth century syntheses of OT theology.[3] It would be easy to dismiss the matter as simply an academic debate, but there are practical ramifications as well. According to Claus Westermann, "One

---

Author's Note: It is an honor to dedicate this essay to Daniel Block, grateful for his many contributions to Old Testament scholarship and for his warm collegiality during his years at Wheaton College.

1. G. von Rad, *Wisdom in Israel* (Nashville: Abingdon, 1972; German ed. 1970). This continues to be a dominant viewpoint even today, as exemplified by Brevard Childs who also speaks of "the wisdom tradition" in his 1992 biblical theology (*Biblical Theology of the Old and New Testament: Theological Reflection on the Christian Bible* [Minneapolis: Fortress, 1992] 187).

2. R. E. Clements, "Wisdom and Old Testament Theology," in *Wisdom in Ancient Israel: Essays in Honour of J. A. Emerton* (ed. J. Day, R. P. Gordon, and H. G. M. Williamson; Cambridge: Cambridge University Press, 1995) 270; R. E. Murphy, "Wisdom Literature and Biblical Theology," *BTB* 24 (1994) 4; J. L. Crenshaw, "Prolegomena," in *Studies in Ancient Israelite Wisdom* (ed. J. L. Crenshaw; New York: Ktav, 1976) 1.

3. See the survey by C. H. Scobie, "The Place of Wisdom in Biblical Theology," *BTB* 14 (1984) 43–44.

is generally convinced that wisdom texts are unsuited for preaching, religious education, counseling, or liturgy. . . . Perhaps one is unconcerned with wisdom's significance for practical theology because it also has little or no significance for theology."[4]

Recent intertextual studies have tempered this judgment concerning the independence of the wisdom corpus. Will Kynes noted the close relationship between the poetry of Job and the books of Psalms and Isaiah, Moshe Weinfeld identified conceptual parallels between Proverbs and Deuteronomy, and Bruce Waltke highlighted the prophetic features of Lady Wisdom's judgment speech in Proverbs 1. David Clemens claimed Ecclesiastes' dependence on Genesis 1–3, and Jennie Barbour found striking traces of Israelite history in Ecclesiastes.[5]

Nevertheless, it is still common to view the message of Qoheleth as *contrary* to rather than *consonant* with the "Deuteronomic Torah" (Daniel Block's preferred manner of referring to this theological bedrock within the Hebrew Bible). This largely depends, however, on how one understands the relationship between the so-called "Epilogue" of Ecclesiastes (12:9–14) and the remainder of the book. Martin Shields reflects the majority view of scholars, which I will dispute below, in stating that "the epilogist's statements about God . . . reflect an understanding of God that is not echoed in Qoheleth's words," concluding that "[t]hese comments more closely reflect Deuteronomistic thought than wisdom thought and tie the epilogist to traditional Yahwism more

---

4. C. Westermann, "Weisheit und praktische Theologie," *Pastoraltheologie* 79 (1990) 515 (my translation). H.-D. Preuß goes even further, rejecting OT wisdom literature as "pagan thought" that should be denied a place within both Christian and OT theology; see H.-D. Preuss, "Alttestamentliche Weisheit in christlicher Predigt?," in *Questions disputées d'Ancien Testament: Méthode et théologie* (ed. C. Brekelmans; BETL 33; Leuven: Leuven University Press, 1974) 165–81. This is a perspective that would be quite troubling to Daniel Block, the honoree of this collection of essays, who throughout his scholarly career has been just as committed to the Church as to the academy and for whom the suggestion that any portion of the OT would not be pertinent to the Church would be unthinkable. It is also my conviction that the book of Ecclesiastes is highly relevant both to the Church and contemporary society.

5. W. Kynes, *"My Psalm Has Turned into Weeping": Job's Dialogue with the Psalms* (BZAW 437; Berlin: de Gruyter, 2012 [forthcoming]); idem, "Job and Isaiah 40–55: Intertextualities in Dialogue," in *Reading Job Intertextually* (ed. Katharine J. Dell and Will Kynes; Library of Hebrew Bible/Old Testament Studies; New York: T. & T. Clark, 2012 [forthcoming]); M. Weinfeld, *Deuteronomy and the Deuteronomic School* (Oxford: Clarendon, 1972) esp. 244–74; B. K. Waltke, "Lady Wisdom as Mediatrix: An Exposition of Proverbs 1:20–33," *Presbyterion* 14 (1988) 13–15; D. M. Clemens, "The Law of Sin and Death: Ecclesiastes and Genesis 1–3," *Themelios* 19 (1994) 5; see also C. C. Forman, "Koheleth's Use of Genesis" *JSS* 5 (1960) 256–63; J. Barbour, *The Story of Israel in the Book of Qohelet: Ecclesiastes as Cultural Memory* (Oxford: Oxford University Press, 2012).

closely than to the sages about whom he comments."⁶ In other words, he understands *the final editor* of the canonical book of Ecclesiastes, as expressed in the Epilogue, as affirming Deuteronomic theology but at odds with the theology of Qoheleth *the sage*, the dominant voice in the book. In fact, according to Shields, "the epilogist is using Qoheleth's words to demonstrate the bankruptcy of the wisdom movement."⁷

2. Links between Deuteronomy and Ecclesiastes

The purpose of this essay is to examine the various structural, conceptual, and verbal parallels that can be noted between these two books, seeking to demonstrate that the book of Ecclesiastes throughout is compatible with Deuteronomic theology and, at least at one point, draws directly on the book of Deuteronomy. I will begin with *weaker* links and move to *stronger* ones, postponing a discussion of possible implications until the conclusion. Not all parallels that can be noted between Ecclesiastes and Deuteronomy offer clear evidence of literary influence or dependence.

2.1. Incidental Parallels

Craig Bartholomew observes the following five "similarities" between the two books, which may be coincidental and thus will not receive detailed discussion in this essay:⁸

1. Eating and drinking is a dominant motif in Ecclesiastes and Deuteronomy.⁹
2. Eccles. 5:1–7 [4:17–5:6] is akin to the Name theology of Deuteronomy....¹⁰

---

6. M. A. Shields, *The End of Wisdom: A Reappraisal of the Historical and Canonical Function of Ecclesiastes* (Winona Lake, IN: Eisenbrauns, 2006) 96.

7. Ibid., 157.

8. C. G. Bartholomew, *Ecclesiastes* (Baker Commentary on the Old Testament: Wisdom and Psalms; Grand Rapids: Baker, 2009) 368–69 n. 45. Bartholomew also notes two additional parallels omitted here that will be discussed at length later in this essay. One should note, however, that he restricts these comments to a footnote. Bartholomew gives the English versification first, followed by the Hebrew in brackets, the reverse order of the verse listings elsewhere in this essay. The numbering of the individual parallels has been added here.

9. It is noteworthy that Deuteronomy frequently associates eating and drinking with experiencing "satisfaction," using Hebrew שבע (Deut 6:11; 8:10, 12; 11:15; 14:29; 23:25[24]; 26:12; 31:20). Ecclesiastes, to the contrary, emphasizes the inability to be satisfied, using the Hebrew negation לא שבע (Eccl 1:8; 4:8; 5:9[10]; 6:3); Eccl 5:11[12] is the exception.

10. I will discuss Ecclesiastes 5 at length below. Here, however, it is unclear exactly what Bartholomew means by "akin to the Name theology."

3. The exhortation to "beware of anything more than these" in Eccles. 12:12 and that "nothing can be taken away from God's work" in 3:14 is similar to Deuteronomy's exhortation not to add or take anything away from the law. . . .[11]
4. The remembrance motif is common to both Ecclesiastes and Deuteronomy.
5. If the author of Ecclesiastes is keenly aware of Deuteronomy or its theology, then it is possible that "one" in Eccles. 12:11 may be related to "one" in Deut. 6:4.[12]

2.2. Genre and Structure

Michael Fox, who analyzes the book of Ecclesiastes as a "frame-narrative," sees an analogous structure in Deuteronomy.[13] According to Fox, if one excludes what scholars commonly view as later "additions" to the book of Deuteronomy (Deut 4:41–43, 32:48–52, 34:1–12), similar to Ecclesiastes, Deuteronomy is a first-person monologue (by Moses) set in a third-person framework. The narrator speaks about Moses while remaining in the background. To be sure, even if Deuteronomy and Ecclesiastes share a common structure, it does not necessarily follow that the shape of the former influenced the author of the latter.[14] Nevertheless, noting this similar structure can remind the reader that Ecclesiastes is to be understood as a narrative rather than merely "as a collection of proverbs and epigrams each of which . . . is intended to be independently valid."[15] Furthermore, the comparison here with the book of

---

11. The translation and interpretation of Eccl 12:12 is much disputed. It is, at best, conceptually—not verbally—close to the other cited texts. It is true that Eccl 3:14, Deut 4:2, and Deut 13:1[12:32] share the use of the Hebrew verb pair יסף (Hiphil) and גרע 'to add' and 'to subtract'. However, whereas Deuteronomy prohibits Israel from revising his commandments, Ecclesiastes declares the impossibility of modifying God's works. A. Vonach sees here a creative reuse of Deuteronomy's "canon formula" in affirming God's sovereign work ("Gottes Souveränität anerkennen: Zum Verständnis der 'Kanonformel' in Koh 3,14," in *Qohelet in the Context of Wisdom* [ed. A. Schoors; BETL 136; Leuven: Peeters, 1998] 391–97), while C.-L. Seow describes the phrase merely as "language . . . used elsewhere in the Bible for something that is decisive, authoritative, and invariable" (*Ecclesiastes* [AB 18C; New York: Doubleday, 1997] 174). Prov 30:6 offers a more striking parallel to the Deuteronomy texts.

12. That is, "one Shepherd" in Eccl 12:11 and "Yahweh is one" in Deut 6:4.

13. M. V. Fox, "Frame-Narrative and Composition in the Book of Qohelet," *HUCA* 48 (1977) 83–106. Fox credits Menahem Haran with suggesting this parallel to him (ibid., 93 n. 24).

14. One might also suggest that both monologists play a similar role (i.e., as one who "[n]ot only was . . . wise, but . . . also imparted knowledge to the people," Eccl 12:9), although Moses is not explicitly described in this manner.

15. M. V. Fox, *Ecclesiastes* (JPS Bible Commentary; Philadelphia: Jewish Publication Society, 2004) xiii.

Deuteronomy, in which the narrator appears to be in basic agreement with the instructions offered by the first-person monologist (see especially Deuteronomy 34), suggests that, in principle, the same could hold true for Ecclesiastes. This is not the view of Fox, however, who understands the narrator-epilogist as warning against "unorthodox writings like Ecclesiastes," despite "showing respect for Koheleth" and "by no means" repudiating him, a claim to which I will now respond.[16]

2.3. The Concluding Epilogue (Eccl 12:13–14) and Deuteronomy

> 13   סוף דבר הכל נשמע את־האלהים ירא ואת־מצותיו שמור כי־זה כל־האדם
>
> 14   כי את־כל־מעשה האלהים יבא במשפט על כל־נעלם אם־טוב ואם־רע
>
> 13   Now all has been heard; here is the conclusion of the matter: Fear God and keep his commandments, for this is the duty of all mankind.
>
> 14   For God will bring every deed into judgment, including every hidden thing, whether it is good or evil.[17]

The three foundational claims of these verses—that (1) there is value both in revering God and (2) in obeying God's commands, because (3) God's future judgment is certain—in my opinion do not constitute an orthodox corrective, contrary to the view of Shields and others,[18] since they state nothing that the main body of the book has not affirmed previously. First, the value of revering God is emphasized repeatedly by Qoheleth. Reverence for God is a proper response to his eternal, unchangeable actions (Eccl 3:14). Reverence for God will prevent us from uttering frivolous vows (5:5[6]).[19] It also will protect us from the twin dangers of pretentious righteousness and wisdom, and excessive wickedness and folly (7:18), for the situation of the righteous ultimately will be better than that of the wicked, precisely because they revere God (8:12–13).

---

16. Ibid., 83–84. T. Longman III, *Ecclesiastes* (NICOT; Grand Rapids: Eerdmans, 1998) 37–39, shares Fox's assessment. Fox and Longman's negative assessment also rests on whether one translates Eccl 12:12 as warning against *Qoheleth's* words (NJPS) or against "anything in addition to them" (NIV, similarly ESV, NRSV), which is my preference.

17. All biblical citations are from the NIV 2011, unless otherwise noted.

18. See nn. 6–7 above. According to Fox (*Ecclesiastes*, 82), many commentators since the nineteenth century have attributed the Epilogue to a later editor who "supposedly considered Koheleth's words too unorthodox and sought to counteract them with pious assurances and precepts."

19. The similarity between Eccl 5:5–6[6–7] and 12:13 in relating the fear of God to obeying his commandments has led some scholars to label 5:6b[7b] as a redactional gloss. See D. Michel, *Untersuchungen zur Eigenart des Buches Qohelet* (BZAW 183; Berlin: Walter de Gruyter, 1989) 257.

Second, the need to obey God's commands is also affirmed by Qoheleth's teaching. Eccl 5:4–6[5–7] explicitly draws on the law regarding vows from Deut 23:22–24[21–23]. This text warns against disregarding the Deuteronomic instructions by trivializing making vows. In addition, Eccl 8:5 contains a suggestive reference to a שׁוֹמֵר מִצְוָה, literally, 'a command-keeper'. Most commentators understand this expression to refer to the king's commands, since the same verb is used in this respect in Eccl 8:2 ("Obey the king's command"). The general formulation in 8:5, however, literally, "a command-keeper knows no evil thing,"[20] and the parallel continuation of the verse, "but a wise heart knows (or acknowledges) a judgment time" (וְעֵת וּמִשְׁפָּט יֵדַע לֵב חָכָם),[21] permit a broader understanding. Lawbreakers get into trouble; law keepers avoid it.

Third, several passages in Ecclesiastes speak of the certainty of divine judgment. Interpreters of Ecclesiastes dispute whether the referenced "time of judgment" in Eccl 8:5 will occur "under the sun" or *post-mortem*. Following my interpretation of Eccl 8:5–6 as referring to the time of judgment (NJPS: "time of doom"; LXX: "time of judgment" [καιρὸν κρίσεως]), this adjudication occurs *before* death or perhaps *at* death. In Eccl 3:15, the nature of the assertion regarding judgment is beset with translation questions, though the NIV's rendering of וְהָאֱלֹהִים יְבַקֵּשׁ אֶת־נִרְדָּף as "and God will call the past to account" sounds *post-mortem*.[22] The NJB translation, "God seeks out anyone who is persecuted," makes good sense of the Hebrew but does not fit the context as well as the NIV, since 3:14 emphasizes that God's actions are not subject to the limitations of time and 3:16–17 speak of judgment. Specifically, 3:17 states that "God will bring into judgment both the righteous and the wicked, for there will be a time for every activity, a time to judge every deed." Here the coming judgment stands in contrast to the present injustice (3:16).

Eccl 5:5[6] ("Why should God be angry at what you say and destroy the work of your hands?"), however, sounds *pre-mortem*, and this

---

20. The phrase "knows no evil thing" in Eccl 8:5 is potentially ambiguous. Most modern translations relate it to the *consequences* of one's action, as in the NASB ("knows no harm") or, more explicitly, the NJPS ("will not suffer from the dangerous situation"). However, the occurrence of "evil thing" in 8:3 suggests that 8:5 either refers to one's involvement in evil *actions* or is an intentional word play.

21. I understand the Hebrew phrase וְעֵת וּמִשְׁפָּט as a hendiadys.

22. Other translations include ESV: "and God seeks what has been driven away"; HCSB: "God repeats what has passed"; NAB: "God retrieves what has gone by"; NLT: "because God makes the same things happen over and over again"; NJPS: "and God seeks the pursued."

is clearly the case with 7:17 ("Do not be overwicked, and do not be a fool—why die before your time?"), and is also likely with 8:12–13 ("I know that it will go better with those who fear God, who are reverent before him. Yet because the wicked do not fear God, it will not go well with them, and their days will not lengthen like a shadow"). Eccl 11:9 ("Follow the ways of your heart and whatever your eyes see, but know that for all these things God will bring you into judgment") is less clear but sounds more *post-mortem*, especially in light of the preceding verse ("However many years anyone may live, let them enjoy them all. But let them remember the days of darkness, for there will be many," v. 8) and the similar formulation of Eccl 11:9 and Eccl 12:14:

Eccl 11:9	Eccl 12:14
על־כל־אלה יביאך האלהים במשפט	האלהים יבא במשפט על כל־נעלם
for all these things God will bring you into judgment	For God will bring every deed into judgment

In sum, regardless of whether or not one considers Eccl 12:9–14 *redactionally* to be a secondary addition to the book, as many scholars do, there is insufficient cause to consider the key assertions of vv. 13–14 to be *theologically* at odds with the rest of the book.[23] And if I have adequately demonstrated the close conceptual relationship between the content of the Epilogue and the main body of the book of Ecclesiastes, then it also would follow that a further demonstration of the close relationship between the Epilogue of Ecclesiastes and Deuteronomy could also indicate a conceptual coherence between the latter and the entire canonical book of Ecclesiastes.[24]

The key affirmation of the Epilogue of Ecclesiastes—namely that reverence for God is a foundational relationship that is closely associated with obeying his commandments—is, in fact, also emphasized in Deuteronomy. The phrase "fear of the LORD/God" occurs eighteen times in Proverbs, five times in Ecclesiastes, and ten times in Job, along with several related expressions, including the one in Eccl 12:13. One cannot simplistically equate this expression in wisdom texts with its

---

23. Fox affirms, succinctly, with regard to the closing admonition to "Revere God and observe His commandments" that "Koheleth would not disagree" (*Ecclesiastes*, 85).

24. Seow concurs that "the perspective of the redactor is not far different from Deuteronomy, where obedience to divine commandments is defined as wisdom," citing Deut 4:6 in support (*Ecclesiastes*, 396).

use outside of the wisdom corpus,[25] for, as Joachim Becker has noted correctly, the fear of God in the OT can be associated with a variety of actions and situations.[26] Nevertheless, Hartmut Gese claims the following:

> In Israel wisdom of necessity consisted in the fear of Yahweh. Human attitudes can be explained in terms of this fear in the same categories as are appropriate in terms of Torah and of prophetic writings. Differences in nuance can be explained by the differences in form between the divine command and wisdom warnings, and by the corresponding differences in *Sitz im Leben*, but *not by a discrepancy in content.*[27]

Most disputed is the use of "fear of God" in Ecclesiastes, which Aarre Lauha distinguishes from that in Proverbs, characterizing the former as trembling "respect for an incomprehensible despot."[28] This characterization, however, is hardly required in Eccl 8:12 where the God-fearer is contrasted with the wicked person who commits "a hundred crimes." More importantly, 12:13 directly links the fear of God to obeying the law, as is also the case implicitly in 5:6[7], which follows the warning against insincere vows in 5:3–5[4–6]. This usage, however, has its closest parallels in Deuteronomy (especially 6:2; see also 4:10–14; 5:29; 6:13, 24; 8:6; 10:12–13, 20; 13:5[4]; 14:23; 17:19; 25:18; 31:12–13). Thus, in at least a few verses in Ecclesiastes, the phrase "the fear of God" not only describes a common Israelite attitude toward God but also entails covenant obedience.

The Hebrew verb שמר 'observe, keep' is used numerous times in Deuteronomy in conjunction with obedience to [the LORD's] commandments, including Deut 4:40, 7:9; 8:2, 11; 13:19[18]; 28:1, 15, 45; 30:10, 16; comparable use in Ecclesiastes is found in Eccl 8:2, 5; 12:13. The most significant corresponding verses in this regard in Deuteronomy are 6:2, 8:6, 13:5[4], and 17:19, although they use several different words to refer to the legal requirements.

- 6:2—"so that you, your children, and their children after them may <u>fear the Lord your God</u> as long as you live <u>by keeping all his decrees and commands</u> (את־כל־חקתיו ומצותיו) that I give you,"

---

25. For example, Gen 22:12; 42:18; Exod 1:21; 14:31; 20:20; Lev 19:14, 32; 25:17; Deut 4:10; 5:26; 6:2, 13, 24; 8:6; 10:12, 20; Josh 4:24; 24:14; 1 Sam 12:14, 24; 2 Sam 23:3; 1 Kgs 18:12; Pss 2:11; 19:10[9]; 111:10; 128:1; Isa 11:3; 33:6.

26. J. Becker, *Gottesfurcht im Alten Testament* (Rome: PBI, 1965). Becker suggests as categories of usage numinous, cultic, ethical, or nomistic.

27. H. Gese, "The Law" in his *Essays in Biblical Theology* (Minneapolis: Augsburg, 1981) 77 (my emphasis).

28. A. Lauha, *Kohelet* (BKAT 19; Neukirchen-Vluyn: Neukirchener, 1978) 17, 70.

- 8:6—"Observe the commands (את־מצות) of the LORD your God, walking in obedience to him and revering him."
- 13:5[4]—"It is the LORD your God you must follow, and him you must revere. Keep his commands (ואת־מצותיו) and obey him; serve him and hold fast to him."
- 17:19—"he is to read it all the days of his life so that he may learn to revere the Lord his God and follow carefully all the words of this law and these decrees (את־כל־דברי התורה הזאת ואת־החקים האלה)."

The close verbal and conceptual relationship between Eccl 12:13–14 and Deuteronomy is clear here. Furthermore, as noted above, Eccl 8:12 contrasts fearing God with doing evil (see also 7:17–18). Within the larger OT wisdom corpus, revering God is repeatedly associated with obeying him or "avoiding evil" (usually expressed in Hebrew as סור/סר מרע). This emphasis occurs in the standard description of Job (Job 1:1, 8; 2:3; compare 28:28), as well as in Proverbs (see Prov 3:7, 8:13, 14:16, 16:17, 24:21). Prov 13:13 uniquely combines the two in promising that "whoever respects a command is rewarded" (וירא מצוה הוא ישלם). As William Brown concludes with respect to Ecclesiastes, "For the epilogist, as for the Deuteronomist, true wisdom is displayed in obedience,"[29] and, in my opinion, the sage Qoheleth would also nod in assent.[30]

Like Ecclesiastes, Deuteronomy contains warnings of impending judgment if God's covenantal laws are not obeyed. This is a primary emphasis in Deut 28:15–68; 29:18–28[19–29]; 30:17–18; 31:16–21, 29; 32:15–25, 40–42. Somewhat surprisingly, the word used several times in Ecclesiastes to refer to divine judgment (משפט) is used in this manner only five times in Deuteronomy in reference to God: Deut 1:17; 10:18; 32:4, 41; 33:21.[31]

2.4. The Law of the Vow in Ecclesiastes and Deuteronomy

The most striking intertextual connection between Ecclesiastes and Deuteronomy, however, does not involve the Epilogue but rather

---

29. W. P. Brown, *Character in Crisis: A Fresh Approach to the Wisdom Literature of the Old Testament* (Grand Rapids: Eerdmans, 1996) 118.

30. This is also the conclusion of G. D. Salyer, who writes that "the implied author stresses what Qoheleth himself stressed; that the commandments of God are important (cf. 5.3–5)" (*Vain Rhetoric: Private Insight and Public Debate in Ecclesiastes* [JSOTSup 327; Sheffield: Sheffield Academic, 2001] 375).

31. The word משפט occurs 37 times in Deuteronomy, the majority of them in the plural and primarily in reference to Israel's laws. Of these, only Deut 32:41 explicitly mentions God's punitive judgment against evildoers, and this text leaves open the identity of God's "enemies."

involves the reuse of the law of the vow from Deut 23:22–24[21–23] in Eccl 5:3–5[4–6].

Eccl 5:3–5[4–6]	Deut 23:22–24[21–23]
3 כאשר תדר נדר לאלהים אל־תאחר לשלמו כי אין חפץ בכסילים את אשר־תדר שלם	22 כי־תדר נדר ליהוה אלהיך לא תאחר לשלמו כי־דרש ידרשנו יהוה אלהיך מעמך והיה בך חטא
4 טוב אשר לא־תדר משתדור ולא תשלם	23 וכי תחדל לנדר לא־יהיה בך חטא
5 אל־תתן את־פיך לחטיא את־בשרך ואל־תאמר לפני המלאך כי שגגה היא למה יקצף האלהים על־קולך וחבל את־מעשה ידיך	24 מוצא שפתיך תשמר ועשית כאשר נדרת ליהוה אלהיך נדבה אשר דברת בפיך
1. (4) When <u>you make a vow</u> to <u>God</u>,	12. (21) If <u>you make a vow</u> to the LORD your <u>God</u>,
2. <u>do not delay to fulfill it</u>.	13. <u>do not be slow to pay it</u>,
3. He has no pleasure in fools;	14. for the LORD your God will certainly demand it of you
4. fulfill your vow.	15. and you will be guilty of sin.
5. (5) It is better not to make a vow	16. (22) But if you refrain from making a vow,
6. than to make one and not fulfill it.	17. you will not be guilty.
7. (6) Do not let your mouth lead you into sin.	18. (23) Whatever your lips utter you must be sure to do,
8. And do not protest to the temple messenger,	19. because you made your vow freely to the LORD your God with your own mouth.
9. "My vow was a mistake."	
10. Why should God be angry at what you say	
11. and destroy the work of your hands?	

Most commentators acknowledge this extensive and striking verbal parallel, characterizing it in weaker or stronger ways. Duane Garrett views Ecclesiastes 5 as "similar" to Deuteronomy 23; Franz Delitzsch sees here an "echo" of Deuteronomy "in thought and expression"; and according to Roland Murphy the former "resembles" the latter "rather closely." James Crenshaw, Craig Bartholomew, Thomas Krüger, and Michael Fox speak of a "quotation" or "near-quotation," while Iain Provan offers the non-committal comment: "Other biblical passages also touch on this topic."³² Barry Webb and Martin Shields present two polar positions. Webb sees here an indication of Qoheleth's knowledge and affirmation of Torah as divine revelation, since this exhortation about keeping one's vows "presupposes the instruction on this matter in the Torah." Referring to Eccl 4:17[5:1], Webb claims that "to go to the house of God to *listen* is to conform one's behavior to it."³³ Shields, however, argues for Qoheleth's independence from—or even disagreement with—Deuteronomy. On the one hand, Webb may be reading too much into the presumed revelatory nature of all speech within the temple precincts. On the other hand, Shields also goes beyond the text in seeing here an "exhortation to abstain from speaking to God" (in both prayer and making vows), since Qoheleth's God "has little or no interest in the concerns of individuals."³⁴

The fact that these texts begin with two nearly identical Hebrew clauses is a sufficient basis for concluding that there is a relationship of dependence here, and no one has argued that Deuteronomy is borrowing from Ecclesiastes. This initial, almost verbatim, repetition suggests the likelihood that the differences stem from Qoheleth's own modifications of the borrowed legal formulation in order to better fit the new textual context and the author's thematic emphases. Each of these differences (i.e., changes) will now be examined. Lines 1 and 12 differ only in their opening conjunction and in their designation of the deity. The Hebrew conjunction כי used by Deuteronomy is common in legal formulations (see also Deut 23:10[9], 11[10], 25[24], 26[25]), while Ecclesiastes' כאשר parallels the use of the same expression in 4:17[5:1]—"when you go to the house of God." Ecclesiastes makes no use of the *tetragrammaton* throughout the book, so it is not surprising that Deuteronomy's "the LORD your God" is replaced in Ecclesiastes simply with "God." Lines 2 and 13 are identical in the Hebrew, despite being translated divergently, for instance, in the NASB, NIV, and NRSV, except in one respect. Deuteronomy uses the negative adverb לא, whereas

---

32. D. A. Garrett, *Proverbs, Ecclesiastes, Song of Songs* (NAC 14; Nashville: Broadman, 1993) 310; F. Delitzsch, *Commentary on the Song of Songs and Ecclesiastes* (trans. M. G. Easton; Grand Rapids: Eerdmans, 1975 [reprint ed.]) 287; R. E. Murphy, *Ecclesiastes* (WBC 23A; Dallas: Word, 1992) 46; J. L. Crenshaw, *Ecclesiastes* (OTL; Philadelphia: Westminster, 1987) 116–17; Bartholomew, *Ecclesiastes*, 203; T. Krüger, *Qoheleth* (trans. O. C. Dean, Jr.; Hermeneia; Minneapolis: Augsburg Fortress, 2004) 213; Fox, *Ecclesiastes*, 33; I. Provan, *Ecclesiastes / Song of Songs* (NIVAC; Grand Rapids: Zondervan, 2001) 117.

33. B. G. Webb, *Five Festal Garments: Christian Reflections on The Song of Songs, Ruth, Lamentations, Ecclesiastes and Esther* (New Studies in Biblical Theology; Downers Grove, IL: InterVarsity, 2000) 97.

34. Shields, *The End of Wisdom*, 159.

Ecclesiastes uses אל. Prohibitions in Deuteronomy commonly use לא, while Ecclesiastes prefers to use אל.[35]

In the remainder of the parallel texts (lines 3–11 and 14–19), Deuteronomy 23 and Ecclesiastes 5 diverge more significantly; Ecclesiastes 5 is briefer and simpler in several respects. Nevertheless, the same basic elements are found in both texts, offering additional support for the claim of literary dependence. Lines 3 and 14–15 offer comparable motivations for heeding the preceding admonition in terms of the deity's response. Deuteronomy threatens being called to account by God for one's actions (the same phrase occurring in Deut 18:19). In Deuteronomy it is not uncommon for God to announce that he will not leave punishment up to the Israelite judiciary but will instead carry out judgment himself. Ecclesiastes simply labels those who make rash vows as "fools," a common wisdom category. Fools, by definition, are unable to please God by their actions and may provoke divine judgment (see, for example, Eccl 7:17). But when a rash vow is accompanied by excuse-based reneging on what one has promised when confronted by the cultic debt-collector (lines 8–9), divine displeasure turns to anger and punitive destructive action (lines 10–11, which give a vivid description of Deuteronomy's threat in line 14 being executed).[36] Line 4 in Ecclesiastes simply expresses the admonition of line 2 as a positive command, repeating the Piel verb שלם 'fulfill', which also occurs in line 6. This is similar in formulation to 5:1[2] ("Do not be quick with your mouth, do not be hasty in your heart to utter anything before God. God is in heaven and you are on earth, so let your words be few"), in which a twofold admonition is also followed by an explanation and a positive command. Ecclesiastes' positive command in line 4 ("fulfill your vow") corresponds to the wordier command in line 18 in Deuteronomy ("Whatever your lips utter you must be sure to do"), which is followed by another motivational clause.

Lines 5–6 and lines 16–17 along with 19 offer a further rationale for the positive command. Ecclesiastes uses a favored "better than" proverbial formulation (see Eccl 4:6, 13; 6:9; 7:1, 2, 3, 5, 8; 9:4, 16, 18). This can be viewed as a sapiential paraphrasing of Deuteronomy that, in line 17, repeats and negates the expression for incurring guilt from line

---

35. For example, in the immediate context, אל occurs twice in Eccl 5:1[2], once in 5:3[4], twice in 5:5[6], and once in 5:7[8].

36. Hence Seow is misleading when he contrasts Ecclesiastes with Deuteronomy in speaking of the motive clause in Eccl 5:3[4] (lit.: "for there is no pleasure in fools") as "typical of the wisdom tradition's tendency to avoid any language of divine causality" (*Ecclesiastes*, 200).

15 (line 15: וְהָיָה בְךָ חֵטְא 'and you will be guilty of sin'; line 17: לֹא־יִהְיֶה בְךָ חֵטְא 'you will not be guilty'; compare also Deut 15:9 and 24:15). In other words, lines 16–17 describe the "better" option; lines 12–15 the "worse." Deuteronomy thereby explicitly emphasizes the voluntary nature of a vow, reinforcing this in line 19—"because you made your vow freely to the LORD your God with your own mouth," using the cultic term נְדָבָה, which in Deut 12:6, 17; 16:10 designates a "freewill offering." In line 7 ("Do not let your mouth lead you into sin"), Qoheleth may pick up the term "sin" in לַחֲטִיא from the Deuteronomy parallel, since elsewhere Ecclesiastes primarily uses the verb as a participial noun (חוֹטֵא; see Eccl 2:26; 7:26; 8:12; 9:2, 18; the only exception is in 7:20). Both texts emphasize the mouth as the instrument of sin-producing vows. Lines 7 and 19 both refer to "your mouth" (פִּיךָ), while line 10 refers to "your voice" (קוֹלְךָ) and line 18 refers to "your lips" (שְׂפָתֶיךָ). In Ecclesiastes, the expression "your mouth" resumes 5:1[2]: "Do not be quick with your mouth, do not be hasty in your heart to utter anything before God." This sets up an ironic word pair—the fool is both too quick to speak and too slow to act.

Although acknowledging Qoheleth's dependence on the law of the vow in Deuteronomy 23, some commentators view the two texts as expressing different attitudes toward making vows. That is, whereas Deuteronomy emphasizes, even encourages, making vows, Ecclesiastes emphasizes *not* making, even discourages making vows.[37] This goes beyond the textual data, however, since Qoheleth is merely warning against making *rash*, literally, *hasty*, vows (Eccl 5:1[2]), rather than warning against making vows altogether.

What about Shields' stronger claim that the differences in wording between Deuteronomy 23 and Ecclesiastes 5 indicate that Qoheleth is, at most, distancing himself from the Torah or perhaps even unaware of the pentateuchal material?[38] Shields can claim this because he sees no significance involving literary dependence in the closeness of the verbal correspondence and because he reads the divergences between the two texts in light of his conclusions from the book as a whole regarding God's transcendence, inaccessibility, and capriciousness. Instead,

---

37. So Crenshaw, *Ecclesiastes*, 117; Murphy, *Ecclesiastes*, 50; Seow, *Ecclesiastes*, 200. Many scholars see in Eccl 4:17–5:6[5:1–7] a sweeping "Religionskritik" questioning the utility of sacrifices, prayer, and vows.

38. Shields, *The End of Wisdom*, 162. Shields implausibly downplays the significance of the Deuteronomy 23 parallel by arguing that vows "were made throughout the ancient Near East, so the practice in Israel . . . in Qoheleth's time need not have been governed by the stipulations made in the Pentateuch" (ibid.).

I would conclude that Qoheleth has quoted the law of the vow from Deuteronomy 23 to illustrate what can happen when one fails to exercise due caution when approaching the house of God, thereby offering "the sacrifice of fools" (Eccl 4:17[5:1]) rather than listening. The rashly promised vow offering is the fools' sacrifice. Beginning with a near-verbatim quotation in 5:3[4] to signal the Deuteronomic source, the sage then modifies the borrowed text to fit into its new context in 4:17–5:6[5:1–7] and to conform it to wisdom style and emphases.

2.5. Links between Ecclesiastes 5 and the Deuteronomistic History

Ecclesiastes 5 is not only dependent on Deuteronomy 23, but there are also striking intertextual links between this passage and the so-called "Deuteronomistic History." Perdue suggests that Eccl 4:17[5:1] ("Go near to listen rather than to offer the sacrifice of fools, who do not know that they do wrong"), especially the initial clause (וקרוב לשמע מתת הכסילים זבח), alludes to Saul's rash deed, as rebuked by Samuel in 1 Sam 15:22—"Does the LORD delight in burnt offerings and sacrifices as much as in obeying the LORD? To obey is better than sacrifice, and to heed is better than the fat of rams." Two words used twice in 1 Sam 15:22 (זבח 'sacrifice', שמע 'obey' [lit. 'hear']) also occur in Eccl 4:17[5:1], in addition to the expression "Does the LORD delight . . . ?" (החפץ ליהוה), which parallels "there is no pleasure" (אין חפץ) in Eccl 5:3[4].[39] The use of the term שגגה 'mistake' in Eccl 5:5[6] may be a further intertextual link to the OT legal material (to Leviticus 4–5 or Numbers 15 where it also occurs repeatedly, rather than to Deuteronomy), but J. Barbour suggests, instead, that it is an additional allusion to Saul's foolish reign (see Eccl 10:5—"the sort of error [also שגגה] that arises from a ruler"), since Saul admits in 1 Sam 26:21, "Surely I have acted like a fool and have been terribly wrong" (NIV); "have committed a serious error" (NASB; Heb. שגה).[40] These verbal links to 1–2 Samuel and to pentateuchal legislation lend support to the disputed claim that Ecclesiastes is theologically "mainstream" rather than "unorthodox."

---

39. L. G. Perdue, *Wisdom and Cult: A Critical Analysis of the Views of Cult in the Wisdom Literatures of Israel and the Ancient Near East* (SBLDS 30; Missoula, MT: Scholars) 182. Perdue incorrectly lists the parallel verse as 1 Sam 15:27.

40. See the more detailed study of this parallel by J. Barbour (" 'Like an Error which Proceeds from the Ruler': The Shadow of Saul in Qoheleth 4:17–5:6," in *Thinking Towards New Horizons: Collected Communications to the XIXth Congress of the International Organization for the Study of the Old Testament, Ljubljana 2007* [ed. M. Augustin and H. M. Niemann; Frankfurt am Main: Peter Lang, 2008] 121–28).

2.6. Additional Links between Ecclesiastes 5 and Deuteronomy

The enigmatic reference to a dream in Eccl 5:2, 6[3, 7] has also prompted scholars to seek to identify an intertextual allusion here: "Much dreaming and many words are meaningless.... Therefore fear God." Given our focus on intertextual connections with Deuteronomy, one finds attractive C. Gutridge's suggestion that the "comparison in Qoh. 5.3, 7 of dreaming with talking too much seems to imply that false (and maybe even superfluous) words are as odious as the false dreams of Deut. 13.1–5."[41] In comparing these two texts, it is interesting to note that in both Eccl 4:17–5:6[5:1–7] and Deut 13:2–6[1–5], dreams and words (of the prophet in Deuteronomy 13) are contrasted with revering God and keeping his commands.[42]

There are additional possible intertextual links between Eccl 4:17–5:6 [5:1–7] and Deuteronomy. "God is in heaven and you are on earth" in 4:17[5:1] parallels Deut 3:24 and 4:39 ("Acknowledge and take to heart this day that the LORD is God in heaven above and on the earth below"). Antoon Schoors is quite certain about the nature of the intertextuality here: "There can be no doubt that Qoheleth here deliberately adapts Deuteronomy 4:39 converting a saying about God's unicity [sic for "ubiquity"?] in heaven and on earth into a sharp contrast between God and man."[43] Whereas Deuteronomy's God is active "in heaven *and* on earth," Qoheleth's God is remote and unreachable.[44] Deut 26:15 and 33:26, however, similarly emphasize only God's heavenly location, while Qoheleth repeatedly notes God's involvement with those on earth, emphasizing the good gifts—as well as the burdens—he gives to humanity (Eccl 2:26, 5:18[19], 6:2, 8:15, 12:7). The "anger" of God aroused by insincere vows, according to Eccl 5:5[6] (יִקְצֹף), is also mentioned in Deut

---

41. C. A. Gutridge, "The Sacrifice of Fools and the Wisdom of Silence: Qoheleth, Job and the Presence of God," in *Biblical Hebrews, Biblical Texts: Essays in Memory of Michael P. Weitzman* (ed. A. Rapoport-Albert and G. Greenberg; JSOTS 333; The Hebrew Bible and its Versions 2; Sheffield: Sheffield Academic, 2001) 86–87.

42. This suggestion is more convincing than that of H. Tita, who sees in this passage an intertextual allusion to the narrative of Solomon's dream in Gibeon (1 Kgs 3:5, 15) (H. Tita, "Ist die thematische Einheit Koh 4,17–5,6 eine Anspielung auf die Salomo-Erzählung?" *BN* 84 [1996] 87–102. The "dream" in Ecclesiastes 5 appears to be used negatively, since it is associated in v. 6[7] with what is "meaningless" (Heb. הבל), while Solomon's dream is to be viewed positively. See also R. Fidler, who instead sees the Jacob-Bethel dream tradition as the primary intertextual referent here (R. Fidler, "Qoheleth in 'The House of God': Text and Intertext in Qoh 4:17–5:6 [Eng. 5:1–7]" *Hebrew Studies* 47 [2006] 7–21).

43. A. Schoors, "(Mis)Use of Intertextuality in Qoheleth Exegesis," in *Congress Volume Oslo 1998* (ed. A. Lemaire and M. Sæbø; SVT 80; Leiden: Brill, 2000) 51.

44. See, for example, Lauha, *Kohelet*, 98–99.

1:34; 9:7, 8, 19, 22; 29:27[28], there provoked by Israel's rebellious disobedience and doubt. According to Deuteronomy, divine wrath threatened to destroy God's people; according to Ecclesiastes, divine wrath can result in the destruction of the "work of your hands" (את־מעשׂה ידיך). Deuteronomy uses the same expression to describe the product of human activity in Deut 16:15 and 24:19 (both also in the plural), as well as the similar expression using the singular "hand" (see Deut 2:7, 14:29, 28:12, 30:9, all references using כל 'all'). None of these three examples involve strong verbal links with Deuteronomy, but each nevertheless contributes to the overall impression that Ecclesiastes resonates with various aspects of Deuteronomic theology.

3. Conclusion

Taken together, the intertextual connections that I have discussed suggest that the book of Deuteronomy was quite influential on the thinking of both Qoheleth and the final author/editor of the book of Ecclesiastes. Why would a sage cite the law of the vow from Deuteronomy 23? The juxtaposition of Eccl 4:1–16 with 4:17–5:6 [5:1–7] may provide a hint. Eccl 4:1–16 is a gloomy section that describes societal fractures without offering any solutions or even mentioning God, while 4:17–5:6 [5:1–7] mentions God six times and employs imperative verb forms for the first time in the book. Perhaps by this juxtaposition Qoheleth may be indicating that the addressee of his book may be moved, like Jephthah in Judges 11, to utter a vow in order to leverage God's assistance in the midst of a puzzling and impersonal world, prompting the first admonition issued in the book. This would parallel the additional warnings in 7:16–17 against resorting to the kind of extreme behavior that will not protect against injustice but might instead provoke divine punishment.

Is Qoheleth's world a moral chaos in which one cannot know anything for certain, as often claimed, or does it rather operate according to the Deuteronomic pronouncements regarding covenantal blessings and curses? It would go beyond the scope of this essay to seek to address this fully here, and there may be insufficient textual evidence in Ecclesiastes for a definitive answer to this question. This study, at least, has argued that Qoheleth and the book of Ecclesiastes as a whole affirm some central covenantal claims of the book of Deuteronomy. It is clear, for example, that disobeying the instructions in Deuteronomy 23 regarding making vows can bring an *individual* under divine judgment, because, in the words of Qoheleth, "it will go better with those who fear God" but "it will not go well with" the wicked (Eccl 8:12–13). In the meantime, the authors of both Deuteronomy and Ecclesiastes[45] strongly urge their listeners to rejoice before God as they enjoy his everyday blessings of food and drink, spouse, and life itself: "There, in the presence of the LORD your God, you and your families shall eat and shall rejoice in everything you have put your hand to, because the LORD your God has blessed you" (Deut 12:7); "Go, eat your food with gladness, and drink your wine with a joyful heart, for God has already approved what you do" (Eccl 9:7).[46]

---

[45]. In light of the Solomonic persona that clearly underlies Qoheleth's description in Ecclesiastes 2–3 of his efforts and achievements, it is intriguing to note that the Solomonic era is characterized in 1–2 Kings as a time when "they ate, they drank and they were happy" (1 Kgs 4:20).

[46]. See also Deut 12:12, 18; 14:26; 16:11, 14, 15; 24:5; 26:11; 27:7; 33:18; Eccl 2:10; 3:12, 22; 5:18–19[19–20]; 8:15; 10:19; 11:8–9.

The Influence of Deuteronomy on Intercessory Prayers in Ezra and Nehemiah

Gary V. Smith

The purpose of this study is to discover how the theology of Deuteronomy impacted the writings of Ezra and Nehemiah.[1] Since the text of Ezra–Nehemiah does not always indicate when it is alluding to a passage in the Torah, the first goal will be to set some criteria that will help identify when a later author is depending on another text. Next, it will be important to identify the importance of the Torah in Jerusalem at the time of Ezra and Nehemiah.[2] This will provide a general impression about the Israelite's knowledge of God's statutes and the importance of the "Law of Moses" in the ministry of Ezra and Nehemiah. Then the intercessory prayers in Ezra 9:1–15 and Neh 1:5–11 will be examined to discover if they have any verbal similarities with phrases in Deuteronomy. This should indicate (a) how much and what part of the theology

---

Author's Note: It was a pleasure to teach with Daniel Block for 22 years (10 in Canada at Winnipeg Bible College and Seminary and 12 at Bethel Theological Seminary). His enthusiasm for research, teaching, and preaching has been an example to us all. May this brief study further his emphasis on the key role Deuteronomy played in the life of the righteous Israelite, in later writers' theological conception of Israel's covenant relationship with God, and in our own devotion to the great and awesome God portrayed in Deuteronomy.

1. This article is based on the assumption that the author of Ezra–Nehemiah was not the Chronicler and that both books were written by one person using the Ezra and Nehemiah memoirs. This conclusion was reached on the basis of the evidence provided by S. Japhet, "The Supposed Common Authorship of Chronicles and Ezra–Nehemiah Investigated Anew," *VT* 18 (1968) 330–71 and H. G. M. Williamson, *Israel in the Book of Chronicles* (Cambridge: Cambridge University Press, 1977) 5–15.

2. The exact content of the "Law of Moses" will not be addressed; it will be assumed that it contained basically what is found in the Pentateuch today. H. G. M. Williamson critiques the views of U. Kellermann, who thinks that this "law book" was Deuteronomy and that it did not contain any narrative accounts, and C. Houtman, who thinks the laws were of a character different from the Pentateuch (*Ezra, Nehemiah* [WBC; Waco: Word: 1985] xxxvii–xxxix). Williamson rejects both approaches and accepts the idea that the "laws of Moses" was "similar to, if not identical with, our Pentateuch" (xxxix).

345

of Deuteronomy influenced these prayers, and (b) how the theology of Deuteronomy was adapted or recontextualized in this new setting.

1. Criteria for Defining Verbal Connections

It is sometimes difficult to prove that an author is consciously quoting from another text. Explicit markers for inner-biblical references are rare in the Hebrew Bible. In a few cases, a biblical author will actually tell the reader that he is referring to words from another scroll (e.g., Jer 26:18 quotes from Micah's message in Mic 3:12).[3] In other cases, the author may introduce a quotation with לאמר 'saying'.[4] Most often, however, the literary or theological influence is unannounced. Modern concepts of making an exact quotation were not a literary ideal that weighed heavily on the minds of biblical authors, so modern standards cannot be applied to biblical quotations. Therefore, scholars must examine the "verbal similarities" between two different texts to find evidence of literary borrowing. These may include instances of extensive verbal correspondence as well as examples where an author merely makes a brief allusion to what is written in another text. An allusion is present when an author refers to ideas or terms from an earlier text, but does not provide an extended reproduction of its words.[5]

After analyzing a number of verbal similarities, it becomes apparent that an author may choose to appropriate language from an earlier text in a few ways. He (or she) may draw ideas or language directly from another scroll, or he may simply make a general reference from memory to an idea found in another scroll, but not an exact reproduction. In some instances a theological concept may draw its inspiration from earlier writings, but the later author may purposely change the language or idea in the process of recontextualizing to the new situation in a later period. Of course, a phrase or a theological idea may coincidentally resemble another text (particularly formulaic phrases or common themes) without the author's direct consciousness of the wording or

---

3. Compare the reference to Jer 25:11 or 29:10 in Dan 9:2, where Daniel refers to the seventy years from "the word of the LORD to Jeremiah the prophet" (Dan 9:2).

4. Neh 1:8, considered below, calls God to "remember the word which you commanded your servant Moses, saying," implying that an allusion or quotation of what Moses said would come after the word לאמר 'saying'.

5. See E. Miner, "Allusion," *The New Princeton Encyclopedia of Poetry and Poetics* (ed. A. Preminger and T. V. F. Brogan; Princeton, NJ: Princeton University Press, 1993) 38–39. Although it is impossible to enter the minds of authors to understand how conscious they were of the allusions they were making, it is possible to make general conclusions based on the texts they produced. If several words in a phrase are the same, one can be fairly certain that the author was dependent on the earlier text.

content of the other passage. Although it may not always be possible to identify the exact nature of the connection between two similar passages, when several words are identical in both texts, one can propose some level of literary and theological influence.

Several scholars have established guidelines for approaching verbal parallels. Richard Hays proposed seven practical tests that can be applied to instances of similar language in order to identify one as an allusion from an earlier text.[6]

1. Availability: Did the author have access to this source text?
2. Volume: How extensive is the explicit repetition?
3. Recurrence: Are there recurrent places where the texts are the same?
4. Thematic Coherence: Do the words mean the same thing in both passages?
5. Historical Plausibility: Would the later text be understood as echoing the earlier one?
6. History of Interpretation: Do others recognize this as an allusion?
7. Satisfaction: Does this allusion help one understand the surrounding narrative?

These criteria help establish purposeful borrowing, but they do not enable one to identify why a later author might wish to make an allusion to an earlier document. Benjamin Sommer has suggested that an author may want to make an allusion: (a) to acknowledge an earlier idea or assert influence on the point he was making; (b) to affirm his closeness to (agreement) or distance from (disagreement) an earlier idea; (c) to affirm a knowledge base shared with an audience; or (d) to display his erudition.[7] In his study of Isaiah, Sommer found instances of typological links and echoes, as well as examples where earlier texts were reversed, prophecies were repeated (sometimes with historical recontextualization), and prophecies were declared fulfilled. But some of Sommer's specific examples of allusions in Isaiah are problematic

---

6. R. B. Hays, *Echoes of Scripture in the Letters of Paul* (New Haven, CT: Yale University Press, 1989), 29–32. Some of these criteria (points 4 and 5) are difficult to determine. For example, how can one determine if readers would understand one text as echoing another? Is it not the author's understanding of the echoing factor that is the real issue, not the understanding of different audiences (some might understand an echo, while others would not).

7. Sommer, *A Prophet Reads Scripture*, 219–20; idem, "Allusions and Illusions: The Unity of the Book of Isaiah in Light of Deutero-Isaiah's Use of Prophetic Tradition," *New Visions of Isaiah* (ed. R. F. Melugin and M. A. Sweeney; JSOTSup 214; Sheffield: Sheffield Academic Press, 1996) 156–86, where examples of various kinds of reworked allusions are found in Isaiah.

because his method of identifying verbal similarities is based on four stylistic characteristics that do not always function as strong indicators of an allusion.[8] In addition, it should be expected that some similarities between two passages will be coincidental and not conscious reproductions of another text, while other similarities can be attributed to the use of formulaic language rather than one author quoting another.

Three steps need to be taken when examining passages that appear to include verbal similarities with other texts. First, one should illustrate or identify the characteristics of the similarities (e.g., grammatical, syntactical, semantic, length of quote). Second, one should attempt to hypothesize the direction of borrowing, even though there is a great danger of circular reasoning and a deceptive tendency to base conclusions on theological assumptions. Sometimes phrases, ideas, words, or stylistic patterns that are characteristic of one source, but not of the other, can point to the original source of a phrase. Third, one should identify the purpose for including this similar phrase in the later text. Was it included (a) to prove a point based on an earlier authoritative tradition; (b) to enhance the authority of the later speaker by showing that an earlier text/author approves of the same idea; (c) to claim the continuing validity of an idea in a new situation; (d) to reverse an outdated idea; or (e) to reinterpret or recontextualize an idea in a new historical or theological setting?[9]

Richard Schultz's thorough study of different ways scholars have dealt with quotations concluded that all verbal parallels involve some level of interpretation "since recontextualization inherently changes the meaning of words quoted."[10] In the new literary location, these words and phrases are being used in a different literary context and in a different historical situation. This may happen because what was originally said to an individual may later be applied to a nation (appli-

---

8. Ibid., 64–66, 93–96. The stylistic features Sommer identifies include the following (a) the breaking up of a pattern into two parts; (b) sound plays; (c) word plays; and (d) parallel word pairs, but some of these features produce "allusions" which are quite subjective and very questionable.

9. Some who have written on the exegetical reinterpretation of later authors include F. F. Bruce, "The Earliest Old Testament Interpretation," *OTS* 17 (1972) 37–52; P. Grech, "Interprophetic Reinterpretation and the Old Testament," *Augustinianum* 9 (1969) 235–30; R. Gordis, "Midrash in the Prophets," *JBL* 49 (1930) 417–22; M. P. Miller, "Targum, Midrash, and the Use of the Old Testament in the New Testament," *JSJ* 2 (1971) 29–82; G. V. Smith, "Paul's Use of Psalm 68:18 in Ephesians 4:8," *JETS* 18 (1975) 181–89; M. Fishbane, *Biblical Interpretation in Ancient Israel* (Oxford: Clarendon, 1985).

10. R. Schultz, *The Search for Quotations: Verbal Parallels in the Prophets* (JSOTSup 180; Sheffield: Sheffield Academic Press, 1999), 213.

cation variation), a statement may be changed into a command (grammatical variation), the setting of the audience is different (historical variation), the words will be used in a different literary environment (contextual variation), or a prayerful wish may be transformed into an eschatological promise (genre variation). Schultz's criteria for identifying a quotation include (a) "verbal and syntactical correspondence" between phrases in both texts and (b) "contextual awareness, including interpretive use," because awareness of the context of the borrowed phrase is essential to understanding how the phrase is being used in its new context.[11] He recommends both a diachronic approach that takes into consideration historical factors that influenced the quotation and a synchronic approach that pays attention to literary factors, the function of the quotation in its larger context, and the rhetorical impact of this persuasive technique.[12]

Some of these factors will be employed in the study of allusions from Deuteronomy in Ezra–Nehemiah, but before this issue is addressed, it is necessary to understand the role of the Torah in the life of the exiles during the time of Ezra–Nehemiah. Did these people have a copy of the Law of Moses to quote from and was it an authoritative source of information that Ezra and Nehemiah might draw on to guide them in their ministry? This information helps one become aware of the broader contextual use of the Torah outside of passages where it is quoted, and this evidence should provide valuable hints about the direction of borrowing.

2. The Importance of the Law of Moses

The likelihood of accurately identifying verbal allusions to an earlier text is increased in those places where there is concrete knowledge that the author had access to the document that may be quoted and that the audience was familiar with the scroll perhaps being used. In addition, the likelihood of discovering the direction of the borrowing is increased in those passages where the author is known to have access to an earlier scroll. Thus a possible allusion to something in Deuteronomy becomes a much greater probability if it can be shown that Ezra and Nehemiah had a copy of the Torah and if they read from it in public gatherings.

As one follows the story line of the historical events in these postexilic books, one discovers that the Hebrew people living in the province of Jehud (Judah) consulted the Law of Moses soon after they arrived back

---

11. Ibid., 222–27.
12. Ibid., 227–37.

from exile in Babylon (around 537 B.C.E.) as well as much later in the time of Ezra (458 B.C.E.) and Nehemiah (445 B.C.E.). For example, in the seventh month after the return to Jerusalem (possibly 536 B.C.E.), the people decided to build an altar in Jerusalem and offer sacrifices to God following the instructions "written in the law of Moses" (3:2).[13] This indicates an early dependence on a written source, but no specific locutions are quoted in this context. Later the leaders gathered the people together to celebrate the Feast of Booths and offered the appropriate daily sacrifices "according to the ordinances" (3:4) in the law, indicating the contemporary authority of the Torah and the people's knowledge of what it said. Later when the congregation celebrated the dedication of the temple building, the leaders appointed priests and Levites to carry out the worship at the temple according to what was "written in the book of Moses" (6:18).[14] All these examples demonstrate a strong dedication to maintaining the covenant relationship with God, a reverence for the authority of the law, and a practical dependence on the instructions that were written in the Torah.

Later when Ezra returned to Jerusalem (445 B.C.E.) one would expect to find literary connections between the Torah and what Ezra said and did, because he was a "scribe skilled in the law of Moses" (7:6, 11, 21) and his whole life was involved with studying, practicing, and teaching the statues and ordinances found in the "law of the LORD" (Ezra 7:10). The king also instructed Ezra to appoint judges who "know the laws of your God," and Ezra was to teach God's statues to any judges who were ignorant of these laws (7:25) because everyone was required to follow "the law of your God and the law of the king" (7:26). Later when interceding for those who had married foreign wives, Ezra identified sin as "forsaking your commandments" (9:10; cf. 9:14). Furthermore, when the people repented and desired to renew their covenant with God, they knew that this had to "be done according to the law" (10:3). All these examples suggest more than a passing familiarity with the

---

13. T. Eshkenazi observed that "The repetition of 'as it is written' in Ezra 3:4 [and 3:2b] stresses the theme of compliance with the definitive written documents" (*In an Age of Prose: A Literary Approach to Ezra–Nehemiah* [Atlanta: Scholars Press, 1988] 58). I emphasize that the people needed to offer sacrifices at the right place, on the right kind of altar, with the right kind of sacrifices, offered by the right priests (*Ezra, Nehemiah, Esther* [Cornerstone Biblical Commentary; Carol Stream: Tyndale House, 2010] 38). The only way the people could get everything right was to read the Law of Moses to find out what it specified.

14. M. Breneman concludes that these many references to the law point to "the centrality of God's revelation in 'the law of Moses'" (*Ezra, Nehemiah, Esther* [NAC; Nashville: B&H, 1993] 53).

law of God, plus a strong commitment to the practical application of the teachings of the Torah in this postexilic setting.

Later around 445 B.C.E., Nehemiah served in the political role as governor, not as a teacher of the law, so there are not as many references to the Torah in his memoirs. Nevertheless, his prayer in chapter 1 implies a general knowledge of the law of Moses because he connects the people's corrupt action with "not keeping the commandments, the statutes, or the ordinances which you gave to your servant Moses" (Neh 1:7).[15] Later Ezra the scribe took the scroll of the law and read to the people from early morning until midday (8:1–2), while the Levites explained the law to the people, probably using the more familiar Aramaic language (8:7–8). This brought weeping and revival because the people heard the words of the law and realized they were not obeying what God said (8:9). The next day Ezra read more of the Torah concerning the Feast of Booths (8:13), and he continued to read portions of the law of God every day for the rest of the feast (8:18). On the twenty-fourth day the reading of the law lasted a fourth of the day and the rest of the time was spent confessing their sins and worshiping God (9:1–3). In the long prayer in chapter 9, the author remembers that God gave the law at Mount Sinai (9:13–14) and the people's sin is identified as "not listening to your commandments" (9:16, 29), "casting your law behind their backs" (9:26), and not "paying attention to your commandments" (9:34). This revival led to the people taking "a curse and an oath to walk in God's law, which was given through Moses" (10:29) and supporting the worship at the temple by bringing the firstborn of their sons and cattle to God as instructed in the law (10:36, 12:44). Finally, at some point they read Deut 23:3–5 about the exclusion of Ammonites and Moabites, so they acted upon these instructions and excluded them (Neh 13:1–3).

This evidence from the memoirs of Ezra and Nehemiah demonstrates that Israel's leaders had a copy of the Torah scroll, and they actively promoted respect and obedience to it. Since Ezra was a teacher of the law, he frequently read God's laws in public and explained the importance of God's instructions to his postexilic audience. Nehemiah did not read the law publicly in any of these accounts, probably because that was not his role or responsibility. However, he often instructed and corrected the people when they acted contrary to the law. Though the present memoirs of Nehemiah never record him justifying his actions

---

15. I have commented elsewhere: "The prayer is heavily dependent on phrases from the book of Deuteronomy . . . demonstrating Nehemiah's extensive knowledge of the writings of Moses" (*Ezra, Nehemiah, Esther*, 106).

as governor based on Torah instruction (Neh 5:1–10, 13:10–29),[16] it is very evident that he knew what it said and aggressively forced people to follow what it said (13:15–22).

With this much emphasis on the law of Moses, one might expect that the memoirs of Ezra and Nehemiah might allude to passages from the law of Moses that they had recently read. Unfortunately, when this happens, neither leader indicates where they are reading in the Torah, so the interpreter is left to guess between likely passages. Nevertheless, these narratives make it abundantly clear that the Torah would be a likely source for some allusions, for it meets the criteria of availability, recurrent usage, thematic cohesion, and historical plausibility. The presence of the Torah in the Postexilic Period and the teaching role of Ezra make it evident that the borrowing direction was from the Torah to the writings of Ezra and Nehemiah. Although there are not that many direct quotations from the Torah in Ezra–Nehemiah, there is a concentration of theological ideas from Deuteronomy in the intercessory prayers of these two leaders.

3. Ezra's Intercessory Prayer (Ezra 9:5–15)

The historical setting of Ezra 9 is probably three days before the twentieth day of the ninth month (10:9), or about four and a half months after Ezra's arrival on the first day of the fifth month (7:9, 8:33). These four-and-a-half months were probably spent traveling around to various neighboring satraps delivering the king's instructions (8:36).[17] The reason for Ezra's prayer in this chapter was because "the people, the priests, and the Levites did not separate themselves from the people of the land," but intermarried with them (9:1–2), contrary to the direct command of God (alluding to the instructions in Deut 7:1–5). The

---

16. It is difficult to make any statements about Nehemiah because arguments from silence prove nothing. He may have used the law to justify his acts but never bothered to put this information in his memoirs. Surely his opposition to charging interest in chapter 5 and his strong insistence on not working on the Sabbath in chapter 13 were heavily influenced by what the law of Moses required.

17. F. C. Fensham discusses various solutions to the question, why did Ezra not know about this theological problem before the fourth month? (*The Books of Ezra and Nehemiah* [NICOT; Grand Rapids: Eerdmans, 1982] 123–24). Fensham believes Ezra did not attend to these problems earlier because he was traveling and not in Jerusalem, while J. M. Myers takes "those events" in Ezra 7:36 to refer to the ceremonies related to the Feast of Booths and believes that Ezra considered what to do about the mixed marriages for four months and now in chapter 9 he takes action on this problem (*Ezra, Nehemiah* [AB; Garden City, NY: Doubleday, 1965] 76). L. H. Brockington suggests the possibility that Neh 8:1–18 could be chronologically placed just before chapter 9 (*Ezra, Nehemiah, Esther* [NCB; London: Oliphants, 1969] 89).

Israelites were to be a holy people (Ezra 9:2, Exod 19:6, Deut 7:6), but some of them were unfaithful to their covenant commitments and married pagan foreigners. Ezra was shocked, astonished, and appalled at this news, so he tore his garments and pulled out some of his hair (9:3). Then at the time of the evening sacrifice (9:5) Ezra began to pray.

The genre of this prayer is a confession of sins, but it is uniquely structured to fit the circumstances of the exiles at this time.[18] The structure of this prayer includes the following: (a) a general confession of past sins that resulted in exile (9:6–7); (b) thankfulness for God's grace in allowing the beginning of a restoration at the present time (9:8–9); (c) a specific confession of their present sin of intermarriage with pagans (9:10–12); (d) a hortatory call to avoid additional divine anger (9:13–14), and (e) a doxology of praise to God (9:15). Since Deuteronomy does not contain a series of prayers of confession of sins, the author has not borrowed from that genre of material in Deuteronomy. Nevertheless, theological ideas from Deuteronomy are quoted in Ezra 9:11–12.

There are two explicit linguistic indications that Ezra is quoting an earlier text in this prayer. First, Ezra uses first-person singular pronouns ("I, we, our") throughout the prayer in 9:6–10, 13–15, but in 9:11–12 he uses second-person pronouns ("you, your"). This change in pronouns sets 9:11–12 apart as different from the rest of the prayer. Second, at the beginning of 9:11 Ezra formally indicates that he is quoting what God spoke though the prophets and introduces this material with "saying" (לאמר). Since Ezra attributes this teaching to the prophets, rather than any one prophet, one might expect this to be a formulaic comment made by several prophets rather than a quotation from one book. But these verbal similarities are classified not as a prophecy in this context, but as one of "God's commandments" in 9:10. An examination of the vocabulary and phraseology in 9:11–12 will illustrate the verbal similarities found in Ezra's prayer. The following comparison of words and phrases indicates places where earlier authors used similar language, especially phrases found in Deuteronomy.

1. In Ezra 9:11 the phrase הארץ אשר אתם באים לרשתה 'the land that you are entering to possess it' finds a strong basis in Deuteronomy, where it occurs twelve times with numerous slight variations from the text of Ezra. The closest example is Deut 4:5: הארץ אשר אתם באים שמה לרשתה. Variations include הארץ אשר אתה בא שמה לרשתה (Deut 7:1; 11:10, 29;

---

18. The prayer is unique because there is no petitioning for forgiveness of sins or for salvation from punishment; plus, as much as it is directed toward God, it has a certain hortatory character that is aimed at the ears of those listening to Ezra pray.

23:21; 30:16), האדמה אשר אתה בא שמה לרשתה (28:21, 63), and הארץ אשר אתם עברים שמה לרשתה (4:14, 6:1, 11:8, 11:11). The only thing that could have made this a more perfect match would be to include שמה 'there', which is so characteristic of this phrase in Deuteronomy. This variation may indicate the Ezra was not slavishly tied down by the text he was quoting, but expressed these ideas in good postexilic idioms that preserved the essence of the material.[19] The purpose of this quotation was likely to affirm his agreement with the Torah, which was considered authoritative by the community. By recontextualizing this belief in his postexilic setting, he was challenging the audience to affirm that the postexilic community (just like their ancestors who came up from Egypt) had entered into the land that God gave to his people as their possession. Thus the same divine requirements in the Torah were applicable to both groups. The historical setting has changed, but in this new situations God assured his covenant people that he intended for them to possess the same land.

2. The phrase "an unclean (נדה) land with unclean (נדה) peoples of the lands" has no exact parallel, but the vocabulary of uncleanness is characteristic of Leviticus 12 (unclean food), Leviticus 15 (unclean discharges), and Numbers 19 (unclean dead bodies).[20] The more common term for uncleanness is טמא (Lev 18:24–30), which appears at the end of Ezra 9:11. This word choice may be due to Ezra's priestly background and education.

3. The phrase "peoples of the lands" in Ezra 9:11 (עמי הארצות) is a common postexilic formula that refers to non-Israelites living around Jerusalem in the historical era of Ezra–Nehemiah (cf. Deut 28:10). The use of this term recontextualizes earlier references to the vile behavior and uncleanness of the Canaanite and Amorites that lived in the land when the Israelites originally entered the land (Lev 18:6–30, 20:22–27). The problem of spiritual uncleanness is basically the same, though the ethnicity of the people is different and the sins that brought about this uncleanness may vary from one group to the other.

4. Classifying the evil deeds of the nations (9:11) as "abominations" (תבעות) alludes to common terminology in Deuteronomy (7:25; 12:31; 13:15[14]; 17:1, 4; 18:9, 12; 22:5; 23:19[18]; 24:4; 25:16; 27:15) and in Prov-

---

19. It is hard to know if this change was purposeful or accidental, if it represents a later style of speaking, or if it is a simple attempt to avoid unnecessary repetition.

20. In Leviticus 15 נדה 'uncleanness, defilement' usually refers to a woman's time of menstruation, which made her unclean, and in Leviticus 19 it refers to "impure" water; as such, Ezra's word choice here is unusual. In 2 Chr 29:5 this word describes the "uncleanness" of the temple due to Ahaz's defilement of the temple area.

erbs (6:16; 11:1, 20; 12:22; 15:8, 9, 26; 16:5, 12). Since Ezra–Nehemiah is not a wisdom text, it seems more likely that these authors were drawing on the usage of this term in Deuteronomy. The author could have chosen many different terms to describe the iniquity of the Samarians, who worshiped pagan gods as well as the God of the Israelites (Ezra 4:1–5). But since the word "abominations" (תועבות) in Deuteronomy frequently refers to the worship of graven images (Deut 7:25, 13:14–15, 17:1–4, 27:15) and terrible pagan rituals like burning children for pagan gods (12:31, 18:9–12), it would be a fitting term to describe the vile practices of the people of the land in Ezra's day.

5. Ezra 9:12 begins, "Do not give your daughters to their sons, and their daughters you shall not take for your sons" (בנותיכם אל תתנו לבניהם ובנתיהם אל תשאו לבניכם), which is very similar to Deut 7:3, "You shall not give your daughters to their sons, and their daughters you shall not take for your sons" (בתך לא תתן לבנו ובתו לא תקח לבנך). This clause appears to be an extended allusion that rises to the level of being a modified quotation. Most of the terms are the same, though the subject of the verbs and the pronominal suffixes are singular in Deuteronomy (referring to the nation as a whole), but plural in Ezra because he wanted to apply these words to the individuals who had committed these sins. These grammatical changes, plus the use of a different verb (לקח 'to take') indicate that making an exact copy (a modern definition of a quotation) was not Ezra's main desire; instead, he was motivated to communicate these thoughts in terms that people would easily recognize as deuteronomic. The purpose of this quotation was probably to affirm his commitment to the marriage principles and theological standards found in the Torah. Time and historical circumstances had changed, but the essence of God's instructions about marriage remained essentially the same.

6. The next clause in Ezra 9:12 is the phrase ולא תדרשו שלמם וטובתם עד עולם 'you shall not seek their peace and prosperity forever', which is nearly identical to Deut 23:7[6] לא תדרש שלמם וטבתם כל ימיך לעולם 'you shall not seek their peace and prosperity all your days, forever'. This too qualifies as a quotation, which further affirms Ezra's dependence on and consistency with Mosaic theological teachings, but these instructions meant two quite different things. In Deuteronomy this meant that the Israelites should kill all the Canaanites when they enter the land, because if they intermarried with them and sought to have peace with them, this might encourage some Israelites to worship their pagan gods (7:1–7). But in Ezra's day there are no instructions to annihilate completely the Samarians living in the land around Jerusalem; instead,

this command implies that those Israelites who returned from exile in Babylon should not allow the Samarians to help them build the new temple in Jerusalem (4:1–5) and that they should not intermarry with any of the non-Israelite people living in the territory surrounding Jerusalem (9:1–4). The means of accomplishing God's will had changed, but the principle of not seeking to further the prosperity of non-Israelites was still valid, for Deuteronomy clearly states that this standard should remain in effect "all your days, forever."

7. Next in Ezra 9:12 comes the phrase למען תחזקו 'in order that you may be strong', which is the same as a phrase in Deut 11:8. Ezra was identifying the needs of his generation with similar problems in an earlier setting when the Israelites first came into the land, and he saw a similar need for God's strengthening. Brief phrases like this tend to be rather formulaic, so some might argue that it is not an allusion to anything from Deuteronomy. Nevertheless, since Ezra was reading from Deuteronomy at that time and the identical phrase is found in the midst of other allusions from Deuteronomy, it seems likely that this phrase was derived from the same source as the other allusions.

8. There are no exact parallels to the last two clauses in Ezra 9:12: ואכלתם את טוב הארץ והורשתם לבניכם עד עולם 'and you shall eat the good (things) of the land, and you shall cause (it) to be a possession for your children forever', though Deut 6:10–11, 8:7–10, and 15:11 describe the good things the nation will inherit. Also, in several places Deuteronomy refers to their sons possessing the land forever. These include Deut 12:28, למען ייטב לך ולבניך אחריך עד עולם 'in order that it may go well with you and your children after you forever', and 6:18, ועשית הישר והטוב בעיני יהוה למען ייטב לך ובאת וירשת את הארץ הטבה 'do the right and good thing in the eyes of the LORD that it may go well with you and that you may possess the good land'. In this case the phrase in Ezra alludes to ideas in Deuteronomy, but it is appropriated creatively for a new purpose. Ezra seems to use this deuteronomic language as a motivation for changing the people's behavior. The earlier generations failed to follow God's instructions on marriage and their children did not inherit the land forever; instead, they lost the land and went into exile. Now this new postexilic generation has an opportunity to see this promise fulfilled in their day, if they listen to and follow the stipulations of the Mosaic covenant.

The verbal allusions to Deuteronomy in Ezra's prayer demonstrate that Ezra was primarily thinking about what the prophet Moses said. Several of his references to Deuteronomy can be classified as verifiable quotations. Others should probably be considered allusions, since there is no exact word-for-word comparison but only an amalgamation of ideas from Deuteronomy. Ezra's decision to use Moses' warning makes good theological sense in the context of this prayer of confession because the shame, guilt, and iniquities of the past era before the exile (9:7) were similar to the nation's present guilt (9:13). In both situations the people ended up forsaking God's commandments by not remaining separate from the unclean people living in Canaan (9:11–12, 14). Consequently, it is logical to think that a judgment similar to the past destruction of Judah (9:9) would lie somewhere in the near future (9:14–15) if the people do not confess their sins.

The parallelism between the two events gives robust theological and logical strength to the hortatory argument of the prayer. By reusing these past instructions from Moses and making them applicable to the present generation after the exile, Ezra has recontextualized the authoritative teaching of Moses to this new setting and applied them to the difficult situation the nation was facing during his ministry. The positive audience response to this prayer (10:1–4) testifies to the power of Ezra's rhetorical appeal, the authoritative status of the traditions he employed to support his argument, the validity of Ezra's recontextualization of these teachings, and the audience's acceptance of the applicability of these covenant traditions to their present situation.

4. Nehemiah's Intercessory Prayer (Neh 1:5–11)

The setting of Nehemiah's prayer is in the Persian citadel of Artaxerxes I at Susa around 445 B.C.E., in the twentieth year of the king's reign. As recently as three years earlier in 448 B.C.E. Artaxerxes I put down a rebellion by Megabyzus, the satrap of the Province beyond the River, but it is unknown if this involved or had any impact on the Israelite remnant that was living around Jerusalem.[21] That possibility is suggested by the report of an earlier attempt to rebuild the walls of Jerusalem in the reign of Artaxerxes I (Ezra 4:7–23). Not long after this rebuilding project started, the local officials successfully stopped this attempt to rebuild the walls of Jerusalem. It is impossible to make a direct connection between these events and the prayer of Nehemiah because it is not known if the events in Ezra 4:7–23 happened before, during, or after Megabyzus' revolt. Hanani describes the present state of the wall in Jerusalem by reporting that "the wall of Jerusalem is broken down and its gates are burned with fire" (Neh 1:2–3). He does

---

21. Fensham explains the revolt of Megabyzus against the Persians (*Ezra and Nehemiah*, 15–16, 149).

not say if these walls were destroyed by the Babylonian forces under Nebuchadnezzar in 587 B.C.E. (Jer 39:8, 2 Kgs 25:10) or if these walls were ruined after the stoppage of work on the wall in Ezra 4:21, 23.[22] In either case, because of instances of rebellion by people like Megabyzus, one can understand why Artaxerxes I would want to send a trusted person like Nehemiah to secure control of this part of his kingdom and make Jerusalem a Persian stronghold in the area (2:6–8).

F. C. Fensham identifies the genre of the prayer in 1:5–11 as a community lament, but it lacks the key element of lament or complaints (about his problems, about his enemies, or about God), so it might be better to call this a prayer of confession or intercession.[23] This fits the general flavor of 1:5–10, but the tone of this prayer is much more optimistic than Ezra's prayer. Another unique factor in this prayer is found in 1:11, where Nehemiah makes his personal request for God to assist him when he speaks to the king about the conditions in Jerusalem. The structural organization of the prayer includes the following elements: (a) an invocation or address to God (1:5); (b) an appeal for God to hear (1:6a); (c) a confession of sin (1:6b–7); (d) a petition for God to remember his covenant (1:8–10); and (e) a personal request for divine favor (1:11).

There are several allusions to earlier texts in the Torah in this prayer, but the most obvious one is introduced in 1:8–9 where Nehemiah asks God to remember what he earlier said to Moses. This allusion is introduced by לאמר 'saying' and includes subject and object pronouns referring to the second person "you," similar to what was found in Ezra 9:11–12. Another similarity between these prayers is that both Ezra and Nehemiah identify with their community, so they confess "our" sins (Neh 1:6b–7). An examination of the verbal similarities in this prayer will indicate which earlier texts Nehemiah alludes to in this prayer, especially those that come from Deuteronomy.

Neh 1:5 states, "O LORD, the God of heaven, the great and awesome God, who keeps the covenant and steadfast lovingkindness for those who love him and keep his commandments" (יהוה אלהי השמים האל הגדול והנורא שמר הברית וחסד לאהביו ולשמרי מצותיו). Similar language is found in Deuteronomy:

---

22. Williamson notes that the Persians caused the work to stop, but there is no record about what was done with the parts of the wall they had rebuilt (*Ezra, Nehemiah*, 64). D. J. A. Clines suggests that "it is reasonable to suppose" that they commanded that the rebuilt sections of the wall should be destroyed and that Neh 1:3 is referring to these ruins (*Ezra, Nehemiah, Esther* [NCBC; Grand Rapids: Eerdmans, 1984] 136).

23. Fensham calls this a lament (*Ezra and Nehemiah*, 153), while Breneman calls this a prayer of repentance (*Ezra, Nehemiah, Esther*, 171). C. Westermann suggests that the prayer of repentance took the place of the community lament in the postexilic era (*The Psalms: Structure, Content, and Message* [Minneapolis: Augsburg, 1980] 31).

The Influence of Deuteronomy on Intercessory Prayers

Deut 7:9	
יהוה אלהיך הוא האלהים האל הנאמן שמר הברית והחסד לאהביו ולשמרי מצותו	The LORD your God, he is God, the faithful God, who keeps covenant and his steadfast lovingkindness to those who love him and keep his commandments.
Deut 7:21	
יהוה אלהיך בקרבך אל גדול ונורא	The LORD your God is in your midst, he is a great and awesome God.
Deut 10:17	
כי יהוה אלהיכם הוא אלהי האלהים ואדני האדנים האל הגדל הגבר והנורא	For the LORD your God, he is God of gods and the Lord of lords, the great, the mighty and awesome God.

Although no passage in Deuteronomy was quoted verbatim, it is clear that Nehemiah's word choice was heavily influenced by common terminology from Deuteronomy. Nehemiah's purpose was to focus on the greatness of God and the great things he has done for his people (the return from exile was in some ways similar to the exodus from Egypt). In doing so he provided a connection between the attributes of the postexilic concept of the "God of heaven" and the preexilic covenant God of Deuteronomy. Similar phrases about God being "great and awesome" are found in Neh 4:8[14], 9:32, and Dan 9:4; and similar phrases about God being one "who keeps covenant and steadfast lovingkindness" in Deut 5:10, 1 Kgs 8:23, 2 Chr 6:14, and Dan 9:4. "God of heaven" is used four times in the first two chapters of Nehemiah (1:4, 5; 2:4, 20) and it is part of common formulaic postexilic terminology. In recontextualizing these phrases to his own situation, Nehemiah probably considered himself as one of those "who love him and keep his commandments," so this opening section of the prayer lays down his optimistic expectation that God would "keep his covenant and steadfast lovingkindness" with Nehemiah in the future.

2. Neh 1:6 says תהי נא אזנך־קשבת ועיניך פתוחות לשמע אל תפלת עבדך 'let your ears be attentive and open your eye to hear the prayer of your servant' is similar to 1:11 אנא אדני תהי נא אזנך־קשבת אל־תפלת עבדך 'O Lord, let your ears be attentive to hear the prayer of your servant'. These repeated phrases reveal the central focus of Nehemiah's concern in this intercessory prayer. Similar phrases are found in 1 Kgs 8:28–29, 2 Chr 6:40, and 7:15, when Solomon interceded for his people at the dedication of the first temple, and this may be the original source of Nehemiah's terminology. The short phrase ומתודה על־חטאות בני־ישראל 'confessing the

sins of the sons of Israel' (Neh 1:6) is like ומתודה חטאתי וחטאת עמי ישראל 'confessing my sins and the sins of the people of Israel' (Dan 9:20) and appears to be formulaic language used in postexilic confessions of sin.

3. In Neh 1:7 Nehemiah describes the people's sin as failure to keep "the commandments, the statutes, and the ordinances" (את־המצות ואת־החקים ואת־המשפטים), the very three words that Deut 5:31 and 6:1 exhort Israel to keep: המצוה החקים והמשפטים 'the commandments, the statutes and the ordinances'. Since this listing is so rare, this phrase appears to be a clear example of a quotation from Deuteronomy. Nehemiah wants to assert the authority of God's past revelation to Moses, so he uses language from Deuteronomy that summarizes all of God's instructions. Finally, the short phrase "which you commanded Moses your servant" (אשר צוית את־משה עבדך) in 1:7 and also 1:8 claims these words have the authority of Moses. By this statement Nehemiah admits that these Mosaic instructions still are applicable to himself and to the present generation of people living in Jerusalem.

4. The source of the quotation from Moses in Neh 1:8 does not exactly fit any one passage. "I will scatter you among the people" (אני אפיץ אתכם בעמים) is similar to both והפיץ יהוה אתכם בעמים 'The LORD will scatter you among the peoples' in Deut 4:27 and והפיצך יהוה בכל העמים 'The LORD will scatter you among all the peoples' in Deut 28:64. The grammatical changes from third person in Deuteronomy to first person are relatively minor, so there is little doubt about the source of this quotation.[24] The past scattering of the people into exile in 587 B.C.E. would verify in the minds of the audience that these earlier words were true; it happened just like Moses predicted so this was no empty threat.

5. Most of Neh 1:9 alludes to ideas from Deut 30:2, 4 as the following comparisons suggest. Nehemiah says, "If you return to me and keep my commandments and do them, and if you should be scattered to the end of the heaven, I will gather them from there and bring them." This is similar to Deut 30:2a, 4: "If you return unto the LORD your God and obey his voice according to everything I am commanding you this day. . . . If you should be scattered to the ends of the earth, from there the LORD your God will gather you and from there he will take you." The comparison below illustrates the verbal similarities and differences between Deuteronomy and Nehemiah's prayer.

---

24. Ezekiel as well cites Deuteronomy's warnings of exile, notably in Ezek 20:23, where he also changes the subject from third person to first person (see J. Gile, "Deuteronomy and Ezekiel's Theology of Exile," in this volume).

The Influence of Deuteronomy on Intercessory Prayers

Neh 1:9a	ושבתם אלי	ושמרתם	מצותי ועשיתם אתם
Deut 30:2a	ושבת עד יהוה אלהיך ושמעת בקלו ככל אשר אנכי מצוך היום		
Neh 1:9b	אם יהיה נדחכם בקצה השמים משם אקבצם		והביאתים
Deut 30:4	אם יהיה נדחך בקצה השמים משם יקבצך יהוה אלהיך ומשם יקחך		

Neh 1:9a	ESV: "but if you return to me and keep my commandments and do them"
Deut 30:2a	ESV: "and return to the LORD your God … and you obey his voice in all that I command you today"
Neh 1:9b	ESV: "though your outcasts are in the uttermost parts of heaven, from there I will gather them and bring them"
Deut 30:4	ESV: "If you outcasts are in the uttermost parts of heaven, from there the LORD your God will gather you, and from there he will take you"

These similarities suggest that Nehemiah was summarizing the theological issues from Deuteronomy in order to show that God faithfully did what he said he would do after scattering his people. The threat of scattering was proven true by the exile and the gathering was being fulfilled by the return of many exiles to Jerusalem. Nehemiah seems to be affirming and aligning himself with what God has said and done. He is not so much interested in the scattering, but in God's promise to gather.

6. The phrase אל המקום אשר בחרתי לשכן את שמי שם 'unto the place where I have chosen for my name to dwell there' in Neh 1:9c is characteristic of Deuteronomy, appearing in Deut 12:5, 11, 14, 26; 14:24, 25; 16:6; 17:8, 10; 18:6; 26:2, 9. This quotation focuses the audience's attention on what God promised about Jerusalem, the place of the temple where his presence dwells. This is one of the few passages that might be used to assert that the presence of the glory of the Lord that dwelt in the tabernacle (Exod 40:34–35) and the first temple (1 Kgs 8:10–11) was expected to dwell in the new temple built in Jerusalem after the exile.

7. The expression פדית בכחך הגדול ובידך החזקה 'you redeemed with your great power and with your outstretched hand' in Neh 1:10 is similar to Deut 9:26: פדית בגדלך אשר הוצאת ממצרים ביד חזקה 'you redeemed though your greatness, whom you brought out of Egypt with your strong hand" (cf. Exod 32:11, Deut 7:8, 9:29). Here Nehemiah compares God's great redemption of his people from Egypt in the first exodus and reapplies this idea to the new people who were redeemed from Babylon by God's great power.

These verbal connections between Deuteronomy and Nehemiah's prayer demonstrate that Nehemiah was heavily influence by the book of Deuteronomy, especially in Neh 1:8–9 where phrases are introduced as the words which Moses spoke. The comparison of Nehemiah's phraseology in Neh 1:9, "unto the place where I have chosen for my name to dwell," shows a strong dependence on the theology and wording of Deuteronomy. Several of his references to Deuteronomy can be classified as allusions because they are not an exact word for word quotation, but an amalgamation of ideas from Deuteronomy. Allusions to ideas and theological phrases related to Deuteronomy are also found in Neh 1:5–7 and 10. Thus, this whole prayer is soaked in vocabulary and theological concepts that come from a thorough knowledge of what God said in Deuteronomy. In light of this concentrated use of Deuteronomy's theology in this prayer, it is a little surprising that the memoirs of Nehemiah do not record him explicitly justifying his later reforms by quoting Deuteronomy's theology in Neh 5:1–13 (on charging interest) or 13:10–31 (on not giving the Levitical tithe, on working and selling on the Sabbath, and on intermarriage with pagans).[25] It is possible that Nehemiah chose to use his authority as governor to accomplish what he needed to do (since he was not a teacher of the law) or his infrequent use of Mosaic instructions may be due to the fact that the words of Moses were not very authoritative for many rebellious Israelites at this time. If this was the case, then an appeal to the theology of Deuteronomy would not have carried much if any rhetorical weight.

5. Deuteronomy's Theological Influence

A comparison of these two prayers shows that Ezra emphasizes the theology that Israel is sinful, guilty, and needs to confess her sins (Ezra 9:6–7, 13–15), while Nehemiah spends much less time confessing the nation's sins (Neh 1:7). Both prayers recognize that the people did not keep the laws given by Moses. Both prayers make observations about the past and about the present state of the nation, and both also look to the future. Ezra seems to be much more pessimistic about the past and the present, and has great fears that another great judgment of the

---

25. As a matter of history, the silence of the Nehemiah memoirs about his lack of use of Deuteronomy's theology merely means we do not have any record on this issue. Arguments from silence do not prove this issue one way or the other. He may have used the theology of Deuteronomy, but chose not to include that in his memoirs. The wording of Neh 13:25b certainly demonstrates that he was acting on the basis of Deut 7:3, though he never states in this context that Deuteronomy was the basis or source of his statement about "not giving your daughters to their sons."

nations looms in the near future. In contrast, Nehemiah seems to be much more optimistic, emphasizing God's greatness, steadfast lovingkindness, and preservation of the covenant (Neh 1:5). Nehemiah believes God will gather more of his people from the far corners of the world (1:9), because these are God's people (1:10) and because he has the power to redeem them. He expects a positive answer because God gives success to those who fear him (1:10).

The difference in attitude in these two prayers could be due to the historical events taking place in the social location of each man. In addition, there are some differences in the theological relationship between God and his people in these two different settings. Ezra was present in Jerusalem with the Israelites who had intermarried with the pagan people of the land, while Nehemiah was in Susa and realized that with God's help he might be able to change the future situation in Jerusalem through his relationship with the king (Neh 1:11). Nehemiah emphasizes the positive theological ideas that God keeps his covenant and God acts in steadfast love and power (1:5). He foresees the possibility of more people returning to Jerusalem (1:9), and he focuses on the wonder-working power of God that redeemed Israel in the past (1:10).

Ezra remembers only a brief time of seeing God's steadfast lovingkindness when the Persian king was gracious in allowing a brief revival of the nation (Ezra 9:9). Ezra's theological emphasis is on the shame, embarrassment, guilt, plunder, abominations, evil deeds, plus the anger of God. He even views the small reviving of the nation that has happened so far as a situation in which the people are still "slaves" in bondage to the Persians (9:9). Indeed, he is so pessimistic that he believes the nation was punished far less than it deserves (9:13), so he expects that this latest abomination might lead to a situation in which there will not even be a remnant of Israel left (9:14). It may be that this severe pessimism was adopted by Ezra as a preferable rhetorical style in order to motivate the listeners to understand the seriousness of their sins and to address this shameful situation head on (10:1–3).

Both of these theological emphases are based on ideas in Deuteronomy, for a positive covenant relationship engendered great hope because of the greatness of God's grace, power, and promises. Nevertheless, the other side of the coin is that covenant breaking holds out the expectation of devastating destruction for those who do not keep God's commandments and do not repent. Deuteronomy's explanation of the covenant puts these two ideas side by side. When the blessings are listed, they are balanced with warnings and curses for those who do not keep the covenant (Deut 6:10–11 vs. 12; 8:7–10 vs. 11–14; 11:26a, 27 vs. 11:26b, 17; 27:15–26 and 28:15–66 vs. 28:1–14, 67–68; and notably in 30:15–20). Deuteronomy predicted a future time of scattering of guilty unrepentant sinners to the ends of the earth, and Ezra recognized that Israel's past history of being scattered was a fulfillment of the covenant curses. Since the Israelites have now returned and are once again committing the same sins again, Ezra's emotional prayer of confession was aimed at those who were about to be judged again if they did not repent. He knew from Deuteronomy that repentance was necessary, if there would ever be any hope for the small remnant to escape another exile and stay in the land that God promised to his people (Deut 4:25–31, 28:58–68, 30:1–4). The situation of Ezra's audience determined how he should pray and the level of hope he should project concerning the future. The positive response of the audience in chapter 10 suggests that Ezra made a wise choice of words in his prayer. Those who gathered around Ezra comprehended the seriousness of their sin (10:1), which is exactly what they needed to do to remove their guilt (10:2a). The passionate prayer of this man accomplished much.

The negative and the positive sides of the covenant relationship in Deuteronomy are equally important; the key is to know the needs of the audience so that one can emphasize what is needed at the proper time. A few years later Nehemiah was not in front of a sinful Israelite audience in Judah, so he did not see the sinful acts that Ezra mentions, nor did he sense the hopelessness that Ezra felt. Nehemiah admitted that past sin was the core problem that resulted in the scattering of the nation of Israel (Neh 1:6–7), but he was much more interested in God's ability to gather his people and do awesome things through his strong outstretched arm (1:10). Deuteronomy's covenant theology provided a sound theological foundation for him to understand both the scattering and the gathering (1:9). Since he was unaware of any specific sin that was preventing God's blessing, similar to Ezra 9:12 (the intermarriage with pagans), Nehemiah takes responsibility for furthering the kingdom's reach by praying for God's new blessings among his people (the building of the walls of Jerusalem). His desire was for God to take away the reproach of the remnant in Jerusalem, for that was the spiritual need he was aware of (Neh 1:2–3). Thus one learns that at times God's people need to be shamed, humbled, and convicted of sin so that they will repent, but at other times they need to be uplifted and reminded of God's greatness and power so that they will have hope. In addition, one learns that a proper application of these verses in Deuteronomy requires a level of sensitivity to the rhetorical situation and relevant parallel circumstances of the audience.

Testing God's Son
Deuteronomy and Luke 4:1–13

GRANT R. OSBORNE

1. Introduction

The Synoptic Gospels include a triple-tradition event that is often tagged the "temptation narrative" (Mark 1:12–13, Matt 4:1–11, Luke 4:1–13),[1] but this title is a slight misnomer. The temptation centers only on Satan's part, and the devil is actually a tool of God in this story. As I. Howard Marshall points out, "The devil's role falls within the purpose of God."[2] Susan Garrett says, "It was (the spirit of) God who put Jesus into the wilderness to be tested. God has declared Jesus to be his son, and now God arranges for Satan to test Jesus to see whether he is worthy of that assessment."[3]

The actant throughout is God, as seen in the literary development of this initiation phase of Jesus' ministry. In Jesus' baptism God spoke from heaven for the first time and declared Jesus to be his "beloved son," echoing Ps 2:7, and the Holy Spirit descended on him "in bodily form like a dove" (Luke's emphasis [3:22], most likely to show this was

---

Author's Note: I began my teaching career with Dan Block in 1973–74 at Winnipeg Bible College and Theological Seminary. I have watched with pleasure his meteoric rise as one of the stellar OT scholars of our time. Thus it is a special privilege to dedicate this study to him. He has spent the last few years especially centered on Deuteronomy, and one of the premier uses of Deuteronomy in the NT takes place at the testing of Jesus as Son of God in Luke 4.

1. J. Nolland says, "The account is primarily concerned with identifying what constituted Satanic temptation for Jesus, affirming the fact of Jesus' steadfastness and reflecting on the significance of his success" (*Luke 1–9:20* [WBC 35A; Dallas: Word, 1989] 177). While I affirm that this is part of the message of the story, I do not believe it is the central theme.

2. I. H. Marshall, *The Gospel of Luke: A Commentary on the Greek Text* (NIGNTC; Grand Rapids: Eerdmans, 1978) 169.

3. S. R. Garrett, *The Temptations of Jesus in Mark's Gospel* (Grand Rapids: Eerdmans, 1998) 59. Garrett (pp. 20–49) provides an excellent discussion of God as the agent of testing and Satan as an agent of testing in Judaism. She concludes that God is in ultimate control, with Satan as "commander of the forces of chaos" (p. 49) and trying to do as much harm to God as possible.

an objective, true event and not just a visionary experience). There is a Trinitarian emphasis as the Son is anointed, not just by John the Baptist but by the Father and the Spirit. Jesus is announced by the Father and empowered by the Spirit to begin his ministry. The impelling presence of the Spirit behind Jesus' journey into the wilderness is stressed in Mark (1:12, "the Spirit sent him out") and Matthew (4:1, "led by the Spirit"), but Luke gives a double emphasis in 4:1, for as he is "led by the Spirit" and does so "full of the Spirit." As David Garland brings out, other instances of "filled with the Spirit" in Luke–Acts use the passive form of the verb to point to God as the giver of the Spirit (e.g., Luke 1:15, 41, 67; Acts 2:4; 4:8; 13:9), but with Jesus the adjective is utilized, meaning that Jesus is "the bearer of the Spirit and is anointed by the Spirit."[4] God is in charge of this scene, and he and the Spirit are testing the Son.

The literary form of this narrative is also a matter of debate. Since Rudolf Bultmann, it has been common to call this a haggadic midrash on Deuteronomy 6–9,[5] perhaps created by a later Christian scribe as a reflection on the Shema in Deut 6:5.[6] However, this is an overstatement, for Deuteronomy, while central, does not define the story as a whole. It is closer to see this as an example of a rabbinic dialogue form in which Scripture passages control the debate.[7] Many like Bultmann prefer to see this as one category, but these are slightly different sub-genres, and I prefer to keep them separate. There are some who doubt that the rabbinic dialogue form applies here on the grounds that this is a confrontation between Jesus and Satan rather than a scriptural debate.[8] However, especially in the third temptation Satan uses Ps 91:11–12, and Jesus responds with Deut 6:16. In both of the other temptations Jesus responds with Deut 8:3 and 6:16, respectively. Therefore, the rabbinic dialogue form provides a viable sub-genre for the story. Moreover, while there is a haggadic dimension, this is not a fictional event, as I will be arguing below.

---

4. D. Garland, *Luke* (ZECNT; Grand Rapids: Zondervan, 2011) 178–79.

5. R. Bultmann, *The History of the Synoptic Tradition* (trans. J. Marsh; 2nd ed.; Oxford: Blackwell, 1968) 254–57.

6. B. Gerhardsson, *The Testing of God's Son (Matt 4:1–11 & Par.): An Analysis of an Early Christian Midrash* (ConBNT 2.1; Lund: Gleerup, 1966) 7–18.

7. For example, *Sifre Deut* 307, a rabbinic debate; b. Sanh. 89b, between Abraham and Satan; *Deut Rab.* 11:5, between Moses and the Angel of Death. See C. A. Kimball, *Jesus' Exposition of the Old Testament in Luke's Gospel* (JSNTSS 94; Sheffield: JSOT Press, 1994) 95; H. A. Kelly, "The Devil in the Desert," *CBQ* 26 (1964) 190–220; N. H. Taylor, "The Temptation of Jesus on the Mountain: A Jewish Palestinian Polemic against Agrippa I," *JSNT* 83 (2001) 36.

8. Marshall, *Luke*, 166; D. L. Bock, *Luke 1:1–9:50* (BECNT; Grand Rapids: Baker, 1994) 367.

Luke places his genealogy here (unlike Matthew) and reverses the order of Matthew (who moves from Abraham up to Jesus) by proceeding from Jesus down to Adam in order to show Jesus not so much as royal Messiah (naming Nathan rather than Solomon and omitting most of the royal names of Matthew's list) but to stress first his human identity[9] and second his identity as "son of Adam, son of God." This Adamic dimension will be explored further below. Suffice it to say that the entire history of humanity is caught up and emancipated in Jesus the final and true "Son of God." The triadic emphasis on Jesus as "Son of God" in the baptism, genealogy, and testing narratives is a highlight of Luke's story. Further, Jesus undergoes the same testing as Israel did in the wilderness and as God's chosen people did throughout the OT. Abraham was tested by the "binding of Isaac" incident (Genesis 22), Moses was tested in the wilderness of Midian (Exodus 2–3), and Job was tested throughout his story.[10] Now Jesus is tested in the wilderness to see if he will be obedient and faithful to his Father.

2. Typological Motifs

There are three promise-fulfillment themes in Luke 4:1–13. These are often presented as competing paradigms, but I will argue that all three are present here and will list them in order of ascending importance (from the least to the greatest emphasis).

2.1. Jesus as a New Adam

The Adamic connection is the least pronounced of the analogies, but it is nevertheless present. In fact, Craig Evans sees the Adamic motif as the primary "new significance" of Luke's story here: "Whereas the first son of God fell into sin because of his failure to obey the command of God, the second Son of God remained faithful to God's commands."[11] While Craig Evans overstates the centrality of the Adamic typology, it is still present. Don Garlington sees two bases of this: (1) the presence of new creation ideas in the baptism account, as Jesus' coming inaugurates a new world order; (2) Luke's deliberate placement of his genealogy between the baptism and testing narratives, thereby "merging the phrase 'Son of God' with Adam (3:38)."[12] Adam and Eve went through the same temptations as Jesus. In Gen 3:6 as the result of the

---

9. F. Bovon, *Luke 1:1–9:50* (Hermeneia; Minneapolis: Fortress, 2002) 137.
10. See Garrett, *Temptations*, 59–60.
11. C. A. Evans, *Luke* (NIBC; Peabody, MA: Hendrickson, 1990) 67.
12. D. B. Garlington, "Jesus the Son of God: Tested and Faithful," *BSac* 150 (1994) 288. See also A. Feuillet, "Le récit lucanien de la tentation (Lc 4, 1–13)," *Bib* 40 (1959) 613–31.

serpent's "crafty" seduction, Eve saw that the forbidden fruit was "good for food" (similar to the first temptation), "pleasing to the eye" (similar to the second temptation), and "desirable for obtaining wisdom" (similar to the third temptation).[13] Justo Gonzales says, "Jesus is tempted in the wilderness much as Adam was tempted in the Garden" so that "the entire passage reminds us of" Adam's temptation.[14] Joseph Fitzmyer calls all attempts to establish a "New Adam motif" here "highly eisegetical" since it lacks direct textual evidence from Luke; instead he strongly prefers Israel typology here.[15] However, this is too disjunctive, and while secondary to the True Israel typology, the Last Adam theme is still present in this pericope.

2.2. Jesus as the New Moses

This is more pronounced in Matthew, where in the third temptation the devil took Jesus "on a very high mountain" (Matt 4:8), probably recalling Moses on Mount Nebo as he surveyed the promised land (Deut 34:1–4). Satan would then be offering Jesus what Moses failed to receive and more than Moses could ever conceive.[16] This motif is not so strong in Luke, which says simply that "the devil led him up to a high place" at the same place in this temptation (Luke 4:5). Still, the language in Luke 4:5 echoes Deuteronomy in that Satan's "showing" Jesus the world's kingdoms reflects Deut 34:1 where God "showed (Moses) the whole land." As William Stegner points out, "Luke's account quotes two additional words from the context—'all' and 'this'—found in Deut 34:1b and 4a, respectively."[17] This is even more pronounced in Jesus' forty-day fast mentioned in Luke 4:2, reflecting as it does Moses' forty-day fast at the giving of the Decalogue in Exod 34:28 and Deut

---

13. See the chart in G. R. Osborne, *Matthew* (ZECNT; Grand Rapids: Zondervan, 2010) 137. It is important to add my comment there: "Again it must be said that this is not intended by Matthew [or Luke here] and the parallels are theological rather than textual, but they are interesting." This is true also because these temptations are also paralleled by Israel in Deuteronomy 6–8.

14. J. L. Gonzales, *Luke* (BTCB; Louisville: Westminster John Knox, 2011) 56.

15. J. A. Fitzmyer, *The Gospel according to Luke I–IX* (AB 28; Garden City, NY: Doubleday, 1981) 512.

16. On the New Moses motif in Matthew, see D. C. Allison, *The New Moses: A Matthean Typology* (Minneapolis; Fortress, 1993). On this motif in Matt 4:8 see Gerhardsson, *Testing*, 62–64; D. A. Hagner, *Matthew* (2 vols.; WBC 33 A–B; Dallas: Word, 1993) 68; C. S. Keener, *A Commentary on the Gospel of Matthew* (Grand Rapids: Eerdmans, 1998) 41.

17. W. R. Stegner, "The Use of Scripture in Two Narratives of Early Jewish Christianity (Matthew 4.1–11; Mark 9.2–8)," *Early Christian Interpretation of the Scriptures of Israel: Investigations and Proposals* (ed. C. A. Evans and J. A. Sanders; JSSNTS 148; Sheffield: Sheffield Academic, 1997) 102.

9:9. Here Jesus "ate nothing," recalling Moses who "ate no bread and drank no water" in the Deuteronomy passages. In Deuteronomy Moses was fasting to prepare himself to receive revelation from God. In this instance Satan times his approach to the moment when Jesus is at his weakest and tries to take over God's role as revelatory agent.[18] Thus, Moses typology is an important ingredient in the story.

2.3. *Jesus as True Israel*

This is the primary motif and the central element, though it does not rule out the other two. Jesus deliberately chose his three responses from Deuteronomy 6–8, and each one recalls an incident in which Israel was tested in the same way as Jesus but failed the test. Jesus sees himself standing in the place of the nation as True Israel. As stated earlier, this scene centers on Jesus as Son of God, and in this he is the antitype of Israel, God's Son (e.g., Exod 4:22, Jer 31:9, Hos 11:1). As Birger Gerhardsson says, "The theme 'son of God' was deeply rooted in the traditional religious ideology of Israel. It was a favourite variant of the election and covenant themes," with Israel "thinking of itself as a chosen people, and as God's covenant people and as God's son."[19] Sonship connotes faithfulness and obedience. Israel failed on both scores, but Jesus as ideal Israel passes the test and becomes the faithful Son. R. T. France shows how central this typology is in the pericope: (a) both Israel and Jesus suffer hardship and hunger inflicted by God, with the forty days of Jesus' fast reflecting the forty years of Israel in the wilderness; (b) both endure the testing of a son (cf. Exod 4:22, Deut 8:5) intended to teach trust and obedience; (c) each of the three temptations as well as Jesus' responses follow this type/antitype pattern, so Jesus saw himself as True Israel being tested before his great messianic mission.[20] Jesus relived Deut 8:2, where Moses extolled the people to "remember how the LORD your God led you all the way in the wilderness these forty years, to humble and test you in order to know what was in your hearts, whether or not you would keep his commands."

It must be stressed that this is a messianic scene. Jesus is being tested not only as God's Son but also as the chosen Messiah who is about to begin his messianic mission to Israel and to the world.[21] All three Synoptic Gospels center on Jesus' coming as Messiah in their introductions. Mark

---

18. See Garland, *Luke*, 180.
19. Gerhardsson, *Testing*, 21.
20. R. T. France, *Jesus and the Old Testament: His Application of Old Testament Passages to Himself and His Mission* (Downers Grove, IL: InterVarsity, 1971) 51–53.
21. See also Kimball, *Exposition*, 90.

1:1 declares "the beginning of the good news about Jesus the Messiah, the Son of God," and Matt 1:1–7 starts with his genealogy presenting Jesus as the royal Davidic Messiah. Luke is not quite as direct but records very early the angel Gabriel telling Mary that her child would be "Son of the Most High" to whom God would give "the throne of his father David" and that "his kingdom will never end" (1:32–33). Luke also emphasizes three times Jesus' messianic nature. At Jesus' birth (2:11) the angel tells the shepherds that the "Savior" born is "the Messiah, the Lord." In 2:26 Simeon relates that the Holy Spirit had revealed to him that he would not die before seeing "the Lord's Messiah." And in 3:15–18 the Baptist relates that he is not the Messiah but rather has come to prepare for that greater One. In short, the testing of God's Son centers on Jesus beginning his messianic mission with victory over Satan and faithful obedience to his Father.

3. The Three Temptations: Introductory Issues

There are clearly two different renditions of the testing narrative: the short version in Mark 1:12–13 that narrates only the basic story of Jesus in the wilderness tempted by Satan; and the longer version of Matt 4:1–11 and Luke 4:1–13 that includes details on the three temptations themselves, commonly identified as part of the Q tradition. A few believe that these are separate traditions,[22] but the majority see the similarities between Luke and Mark (the impelling Spirit, the wilderness, tempted by Satan) and conclude correctly that Luke has combined Mark and Q.[23]

A more difficult question is the order of the temptations, for Matthew and Luke reverse the second and the third, with the result that Matthew concludes with the temptation on the high mountain and Luke with that on the pinnacle of the temple. It is commonly thought that Luke reversed Matthew for redactional reasons, since Jerusalem and the temple play so large a part in his Gospel and the book of Acts. Yet in Matthew mountains as the place of revelation and the glory of God are equally prominent,[24] so Robert Stein concludes that on the basis of redaction "which order is the original is uncertain."[25] Still, for several reasons Matthew is most likely the original order. It is Matthew,

---

22. See Taylor, "Temptation," 29.
23. See, for example, Marshall, *Luke*, 166–67; Fitzmyer, *Luke*, 506–7. Bovon says Mark's influence is "weak" but still present (*Luke*, 139).
24. See T. L. Donaldson, *Jesus on the Mountain: A Study in Matthean Theology* (JSNTSS 8; Sheffield: JSOT Press, 1985).
25. R. H. Stein, *Luke* (NAC; Nashville: Broadman, 1992) 145.

not Luke, who presents the Deuteronomy quotations in reverse order of the original (Deut 8:3 in 4:4; Deut 6:16 in 4:7; Deut 6:13 in 4:10). There is also a geographic/spatial progression in Matthew from the wilderness plain to the pinnacle of the temple to the high mountain. Luke has his own progression, changing the natural order of Q in order to climax with the temple temptation.

Luke's order quite possibly also intends to follow the development of Psalm 106, which after Psalm 105 on God's unending faithfulness to his people centers on Israel's failure to respond to God's good and mighty acts. After tracing God's wondrous deeds and saving power, the psalmist then recounts the extent of Israel's unbelief and rebellion (106:13–43). The bread temptation reenacts 106:13–15 that recounts Israel's murmuring over the manna and the quail in the wilderness (Exodus 15–17). The temptation to bow down before Satan reenacts Ps 106:19–23 and the incident over the golden calf in Exodus 32. The temptation to throw himself off the pinnacle of the temple reenacts Ps 106:32–33, which recounts the waters of Meribah when Moses hit the rock and disobeyed the Lord. The same order is followed by Paul in 1 Cor 10:6–9 as he traces the history of Israel's rebellion from eating and drinking (v. 7a) to idolatry (v. 7b) to testing God/Christ (v. 9).[26] It is possible that this order followed an early Christian catechetical tradition, but that is difficult to prove, and the Matthean order (as said above) is more likely original.

The question of history is also a critical issue. It is quite common to assume that this story was a fictional story made up by the early church to sum up the types of temptations they endured (the ethical side) and also to explain why Jesus never performed miracles to benefit himself (the Christological side). As stated above, form-critically the narrative is called a "haggadic midrash" written by a later Christian scribe.[27] Others, however, are not quite so quick to label this a fictive creation. Fitzmyer, for example, considers it impossible to establish the final historicity of the scene but finds it "difficult to ascribe the fantastic details to a communal popular imagination," as if the followers who had come to "venerate Jesus as the Son of God" could "fabricate" these kind of "fantasies ... out of whole cloth."[28] John Nolland has no problem

---

26. See H. F. G. Swanston, "The Lukan Temptation Narrative," *JTS* 17 (1966) 71; Evans, *Luke*, 68; Garland, *Luke*, 178.

27. See Bultmann, *Tradition*, 254–57; Gerhardsson, *Testing*, 11–13; P. Pokorny, "The Temptation Stories and Their Intentions," *NTS* 20 (1974) 115–27; W. R. Stegner, "The Temptation Narrative," *Biblical Review* 35 (1990) 5–17; Davies and Allison, *Matthew*, 1:353.

28. Fitzmyer, *Luke*, 509.

tracing the basic story back to Jesus himself.[29] There are several reasons for its basic veracity. The criterion of multiple attestation (it appears in Mark and Q) means it crosses the spectrum of NT witnesses. The criterion of plausibility speaks to the unlikelihood that it would be created by the early church. Darrell Bock states that it must go back to Jesus himself, for there are no parallels elsewhere to point to later creation.[30] If there is a personal devil, and if Jesus existed, such a confrontation makes perfect sense.

Others label it a true story but one that relays a purely psychological experience, as Jesus meditated on the meaning of his call at the baptism. The appearance of the devil then would be mental, as Jesus pictured his inner turmoil over his messianic mission as a conflict with Satan. While such is possible, of course, there is little evidence of that in the story itself, as the details of the story take place in the real world "as a battle between real beings.... The encounter is much more serious than a mere issue of internal psychological reflection. Whatever form the confrontation took, it was clear that two personalities were in the ring of battle."[31] There is a visionary element when the devil shows Jesus the kingdoms of the world (Luke 4:5), but that does not define the entire narrative.

4. The Deuteronomic Basis for This Episode

C. H. Dodd provided the important dictum that a NT quote from the OT often presupposes the entire context in which the quote is found.[32] This is certainly true here, as Deuteronomy provides the theological core for this periscope. The book of Deuteronomy centers around a series of addresses that Moses made on the plains of Moab just as Israel was on the verge of entering the promised land. In them Moses reiterates the Torah given on Sinai (usually called Horeb in Deuteronomy), and in them he emphasizes how the daily conduct of the people must reflect God's laws. There are frequent warnings from the wilderness failures of the nation resulting in their failure to enter the promised land, and this leads to a call for covenant renewal and a new faithfulness in obeying the stipulations of Torah. Gordon McConville calls Deuteronomy a

---

29. Nolland, *Luke*, 177. See also L. Schiavo, "The Temptation of Jesus: The Eschatological Battle and the Ethic of the First Followers of Jesus in Q," *JSNT* 25 (2002) 142–43, who thinks this is a reflection of Jesus' own experiences of temptation, probably towards the end of his ministry.

30. Bock, *Luke*, 364. See also Hagner, *Matthew 1–13*, 63; Keener, *Matthew*, 136–37.

31. Bock, *Luke*, 371. See also Marshall, *Luke*, 168.

32. C. H. Dodd, *According to the Scriptures: The Sub-structure of New Testament Theology* (London: Collins, 1952) 126–33.

"constitution for Israel" with the Torah a grace-gift from God intended to protect his people and enable them to live under his grace and mercy. Thus the central element is a religion of the heart flowing out of love for Yahweh and heart-worship.[33] Daniel Block stresses the significance of Deut 6:20, where Moses asks how the people will respond when their children ask about the meaning of the laws. In other words, the faith of the earlier generation must be transmitted to later generations, and they must be taught that the regulations actually provide a way of responding to the grace of God and his salvific gifts to his people. They are not a set of duties but a means of covenant expression, a way of life under the merciful suzerainty of Yahweh.[34]

Deuteronomy 6–8 is part of the larger section of the book beginning with 4:44 in which Moses expounds the laws to the people (4:44–26:19). He identifies it with the law proclaimed at Horeb/Sinai (4:45). Moses is calling for a renewal of the covenant as a present contract reenacted with the people as an ongoing relationship (5:2–3). Interestingly, Moses then begins with the Decalogue (5:6–21) as "the legal aspect of the covenant relationship in a sense similar to the role a wedding contract plays in a marriage. A marriage may be legalized by a marriage license, but it is a true marriage only when the legal terms of the contract are representative of a love leading to and maintaining the marital relationship."[35] In short, these "ten words" in one sense are commandments that should be obeyed but in a deeper sense depict a loving response to the redeeming grace of God shown in the exodus from Egypt and in his gift of covenant to the nation. The people can have only one proper response, to obey and walk unswervingly on the basis of the covenant stipulations given by God (5:32–33).

Deuteronomy 6–8 flow out of this covenant perspective. We begin with the Shema (6:4–9), which can be described as a "call to covenant love"[36] and a demand for covenant faithfulness.[37] The creedal affirmation, "The LORD our God, the LORD is one" (יהוה אלהינו יהוה אחד) speaks

---

33. J. G. McConville, "Deuteronomy, Book of," in *Dictionary of the Old Testament: Pentateuch* (ed. T. D. Alexander and D. W. Baker; Downers Grove, IL: InterVarsity, 2003) 187–91.

34. D. I. Block, "The Grace of Torah: The Mosaic Prescription for Life (Deut 4:1–8; 6:20–25)," *BSac* 162 (2005) 17–19; repr. in idem, *How I Love Your Torah, O LORD! Studies in the Book of Deuteronomy* (Eugene, OR: Cascade, 2011) 1–20.

35. P. C. Craigie, *The Book of Deuteronomy* (NICOT; Grand Rapids: Eerdmans, 1976) 149–50.

36. D. I. Block, *Deuteronomy* (NIVAC; Grand Rapids: Zondervan, 2012) 180, building on J. S. DeRouchie, *A Call to Covenant Love: Text Grammar and Literary Structure in Deuteronomy 5–11* (Piscataway, NJ: Gorgias, 2007).

37. J. G. McConville, *Deuteronomy* (Apollos Old Testament Commentary; Downers Grove, IL: InterVarsity, 2002) 139.

in one sense of the integrity, uniqueness, and unity of the one and only God who alone has power over the nations,[38] yet in another and perhaps greater sense, provides a call to covenant commitment and can be translated, "Our God is Yahweh, Yahweh alone!"[39] This provides the theme for all of chapters 6–8. The rest of chapter 6 develops the motif of the command to total obedience and loyalty to Yahweh, serving (תעבד) him alone (6:13), reminding them first of God's oath to the patriarchs (v. 10b) and then of his delivering the people from the Egyptians (vv. 12, 21–23) as proof that God would give them a bountiful land as their inheritance (vv. 10b–11). However, in return he demands their unswerving faithfulness and exclusive loyalty. The first section (6:10–19) revolves around three warnings: "dangerous prosperity (v. 12, 'be careful lest you forget'), foreign religions (v. 14, 'do not go after'), and doubt about God's will to punish (v. 16, 'do not put God to the test'),"[40] with Israel's failure in the wilderness as the prime example. The second section (6:20–25) begins with the child's ritual query, "What is the meaning of the stipulations (העדת)?" (cf. Exod 13:14) followed by Moses' (the father's) creedal response, again reminding them of the exodus deliverance (vv. 21–23) and then commanding them once more to obey all the decrees of Torah (vv. 24–25). Israel's continued prosperity depends entirely on their covenant commitment to Yahweh. A critical theme is that of memory (vv. 7–9, 12, 20–21), transmitting the sacred events and the duties to worship Yahweh from generation to generation.

Deuteronomy 7 continues this theme but moves from the internal problem of disobedience (ch. 6) to the external problem of the Canaanite nations. This passage is in one way a virtual midrashic-style exposition of Exod 23:20–33, providing theological commentary on the double command not to worship the gods of the Canaanites but instead to destroy them lest they seduce the Israelites into idolatry. Since Yahweh alone is God (Deut 6:4–9), Israel must remove all vestiges of the pagan gods from their land. There were to be no political treaties or mixed marriages, since either would turn their children from Yahweh (7:1–5). As a holy and chosen people, ransomed from slavery to Egypt (vv. 6–8), the people must respond to the covenant God who loves them (vv. 9–10a, 12b–13) by utterly keeping his commands, including the command to destroy his enemies (vv. 10b–12a). The future blessing,

---

38. Craigie, *Deuteronomy*, 169; McConville, *Deuteronomy*, 141.

39. D. I. Block, "How Many Is God? An Investigation into the Meaning of Deuteronomy 6:4–5," *JETS* 47 (2004) 193–212; repr. in *How I Love Your Torah*, 73–97

40. R. D. Nelson, *Deuteronomy: A Commentary* (OTL; Louisville: Westminster John Knox, 2002) 92.

health, and prosperity of the nation are contingent upon their faithful obedience (vv. 12–16). The final section responds to a rhetorical question (v. 17, "How can we drive out such stronger nations?") by reminding them that the God who defeated the Egyptians will doubtlessly destroy their enemies (vv. 18–24). Their responsibility is to have nothing to do with the idols but to detest them (vv. 25–26). All in all, chapter 7 with its principle of *ḥerem* against the enemies of God flows out of the absolute demand for covenant faithfulness to Yahweh alone.

The final of the three chapters (Deuteronomy 8) returns to the internal life of the Jewish people, tracing now the danger of forgetting God due to their prosperity in the land he has given them. The answer is to remember the grace of God they had experienced. As Peter Craigie observes, there is a double contrast—remember/forget and wilderness/promised land.[41] When they are tempted to forget God in the midst of the blessings of the land, they must remember the wilderness generation who suffered divine judgment due to their failures. Many follow Norbert Lohfink's chiastic organization of this chapter:[42]

A	Exhortation (v. 1)	
B	Wilderness (vv. 2–6)	
C	Arable land (vv. 7–10)	
D		Exhortation: Do not forget (v. 11)
C'	Arable land (v. 12–13)	
B'	Wilderness (vv. 14–17)	
A'	Exhortation (vv. 18–20)	

The importance of remembering God's provision and commands has already been seen earlier (6:7, 12; 7:9, 18), and it forms the core of chapter 8 as well. Block notes five parallels with chapter 6 that show the structural integrity of the whole unit: the context of the test (the land promised, 6:10a // 8:1), the nature of the test (limitless prosperity, 6:10b–12 // 8:7–10), the wrong response (forgetting Yahweh, 6:12 // 8:17), the right response (fearing/remembering Yahweh, 6:13–14 // 8:18), and final warning (elimination from the land, 6:15 // 8:19–20).

The first section (Deut 8:1–6) is framed by commands to do/keep the commands (vv. 1, 6) and calls the people to "remember" (וזכרת) (v. 2) the wilderness wanderings in which God both tested and provided for his people, demanding that they exercise the "discipline" (vv. 2, 5) that

---

41. Craigie, *Deuteronomy*, 184.
42. N. Lohfink, *Höre Israel: Auslegung von Texten aus dem Buch Deuteronomium* (Düsseldorf: Patmos, 1965) 76 (so Craigie, McConville, Block).

they had learned. The next part (8:7–10) builds on the promise to possess the land in verse 1 and describes in glowing terms the beauty and bounty of the land promised to them. Then 8:11–17 describes the danger of forgetting (תשכח) Yahweh and centering only on the prosperity of the land, ignoring that all they have was given them by God. Yahweh is described (vv. 14–16) as the one who brought them out of Egypt, who led them through all the wilderness trials, who gave them water from the rock, and who fed them with manna. They must interpret the future good they will experience in the land on the basis of the past good they have already experienced from God. The conclusion is found in 8:18–20, warning them that if they forget all Yahweh has done, they will perish like the nations of the earth.

We should mention the following chapters, especially Deuteronomy 9–11, as they provide further context for this material and are the final part of the first major section of instructions in the book, chapters 5–11. In this final section the same general theme is developed: Israel in the present is warned on the basis of Yahweh's past faithfulness and its past unfaithfulness and resultant suffering that in the future it must teach its children to remember God's gracious mercy and both follow and obey all that the Lord has said. Chapter 9 traces Israel's rebellion, recalling the golden calf incident of Exodus 32–34 to demonstrate its stubbornness, self-centeredness, and apostasy. As they are set to enter the promised land, they must realize that it will be theirs on the basis of the grace and mercy of God, not through any righteousness of their own (Deut 9:3–6). They repeatedly turned from God (vv. 7–24), and it was only the intercession of Moses for God's forgiveness and mercy that stayed his mighty hand (vv. 25–29). God's grace is demonstrated in a second giving of the two stone tablets and their being placed in the ark (10:1–10). The necessary results occur in 10:11–11:1 via a further series of commands for Israel to fear and obey Yahweh (10:12a, 20), love and serve him (10:12b, 20; 11:1), keep his commands (10:13), refuse to be stiff-necked (10:16), swear by his name (10:20b), and praise him (10:21). All of this must result from remembering his mighty acts of covenant mercy and love (10:14–22, 11:2–7). In 11:8–17 the people are reminded again to obey, love, and serve Yahweh (vv. 8, 13), but now the focus is upon the future prosperity and fertility of the land. The God of the past will continue to provide for his people as they take over the land, but they must turn their hearts continually to him in order to experience his blessings. There are two concluding paragraphs: (1) 11:18–25 sums up all that has been said about Israel teaching their children to obey, love, and serve Yahweh so that all this can be theirs; (2) 11:26–32 promises a blessing for those who listen and a curse upon those who refuse to listen.

5. The Three Temptations in Light of their Deuteronomic Setting

5.1. Temptation One: Provide Food for Yourself

The first temptation (Luke 4:2–4) occurs when the devil of the wilderness (= the ancient serpent of Genesis) challenges the hungry Jesus to place physical needs above the will of God. Every element of the setting relates to this opening salvo. There is a chiastic pattern in verses 1–2a where (A) Jesus is led by the Spirit (B) into the wilderness where (B') he is for forty days (A') tempted by the devil. The two protagonists are clearly identified: the Spirit who fills and leads Jesus versus the devil who tries to sidetrack Jesus from his Spirit-sent mission. Jesus has clearly been filled since the Spirit descended on him "in bodily form" (3:22), and the oneness of Jesus with the Spirit is emphasized. The fact that Jesus "was being led" (dramatic imperfect ἤγετο) throughout the forty-day period (the "forty days" modifies "led" and "tempted") as well as enduring the temptations demonstrates that Jesus was endowed by the Spirit through every aspect of the events in 4:1–13.[43]

It is clear that the *diabolos* (διαβόλου, the Greek form of the Hebrew *satan* [שטן] for the "adversary" or "accuser" of God and his people) appears merely as the opponent and does not control the action. His task is πειραζόμενος (a present participle depicting its ongoing nature) with its double-meaning of "tempting" (from the devil's side) and "testing" (from God's side). It makes sense for the "devil" to be the one tempting Jesus here, for in the OT he occasionally accused and incited God's people (1 Chr 21:1, Zech 3:1), and he frequently did so in Second Temple Jewish literature (e.g., *1 Enoch* 40:7, 54:6; *Jub.* 1:20; 17:15–18; *T. Ab.* 16a; CD 4:12–13). The "forty days" was the traditional time for a test of God's servants, with both Moses (Exod 34:28, Deut 9:9) and Elijah (1 Kgs 19:8) experiencing forty-day fasts and Israel going through forty years of wandering in the wilderness (especially Deut 8:2). The latter provides the primary (though not exclusive) typology here, as we will see, for Jesus reenacts the "sons of God," Israel (see earlier on Jesus as "True Israel"), facing the testing of their wilderness experience.[44] As Marshall

---

43. See Garlington, "Tested and Faithful," 286.
44. Bovon (*Luke*, 142) points out that temptation played no part in Moses' forty day fast, and that it took place in a context of the giving of the law, with Moses' face made radiant, a greater parallel with Jesus' transfiguration than with the incident here. Num

says, "A period of days is regarded as the appropriate counterpart for a single man to a period of years to a nation."[45] So where Israel failed in their forty-year wilderness test, Jesus will here succeed.

Like Matthew, Luke places a great deal of emphasis on the fasting and its results, describing Jesus in Luke 4:2b as eating "nothing during those days, and at the end of them he was hungry" (cf. Deut 8:3 regarding Israel, "He humbled you, causing you to hunger"). While Matt 4:2 explicitly mentions Jesus "fasting," Luke's "ate nothing" (οὐκ ἔφαγεν οὐδὲν) is the semantic equivalent and strengthens the picture of Jesus rejecting all food. In Luke there is a parallel with Exod 34:28 and Deut 9:9 where Moses "ate no bread and drank no water" before receiving the law, so that "as Jesus is poised to begin his ministry, his abstinence from food is not an act of penitence but part of his preparation to receive God's guidance."[46] There may be a slight Adam typology as well, for Adam had not fasted and could eat from any tree in paradise save one yet still surrendered to temptation, while Jesus was in the wilderness and had eaten nothing but still conquered his temptation.[47]

The devil tries to use the situation of Jesus' hunger to his own advantage. We must note at the outset that Satan does not doubt Jesus' status as Son of God. That was not only proclaimed to Mary (Luke 1:32, "He will be great and will be called the Son of the Most High"; 1:35, "the holy one to be born will be called the Son of God") but also declared by God at the baptism (3:22b, "You are my Son, whom I love"), and then confirmed by Luke via Jesus' genealogy ("the son of Adam, the son of God," 3:38). The first and third temptations focus on Jesus' sonship, so it is a core aspect of this pericope. Satan's challenge thus begins with acknowledgement of that fact, "If (εἰ, condition of fact)," meaning in effect, "I know you are God's Son, you know you are God's Son, so now prove it by using your power to meet your need." The temptation is subtle, but in essence it means to use his office selfishly, to follow his own path rather than God's will. As Nolland puts it, "The Devil suggests that Sonship is a privilege to be exploited."[48]

The title itself center's on Jesus' unique filial relationship to God as his Father. The devil wants him to ignore the God-Son relationship and center only on his own desires. His point is that divine royalty should

---

14:34 equates forty years typologically with forty days. On typology in this scene, see Stegner, "Use of Scripture," 103–5.

45. Marshall, *Luke*, 169. See also Gerhardsson, *Testing*, 41–43.
46. Garland, *Luke*, 180.
47. Bock, *Luke*, 371, from W. Hendriksen, *Exposition of the Gospel according to Luke* (Grand Rapids: Baker, 1978) 233–34.
48. Nolland, *Luke*, 169.

never suffer want, so Jesus should take advantage of his position. However, God demanded that Jesus exercise his sonship to be suffering Servant, and the question is whether sonship is to be defined through privilege or obedience. To change "the stone into bread" would entail using his power to redo the wilderness miracle of Exodus 16 and not just to replace the wilderness rocks with manna from heaven but to turn the rocks themselves into bread, thereby producing an even greater miracle. Both the manna miracle (Exodus 16) and the water from the rock (Exodus 17; Numbers 20) are intended here. In Ps 114:8 it is Yahweh who is to "turn the rock into a pool," and the question is whether Jesus will wait for God's timing to provide for him. The problem is that it would not be a God-performed miracle but a selfish act, thus obviating the real meaning of Jesus' sonship.

Jesus' response stems from Deut 8:3, looking upon himself in his sonship as True Israel facing the wilderness challenge. As stated above, the context of Deuteronomy 8 centers on the danger of forgetting the grace of God as Israel enters the promised land and calls on the people to remember the wilderness experience and commit themselves to avoiding past failures in their future tests. The section in which this command is found (8:1–6) demands that they remember God's provision which they had experienced in the wilderness and rekindle the discipline to obey his commands. Jesus shows that he is fully aware of what the devil is doing. That tactic worked with Israel; it would not succeed with Jesus. He is God-centered and refuses to allow earthly needs to dictate his responses to life's situations, unlike Israel. In this spiritual battle, Jesus intends to emerge victorious.

The introductory γέγραπται is a traditional formula that means 'God has said' and emphasizes the divine origin of a truth. The saying is not just a principle but also an oracle from God, and it constitutes final truth. Israel's hunger led to rebellion and complaint (Exod 15:24, 16:2–3) because the peoples' physical needs had priority over following and trusting God. Jesus relives Israel's dilemma and reenacts the peoples' conflict. Gerhardsson says, "The real nature of the sin of craving is here revealed. Discontent with the divine nourishment provided during the wilderness period is characterized as unbelief, lack of trust (*emonah*), as a violation of the basic obligation of the covenant."[49] Jesus centers on his humanity, and as a person (ὁ ἄνθρωπος) he like Israel must not define his existence by "bread alone" (ἄρτῳ μόνῳ). In Deuteronomy 8 God has repeatedly made provision for the needs of his people and asks them

---

49. Gerhardsson, *Testing*, 47.

to depend on him and his covenant promises. If Jesus were to use his power to meet his needs for himself, he would be leaving the Father out of the picture and in effect denying his sonship. It would constitute a declaration of independence with catastrophic implications. Luke has shortened the quotation (Deut 8:3 = Matt 4:4, "Man shall not live on bread alone, but on every word that comes from the mouth of God"), probably to focus entirely on the temptation itself.[50] It is common to interpret this as Jesus "rejecting miracles," refusing to perform the miracles of Moses. The point would then be that he used miracles only to help others not selfishly to serve himself.[51] While there is some validity in this, it is peripheral and not the main point. Primarily, Jesus as Son is obedient to his Father and trusts all his needs to him.[52]

5.2. Temptation Two: Control the Kingdoms of the World

The second temptation (Luke 4:5–8) occurs when the devil tries to seduce Jesus into idolatry by promising him what would one day be his anyway: authority over the world's kingdoms. Luke begins differently than Matthew, who sets the scene on "a very high mountain," with Sinai imagery very visible. Luke has the devil "leading him up" (ἀναγαγών), with no mention of a high place, possibly to reserve the imagery for the final scene on "the highest point of the temple" (4:9).[53] The emphasis here is on time ("in an instant," also a Lukan redactional addition) more than place, to emphasize the visionary nature of the temptation[54] and to provide a seamless movement to the climax in Jerusalem and the temple in Luke's rendition.[55] What the devil shows Jesus in the vision is "all the kingdoms of the world," with Luke's οἰκουμένης referring to the "inhabited world" rather than the geographical "world" (κόσμος) of Matt 4:8, perhaps to bring out more strongly the universal or comprehensive nature of the offer.[56] Satan promises Jesus power over every

---

50. Redaction critics spend a great deal of time on whether the longer (of Matthew) or the shorter (of Luke) version was "original," but such questions are nearly always too speculative to be helpful. As Bock (*Luke*, 385) concludes, "The differences may illustrate only that slightly distinct, but similar, sources have been used, since there is no clear evidence that one or the other is original."

51. See Bovon, *Luke*, 143.

52. France, *Jesus and the Old Testament*, 52.

53. Garland, *Luke*, 181.

54. So Kimball, *Exposition*, 93; H. Schürmann, *Das Lukasevangelium* (Freiburg, 1990), 210; Fitzmyer, *Luke*, 515. Hester calls this "suprahistorical, to emphasize the cosmic scope of the vision" ("Luke 4:1–13," *Int* 31 [1977] 55).

55. Nolland, *Luke*, 179; Bock, *Luke*, 375.

56. Bovon, *Luke*, 143. Fitzmyer, *Luke*, 516; Schürmann, *Lukasevangelium*, 211; Marshall, *Luke*, 172; Taylor believes Luke may have in mind primarily the Roman Empire ("Temptation of Jesus," 37).

person in the world. The scene is reminiscent of Deut 34:1–4 where, just prior to his death, Moses climbs to the top of Pisgah across from Jericho and is shown by Yahweh "the whole land." The devil elevates this to "all the kingdoms."

We should also note that the devil offers Jesus "all (πάσας) this authority," claiming universal power over this world. This is expanded in Luke 4:6 to "all their authority and splendor (δόξαν)," and the arrogant claim is, "it has been given (παραδέδοται, a divine passive) to me, and I can give it to anyone I want to." The question is whether the devil has the very authority he claims. Satan is called "the god of this age" in 2 Cor 4:4, probably meaning "the god who rules over this age" as opposed to the final Age that will come at the Day of the Lord.[57] He is also called "the ruler of the kingdom of the air" in Eph 2:2 (cf. "the rulers of this age" in 1 Cor 2:6) and "the prince of this world" in John 12:31, 14:30, and 16:31 (ἄρχων is used in both the Ephesians and Johannine passages). The devil is not offering ultimate, eternal authority but temporal, earthly authority. Demonic powers were said to control the nations of the world (Dan 10:13, 20–21; *Jub.* 35:17; *T. Job* 8:1–3). While God is the ultimate authority, he had allowed Satan certain dominion over this world (note "it has been given to me"), and Satan is offering this to Jesus. So it is a real, though not final, offer.[58]

The temptation also is real. God would in the future give Jesus the Son of Man dominion over this world (Dan 7:13–14; cf. Ps 2:8; Rev 11:15, 22:1–2); and the Son would have "all authority in heaven and earth" (Matt 28:18), but not at this time. In Jesus' incarnation and mission he came to be suffering Servant and to yield his life as a "slave" (Phil 2:6–8). So Satan was offering Jesus a shortcut to glory, a "crossless path to messiahship."[59] It would constitute Jesus as a political Messiah seizing power with no recourse to God. To accept this would mean Jesus has switched his loyalty/allegiance from his Father to the devil.

The requirement is to "worship" the devil, with προσκυνήσῃς meaning to bow down and worship Satan as Jesus' new god. This has always been Satan's goal and comes to culmination in the plan of the false

---

57. See M. J. Harris, *The Second Epistle to the Corinthians: A Commentary on the Greek Text* (NIGNTC; Grand Rapids: Eerdmans, 2005) 328.

58. Bovon (*Luke*, 144) gives another view: "But the devil is also a liar, and Luke may well accept in a different context the Hebrew Bible belief in God as the source of political authority." This is correct in one sense, but Satan is claiming here that God has delegated ("given") that authority to himself. On this issue, see D. Rudman, "Authority and Right of Disposal in Luke 4:6," *NTS* 50 (2004) 77–86, who brings out the Danielic background behind God's handing this evil world over to the cosmic powers.

59. Stein, *Luke*, 147.

trinity in Revelation (the dragon, the beast, the false prophet, Rev 16:13) to coerce the whole world to worship him rather than God (Rev 13:3–4, 8; 14:11; 16:2; 19:20). There is a great deal of Israel typology in this as well. The opening commandments of the Decalogue in Deut 5:6–8 state, "I am the LORD your God.... You shall have no other gods before me." In Deut 6:10–15 God promises Israel remarkable prosperity in the new land but warns them not to forget him (v. 12) or to "follow other gods" (vv. 14–15). This theme is expanded in Deuteronomy 7, which warns the nation as it is about to enter the promised land not to allow prosperity within the land to seduce it into idolatry. The danger is that the nations "turn your children away from following me to serve other gods" (7:4). The blessings of God and the future prosperity of the Israelites (vv. 12–15) is dependent on their obedience to God's demands that they refuse to follow the pagan peoples and destroy those who have set themselves against Yahweh (v. 16). This continues in Deut 8:11–17 as the people are warned not to forget God (vv. 11, 14, 17) and allow the fertility of the land to lead them to serve other gods (v. 19).[60]

This Deuteronomic background leads naturally into Jesus' response from Deut 6:13, "It is written, 'Worship the LORD your God and serve him only.'" This is in complete antithesis to Satan's request, "worship me," and reflects the Shema of Deut 6:4: "Our God is Yahweh, Yahweh alone" (see above). God alone is worthy of worship. The quote comes from the first section after the Shema (Deut 6:10–19), which reminds the people it was Yahweh alone who brought them out of Egypt and gave them the fertile land and then warns them not to commit rebellion and idolatry as at Massah (Exodus 17). Gerhardsson states that in Jewish writing "the worship of the calf could sometimes be considered as Satan worship even in this literal sense" (of Satan being in the golden calf).[61] Once more, Israel failed in this very thing, but Jesus God's Son will remain faithful to his Father.

5.3. Temptation Three: Prove God's Faithfulness

The third temptation in Luke (4:9–12) provides the capstone to the three, as the devil tries to talk Jesus into misusing for his own sake God's scriptural truths, to "test God to see if he will prove true to his promise in the Old Testament."[62] This might also involve a visionary experience

---

60. So Gerhardsson, *Testing*, 64–65, in an excellent section entitled "Riches and Idolatry" where he looks at the Deuteronomic material as background to the second temptation.
61. Ibid., 65.
62. France, *Jesus and the Old Testament*, 52.

since Jesus and Satan travel alone with no witnesses[63] to the very pinnacle of the temple, probably the southeast side with the Kidron ravine hundreds of feet below, a drop so steep that people would get dizzy looking over it (Josephus, *Ant* 15:411–12). There the devil tempts Jesus to challenge God to prove his protection of a righteous man; there are no spectators, so this would be a purely personal test.[64] Fitzmyer sees messianic overtones in this due to a rabbinic saying preserved in *Pesiqta rabbati* 36: "When the King, the Messiah, reveals himself, he will come and stand on the roof of the temple."[65] Satan once more acknowledges Jesus as "Son of God" (again utilizing the first class condition εἰ, assuming the reality of the claim) and then asks Jesus to prove it by "throwing" himself "down from" the pinnacle. On the surface such a thing seems illogical, even ridiculous, a pathetic suicide. The key of course is that Jesus as Son of God can expect his Father to save him from such a fate.

Satan then quotes Ps 91:11–12 to make his case. Jesus has twice turned the devil aside by quoting Scripture, so the devil now uses the same ploy against Jesus. Psalm 91 is part of a threefold series that begins Book IV of the Psalter (Psalms 90–106) dealing with the tragedy of the exile. Surrounding Psalm 91 are Psalm 90, called in the superscription "a prayer of Moses" and centering on the Lord as the everlasting God who provides a dwelling place for his people, and Psalm 92, a "song for the Sabbath" that calls upon the righteous to proclaim the wondrous deeds of God. In the middle of these themes, Psalm 91 celebrates God as "my refuge and my fortress" (v. 2) and prays for divine protection from the vagaries of life. It is a wisdom psalm that "encourages the godly to pursue the path of godliness and holds out the many promises of God's protection and blessings."[66] "Many would see this as a liturgical psalm that anticipates God's protection in the temple worship (Tate 1990: 450–51), and it is this theme of divine protection that emerges in Satan's testing of Jesus."[67] Luke Johnson brings out the *a fortiori* argument: the

---

63. So Bock, *Luke*, 378.

64. Bovon (*Luke*, 144) sees this as possibly "a priestly temptation on the heels of a prophetic and a kingly temptation." This is interesting, but there is little indication of such a reading in the text.

65. Fitzmyer, *Luke*, 517; so also Kimball, *Jesus' Exposition*, 94. This is challenged by Marshall, *Luke*, 173, on the grounds that there is no hint in Jewish speculation that the Messiah would prove himself by leaping from the temple's roof.

66. W. A. VanGemeren, *Psalms* (Expositor's Bible 5; Grand Rapids: Zondervan, 2008) 696.

67. D. W. Pao and E. J. Schnabel, "Luke," in *Commentary on the New Testament Use of the Old Testament* (ed. G. K. Beale and D. A. Carson; Grand Rapids: Baker, 2007) 284. They

God who would keep David from "stubbing his foot" would even more protect the Messiah, his Son, were he to tumble from the parapet of the temple.[68] Ps 91:1–10 promises divine protection to those who will find "refuge" (מחסה) in "the Most High" (vv. 2, 4, 9). Verses 11–13 then tell what form that protection will take: the angels as guardians (v. 11), being lifted up in the hands of angels (v. 12), deliverance from enemies (personified in dangerous beasts, v. 13). But the emphasis in the psalm is not upon the fact and the extent of the protection but on the responsibility of the righteous to shelter within the Most High God.[69] David Pao and Echkhard Schnabel see a further important nuance. The protection from "pestilence that stalks in the darkness" (v. 6) in the LXX (= Psalm 90 LXX) refers to "the noonday demon" and in Jewish tradition refers to deliverance from the cosmic powers. "Thus the use of this psalm by Satan in the temptation narrative is striking because the divine power offered to Jesus is actually one to be used against the evil one."[70]

Jesus' response in Luke 4:12 stems from Deut 6:16, which as we said in the previous passage occurs in a context warning the Israelites that when they enter the land, they must fear Yahweh and serve him only, lest his divine wrath "burn against" them (Deut 6:15a) as it did at Massah, when they "tested" him and were destroyed (vv. 15b–16). In Exod 17:1–7 the people refused to trust God for water but grumbled and complained so that the place was named "Massah" ("testing") and "Meribah" ("quarreling"). Israel had "tested" God, bringing on itself God's white-hot anger. Jesus refuses to do so and therefore succeeds where Israel sinned. According to France, "Jesus saw himself as God's Son, undergoing prior to his great mission as Messiah the testing which God had given to his 'son' Israel before the great mission of the conquest of Canaan.... The history is taken up by him and carried to its fulfillment."[71] Jesus is the faithful, obedient Son who refuses to put God to the test, who refuses to reenact Israel's failure to trust God for its needs. If Jesus were to jump from the pinnacle, he would in effect be refusing to trust God and demanding proof of God's protecting presence whenever he wished it. Further, Jesus is willing to die if such were

---

allude to M. E. Tate, *Psalms 51–100* (WBC 20; Dallas: Word, 1990).

68. L. T. Johnson, *The Gospel of Luke* (Sacra Pagina; Gollegeville, MD: Liturgical, 1991) 74. It has sometimes been thought that by omitting "in all your ways" from the psalm passage, Satan was twisting its meaning, but it is more likely the phrase is omitted because it is not essential to the meaning of the passage. See Bock, *Luke*, 381.

69. See VanGemeren, *Psalms*, 699–700.

70. Pao and Schnabel, "Luke," 285.

71. France, *Jesus and the Old Testament*, 53.

God's will, so in this sense this final temptation readies Jesus for his martyrdom on the cross. He will not demand rescue from death.

The devil, now defeated and at the end of "all this tempting," is forced to leave Jesus "until an opportune time" (ἄχρι καιροῦ, Luke 4:13). Satan had used up every bit (πάντα) of his ammunition and could only slink away in "concession of defeat and concomitant shameful withdrawal"[72] until another chance presented itself. Jesus enters his mission with an absolute victory over Satan. The oft-stated view that Satan is silenced until the passion events[73] is overdone, for there is demonic activity throughout Luke (and "Satan" is mentioned in 10:18, 11:18, and 13:16). Still, there is some truth in this, as the activity of Satan increases greatly as the passion events unfold (Luke 22:3, 31, 53). Probably, "Luke sees the ministry of Jesus as a period of victory over Satan and his demons,"[74] and this represents his defeat at the hand of Jesus.

6. Theological Implications

For years I have thought the message of this pericope was entirely Christological with no hint of discipleship. This was an over-reaction on my part because I grew up hearing messages from this text proclaiming, "Memorize Scripture, and you can defeat Satan every time" (a poorly conceived discipleship interpretation), ignoring the Son of God Christology and the setting of this passage. So for the last thirty years I have declared it entirely a passage about Jesus beginning his ministry with a defeat of the devil. That certainly is the primary thrust, but after further study and a deeper look at the important contribution of the Deuteronomic material, I now see an essential secondary thrust as well, centering on Jesus as True Israel demonstrating the defeat of temptation for the New Israel he is establishing. I will now summarize the Victorious Son and True Israel themes that I see present in the passage.

6.1. The Primary Theme: Victory over the Cosmic Powers

Jesus is the Divine Warrior who engages the devil in open combat and defeats him utterly in a "war of words," thereby proving himself to be the Son of God and beginning his ministry as the ultimate Victor.[75] This is especially true of Luke, who in 4:13 has the devil leaving in

---

72. Green, *Luke*, 196.
73. So H. Conzelmann, *The Theology of St. Luke* (New York: Harper, 1960) 28, who calls this a "Satan free" period.
74. Marshall, *Luke*, 174.
75. On the theme of Divine Warrior, see T. Longman III and D. G. Reid, *God Is a Warrior* (SOTBT; Grand Rapids: Zondervan, 1995).

defeat, looking for another "opportune time" in the future. Luigi Schiavo makes an excellent argument for this scene constituting an "eschatological battle" that makes use of the ancient "combat myth" in which two "divine beings" wage war to gain dominion over this world.[76] He sees this as the background to Jesus' conflict with Satan over "the three nets (or kinds of activity) of Belial" taking place in the three temptations.[77] While overstating his case somewhat, Schiavo is correct in seeing an eschatological battle for hegemony between Satan and Jesus, what Joel Green calls "a clash of cosmic proportions."[78]

Jesus begins his ministry as "Christus Victor," the Son of God who has won the battle over Satan and will conduct his entire ministry as a "binding of Satan" (Luke 11:21–22 = Mark 3:27). In this narrative Jesus wins the battle by refusing to take charge of his own destiny but instead by becoming the faithful, obedient Son who conducts his life according to the will of his Father. This will become especially true in his passion, where the activity of Satan will rise to new heights, yet Jesus will conquer his own inner temptations (especially at Gethsemane) and walk the path of obedience to the cross. He will indeed experience honor, glory, and dominion, but it will come through his surrender of himself as the atoning sacrifice for sin and thereby make it possible for sinners to find forgiveness and life with God. Through humbling himself (Phil 2:6–8) he then receives exaltation and worship from his Father (2:9–11). That is his victory and the ultimate "demise of the devil."[79]

6.2. The Secondary Theme: Jesus as True Israel Providing the Model for New Israel

The Adamic Christology in this section (arising out of Luke 3:38 as the lead-in to the narrative) shows that there is definitely an exemplary dimension to this story. Jesus as Last Adam makes it possible to reverse the failure of Adam (and Eve) and find victory over human frailty and tendency to sin (cf. 1 Cor 10:13). Also, the likelihood that Jesus viewed himself as True Israel reenacting the wilderness temptations shows that Jesus was preparing the way for his followers, New Israel, to win the

---

76. Schiavo, "Eschatological Battle," 148, building on A. Y. Collins, *The Combat Myth in the Book of Revelation* (Missouls, MT: Scholars, 1976) 19. Schiavo finds parallels in the Cycle of Baal; Michael in Dan 12:1; IQM 1:13–15, 17:5–8; Rev 12:7–9; the Son of Man in Dan 7:13–14, *1 Enoch* 45–46; Melchizedek in 11Q13 2:13–25 ("Eschatological Battle," 149–53). See also Garrett, *Temptations*, 36–40.

77. Schiavo, "Eschatological Battle," 153–55.

78. Green, *Luke*, 192.

79. See S. Garrett, *The Demise of the Devil: Magic and the Demonic in Luke's Writings* (Minneapolis: Fortress, 1989).

battle over temptation as well. As Bock says, "The issues of the test are fundamental ones that can be repeated for anyone," so that these are representative temptations that can be overcome by all who are faithful and obedient to God.[80]

---

80. Bock, *Luke*, 383. See also Stein, *Luke*, 150.

Paul's Reading of Deuteronomy
Law and Grace

Douglas Moo

The book of Deuteronomy has had a significant influence on the letters of Paul. Quotations are the most obvious evidence of this impact. Paul quotes Deuteronomy 13 times:[1]

- Rom 7:7 = Deut 5:21 (and/or Exod 20:17)
- Rom 10:6–8 = Deut 30:11–14
- Rom 10:19 = Deut 32:21
- Rom 11:8 = Deut 29:3 (2:4 LXX; mixed with Isa 29:10)
- Rom 12:19 = Deut 32:35
- Rom 13:9 = Deut 5:17–21 (and/or Exod 20:13–17)
- Rom 15:10 = Deut 32:43
- 1 Cor 9:9 = Deut 25:4
- 2 Cor 13:1 = Deut 19:15
- Gal 3:10 = Deut 27:26
- Gal 3:13 = Deut 21:23
- Eph 6:2–3 = Deut 5:16 (and/or Exod 20:12)
- 1 Tim 5:18 = Deut 25:4

Only Isaiah (22 times) and the Psalms (19 times) are quoted by Paul more often; Genesis is tied with Deuteronomy at 13. The 13 quotations can be grouped into four categories.

Author's Note: I offer this essay to my friend and colleague, Dan Block. He will not agree with everything in this essay (indeed, I fear that he may not agree with much of it!), but I trust that he will forgive me for my overly Pauline reading of his beloved Deuteronomy.

1. Paul marks 11 of these as quotations by using an introductory formula. The two without such an introductory formula—the references to the Decalogue in Rom 13:9 and to the "two or three witnesses" principle in 2 Cor 13:1—are clearly intended to be quotations (although it is impossible to know whether, in Rom 13:9, Paul depends on Exodus or Deuteronomy, on both, or on neither [if he quotes from memory]). See E. E. Ellis, *Paul and the Old Testament* (Grand Rapids: Baker, 1957) 150–54; R. N. Longenecker, *Biblical Exegesis in the Apostolic Period* (Grand Rapids: Eerdmans, 1975) 108–11; D.-A. Koch, *Die Schrift bei Paulus: Untersuchungen Zur Verwendung Und Zum Verständnis Der Schrift Bei Paulus* (BHT 69; Tübingen: Mohr-Siebeck, 1986) 33. These scholars, and others, come up with different numbers because of the inherent subjectivity in identifying quotations (as opposed to allusions) and because of the difficulty of how to count combination quotations.

(1) Paul cites commandments from Deuteronomy as relevant in some way to the conduct of Christians. He quotes three times from the Decalogue (Deut 5:16 in Eph 6:2–3; Deut 5:17–21 in Rom 13:9; Deut 5:21 in Rom 7:7); he twice applies the "don't muzzle the ox" command from Deut 25:4 to the support of Christian ministers (1 Cor 9:9 and 1 Tim 5:18); and he cites the "two or three witnesses" requirement from Deut 19:15 as a warning to the Corinthians (2 Cor 13:1).[2]

(2) Paul cites the Lord's claim that he is the one who "avenges" (Deut 32:35a) to ground his exhortation to believers to refrain from taking revenge (Rom 12:19).

(3) Paul uses the declaration in Deut 21:33 that a curse falls on executed criminals whose bodies are "hung on a tree" to elaborate his claim that on the cross Christ took on himself "the curse of the law" (Gal 3:13).

(4) Paul cites three passages from Deuteronomy to support his particular reading of the history of salvation. He repeats the warning about violating any of the commandments in Deuteronomy (Deut 27:26) to warn believers about seeking justification by means of "the works of the law" (Gal 3:10); he uses language from Moses' claim about the "nearness" of God's law to describe his own gospel message (Deut 30:11–14 in Rom 10:6–8); and he uses language from "the Song of Moses" (or, as Dan Block would prefer, "the Song of Yahweh") to characterize his own day, when the "nations" (or "Gentiles") have joined with Israel in rejoicing in God's faithfulness (Deut 32:43 in Rom 15:10[3]).

Paul therefore quotes Deuteronomy for parenetical, theological (in the service of parenesis), christological, and salvation-historical purposes—a breadth of usage that testifies further to the influence of Deuteronomy on his theology and teaching.

---

2. The way in which Paul considers these commandments to be relevant to his Christian audience is quite disputed. For an overview of my view, see D. J. Moo, "Jesus and the Authority of the Mosaic Law," *JSNT* 20 (1984) 3–49; idem, "The Law of Christ as the Fulfillment of the Law of Moses: A Modified Lutheran View," in *The Law, the Gospel, and the Modern Christian: Five Views* (Grand Rapids: Zondervan, 1993) 319–76. You may contrast this with the view of this volume's honoree in D. I. Block, "Preaching Old Testament Law to New Testament Christians," in idem, *The Gospel According to Moses: Theological and Ethical Reflections on the Book of Deuteronomy* [Eugene, OR: Cascade, 2012] 104–36; first published in *Hiphil (Scandinavian Evangelical E-Journal)* 3 (2006) 1–24, and subsequently published in three parts in *Ministry* 78.5 (2006) 5–11; 78.7 (2006) 12–16; 78.9 (2006) 15–18.

3. This is not the place to enter into the difficult textual issues in Deut 32:43. Paul, at least—as is his habit—quotes the LXX. For a helpful assessment of the textual problem that views Paul's quotation as deriving from the most original textual tradition, see D. I. Block, "Text Critical Issues in Deuteronomy 32:43," in idem, *How I Love Your Torah, O LORD! Studies in the Book of Deuteronomy* (Eugene, OR: Cascade, 2011) 185–88.

Although not as obvious, the many allusions to Deuteronomy that Paul weaves into his own teaching are also important indicators of his concern with this book. But perhaps even more important, though more difficult to pin down, is the impact of Deuteronomy's overall theological perspective on Paul's understanding of salvation history and its culmination in Christ.[4]

In this essay, I will focus on two of Paul's quotations of Deuteronomy—Deut 27:26 in Gal 3:10 and Deut 30:12–14 in Rom 10:6–8. The analyses of these Pauline passages will demonstrate this larger contextual reading of Deuteronomy as a whole.

Deuteronomy 27:26 in Galatians 3:10[5]

Paul's quotation of Deut 27:26 comes toward the beginning of the great central argument of Galatians (3:1–5:12). This argument is framed by two passages of rebuke and exhortation (3:1–6, 5:1–12). In 2:15–21, which is a key transitional passage between the opening section and this central section of the letter, Paul briefly delineates the gospel. This next part of the letter is a prolonged defense of that gospel. Especially important in this defense is the key distinction that Paul first introduces in 2:16: "works of the law" vs. "Christ faith." This antithesis is a thread that weaves together the disparate subjects of this part of the letter. In the opening passage, in which Paul sets the tone for the argument to follow, he confronts his readers with this fundamental issue: did they experience the Spirit by "the works of the law" or by "the hearing that accompanies faith" (3:2, 5)? This contrast, stated with several different combinations ("law," "doing" vs. "faith," "believing," "[Jesus] Christ faith") surfaces repeatedly in the argument that follows.

Narrowing our focus one more step brings us to Gal 3:7–29, a discrete section that is bracketed by a concern to show that the Abrahamic promise was intended all along to include Gentiles, a situation that has come to pass "in Christ." At the same time, and with equal importance, Paul continues to develop the key contrast he introduced in 2:16 and which becomes the basis for his exhortation in 3:1–6: "works of the law"/"law" vs. "Christ faith" as the means of becoming the sons of Abraham. Having expounded the positive side of this antithesis in 3:7–9 (one is justified and receives the Abrahamic blessing by faith),

---

4. See, for the influence on Paul of "the Deuteronomic view of Israel's history," J. M. Scott, "Paul's Use of Deuteronomic Tradition," *JBL* 112 (1993) 645–65.

5. The section that follows is built heavily on my treatment of this text in my forthcoming commentary on Galatians (BECNT; Grand Rapids: Baker, 2013 [forthcoming]).

Paul turns in 3:10–14 to the negative side (those who seek to relate to God by works of the law/law are under a curse). It is at this point that Paul quotes Deut 27:26.

The γάρ 'for' suggests that Gal 3:10 explains an implied negative counterpart to v. 9: "those who are of faith" inherit the Abrahamic blessing *and not "those who are of works of the law"* because. . . .[6] Specifically, Paul claims, Ὅσοι . . . ἐξ ἔργων νόμου εἰσίν, ὑπὸ κατάραν εἰσίν: "as many as are out of the works of the law, are under a curse."[7] The word ὅσοι, in contrast to οἱ [ἐκ πίστεως] in v. 9, expresses "an element of 'uncertainty' or 'potentiality' regarding the membership" of this group.[8] Paul is, in effect, warning the Galatians about joining this group. To be "under a curse" is to be under God's judgment for failure to live up to his covenant requirements. Reference to "curse," and especially to the blessing/cursing contrast, draws attention to Deuteronomy 27–30, where Moses sets before the people of Israel the alternatives of blessing for covenant faithfulness and cursing for unfaithfulness (19 of the 48 LXX references to ἐπικατάρατος 'cursed' occur in these chapters; and six of the 46 references to κατάρα 'curse'). It is no surprise, then, that Paul quotes from these chapters in Gal 3:10b. His base text is clearly Deut 27:26, the climax and summary of a series of curses for various sins. Paul's version of the text differs slightly from both the LXX and the MT.[9]

MT	LXX	Paul
ארור אשר לא־יקים את־דברי התורה־הזאת לעשות אותם	ἐπικατάρατος πᾶς ἄνθρωπος ὃς οὐκ ἐμμενεῖ ἐν πᾶσιν τοῖς λόγοις τοῦ νόμου τούτου τοῦ ποιῆσαι αὐτούς	ἐπικατάρατος πᾶς ὃς οὐκ ἐμμένει πᾶσιν τοῖς γεγραμμένοις ἐν τῷ βιβλίῳ τοῦ νόμου τοῦ ποιῆσαι αὐτά
"Cursed be the one who does not uphold the words of this law to do them"	"Cursed be every person who does not remain in all the words of this law to do them"	"Cursed be everyone who does not remain in all that is written in the book of the law to do them"

The differences between Paul's wording and the LXX are minor: he omits LXX ἄνθρωπος (which has no explicit Hebrew equivalent), drops

---

6. F. Mussner, *Der Galaterbrief* (5th ed.; HTKNT 9; Freiburg: Herder, 1988) 223.

7. Quotations from Scripture, unless indicated otherwise, are my own translation.

8. C. D. Stanley, "'Under a Curse': A Fresh Reading of Galatians 3:10–14," *NTS* 36 (1990) 498.

9. Single underline indicates divergence from the Hebrew; double underline from the Greek; dotted underline from both.

the ἐν after ἐμμενεῖ, substitutes τοῖς γεγραμμένοις ἐν τῷ βιβλίῳ for τοῖς λόγοις, and uses the neuter plural αὐτά in place of the masculine plural αὐτούς. The importance of doing everything written in this law/book of this law is repeatedly stressed in Deuteronomy:[10]

- Deut 28:61: "The LORD will also bring on you every kind of sickness and disaster not recorded in this Book of the Law, until you are destroyed."
- Deut 29:20[21]: "The LORD will single them out from all the tribes of Israel for disaster, according to all the curses of the covenant written in this Book of the Law."
- Deut 29:26[27]: "Therefore the LORD anger burned against this land, so that he brought on it all the curses written in this book."
- Deut 30:10: "if you obey the LORD your God and keep his commands and decrees that are written in this Book of the Law and turn to the LORD your God with all your heart and with all your soul . . ."[11]

Of possible interpretive significance is one key difference between the MT, on the one hand, and both the LXX and Paul on the other: the occurrence of πᾶσιν ("all") in the Greek. However, because similar passages in the MT of Deuteronomy have an "all" (e.g., Deut 6:24), it is likely again that Paul (or the LXX before him) have simply assimilated the wording of Deut 27:26 to these other texts.[12] On the whole, then, the textual differences probably have no interpretive significance.[13]

While obviously citing Deut 27:26, then, there is every reason to suspect that Paul views this verse as an expression of a key theological thrust of Deuteronomy: that continued enjoyment of the blessing of God in the land of Israel is dependent on the people's faithful obedience to the law of Moses, while a failure to do that law would result in curse and exclusion from the land. Paul connects this quotation to his claim in the first part of the verse with a γάρ 'for', showing that this quotation explains or grounds that claim. How to understand the logical relationship between the two parts of the verse is quite controversial. And a

---

10. U. Heckel, *Der Segen im Neuen Testament* (WUNT 2.15; Tübingen: Mohr Siebeck, 2002) 129.

11. On this theme in Deuteronomy, see M. Noth, *The Laws in the Pentateuch and Other Essays* (Edinburgh: Oliver & Boyd, 1966).

12. Note also that the *Sam. Tg.*, *Lev. Rab.* 25, and *y. Soṭah* 21d include a comparable word in their quotations of this verse.

13. Contra, e.g., Koch, *Die Schrift*, 120, 164; C. D. Stanley, *Paul and the Language of Scripture: Citation Techniques in the Pauline Epistles and Contemporary Literature* (SNTSMS 69; Cambridge: University Press, 1992) 239; R. Hays, "Galatians," *NIB* 11:258.

decision about this matter is important, because the verse is a kind of linchpin in the argument of Galatians 3. Its interpretation determines—and, perhaps, more often, is determined by—the nature of the larger argument that Paul is making in these verses.

The problem created by this verse is a well-known one, identified as long ago as Luther: the quotation in the second part of the verse seems to prove just the opposite of what Paul says in the first part of the verse.[14] Deut 27:26 encourages people to obey the law as a means of avoiding the curse. Yet Paul claims that it is just those people who are bound up with law who suffer that curse. An initial response to this problem is to note that Paul refers not to people who are doing the law but to people who are "out of works of the law" (ἐξ ἔργων νόμου). As the parallel with "those who are out of faith" (οἱ ἐκ πίστεως) in Gal 3:9 (and cf. vv. 7, 8, 11, 12) suggests, the phrase refers not to those who "do the law" but to those who are somehow identified with the law. This identification with the law has usually been taken to refer to people who, as Aquinas put it, "trust in the works of the Law and believe that they are made just by them."[15] The ἐξ would then have the instrumental force that it appears to have in parallel texts (2:16; 3:2, 5), and the ὅσοι would have the rhetorical effect of warning the Galatians about taking this step. On this reading of the initial clause, the quotation functions as the statement of a principle that explains why the curse comes on such people: *everything* that is written in the law must be done if the curse is to be avoided.

But one more logical step is necessary if this principle is to ground Paul's claim: the assumption that no one can, in fact, do *everything* that is written in the law. Put in the form of a syllogism, the logic of Gal 3:10 would then look like this:

> Only those who do everything written in the law will escape the curse (v. 10b);
>
> *No one can do everything written in the law* (assumed);
>
> Therefore: No one who depends on doing the law will escape the curse (v. 10a).

This way of making Paul's argument work has been the traditional approach to this verse and continues to be held by a significant number of interpreters.[16] But a rival interpretation has gained considerable

---

14. *Lectures on Galatians* 1535, Chapters 1–4 (Luther's Works 26; Saint Louis: Concordia, 1963) 252.

15. See J. Riches, *Galatians through the Centuries* (Oxford: Blackwell, 2008) 173.

16. Among older interpreters: Ambrosiaster, who comments on 3:10, "The commandments are so great that it is impossible to keep them" (cf. G. Bray, *Ambrosiater:*

support in recent years.[17] Rather than being an implicit statement of a principle, Paul's quotation, according to these scholars, is historically oriented. The text serves to summarize the state of Israel as a people in Paul's day: under a curse because of persistent covenant disobedience. Advocates of this interpretation argue that "those who are out of the works of the law" refers to people "whose identity is derived from works of the Law"[18]: the ἐξ would then function as it does in 2:12, where τοὺς ἐκ περιτομῆς means "belonging to the group of people who are circumcised."[19] Paul would then be reminding the Galatian Gentiles of the unfortunate situation of Israel before God as a means of warning them not to join Israel by undertaking "works of the law." Should the Galatians identify with Israel by taking on the distinctive "markers" of Judaism—"the works of the law"—they would fall under the curse

---

Commentaries on Galatians-Philemon [Ancient Christian Texts; Downers Grove, IL: InterVarsity, 2009] 16). Chrysostom is explicit about this in his comments on 3:10: ". . . here again he establishes his point by a text which concisely states both points: that no man has fulfilled the Law (wherefore they are under the curse), and, that Faith justifies" (*Comm. Gal.*, on 3:10 [*NPNF* 13:26]). See also comments on 2:17, 19; 3:2, 12; 5:2. See also, e.g., Luther, *Lectures on Galatians* 1535, Chapters 1–4, 253; J. B. Lightfoot, *Saint Paul's Epistle to the Galatians: A Revised Text with Introduction, Notes, and Dissertations* (7th ed.; London: MacMillan and Co., 1881) 137; E. de W. Burton, *A Critical and Exegetical Commentary on the Epistle to the Galatians* (ICC; Edinburgh: T. & T. Clark, 1921) 164. Among more recent scholars, see especially T. R. Schreiner, "Is Perfect Obedience to the Law Possible? A Re-examination of Galatians 3:10," *JETS* 27 (1984) 151–60; and see also, e.g., F. F. Bruce, *The Epistle to the Galatians: A Commentary on the Greek Text* (NIGTC; Grand Rapids: Eerdmans, 1982) 159; Mussner, *Der Galaterbrief*, 224–26; R. N. Longenecker, *Galatians* (WBC 41; Dallas: Word, 1990) 117–18; H. Hübner, *Law in Paul's Thought: A Contribution to the Development of Pauline Theology* (Edinburgh: T. & T. Clark, 1984) 18–19; B. W. Longenecker, *The Triumph of Abraham's God: The Transformation of Identity in Galatians* (Edinburgh: T. & T. Clark, 1998) 134–42; G. Waters, *The End of Deuteronomy in the Epistles of Paul* (WUNT 2:221; Tübingen: Mohr Siebeck, 2006) 93–100; S. Kim, *Paul and the New Perspective: Second Thoughts on the Origin of Paul's Gospel* (Grand Rapids: Eerdmans, 2002) 139–52.

17. In fact, several alternative explanations have been put forward, but the two above are the most popular and the most likely. However, I should briefly mention the view of J. Dunn, which has its starting point in his interpretation of "works of the law" in terms of a law-doing distinctive to Judaism and thus inherently antagonistic to Gentiles. It is, then, those who insist on maintaining these Jewish boundary markers who are missing the true intent and purpose of God's law to include Gentiles. They do not "remain in the law" as re-configured in Paul's interpretation and thus fall under the curse (esp. J. D. G. Dunn, *The Epistle to the Galatians* [Peabody, MA: Hendrickson, 1993] 171–73; cf. also J. R. Wisdom, *Blessing for the Nations and the Curse of the Law* [WUNT 2.113; Tübingen: Mohr Siebeck, 2001]).

18. Hays, "Galatians," 258.

19. See, e.g., T. D. Gordon, "Abraham and Sinai Contrasted in Galatians 3:6–14," in *The Law is Not of Faith: Essays on Works and Grace in the Mosaic Covenant* (ed. B. D. Estelle, J. V. Fesko and D. VanDrunen; Phillipsburg, NJ: Presbyterian and Reformed, 2009) 240–58.

that hangs over Israel.[20] This interpretation fits neatly into the more narratival reading of Paul's argument in this part of Galatians that has gained support in recent years. Yet I think there are good reasons for preferring the "traditional" view—although modified a bit in terms of the more historical approach.[21]

Particularly important is the much-debated phrase, "works of the law." While I cannot develop the argument here, this phrase is a general way of referring to "doing" the law. It does not mean identification with the law or the possession of the law: the "works" in the phrase is significant.[22] In this context, moreover, it is just this "doing" that Paul emphasizes, both in the quotation—what is written in the book of the law is to be done (τοῦ ποιῆσαι αὐτά) and in Gal 3:12—"the one who *does* [the commandments] will live by them" (Lev 18:5; my emphasis).[23] The same emphasis is found in 5:3: "Now I testify again to every man who wants to be circumcised that he is obligated *to do* the whole law" (again, my emphasis). While the "law" in view is, of course, the law of Moses, and much of Paul's argument in Galatians rests on the contrast between the era of the law and the era of fulfillment in Christ,[24] this verse, in its context, suggests that Paul is also concerned with the fundamental

---

20. See esp. Stanley, "Under a Curse," 481–511; J. M. Scott, "'For as Many as Are of Works of the Law Are under a Curse' (Galatians 3:10)," in *Paul and the Scriptures of Israel* (ed. C. A. Evans and J. M. Sanders; JSNTSup 83; Sheffield: Sheffield Academic Press, 1993) 187–221; N. T. Wright, *The Climax of the Covenant: Christ and the Law in Pauline Theology* (Philadelphia: Fortress, 1993) 141–48; cf. also Hays, "Galatians," 258; F. Thielman, *From Plight to Solution: A Jewish Framework for Understanding Paul's View of the Law in Galatians and Romans* (NovTSup 61; Leiden: Brill, 1989) 66–69; J. P. Braswell, "'The Blessing of Abraham'" Versus 'The Curse of the Law': Another Look at Gal 3:10–13," *WTJ* 53 (1991) 74–76; A. Caneday, "'Redeemed from the Curse of the Law': The Use of Deut 21:22–23 in Gal 3:13," *TJ* 10 (1989) 192–95; W. Dumbrell, "Abraham and the Abrahamic Covenant in Galatians 3:1–14," in *The Gospel to the Nations: Perspectives on Paul's Mission in Honour of P. T. O'Brien* (ed. P. Bolt and M. Thompson; Downers Grove, IL: InterVarsity, 2000) 23–25, 27–29; and, in modified form, D. I. Starling, *Not My People: Gentiles as Exiles in Pauline Hermeneutics* (BZNW 184; Berlin: de Gruyter, 2011) 49–52.

21. For many of the points I make below, see esp. Schreiner, "Is Perfect Obedience to the Law Possible?"; ibid., "Paul and Perfect Obedience to the Law: An Evaluation of the View of E. P. Sanders," *WTJ* 47 (1985) 257–66.

22. See D. J. Moo, "'Law,' 'Works of the Law,' and Legalism in Paul," *WTJ* 45 (1983) 73–100.

23. M. Silva, *Interpreting Galatians: Explorations in Exegetical Method* (2nd ed.; Grand Rapids: Baker, 2001) 259–60; A. A. Das, *Paul, the Law, and the Covenant* (Peabody, MA: Hendrickson, 2001) 151–53; R. H. Gundry, "Grace, Works, and Staying Saved in Paul," *Bib* 66 (1985) 15–32.

24. Dumbrell ("Abraham," 23–25), therefore, suggests that the implied premise in Paul's argument is: "since the era of the Mosaic covenant has now ended." Because the coming of Christ had ended the covenant and its associated provisions for atonement,

issue of "doing." A simple claim that Christ has superseded the law may be adequate for Paul's purposes; but we might expect him to push farther and ask why it was necessary for Christ to supersede the law. In other words, while much of Paul's argument in this letter could be summarized as "doing is wrong because (and when) it is tied to an outmoded law," Paul here suggests that he has moved to a deeper and more universal issue: "doing is wrong because a doing that is adequate to please God is impossible." This argument, central to Reformation soteriology, is, I think, present in our text. Another reason to prefer the traditional interpretation is the text that Paul quotes. There are many OT texts, even some from Deuteronomy 27–30 (e.g., 29:26[27]) that refer more clearly and obviously to the curse that fell on Israel. Paul, instead, selects a text that focuses on individuals—"everyone who" (πᾶς ὅς)—and on their consistent obedience—"remain ... to do" (ἐμμένει ... ποιῆσαι).[25] The quotation serves perfectly as a way of reminding the Galatian Christians of a central principle in the law: that blessing and cursing depend on doing.[26]

A major objection to this traditional interpretation is the need to assume a critical point: the impossibility of fulfilling the law. Not only must we assume this step in the logic, but the assumption is one, it is argued, that neither Paul's argument in Galatians nor his Jewish milieu can justify. The first point to make in response to this objection is that both views require that a central element in the argument be assumed: the inability to fulfill the law on the traditional view and identification with Israel on the revisionist view. Nevertheless, revisionists argue that the assumption they make is much more likely than what is required in the traditional view. For the idea that humans could not do the law perfectly was not, it is argued, a common teaching in the Judaism of Paul's day; nor does Paul clearly teach it anywhere else. How could he then assume that his readers would infer it?

In fact, the assumption is not nearly as unlikely as it might appear. If the Galatian Christians had even a cursory acquaintance with the OT, they would readily have assumed this point. The failure of the Israelites

---

identification with that covenant by means of "the works of the law" inevitably puts a person under the curse.

25. The infinitive ποιῆσαι might indicate result but should probably be taken closely with ἐμμένει in a single verbal idea: "keep on doing" (NET); or, better, "remain in by doing."

26. On the theology and significance of blessing and cursing in Deuteronomy 27–30, see esp. Waters, *The End of Deuteronomy*, 29–77, who questions whether a single clear perspective can be read from these chapters.

to "confirm" the covenant God made with them by obeying the law is clearly predicted within Deuteronomy itself (31:14–29) and becomes the leitmotif of Israel's history. God sends his people into exile because "[a]ll Israel has transgressed your law and turned away, refusing to obey you" (Dan 9:11). This history reveals, then, innate human failure to remain consistently oriented toward God and his law, a situation to be remedied only by God's intervention to transform human beings, replacing the "heart of stone" with a "heart of flesh" and sending his Spirit to enable his people to produce the obedience that he expects (Ezek 36:24–28). It is precisely this innate human inability to do God's law that Paul himself elaborates in Rom 7:14–25: the Jew is in despair because he or she is unable to "do" the good law of God that God gave Israel. The law cannot bring the life it promises (7:10) because it "was weakened by the flesh" (8:3).[27] Granted, then, the massive OT witness to the problem of human inability to do the law, a viewpoint that Paul explicitly takes over in his other letters, it is hardly an arbitrary "reading into" this passage in Galatians to think that Paul assumes it here.

Nor does Paul's Jewish context render such an assumption improbable. There is considerable confusion about just what the Jewish view was and how it might relate to Paul's argument. Sanders's summary of the Jewish viewpoint may be taken as representative: "the law is not too difficult to be satisfactorily fulfilled; nevertheless more or less everybody sins at some time or other . . . ; but God has appointed means of atonement which are available to all."[28] As Sanders notes, the Jewish view was *not* that human beings could perfectly "do" the law, in the sense of successfully obeying all its commandments. Jewish claims that the law could be "done" mean, in effect, that a Jew can be viewed as being free of condemnation for inevitable transgressions by taking advantage of the provision for forgiveness via sacrifice included in that same law (and it is possible that this is what Paul means when he claims that, as a Jew, he was "faultless" with respect to the "righteousness based on the law" [Phil 3:6]).

Against this Jewish background, there are two ways to understand Paul's language about the need to do all the law. First, he might mean that the requirement to undertake the whole law involves not only obedience to the commandments in general but also reliance on the law's provisions for atonement via sacrifice. The general reference to "doing all the law" in Gal 5:4 could have this sense. But 3:10, especially granted

---

27. For this reading of Romans 7, see D. J. Moo, *The Epistle to the Romans* (NICNT; Grand Rapids: Eerdmans, 1996) 442–51.

28. E. P. Sanders, *Paul, the Law, and the Jewish People* (Minneapolis: Fortress, 1983) 28.

the context in Deuteronomy from which Paul draws this language, is less susceptible to such a meaning. And, of course, it is well known that Paul generally ignores, for whatever reason, provisions for sacrifice and worship in his discussion of the law.

The second interpretation is, then, more likely: Paul assumes that the sacrifice of Christ has rendered the OT provisions for atonement null and void (see Gal 1:4; 3:1, 13). The fact that Paul never touches on this matter in Galatians suggests that the definitive nature of Christ's atoning sacrifice was common ground with his opponents. In the time after Christ, then, one is faced with two, and only two, options: find justification in Christ by faith; or find justification through the law, a justification that can now, apart from the provision of sacrifice, be secured only by doing "all" the law.[29]

My reading of Paul's appeal to Deut 27:26 in Gal 3:10 has important implications for the wider argument of the letter. Many recent interpreters, especially (though not exclusively) those associated with the "new perspective," argue that Paul's polemic against the law in Galatians is entirely salvation-historical and sociological. The Galatian Gentiles are not to put themselves under the law because the era of the law has ended and because the law, given to Israel as her own covenant document, excludes Gentiles. The former point is no doubt an important part of Paul's argument in Galatians. Yet the logic I have argued for in Gal 3:10 suggests that, while not as evident in Galatians as in Romans, the underlying anthropology of human inability to do the law is also present in Galatians.[30] "Works of the law," like any other human "work," always fall short of what God expects of his creatures,

---

29. See esp. A. A. Das, *Paul, the Law, and the Covenant* (Peabody, MA: Hendrickson, 2001) 215–22; and also T. Laato, "Paul's Anthropological Considerations: Two Problems," in *Justification and Variegated Nomism, Vol. 2: The Paradoxes of Paul* (ed. D. A. Carson, P. T. O'Brien, and M. A. Seifrid; Tübingen: Mohr Siebeck, 2004) 343–46.

30. This is the critical issue in assessing the ultimate theological significance of the argument in Galatians. This point is recognized by, among others, B. Matlock and A. A. Das. Matlock says, ". . . the question it [the New Perspective] brings, particularly to Paul's Epistles to the Galatians and Romans, concerns Paul's overall argumentative context: is there, in Paul, a principled contrast between 'doing' (the law) and 'believing' (the gospel), or is the contrast between an 'exclusive' (a Jewish law) and an 'inclusive' (a universally accessible faith) approach to God's saving prerogatives?" (*Unveiling the Apocalyptic Paul: Paul's Interpreters and the Rhetoric of Criticism* [JSNTSup 127; Sheffield: Sheffield Academic, 1996] 436). And Das claims: "The perceived overemphasis on the boundary-marking 'works of the Law' has become the most prominent defining feature of this 'new perspective' on Paul. The pivotal question, then, is whether Paul's critique of the 'works of the Law' is limited to their boundary-marking function or whether his critique is articulated also in terms of human accomplishment" ("Paul and Works of Obedience in Second Temple Judaism: Romans 4:4–5 as a 'New Perspective' Case Study," *CBQ* 71 [2009] 796).

leaving incorporation into Christ by faith as the only means of achieving righteousness. This way of reading the logic of Galatians follows a long line of interpreters—a line, it should be emphasized, that extends beyond the Reformers to at least as far as Chrysostom, who regularly introduces this point about human inability into his homilies on Galatians. S. Westerholm puts the point well: "The fundamental question addressed by Galatians thus is not 'What is wrong with Judaism (or the Sinaitic law)?' but 'What is wrong with humanity that Judaism (and the Sinaitic law) cannot remedy?'"[31] A distinction between human doing and human believing, while not the focus in the letter, does underlie the argument of Galatians.

Deuteronomy 30:11–14 in Romans 10:6–8

The debate over Paul's application of Deut 27:26 in Gal 3:10 pales in comparison with the tempest that rages over his use of language from Deut 30:11–14 in Rom 10:6–8. In Deut 30:11–14, Moses proclaims the "nearness" of God's law as a means of exhorting the people to obey it. Paul appears to force these verses from Deuteronomy to mean virtually the opposite of what they appear to be saying: he applies them to Christ and the gospel, *in contrast to the law*. The passage is therefore regularly cited as one of the most extreme examples of the NT authors' forceful and arbitrary squeezing of the OT into the mold of the gospel.[32]

Paul's appeal to Deut 30:11–14 comes in the midst of a passage (Rom 9:30–10:13) that has at its heart a contrast between two kinds of 'righteousness' (δικαιοσύνη):

1. "the righteousness based on faith" versus "the law of righteousness" (9:30–31);
2. "the righteousness of God" versus "their own righteousness" (10:3);
3. "the righteousness based on the law" versus "the righteousness based on faith" (10:5–6).

In the wider context (9:30–10:21) Paul offers an explanation for the surprising turn in salvation history: Gentiles, who were "not a people"

---

31. S. Westerholm, *Perspectives Old and New on Paul: The 'Lutheran' Paul and His Critics* (Grand Rapids: Eerdmans, 2004) 381; see also, esp. M. Silva, "Faith Versus Works of the Law in Galatians," in *Justification and Variegated Nomism, Vol. 2: The Paradoxes of Paul*, 217–48; Gundry, "Grace," 15–32; Kim, *New Perspective*, 61–75.

32. R. Hays opens his innovative and influential book on Paul's hermeneutics with this text, citing it as a particularly clear instance of Paul's hermeneutical freedom (*Echoes of Scripture in the Letters of Paul* [New Haven, CT: Yale University Press, 1989] 1–5); see also R. N. Longenecker, *Introducing Romans: Critical Issues in Paul's Most Famous Letter* (Grand Rapids: Eerdmans, 2011) 239.

are becoming the people of God while only a remnant of Israel is being saved (9:24–29). In the first phase of his argument in chapters 9–11 (9:6b–29), Paul traces this state of affairs to the sovereign determination of God. In 9:30–10:21, by contrast, he argues that the failure of Israel to respond to God's grace in the gospel is at fault. The manifestation of God's eschatological righteousness in Christ has been met by Gentiles with faith but by Israel (generally) with disobedience and unbelief. Gentiles are being included in God's true spiritual people because they have embraced the eschatological revelation of God's righteousness in Christ, a righteousness that is now available to anyone who believes (10:4b, 11–13). Most Jews, on the other hand, are finding themselves outside this true people of God because they are wrongly preoccupied with another, false, kind of righteousness. They have persisted in seeking to work out their relationship with God through the law (9:31; 10:3, 5) and the works it demands (9:32a; 10:5). They have therefore missed the true focus of salvation history, "stumbling" over Jesus Christ (9:32b–33), the embodiment of God's righteousness (10:3), climax (τέλος) of the law (10:4), and focus of God's word of grace in the new age of redemptive history (10:6–8).[33]

Rom 10:5–13 exposit the final words of v. 4: "so that there might be righteousness for everyone who believes."[34] Paul begins by citing Scripture to explain the connection between righteousness and faith. He cites Lev 18:5: "the person who does these things will find life through them" (ὁ ποιήσας αὐτὰ ἄνθρωπος ζήσεται ἐν αὐτοῖς).[35] These words capture

---

33. In this passage, Paul's criticism of the Jews with respect to the law is mainly salvation-historical: they have failed to see that its era has come to an end. (Contrast Paul's earlier treatment of the Jews [Rom 2:1–3:20], which focuses on their inability to fulfill the law because he is there looking at the situation before Christ; cf. U. Wilckens, *Der Brief an die Römer* [3 vols.; EKKNT; Neukirchen/Vluyn: Neukirchener, 1978–81] 2.102.) But this is not Paul's only basis for criticism of the Jews in these verses (contra, e.g., Sanders, *Paul, the Law and the Jewish People*, 37–38). Paul also makes clear that Israel's failure to perceive the shift of salvation history in Christ is bound up with her myopic preoccupation with the law and its works. Criticism of the Jews for "legalism," the attempt to secure a relationship with God through doing the law, is part and parcel of this text (cf. T. R. Schreiner, "Israel's Failure to Attain Righteousness in Romans 9:30–10:3," *TJ* 12 [1991] 215–20; T. Laato, *Paulus und das Judentum: Anthropologische Erwägungen* [Abo: Abo Academy, 1991] 250–54; R. H. Bell, *Provoked to Jealousy: The Origin and Purpose of the Jealousy Motif in Romans 9–11* [WUNT 2.63; Tübingen: Mohr Siebeck, 1994] 187–91).

34. See particularly C. T. Rhyne, *Faith Establishes the Law* (SBLDS 55; Chico, CA: Scholars, 1981) 110–11; cf. also F. W. Maier, *Israel in der Heilsgeschichte nach Röm 9–11* (BZ 12.11/12; Münster: Aschendorff, 1929) 467; E. Käsemann, *Commentary on Romans* (Grand Rapids: Eerdmans, 1980) 284.

35. Paul, as usual, follows the LXX, introducing minor stylistic changes required by his taking the clause out of its context. The LXX straighforwardly translates the Hebrew in Lev 18:5 (אשר יעשה אתם האדם וחי בהם).

a central role of the law as it is presented in the Pentateuch: by obeying its commandments, people may find "life," peaceful, secure, and bountiful existence in the land of promise.[36] The verse is cited in this sense regularly in later parts of the OT and in Judaism (Ezek 20:11, 13, 21; Neh 9:29; CD 3:14–16; 4Q266; Philo, *Prelim. Studies* 86–87; *LAB* 23:10; *Pss. Sol.* 14:1–2; and cf. Luke 10:28).[37] As in Gal 3:12, then (where Paul cites the same verse), the quotation of Lev 18:5 touches on what, for Paul at least, is fundamental to the law of Moses: it is something to be "done"; it demands "works."[38] Any "righteousness," then, that is derived from the law will be a righteousness that is based on human doing. Such a righteousness, as Paul has already shown (Rom 9:31–32a, 10:3), is a phantom righteousness, for it cannot bring a person into relationship with a holy God.

If the Jews would only see the message of the OT as Paul sees it, they would recognize that the OT itself proclaims the indispensability of faith—the very message that Paul and the other apostles are preaching. This is the point that Paul is making by means of his references to Deut 30:12–14 in Rom 10:6–8. But what are we to make of this appeal to Scripture? Is Paul's interpretation a simple *tour de force* by which he arbitrarily reads faith and the gospel into a text that has nothing to do with them? Let us first see how Paul integrates references to Deuteronomy into his argument (see table, p. 403). The δέ at the beginning of v. 6 is adversative: as the context makes clear, "the righteousness of

---

36. The ב before הם 'them' (e.g., "the decrees and the laws") is instrumental ("by them") not locative ("in them"). See, e.g., G. J. Wenham, *The Book of Leviticus* (NICOT; Grand Rapids: Eerdmans, 1979) 253; P. M. Sprinkle, *Law and Life: The Interpretation of Leviticus 18:5 in Early Judaism and in Paul* (WUNT 2:241; Tübingen: Mohr Siebeck, 2008) 28–34; contra, e.g., W. C. Kaiser, Jr., "The Book of Leviticus" in *NIB* 1:1125; ibid., "Leviticus 18:5 and Paul: 'Do This and You Shall Live (Eternally?),'" *JETS* 14 (1971) 19–28; N. Chibici-Revneanu, "Leben im Gesetz: Die paulinische Interpretation von Lev 18:5 (Gal 3:12; Röm 10:5)," *NovT* 50 (2008) 105–19.

37. S. J. Gathercole ("Torah, Life, and Salvation: Leviticus 18:5 in Early Judaism and the New Testament," in *From Prophecy to Testament: The Function of the Old Testament in the New* [ed. C. A. Evans; Peabody, MA: Hendrickson, 2004] 126–45) and Sprinkle (*Law and Life*, 34–130) have shown that most of these texts (the only clear exception being the Philo passage) interpret the verse as a soteriological promise. Note also rabbinic texts such as *t. Shabb.* 15.17: "The commands were given only that men should live through them, not that men should die through them" (cf. E. E. Urbach, *The Sages: Their Concepts and Beliefs* [2 vols.; Jerusalem: Magnes, 1979] 1:424–26). Both Targum Onkelos and Targum Pseudo-Jonathan paraphrase the Hebrew with the language of "eternal life."

38. I bypass here the question of the appropriateness of rendering Hebrew תורה by Greek νόμος. The NT authors, at least, choose not to "correct" the LXX at this point, suggesting that they do not find anything fundamentally inappropriate about the lexical equivalence.

Romans 10	MT	LXX
(6) But the righteousness that is by faith says:	Deut 9:4 After the Lord your God has driven them out before you,	Deut 9:4
Do not say in your heart (μὴ εἴπῃς ἐν τῇ καρδίᾳ σου) "Who will ascend into heaven?"	**do not say in your heart** (אל־תאמר בלבבך) "The Lord has brought me here to take possession of this land because of my righteousness"	μὴ εἴπῃς ἐν τῇ καρδίᾳ σου
	Deut 30:11–14 For this commandment, that I am commanding you today, is not too difficult for you or too far. It is not in heaven as though you should say	
(τίς ἀναβήσεται εἰς τὸν οὐρανόν;)	**"Who will go up for us to heaven to bring it to us** (מי יעלה־לנו השמימה) so that we might hear it and do it?" And it is not beyond the sea as though you should say	τίς ἀναβήσεται ἡμῖν εἰς τὸν οὐρανὸν
that is, to bring Christ down		
(7) or, "Who will go down into the abyss?" (τίς καταβήσεται εἰς τὴν ἄβυσσον)	**"Who will go across for us to the other side of the sea** (מי יעבר־לנו אל־עבר הים)	τίς διαπεράσει ἡμῖν εἰς τὸ πέραν τῆς θαλάσσης
	[Ps 107:26a They mounted up to the heavens and went down to the depths (יעלו שמים ירדו תהומות)]	[Ps 106:26 ἀναβαίνουσιν ἕως τῶν οὐρανῶν καὶ καταβαίνουσιν ἕως τῶν ἀβύσσων]
that is, to bring Christ up from the dead.	and bring it to us so that we might hear it and do it?"	
(8) But what does it say?		
The word is near you, in your mouth and in your heart, (ἐγγύς σου τὸ ῥῆμά ἐστιν ἐν τῷ στόματί σου καὶ ἐν τῇ καρδίᾳ σου),	**For the word is very near to you, in your mouth and in your heart** (כי־קרוב אליך הדבר מאד בפיך ובלבבך)	ἔστιν σου ἐγγὺς τὸ ῥῆμα σφόδρα ἐν τῷ στόματί σου καὶ ἐν τῇ καρδίᾳ σου
	that you might do it.	
that is the word of faith that we are preaching.		
	(*t. Neof.*: Neither is the law beyond the great sea that one may say: would that we had one like the prophet Jonah who would descend into the depths of the Great Sea and bring it up for us.)	

the law" (v. 5) stands in contrast to the "righteousness of faith."[39] Paul follows the biblical pattern of personifying activities and concepts that are closely related to God by claiming that the "righteousness of faith speaks."[40] As the chart above reveals, Paul's introductory warning, "Do not say in your heart," is taken from Deut 9:4. These words gain particular force in light of the context from which Paul takes them. In Deut 9:4–6 Moses warns the people of Israel that when they have taken possession of the land into which God is bringing them, they must not think that they have earned it because of "their own righteousness." Paul therefore adds implicit biblical support to his criticism of the Israel of his day for its pursuit of their own righteousness (Rom 10:5 with Deut 9:4). Following the introductory allusion to Deut 9:4 are three quotations from Deut 30:12–14, each with its accompanying interpretation. These interpretations are introduced with the phrase "that is" (τοῦτ' ἔστιν), which some think Paul uses to signal his intention to pursue a "pesher"-style exegesis, the mode of interpretation typical of the DSS community (the Greek phrase is similar to the familiar interpretive gloss in the scrolls, פשרו 'its interpretation [is]'.[41] But this connection is not clear.[42]

The first selection from Deuteronomy 30 is the question "Who will ascend into heaven?" These words are taken from a larger question in

---

39. A few scholars think the δέ indicates continuity between vv. 5 and 6, either in the sense that "the one who does these things" in v. 5 is Christ, whose obedience provides the foundation for the righteousness of faith (K. Barth, *CD* II.2, 245; A. J. Bandstra, *The Law and the Elements of the World: An Exegetical Study in Aspects of Paul's Teaching* [Kampen: Kok, 1964] 103–5; C. E. B. Cranfield, *A Critical and Exegetical Commentary on the Epistle to the Romans* [vol. 2; ICC; Edinburgh: T & T Clark, 1979] 521; W. S. Campbell, "Christ the End of the Law: Romans 10:4," *Studia Biblica* III [1978] 77–78; M. Barth, *The People of God* [JSNTSup 5; Sheffield: JSOT Press, 1983] 39) or in the sense that the true "doing" of the law is nothing but faith (G. E. Howard, "Christ the End of the Law: The Meaning of Romans 10:4ff.," *JBL* 88 [1969] 333–36; D. P. Fuller, *Gospel and Law: Contrast or Continuum?* [Grand Rapids: Eerdmans, 1980] 66–68; F. Flückiger, "Christus, des Gesetzes τέλος," *TZ* 11 [1955] 153–57; R. Bring, *Christus und das Gesetz* [Leiden: Brill, 1969] 54; R.Badenas, *Christ the End of the Law: Romans 10*:4 in Pauline Perspective [JSNTSup 10; Sheffield: JSOT Press, 1985] 120–25; N. T. Wright, *Climax of the Covenant*, 245).

40. Wisdom (Prov 8:21–36); the Word (Isa 55:10–11). For similar personifications of "righteousness," see Ps 85:10–13 and Isa 45:8. As J. D. G. Dunn notes, this last verse might be significant for Paul since he has perhaps alluded to Isa 45:9 in Rom 9:20–21 (*Romans 9–11* [WBC 38B; Waco, TX: Word, 1989] 602).

41. The word is found frequently in 1QpHab and 1QpNah; for the connection with Romans, see, e.g., E. Lohse, *Der Brief an die Römer* (KEK; Göttingen: Vandenhoeck & Ruprecht, 2003) 294.

42. The Greek phrase τοῦτ' ἔστιν is widely used in the LXX, Philo, and the NT to introduce an explanation; there is little reason to think that it deliberately echoes the DSS (see esp. M. A. Seifrid, "Paul's Approach to the Old Testament in Rom 10:6–8," *TJ* 6 [1985] 29–34; Koch, *Die Schrift*, 229–30).

Deuteronomy that denies any need to go into heaven to gain access to God's law so that the people might obey it. Paul applies it to Christ. Some interpreters think that Paul is asking about the need to bring the ascended Christ down,[43] but it is more likely that he refers to the incarnation.[44] Christ has already come down from heaven and taken on human flesh in order to redeem humans; no one has to go into heaven to bring him down. God, from his side, has acted to make himself and his will for his people known; his people now have no excuse for not responding.

Paul's second use of Deuteronomy 30 language comes in Rom 10:7 and is quite parallel to the first. Again Paul asks a question, "Who will descend into the deep?" and adds a christological explanation: "that is, to bring Christ up from the dead." If Paul's quotation in v. 6, however, straightforwardly followed the text of Deuteronomy, this second quotation differs significantly: Deut 30:13 asks about "crossing the sea." This difference has led some scholars to think that Paul may here be quoting Ps 107:26 rather than Deut 30:13.[45] But this is unlikely, since Paul's language is generally parallel to that of Deuteronomy and since it is sandwiched between two other references to Deuteronomy 30. In fact, the "sea" and the "abyss" were somewhat interchangeable concepts in the OT and in Judaism;[46] and some Aramaic paraphrases of the

---

43. E.g., O. Michel, *Der Brief an die Römer* (5th ed.; KEKNT; Göttingen: Vandenhoeck & Ruprecht, 1955), 328; Käsemann, *Romans*, 288; Dunn, *Romans 9–11*, 605; T. Holland, *Romans: The Divine Marriage. A Biblical Theological Commentary* (Eugene, OR: Pickwick, 2011) 348–49.

44. This is the interpretation of most church fathers; and see also, among modern interpreters, J. Murray, *The Epistle to the Romans* (vol. 2; NICNT; Grand Rapids: Eerdmans, 1965) 53; C. K. Barrett, *A Commentary on the Epistle to the Romans* (HNTC; San Francisco: Harper & Row, 1957) 199; J. Fitzmyer, *Romans* (AB; New York: Doubleday, 1993) 590; N. T. Wright, "Romans," *NIB* 10:663. The sequence "come down" (v. 6) and "go up" (v. 7) reflects the common early Christian kerymatic sequence of Christ's incarnation and resurrection (see Phil 2:6–11, 1 Tim 3:16; and cf. E. Schweizer, "Zur Herkunft der Präexistenzvorstellung bei Paulus," *EvT* 19 [1959] 67–68).

45. See, e.g., Fitzmyer, *Romans*, 590. Ps 107:26 refers to those whom God has redeemed from trouble (cf. v. 2): "They mounted up to heaven, they went down to the depths; their courage melted away in their calamity" (see the chart above).

46. In the LXX, ἄβυσσος almost always translates תהום, which usually refers to the deep places of the sea (BDB), but which in later Judaism was also used of the depths of the earth and the place where evil spirits are confined (J. Jeremias, *TDNT* 1:9). On the equivalence of the terms, see esp. J. Heller, "Himmel- und Höllenfahrt nach Römer 10, 6–7," *EvT* 32 (1972) 482; on similar rabbinic traditions, see A. M. Goldberg, "Torah aus der Unterwelt? Eine Bemerkung zu Röm 10,6–7," *BZ* 14 (1970) 127–31. In the NT, "abyss" refers to the place where (evil) spirits dwell and are confined (Luke 8:31; Rev 9:1–2, 11; 11:7; 17:8; 20:1, 3).

Deut 30:13 used the language of the abyss.⁴⁷ Paul has probably, then, under the influence of these texts, shifted the horizontal imagery to a vertical imagery that better suits his application.⁴⁸ As he could use the fact of the incarnation to suggest the foolishness of "going into heaven" to bring Christ down, so now he can use the fact of the resurrection to deny any need to "go down to the abyss" to bring Christ up from "the realm of the dead."

In Rom 10:6–7, Paul uses language from Deuteronomy 30 to indicate what the "righteousness of faith" does *not say*. Now, in v. 8, he continues to plunder Deuteronomy 30 to show what this righteousness *does* say: "The word is near you; it is in your mouth and in your heart." Paul's Greek follows the LXX of Deut 30:14 closely (which in turn straightforwardly renders the Hebrew; again, see the chart above). Significant, however, is Paul's omission of the concluding words in Deuteronomy: "so that you may obey it" (that is, "what I [Moses] am commanding you today"—Deut 30:11). Paul is therefore able to apply these words to "the message concerning faith that we proclaim."

What are we to make of this startling "shift of application"?⁴⁹ How can Paul take a text that enjoins obedience to the law of God and apply it to the message of the gospel of righteousness by faith? Is he arbitrarily twisting the Scriptures to fit his theology of the gospel? And, if so, what happens to the unity of Scripture? When I worked on this passage in preparation of my commentary on Romans in the early 1990s, I was frustrated in my attempt to provide a neat and satisfactory answer to this question—specifically, an answer that would both interpret Romans 10 accurately and explain the legitimacy of Paul's appeal to Deuteronomy.⁵⁰ I seized on this invitation as an opportunity to return to the issue and see if I could do any better.

---

47. *Targum Neofiti* reads, "Neither is the Law beyond the Great Sea that one may say: Would that we had one like the prophet Jonah who would descend into the depths of the Great Sea and bring it up for us" (the translation is from M. McNamara, *The New Testament and the Palestinian Targum to the Pentateuch* [AnBib 27; Rome: Pontifical Biblical Institute, 1966] 370–78). It may also be significant for Paul's application of the language to the resurrection of Christ that Jonah 2:3–10 uses both מים 'sea' and תהום 'abyss' in parallel of the prophet's experience in the belly of the great fish (see Matt 12:40).

48. Stanley, *Paul and the Language of Scripture*, 131.

49. For the language of "shift of application," see my *The Old Testament in the Gospel Passion Narratives* (Sheffield: Almond, 1983; reprint: Eugene, OR: Wipf & Stock) 51–55.

50. The concern for "legitimacy" in the NT interpretation of the OT is a direct by-product of a high view of Scripture. For a recent consideration of this important issue, see D. J. Moo and A. D. Naselli, "The Problem of the New Testament's Use of the Old Testament," in vol. 1 of *"But My Words Will Never Pass Away": The Enduring Authority of the Christian Scriptures* (2 vols.; ed. D. A. Carson; Grand Rapids: Eerdmans, forthcoming); see

What are our options? First, we could deny that there is a problem. The problem disappears if, in fact, Paul has no intention of claiming the authority of the Deuteronomy text for his own teaching. He may simply be borrowing language from Deuteronomy—language that, as we will see below, had become somewhat proverbial—to make his point about Christ and the gospel.[51] It is certainly unfair to label this approach a desperate measure to get around a problem. Certain elements of the text at least suggest this is not an unreasonable option. Paul does not use a traditional "introductory formula" (e.g., γέγραπται 'it is written') to introduce his quotations from Deuteronomy. Rather, he puts the language of Deuteronomy in the mouth of personified "righteousness of faith." As we have seen, Paul cites fragments from Deut 30:12–14; and, in one case, he changes the wording of the fragment he quotes significantly. Moreover, he introduces his explanations of the Deuteronomy fragments with an expression ("that is") that he never elsewhere uses to connect scriptural citations to his own conclusions. I am more open to this approach than I was twenty years ago: the combination of unusual, even unprecedented, features in Paul's appeal to the words of Deuteronomy may, indeed, imply a certain "distance" from strict interpretation of the text.[52] Nevertheless, it is hard to avoid the impression that Paul is intending, to some degree, to appeal to the authority of Deuteronomy for the points he is making here. More interpreters agree.[53]

Second, we could at least lessen the degree of difference between Paul and Deut 30:11–14 if these verses are a prediction of the new covenant. This paragraph occurs toward the end of the presentation of the Moabite covenant in Deut 28:69–30:20[29:1–30:20].[54] Moses' warning about the consequences of the failure of the people to ratify the

---

also D. J. Moo, "Paul's Univeralizing Hermeneutics in Romans," *Southern Baptist Journal of Theology* 11 (2007) 62–90.

51. W. Sanday and A. C. Headlam, *A Critical and Exegetical Commentary on the Epistle to the Romans* (ICC; Edinburgh: T & T Clark, 1902) 287; C. Hodge, *Commentary on the Epistle to the Romans* (Grand Rapids: Eerdmans, 1950) 338; Fitzmyer, *Romans*, 588; H. Hübner, *Gottes Ich und Israel: Zum Schriftgebrauch des Paulus in Römer 9–11* (FRLANT 136; Göttingen: Vandenhoeck & Ruprecht, 1984) 86–91; Longenecker, *Biblical Exegesis*, 121–23.

52. R. E. Ciampa appropriately views Paul's use of Deuteronomy to lie somewhere between "straight" exegesis and the mere use of Deuteronomic language to make a point ("Deuteronomy in Galatians and Romans," in *Deuteronomy in the New Testament* [ed. M. J. J. Menken and S. Moyise; London: T & T Clark, 2007] 107). Calvin, similarly, claims that Paul's purpose is not "strictly to explain this passage" but "apply it to the explanation of his present subject" (*Romans*, 389).

53. See, e.g., Stanley, *Paul and the Language of Scripture*, 129.

54. J. G. McConville, *Deuteronomy* (Apollos Old Testament Commentary 5; Downers Grove, IL: InterVarsity, 2002) 423.

covenant by their consistent obedience to the law turns into a semi-realistic prediction of failure. By the end of chapter 29, warning about the curse has become a description of the curse that will, indeed, come. In 30:1–10, then, Moses pictures the people in exile and predicts that through their own "turning" God would himself effect a "turning," accomplishing for them the "circumcision of the heart" that Moses required of the people (10:16) but that they have proved incapable of doing for themselves (v. 6). After this prediction of future restoration, most interpreters think that Moses returns in vv. 11–14 to the present, exhorting the people of his day to obey the law. But a significant minority of interpreters argues that vv. 11–14 continue the future focus of vv. 1–10. It is at this time, when God himself circumcises the hearts of his people, that he will bring his word near to Israel (v. 14). Paul would therefore legitimately be applying Lev 18:5 to the Old Covenant and Deut 30:11–14 to the New, when God writes his law on the hearts of his people (Jer 31:31–34).[55] I wish I could interpret Deut 30:11–14 this way: it would, indeed, considerably diminish the apparent dissonance between this text and Paul's application. But I am not sure that I can. Most interpreters of Deuteronomy argue that the characteristic language of "today" in v. 11 suggests that the implied tense in vv. 11–14 shifts back to the present—from future prediction in vv. 1–10 to exhortation about the present in vv. 11–14.[56] Reluctantly, then, I must reject this option.

A third attempt at explaining Paul's interpretive approach appeals to the appropriation of Deut 30:11–14 in some other early Jewish texts. In

---

55. See esp. P. A. Barker, *The Triumph of Grace in Deuteronomy: Faithless Israel, Faithful Yahweh in Deuteronomy* (Paternoster Biblical Monographs; Waynesboro, GA, 2004) 168–90; and also S. R. Coxhead, "Deuteronomy 30:11–14 as a Prophecy of the New Covenant in Christ," *WTJ* 68 (2006) 305–20; B. D. Estelle, "Leviticus 18:5 and Deuteronomy 30:1–14 in Biblical Theological Development: Entitlement to Heaven Foreclosed and Proffered," in *The Law is Not Of Faith*, 123–37; J. G. Millar, *Now Choose Life: Theology and Ethics in Deuteronomy* (NSBT 6; Downers Grove, IL: InterVarsity, 1998) 94, 174–75; J. Sailhamer, *The Pentateuch as Narrative* (Grand Rapids: Zondervan, 1992) 473. This view is assumed (though not argued) by Wright, "Romans," 659–60 ("restoration after the exile"). Other scholars, while admitting that Deut 30:11–14 focuses on the Israelites of Moses' day, note that the future orientation of vv. 1–10 would inevitably have opened up a reading of vv. 11–14 as also having relevance to the future (e.g., McConville, *Deuteronomy*, 429; T. R. Schreiner, *Romans* [BECNT; Grand Rapids: Baker, 1998] 558).

56. E.g., S. R. Driver, *A Critical and Exegetical Commentary on Deuteronomy* (ICC; New York: Charles Scribner's Sons, 1916) 330–31; McConville, *Deuteronomy*, 429; E. J. Woods, *Deuteronomy* (TOTC; Downers Grove, IL: InterVarsity, 2011) 294; W. Brueggemann, *Deuteronomy* (Abingdon Old Testament Commentaries; Nashville: Abingdon, 2001) 267–68; C. J. H. Wright, *Deuteronomy* (NIBC; Peabody, MA: Hendrickson, 1996) 290–91; J. H. Tigay, *Deuteronomy* (JPS Torah Commentary; Philadelphia: Jewish Publication Society, 1996) 286. Most commentators do not even mention the alternative.

Bar 3:29-30, language from Deut 30:11-14 is applied to wisdom: "Who went up into heaven and received her [wisdom] and brought her down from the clouds? Who travelled beyond the sea and found her and will buy her for precious gold?" Wisdom is associated with "the commandment of life" in Bar 3:9, relying on a widespread tendency to identify torah and wisdom in Judaism. Paul, in his turn, identifies Christ with wisdom. Therefore, in light of Christ being the *telos* of the law, it would make sense for Paul to use language from a passage that was associated with wisdom with respect to Christ.[57] However, Paul's reliance on the Baruch text is not clear;[58] and the association of Christ with wisdom is perhaps neither as widespread nor as important to Paul's Christology as some have made it.[59] Moreover, while dependence on this Jewish tradition may help explain why Paul uses Deuteronomy in the way that he does, it does not help us at all with the "legitimacy" question.[60]

Fourth, we could widen our horizons and seek to understand how Paul's use of Deuteronomy might cohere with a broad reading of the

---

57. See esp. M. J. Suggs, "'The Word is Near You': Romans 10:6-10 within the Purpose of the Letter," in *Christian History and Interpretation: Studies Presented to John Knox* (ed. W. R. Farmer, C. F. D. Moule, and R. Niebuhr; Cambridge: Cambridge University Press, 1967) 289-312. Many scholars find this background to be at least part of the explanation for Paul's application; see, e.g., S. Kim, *The Origin of Paul's Gospel* (Grand Rapids: Eerdmans, 1981) 130-31; E. J. Schnabel, *Law and Wisdom from Ben Sira to Paul: A Tradition-historical Enquiry into the Relation of Law, Wisdom, and Ethics* (WUNT 2.16; Tübingen: Mohr Siebeck, 1985; reprint: Eugene, OR: Wipf & Stock, 2011) 248-49; Hays, *Scripture*, 78-81; Koch, *Der Schrift*, 153-60; B. Witherington (with D. Hyatt), *Paul's Letter to the Romans: A Socio Rhetorical Commentary* (Grand Rapids: Eerdmans, 2004) 262. E. E. Johnson thinks that there is contact with Baruch but that Paul simply identifies wisdom with the gospel (*The Function of Apocalyptic and Wisdom Traditions in Romans 9-11* [SBLDS 109; Atlanta: Scholars, 1989] 133-37). Deut 30:11-14 figured in other Jewish writers also; Philo, for example, applied the text to the search for "the good" (*On the Posterity of Cain* 84-85; *Change of Names* 236-37; *Rewards and Punishments* 80; *Virtues* 183; see esp. P. J. Bekken, "Paul's Use of Deut. 30,12-14 in Jewish Context. Some Observations," in *The New Testament and Hellenistic Judaism* (ed. P. Borgen and S. Giversen; Peabody, MA: Hendrickson, 1995) 53-81.

58. As Seifrid points out, Paul's text is closer to Deuteronomy than to Baruch ("Paul's Approach," 20-23). Moreover, the language of ascending to heaven and crossing the sea (or going down into the abyss) became somewhat proverbial (see *Jub.* 24:31; *4 Ezra* 4:8; *b. B. Meṣ.* 59b).

59. For an extreme expression of doubt on this point, see G. D. Fee, *Pauline Christology: An Exegetical-Theological Study* (Peabody, MA: Hendrickson, 2007) 594-619.

60. See the perceptive comments on this by Hays: "The more closely Paul's methods can be identified with recognized interpretive conventions of first-century Judaism, the less arbitrary and more historically understandable they appear; however, at the same time, such historical explanations of Paul's exegesis render it increasingly difficult to see how interpretations that employ such methods can bear any persuasive power or normative value for that mythical creature of whom Bultmann spoke with such conviction: modern man" (*Echoes of Scripture*, 8-9).

theology of Deuteronomy as Paul sees it to have come to fruition in Christ. In 1996 I wrote the following:

> The best explanation for Paul's use of the Deut 30 text is to think that he finds in this passage an expression of the grace of God in establishing a relationship with his people. As God brought his word near to Israel so they might know and obey him, so God now brings his word "near" to both Jews and Gentiles that they might know him through his Son Jesus Christ and respond in faith and obedience. Because Christ, rather than the law, is now the focus of God's revelatory word (see 10:4), Paul can "replace" the commandment of Deut 30:11–14 with Christ. Paul's application of Deut 30:12–14, then, is of course not a straightforward exegesis of the passage. But it is a valid application of the principle of that passage in the context of the development of salvation history. The grace of God that underlies the Mosaic covenant is operative now in the New Covenant; and, just as Israel could not plead the excuse that she did not know God's will, so now, Paul says, neither Jew nor Gentile can plead ignorance of God's revelation in Jesus Christ.[61]

I think this basic approach can be strengthened and elaborated by appeal to two theologically sophisticated assessments of Deuteronomy and its relationship to Paul.

The first is from an OT scholar noted for his work on Deuteronomy, Gordon McConville. McConville argues, broadly, that Deuteronomy offers "a sophisticated theological reflection" on the tension between law and grace, between exhortations to Israel that appear to assume her ability to respond and confirm the blessing of God and expressions of pessimism that suggest that Israel is "constitutionally incapable of choosing the way of life." This tension emerges particularly clearly in Deuteronomy 30: vv. 1–10 look to God to reverse the curse that will inevitably fall on Israel, while vv. 11–14 appear to assume Israel's responsibility for her own fate.[62] Ultimately, McConville suggests, the exhortation gains validity only as the response to a new work of God's grace.

---

61. Moo, *Romans*, 653. For similar approaches, see J. Calvin, *Commentaries on the Epistle of Paul the Apostle to the Romans* (Grand Rapids: Eerdmans, 1947) 389; F. L. Godet, *Commentary on Romans* (Grand Rapids: Kregel, 1977) 379; Murray, *Romans*, 2:52–53; Cranfield, *Romans*, 2:526; Seifrid, "Paul's Approach," 35–37; D. O. Via, "A Structuralist Approach to Paul's Old Testament Hermeneutic," *Int* 28 (1974) 215–18.

62. G. J. McConville, *Grace in the End: A Study in Deuteronomic Theology* (Grand Rapids: Zondervan, 1993) 63–64, 133–34, 138. I hope that my failure to interact with McConville in my commentary was because the book was not published in time for me to take it into account.

A second reflection on the relationship between Paul and Deuteronomy is found in Francis Watson's stimulating study of Paul's appropriation of themes within the Pentateuch for his distinctive law/gospel emphasis.[63] Watson argues that "Paul's fragmentary exegetical statements do indeed stem from a broad construal of the narrative shape of scripture, and that fundamental scriptural themes function as hermeneutical keys."[64] Watson therefore considers Paul's use of Deut 30:11–14 within a broader reading of Deuteronomy (and ultimately of the Pentateuch). Paul, Watson argues, is engaged in debate with other Jews of his day about the ultimate meaning of Deuteronomy, a book that ends with a "severe internal tension": a tension "between conditional statements, which imply that the choice between blessing and curse, life and death is genuinely open, and statements of prophetic denunciation, in which the realization of the curse has become a certainty."[65] Many of Paul's Jewish contemporaries read Deut 30:11–14 as proclaiming that God's restoration of his people would occur via the law. Paul cannot accept this reading of the text, and so he re-interprets it.[66] Moses' "over-optimistic claim . . . stands in need of correction." But this "correction" is not simply (or only) an arbitrary imposition on the meaning of Deuteronomy from a later, christologically oriented perspective: it is a correction that Moses himself suggests with his focus on the primacy of divine action in chapter 32.[67] Here, beyond the threat of curse in chapters 27–29 and the illusory promise of a new start by means of the law (ch. 30), Moses speaks of an unconditional work of God, a focus that resembles the unconditional promise to Abraham on which Paul puts so much stress.[68]

As the title of McConville's book puts it, then, Deuteronomy is about "grace in the end." Paul is convinced that this grace is manifest in Christ, being made available to both Jew and Gentile on the same terms: faith. His claim that the "near" word is to be found in Christ and the gospel proclamation about him is at the same time a faithful reading of Deuteronomy and an extension of the meaning of Deuteronomy in light of

---

63. F. Watson, *Paul and the Hermeneutics of Faith* (London: T & T Clark, 2004). He discusses Deuteronomy on pp. 415–513.
64. Ibid., 17.
65. Ibid., 429.
66. Ibid., 454.
67. Ibid., 439. I do not endorse the language of "correction" that Watson uses here.
68. Ibid., 453. D. Lincicum (*Paul and the Early Jewish Encounter with Deuteronomy* [WUNT 2.284; Tübingen: Mohr Siebeck, 2010] 157–67) follows Watson to the extent that he, too, stresses that Paul reads Deuteronomy from back to front, finding the focus on divine initiative in ch. 32 to be the key to his reading.

the movement of redemptive history. Paul's appeal to Deut 30:11–14 exhibits the "deeper meaning" approach that typifies his (and other NT authors') reading of the OT. The word that brings the fulfillment of the promise, the "grace that lies beyond exile," is not the torah, limited as it was in its effectiveness because of human sin, but a "new" word of God that itself provides for the true fulfillment of the torah—a fulfillment that, in my view, Christians experience not in their own always imperfect obedience, but in their union with Christ, who has fulfilled the torah on our behalf (Rom 8:4).[69]

Conclusion

Paul's appeal to Deut 27:26 in Gal 3:10 and Deut 30:11–14 in Rom 10:6–8 shows that he finds in Deuteronomy both law and grace. The torah given to Israel reveals to the people (and to us!) the character of God and sets forth God's will for the people with whom he has entered into covenant. That torah, however, as Moses anticipates and as the history of Israel tragically demonstrates, could not be fulfilled by people whose hearts, because of sin, were "hard." Paul finds in the warning about a curse that would fall on failure to uphold all the torah a principle about "law" in general: it makes demands that, because they cannot be met, confirms people in the death they have already chosen. But Deuteronomy also proclaims grace: grace in the very existence of Israel as a people chosen by God, grace in God's willingness to reveal his will to this people but, ultimately, a final and transcendent act of grace that restores God's people after their sin and exile. This is the grace that Paul finds to be proclaimed in the "near word" of Deut 30:11–14.

---

69. My appeal to Rom 8:4 for this point is certainly not uncontested (to put it mildly!); but I still think it is the best understanding of the verse (see my *Romans*, 481–85).

PART 3

The Lasting Significance of Deuteronomy

Making the Ten Count
Reflections on the Lasting Message of the Decalogue

JASON S. DEROUCHIE

Throughout history, few OT texts have had as much impact on the church as the Ten Words (Exod 20:2–17 // Deut 5:6–21).[1] In an earlier essay in this volume titled "Counting the Ten," I argued that a modified version of the Catholic-Lutheran numbering of the Decalogue is most faithful to the discourse grammar and finds strong support from the perspective of style, semantic content, and cantillation (Fig. 1, p. 416). However, knowing how to count the Ten means nothing if we fail to make them count.

Author's Note: Dan Block loves God and his church, and it was because Dan's solid scholarship was matched by this love that I accepted his invitation to do my doctoral studies under his watchful, fatherly care. While the body of my dissertation approached Deuteronomy in order to better understand discourse grammar, Dan stressed from the very beginning that my work also had to show the exegetical payoff of my discoveries in the interpretation of the biblical text. I forever will remain grateful to God and Dan for my years under this man's masterful tutelage, which set fresh trajectories for my life and scholarship and grounded my commitment to engage academic ministry for the glory of God and for sake of the church.

1. On this, see most recently J. P. Greenman and T. Larsen, eds., *The Decalogue through the Centuries: From the Hebrew Scriptures to Benedict XVI* (Louisville: Westminster John Knox, 2012). The influence of the Decalogue on the church naturally grows out of its central place in the OT. The Ten Words are the first written material in Scripture specified as authoritatively binding (but note Gen 5:1 and Exod 17:14), and they are the only portion of Scripture that we are told was "written with the finger of God" (Exod 31:18; Deut 9:10; cf. Exod 24:12, 32:15–16; Deut 5:22). They are classified as "the words of the covenant" (Exod 34:27–28), which highlights how they and all the rest of Scripture that develops from them were not the decrees of a distant dictator but the loving instructions of a covenant father to his vassal children, all designed to sustain relationship in the context of freedom. The Ten Words are the only part of the Bible that was placed in the ark of the covenant (Exod 40:20–21; cf. 25:21–22, Deut 10:1–5; Heb 9:4), and they stand in a foundational position at the head of all other instructions in Exodus and Deuteronomy. They are also echoed throughout Scripture as a summary of what it means to love God and neighbor (see Hos 4:2; Jer 7:9; Pss 50:16–23, 81:9; Matt 5:21, 19:18; Mark 10:19; Luke 18:20; Rom 13:9). All these elements display the unique role the Ten Words played among those faithful to Yahweh.

Fig. 1. A Modified Catholic-Lutheran Numbering of the Ten Words

1. I am Yahweh. . . . Never other gods (Exod 20:2–6 // Deut 5:6–10)
2. Never bear Yahweh's name in vain (Exod 20:7 // Deut 5:11)
3. Remember (/Observe) the Sabbath (Exod 20:9–11 // Deut 5:12–15)
4. Honor your parents (Exod 20:12 // Deut 5:16)
5. Never murder (Exod 20:13 // Deut 5:17)
6. (And) Never commit adultery (Exod 20:14 // Deut 5:18)
7. (And) Never steal (Exod 20:15 // Deut 5:19)
8. (And) Never bear false witness (Exod 20:16 // Deut 5:20)
9. (And) Never covet your neighbor's house (/wife) (Exod 20:17a // Deut 5:21a)
10. (And) Never covet (/desire) your neighbor's wife, etc. (/house, field, etc.) (Exod 20:17b // Deut 5:21b)

As a step toward this end, the present essay seeks to reflect theologically on the message and lasting significance of the Ten Words, specifically in relation to my enumeration as highlighted in the previous essay. No attempt can be made here at a full analysis, so my comments are designed to set a trajectory for further contemplation and application.[2]

1. The Ten Words and Bearing God's Image

Before unpacking some of the theological implications of my numbering of the Decalogue, we will be served by meditating on the revealed significance of the Ten Words for Israel. According to David, "the law, testimony, precepts, commandment, fear, and rules" that are "perfect, sure, right, pure, clean, and true" are all *"of Yahweh,"* finding their source in him and displaying qualities comparable to his own (Ps 19:7–9). In this vein, Nehemiah characterized the Decalogue and other Sinai instruction as "right rules and true laws, good statues and commandments" (Neh 9:13). Similarly, Paul portrayed God's law as "the embodiment of knowledge and truth" (Rom 2:20), and "holy, righteous, and good" (7:12). These texts connote that Yahweh's *torah* manifests his character. They also suggest that humbly heeding his instruction would result in putting God on display.

Yahweh himself stressed this connection when he charged Israel at Sinai, "If you will indeed heed my voice and keep my covenant . . . then you shall be to me . . . a holy nation" (Exod 19:5–6). By heeding Yah-

---

2. For two recent and very useful summaries that wrestle more broadly with the message and lasting significance of the Ten Words for the church, see D. K. Stuart, *Exodus* (NAC 2; Nashville: B&H, 2006) 438–73; and D. I. Block, *Deuteronomy* (NIVAC; Grand Rapids: Zondervan, 2012) 158–74.

weh's instructions, Israel would fulfill the later charge, "You shall be holy, for I Yahweh your God am holy" (Lev 19:2; cf. 11:44–45; 20:7, 26; 1 Pet 1:16). Moses too emphasized the link between God's commands and the display of God's character when he disclosed the revealed goal of the Ten Words: "Do not fear, for God has come to test you, that the fear of him may be before you, that you may not sin" (Exod 20:20). Through the Decalogue, humans are to encounter God in such a way that inspires both worship and the parade of his worth and wisdom through surrendered, satisfied lives.

In this light, it seems significant that the Ten Words were the only Scripture placed in the ark of the covenant within the holy of holies, directly where a sculptured god would have rested in the temples of Israel's neighbors (Exod 40:20–21; cf. 25:21–22, Deut 10:1–5).[3] For Yahweh, his image would not and could not be mediated through idols of wood or stone. Instead, he purposed that his image would be evident in his people's living out of the Decalogue. As Peter Gentry has proposed, "This is why there could be no image at the centre of Israel's worship—God wanted the commands or instructions in the ark to be imaged in one's actions: this was the divine character embodied in human lives!"[4]

God's original blessing-commission of humanity called for God-dependent families to populate and oversee the earth—reflecting, resembling, and representing the Creator as his appointed image bearers (Gen 1:26–28; cf. 5:1–3).[5] This portrayal of royal and priestly sonship under Yahweh is then picked up in the mission of Israel, God's "son" (Exod 4:22–23), who was appointed to serve as the agent through whom the world would be blessed, overcoming the curse of Genesis 3 (Gen 12:3; cf. 3:15, 22:17b–18). In the context of the whole world, Israel was

---

3. It is also noteworthy that the Levites were to place Moses' collection of sermons in Deuteronomy 1–30 *beside* the ark of the covenant as perpetual witness against Israel (Deut 31:26). That is, because "the Book of the Law" as a whole clarifies the makeup of and means for a God-centered life, it would by nature expose Israel's anticipated rebellion (31:16–21, 27–29).

4. P. J. Gentry and S. J. Wellum, *Kingdom through Covenant: A Biblical-Theological Understanding of the Covenants* (Wheaton, IL: Crossway, 2012) 190 n. 23.

5. For more on this view of the blessing-commission in Genesis, see J. S. DeRouchie, "The Blessing-Commission, the Promised Offspring, and the *Toledot* Structure of Genesis," *JETS* 56 (2013) 219–47; cf. C. M. Kaminski, *From Noah to Israel: Realization of the Primaeval Blessing after the Flood* (JSOTSup 413; New York: T. & T. Clark, 2004). For a helpful discussion of the meaning of divine image bearing as royal sonship expressed through kinship, kingship, and cult, see C. L. Beckerleg, *The "Image of God" in Eden: the Creation of Mankind in Genesis 2:5–3:24 in Light of the* mīs pî pīt pî *and* wpt-r *Rituals of Mesopotamia and Ancient Egypt* (PhD diss., Harvard University, 2009) esp. 161–244, 289–92; cf. M. G. Kline, *Kingdom Prologue: Genesis Foundations for a Covenantal Worldview* (Overland Park, KS: Two Ages, 2000) 45–46; Gentry and Wellum, *Kingdom through Covenant*, 189–209.

commissioned to serve as a "kingdom of priests and a holy nation," which would be accomplished only as they would "heed my voice, and keep my covenant, and be to me a treasured possession among all the peoples" (Exod 19:5–6; cf. Deut 4:5–8, 26:18–19).[6]

That the Decalogue was to play a central role in Israel's God-imaging mission is suggested by the link between Yahweh's invitation for Israel to "heed my voice and keep my covenant" (Exod 19:5) and the statement "God spoke all these words" (20:1) at the head of the Decalogue. The Ten Words, therefore, appear to supply not only the essential content for Israel's covenant obedience but a key means for Israel to fulfill her royal, priestly mission in the world (19:6).[7] As Israel would freely and dependently pursue covenant obedience, celebrating Yahweh's nearness and treasuring his just requirements, God's will and character and rule would be put on display (i.e., imaged), portraying a wisdom that would be attractive to once enemy nations (Deut 4:5–8, 26:18–19) and resulting in God's blessing reaching those once far off (Gen 12:3, 18:18, 22:17b–18, 26:4, 28:14).[8]

---

6. As far back as the LXX, interpreters of Exod 19:5–6 have treated the apodosis of the complex conditional sentence to begin with the clause regarding Israel's being a "treasured possession." However, an apodosis in a two-element syntactic construction is almost always signaled by a shift in grammar, whether through a change in word order, participant, verb form, or the like. In Exod 19:5–6, no shift is apparent until v. 6, where an unnecessary 2mp pronoun (ואתה) is used for emphasis at the front of the clause: "*then you* shall be to me a kingdom of priests and a holy nation." In contrast, in v. 5, the initial infinitive absolute + *yiqtol* (שמוע תשמעו) 'you shall surely hear/heed') is followed by two *weqatal* forms (ושמרתם 'and you shall keep' and והייתם 'and you shall be'), which simply appear to carry forward the conditional protasis: "And now, if *you will indeed heed* unto my voice, *and keep* my covenant, *and be* to me a treasured possession from all people, for all the earth is mine, then you will be to me a kingdom of priests and a holy nation." For a helpful overview of this text (though with a traditional view of the protasis-apodosis relationship), see J. A. Davies, *A Royal Priesthood: Literary and Intertextual Perspectives on an Image of Israel in Exodus 19:6* (JSOTSup 395; London: T. & T. Clark, 2004); cf. Gentry and Wellum, *Kingdom through Covenant*, 309–27.

7. B. S. Childs, *The Book of Exodus* (OTL; Louisville: Westminster, 1974) 371. For a helpful, balanced, and faithful assessment of the role of the Decalogue in ancient Israel as witnessed to in the OT, see D. I. Block, "Reading the Decalogue Right to Left: The Ten Principles of Covenant Relationship in the Hebrew Bible," in idem, *How I Love Your Torah, O LORD! Studies in the Book of Deuteronomy* (Eugene, OR: Cascade, 2011) 21–55. Block argues that, more than the Decalogue, Deuteronomy as a whole played the most foundational role in shaping a Yahwistic worldview and the Scriptures.

8. Davies believes that Israel's priestly role in Exod 19:6 does not include a missional view toward the nations (*Royal Priesthood*, 89–100). However, while the priestly role is certainly focused on drawing near to Yahweh in worship (see Exod 19:22), the explicit contextual markers "among all peoples" and "for all the earth in mine" in Exod 19:5, along with the metanarrative of God's kingdom program laid out in the Pentateuch, suggest that Israel's worship of Yahweh through surrendered lives was to be the key means

The Ten Words together supply a portrait of the ideal old covenant-keeper fulfilling his role as the image of God, which in Deuteronomy finds its closest embodiment in the anticipated king (Deut 17:18–20). Far from replacing Yahweh, Israel's king was to be a man under authority, a man of the Book, who would lead the people as an overflow of his own surrendered life to God.[9] In view of this connection, it is not a stretch to see the Decalogue's multi-orbed call to love God and neighbor as a visual anticipation of the character and behavior of the Pentateuch's expected God-imaging, curse-overcoming, male, royal offspring (Gen 3:15, 22:17b–18, 24:60, 49:8–10; Num 24:7, 17–19).[10] This seed of the woman and of Abraham from the line of Judah is hoped for throughout the rest of the OT (e.g., 2 Sam 7:12–13; Ps 72:4, 9, 17; Jer 23:5–6; Ezek 34:23–24; Isa 9:6–7), and the NT identifies him as Jesus Christ (Luke 1:68–79; Acts 3:25–26; Gal 3:8, 13–14), who is "the image of the invisible God" (Col 1:16; cf. 2 Cor 4:4, Heb 1:3). Scripture portrays Jesus as the last Adam, the true Israel, God's royal-priest Son, whose perfect obedience of faith in his life and death completely fulfilled the law and thus secured eternal blessing for the elect (Rom 5:18–19, Phil 2:8, Heb 5:8). The meeting of the law's legal demands is one way in which Christ Jesus stands as the fulfillment and *telos* of the law of the Decalogue (Matt 5:17, Rom 10:4; cf. Eph 2:15, Col 2:13–15).

Furthermore, just years before Judah fell to Babylon in 586 B.C., Jeremiah began to foretell a new covenant that would grow out of the ashes of divine judgment. The earliest hints come in Jer 3:11–4:4, where the prophet promises that God will forgive the northern and southern kingdom's sins if they will but repent and return to him. In this context, Yahweh declares that, in this eschatological age, "the ark of the covenant of Yahweh . . . shall not come to mind or be remembered

---

by which God's kingdom would expand and the global curse would ultimately be reversed (so too Gentry and Wellum, *Kingdom through Covenant*, 321; cf. W. J. Dumbrell, *Covenant and Creation: A Theology of the Old Testament Covenants* [Carlisle, UK: Paternoster, 1984] 89–90).

9. See D. I. Block, "The Burden of Leadership: The Mosaic Paradigm of Kingship (Deut 17:14–20)," *BSac* 162 (2005) 259–78; repr. in idem, *How I Love Your Torah*, 118–39.

10. For an argument that the Genesis texts truly anticipate a single, male, royal deliverer and for an overview of how these texts are developed in the rest of Scripture, see J. S. DeRouchie and J. C. Meyer, "Christ or Family as the 'Seed' of Promise? An Evaluation of N. T. Wright on Galatians 3:16," *SBJT* 14.3 (2010) 36–48; see also J. Collins, "A Syntactical Note (Genesis 3:15): Is the Woman's Seed Singular or Plural," *TynBul* 48.1 (1997) 139–48; T. D. Alexander, "Further Observations on the Term 'Seed' in Genesis," *TynBul* 48.2 (1997) 363–67; C. J. Collins, "Galatians 3:16: What Kind of Exegete Was Paul?" *TynBul* 54.1 (2003) 75–86; J. Hamilton, "The Seed of the Woman and the Blessing of Abraham," *TynBul* 58.2 (2007) 253–73.

or missed," that Jerusalem, not the ark, "shall be called the throne of Yahweh," and that this city will be the habitation of both the restored remnant of united Israel (3:14) and a remnant from the nations, who "shall no more stubbornly follow their own evil heart" (3:16–17). What is the connection here?

Kevin J. Youngblood helpfully reflects on the significance of the ark's absence: "Since this was the box that housed the copy of the covenant document, the implications of its loss should be catastrophic as it was in DtH (1 Sam 4–6). Instead, Yhwh says, no ark will be necessary in the future. Why not? Because Jer 31:31ff indicates that the new covenant document will be stored, not in a piece of cultic furniture but in the very hearts of Yhwh's people."[11] In Jeremiah's day, Judah had sin, not the Decalogue, "engraved on the tablet of their heart" (Jer 17:1). However, the prophet envisions a new covenant wherein all members will have God's law, synthesized in the Ten Words, etched on their hearts (Jer 31:33).[12] That is, as pointed to in the fact that Jerusalem will be both Yahweh's throne and the dwelling place of all the redeemed (3:14, 17; cf. 12:16, 30:8–9; Rev 21:2, 9), God's people would become the ark, housing within them the law and enjoying on their lives the manifestation of Yahweh's presence (Ezek 36:27, 37:14, 27). Yahweh would teach every member of the restored remnant (Jer 31:34, Isa 2:3, 54:13; cf. John 6:45–46, 1 Cor 2:13, 1 Thess 4:9, 1 John 2:20–21), ultimately through his Messiah (Isa 42:4, 51:4; cf. Matt 28:20), with the result that every covenant member would faithfully follow the Lord, rightly imaging God's character and worth within the world (Jer 31:34; cf. 22:15–16 with 9:24).

According to Jeremiah, in Israel's return to the Lord, their God-given mission of serving as an agent of blessing to the nations would be fulfilled, as the nations would declare themselves blessed in Yahweh (Jer 4:1–2; cf. Gen 22:18; 26:4). Those once "evil neighbors" (Jer 12:14) would "learn the ways of my people" and in turn "be built up in the midst of my people" (12:16). Those once "foreigners" who served with Babylon against God's people (31:8) would now "serve Yahweh their God and David their king" (31:9), enjoying all the fruits of the new covenant. Paul draws on all these images in 2 Cor 3:3, when he writes to the predominantly Gentile believers in Corinth, "And you show that you are a letter from Christ delivered by us, written not with ink but the Spirit of

---

11. K. J. Youngblood, "Beyond Deuteronomism: Jeremiah's Unique Theological Contribution" (paper presented at Lipscomb University, 2009) 11. I was first directed to this quote in Gentry and Wellum, *Kingdom through Covenant*, 507.

12. This was experienced in the old covenant, but only among the remnant few (see Prov 3:3, 7:3; Isa 51:7; Pss 37:31, 40:9[8], 119:11).

the living God, not on tablets of stone but on tablets of human hearts" (cf. Rom 2:15, 29; Ezek 11:19, 36:26–27). For Paul, Jeremiah's vision of the Decalogue embodied in human lives is seeing its manifestation in the church of Jesus Messiah.

With these elements in mind and toward a goal of grasping what imaging God through the Decalogue meant for Israel and Christ and what it ultimately means for us, we will now direct our attention to the Decalogue itself. Specifically, we will unpack three features of the Decalogue's message that are highlighted by a modified Catholic-Lutheran enumeration.

2. Theological Reflections on the Decalogue's Numbering

2.1. Word One—An Answer to Israel's Most Fundamental Ideological Question

The majority Jewish position regards the statement "I am Yahweh your God" (Exod 20:2 // Deut 5:6) as the first Word of the Ten, and the Orthodox-Reformed understanding holds that the injunctions "There shall never be to you other gods" (Exod 20:3 // Deut 5:7) and "You shall never make a carved image" (Exod 20:4[–6] // Deut 5:8[–10]) are distinct Words. In contrast to both of these approaches, the modified Catholic-Lutheran numbering treats as the first Word all the first-person address that runs from the initial indicative "I am Yahweh your God" through the phrase "those who love me and keep my commandments."

The initial statement and three prohibitions that make up the first Word together clarify one of Israel's most fundamental ideological questions—how should we perceive and, by implication, approach the God who has saved us? Before any directive is given, the first Word begins with an indicative declaration that the one speaking from the midst of the fire was none other than "Yahweh your God," who rescued Israel from the bonds of slavery in Egypt (Exod 20:2 // Deut 5:6). While most directly connected to the initial injunction that follows,[13] this statement places all the Ten Words in the context of freedom and identifies Yahweh as the great giver. All obedience, therefore, is done in light of the experience of past grace and in the hope of the promise of future grace that could naturally be expected to flow from Yahweh's

---

13. This link between the statement "I am Yahweh your God" in Exod 20:2 // Deut 5:6 and the initial injunction "There shall not be to you other gods before me" in Exod 20:3 // Deut 5:7 is established through the 1cs pronominal suffix at the end of the prepositional phrase על־פני 'before *me*' (lit. 'on my face'). For more on this, see DeRouchie, "Counting the Ten," §2.3.1.

benevolence.¹⁴ The ground clause that follows says just as much, for the fruit of Yahweh's jealousy for his people's affection overflows in his "showing steadfast love to thousands of generations of those who love me and keep my commandments" (Exod 20:6 // Deut 5:10). Yahweh, the compassionate and gracious God, has acted on Israel's behalf, and it is this God who declares, "there shall never be to you other gods before me" (Exod 20:3 // Deut 5:7).

In all likelihood, this initial charge relates *not* to Yahweh having highest priority or rank among many (though this is a justified implication of the meaning) but to his status as the only sovereign, the one who acts alone, not as the head of a pantheon of rival deities but as the sole and ultimate power in the universe.¹⁵ This view is suggested by the fact that whenever the preposition על־פני 'before' bears a personal object in the Hebrew Bible, the meaning is always spatial, thus implying that the stress in this text is that Yahweh has no peers in his presence.¹⁶ Yahweh does not share power, authority, or jurisdiction with any other.¹⁷

Elsewhere it is clear that Yahweh does act within a heavenly assembly: "God has taken his place in the divine council; in the midst of the gods he holds judgment" (Ps 82:1; cf. 1 Kgs 22:19–22; Jer 23:18; Isaiah 6; Ps 89:6, 8[5, 7]; 95:3; Job 1:6–12; 2:1–7). Members of the divine court are variously referred to as "messengers/angels" (מלאכים), "gods" (אלהים), "the sons of the gods" (בני־האלהים), and "holy ones" (קדשים), and Job 1–2 make clear that "the satan" (השטן) himself is part of this group. What is also apparent, however, is that none of these angels or "gods" is equal to Yahweh; indeed they are all subordinate and subservient to him, serving him (1 Kgs 22:19), bowing to him (Ps 29:2), obeying him (103:20–21), and praising him (148:2–5).¹⁸ Yahweh is "a great King above all gods"

---

14. Comparably, in light of the salvific antitype to Israel's temporal deliverance from Egypt, Paul asserts in Rom 8:31–32: "If God is for us, who can be against us? He who did not spare his own Son but gave him up for us all, how will he not also with him graciously give us all things?" Past grace grounds the hope of future grace.

15. See J. H. Walton, "Interpreting the Bible as an Ancient Near Eastern Document," in *Israel—Ancient Kingdom or Late Invention? Archaeology, Ancient Civilizations, and the Bible* (ed. D. I. Block; Nashville: B&H Academic, 2008) 305–9. Similarly, C. J. H. Wright asserts, "The fundamental thrust of the verse is not Yahweh's sole deity, but Yahweh's sole sovereignty over Israel" (*Deuteronomy* [NIBC; Peabody, MA: Hendrickson, 1996] 68, now published in the Understanding the Bible Commentary Series by Baker).

16. Gen 11:28; 23:3; 32:22; 50:1; Exod 33:19; Lev 10:3; Num 3:4; 1 Kgs 9:7; 2 Kgs 13:14; Ezek 32:10; Ps 9:20; Job 4:15; 21:31 (so Walton, "Interpreting the Bible as an Ancient Near Eastern Document," 307).

17. Walton, "Interpreting the Bible as an Ancient Near Eastern Document," 308.

18. See W. R. Garr, *In His Own Image and Likeness: Humanity, Divinity, and Monotheism* (Culture and History of the Ancient Near East 15; Leiden, Netherlands: Brill, 2003) 69–70; Gentry and Wellum, *Kingdom through Covenant*, 204.

(95:3). Even the satan in the book of Job can only do what God allows.[19] Thus Moses could declare, "Yahweh your God is God of gods and Lord of lords, the great, the mighty, and the awesome God" (Deut 10:17).[20] The call of the Decalogue's first Word is for Israel to recognize that Yahweh stands alone and that, while he works through spiritual agents, he is not the first among equals but is rather the sole ultimate mover who alone is worthy of worship. He is both ontologically and functionally transcendent.

This interpretation, then, allows the initial charge to lead naturally into the explanatory statements regarding (1) the crafting of a sculptured image and (2) the worship and service of other gods (Exod 20:4–6 // Deut 5:8–10). What is striking here is that the truth of Yahweh's preeminence over all is not left as a theological abstraction; rather the implications for Israel's every day life are made explicit by the two injunctions.

First, Yahweh's transcendence both in being and function requires that human-made idols hold no place in Israel's existence. As is still common practice in parts of the world, ancient nations, especially from Mesopotamia and the Levant, regularly associated their gods with manufactured idols. Thus we read in the OT of "gods of silver and gold" (Exod 23:20; cf. 32:23–24), of "molten gods" (Lev 19:4), of "gods put in the shrines" (2 Kgs 17:29), of "gods of wood and stone" (19:18), and of "removing (foreign) gods" (Gen 35:4; Josh 24:14, 23; Judg

---

19. Thus Yahweh declares to the satan: "Behold, all that [Job] has is in your hand; only against him do not stretch out your hand" (Job 1:12), and again, "Behold, he is in your hand; only spare his life" (2:6). The satan could only do what God permitted him to do. It is in this context, I believe, that Paul could say that "a thorn was given me in the flesh, a messenger of Satan to harass me, to keep me from becoming conceited" (2 Cor 12:7). At one level, the apostle's suffering was from Satan, but at a higher level it was from one who was concerned about keeping him humble, the one who would intentionally make Paul weak so that the divine power could be perfected as the power of Christ rested upon him (12:9). Comparably, Paul asserted that his having undergone intense persecution even to the point of death "was to make us rely not on ourselves but on God who raises the dead" (1:9). Paul's was convinced that God was the ultimate mover in his suffering, even though Satan was certainly involved.

20. Paul echoes this passage when he asserts in 1 Cor 8:4–6: "Therefore, as to the eating of food offered to idols, we know that 'an idol has no real existence,' and that 'there is no God but one.' For although there may be so-called gods in heaven or on earth—as indeed there are may 'gods' and many 'lords'—yet for us there is one God, the Father, from who are all things and for whom we exist, and one Lord, Jesus Christ, through whom are all things and through whom we exists." Later, with an echo of Deut 32:17, he identifies real demonic forces behind every idol (10:19–20): "What do I imply then? That food offered to idols is anything, or that an idol is anything? No, I imply that what pagans sacrifice they offer to demons and not to God. I do not want you to be participants with demons."

10:16; 1 Sam 7:3; 2 Chr 33:15).[21] Graven images were believed to mediate the presence of the gods, and by them humans served the needs of the gods.[22] Yahweh has no needs but indeed supplies everything as he governs heaven and earth (Deut 4:39, 32:39; cf. Acts 17:25). Furthermore, Yahweh encounters his creation through his Spirit-presence and not through idols (Deut 4:15–18).

Second, Yahweh's supremacy over all necessitates that Israel never worship or serve anything other than him (Exod 20:5 // Deut 5:9). The practical import here is vast. Powers and pleasures abound in this world that vie for attention and allegiance. Indeed, they can even be viewed as being controlled by demons (Deut 32:17, 1 Cor 10:19–20)! Yet in this world where God alone holds absolute supremacy, honor and thanksgiving must ultimately be given to him alone (Rom 1:21).

The first Word of the Ten includes three prohibitions, the second and third of which develop the implications of the first. A ground clause then follows, which appears to support all three injunctions, which should be kept *because* Yahweh is jealous (Exod 20:5 // Deut 5:9). Yahweh's jealousy is intimately connected to his character (Exod 34:14),[23] and a survey of the portrayal of God in Scripture suggests that this jealousy is just, necessary, and loving. It is a *just* jealousy because, as we have seen, he alone is preeminent over all things and is therefore worthy of utmost worship (Exod 34:14, Deut 32:39, Rom 11:36, Col 1:16). It

---

21. "And you have praised the gods of silver and gold, of bronze, iron, wood, and stone, which do not see or hear or know, but the God in whose hand is your breath, and whose are all your ways, you have not honored" (Dan 5:23). For more on the view and portrayal of gods in the ancient Near East, see D. I. Block, *The Gods of the Nations: Studies in Ancient Near Eastern National Theology* (Evangelical Theological Society Studies; 2nd ed.; Grand Rapids: Baker, 2000).

22. See Walton, "Interpreting the Bible as an Ancient Near Eastern Document," 309–13. In contrast to Walton's interpretation of the injunction against idolatry, the idea of God's transcendence seems apparent in the text both in Exodus, where the Words are given in the context of a theophany, and in Deuteronomy, where the commandment against image making echoes the very language of chapter 4 where Israel is charged thus: "Since you saw no form on the day that Yahweh spoke to you at Horeb out of the midst of the fire, beware lest you act corruptly by making a carved image for yourselves in the form of any figure, the likeness of male or female, the likeness of any animal that is on the earth, the likeness of any winged bird that flies in the air, the likeness of anything that creeps on the ground, the likeness of any fish that is in the water under the earth.... Take care, lest you forget the covenant of Yahweh your God, which made with you, and make a carved image, the form of anything that Yahweh your God has forbidden you. For Yahweh your God is a consuming fire, a jealous God" (Deut 4:15–18, 23–24).

23. In light of the fact that Exodus stresses the name of God is Yahweh (Exod 3:14–15), I translate Exod 34:14, "for you shall worship no other god, for Yahweh is jealous with respect to his name; he is a jealous God."

is a *necessary* jealousy because if Yahweh, as sovereign of the universe, allowed his glory to be given to another, declaring something else worthy of highest praise, he would stop being God and all the world would come to an end (Isa 42:8, 48:11; Job 34:14–15; cf. Heb 1:3). Finally, it is a *loving* jealousy because Yahweh alone can save (Isa 43:10–11; 45:21; Hos 13:4) and has saved Israel (Exod 20:2 // Deut 5:6) and because he alone can satisfy with full joy for the longest amount of time (Ps 16:11, Matt 13:44, John 15:10–11). In the words of the prophet Samuel, "Do not turn aside from following Yahweh, but serve Yahweh with all your heart. And do not turn aside after empty things that cannot profit or deliver" (1 Sam 12:20–21).

At the end of the first Word, we are told that God's zeal for his own renown gives rise to great wrath toward disloyalty (unto the third and fourth generation) and even greater love toward the faithful (unto a thousand generations). What motivation are the promises of God, which Peter declares are given "so that through them you may become partakers of the divine nature, having escaped from the corruption of the world because of sinful desire" (2 Pet 1:4)! Believing the promises of future curse would discourage Israel's disobedience, whereas faith in future blessings would motivate love for God seen in obedience.[24]

In the Decalogue's first Word, Yahweh is portrayed as the only savior, sovereign, and satisfier of Israel who therefore deserves highest praise. God's singular being and function bore radical implications for Israel's daily existence, and they continue to bear comparable implications for our own. As Paul declares in 1 Cor 8:4–6: "We know that 'an idol has no real existence' [citing Isa 41:24] and that 'there is no God but one' [citing Deut 4:35, 36]. For although there may be so-called gods in heaven or on earth—as indeed there are many 'gods' and many 'lords' [alluding to Deut 10:17]—yet for us there is one God, the Father, from whom are all things and for whom we exist, and one Lord, Jesus Christ, through whom are all things and through whom we exist."

2.2. Two Groupings: Love for God and Love for Neighbor

The Decalogue witness two groupings of commands. We have observed that the first four Words each include reference to "Yahweh your God" and thus bear an explicit Godward-focus not apparent in the last six. The stylistic shift seems intentional and likely supports the traditional view that the Decalogue opens with a focus on love for God

---

24. For more on this theme, see J. Piper, *Future Grace: The Purifying Power of the Promises of God* (rev. ed.; Sisters, OR: Multnomah, 2012).

(Words 1–4) and ends with a focus on love of neighbor (Words 5–10) (cf. Mark 12:30–31, Rom 13:9). Foundational to Israel's covenant with Yahweh is a radical God-entranced vision that relates to their worldview and worship (Word 1), their daily witness (Word 2), their weekly schedule (Word 3), and their family relationships (Word 4). Indeed, their love for God is to cover "all," as is later highlighted in the supreme commandment (Deut 6:5). I will comment briefly on these four spheres, clarifying how each Word primarily addresses love for God. More attention is given to the Words related to Sabbath keeping and to honoring one's parents, for their role in expressing love for *God* may be less clear.

2.2.1. Recognize Yahweh Is One

In the first Word, Yahweh alone stands as Israel's redeemer, the decisive ruler over all, who has no needs and who is worthy of sole worship, all in light of his jealousy (Exod 20:2–6 // Deut 5:6–10). To love God is to affirm his sovereignty over all and to recognize the implications of his supremacy in all of life. Because I have already expanded on this Word above, I will move ahead.

2.2.2. Bear Yahweh's Name Well

In Word two, Yahweh will hold every covenant member accountable for his or her lifestyle and witness as an emissary of God (Exod 20:7 // Deut 5:11).[25] While in popular circles, "bearing Yahweh's name in vain" is often understood to denote casual, crass, or disrespectful use of God's name in speech, there is likely much more at stake. Specifically, those "bearing" the name are those "called by Yahweh's name" (Deut 28:10, Dan 9:19), who have had his name "placed" on them (Num 6:27), and who claim Yahweh as their own (Isa 44:5). To keep God's word and to remain in the faith is to "hold fast" to God's name and not to "deny" it (Rev 2:13, 3:8), whereas to portray a warped view of Yahweh's power, will, and worth through poor judgment and rebellious behavior is to "profane" his name (Ezek 36:22–23). "Bearing Yahweh's name" is about the image of God in human lives; it is about one's witness in the world. Those bearing God's name are called upon to reflect, resemble, and represent the Lord through covenant obedience, whether in public or

---

25. What follows is my own theological developments on some initial thoughts first expressed to me by D. I. Block. He has now developed his own thinking in what it means "to bear Yahweh's name" in two essays: Block, "Bearing the Name of the LORD with Honor," *BSac* 168 (2011) 20–31 (repr. in idem, *O How I Love Your Torah*, 61–72); and idem, "No Other Gods: Bearing the Name of YHWH in a Polytheistic World," in idem, *The Gospel according to Moses: Theological and Ethical Reflections on the Book of Deuteronomy* (Euguene, OR: Cascade, 2012) 237–71.

in private. As Moses asserted in Deut 28:9–10: "Yahweh will establish you as a people holy to himself, as he has sworn to you, if you keep the commandments of Yahweh your God and walk in his ways. And all the peoples of the earth shall see that you are called by the name of Yahweh, and they shall be afraid of you." Image bearers who have surrendered to Yahweh's claim on their lives must live for the fame of God's name, and this is done significantly by seeing the principles laid out in the Decalogue embodied in one's life. This is the point of the second Word.

Intriguingly, the book of Revelation portrays all of humanity as having one of two identifying marks: one group has the Lamb's "name and his Father's name" written on their foreheads (Rev 14:1; cf. 3:12; 22:4), and the other has "the mark of [the beast's] name" written on the hand or forehead (14:11; cf. 13:16–17). G. K. Beale has argued for the likelihood that "the mark of the name" in Revelation is figurative and not physical and relates to spiritual identification with either God and Christ or the Satanic beast. Beale's discussion on Rev 13:16–17 is worth an extended citation.

> Since the seal or name on the true believers is invisible, so also is the "mark" on the unbeliever. That the two are parallel in being spiritual in nature and are intended to be compared is evident from the immediately following mention of God and Christ's name "written on the foreheads" of the saints (14:1). Those who have believed in Jesus have been identified with him and are protected by the power of his name against ultimate deception. His name is none other than his very presence with them (as 22:4 makes explicit). Their refusal to identify with the beast will result in suffering and even death, but they will have the ultimate reward of eternal life (so 20:4). Those not trusting in Christ are identified with the beast, are under the devil's power, and are unable to avoid deception by the beast (. . . 2:17). While identification with the beast given them temporary prosperity in this life, they will ultimately be punished with eternal death (. . . 14:9–11). . . .
>
> That the mark of the name is figurative and not literal is evident from the 'blasphemous names' on the head of the beast (13:1), which figuratively connote false claims to earthly divine kingship. Likewise, the point of saying that the beast's worshipers have his name written on their heads is to underscore the fact that they pay homage to his blasphemous claims to divine kingship. Just as the seal and the divine name on believers connote God's ownership and spiritual protection of them, so the mark and Satanic name signify those who belong to the devil and will undergo perdition.[26]

---

26. G. K. Beale, *The Book of Revelation* (NIGTC; Grand Rapids: Eerdmans, 1999) 716.

Beale also notes, "The mark may also connote that the followers of Christ and the beast both are stamped with the image (i.e., character) of their respective leaders."[27] This latter point would fully align with my own assessment above, but the additional comments drawn out by Beale are also helpful.

Deuteronomy teaches that the charge of the Shema ("Hear, O Israel: *Yahweh* our God, *Yahweh* is one. And you shall love *Yahweh* your God with all . . . ," Deut 6:4–5) should radically influence one's heart, behavior, and worldview: "And these words that I command you today shall be on your heart. . . . And you shall bind them as a sign on your hand, and they shall be as frontlets between your eyes" (6:6, 8).[28] In short, *Yahweh*-centeredness was to be the identifying feature of one's life. To bear the name of Yahweh necessitated a radically dependent, God-honoring existence.

While the majority of Israel's history was scathed with rebellion, Zechariah anticipated a day when Yahweh's name would be rightly honored and displayed: "And Yahweh will be king over all the earth. On that day Yahweh will be one and his name one" (Zech 14:9). Here Zechariah foresees a time when the whole world will celebrate Yahweh's singularity—when the bearers of Yahweh's name will perfectly display Yahweh's character. In this day, "no longer will there be anything accursed, but the throne of God and of the Lamb will be in it, and his servants will worship him. They will see his face, and his name will be on their foreheads" (Rev 22:3–4).

2.2.3. Keep the Sabbath to Yahweh

In what way is the Sabbath commandment principally about love for God? Jesus' assertion that "the Sabbath was made for man" (Mark 2:27) finds support in the wording of the Decalogue, which calls all household heads to give rest to all persons and beasts under their care. Nevertheless, the text stresses that Sabbath keeping was to be performed "to Yahweh your God" (Exod 20:10 // Deut 5:14), which establishes the radical God-centeredness of Israel's 6 + 1 pattern of existence.[29] Yah-

---

27. Ibid.

28. That "hands" and "eyes" in Deut 6:8 is shorthand for behavior and worldview is suggested by the pairing of these two nouns elsewhere in the OT, where they clearly point to action and perception. For example, in Deut 21:7, the elders of a city speak in response to an unsolved murder: "Our hands did not shed this blood, nor did our eyes see it shed." Similarly, Beale writes, "The 'forehead' represents ideological commitment and the 'hand' the practical outworking of that commitment" (*The Book of Revelation*, 717).

29. D. I. Block argues that the Sabbath ordinance is transitional, pointing to love for God in the Exodus version (addressing "the divine right to the Israelite's time/life") but

weh designated the Sabbath as the Mosaic Covenant's "sign" (אוֹת, Exod 31:13, 17), which most likely meant that it would either prove to Israel something about God or remind Israel in some way about their missional identity. In this latter light, the Sabbath may also have served to represent for Israel a hopeful future reality.[30] As will be seen, all these potential aspects of the Sabbath bear a God-exalting stamp.

Yahweh clarified for Moses that the purpose of the Sabbath sign was that Israel might "know that I am Yahweh, who sanctifies you" (Exod 31:13; cf. Ezek 20:12, 20). In Israel's journey from the exodus to Mount Sinai, it was shown that the Sabbath would test Israel's obedience and nurture their trust in Yahweh as their great provider, the one from whom, ultimately, all daily bread comes (Exod 16:4–5, 23–26; cf. Acts 17:24–25). Keeping the Sabbath, therefore, would in time prove that Yahweh alone is the sanctifier. The Sabbath would magnify Yahweh as the supplier of all things and would nurture trust in this truth within God's people.

Yet the Sabbath's connection to the original creation week (Exod 20:11, 31:17) and the exodus (Deut 5:15) suggests that the function of the Sabbath was also to remind Israel in some way about their identity and purpose as a people in relation to the whole world. For God, the culmination of the original creation week was not a rest of laziness but of sovereignty, wherein the Great King, having established the sacred space of his kingdom, sat enthroned, enjoying peace with all he had made (Gen 2:1–3; cf. Ps 132:7–8, 13–14).[31] While mankind's rebellion at

---

to love for neighbor in the Deuteronomic version (addressing the right of all household members "to human treatment from their head") ("'You Shall Not Covet Your Neighbor's Wife': A Study in Deuteronomic Domestic Ideology," in idem, *The Gospel according to Moses*, 146 with notes 27 and 29 [orig. printed in *JETS* 53 (2010) 449–74]). While I affirm these aspects, the stylistic use of "Yahweh your God" in Words one through four must still be accounted for structurally, and this is why I have suggested that Words one through four are principally focused on love for God. Nevertheless, none can question that every Word is in some sense an expression of love for God and for neighbor, because the latter should always be a fruit of the former and because neighbors can only truly be loved when we love God.

30. M. V. Fox has observed that "signs" in the Hebrew Bible fulfill at least one of three functions: (1) to prove the truth of something (e.g., Isa 38:7–8); (2) to symbolize or represent a future reality by virtue of resemblance or conventional association (e.g., Ezek 4:1–3); or (3) to rouse knowledge of something, whether by (a) identifying (e.g., Josh 2:12) or (b) reminding (Exod 13:9) ("The Sign of the Covenant: Circumcision in the Light of the Priestly "ôt Etiologies," *RB* 81 [1974] 557–96). I believe the "sign" nature of the Sabbath bears the primary functions of 1 and 3b and the secondary function of 2.

31. Walton identifies six aspects related to the notion of divine rest in the ANE ("Interpreting the Bible as an Ancient Near Eastern Document," 319–22): divine rest (1) was disturbed by rebellion, (2) achieved after conflict, (3) achieved after order-bringing acts

the fall did not remove God's right and authority over all things, it did alter the state of universal peace. As such, within the Pentateuch, the 6 + 1 pattern of creation is used not simply as a portrait of what was but as an image of the ideal for which the world is to long, and this ideal becomes attached directly to Israel's mission as the agent of curse reversal and global blessing (Gen 12:3, 18:18, 22:17b–18, 26:4, 28:14; cf. Exod 19:4–6; Deut 4:5–8, 26:18–19).[32] The Sabbath was to serve as a reminder to Israel of their mission, and it in turn represented a future reality for which Israel and the world were to hope.

More specifically, Israel's Sabbath identity is directly linked with the purpose of humanity at creation—namely, for God-imaging families to expand and rule the earth (Day 6, Gen 1:26–28) in a way that would culminate in the world being reconciled and at rest with its Creator King (Day 7). As a marker of Israel's mission, the Sabbath reminded Israel of her need for sustained devotion (i.e., to image God), for by covenant loyalty alone was God put on display in the midst of the world: "If you heed my voice ... then you shall be to me a kingdom of priests and a holy nation" (Exod 19:5–6; cf. Deut 4:5–8).[33] Yet the Sabbath itself was a means for proving that Yahweh alone was the source of Israel's holi-

---

of creation, establishing order; (4) achieved in the temple; (5) characterized by ongoing control and stability; and (6) achieved by the gods creating people to work in their place and on their behalf. Scripture's portrayal of Sabbath rest is distinct in that humanity's work is never viewed as replacing or benefiting God but is rather understood to be made possible by God himself (Deut 4:39, Acts 17:24–25). A parallel is seen in the fact that the original Sabbath of God and the temple building of the ancient world "represent the same moment in the divine life, one of exaltation and regal repose" (cited by Walton on p. 322 from J. D. Levenson, "The Temple and the World," *JR* 64 [1984] 275–98, quote from 288).

32. In this regard, the words of W. J. Dumbrell regarding Gen 2:1–3 are significant: "By the divine rest on the seventh day the goal of creation is indicated, a goal which will be maintained notwithstanding sustained human attempts to vitiate it. Not only does the seventh day rest note the goal to which creation points, but is the call to man to begin history holding firmly to the view that the 'goal of creation, and at the same time the beginning of all that follows, is the event of God's Sabbath freedom, Sabbath rest and Sabbath joy, in which man, too, has been summoned to participate.' ... On the sabbath ... Israel is to reflect upon the question of ultimate purposes for herself as a nation, and for the world over which she is set. For in pointing back to creation, the Sabbath points also to what is yet to be, to the final destiny to which all creation is moving" (*Covenant and Creation*, 34–35; here Dumbrell cites Karl Barth, *Church Dogmatics*, 3/1 [Edinburgh: T. & T. Clark, 1958] 98).

33. Similarly, in Genesis 12, the promise that "in you all the families of the earth shall be blessed" (v. 3) is grammatically contingent on the fulfillment of the imperative "and you shall be a blessing" (v. 2), something completely realized only in Christ, the true Israel (Gal 3:8, 14) (see P. R. Williamson, *Sealed with an Oath: Covenant in God's Unfolding Purpose* [NSBT 23; Downers Grove, IL: InterVarsity, 2007] 78–79; Gentry and Wellum, *Kingdom through Covenant*, 230–34).

ness (the first function of the Sabbath "sign," Exod 31:13; cf. 33:16). As such, Yahweh would receive all the glory in Israel's fulfilling their covenantal purposes of blessing transmission to the nations.[34] That is, by participating in Yahweh's sovereign rest through celebrating the Sabbath, Israel would nurture the type of God-centeredness that would ultimately bring about the exaltation of *God* among the peoples of the world.[35] The Sabbath, by nature, was kept *to Yahweh*.

As the sign of the covenant between Yahweh and Israel, the Sabbath's placement on the last day of the week signaled that rest in Yahweh's Sovereignty was the goal of Israel's missional makeup. Their weekly Sabbath would typify the future rest they would find in the promised land (Exod 33:14, Deut 12:9–10, Josh 1:13, 2 Sam 7:1). Furthermore, this partial and temporary rest would itself point ahead to the ultimate kingdom rest that has been secured for all who are in King Jesus (Ps 95:7–11, Matt 11:28–29, Heb 4:8–11 with 3:14) and that will be fully enjoyed in the age to come (Rev 14:13; chs. 21–22; cf. Isa 56:1–8; 61:2; 66:22–23).

For OT Israel, Sabbath was the climax of each week and symbolized sovereign rest as the goal of life. In contrast, for the believer in Christ Jesus, fulfillment of God's sovereign rest has been inaugurated, the "shadow" finding its "substance" in Christ (Col 2:16–17), so that we already enjoy peace under the Lordship of God seven days a week (Matt 11:28–29, Heb 4:8–11; cf. Rom 15:5–6). In light of this eschatological shift secured for us in Jesus' resurrection on a Sunday (Matt 28:1; Mark 16:2, 9; Luke 24:1; John 20:1), corporate worship has shifted to the first day of the week (Acts 20:7, 1 Cor 16:2) in order to picture the inaugurated nature of our rest that we enjoy through the remaining week

---

34. This element is further highlighted when, after the golden calf episode, Moses stresses the need for Yahweh's presence with Israel (Exod 33:15–16): "If your presence will not go with me, do not bring us up from here. For how shall it be known that I have found favor in your sight, I and your people? Is it not in your going with us, so that we are distinct, I and your people, for every other people on the face of the earth?" Yahweh alone made Israel different, keeping them from sin and enabling their mission (19:5–6, 20:20). Comparably, at the original creation, the commission to populate and oversee the earth was placed in the context of and made dependent on God's "blessing" (Gen 1:28) (see DeRouchie, "The Blessing-Commission, the Promised Offspring, and the *Toledot* Structure of Genesis"). For more on Yahweh as the sanctifier, see Lev 20:8; 21:8, 15, 23; 22:9, 16, 32.

35. Walton helpfully notes ("Interpreting the Bible as an Ancient Near Eastern Document," 322): "When commanded to share the rest of God on the Sabbath, it is not to participate in it per se, but to recognize His work of bringing and maintaining order. God's rest symbolizes His control over the cosmos, which His people recognize whenever they yield to Him the day they could have used to provide for themselves."

and to heighten hope for full consummation of that rest when Christ returns, overcoming all evil and removing all pain and death (Rev 21:4, 22:3). Our present enjoyment of Sabbath rest every day magnifies the curse-overcoming work of Christ, even as we continue to pray, "Your kingdom come . . . on earth as it is in heaven" (Matt 6:10).

2.2.4. Honor Your Parents

Finally, in Word four, Yahweh commands the honor of one's parents (Exod 20:12 // Deut 5:16), a statement that Paul himself quotes in Eph 6:1–3 and to which he likely alludes in 1 Tim 5:3. The deuteronomic version stresses that Yahweh himself gave this instruction, and both Exodus and Deuteronomy include the gift of the land from "Yahweh your God" as a motivator for obedience. Recognizably, this commandment is the only one of the first grouping that relegates the phrase "Yahweh your God" solely to a subordinate clause—a fact that may suggest that the commandment itself is transitional, bridging the focus between the call to love God and the call to love neighbor.[36] Nevertheless, the explicit use of the phrase and the extended length of the commandment place it principally within the first grouping that bears a Godward focus.

To speak of honoring one's parents as an expression of love for God rather than neighbor may seem strange. However, because parents are consistently portrayed in the OT as the principal agents of discipleship, hearing and heeding them is fundamental to preserving the mark of Yahweh in the community.[37] The command to honor one's parents is principally about honoring God!

Elsewhere, Scripture stresses that parents are the ones who should model God-centeredness and set the tenure of the home, affirming Yahweh's singularity and his call to life-encompassing love (Deut 6:6–9;

---

36. Support for treating the commandment for honoring one's parents as transitional is perhaps seen in Jesus' including it in a list with other commandments from the second section of the Decalogue: "If you would enter life, keep the commandments. . . . You shall not murder, You shall not commit adultery, You shall not steal, You shall not bear false witness, Honor your father and mother, and, You shall love your neighbor as yourself" (Matt 19:17–19).

37. Two millennia ago, Philo (*Decal.* 12.51) commented on the Decalogue's initial grouping: "the beginning is the God and Father and Creation of the universe; and the end are one's parents, who imitate his nature, and so generate the particular individuals" (*The Works of Philo* [updated ed.; trans. C. D. Younge; Peabody, MA: Hendrickson, 1993] 522). Similarly, D. N. Freedman asserts that the ordinance to honor one's parents is likely part of the first unit because the home is the principle means through which God will be exalted (*The Nine Commandments: Uncovering the Hidden Pattern of Crime and Punishment in the Hebrew Bible* [New York: Doubleday, 2000]). Cf. M. Greenberg, "The Decalogue Tradition Critically Examined," in *The Ten Commandments in History and Interpretation* (trans. M. Shorashim; ed. B.-Z. Segal and G. Levi; Jerusalem: Magnes, 1985) 112.

cf. 11:19). Parents should clarify the role of obedience and its relationship to past and future grace (6:20–25), and out of a passion to preserve the fame of God's name into the future generations, parents must teach their children the commands and thus help them to "set their hope in God and not forget the works of God" (Ps 78:7; cf. Judg 2:10). The NT charges fathers in particular to raise their children "in the discipline and instruction of the Lord" (Eph 6:4).

In contrast to these texts, the Decalogue directs its instruction about family life to the inferior not the superior, to the progeny not the parent (cf. Lev 19:2). At least two elements related to loving God are probably highlighted by this shift. First, good teaching and modeling must still be met with a proper response, and this is a mark of love for God. Like the book of Proverbs, which calls children to pursue the ways of God as taught by their parents ("Hear my son, your father's instruction, and forsake not your mother's teaching," Prov 1:8), so too the Decalogue stresses how love for Yahweh will characterize the community only when children recognize their part in joyful surrender to their God-placed parental authority. It is from this perspective that Paul charged Timothy as an adult son: "Continue in what you have learned and have firmly believed, knowing from whom you learned it and how from childhood you have been acquainted with the sacred writings, which are able to make you wise for salvation through faith in Christ Jesus" (2 Tim 3:14–15). By treasuring and applying the scriptural truths that were taught him as a young boy, Timothy would honor God by continuing to honor his mother and grandmother, from whom he received his instruction (1:5; cf. Eph 6:1–3).

A second way honoring one's parents is shown to be about loving God is evident in how respect and care for one's relatives is considered central to the works of faith that display one indeed knows God (see Titus 1:16). Along with the Decalogue's call to honor one's father and mother, the Pentateuch asserts that striking or cursing one's parents should result in death (Exod 21:15, 17; cf. Lev 20:9) and that anyone who dishonors father or mother is cursed (Deut 27:16). Jesus drew on these texts with the Decalogue commandment in order to highlight that when adult children fail to care for their parents, they are "rejecting the commandment of God" (Mark 7:9–13). That is, dishonor of father and mother is rebellion against the Lord!

Even more directly, with apparently some of the same OT texts in mind,[38] Paul stresses that biological family members bear the first

---

38. The link with the fourth Word is made in 1 Tim 5:3, where Paul urges Timothy to "honor widows who are truly widows." While the call to honor one's parents has most

responsibility to care for elderly relatives, and that failing to do so is to turn away from God.[39] When adult children "make some return to their parents" by meeting practical concerns in their times of need, God is "pleased" and "godliness" is shown (1 Tim 5:4). However, "if anyone does not provide for his relatives, and especially for members of his household, he has denied the faith and is worse than an unbeliever" (5:8; cf. Jas 1:27).

2.3. The Decalogue's Call for Servant Leadership, Not Male Domination

A third area of theological significance related to my modified Catholic-Lutheran numbering of the Decalogue is associated with the commands related to coveting. Changes made to the deuteronomic Decalogue suggest that after forty years in the wilderness Moses is intentionally shaping a polemic against headship abuses in the community. One of the major alterations made to the deuteronomic version of the Decalogue was the removal of the wife from the list of household members in the final injunction against evil desire (Deut 5:21b; cf. Exod 20:17b). Moses does not explicitly state the purpose behind his change. However, in light of the stress throughout Deuteronomy on the rights of the vulnerable, especially women, Daniel Block is likely correct to see in the deuteronomic version of the Decalogue "a deliberate effort to ensure the elevated status of the wife in a family unit and to foreclose any temptation to use the Exodus version of the command to justify men's treatment of their wives as if they were mere property, along with the rest of the household possessions."[40] The Decalogue affirms

---

immediate applicability to biological relatives (as is clear from Paul's argument that follows), he has no hesitation calling the household of God to abide by comparable principles. Thus Timothy should encourage older men "as you would a father, younger men as brothers, older women as mothers, younger women as sisters, in all purity" (5:1–2). Instructions directly related to the human household find broader applicability within the household of faith (see Gal 6:10; cf. P. H. Towner, *The Letters to Timothy and Titus* [NICNT; Accordance electronic ed.; Grand Rapids: Eerdmans, 2006] 338).

39. Most certainly Paul is also drawing on the numerous OT texts that highlight the need to care for the widow (e.g., Exod 22:22; Deut 24:17, 19–21; 26:12; Isa 1:17), all in order to be like God (Deut 10:18–19).

40. Block, "'You Shall Not Covet Your Neighbor's Wife'," 156. Block notes Deuteronomy evinces a high concern for widows (Deut 10:17–18 et passim), invites women to participate in worship (12:12 et passim), requires the manumission of female slaves (15:12), exempts new husbands from military service (20:7), guards the rights of captive brides and second-ranked wives (21:10–14, 15–17), stresses the authority of the mother over a rebellious child (21:18–21), protects a wife who is falsely accused of lying about her virginity (22:13–21), assumes the innocence of rape victims (22:23–29), shields divorced

the patricentric nature of Israelite society; it is not addressed to priests or rulers but to male heads of households that enjoy wives, children, household servants, and property.[41] With this, the Ten Words emphasize that household heads are under God and that they lead principally by loving God and by serving, honoring, and looking out for their family members and neighbors. That is, biblical leaders are characterized by preserving *others'* rights and not their own. Love of others and not love of self is what drives the Decalogue.

In Scripture, human "rights" (or a neighbor's desert of our love) are a natural and necessary fruit of being made in God's image. In a way distinct from any other creature, humans bear a capacity to reflect, resemble, and represent God, and this alone establishes human worth and clarifies why the murder of the innocent demands the death of the perpetrator, "for God made man in his own image" (Gen 9:6).[42] In Section 1, I highlighted how the instructions of the Decalogue display the character of God that is to be embodied in the life of the faithful. The language of other people's "rights" now draws attention to the fact that every one of the Ten Words is shaped with the deepest conviction that Yahweh and his image are of highest value in the universe. The Decalogue is about God not only in the way the laws themselves portray his character but also in the way they display his worth by calling humans to respect his divine rights and the rights of all those bearing his image.

Following the Catholic-Lutheran numbering, Block depicts as follows what he terms the "Deuteronomic Bill of *Others'* Rights":[43]

---

women from abuses from their previous husband (24:1–4), and secures the integrity of families and estates through levirate marriage (25:5–10) (ibid., 160–67). Cf. M. Weinfeld, *Deuteronomy and the Deuteronomic School* (Oxford: Oxford University Press, 1972; repr. Winona Lake, IN: Eisenbrauns, 1992) 282–92; idem, *Deuteronomy 1–11* [AB 5; New York: Doubleday, 1991] 318.

41. I use patricentric as opposed to patriarchal because the latter term is often used pejoratively. On the biblical vision of Israel's society being centered on the father as servant leader as opposed to dominated by a father as self-exalting dictator, see D. I. Block, "Marriage and Family in Ancient Israel," in *Marriage and Family in the Biblical World* (ed. K. M. Campbell; Downers Grove, IL: InterVarsity, 2003) 33–102.

42. My student Matthew Rowley has established the following syllogism that clarifies why the concept of human rights is nonsensical apart from beliefs in God and in humans being made in the divine image: If we give up the biblical God, then we give up the *imago dei*. If we give up the *imago dei*, then we give up inherent or conferred human worth. If we give up human worth, then we give up human worth violations (since a worthless thing can't be violated). If we give up human worth violations, then there is no real enforceable wrong done by a human to another human.

43. On this feature of the Ten Words, see Block, "'You Shall Not Covet Your Neighbor's Wife'," 145–46.

1. Yahweh's right to the Israelites' exclusive allegiance.
2. Yahweh's right to proper representation (Israel bears his name).
3. Household members' rights to humane treatment from the head.
4. Parents' right to respect from progeny.
5. The next person's right to life.
6. The next person's right to sexual purity.
7. The next person's right to property.
8. The next person's right to honest and truthful testimony.
9. The next person's right to a secure marriage.
10. The next person's right to enjoy property without fear that a neighbor may want it for himself.

The Israelite community was a collection of families, and at the center of each was the father. The layout of the Decalogue defines his role as leader principally as love for God and neighbor—not self-exalting but other-serving. By focusing on the rights of others, the Ten Words as a whole and the deuteronomic version in particular confront present or potential pride, self-elevating power, and abuses by a household head toward God, wives, other household members, and property.[44] And if the head could love Yahweh and neighbor rightly, the rest of the community would follow in line.

3. Conclusion

Yahweh gave Israel ten Words, which were to be embodied in the lives of God's people as part of the display of God's worth and character in the context of the world. In this framework, the Decalogue naturally finds its place within the numerous biblical calls to intentional family and community discipleship from generation to generation, that all might "set their hope in God and not forget the works of God but

---

44. W. L. Moran has observed some significant parallels in Akkadian literature to the coveting commandments and on this basis has argued that there is no theological significance to the "wife" being separated from the list of other household members ("The Conclusion of the Decalogue [Ex 20,17 = Dt 5,21]," *CBQ* 29 [1967] 548–52). He does not, however, give any clarity as to why the wife stands in a completely different position in Deuteronomy. In contrast, Block's argument that Deuteronomy's domestic ideology drives the shift is not bound by the same higher-critical presuppositions, takes more account of the Deuteronomic context, and, I believe, effectively proves that the separation of the "wife" from the rest of the household list in Deut 5:21 is indeed part of Moses' emphatic attempt to awaken a higher respect for the place of the wife within Israel's faith community. For a detailed analysis of all relevant texts in Deuteronomy related to the role and restrictions of the head of household, see R. Josberger, *Between Rule and Responsibility: The Role of the 'āb as Agent of Righteousness in Deuteronomy's Domestic Ideology* (PhD diss., The Southern Baptist Theological Seminary, 2007); see also idem, "For *Your* Good Always: Restraining the Rights of the Victor for the Well-being of the Vulnerable (Deut 21:10–14)," in this volume.

keep his commandments" (Ps 78:7; cf. Exod 13:14–16; Deut 6:7, 20–25; 11:19).[45] Furthermore, the covenantal Ten Words also become central to Israel's mission of drawing the nations to Yahweh (Gen 12:3; Exod 19:5–6 with 33:16; Deut 4:5–8; 26:17–19).

Significantly, Moses himself believed that the Decalogue and all the rest of his instruction in Deuteronomy would have lasting significance in the eschatological era now associated with the new covenant.[46] Moses made this clear in chapter 30, when he declared that, in the eschatological age of heart-transformation and divine-enablement, Yahweh's restored people would "return and heed God's voice and keep all his commandments *that I command you today*" (Deut 30:8; cf. 30:2 with 4:30–31; Jer 12:16; 31:33; Ezek 36:27). While it is beyond the scope of this paper to clarify fully how this is rightly accomplished, the Decalogue clearly matters for the church.

Nevertheless, because the Ten Words originally supplied a written witness to the *old* covenant, which has now been superseded by the new, they apply to Christians *not directly* but only through Christ and in light of his eschatological new covenant work. My treatment of the Sabbath command above provides a case in point. The sovereign rest of God bound up in the Sabbath law finds its ultimate fulfillment *in Christ*, and believers heed the Sabbath command in so far as they are daily satisfied and resting in all God is for them in Jesus.[47]

---

45. As one considers why Yahweh gave *ten* Words and not nine or eleven, at least two reasons are immediately suggested. First, as P. J. Gentry has observed, the association of ten precepts with the term "words" at the head of the Decalogue (Exod 20:1; cf. Exod 34:28; Deut 4:13; 10:4) is likely an echo of the original creation account, wherein the verb ויאמר 'and he said' occurs exactly ten times (see Gen 1:3, 6, 9, 11, 14, 20, 24, 26, 28, 29) (Gentry and Wellum, *Kingdom through Covenant*, 327–28). Just as God's original relationship with his creation was established through ten consecutive words (cf. Heb 1:3), so too would his covenantal relationship with Israel be fully dependent on Ten Words. As Gentry states, "It is . . . Ten Words that brings about the birth of the nation. Like the creation, Israel as a nation hangs upon the Ten Words for her very being" (328). Second, it seems probable that Yahweh intentionally spoke them in a way that could easily be passed on to others, even using one's ten fingers (or toes).

46. P. S. Ross recently published an extensive argument for the classic threefold division of the law, with only the moral law having lasting relevance in the new covenant age (*From the Finger of God: The Biblical and Theological Basis for the Threefold Division of the Law* [Fearn, Ross-shire, Scotland: Christian Focus, 2010]). For a recent review article that identifies both strengths and weaknesses with Ross's case and helpfully posits an alternative view that supports the central thesis of the present study, see D. A. Carson, "The Tripartite Division of the Law: A Review of Philip Ross, *The Finger of God*," in *From Creation to New Creation: Biblical Theology and Exegesis—Essays in Honor of G. K. Beale* (ed. D. M. Gurtner and B. L. Gladd [Peabody, MA: Hendrickson, 2013], 223–36).

47. For more on this, see this paper's appendix: "A Note on the Christian's Relationship to Old Testament Law."

Together the Ten Words supply expressions of God's eternal wisdom and righteousness and of the heights and depths of love for God and neighbor. They embody timeless ethical principles that every believer needs to grasp and heed and that can only be rightly grasped and heeded today in relation to the fulfillment in Jesus. The Decalogue anticipates the very image of God now seen in the face of Christ (John 12:45; 14:9; Col 1:15; Heb 1:3). God is a consuming fire (Heb 12:29), blazing in jealousy for the fame of his name. We must, therefore, stand in reverence and awe of the vision of God in the face of Christ, passionately and progressively pursuing his ways, even as we await the day of glory when the righteous will be made perfect (Heb 12:23, 28; cf. 2 Cor 4:6).

In an attempt to help my own children display more purely the image of God seen in the face of Christ, my wife and I put the Ten Words to song. I conclude with it here as a challenge to the reader to begin counting the Ten and making the Ten count.[48]

> I am Yahweh your God, / who saved you all from slavery.
> I have Ten Words to guide your way / so you can follow me.
>
> The first four focus on loving me; / the others on your neighbor.
> Some point in both ways, / and all protect from danger.
>
> First, worship only me; / no other gods allowed.
> Second, represent me well / in private or in crowd.
>
> Third, observe the Sabbath day, / allowing all to rest.
> Fourth, honor Dad and Mom; / believe I want your best.
>
> Fifth, respect human life. / Sixth, respect marriage.
> Seventh, respect others' stuff. / Eighth, respect the truth.
>
> The Ninth and Tenth call to covet not / wife or household.
> We've counted to Ten; we've come to the end. / God is Lord of all.

4. Appendix: A Note on the Christian's Relationship to Old Testament Law

Highly debated are questions about the relationship of the old and new covenants in general and of the Christian's relationship to OT law in particular.[49] The following significant convictions govern my own approach as a Christian to OT law:

---

48. We used the familiar melody of "Row, Row, Row Your Boat" for easy memorization.
49. See W. G. Strickland, ed., *The Law, the Gospel, and the Modern Christian* (Grand Rapids: Zondervan, 1991); reprinted as *Five Views on Law and Gospel* (1996). Three recent volumes in biblical theology that generally reflect the sentiments of the present author are T. Wells and F. Zaspel, *New Covenant Theology: Description, Definition, Defense* (Frederick,

1. Christians are no longer under the old covenant as a written legal code (Acts 15:10, 19; Gal 5:1–12; Eph 2:14–16), which brought forth an age of death to the majority of Israel who retained hard hearts and which has now been transcended through the eschatological, new covenant work of Christ (Gal 3:25; cf. 2 Cor 3:6–8, 11; Heb 7:12; 8:13; 10:9), who provides freedom from the law's condemning power and supplies all the righteousness that the law requires (Rom 3:21–26; Phil 3:8–9; Col 2:13–14).
2. The entire OT finds its fulfillment in Christ, and therefore "every detail" of the Mosaic law is to be done and taught by Christians only in keeping with its fulfillment in Jesus (Matt 5:17–20; cf. Luke 16:17; Rom 3:21, 31; 10:4).[50] While Christians are not bound to the old covenant, we do not abandon the OT law. However, we appropriate it only through Christ and in light of the teaching of his apostles, which together alone ground and sustain the church (Acts 2:42; Eph 2:20; cf. Matt 7:24–27; 17:5; 28:20; John 16:12–14; 17:8, 18, 20; 2 Thess 2:15; Heb 1:1–2).
3. The OT laws encapsulate a temporal expression of love for God and neighbor that, when read in light of and through the completed work of Christ, should now serve as wise guides for believers across all cultures and times (Deut 30:6; Matt 7:12; Rom 13:8–10; Gal 5:14; 6:2; cf. Lev 19:18, 34; Deut 6:5; 10:12–19; Matt 22:37–40). While Christians are not obligated to keep the Mosaic law itself, they must benefit from old covenant instruction in the way that it finds fulfillment in and informs "the law of Christ," "perfect law," "law of liberty," or "royal law" (1 Cor 9:20–21; Gal 6:2; Jas 1:25; 2:8, 12; cf. Matt 5:17–20; 28:19). In this way, the OT law becomes useful "for teaching, for reproof, for correction, and for training in righteousness" (2 Tim 3:16; cf. Rom 4:23; 13:9; 15:4; 1 Cor 9:9; 10:11; Eph 6:1–3; 1 Tim 5:18; 1 Pet 1:15–16; 1 John 5:21).[51]

MD: New Covenant Media, 2002); J. C. Meyer, *The End of the Law: Mosaic Covenant and Pauline Theology* (NAC Studies in Bible and Theology; Nashville: B&H Academic, 2009); and Gentry and Wellum, *Kingdom through Covenant*; see also D. Moo, "The Law of Christ as the Fulfillment of the Law of Moses," in *The Law, the Gospel, and the Modern Christian* [ed. W. G. Strickland; Grand Rapids: Zondervan, 1991], 319–82; T. R. Schreiner, *40 Questions about Christians and Biblical Law* (Grand Rapids: Kregel Academic & Professional, 2010).

    50. For this view, see F. Zaspel's discussion in Wells and Zaspel, *New Covenant Theology*, 77–160, esp. 126–27, 157–60.

    51. For examples of a principlizing approach to OT law, see W. C. Kaiser Jr., *Toward Old Testament Ethics* (Grand Rapids: Zondervan, 1983); idem, "A Principlizing Model," in *Four*

4. The familial, social, economic, and political structures of Yahwistic Israel as revealed in the OT bore a missional purpose and were intended to provide a contextual paradigm of the values God desires for all peoples and in all times (Gen 26:5; Exod 19:4–6; Deut 4:5–8; 26:16–18; 30:6, 8; Jer 12:16; Ezek 36:23, 27; Isa 2:3; 42:4; 51:4; Rom 2:13–14, 26; 3:31; 7:12; 8:4; 13:8; 1 Cor 9:21; Gal 6:2; Jas 1:25; 2:12).[52]

5. The church and the new creation stand in a divinely orchestrated typological relationship with earlier events, peoples, and structures that allows for ethical teaching from the OT to be done through a redemptive-historical, textually grounded, Christological lens (Rom 5:14; 1 Cor 10:6, 11; Col 2:16–17; Heb 8:5; 9:24; 1 Pet 3:21).[53]

Views on Moving Beyond the Bible to Theology (ed. G. T. Meadors; Grand Rapids: Zondervan, 2009) 19–50; J. D. Hays, "Applying the Old Testament Law Today," *BSac* 158.1 (2001) 21–35.

52. For more on this point, which may be called a principlizing-paradigmatic approach, see C. J. H. Wright, *Old Testament Ethics for the People of God* (Downers Grove, IL: InterVarsity, 2011) 62–74, 182–211, 314–25; cf. W. Janzen, *Old Testament Ethics: A Paradigmatic Approach* (Louisville: Westminster John Knox, 1994); E. A. Martens, "How Is the Christian to Construe Old Testament Law?" *BBR* 12.2 (2002) 199–216; D. I. Block, "Preaching Old Testament Law to New Testament Christians," in *The Gospel according to Moses*, 104–46, esp. 133–36; orig. published in *Hiphil (Scandinavian Evangelical E-Journal)* 3 (2006) 1–24, and subsequently published in three parts in *Ministry* 78.5 (2006) 5–11; 78.7 (2006) 12–16; 78.9 (2006) 15–18.

53. For more on this, see Gentry and Wellum, *Kingdom through Covenant*, 94–95, 101–8, 606–8; cf. R. Davidson, *Typology in Scripture: A Study of Hermeneutical TUPOS Structures* (Andrews University Seminary Doctoral Dissertation Series 2; Berrien Springs, MI: Andrews University, 1981); D. Moo, "The Problem of *Sensis Plenior*," in *Hermeneutics, Authority, and Canon* (ed. D. A. Carson and J. D. Woodbridge; Grand Rapids: Zondervan, 1986) 175–212; G. K. Beale, "Did Jesus and His Followers Preach the Right Doctrine from the Wrong Text?" *Themelios* 14 (1989) 89–96; reprinted in *The Right Doctrine from the Wrong Text? Essays on the Use of the Old Testament in the New* (ed. G. K. Beale; Grand Rapids: Baker, 1994) 387–404; R. Lintz, *The Fabric of Theology: A Prolegomenon to Evangelical Theology* (Grand Rapids: Eerdmans, 1993) 304–10; G. P. Hugenberger, "Introductory Notes on Typology," in *The Right Doctrine from the Wrong Text?* 331–41; D. A. Carson, "Mystery and Fulfillment: Toward a More Comprehensive Paradigm of Paul's Understanding of the Old and the New," in *Justification and Variegated Nomism: Volume 2—The Paradoxes of Paul* (ed. D. A. Carson et al.; Grand Rapids: Baker, 2004) 393–436, esp. 404.

Welcoming the Stranger
Toward a Theology of Immigration in Deuteronomy

M. Daniel Carroll R.

"Cursed is anyone who withholds justice from the foreigner, the fatherless or the widow."
Then all the people shall say, "Amen!" (Deut 27:19, NIV)

1. Introduction

It is estimated that presently there are over 210 million migrants worldwide.[1] People move as individuals, as families, or as larger population groups for many reasons—to escape armed conflict, to flee political, religious or ethnic persecution, to seek relief from hunger or disease, or to secure more secure employment. The multiple pressures on nation states that have absorbed these outsiders have triggered internal debates about ethnic identity, social coherence, economic viability, law enforcement, national security, and accessibility to medical care and education. We are witnessing a new socio-economic and cultural reality created by an increasingly complex and multidimensional globalization.[2] In response, migration studies and research on diaspora and transnationalism are booming in the disciplines of anthropology and sociology.[3]

Author's Note: It is a pleasure to offer this essay in honor of a respected scholar and friend, Dan Block, someone who is committed to the study of the Old Testament—in particular Deuteronomy—and to a life faithful to its truth.

1. International Organization for Migration (http://www.iom.int/jahia/Jahia/about-migration/facts-and-figures/lang/en; last accessed June 4, 2012). This figure in part is drawn from the United Nations Department of Economic and Social Affairs.

2. See, e.g., T. J. Hatton and J. G. Williamson, *Global Migration and the World Economy: Two Centuries of Policy and Performance* (Cambridge, MA: MIT Press, 2005); C. B. Brettell and J. F. Hollifield, eds., *Migration Theory: Talking Across Disciplines* (2nd ed.; New York: Routledge, 2008); S. Castles and M. J. Miller, *The Age of Migration: International Population Movements in the Modern World* (4th ed.; New York: Guilford, 2009).

3. For helpful introductions, see J. Clifford, "Diasporas," *Cultural Anthropology* 9, no. 2 (1994) 302–38; S. Dufoix, *Diasporas* (trans. W. Rodarmor; Berkeley, CA: University of California Press, 2008); and journals, like *Diaspora: A Journal of Transnational Studies*, *Journal of Ethnic and Migration Studies*, and *International Migration Review*.

This massive displacement of populations also has generated a growing field in mission circles: diaspora missiology.[4] It views the unreached peoples of these communities as untapped areas for ministries of proclamation, mercy, and church-planting. At the same time, there is interest in gauging the potential impact on their host societies of those diaspora communities who claim the Christian faith and their possible involvement in the worldwide mission of the Church. Denominations have begun to invest in leadership training and the publication of materials in the languages of these newcomers.

Interestingly, while their presence has spawned creative *ministry involvement* with immigrant groups, many Christians wrestle *theologically* and *politically* with the phenomenon of immigration. Many are conflicted, torn between an impulse toward charitable hospitality on the one hand and a commitment to support current immigration legislation as law-abiding citizens on the other. Sadly, a general lack of exposure to what the Bible might have to say about the issue characterizes this confusion. For those who hold the Bible as fundamental to faith and practice, it is important that the Bible be allowed to speak to the topic in order to explore how it might inform a genuinely Christian position on the matter. This is a particularly urgent matter, since gracious welcoming of the sojourner is a significant matter in Old Testament Law (Exod 23:9; Lev 19:18, 33–34; Deut 10:17–19).[5] Migration also is a central metaphor for the Christian life (1 Pet 1:1, 2:11).

Scholarly work on ethnicity in ancient Israel and on Old Testament diaspora texts and backgrounds is growing,[6] some of which make con-

---

4. E.g., E. Wan, ed., *Diaspora Missiology: Theory, Methodology, and Practice* (Seattle: CreateSpace, 2012); S. Ybarrola, "Anthropology, Diasporas, and Mission," *Mission Studies* 29, no. 1 (2012) 79–94. The Lausanne Committee for World Evangelization has hosted consultations on diaspora (http://www.lausanne.org/en/gatherings/issue-based/diasporas-2009.html; last accessed June 4, 2012) and has produced *Scattered to Gather: Embracing the Global Trend of Diaspora* (Manila: LifeChange, 2010); cf. the Vatican's Pontifical Council for the Pastoral Care of Migrants and Itinerant People at http://www.vatican.va/roman_curia/pontifical_councils/migrants/index.htm; last accessed June 4, 2012.

5. In *Making Wise the Simple: The Torah in Christian Faith and Practice* (Grand Rapids: Eerdmans, 2005), J. W. H. van Wijk-Bos makes concern for the stranger central to the ethos of the Torah.

6. E.g., M. G. Brett, ed., *Ethnicity & the Bible* (Biblical Interpretation Series 19; Leiden: Brill, 1996); K. L. Sparks, *Ethnicity and Identity in Ancient Israel: Prolegomena to the Study of Ethnic Sentiments and Their Expression in the Hebrew Bible* (Winona Lake, IN: Eisenbrauns, 1998); A. E. Killebrew, *Biblical Peoples and Ethnicity: An Archaeological Study of Egyptians, Canaanites, Philistines, and Early Israel 1300–1100 B.C.E.* (SBLABS 9; Atlanta: Society of Biblical Literature, 2005); K. E. Southwood, *Ethnicity and the Mixed Marriage Crisis in Ezra 9–10: An Anthropological Approach* (Oxford Theological Monographs; Oxford: Oxford University Press, 2012).

nections to the experiences of contemporary immigrant communities.[7] In fact, there is much related to migration throughout the Old Testament that can contribute to the articulation of a substantive biblical position on immigration.[8] This essay will concentrate on Deuteronomy. It is divided into three major parts. The first engages the prospect of appealing to Deuteronomy as a viable resource for the contemporary moral and civil debate. The second section presents the relevant material on immigration in Deuteronomy. The third suggests ways in which this might be brought to bear on the modern context. The complexity of the topic and the challenges to understanding fully the biblical data are the reason this essay is suggestive, a step "toward" a theology of immigration from this Pentateuchal book.

2. Deuteronomy: A Resource for a Theology of Immigration?

Deuteronomy has a good number of verses that refer to the outsider. These are the focus of the next section. A prior consideration concerns whether the book should be consulted for contributing to a theology of immigration. There are voices that decry the appeal to Deuteronomy for ethics. Doubts about its usefulness arise from the conviction that the book is fundamentally flawed as an ethical resource.

To begin with, there is the indisputable historical fact that Deuteronomy has been employed to sanctify unjust ideologies and regimes. For instance, it provided part of the biblical foundation for the Afrikaner theology of apartheid in South Africa (see Deut 7:3–4, 23:2–8, 29:9–11, 32:8).[9] Robert Jewett and John Lawrence ground the conviction of the United States as a special virtuous people in what they call the "Deuteronomistic principle" of Deuteronomy 28, where material blessing and

---

7. E.g., G. L. Cuellar, *Voices of Marginality: Exile and Return in Second Isaiah and the Mexican Immigrant Experience* (American University Series VII/271; New York: Peter Lang, 2008); J.-P. Ruiz, *Reading from the Edges: The Bible & People on the Move* (Maryknoll, NY: Orbis, 2011).

8. Among the several publications of the author on the topic, note M. D. Carroll R., *Christians at the Border: Immigration, the Church, and the Bible* (Grand Rapids: Baker, 2008; translated as *Cristianos en la frontera: La inmigración, la Iglesia y la Biblia* [Lake Mary, FL: Casa Creación, 2009]); idem, "Aliens, Immigration, and Refugees," in *Dictionary of Scripture and Ethics* (ed. J. Green et al.; Grand Rapids: Baker, 2011) 53–58; idem, "Looking at the Challenges of Immigration Through a Missional Lens," in *Missional Ethics: Biblical and Theological Perspectives* (ed. J. Rowe and A. Draycott; Downers Grove, IL: InterVarsity, 2012) 258–77.

9. F. Deist, "The Dangers of Deuteronomy: A Page from the Reception History of the Book," in *Studies in Deuteronomy in Honour of C. J. Labuschagne on the Occasion of His 65th Birthday* (ed. F. García Martínez et al.; VTSup 53; Leiden: Brill, 1994) 13–29.

victory are contingent on faithfulness to God. They trace this mythic worldview of being a uniquely chosen nation to declarations John Winthrop pronounced in 1630. This self-righteous confidence persists to the present day, they argue, even though in a more secular version.[10] Unfortunate appropriations of Deuteronomy could be multiplied. History is littered with biblically based claims of divine support for selfish gain and oppression. This reality is pertinent to our topic, as these negative attitudes and policies have been directed at the "other," often those of another race, culture, or homeland. In these reflections, it is important to decide whether the book itself is abusive or whether the issue lies rather with its inappropriate use. As we will see, the book is generally favorable to the one who enters into the community of Israel.

In addition to historical examples of segregationist interpretation, today there are views that combine socio-historical reconstructions and ideological criticism with hypotheses about the redactional history of Deuteronomy in order to argue that the book is problematic.[11] Harold Bennett argues that its charitable laws are not as sensitive to the needs of the vulnerable (including the outsider) as they might appear at first glance. He argues that these measures originally were designed to protect the financial interests of a struggling religious elite in the Northern Kingdom (the Yahweh-alone movement of ninth century B.C.E. Israel), which opposed the state religion of the Omride regime and the popular religion of the masses.[12] In similar fashion, Douglas Knight recently has suggested that these laws were the creation of urban elites to manipulate the rural poor.[13] The strength of these sorts of positions, of course, depends on the quality of their historical, sociological, and ideological reconstruction and the depth of understanding of the sociology of literature.[14] It also depends on how well they have dealt with the material in Deuteronomy.

---

10. R. Jewett and J. S. Lawrence, *Captain America and the Crusade against Evil* (Grand Rapids: Eerdmans, 2003) 273–93.

11. On a broader scale, in *Glimpses of a Strange Land: Studies in Old Testament Ethics* (OTS; London: T. & T. Clark, 2001), C. S. Rodd discounts the entire Old Testament as too limited to its ancient context to be of use for ethics today.

12. H. V. Bennett, *Injustice Made Legal: Deuteronomic Law and the Plight of Widows, Strangers, and Orphans in Ancient Israel* (Grand Rapids: Eerdmans, 2002).

13. D. A. Knight, *Law, Power, and Justice in Ancient Israel* (Library of Ancient Israel; Louisville: Westminster John Knox, 2011) 9–86, 153–54, 217–22; cf. M. Sneed, "Israelite Concern for the Alien, Orphan, and Widow: Altruism or Ideology?" *ZAW* 111, no. 4 (1999) 498–507.

14. See evaluative criteria in M. D. Carroll R., "Social-Scientific Approaches," in *Dictionary of the Old Testament: Prophets* (ed. M. Boda and J. G. McConville; Downers Grove, IL: InterVarsity, 2012) 734–47.

Another current challenge to any effort to draw ethical guidance from the Old Testament concerns the exclusionary violence that seems to be sanctioned in its pages. Even those who generally are positively disposed to the Old Testament as authoritative for the Church question the text. Eric Seibert includes Deuteronomy's laws of war, especially against the native population in the Conquest (Deuteronomy 7 and 20), among the difficult passages that he says communicate an unacceptable portrait of God. His solution to this theological quandary is a "christocentric hermeneutic": the God that Jesus presents in the Gospels is the norm for discerning which parts of the Old Testament truly reflect his person.[15] Rob Barrett and Caryn Reeder offer careful literary readings of Deuteronomy's texts of violence in conversation with its ancient background and modern culture. Barrett deals with passages that contain Yahweh's threats of wrath against Israel (chs. 4, 9–10, 13, 28, 32), while Reeder studies those that command the execution of household members for certain unacceptable acts (13:7–12[6–11], 21:18–21, 22:13–21). Both, however, are more affirming of the Old Testament than Seibert. Barrett calls his approach one of "engagement and sympathy"; Reeder calls hers a "hermeneutics of trust."[16]

There are laws in Deuteronomy concerning outsiders that appear discriminatory. For example, various ethnic groups are barred from the assembly for several generations (Deut 23:4–9[3–8]). These passages raise questions about the value of what Deuteronomy might have to say about migration and the treatment of those who have migrated into the community of faith. Is there an openness to the sojourner (if so, how much and why?), or does Deuteronomy present an exclusionary perspective that would raise questions about its viability for moral guidance today?

The point to be made at this juncture is that probing Deuteronomy for ethics is no simple matter. A survey of its teaching follows in the next section, but these moral challenges cannot be ignored. How then are we to utilize Deuteronomy as a basis for a theology of immigration that is grounded in a commitment to the text—one that approaches the

---

15. E. A. Seibert, *Disturbing Divine Behavior: Troubling Old Testament Images of God* (Minneapolis: Fortress, 2009). E. W. Davies surveys various approaches dealing with difficult passages in the Old Testament in *The Immoral Bible: Approaches to Biblical Ethics* (London: T. & T. Clark, 2010).

16. R. Barrett, *Disloyalty and Destruction: Religion and Politics in Deuteronomy and the Modern World* (LHBOTS 511; London: T. & T. Clark, 2009); C. A. Reeder, *The Enemy in the Household: Family Violence in Deuteronomy and Beyond* (Grand Rapids: Baker, 2012).

book's teaching through "engagement and sympathy" and "trust," (to use Barrett and Reeder's labels)? That is the concern of the third section.

Along with the need to grapple with the content of Deuteronomy, it is necessary to specify the text to be studied if one does embrace the book for ethics. What follows does not attempt to locate its teaching along some diachronic continuum.[17] Instead we will work with the received, or canonical, form of Deuteronomy that is the Scripture of the Church. I am interested in the Old Testament for Christian ethics, especially in its role as Scripture for the moral life of Christian communities. The canonical shape is the only text these communities know and own.[18] Therefore, I will not engage hypotheses about the possible provenance of the document and the hypothetical steps in its production,[19] even though it is an important dimension of scholarly discourse

---

17. Such as C. van Houten, *The Alien in Israelite Law* (JSOTSup 107; Sheffield: Sheffield Academic Press, 1991); J. E. Ramírez Kidd, *Alterity and Identity in Israel: The GR in the Old Testament* (BZAW 283; Berlin: de Gruyter, 1999).

18. See M. D. Carroll R., *Contexts for Amos: Prophetic Poetics in Latin American Perspective* (JSOTSup, 132; Sheffield: Sheffield Academic Press, 1992) 140–75; idem, "Ethics and Old Testament Interpretation," in *Hearing the Old Testament: Listening for God's Address* (ed. C. G. Bartholomew and D. J. H. Beldman; Grand Rapids: Eerdmans, 2012) 204–30; cf. idem and D. L. Bock, "The Bible and Ethics," in *The Oxford Handbook of Evangelical Theology* (ed. G. R. McDermott; Oxford: Oxford University Press, 2010) 371–88.

19. There are several scholarly options about its origins, although all admit that the book contains early material. These include: (1) Late Bronze Age (see, e.g., K. A. Kitchen, *On the Reliability of the Old Testament* [Grand Rapids: Eerdmans, 2003] 283–306; P. T. Vogt, "'These Are the Words Moses Spoke': Implied Audience and a Case for Pre-Monarchic Dating of Deuteronomy" in the present volume); (2) the Assyrian period of the 7th century, including the Josianic reform (see J. G. McConville, *Deuteronomy* [Apollos OT Commentary 5; Leicester: Apollos; Downers Grove, IL: InterVarsity, 2002] 21–41; idem, *God and Earthly Power—An Old Testament Political Theology: Genesis—Deuteronomy* [LHBOTS 454; London: T. & T. Clark, 2006] 28–29; B. M. Levinson, "Deuteronomy," in *The Oxford Encyclopedia of the Books of the Bible* [ed. M. D. Coogan; Oxford: Oxford University Press, 2011] 192–209); (3) Josiah's reform in the last quarter of the 7th century (see, e.g., F. Crüsemann, *The Torah: Theology and Social History of Old Testament Law* [trans. A. W. Mahnke; Edinburgh: T. & T. Clark, 1996] 207–15; M. D. Coogan, *The Old Testament: A Historical and Literary Introduction to the Hebrew Scriptures* [New York: Oxford University Press, 2006] 173–90); (4) the Postexilic, or Persian, Period (see, e.g., S. E. Balentine, *The Torah's Vision of Worship* [OBT; Minneapolis: Fortress, 1999]; J. W. Watts, ed., *Persia and Torah: The Theory of Imperial Authorization of the Pentateuch* [SBLSS; Atlanta: Society of Biblical Literature, 2001]; E. Otto, "Anti-Archaemenid Propaganda in Deuteronomy," in *Homeland and Exile: Biblical and Ancient Near Eastern Studies in Honour of Bustenay Oded* [ed. G. Galil, M. Geller, and A. Millard; Leiden: Brill, 2009] 547–58). For surveys, see the commentaries. Deuteronomy itself suggests a process of compilation (see D. I. Block, "Recovering the Voice of Moses: The Genesis of Deuteronomy," *JETS* 44 [2001] 385–408, reproduced with excurses in idem, *The Gospel According to Moses: Theological and Ethical Reflections on the Book of Deuteronomy* [Eugene, OR: Cascade, 2012] 21–67).

on the book. Our attention is directed elsewhere. Other scholars, who have worked on Deuteronomy for contemporary ethics, have made the same choice.[20]

3. The Sojourner in Deuteronomy

The Old Testament has several terms for outsiders. This essay will concentrate on one in particular, גר.[21] The גר, often translated in English translations (although not consistently) as 'sojourner' or 'alien',[22] was someone who had moved from a different part of the country or from elsewhere.[23] Most occurrences refer to the latter. This Hebrew word occurs twenty-two times in Deuteronomy.[24]

In the ancient world sojourners were in a vulnerable and precarious position. In that context most help in time of need would come through extended family, but sojourners were separated from this familial network. They would have been forced to be dependent upon the host population for charitable aid. In addition, these outsiders probably would have had a considerably difficult time acquiring land, a key economic factor for sustenance and survival in a peasant agrarian social world like Israel's.[25] The law of Moses and custom stipulated that land

---

20. E.g., McConville, *God and Earthly Power*, 1–29; J. G. Millar, *Now Choose Life: Theology and Ethics in Deuteronomy* (Grand Rapids: Eerdmans, 1998); cf. C. J. H. Wright, *Old Testament Ethics for the People of God* (Downers Grove, IL: InterVarsity, 2004); van Wijk-Bos, *Making Wise the Simple*.

21. See, e.g., D. I. Block, "Sojourner," *ISBE*, 4:561–64; D. Kellermann, "גור *gûr*," *TDOT* 2:439–49; A. H. Konkel, "גור", *NIDOTTE* 1:836–39; R. J. D. Knauth, "Alien, Foreign Resident," *DOTP*, 26–33; van Houten, *The Alien in Israelite Law*; R. Rendtorff, "The Ger in the Priestly Laws of the Pentateuch," in *Ethnicity in the Bible* (ed. M. G. Brett; Biblical Interpretation Series 19; Leiden: Brill, 1995) 77–87; R. Kidd, *Alterity and Identity in Israel*. Two other Old Testament terms are תושב, which does not appear in Deuteronomy, and נכרי, which occurs five times (Deut 14:21, 15:3, 17:15, 23:21, 29:21). The נכרי seems to be an individual, who does not integrate into Israelite society. Some suggest that they were foreign merchants.

22. Other translations include "resident alien," "stranger," or "foreigner." CEB renders it "immigrant." We will use "sojourner" for these individuals in the rest of the essay.

23. The noun גר and verb גור 'to sojourn, dwell as an alien' occasionally are used to describe Israel's position before God (e.g., Lev 25:23, 1 Chr 29:15; cf. Deut 26:5).

24. Deut 1:16; 5:14; 10:18, 19 (twice); 14:21, 29; 16:11, 14; 23:8; 24:14, 17, 19, 20, 21; 26:11, 12, 13; 27:19; 28:43; 29:10; 31:12. The verb גור I ('sojourn') occurs in 18:6 and 26:5.

25. For the peasant world of ancient Israel, although from different perspectives, see W. R. Domeris, *Touching the Heart of God: The Social Construction of Poverty among Biblical Peasants* (LHBOTS 466; New York: T. & T. Clark, 2007); E. F. Davis, *Scripture, Culture, and Agriculture: An Agrarian Reading of the Bible* (Cambridge: Cambridge University Press, 2009); Knight, *Law, Power, and Justice in Ancient Israel*, 115–56; cf. P. J. King and L. E. Stager, *Life in Biblical Israel* (Library of Ancient Israel; Louisville: Westminster John Knox, 2001) 85–200.

was to remain in the family and be passed through the male heir (Num 27:1–11, 36:1–12; cf. 1 Kgs 21:1–3). Obviously, this eliminated opportunities for the sojourner.[26] They would have had to seek employment on Israelite farms. Outsiders, too, are susceptible to suffering discrimination and marginalization at the hands of the native-born in day-to-day affairs and legal matters. In all kinds of ways, then, the sojourner was at the mercy of the Israelites. How does Deuteronomy respond to these realities?[27]

3.1. Positive Laws for the Sojourner

We can classify the pertinent verses in several basic categories. To begin with, concerning the immediate need for provision, Deuteronomy's laws allow for the sojourner, along with others who were particularly at risk (the poor, widows, and orphans),[28] to gather from the fields and glean from the olive trees and vineyards at harvest time (Deut 24:19–21). There also was a triennial tithe of produce for these groups, along with the Levites (14:29; 26:12–13).

Second, Deuteronomy addresses issues of labor. The גרים 'sojourners' were to be granted the Sabbath rest along with the rest of the household (Deut 5:14). The household was central to Israelite life and identity, and the welfare of its members was a fundamental ethical expectation.[29]

---

26. In addition to the sources cited in n. 25, see D. L. Baker, *Tight Fists or Open Hands: Wealth and Poverty in Old Testament Law* (Grand Rapids: Eerdmans, 2009) 15–107. Lev 25:47 represents an exceptional case of land in the possession of the foreigner (cf. Deut 28:43–44).

27. In addition to the sources cited in *supra*, n. 21, note D. E. Gowan, "Wealth and Poverty in the Old Testament: The Case of the Widow, the Orphan, and the Sojourner," *Int* 41, no. 4 (1987) 341–53; P. D. Miller, "Israel as Host to Strangers," in *Israelite Religion and Biblical Theology: Collected Essays* (JSOTSup 267; Sheffield: Sheffield Academic Press, 2000) 548–71.

28. In addition to this grouping, one could also mention the sensitivity to the blind (27:18), slaves (23:15–16), and even domestic animals (5:14; 22:1–4, 6–7; 25:4). For more on Deuteronomy's approach to the disadvantaged, see in this volume R. Josberger, "For *Your* Good Always: Restraining the Rights of the Victor for the Well-being of the Vulnerable (Deut 21:10–14)"; M. Theocharous, "Stealing Souls: Human Trafficking and Deuteronomy 24:7."

29. C. Meyers, "The Family in Early Israel," in *Families in Ancient Israel* (ed. L. G. Perdue et al.; The Family, Religion, and Culture; Louisville: Westminster John Knox, 1997) 1–47; King and Stager, *Life in Biblical Israel*, 21–84; D. I. Block, "Marriage and Family in Ancient Israel," in *Marriage and Family in the Biblical World* (ed. K. M. Campbell; Downers Grove, IL: InterVarsity, 2003) 33–102; cf. Wright, *Old Testament Ethics*, 327–62. Also note the "brother" language applied in Deuteronomy to fellow Israelites. See, McConville, *God and Earthly Power*, 92–95; W. J. Houston, "'Open your hand to your needy brother': Ideology and Moral Formation in Deut. 15:1–18," in *The Bible in Ethics* (ed. J. W. Rogerson, M. Davies, and M. D. Carroll R.; JSOTSup 207; Sheffield: Sheffield Academic Press, 1995)

The sojourners are included in this care. The Israelite kinship group was to extend to them the basic rights of the native born. The fact that they are said to be "at the gate" (likely of a town or of the collection of households comprising a village) and are listed with other individuals and animals of the household suggests that they were day laborers. Perhaps they gathered at the gate and then were brought into family contexts to work. Taking unfair advantage of foreign labor was (and is) a real temptation, and the next verse reminds the Israelites of their own experience in Egypt (5:15). In 24:14–15 the call for the payment of wages before sunset could imply that work would have been on a day-to-day basis. Late or exploitative compensation would have been disastrous for such needy people. Once again, there is a motive clause. It, too, points to Israel's experience in Egypt: God will respond to the cry of the needy, as he had done so many years before on their behalf (see Exod 2:23–25).

Third, Deuteronomy addresses legal matters. Outsiders naturally fear unfair disadvantage in the adjudication of legal cases because they must compete with the native-born and are sentenced by them. The narrative introduction of Deuteronomy harks back to Moses' delegation of decision-making in Exodus 18 and to his injunction to be impartial in judgment to both the Israelite and the גר (Deut 1:16–17). Two passages dealing with justice connect the sojourner to the widow and the orphan (24:17–18, 27:19). In the former, appeal again is made to the injustices of Egypt; in the latter, to deprive justice from any of these groups is to incur a curse. Righteousness (צדקה) and justice (משפט) were to characterize the legal ethos of Israel.

Fourth, there are provisions to allow participation in worship. Sojourners are invited (with the other vulnerable groups) to take part in the feasts of Weeks (*Shavuot*, Deut 16:11), Booths (*Sukkot*, 16:14), and First Fruits (26:11). The Sabbath has already been mentioned. The command to permit their involvement in Israel's religious ceremonies is significant. It grants the גרים entry into another arena at the core of the community's identity (along with the family). They could come into Israel's sacred spaces, embrace its symbols, and engage in its holy activities, all of which together defined and structured that community and provided its rhythms and the meaning of life. The גרים also were to gather periodically to hear the reading of the law in order to fear and obey Yahweh (31:9–13), an orientation necessary for anyone to integrate into a different social construction of reality. This exercise would

---

296–314; idem, *Contending for Justice: Ideologies and Theologies of Social Justice in the Old Testament* (rev. ed.; London: T. & T. Clark, 2008) 179–90.

make Israel's way of life clearer to newcomers and their children, as well as secure their allegiance to that context and its norms. Involvement in the cult and at the reading of the law also would have carried expectations for sojourners on the part of Israelites. Sojourners would have to acquire Israel's language to comprehend that reading and to make informed adjustments to the various spheres of their new context.

The breadth of this legislation is impressive. The question that naturally surfaces is the following: Why should Israel welcome these outsiders? Deuteronomy offers at least three reasons. The most repeated was the recollection of Israel's tragic experience in Egypt. Several injunctions concerning the גרים are coupled with a call to remember the past.[30] What cannot be missed is that this memory of oppression included life under a brutal legal system of a people, whose gods and religion legitimized the exploitation of immigrants and their labor.[31] In other words, the historical memory was caused by the unjust laws of a cruel culture. It must not be so in Yahweh's new society, Israel.

The role of collective memory (the verb זכר) is an important theme in Deuteronomy.[32] The people's history was to be periodically rehearsed and reenacted in home and cult (in processions, the celebration of the feasts, the making of booths, and song), because it was foundational to defining Israel's responsibilities of faithfulness to Yahweh and of charity toward others. In these rituals, memory is made tangible at individual, familial, and community levels. These practices (and here I am thinking of the meaning of practices in virtue ethics)[33] were to inculcate and transmit those memories across generations.

In *The End of Memory*, Miroslav Volf contemplates how to deal with memories that hurt and haunt us.[34] There is the need to grapple with the wrongs endured, but also the challenge to discern the grace of God in the midst of that experience then, in the present, and into the future.

---

30. Deut 5:15; 10:19; 16:12; 24:18, 22; cf. 26:6–10. This motivation is not limited to the treatment of the sojourner; it is applied to the treatment of other unfortunate groups.

31. For details on the oppression of Semites in Egypt during the New Kingdom period, see J. K. Hoffmeier, *Israel in Egypt: The Evidence for the Authenticity of the Exodus Tradition* (New York: Oxford University Press, 1996) 112–16. Scenes of bricklaying by Semites appear on the walls of the tomb of the vizier Rekhmire (*op. cit.*, fig. 8, 9).

32. As is the danger of forgetting (שכח). The relevant passages are Deut 4:9, 23; 6:12; 8:11, 14, 19; 9:7; 25:19; 26:13; 31:21; 32:18.

33. For a foundational discussion of this feature of virtue ethics, see A. MacIntyre, *After Virtue: A Study in Moral Theory* (2nd ed.; Notre Dame: University of Notre Dame Press, 1984), 186–203. Also G. Mikoski, "Practices," in *Dictionary of Scripture and Ethics* (ed. J. B. Green; Grand Rapids: Baker, 2011) 613–17.

34. M. Volf, *The End of Memory: Remembering Rightly in a Violent World* (Grand Rapids: Eerdmans, 2006). He discusses the Exodus on pp. 103–11.

Ideally, one can redeem that memory and even the perpetrator of the evil. In the divine demand to remember the exodus, the people are to turn those ancient stories of long and terrible suffering and the subsequent experience of redemption into the basis of their ethical treatment of the "other." Israel cannot, should not, must not forget its history, if it desires to be the people of Yahweh. In Egypt, negative attitudes generated unfortunate laws. To forget those cultural and legal realities would lead to their becoming like that very past which they hated, with others as the victims. Though not in the personal experience of those standing at the Jordan, they and every subsequent generation were to look back to inform a perspective pleasing to Yahweh and beneficial to others.[35]

Another motivation to show kindness to the outsider is that to do so would yield bountiful crops by God's hand (Deut 14:29, 16:15, 24:19, 26:15). This second reason moves us to the third and most weighty impetus: the love of God for the sojourner. Leviticus 19 contains the well-known command to "Love your neighbor as yourself," which is connected later in that same chapter to the love of the sojourner (Lev 19:18, 33–34). Deuteronomy has its love verse too, but instead of connecting care for the גר to the love of self, Israel is called to mimic the love of God. Yahweh executes justice for the widow and orphan and loves the גר, and does so in material ways, with food and garments (Deut 10:18–19). This provision would have to come through his people. Charity towards sojourners was an expression of the love of God and proof of a circumcised heart (10:16). It makes sense then that sojourners would be invited to come to the sanctuaries and share in the worship of this unique God, who loved them. Part of the attractiveness of Yahweh was the laws of Israel, including those reaching out to the outsider (4:5–8).[36]

There are also broader theological themes that frame the attitude of graciousness toward sojourners. First, the central section of the book (Deut 16:18–18:22), which lists the qualifications and duties of the leadership (judges, priests, kings, prophets), counters the centralization and abuse of power. This is especially notable, when the passage about kings (17:14–20) is set against the backdrop of ancient Near Eastern thought. Israel's kings were to be subordinate to the demands of *torah* and the pursuit of the common good. They were not to accumulate the

---

35. For more on Deuteronomy's appropriation of the past for Israel's present ethics, see J. Hwang, *The Rhetoric of Remembrance: An Investigation of the "Fathers" in Deuteronomy* (Siphrut 8; Winona Lake, IN: Eisenbrauns, 2012).

36. Interestingly, there is almost nothing in extra-biblical ancient law codes pertaining to the sojourner.

trappings of royalty (armies, harems, and wealth), nor were they to think themselves better than others. This leveling posture was to be embedded in the political fabric of that society.[37] It sets a tone and level of equality that coheres with the value placed on the disadvantaged, among whom were counted the sojourners.

In addition, acceptance of outsiders in Deuteronomy must be placed alongside the surprisingly negative appraisal of Israel. The historical prologue is not shy about pointing out the rebelliousness of Israel (Deut 1:26–40; cf. 9:6–7, 13, 27). This people was chosen not because it was great, but by the unmerited grace of God (7:7–8). Moses challenges those of the present generation to respond properly to his admonitions and so choose life and avoid the mistakes of their ancestors (30:19; cf. 5:3).[38] Future generations would have to make the same decision, and their decisions would determine if they experienced blessings or curses (ch. 28; 30:1–10) and fulfilled their calling as God's treasured possession (26:16–19).[39] The facts of their history and these warnings reveal the fault lines in the national character. Israel must steer clear of the self-deceptive temptation of thinking itself superior to other peoples, including those who had come to live in their midst.

Literary details in the pentateuchal narrative indicate that the moral demands of the law predate Moses and are connected to creation and Abraham.[40] In other words, the values in the law and the obligations towards others are linked with what is expected of humanity in general. They are woven into what we label "natural law." The moral appeal concerning the sojourner, then, can be said to be deep and broad, not limited only to this particular covenant relationship. This may be a rea-

---

37. E.g., McConville, *Deuteronomy*, 293–96, 304–6; Wright, *Old Testament Ethics*, 229–39; P. T. Vogt, *Deuteronomic Theology and the Significance of Torah: A Reappraisal* (Winona Lake, IN: Eisenbrauns, 2006) 204–26; J. A. Berman, *Created Equal: How the Bible Broke with Ancient Political Thought* (Oxford: Oxford University Press, 2008), 51–80; D. I. Block, "The Burden of Leadership: The Mosaic Paradigm of Kingship (Deut. 17:14–20)," *BSac* 162, no. 3 (2005) 259–78, reproduced in idem, *How I Love Your Torah, O LORD! Studies in the Book of Deuteronomy* (Eugene, OR: Cascade, 2011) 118–39; idem, "Leader, Leadership, OT," in *New Interpreter's Dictionary of the Bible* (ed. K. D. Sakenfeld; 5 vols.; Nashville: Abingdon, 2008) 3:621–26.

38. Note the repetition of "today" in, e.g., 4:8, 39, 40; 6:6; 11:2, 13; 29:11–12[12–13]; 30:15–16.

39. D. I. Block, "The Privilege of Calling: The Mosaic Paradigm for Missions (Deut. 26:16–19)," *BSac* 162.4 (2005) 387–405, reproduced in idem, *How I Love Your Torah*, 140–61.

40. McConville, *God and Earthly Power*, 76–78; T. E. Fretheim, *God and World in the Old Testament: A Relational Theology of Creation* (Nashville: Abingdon, 2005) 133–47; J. K. Bruckner, *Implied Law in the Abraham Narrative: A Literary and Theological Analysis* (JSOTSup 335; Sheffield: Sheffield Academic Press, 2002); cf. Wright, *Old Testament Ethics*.

son that Israel's law could strike a cord with the surrounding peoples (Deut 4:5–8).

3.2. The Negative Laws

Deuteronomy offers an impressively positive orientation to outsiders that is grounded in its history and theology and formalized in its laws. This orientation to the גרים, however, is not completely uniform. For example, one of the curses listed in the litany of disasters as divine judgment for disobedience is, "The foreigners who reside among you will rise above you higher and higher, but you will sink lower and lower. They will lend to you, but you will not lend to them. They will be the head, but you will be the tail" (Deut 28:43–44 NIV). Evidently, there could be shame in being beneath an outsider. This curse is a reversal of the blessing found in 28:12–13, so perhaps the intent is to communicate that in judgment the usual social order would be turned on its head (cf. Isa 3:12; Lam 5:8). Deut 29:11 describes the גר as one who cuts firewood and draws water, which may reflect their dependency on the Israelites. This verse portrays this as their duty "in the midst of the camp," conceivably before the settlement in the land. Whatever the intent or the context, the expectation of these passages is that sojourners occupied a lower station (cf. 14:21).

Perhaps the most difficult verses regarding the outsider are Deut 23:4–9[3–8].[41] Verses 4–7[3–6] deal with the Ammonites and Moabites; verses 8–9[7–8] refer to the Edomites and Egyptians. The first pair, the Ammonites and the Moabites, is not to enter the קהל 'assembly' *of Yahweh* (commanded twice in v. 4[3]) until the tenth generation. Ten is a symbolic number, so it does not have to be taken literally; it means a long time (reinforced in v. 7[6], lit. "all your days until forever"). In contrast, the Israelites are not to "abhor" (תעב) the Edomites nor the Egyptians, who are restricted until the third generation (another symbolic number) from the קהל. In both cases the passage appeals to historical memory.

To begin with, the קהל *of Yahweh* must be identified.[42] In light of the rest of the book, several interpretive options can be eliminated. It cannot refer to Israelite society *in toto*, as this is contradicted by legislation that grants גרים permission to become part of the community. Some be-

---

41. The following discussion follows the Hebrew verse enumeration; the verses of the English versions are in brackets.

42. This is the only chapter in which the phrase appears. Elsewhere it is simply קהל (5:22, 9:10, 10:4, 18:16, 31:30). The verb of the same root (Hiphil) means "to assemble" (4:10; 31:12, 28). For the options cited in this paragraph, see the commentaries.

lieve the term means religious gatherings of Israel, but this does not make sense either in light of the explicit reference to feasts in which sojourners can share.[43] The reference must be to a particular kind of assembly, possibly a civic gathering of landed males, where certain decisions had to be made, perhaps related to war (Deut 23:10–15[9–14] deals with matters related to war). What is in view here, therefore, is not entry into the community or worship, but rather levels of citizenship participation.

The reasons given for exclusion are connected to historical memory. This is where we meet a surprise. What is cited is not what is mentioned earlier in Deuteronomy. Elsewhere Yahweh commands Israel not to engage Moab and Ammon in battle and to pass through in peace, since he had given those nations their own land and earlier helped them displace other peoples (Deut 2:8b–12, 29 and 2:19–21, respectively; cf. 32:8). Deut 23:5[4], however, recalls Balaam's effort to curse Israel, an event not mentioned in the historical prologue of chapters 1–4. Strangely, in the Numbers 22–24 account, Ammon plays no part.[44]

In addition, the oft-repeated warning not to forget the negative experience as slaves in Egypt is set aside in Deut 23:8[7] to remind Israel that it had been a גר there. The implication is that the stay in Egypt was positive, or at the very least that there had been some level of acceptance there. The memory of unfavorable life in Egypt is used in other passages to foster positive attitudes toward the outsider. Here, this is replaced with an affirming spin, maybe referring to Jacob's arrival there in Genesis 46–47 (cf. Deut 26:5). Here, they are to welcome the perpetrators of their misfortunes. The memory associated with Edom is also historical, but it is of a different sort. It is an appeal to common ancestry: the Edomite is "your kinsman" (אחיך). This idea does appear in the historical prologue (Deut 2:4), where, as in the case of Moab and Ammon, Israel is told not to fight them; Yahweh had given the Edomites their territory (2:5–8a, 12, 29). Interestingly, in both pairings the apparent exclusion of other groups is coupled with the historical prologue's detailing Yahweh's work on their behalf. Even this marginalization, then, is not as simple as a quick reading might suggest.

In any case, these laws give a different picture about attitudes toward those of other ethnicity and backgrounds. How then is this wide span of Deuteronomy's teaching to be understood and evaluated? It is

---

43. Perhaps the reference is to a specialized religious gathering, if vv. 3–4[2–3] are interpreted cultically.

44. Some scholars link the pairing of Moab and Ammon here to the story of incest in Gen 19:30–38.

overwhelmingly charitable, with the exception of several exclusionary verses. Can it be appropriated for contemporary society?

4. Lessons for Immigration from Deuteronomy

If the conviction is that Deuteronomy's teaching is relevant for the people of God and for the world, then the challenge is to employ suitable means to draw out appropriate lessons.[45] The following discussion will use two standard methods[46] and then offer additional perspectives that can complement these and respond more adequately to the implications of the problematic passages.

4.1. Deuteronomy, an Enduring Text

One common way to bring Old Testament law into the modern context is the principle approach, which is championed by Walter Kaiser and many others.[47] This stance begins with the recognition that this legislation was given to a covenant people in another time and place. With the coming of Christ and the birth of the Church, the new people of God does not stand in exactly the same relationship before him as did ancient Israel. All strands of the Christian faith agree that things changed with the ministry of Jesus, even though opinions differ regarding the degree of continuity or discontinuity between the Church and Israel and, consequently, of the implications for Christian daily life, ethics, and worship.

The principle approach contends that, in spite of the temporal, cultural, and theological (however defined) distance from Old Testament laws, there is truth in these texts that transcends those barriers (e.g., Matt 5:17–20, 23:23, 1 Cor 10:1–13, 2 Tim 3:15–17, Heb 11:39–12:1).

---

45. This task is inseparable from the perennial Christian debate about how to utilize the Old Testament law. For surveys of evangelical positions, see, e.g., J. S. Feinberg, ed., *Continuity and Discontinuity: Perspectives on the Relationship Between the Old and New Testaments—Essays in Honor of S. Lewis Johnson, Jr.* (Wheaton, IL: Crossway, 1988); G. L. Bahnsen et al., *Five Views on Law and Gospel* (Grand Rapids: Zondervan, 1996); cf. Wright, *Old Testament Ethics*, 378–414.

46. For a helpful overview of the several ways evangelicals move from biblical text to modern context, see W. C. Kaiser Jr. et al., *Four Views on Moving Beyond the Bible to Theology* (Grand Rapids: Zondervan, 2009). Also note the surveys in C. H. Cosgrove, *Appealing to Scripture in Moral Debate: Five Hermeneutical Rules* (Grand Rapids: Eerdmans, 2002); E. W. Davies, *The Immoral Bible: Approaches to Biblical Ethics* (London: T. & T. Clark, 2010).

47. E.g., W. C. Kaiser, Jr., *Toward Old Testament Ethics* (Grand Rapids: Zondervan, 1983); idem, "A Principlizing Model," in Kaiser et al., *Four Views on Moving Beyond the Bible to Theology*, 19–50; J. D. Hays, "Applying the Old Testament Law Today," BSac 158, no. 1 (2001) 21–35; W. W. Klein, C. L. Blomberg, R. I. Hubbard, Jr., *Introduction to Biblical Interpretation* (rev. ed.; Nashville: Thomas Nelson, 2004) 406–25.

Aware of the differences in audience and circumstances of that time, one first identifies the meaning of a particular law in its original context and then seeks a universal principle undergirding that particular law. This transferable cross-cultural principle subsequently is applied in a specific way now. Oftentimes this is correlated with New Testament teaching.

A second approach is the paradigm method of Christopher Wright.[48] His conviction is that "God's relation to Israel in their land was a deliberate reflection of God's relation to humankind on earth."[49] In other words, in its familial, social, economic, and political structures this chosen people were to be a concrete contextual model, or paradigm, of the values that God desires for all peoples across the ages in their distinct settings (Deut 4:5–8). It is not that the nations were (or are) to imitate Israel's particularities—their own embodiments of God's design necessarily would differ—but rather that its life ideally could be a window into God's will for all societies.[50] Accordingly, Israel would function as a priest to the nations (Exod 19:4–6). This view takes us beyond the more personal application tendencies of the principle approach to consider the possible insights that Israel's laws and structures can have at broader community levels.

Wright extends this approach by suggesting that Jesus and the New Testament messianic community fulfill Old Testament hopes and structures, and thereby stand in a typological relationship with Israel. At the same time, there are eschatological pointers and lessons to be drawn between the Old Testament and the new earth and redeemed humanity at the end of the age. Wright employs the Jubilee laws as his example through his three stages of relevance (paradigmatic, typological, and eschatological).

These two approaches are useful as means for discerning abiding teaching from Deuteronomy. Here I mention three lessons that can be drawn for immigration legislation and then add one observation. A foundational point concerns the commitment to help the vulnerable,

---

48. Wright has used this approach in various publications. See recently Wright, *Old Testament Ethics*, 62–74, 182–211, 314–25. For another paradigm approach, see W. Janzen, *Old Testament Ethics: A Paradigmatic Approach* (Louisville: Westminster John Knox, 1994); cf. E. A. Martens, "How Is the Christian to Construe Old Testament Law?" *BBR* 12, no. 2 (2002) 199–216. Note the critiques of J. Rogerson, *Theory and Practice in Old Testament Ethics* (ed. M. D. Carroll R.; JSOTSup 405; London: T. & T. Clark, 2004) 34–37; Davies, *The Immoral Bible*, 101–19.

49. Wright, *Old Testament Ethics*, 183.

50. Compare the interplay between natural morality, the imperatives of redemption, and structures of grace in Rogerson, *Theory and Practice in Old Testament Ethics*.

which includes sojourners, or immigrants. It is noteworthy that they are categorized with others whose lives were precarious: the poor, widows, and orphans. That is, for the biblical text, the most important realities are the instabilities and insecurity of the immigrants' existence. Deuteronomy responds to their elemental human needs for food, dignified work, and a fair treatment in the judicial system. This is a crucial perspective today, when many evaluate immigrants and their plight primarily through the criterion of *legal status*. In sharp contrast, the law treats them above all as disadvantaged *persons*.[51]

A second lesson is the need for appropriate legislation to meet these needs. This is where Wright's paradigm approach is suggestive. Deuteronomy contains laws that correspond to its agrarian world. The challenge today is to envision legislation that reflects the transcendent values expected of all humanity (those creation values made concrete in Israel's laws) that would be suitable to the realities of the twenty-first century. It also is crucial to appreciate that the previous principle is the base line for elaborating that legislation. That is, the laws of Deuteronomy are sensitive to the plight of sojourners. The legislation is not punitive, something that often is the case in the contemporary scene. Rather, charity and openness toward these needy persons, not harshness and rejection of foreigners, are characteristics of the Deuteronomic legislation.

A third lesson deals with the motivations behind whatever laws are put into place. First, there is historical memory. The law warns the descendants of immigrants not to forget their immigrant heritage. Otherwise they will mistreat newcomers and become like those who committed injustice against one's ancestors. Everyone (except Native Americans) in the United States has immigrant roots. The problem is that the country suffers from collective amnesia. Forgotten are the discrimination against Germans in the mid-nineteenth century, the cruelty of the Chinese Exclusion Act of 1882 (not rescinded until 1943), the quotas on the Irish and Italians largely because of their Catholic faith and their marginalization in inner-city ghettoes, the exploitation of African labor and the century of segregation after the Civil War, the incarceration of Japanese Americans in World War II, and the mistreatment of Hispanics over the last one hundred years. The socio-economic exploitation and the pressures on past immigrant communities no longer

---

51. In *The Immigration Crisis: Immigrants, Aliens, and the Bible* (Wheaton, IL: Crossway, 2009), J. K. Hoffmeier argues that the Old Testament legislation applies only to legal immigrants. This is too narrow an interpretation of the evidence.

come to mind, so those negative attitudes raise their ugly head again. This country would do well to rehearse its immigrant history as it formulates its immigration laws.

The other motivation, for those who claim the Christian faith, lies in the stark decision to incarnate the love that Yahweh has for the immigrant or reject the call of Deuteronomy 10. God desires to feed and clothe these vulnerable persons, and this must be done through his people. The Christian Church should grasp the connection between the love of God and the welcoming stance toward immigrants, particularly in regard to worship. Charitable actions and sharing worship with them go hand-in-hand. How might the Christian Church extend divine care for sojourners in tangible ways as individual believers, congregations, and national bodies and bring them to know Yahweh and worship him? Dare it proclaim the love of God toward humanity and deny his explicit love for the sojourner?

My observation concerns immigrant assimilation. As mentioned earlier in this essay, the expectation in Israel surely would have been that sojourners would integrate into that society linguistically, religiously, culturally, and legally. This is a reasonable presumption of a host community, and the Law facilitates that process. The book of Ruth recounts the complexities this process poses for the immigrant. What many do not comprehend—and this is tied to the historical memory principle—is that this is a difficult and painful transition that takes time. There is a growing body of literature and social science studies that reveal this reality.[52]

These are a few of the principles on immigration that can be gleaned from Deuteronomy. But what is one to do with the negative laws, such as Deut 23:3–8?

4.2. *Deuteronomy, a Situated Text*

The more exclusionary texts testify to the fact that Deuteronomy is a text of its time. As explained above, these contextual limitations lead some to critique the Old Testament. Those who defend the ethical viability of the law, however, often respond by appealing to the concept of *theological* and *hermeneutical* progressive revelation.

The premise is that the Bible's teaching is not static, that there are trajectories of ethical development. Kaiser incorporates this feature

---

52. See, e.g., my discussion in *Christians at the Border*, 39–48; cf. the ongoing work of the Pew Hispanic Center (http://www.pewhispanic.org/; last accessed June 6, 2012). Autobiographic accounts, fictional stories, and sociological and anthropological studies are appearing constantly.

into his discussion of principles; Wright's system is based on these trajectories across the Testaments. This movement has been worked out with issues such as the role of women and slavery.[53] The same could be done with immigration. One can chart development from these laws (both positive and exclusionary) to the incorporation of the Moabitess Ruth into Bethlehem and the prophetic hope of inclusion (Isa 56:6),[54] and ultimately to the New Testament, where Jesus embraces the marginalized, Paul declares that in Christ there is neither Jew nor Greek (Gal 3:28) and that believers are citizens of a heavenly kingdom (Phil 3:20; cf. Heb 13:14), and Peter likens Christian faith to migration (1 Pet 1:1, 2:11). A comprehensive biblical discussion on immigration should incorporate the full breath of scriptural teaching.

A complementary approach looks at the issue of these restrictions *anthropologically*. A helpful starting point is to re-conceive for a moment the nature and purpose of the book. McBride has said that Deuteronomy, in particular 16:18–18:22, should be viewed as a "polity" document, "political constitution," or "social charter." That is, it is a divinely given covenant text that lays out a sociopolitical and cultural framework for Israel and details laws for securing the viability and prosperity of its people.[55] It organizes the social world of Israel in its many dimensions, even as it locates the nation historically, exposes its rebellious tendencies, and offers it choices for the future. This perspective underscores that the shape and content of Deuteronomy are related to the ancient world, while it also speaks across the centuries. In other words, one may glean direction today from the values behind its legislation and from the shape of the nation and its politics, its social mores, and the like, but it still belongs to its context. Not surprisingly, it exhibits certain limitations of that time.

---

53. In addition to the sources cited in above, nn. 18, 45, and 46, see esp. W. J. Webb, *Slaves, Women & Homosexuals: Exploring the Hermeneutics of Cultural Analysis* (Downers Grove, IL: InterVarsity, 2001); cf. W. M. Swartley, *Homosexuality: Biblical Interpretation and Moral Discernment* (Scottdale, PA: Herald, 2003).

54. There are cases of exclusion in Ezra 9–10 and Nehemiah 13, but these also reflect a discreet historical context.

55. S. D. McBride, Jr., "Polity of the Covenant People: The Book of Deuteronomy," *Int* 41, no. 3 (1987) 229–44; cf. P. D. Miller, "The Good Neighborhood: Identity and Community through the Commandments," in *Character & Scripture: Moral Formation, Community, and Biblical Interpretation* (ed. W. P. Brown; Grand Rapids: Eerdmans, 2002) 55–72; idem, "'That it may go well with you': The Commandments and the Common Good," in *In Search of the Common Good* (ed. D. P. McCann and P. D. Miler; New York: T. & T. Clark, 2005) 14–40; McConville, *God and Earthly Power*, 85–88; F. Crüsemann, *The Torah*, 234–49. D. T. Olson prefers the notion of "catechesis" in *Deuteronomy and the Death of Moses* (OBT; Minneapolis: Fortress, 1994) 6–14.

This historical horizon is evident in the fact that there are differences in the pentateuchal law codes. It is commonplace to observe an internal dynamic within the law that is visible, for instance, when comparing Deuteronomy with other legal material. Whether this is explained narratively or historically, adjustments and new formulations are apparent.[56] The enduring principles are embodied differently, reshaped, and redirected, yielding suitable changes within the law codes. The point to be made here is that legislation must change as realities shift—then and today. The changing demographics and pragmatic challenges of our day, in this country and around the world, demand the reformation of current immigration laws. It will not do to adamantly defend legislation created for a past that no longer exists. The shifts within the Pentateuch's law codes are situation-specific; at the same time, their adaptability offers a timeless lesson.

My experience in the immigration debate and with immigration legislation leads me to offer one final comment to this notion of Deuteronomy as a dynamic contextual polity document. What I would add is that Deuteronomy also is what I might call *an ethnographic report*.[57] What to us may appear to be a lack of *logical and ethical uniformity* in some of its laws is for me *culturally and ethnically coherent*. Let us return to Deut 23:4–9[3–8]. Note that, whereas many laws in the book deal with the גרים as a socioeconomic group, these verses specify ethnic identity (Moabite, Ammonite, Edomite, Egyptian) and present Israel's history differently.

Permit me to make some parallels to the competing visions of immigration in the United States. On the one hand, we have tales of immigrants coming as pioneers, hard-working people forging a new life, who strove to integrate into American society and contributed to its growth and development. This image is coupled with the impressive symbol of the Statue of Liberty in New York Harbor and the romanticization of Ellis Island. But there also is a more complex side of our

---

56. Note, e.g., the very different approaches of Crüsemann, *The Torah*, 201–75; J. D. Pleins, *The Social Visions of the Hebrew Bible: A Theological Introduction* (Louisville: Westminster John Knox, 2001) 41–91; Fretheim, *God and World in the Old Testament*, 147–56; Baker, *Tight Fists or Open Hands?*; cf. D. I. Block, "'You shall not covet your neighbor's wife': A Study in Deuteronomic Domestic Ideology," *JETS* 53, no. 3 (2010) 449–74, reproduced in idem, *The Gospel According to Moses*, 137–68; J. Hwang, "The Rhetoric of Theophany: The Imaginative Depiction of Horeb in Deuteronomy 9–10" in the present volume.

57. See my comments in "Re-Examining 'Popular Religion': Issues of Definition and Sources. Insights from Cultural Anthropology," in my *Rethinking Context, Rereading Texts: Contributions from the Social Sciences to Biblical Interpretation* (ed. M. D. Carroll R.; JSOTSup, 299; Sheffield: Sheffield Academic Press, 2000) 163–67 [146–67].

immigrant history. The counterpart to Ellis Island on the West Coast is Angel Island in San Francisco Harbor, with its sad accounts of interrogations and lengthy detentions (1910–1940).[58] There is no need to repeat the other dark stories of immigration listed earlier.

Clearly, the history of immigration into this country is conflicting, a mixture of the good and bad, of things to celebrate and others for which repentance awaits. The history of immigrant legislation is also complicated and contradictory, because the interaction between ethnicities, between newcomer and native-born, is never easy or tidy. In spite of all of this confusion, the nation functions (not always in optimum fashion!) and *coheres*, with all of its ethnic tensions and inconsistencies. Current legislation on immigration is neither constant nor quite compatible with previous laws; sometimes they have been unfair, and there have been revisions across the decades to meet new circumstances. U.S. immigration laws are not always logical or clear. They also are laced with ethnic sentiments, and occasionally the ideal tales of our history clash with other realities that impact the national debate. That is, history and ethnicity are part and parcel of legislative deliberations. It was also so in ancient Israel. Deuteronomy is a document in which ethnic realities and attitudes occasionally surface in its sojourner legislation. It reflects a mix of theological truths, various historical memories, and multifaceted ethnic sentiments. It is a complicated legal package.

5. *Conclusion*

The movement of many millions around the world today demands the serious consideration of the Bible's teaching on the topic of immigration. Too many Christians default to arguments devoid of scriptural content or limit that voice to a very few passages. We have offered a summary of Deuteronomy's extensive teaching, which is built upon the experiences of Israel's history and the person of God himself.

The movement from that biblical text to modern society is a challenge, but there is much there that can orient contemporary debates and legislation. The hope is that this essay, at least in some small measure, has demonstrated Deuteronomy's contribution as both a substantive fund of enduring principles and a useful paradigm, with ethical trajectories developed across the canon, as well as a situated testimony of an ancient people under God who wrestled with welcoming the stranger.

---

58. J. Soennichsen, *Miwoks to Missiles: A History of Angel Island* (Tiburon, CA: Angel Island Association, 2001); E. Lee and J. Yung, *Angel Island: Immigrant Gateway to America* (Oxford: Oxford University Press, 2012).

Sermonizing in Deuteronomy, Jeremiah, and the 21st Century

ELMER A. MARTENS

Sermons in the Old Testament? Yes, of course! What are they about, and in what way might they be instructive for modern preaching? An exploratory probe on two sermons, one from Deuteronomy 4 and one from Jeremiah 7, offers answers to these questions. The theological themes highlighted in these two sermons are appropriate for any age, including the present one. Preachers especially, but also teachers of the Bible, can profit by examining the rhetoric and the substance of these two sermons.

Commenting on the book of Deuteronomy, Daniel Block asserts, "This is prophetic preaching at its finest."[1] Decades earlier Gerhard von Rad had already claimed that the genre of the entire book was a sermon.[2] That claim has been widely accepted by scholars, although Bernhard Levinson has recently challenged it.[3] Duane Christensen proposed a song-associated genre for Deuteronomy rather than sermon, but conceded, "It may be correct, with von Rad, to see the book as being shaped by Levitical preaching and put in the form of a cult liturgy,

---

Author's Note: This essay is offered to Professor Daniel Block with high esteem for his energetic and renowned scholarship, his forceful preaching, and with large appreciation for his friendship, our mutual denominational roots, not to mention our common place of origin, Saskatchewan, Canada.

1. D. I. Block, "Deuteronomy, Book of" in *Dictionary for Theological Interpretation of the Bible* (ed. K. J. Vanhoozer; Grand Rapids: Baker, 2005) 168.

2. G. von Rad observes, "Deuteronomy is not divine law in codified form, but preaching about the commandments—at least, the commandments appear in a form where they are very much interspersed with parenesis" (*Studies in Deuteronomy* [trans. D. M. G. Stalker; SBT 9; London: SCM, 1953] 15, see also pp. 66–69).

3. B. M. Levinson, "Reading the Bible in Nazi Germany: Gerhard von Rad's Attempt to Reclaim the Old Testament for the Church," *Int* 62.3 (2008) 238–54. Levinson claims that von Rad's judgment about genre is arbitrary and is influenced by his social situation, namely an attempt to counter the theological faculty at Jena who promoted the Nazi ideology, a tenet of which was to expunge the Jewish aspects of Christianity.

a series of sermons from the lips of Moses shortly before his death."[4] Elizabeth Achtemeier is emphatic: "Given the nature of its message, Deuteronomy probably could have taken no other form than that of preaching, because it is in that activity, above all others, that God confronts his people."[5] Many affirm that Deuteronomy, if not a sermon in its entirety, nevertheless included sermons such as 4:1–40, a focus of this essay.[6]

Though sermons in the Old Testament, as distinguished from oracles, are not numerous, one of the most notable is "The Temple Sermon" of Jeremiah 7.[7] To compare this sermon with the one in Deuteronomy 4 is not only tantalizing as a matter of intellectual curiosity, but bears on preaching practices generally. Both Moses and Jeremiah addressed a culture in the throes of transitions. Given the current cultural transitions, such as from modernism to post-modernism and beyond, and given the current state of church life in North America, the investigation can be expected to speak directly, even if uncomfortably into our times.

1. Heading out to Hear the Sermons

There are good reasons for setting these two sermons—Deut 4:1–40 and Jer 7:1–15—side by side. Each, as noted, is addressed to a people at a critical juncture in their history. Moses' sermon in Deuteronomy is presented as a speech prior to entry into the Promised Land. Much of Jeremiah deals with the threat of the possible expulsion of Israel from the Promised Land, given the imminent Babylonian invasion. Both sermons touch on similar subjects, as we shall see. Taking the larger con-

---

4. D. L. Christensen, "Deuteronomy in Modern Research: Approaches and Issues," in *A Song of Power and the Power of Song* (ed. D. L. Christensen; Winona Lake, IN: Eisenbrauns, 1993) 3.

5. E. Achtemeier, *Deuteronomy, Jeremiah* (Philadelphia: Fortress, 1978) 14.

6. In commenting on Deuteronomy 4, R. Alter spoke of "the ringing language of the sermon" and asserted, "It [Deut 4:1] introduces the grand sermon that concludes this whole preamble to the main body of the book of Deuteronomy (chapters 5–31)" (*The Five Books of Moses: a Translation with Commentary* [New York: W. W. Norton & Co., 2004] 897, 899–900). P. Miller titles Deut 4:9–31 "A Sermon on the Second Commandment" (*Deuteronomy* [Interpretation; Louisville: John Knox, 1990] 57), and M. Weinfeld claims that chapter 4 "actually constitutes an elaborate sermon, the first one in the chain of sermons" (*Deuteronomy 1–11* [AB 5; New York: Doubleday, 1991] 215). J. H. Tigay similarly designates Deut 4:1–40 a sermon (*Deuteronomy* [JPSTC 5; Philadelphia: The Jewish Publication Society, 1996] 40).

7. R. W. L. Moberly adds two other "temple" sermons: Amos 5:18–27 and Micah 3:9–12, which he compares and contrasts with Jeremiah 7:1–15 ("'In God we Trust': The Challenge of the Prophets," *Ex Auditu* 24 [2008] 18–33).

texts into account, there are other correspondences between the books of Deuteronomy and Jeremiah. The subject of "land" is prominent in both books.[8] The two books bracket the story of Israel in the land irrespective of each book's dating. Moreover, the two books are replete with invitations and warnings, some of them clustering around the term "obey" (שמע).[9] Another example of vocabulary common to both is the idiom "evil in God's sight."[10] The metaphor of Egypt as a fiery furnace is found in Deut 4:20 and Jer 11:4, and elsewhere only in 1 Kgs 8:51. The books share a common theology which, to mention only one feature, highlights "covenant."[11] As long since noticed, a wordy, often repetitive style, characterizes both books; scholars speak of Jeremiah's deuteronomistic style.[12] Historically, it is claimed that it was the Book of Deuteronomy or portions of it that were found during Josiah's reign, thus triggering the reform in 622 B.C.[13] It is not without interest that Westminster's series, "Proclamation Commentaries—The Old Testament Witnesses for Preaching," coupled the books of Deuteronomy and Jeremiah in one volume.[14]

Each of these two passages, Deut 4:1–40 and Jer 7:1–15, is a sermon.[15] In simple terms, a sermon is a speech of a religious nature given orally

---

8. The word ארץ 'land' occurs in Deuteronomy 81 times and in Jeremiah 55 times. A. D. H. Mayes observes, "The land is in fact central to Deuteronomy's whole theology" (*Deuteronomy* [NCB; Grand Rapids: Eerdmans, 1979] 79).

9. In Deuteronomy, שמע 'hear' occurs 14 times; in Jeremiah, 20 times.

10. The idiom occurs in Deut 9:18, 17:2, 31:29 and in Jer 7:30, 18:10, 32:30, 44:22, as noted in T. Work, *Deuteronomy* (Grand Rapids: Brazos, 2009) 67.

11. The word ברית 'covenant' occurs 9 times in each book, but if one includes the covenant formula, "I will be your God and you shall be my people," then as J. G. McConville notes, the subject of covenant is prominent in both books. See his articles "Deuteronomy: Theology of" and "Jeremiah: Theology of" in *NIDOTTE* 4:528–37 and 4:755–67.

12. E.g., E. W. Nicholson, *Preaching to the Exiles A Study of the Prose Tradition in the Book of Jeremiah* (Oxford: Basil Blackwell, 1970) 63, 67, 69. Commenting on Jer 7:1–15, R. E. Clements remarks, "The elevated prose of the discourses shows that these are not Jeremiah's own words; they have passed through the minds of editors with close Deuteronomic affiliations" (*Jeremiah* [Interpretation; Atlanta: John Knox, 1988] 44).

13. The claim was enunciated by W. M. L. de Wette in his 1805 dissertation, though already surmised by Jerome. See M. Weinfeld, "Deuteronomy: The Present State of Inquiry," *JBL* 86 (1967) 249–62; repr. as pp. 21–35 in Christensen, ed., *Song of Power*.

14. Achtemeier, *Deuteronomy, Jeremiah*. F. McCurley, the series editor, asks, "Why is it that a Pentateuchal book and a prophetic book appear in the same commentary of this series?" His answer is that since the turn of the century, scholars have recognized many affinities in the language, style and thought of these two books (p. 6). For more on this, see M. Graves' essay in the present volume, "The Enduring Word of the LORD in Deuteronomy and Jeremiah 36."

15. The long-held designation of Jer 7:1–15 as a "sermon" is disputed by J. Lundbom. Lundbom structures the text as three oracles: "Make good your ways" (vv. 3–7), "My

to an audience. The nature of these speeches is often characterized by teaching, explanations, and exhortation. They intend to inform and, more often, to persuade. Each of these two sermons opens with the direct address of the speaker to an audience. Moses begins, "So now, O Israel, hear the statutes . . ." (Deut 4:1). Jeremiah's sermon begins, "Hear the word of the Lord, all you people of Judah . . ." (Jer 7:2b). Each speaker self-consciously delivers his message in response to Yahweh's directive (Deut 4:5; Jer 7:2–3).

Sermons, by their nature, are addressed to specific audiences in a specific circumstance. Moses' sermon is preached on the other side of the Jordan River to Israel, who, following years of wandering, are now prepared to enter the Promised Land (Deut 4:5). The stage is set for final instructions for them to observe "in the land that you are about to enter and occupy" (4:5b). One can infer, somewhat from the sermon itself, that the audience is in a tentative, if not uncertain, mood. Israel lives in the shock wave of having heard the voice of God speak. Moses asks, "Has anything so great as this ever happened or has anything like it ever been heard of?" (4:32b). The people's future is one of uncertainty. How are they to know what awaits them?

By contrast, Jeremiah's sermon addresses an audience milling around the gate of the temple.[16] His sermon confronts a people taken up with a certitude that Jeremiah will declare false. Their theology of God's presence rings with a note of dogmatism: "The temple of the LORD; the temple of the LORD; the temple of the LORD." Such dogmatism about the inviolability of Zion blinds them, Jeremiah will say, to the dangers that are imminent: Babylonian forces are approaching. Jeremiah will challenge a false complacency that derives from entrenched views. Some theologies appropriate for one situation are inappropriate for another! The prospect of expulsion from their land is real.

The status of the two preachers differs, however. Moses is a revered leader who has almost unsurpassed credibility given his record with

---

House a Robbers' Den?" (vv. 8–11), and "Look Again at Shiloh" (vv. 12–15)—each beginning with a messenger formula and defined as units because of inclusios in each. He concludes: "The term 'Temple sermon' for 7:1–15 is then a misnomer and is best abandoned." However, the unity of the text via outline and movement, not to mention the location, speaker and audience and its hortatory style justify the appellation, "sermon." Even he concedes, at least for the first oracle (vv. 3–7) that "It has the ring of a sermon out of Deuteronomy" (*Jeremiah 1–20* [AB 21A; New York: Doubleday, 1999] 461).

16. W. Holladay suggests, "It [the sermon in Jeremiah 7] was uttered in the 'beginning' of the reign of Jehoiakim (v. 1), thus evidently sometime between September 609 and March 608, probably at the feast of booths in September/October 609" ("The Years of Jeremiah's Preaching," *Int* 37 [1983] 149).

the people of God in a forty-year wilderness journey. Jeremiah is a controversial prophet who, one surmises, functions not from the center but from the margins. He is thought of as a conspirator; his own family makes threats on his life (Jer 11:21). Nevertheless, both preachers claim to be authorized spokespersons for Yahweh.

2. In the Audience with Moses and Jeremiah

Let us join the congregation of Israelites to listen first to Moses (see Deut 4:1–40). An immediate impression has to do with the frequency of exhortations clustered around various word forms of שמר, which Robert Alter felicitously translates, *"Be you on the watch."*[17] The exhortations are variations of the theme to listen to and obey the Torah, to follow Yahweh's ways, and not to forget Yahweh's covenant. Two examples are,

- 4:9. "Take care [Niphal impv. of שמר] and watch yourselves closely [Qal impv. of שמר with מאד], so as neither to forget the things that your eyes have seen nor to let them slip from your mind all the days of your life. . . ."
- 4:15–16a. "Watch yourselves closely [Niphal perfect with conjunction of שמר], so that you do not act corruptly."

A series of motivational arguments buttresses these exhortations. Jeffrey Tigay aptly summarizes these: "Like preachers in all ages, he [Moses] advances various types of arguments for observance: history teaches the utility of observance; the laws are just; they secure God's closeness; they make Israel unique; observance will earn the admiration of others; the laws have logical reason; they are the will of the only true God; and they are a prerequisite for wellbeing."[18]

To these reasons for following Yahweh, Moses adds several reminders of key stages in Israel's journey that reinforce, by way of incentives, the call to loyalty to Yahweh. These include (1) the exodus from Egypt (Deut 4:20, 37b); (2) the unforgettable experience at Horeb where Yahweh benevolently declared his covenant but did so in the frightening context of fire blazing from Horeb (4:10–14); (3) the divine purging at Baal of Peor (4:3) and the gift of life for those loyal to Yahweh midst the temptations (4:4); (4) victory over enemies (4:38a); and (5) the gift of land (4:38b). Moses' appeal for devotion to Yahweh is rooted in experience and is decidedly rational.

---

17. Alter, *Five Books of Moses*, 898.
18. Tigay, *Deuteronomy*, 41.

But the appeal to obedience is not made solely in cerebral terms. The passion of the speaker is evident throughout. Moses is the voice of Yahweh. "Keep the commandments," he cries. Moses is the one who is charged with sharing them (Deut 4:2, 5, 14). His rhetorical questions, five of them by one count (NRSV), are charged with emotion: "For what other great nation has a god so near to it as the LORD our God is whenever we call to him?" (4:7), or again, "Has anything so great as this ever happened or has anything like it ever been heard of?" (4:32b). His repeated pleas to keep Yahweh's statutes (4:6a, 15, 40), not to forget the covenant (4:23), and to watch themselves (4:9, 15) together with appeals to teach the coming generations (4:9c, 10c) are pastor-like expressions of deep concern. So earnest is the speaker and so high are the stakes that Moses cries, "I call heaven and earth to witness . . ." (4:26). Those in Moses' audience, and we too, sense the passion of the speaker.[19]

In imagination, we next join the milling crowds in a different space and time. At the entrance gate to the Jerusalem temple, the prophet Jeremiah is raising his voice above the din. Jeremiah pounds away on two points. The first is an admonition, "Amend your ways." The second is a caution, "Don't be deceived."

The two points of the sermon are stated forthrightly (Jer 7:3–4), and then each is elaborated. First, the admonition for listeners to amend their ways is essentially repeated and then pinpointed with specifics, such as doing justice, refusing to oppress the vulnerable in society, and refusing to follow other gods (7:5–7). The second point, a caution and warning about trusting in deceptive words, is likewise restated and then elaborated (7:8–10). The deception consists of claiming God's nearness as symbolized by the temple, on the one hand, while on the other hand continuing in behavior that is clearly ungodly, including violating the commandments not to steal, murder, or commit adultery.

For each of these two points in the sermon, motivation to respond is offered. If the hearers will amend their ways, then Yahweh will both dwell with them (7:3) and allow them to continue in the land (7:7).[20] However, if Judah will continue trusting in the temple as some sort of talisman guaranteeing protection, then it stands to suffer destruction

---

19. Alter identifies a "revivalist fervor" in Moses' recurrent phrase "with all your heart and with all your being" (4:29) (*Five Books of Moses*, 902).

20. Here I follow the NRSV (footnote) and the argument of W. L. Holladay drawing on the Vulgate that the Hebrew of שׁכן in 7:3 is to be pointed as Qal: "so I may dwell with you [וְאֶשְׁכְּנָה אִתְּכֶם]"; and in the second instance (v. 7) drawing on the Masoretic text, i.e., Piel: "I shall let you dwell [וְשִׁכַּנְתִּי אֶתְכֶם] in this place" (*Jeremiah 1* [Hermeneia; Philadelphia: Fortress, 1986] 236–38). Others hold that v. 3 and v. 7 are both about Israel remaining in the land.

even as Shiloh, once Yahweh's dwelling, was destroyed. Indeed, Jeremiah's closing judgment speech includes the pronouncement of Jerusalem's destruction and the people's exile (7:13–15).

Thus Jeremiah offers a sound rationale for a change in behavior and theology. But he is not done. An emotional appeal arises out of Jeremiah's exasperation and frustration. Like Moses, Jeremiah resorts to rhetorical questions, challenging, "Will you steal, murder . . . make offerings to Baal . . . and then come and stand before me in this house, which is called by my name, and say, 'We are safe!'—only to go on doing all these abominations?" (7:9–10). One can imagine Jeremiah, face drawn, forefinger raised, leaning toward his listeners, saying, "You know, I too am watching, says the LORD" (7:11b). For both Moses and Jeremiah, preaching is laced with passion.[21]

3. Post-Sermon Reflections: Analyzing the Rhetoric

Having heard both sermons and being inwardly moved by both, we as listeners pause to reflect. As already stated, pathos is evident in both messages. That observation brings to mind Aristotle's principles for rhetoric: logos, pathos, and ethos.

Logos entails reason. Each of these speakers offers exhortations. Moses' sermon is an appeal to stay the course: remain loyal and be obedient. Jeremiah calls his hearers to change their course. But most significant, each marshals a series of reasons to support his appeal. As noted above, these reasons are rationally based on the premise that actions have consequences. Moses gives as reasons for obedience and loyalty to Yahweh the prospect of a good and fulfilled life guaranteed by Yahweh. Similarly, Jeremiah cites positive consequences: for example, continued occupancy of the land. Each appeals to past experience. By way of warning, Moses cites the loss of life that resulted from disobedience at Baal-Peor. Jeremiah likewise invokes a negative example, Yahweh's destruction of Shiloh, the place where the ark was once housed, and thus where Yahweh dwelt. If the function of preaching is to motivate both faith and obedience, then appeals to logic are essential.

Aristotle urged attention to ethos in persuasive writing or speaking. By "ethos" he had in mind the importance of the speaker or writer's character and credibility. Clearly the words of a respected community leader carry weight, much more so than those of an individual whom

---

21. C. J. Dempsey aims in her slim book to "present Jeremiah as a gifted and skilled preacher whose rhetoric is poetic, passionate, and prophetic" (*Jeremiah: Preacher of Grace, Poet of Truth* [Interfaces; Collegeville, MN: Liturgical, 2007] xvi).

the community sees as duplicitous and flaky. Moses' message is indeed credible, even authoritative. His claim is that Yahweh God has charged him with a certain message. Moreover, his career as leader, spanning forty years, speaks volumes about his own loyalty to Yahweh. His sermon gains in credibility through his vulnerability as he relates Yahweh's judgment on him with the result that he, Moses, will not enter the Promised Land (Deut 4:21–22). Moses' "ethos quotient" is formidable.

As for Jeremiah, his imposing stature is to be measured in part by his boldness in addressing royalty: Jehoiakim, Jehoiachin, and Zedekiah (Jer 22:11–19, 22:24–30, 21:1–7). Jeremiah announced, "Thus says the LORD of hosts, the God of Israel" (7:3). In so doing he spoke with the authority of the commander in chief of the universe. The expression "LORD of hosts [צבאות 'armies']" alludes to the royal status and majesty of Yahweh, but is also associated with the might of a commander or warrior.[22] The gravitas of Yahweh as speaker could not be greater. Beyond this claim, Jeremiah, though a controversial and somewhat marginalized figure, had credibility as a prophet, in part because of the report of his calling to this role (1:4–10). Moreover, later events, such as his tangle with Hananiah the prophet, especially his prediction of Hananiah's death (fulfilled), could not but buttress Jeremiah's claim to be Yahweh's prophet (28:16–17).

The pathos in the sermons has already been mentioned and needs no elaboration. Thus, as a grid for analyzing public speech, Aristotle's three categories—logos, ethos, and pathos—are illuminating. In summary, both "preachers" carry a formidable quality of ethos, exhibit strong pathos, and give priority to matters of logos.[23]

4. Post-Sermon Reflections: Analyzing the Sermons' Substance

The substance of these sermons is as impressive as their style. The question here is one of worldview and theology. What depiction of Yahweh is operative in these sermons?

---

22. The nuance of majesty is expressed in passages such as 1 Sam 4:4, 2 Sam 6:2, Isa 6:3. Yahweh is commander of "hosts" or "armies," an expression that can refer to Israel's militia (1 Sam 17:45), to heavenly beings (1 Kgs 22:19), or to astral bodies (Deut 4:19).

23. For a more extended discussion see M. Avioz, "A Rhetorical Analysis of Jeremiah 7:1–15," *TB* 57.2 (2006) 173–89 and the extensive bibliography there. See also Lundbom, *Jeremiah 1–20*. D. I. Block's first of six propositions on how to preach Ezekiel with authority states, "In order to preach from Ezekiel with authority and clarity, we need to understand the prophet—his character (*ethos*), passion (*pathos*) and argumentation (*logos*)" ("Preaching Ezekiel," in *Reclaiming the Old Testament for Christian Preaching* [ed. J. G. Kent, et. al.; Downers Grove, IL: InterVarsity, 2010] 158).

Both preachers present a God of majesty and mystery. We begin with Moses. Assuming for the moment that in painting Yahweh's portrait we are limited to this sermon alone, several features are noteworthy. Yahweh is a deity who is engaged with his people. Moses is explicit about Yahweh's existence, not evident in a visible form, but clearly evident through his speech at Horeb and his earlier action in Egypt (Deut 4:12–14, 20, 34). "What other nation," Moses asks, "has statutes and ordinances of such high caliber communicated by God himself" (4:8, a paraphrase)? Besides, this deity, Yahweh, is a God near them, on call, unlike the gods of other nations (4:7). As A. D. H. Mayes notes, "This assertion of the nearness of God to Israel is distinctive in the context of a polytheistic world in which the distance separating the high god from man was filled with minor personal deities who could act as intermediaries."[24] Jeremiah has Yahweh asking, though not in this sermon, "Am I a God nearby, says the LORD, and not a God far off?" (Jer 23:23). For Jeremiah, the title Yahweh Sebaoth, the mighty One, captain of cosmic hosts, represents mystery and evokes awe. Both Moses' and Jeremiah's sermons touch on God's grandeur, God's majesty, and, remarkably, also on God's nearness.

> Ask from one end of heaven to the other: has anything so great as this ever happened or has anything like it ever been heard of? Has any people ever heard the voice of a god speaking out of a fire, as you have heard, and lived? Or has any god ever attempted to go and take a nation for himself from the midst of another nation, by trials by signs and wonder, by war, by a mighty hand and an out stretched arm, and by terrifying displays of power, as the LORD your God did for you in Egypt before your very eyes? To you it was shown so that you would acknowledge that the LORD is God; there is no other besides him. (Deut 4:32b–35)

Not only the greatness of Yahweh but also Yahweh's goodness is fundamental to both sermons. For Moses, the implicit goodness of God is evident when, as Moses envisions, the people after deserting Yahweh eventually return to him and discover that Yahweh is "a merciful God, [who] will neither abandon you or destroy you" (Deut 4:31). Yahweh's good purposes have been performed before Israel's eyes. Yahweh delivered his people from Egypt, the iron furnace (4:20), and brought

---

24. Mayes, *Deuteronomy*, 150. N. Lohfink elaborates on the deities' nearness in the ancient Near East by pointing to the names given to deities who were experienced as "near," for example, Iliqriba (from the root קרב 'to be near'). Hence the name Iliqriba signifies, "My God has drawn near me" (*Höre, Israel! Auslegung von Texten aus dem Buch Deuteronomium* [Düsseldorf: Patmos, 1965] 101). Lohfink discusses Deut 4:1–40 on pp. 87–120.

them to the land. "The gift of land is THE prominent good for Israel in Deuteronomy."[25]

Beyond the story of God's goodness is forthright teaching. Moses explains that because Yahweh loved the ancestors, he went to work on Israel's behalf (Deut 4:37). Jeremiah, too, tells of a God whose intention for Israel is good. As Israel aligns herself with Yahweh, Yahweh will continue his presence with his people and stabilize them in the land (Jer 7:3, 7).[26] Even Yahweh's threat that a disaffected people will be exiled is, by virtue of being a warning, a gesture of Yahweh's mercy.

Both speakers highlight God's covenant with Israel. Moses is explicit. At Sinai Yahweh made a covenant with Israel, a fact mentioned several times (Deut 4:13, 23, 31). Moses notes the covenant stipulations (4:5, 13, 14, 15–19, 23, 40) and mentions witnesses (v. 26). Walter Brueggemann states that Deut 4:1–40 offers "the fullest, perhaps most mature covenant theology of the tradition of Deuteronomy."[27] The phrase, "a people of his very own possession" (4:20), is an allusion to the covenant formula, "I will be your God and you will be my people."[28] That formula, which occurs some 20 times in the Bible, appears more frequently in Jeremiah than in any other book (e.g., 7:23; 11:4; 24:7; 30:22; 31:1, 33; 32:38), though not in Jeremiah's temple sermon. But, not often noticed, in Jeremiah's sermon three covenants are invoked without specifically naming them: the Abrahamic (occupancy of the land, 7:7, but also the threat of its loss, 7:15; cf. Deut 4:26–28); the Sinaitic (broken commandments, 7:9); and the Davidic (temple, 7:4). Thus in both sermons Yahweh's covenant with Israel is the context in which the message is cradled.

Closely connected to covenant ideology is occupancy of the land, which serves as something of a litmus test regarding Israel's obedience/loyalty to the covenant. In commenting on Deut 4:25–28, Jeffrey Tigay states, "No other nation has devoted so much of its historical and religious thought to the possession of its land."[29] In their sermons, both Moses and Jeremiah note the possible loss of land, Israel's inheritance. Debates may rage about whether covenants are conditional or uncon-

---

25. Achtemeier, *Deuteronomy, Jeremiah*, 30 (capitalization is hers). See n. 20 above.
26. See n. 20 above.
27. W. Brueggemann, *Deuteronomy* (Nashville: Abingdon, 2001) 50.
28. D. I. Block discusses the formula pointing out the resemblance to the ancient Hebrew marriage formula in the chapter, "The Privilege of Calling: The Mosaic Paradigm for Missions (Deut 26:16–19)," *BSac* 162 (Oct–Dec, 2005) 391–93; repr. in idem, *How I Love Your Torah, O LORD! Studies in the Book of Deuteronomy* (Eugene, OR: Cascade, 2011) 146–48.
29. Tigay, *Deuteronomy*, 52.

ditional, but at least this much can be affirmed: occupancy of the land for Israel is conditioned on their loyalty to Yahweh.

Furthermore, the worldview or theology shared by Moses and Jeremiah is of a God who is lawgiver and who does not wink an eye at evil, be it idolatry or sins of a social nature—injustice, adultery, or murder. God punishes perpetrators of these evils. In his sermon Moses repeatedly refers to statutes (חקים), ordinances (משפטים, Deut 4:1, 5, 8, 14, 40), commandments (מצות, 4:2, 13, 40), and once to the law (תורה, 4:8). The evil of idolatry is noted in two sections (4:15–19, 25–28), punishment for which will come in a scattering of the people. In his sermon, Jeremiah iterates several of the Ten Commandments (Jer 7:9–10), targets idolatry as well as social evils (7:5–7), and, like Moses, spells out dire punishment (7:12), including the specter of expulsion from the land (7:15). One cannot miss the biblical message that Yahweh sooner or later enforces the principle that one reaps what one sows. Breach of covenant is serious. It is with a pronounced passion of disgust—even anger—that Yahweh moves against that which is a blatant affront to his covenant and his holiness.

An unsettling feature in Moses' sermon for some moderns is talk of Yahweh's anger. Moses speaks ominously, "For the LORD your God is a devouring fire, a jealous God" (Deut 4:24). The Hebrew root קנא means both "jealous" and "zealous," as Jeffrey Tigay explains. He quotes Moshe Greenberg, who describes קנא as "the resentful rage of one whose prerogatives have been usurped by, or given to, another."[30] Moses tells his own story of how God was angry with him, as a result of which Yahweh denied him entry into the Promised Land (4:21). Moses warns forthrightly that were Israel to resort to the making of idols, they should know that Yahweh would be provoked to anger (4:25).

Jeremiah's message, while not employing the term "anger" or "wrath," nevertheless breathes Yahweh's exasperation with a people who revel in their salvation while brazenly flaunting Yahweh's commandments (Jer 7:9–10). The rhetorical question is laced with passion: "Has this house, which is called by my name, become a den of robbers in your sight? You know, I too am watching, says the LORD" (7:11). The advice to remember Shiloh is to recall how God summarily destroyed it, and the audience would hear it as an expression of Yahweh's anger. Overall, the book of Jeremiah often touches on the wrath of God.[31]

---

30. Ibid., 65.
31. In Jeremiah, 42 different verses or passages mention or elaborate on God's anger. The term אף 'anger' is found in Jeremiah 24 times, more often than in any other book (e.g.,

So, while both sermons call attention to God's goodness, both sermons are also forthright in speaking about God's retributive action, an action arising from an "impassioned God." The God with whom Israel relates is a God whose passions rise in anger against unholy behavior.

Other theological matters emerge in these sermons: divine election (Deut 4:20, 34, 37), the role of "torah" (Deut 4:5, 40; Jer 7:5–10), the definition of justice and its importance (Jer 7:5), repentance, the symbolism of the temple (Jer 7:4, 8–11), and the responsibility of a given generation to teach successive generations (Deut 4:9c, 10c, 25, 40b). Daniel Block clarifies the vexing question of "law" (better "teaching") in Deuteronomy.[32] Leaning on Deut 4:1–8 (Moses' sermon), Block explains that the Torah [law] was normative (Deut 4:1–2), that it was the key to life (4:3–4), and that knowledge of the Torah was the highest privilege imaginable (4:5–8). The law (teaching) is to be viewed positively as a gift of God's grace. Jeremiah mentions justice; he does not leave it as a general concept but immediately offers specifics as to what it entails. "For if you truly amend your ways and your doings, if you truly act justly one with another, if you do not oppress the alien, the orphan and the widow, or shed innocent blood in this place, and if you do not go after other gods to your own hurt, then I will dwell with you in this place, in the land that I gave of old to your ancestors forever and ever" (Jer 7:5–7). In short, justice is to act honorably toward God and neighbor according to God's standards.

Three other topics that are part of Israel's singular worldview and that are treated in these sermons deserve mention. Note should be taken most especially that for Jeremiah as well as for Moses, worship is not to be divorced from ethical living (Jer 7:9–10; Deut 4:10–14, 4:39–40). Commenting on Deut 4:1–8, Brueggemann asserts: "All through the book of Deuteronomy, the tradition is at pains to hold together *holy presence* and *social practice,* for either alone is inadequate."[33] Nathan MacDonald sees the *peroratio* (Deut 4:32–40) as highly pertinent to the theme of monotheism.[34] C. J. H. Wright stresses the missionary dimen-

---

2:35, 15:14, 33:5). Of the 125 OT occurrences of the word חמה 'rage, wrath', 17 are found in Jeremiah (e.g., 7:20, 25:15, 30:23).

32. D. I. Block, "The Grace of Torah: The Mosaic Prescription for Life (Deut. 4:1–8; 6:20–25)," *BSac* 162 (Jan–Mar, 2005) 3–22; repr. *How I Love Your Torah,* 1–20.

33. Brueggemann, *Deuteronomy,* 53 (italics his).

34. N. MacDonald, offers an extended exegesis of Deut 4:1–40 (*Deuteronomy and the Meaning of 'Monotheism'* [Tübingen: Mohr Siebeck, 2003] 185–204). He explores the themes of divine presence, human obedience, election, and the land in "The Literary Criticism and Rhetorical Logic of Deuteronomy I–IV," *VT* 56.2 (2006) 203–24.

sion of Deuteronomy 4 in a major subsection of a chapter in his book.[35] In summary, an entire worldview is brought to bear on the exhortations (and promises) in both texts. That ideology is Hebraic in nature with clear delineations about the nature of the deity, Yahweh, and Yahweh's relation to the world both in judgment and in salvation.

Such a worldview stands in sharp contrast to that of the surrounding cultures.[36] Moses is at pains to mark out several characterizing differentiations. Israel's wisdom, given its divine origin, is superior to that of other cultures (Deut 4:5). Israel's deity is accessible in contrast to pagan gods often characterized as indifferent (4:7). Israel's deity identifies with his people and communicates with them (4:34). Such a God contrasts with gods of the nations, who are territorial gods.[37] This God's laws are just (צדק) as opposed to arbitrary laws (4:8; cf. Jer 7:5). This God prohibits images of God in wood and stone, which are common in the worship of other nations (Deut 4:15–19, 23, 28; cf. mention of Baal and "other gods" in Jer 7:9). Israel's God prohibits astral worship (Deut 4:19), contra Egyptian practice, for example. Yahweh is a sole god (monotheism) in contrast to polytheism (4:39).[38] Thus, both sermons are theologically loaded.

5. Bringing it Home: Challenges for Today's Preacher

With the modern-day preacher in mind, we ask, "How can today's preacher profit from examining ancient preaching?" That raises the question to what extent past sermons and sermonizing in general are instructive to preachers of another generation. That question could be dismissed on the grounds that these sermons are not recorded for the benefit of homileticians; the messages of Moses and Jeremiah were intended to help listeners of a given time live in faithful devotion to Yahweh and even to warn listeners of the dangers of neglect. Thus, a general modern-day application would be along the lines of encouraging hearers to faithfulness to Yahweh on Yahweh's terms.

---

35. C. J. H. Wright, *The Mission of God: Unlocking the Bible's Grand Narrative* (Downers Grove, IL: InterVarsity, 2006) 375–87.

36. MacDonald observes, "Certainly the religion envisaged by Deuteronomy appears to be sharply differentiated from other ancient Near Eastern religions by its programmatic aniconism, and its emphasis on the words that Yhwh spoke at Horeb" (*Deuteronomy and the Meaning of 'Monotheism'*, 182).

37. Cf. D. I. Block, *The Gods of the Nations: Studies in Ancient Near Eastern National Theology* (rev. ed.; Grand Rapids: Baker, 2000).

38. Cf. A. Rofé, "The Monotheistic Argumentation in Deuteronomy 4:32–40: Contents, Composition and Text," *VT* 35 (1985) 434–45; repr. in idem, *Deuteronomy: Issues and Interpretation* (London/New York: T & T Clark, 2002) 15–24.

Still, these biblical sermons can serve heuristic purposes for the preacher in the 21st century. Hence we move from a comparison of the two biblical sermons to an examination of guidelines that these sermons offer to the modern preacher.[39] The challenges for doing so are several, but five deserve more extended treatment: theological balance, ritual and ethics, use of history, sermon format, and passion.

5.1. Theological Balance: God's goodness; God's anger

Both sermons under investigation contain good news. Moses underlines the wonder and the mystery of God revealing himself and of his love in choosing Israel and of desiring his people's wellbeing.[40] Jeremiah holds out the promise of God's continued presence, as well as his protection. But that good news is balanced with some warnings. Moses warns of the dreaded consequences of apostasy; Jeremiah targets injustice and hypocrisy, warning of expulsion from the land. God is presented both as a good God and, on occasion, as an angry God. Such claims pose intellectual challenges, but von Rad's observation is pertinent: "Good sermons have something of an intellectual adventure about them."[41] Sermons gain in depth and interest as the preacher identifies and addresses tensions in the text.

Do these sermons call for preachers to address tensions such as those posed by Yahweh's wrath, this negative aspect of God's governance? The answer must surely be Yes. However, the preacher is at once cautioned not to overplay the biblical message of God's anger. Paul Scott Wilson, who devotes an entire chapter to "condemnation," wisely remarks, "Condemnation ought to be used with exceeding care." He also counsels that while many things in our world need condemning, entire sermons should not be given to condemnation; rather, it should arise in sub-forms, that is, parts of sermons.[42] Not every sermon must reference God's punitive action, but the overall preaching program in a church must make clear that the Christian message as found in both the Old and New Testaments is not exclusively about God's love. To portray God in balanced fashion is a major challenge. In the light of scriptural teaching, the message of God's negative emotion must not be muted.

---

39. Surprisingly, in a survey of more than twenty books with titles on the order of "Biblical Preaching," I found virtually no discussion of sermons within the Bible.

40. "The authors of Deuteronomy are concerned primarily with the proclamation of the astounding and abundant love of God, by which they wish to awaken in Israel's heart an answering and commensurate love" (Achtemeier, *Deuteronomy, Jeremiah*, 28).

41. G. von Rad, *Biblical Interpretations in Preaching* (trans. John E. Steely; Nashville: Abingdon, 1977) 18.

42. P. S. Wilson, *Setting Words on Fire: Putting God at the Center of the Sermon* (Nashville: Abingdon, 2008) 117–18.

John the Baptist warned his listeners to flee from the coming wrath (Matt 3:7). Jesus said that those disobeying the Son would not see life but must endure God's wrath (John 3:36). Paul declared that wrath and fury will be the portion of those refusing to obey the truth (Rom 2:8). The image in Revelation is of the idolatrous drinking "the wine of God's wrath, poured unmixed into the cup of his anger" (Rev 14:9–10). One can hardly claim to be biblical in one's preaching if a fairly dominant feature of God's action is muted or silenced.

Objection to a presentation of God's anger has recently become loud.[43] Today's listeners to sermons will find that just the mention of God's wrath is distasteful, even objectionable. Pastors are inclined to side-step the subject of God's displeasure and anger in the fear that this will alienate listeners. Given the emphasis on churches being seeker-friendly, talk of God's anger is likely to put people off.

But the preacher can help with some clarifications. First, he or she must not communicate vindictiveness. Human anger is rarely fully righteous and certainly not holy. Yahweh's anger must be differentiated from human anger in that it arises out of purity and is untainted by evil. It is important to stress that God is not to be defined by his wrath and anger. Yahweh is defined by his mercy and compassion, his steadfast love and un-surpassing kindness (Exod 34:6–7). The psalmist, repeating that ancient confession, asserts, "God is good to all" (Ps 145:9). Moses' sermon not only highlights God's anger but also insists, "Because the LORD your God is a merciful God, he will neither abandon you nor destroy you; he will not forget the covenant" (Deut 4:31). Compassion, as well as anger should be seen as Yahweh's responses to human behavior. "In general biblical and theological terms, 'wrath' is what happens when God's good and loving purposes (חסד, ἀγάπη) encounter human complacency and intransigence (stiffness of neck, hardness of heart, impenitence, unbelief)."[44]

A grasp of Yahweh as solicitous for human well-being is clearly the backdrop in both of the OT sermons, and, for that matter, in the entire depiction of God in Scripture. So the preacher will keep the message of Yahweh's love as shown in the gospel to the fore; but, as one committed to the veracity of the entire Scripture, the preacher cannot remain silent about the darker background.[45]

---

43. E.g., R. Schwartz, *The Curse of Cain: The Violent Legacy of Monotheism* (Chicago and London: University of Chicago Press, 1997).

44. Moberly, "Challenge of the Prophets," 32.

45. D. Gowan spells out the balance well: "Preaching from Amos (or from any of the rest of the judgment passages in the prophets) must then emphasize the dark side of

5.2. Worship and Ethics

Both sermons, but especially Jeremiah's sermon, address the possible disconnect between worship and ethics. We read in Jer 7:9–11a:

> Will you steal, murder, commit adultery, swear falsely, make offerings to Baal, and go after other gods that you have not known and then come and stand before me in this house, which is called by my name and say, "We are safe!"—only to go on doing all these abominations? Has this house which is called by my name, become a den of robbers in your sight?

Moberly speaks of the "significant mismatch between their [Israel's] religious practices and their way of living," and hence the "need to hear a challenge that their religious practices have become empty, even offensive, to God."[46]

The ancient disconnect between ritual and behavior is also a modern one. For all that is said about love and unity in the church, the divisions resulting from bickering and backbiting, often on relatively inconsequential issues, are scandalous. Hence the call, "Amend your ways!" Alongside all the buzz about justice, the intrigue and the exploitation by the powerful of the powerless—be these individuals, corporations, the church, or the nations—make it imperative that someone speaking for God call out, "Amend your ways!" For all the talk about Christianity as being about transformation and honorable relationships, the selfishness, greed, and conspicuous consumerism of God's people demand that a voice, as though from heaven speak, "Amend your ways!"

It was one of the tasks of the prophets to identify the shape of evil in the society and to address it. Today's preacher has the task of identifying areas of life in which justice, namely, "honorable relations," are in disrepair. One of these arenas is family life. The gospel message of spiritual power to bring change of character and behavior is virtually undercut by the large percentage of marriages that end in divorce. The biblical message of love, as it becomes operational in a household and in husband-and-wife relationships, is not made sufficiently explicit. Instruction is part of the preacher's task. The one proclaiming God's Word must teach on integrity, forgiveness, and conflict resolution, and that not only in an idealistic way but with attention to unjust behaviors. The preacher has the obligation to identify the shape of today's evil within society and even the church, evils such as corruption, misrepresentation, and obsession with goods.

---

human existence, but without ever forgetting that it is still existence under grace" (*Reclaiming the Old Testament for the Christian Pulpit* [Atlanta: John Knox, 1980] 130).

46. Moberly, "Challenge of the Prophets," 29.

The sermons in Deut 4:1–40 and Jer 7:1–15 are both characterized by stern exhortations. "If you act corruptly by making an idol . . . I call heaven and earth to witness against you today that you will soon utterly perish from the land" (Deut 4:25–26). "Will you steal, murder, commit adultery . . . and then come and stand before me in this house . . . ? You know, I too am watching, says the LORD" (Jer 7:8–11). Similarly, Jesus is known for even harsher words. "If your right hand causes you to sin, cut it if off and throw it away" (Matt 5: 30). It is not enough to speak in generalities. Today's preachers, as did the ancients, should move on to specifics and make their case by offering compelling rationale. C. J. H Wright's comment on the sermon in Deuteronomy 4 is apropos. His parenthetical comment should be heeded: "Many are the motivations in Deuteronomy—it is one of the noted features of the book (as it should be of our preaching)."[47]

But the exhortations are also nurturing, both in Moses' sermon (e.g., "Keep his statutes and his commandments . . . for your own well-being" [Deut 4:40]) and in Jeremiah's (e.g., "If you amend your ways . . . then I will dwell with you" [Jer 7:3]). Evil ways are to be avoided. The path of righteousness is to be followed. Moses reviews some of Israel's history, soliciting Israel to recognize the good in their lives that will come from obedience. If there is reproof and admonition, as there is, the preachers make clear that they are speaking with the interests of the people at heart.

The sermons by Moses and Jeremiah have a counter-cultural ring to them. Should that also be true of twenty-first century preaching? Does modern evangelical preaching assume that Christian faith and American civil religion are compatible? Is there a congenial fit between values of government, such as national security, and Christian belief? Does the system of capitalism easily comport with the biblical principles related to economics and finances? Jeremiah's sermon was provocative to the point of inciting a riot and near lynching because he challenged the people's sacred cow, the temple (Jer 26:1–15).[48] Many centuries later, Stephen's sermon, which rehearsed Israel's stubborn ways and ended (not unlike Jeremiah's) with reference to the temple, resulted in the people's violent reaction (Acts 7:44–54). Careful attention to these sermons makes for serious probing of contemporary preaching where sermons become all too easily an accommodation of current theories and

---

47. C. J. H. Wright, "Preaching from the Law," in *Reclaiming the Old Testament for Christian Preaching* (ed. G. J. R. Kent, P. J. Kissling, and L. A. Turner; Downers Grove, IL: InterVarsity, 2010) 51.

48. It is generally assumed that the incidents reported in Jeremiah 26 echo Jer 7:1–5.

practices. On this topic David Buttrick, a teacher of preachers, has this to say: "I write with urgency. For I am firmly convinced that American churches and American preachers have been frightened into a timid reactionary posture. Afraid, we no longer address public issues or promote public theology, though both are desperately needed."[49]

5.3. Use of Illustrations Drawn from History

Noteworthy in these two sermons is that each employs illustrations drawn from history. Moses reinforces his warnings by calling attention to the events at Baal-Peor (Num 25:1–15). Those destroyed there were following the deities of the surrounding culture in a form of worship that entailed low ethical sexual practices (Deut 4:3–4). Nelson refers to "a thematic pattern of arguing from history" evident in Deuteronomy 4 (as well as Deut 7:7–11, 10:12–22, 11:1–8).[50] Jeremiah cited the historical destruction of the worship center at Shiloh four hundred years earlier to demonstrate that worship rituals without ethical compliance would not guarantee Yahweh's favor (Jer 7:14). Yahweh was not bound to a place of worship, such as the sacred tent in Shiloh or the temple in Jerusalem. Rather, Yahweh would ruin a worship center where the worshippers were no longer single-minded and devout. Both instances cited—Baal-Peor and Shiloh—are illustrations taken from Israel's national history.

Preachers in the 21st century draw illustrations from various venues: nature, novels, films, etc. The use of personal experiences such as that cited by Moses (see Deut 4:21–24; also in 1:37, 3:26) can certainly be effective. Illustrations from history are especially telling. Since history reading is not generally a priority for preachers, more energy may be required to search out appropriate illustrations. The preacher will find that by reaching into national or church history, the message will become more memorable and compelling. Illustrations from church history offer a longitudinal view of life lived under God. The call for today's preachers is to give depth to their preaching by tapping into older biographies, stories, and historical accounts.

---

49. D. Buttrick, *Preaching the New and the Now* (Louisville: Westminster John Knox, 1998) 3.

50. R. D. Nelson, *Deuteronomy. A Commentary* (OTL; Louisville: Westminster John Knox, 2002) 70. Nelson references G. Braulik who outlines the "schema of presentation of evidence" having several characteristic elements, all of which are found in Moses' sermon in Deuteronomy 4: review of history (vv. 32–34, 36–38), consequence for belief (vv. 35, 39), and practical conclusion (v. 40).

As an example of illustrations from history, one might, when speaking about justice, explain that in biblical terms "justice" has to do with honorable relationships. Jesus spoke of the "honorable relationship" that his followers should have with an enemy. His followers were to love even the enemy. To illustrate this kind of "justice" one might adduce the story of Dirk Willems in the 16th century. Arrested by authorities for his Anabaptist beliefs, Willems was incarcerated. He managed an escape but an officer was soon in hot pursuit. The ice in the pond, the "Hondegat," was thin but sufficient to carry across it this man, now light-weight due to his imprisonment. His pursuer, of heavier build, broke through the ice and was in danger of drowning. Willems turned to see, then reversed his course and saved the officer from drowning. He received no thanks. Instead, he was re-arrested, languished in prison, then tried and, before long, burned at the stake.[51]

5.4. Sermon Format Variety

A conventional comment as part of an introduction to a preacher's sermon goes something like this: "My topic is X, and I have three points." The "point" sermon, which is modeled after a lecture, has advantages to be sure, such as clarity and progression, but the liabilities of this preaching format, such as predictability, have been identified as well. Wilson, noting reasons why point preaching has fallen out of favor, observes that such a preaching format implies that the sermon is primarily information, that it is too much like a lecture, that the preacher is more likely to follow a deductive than an inductive approach, and that to some listeners point preaching has a vertical and "sometimes male notion of authority." Wilson correctly observes, however, that "biblical warrant may be found for both propositional [though not specifically three-point] and narrative sermons."[52] As for justification for the point sermon, Jeremiah's temple sermon is ready-made. In this sermon there are two clearly stated emphases: "Amend your ways" and "Don't trust the popular mantra about the temple" (Jer 7:3–4). Here the format is not "three points and a poem" but two points and an announcement. Point sermons once viable, one could argue, are viable still.

---

51. Details at http://www.mbhistory.org/profiles/dirk.en.html (last accessed February 24, 2012).

52. Wilson, *Setting Words on Fire*, 20, 22. Help towards narrative preaching can be found in P. R. House, "Examining the Narratives of OT Narrative: An Exploration in Biblical Theology," *WTJ* 67 (2005) 229–45, in which he treats Deut 1–4 (pp. 232–35). See also J. Sailhamer, *The Pentateuch as Narrative: a Biblical-theological Commentary* (Grand Rapids: Zondervan, 1992).

Moses' sermon, in terms of organization, seems more circular or spiral. Mayes describes it as a "patchwork."[53] The thrust of the sermon is to exhort hearers to remain loyal to Yahweh. The exhortation is given in the context of Yahweh's uniqueness and his covenant with his people. The exhortation, repeated several times, is sometimes amplified by offering motivations showing that to be loyal is a good thing, and sometimes to explicate what loyalty entails, as well as what behaviors are outside loyalty, and sometimes incorporating an example. Rhetorical questions about God's awesome acts are asked initially (Deut 4:7) and reappear toward the conclusion (4:33). Similarly, in the format of poetic parallelism, Moses inveighs against idolatry in the first half of the sermon (4:16–19) and again in the latter half (4:25–28).

It is fair to say, I think, that Moses' sermon is an illustration of a "move" sermon. As Buttrick has explained and advocated, a move sermon takes the shape of a movie film where a scene is introduced, the movie-maker lingers there briefly, and then takes the viewer to another venue. The move sermon does not leave the listener with a series of "points" that can be conveniently numbered, but essentially makes one point. Part of the rationale for a move sermon is that the listeners, especially in the modern media age, have a short attention span. Whatever the advantage to a "move" sermon, today's preacher does well to know that there is high precedent in Scripture for such a sermon and to mark it well in his or her repertoire of sermon formats.[54] Variety of format is clearly important in our times—listeners have been conditioned to such variety in film, TV, and music.

Effective preaching includes other features such as repetition. Both sermons we are exploring could be faulted for undue repetitions were they assessed as written compositions. But these are oral presentations and should be so assessed. The attention of listeners is easily diverted for many reasons. Repeating the major thrust of the message through key, even catchy, phrases or terms is necessary to keep the audience on track. If preachers read their sermons, they need to envision in preparation of their manuscripts not a reading audience but a listening one. Effective communication requires repetition; highly effective communication will couch that repetition creatively.

---

53. Mayes, *Deuteronomy*, 149.
54. D. Buttrick, *Homiletic Moves and Structures* (Philadelphia: Fortress, 1987) 23–53. Other sermon formats appear in Scripture as well, e.g., narrative sermon form, a strongly viable form for moderns, is illustrated in Stephen's sermon in Acts 7. For a concise review of Buttrick's strategies, as well as those of F. Craddock and E. Lowry, see R. O. Bystrom, *Preaching Biblical Sermons: Three Contemporary Strategies* (Winnipeg, MB: Kindred, 2006).

Sermons capitalize on recalling the biblical tradition. Fred Craddock identifies the qualities to be sought in a sermon, one of which is memory. In different ways, through exposition, quotation, allusion, or echo, listeners are reminded of the biblical story. Sermons are enriched and listeners are nourished as the particular message is bathed in the context of the larger biblical story.[55] Both sermons we are exploring illustrate the principle that Craddock enunciates. Moses tells of Horeb and Baal-Peor and exposits the second of the Ten Commandments, even without directly mentioning it. Jeremiah invokes the ancient covenants of Abraham, of David, and of Moses. His listeners hear of Shiloh. "Memory listens, reflects, sifts, and learns; otherwise we deny the present, cut off the future, and halt the growth toward maturity which should characterize the people of God."[56] The challenge for preachers is to integrate into their sermons allusions to Biblical events and texts and thus reinforce the memory of the biblical tradition.

5.5. Sermonizing with Passion

A sermon is not an innocuous affair. The stakes are high. For both Moses and Jeremiah the future of the listeners is dire if the preaching is ignored. On the other hand, if listeners act on the counsel they hear, they stand to do well. No wonder that both Moses and Jeremiah come across as preachers with passion.

But to put it this way is still too bland. Their sermons were more than counsel or invitations to take a certain course of action: they were declarations. Moses called heaven and earth to witness as he forthrightly announced the deadly consequences of ignoring the call to follow God. Not all sermons are built on an "either-or" template, but it is characteristic of these two sermons that the press for a decision was direct. Moses declared, "See, I have set before you today life and prosperity, death and adversity. . . . Choose life so that you and your descendants may live" (sermon in Deut 30:15, 19b). Christian preaching is a matter of the greatest earnestness. A "take-it-or-leave-it" presentation is not in the spirit of the gospel, nor is it in tune with sermons such as those by Moses and Jeremiah.

While not unappreciative of the New Homiletic, which is marked by sermons structured according to the needs of people, with the use of narrative and sensitivity to images, Paul Scott Wilson makes the case for a kind of proclamation where God is at the center. He cites the following as genres of gospel proclamation: testimony, prayer, nurturing

---

55. F. Craddock, *Preaching* (Nashville: Abingdon, 1985) 157–59.
56. Ibid., 158.

exhortation, proclamatory statements, doxology, and celebration.⁵⁷ He insists, "When preaching stops short of proclamation, arguably its main purpose is lost." Proclamation, he says, "is impassioned announcement of God's word in God's name such that God is heard speaking directly to the individual and community...."⁵⁸

The current ethos is one attuned more to "conversation" than to declaration. Granted, there is an important place for conversation, especially in teaching settings, and it is therefore occasionally appropriate in those sermons that are primarily instruction. However, preaching is more than sharing information; it is persuasion. Preaching is a declaration of the way God intersects with us humans in grace and forgiveness. Preaching spells out what is entailed in following Jesus. Good preaching motivates. Good preaching aims at change in ways of thinking. Good preaching has a confrontational edge as it addresses attitudes and actions in need of transformation.⁵⁹ Good preaching shows an awareness of what is at stake and persuasively speaks the word of God into the situation.

6. Conclusion

Ancient sermons by biblical giants such as Moses and Jeremiah still move us. God's Spirit, which was upon them then for effective communication, is still available today for God's servants called to proclaim the word of God. Beyond attending to the enabling power of the Spirit, preachers have reason to think deeply about sermons recorded in the Scriptures. Without question, these sermons both enlighten and inspire preachers of every generation.⁶⁰

---

57. Wilson, *Setting Words on Fire,* chaps. 12–17, pp. 149–223.
58. Ibid., 2, 112.
59. "The purpose of prophetic preaching is to transform the audience's thinking about historical and theological realities, particularly their own spiritual condition, and to bring about change in disposition and action" (Block, "Preaching Ezekiel," 160).
60. I acknowledge with appreciation the interaction and feedback of my colleagues, Professors Lynn Jost, Jon Isaak, and Pierre Gilbert, as well as of my pastor friend, Dean Williams.

The Prophet Who Is Like and Greater Than Moses
A Sermon on Deuteronomy 18:15–22

DANIEL L. AKIN

Introduction

As one walks through the pages of Holy Scripture, the reader discovers an unfolding portrait of God's Messiah that grows in beauty as well as detail. Daniel Block well says, "Although complex, the Old Testament picture of the messiah gains in clarity and focus with time."[1] In other words, it begins broadly but progressively narrows and becomes more specific and precise.

One aspect of this focusing of messianic vision is that later texts open new vistas for looking at earlier texts. As in any good drama, the earlier parts of God's story are given fresh perspective in light of the climax found in the person and work of Jesus described in the New Testament. Reading the beginning in light of the end allows us to see Jesus of Nazareth as the ultimate fulfillment of many Old Testament texts, beginning with God's promise to send a deliverer who would be the seed of a woman and who would crush the head of the serpent (Gen 3:15, Rom 16:20). Similarly, Jesus Christ is understood as the seed of Abraham (Gen 12:1–3, 22:18), descended from the tribe of Judah (49:10), a prophet like Moses (Deut 18:15–17), a Davidic King (2 Sam 7:12–17, Isa 11:1), Yahweh's Anointed (Psalm 2), one whom the Lord delivers from death (Psalms 16, 22), a King-Priest (Psalm 110), virgin conceived (Isa 7:14),

---

Author's Note: My friend Daniel Block has been a gift to the body of Christ. He is absolutely stellar in the classroom and his writings have blessed many including me. He has a unique gift for touching both the mind and the heart when he opens up the Scriptures. Numerous students have informed me that he was one of the best teachers that they ever studied under. I am truly honored to contribute to a volume that appropriately honors one of the Church's premier Old Testament scholars.

1. D. I. Block, "My Servant David: Ancient Israel's Vision of the Messiah," in *Israel's Messiah in the Bible and the Dead Sea Scrolls* (ed. R. S. Hess and M. D. Carroll R.; Grand Rapids: Baker, 2003) 17–56, citation from p. 56.

the Suffering Servant of the Lord (Isa 52:13–53:12), the anticipated Son of Man (Dan 7:13–14), the ruler born in Bethlehem (Mic 5:2), and the pierced one who will cleanse from sin and uncleanness (Zech 12:10–14).

The portrait is breathtaking and overwhelming both in its promise and in its particulars. It is like one has discovered an array of magnificent pearls linked together to form a beautiful necklace that only God could have designed. Each Old Testament text invites careful study and inspection. For our purposes we will focus on the promise found in Moses' exposition of the Torah in the plains of Moab, the promise of a prophet like Moses found in Deut 18:15–22.[2]

Moses addresses the Israelites in preparation for their entrance "into the land that the Lord your God is giving you" (18:9). He warns them that they will be confronted with all sorts of evil ("abominable") practices that they must not follow or emulate (18:9–14). To aid them in faithful devotion to the Lord, God promises to raise up a prophet who would speak the Lord's word to the people—a word they should hear and obey (18:18–19). Though a series of prophets is most likely the thrust of the text,[3] eventually the nation of Israel began to look for and anticipate the prophet *par excellence* "who would be either a messianic figure or the announcer of the Messiah (cf. John 1:21, 25; Acts 3:22; 7:37)."[4] The New Testament testifies to the fulfillment of this anticipated prophet like Moses in the coming of Jesus of Nazareth.[5]

Now, let us walk through Deut 18:15–22 and observe exactly what it is that God says we should understand concerning his gift of the

---

2. It should be noted that the esteemed colleague we honor in this book sees this text differently than do I (see his fine article noted in n. 1). As was the case during the eight years we served together at The Southern Baptist Theological Seminary, we will graciously and respectably disagree, rejoicing in our common love for God's Word and the wonderful challenges it often presents for serious students of Scripture.

3. Virtually all scholars view this in a collective sense. See, e.g., E. Merrill, *Deuteronomy* (NAC 5; Nashville: Broadman & Holman, 1994) 272.

4. Ibid. Merrill notes, "The ambiguity of the individual and collective both being expressed in the grammatical singular is a common Old Testament devise employed to afford multiple meanings or application to prophetic texts." See also W. C. Kaiser Jr., *Toward an Old Testament Theology* (Grand Rapids: Zondervan, 1978) 215–17 (cited in Merrill, *Deuteronomy*, 272 n. 127).

5. C. Erdman states simply: "This promise received its complete fulfillment when God finally spoke through His own Son.... We find in Christ the final antitype of all these Hebrew mediators. He is the divinely appointed Prophet, Priest, and King, whose service is eternal" (*The Book of Deuteronomy* [Grand Rapids: Baker, 1953] 59). Similarly, in preaching a single message on the whole book of Deuteronomy, my good friend M. Dever confidently affirms: "Today we know who that promised prophet is: Jesus Christ. Jesus Christ is the one who speaks God's words perfectly. He is the one sent from God to teach us the way to God" (*The Message of the Old Testament* [Wheaton, IL: Crossway, 2006] 174).

prophets and the ultimate Prophet. What is their purpose? How do we recognize the true prophet from the false prophet? What should be our response to the prophet's words?

Message Outline
Introduction
1. God Raises up His Prophets and We Should Listen to Them (18:15–17)
    1.1. God's prophets speak at God's initiative (18:15)
    1.2. God's prophets speak as God's mediators (18:16–17)
2. God Speaks through His Prophets and We Should Obey Them (18:18–19)
    2.1. God gives the prophets the words to proclaim (18:18)
    2.2. God expects his people to respond (18:19)
3. God Validates His Prophets and We Should Trust Them (18:20–22)
    3.1. False prophets speak lies for other gods (18:20, 22)
    3.2. True prophets speak truth for the one true God (18:21–22)
Conclusion

---

1. God Raises Up His Prophets and We Should Listen to Them (18:15–17)

Our God is a God who speaks. He is a God who takes initiative to communicate with his creation. While we cannot know him exhaustively, we can know him truly and genuinely, because he chooses to speak to us. One means by which God has revealed himself is through his prophets, whom he called to declare a message on his behalf. As Earl Kalland notes, "Being the spokesman for God is the central characteristic of a prophet."[6] Moses highlights two aspects of the occupation of those who speak for God.

1.1. God's Prophets Speak at God's Initiative (18:15)

Moses informs us that it is the LORD (Yahweh) who raises up a prophet (Hebrew *nābî'* 'one who is called [by a god]').[7] The prophetic office is not something people take upon themselves, but is fully and completely established by God's initiative and calling. In John 8:28 the Lord Jesus said of his own prophetic ministry, "When you have lifted up the Son of Man, then you will know that I am he, and that I do nothing on my own authority but speak just as the Father taught me." He spoke, as do all true prophets, only at God's initiative.

---

6. E. Kalland, *Deuteronomy* (EBC 3; Grand Rapids: Zondervan, 1992) 121.
7. Ibid., 123. See also R. D. Culver, "*nābî'*," *TWOT* 2:544–45.

Further, Deuteronomy 18 states that such prophets will be like Moses and come from among the Israelites themselves, "from among you, from your brothers" (cf. 18:20, 22). Moses himself was an Israelite who faithfully declared God's word to his people, and the Israelites were called to listen to him. Similarly, Israel was called to heed God's later messengers: "The LORD your God will raise up for you a prophet like me from among your brothers—it is to him you shall listen" (18:15).

Like the prophets of old, for those of us today called by God to proclaim his word, our mandate is to be text-driven preachers who rightly handle the word of God.[8] Apart from this word we have no message and basis by which to call our people to do anything. As Haddon Robinson well says of preachers: "When they fail to preach the Scripture, they abandon their authority. No longer do they confront their hearers with a word from God."[9] Indeed, they offer only another word of human origin—a word lacking divine authority, power, and substance. As Raymond Brown writes, "The preacher's task is not to confront the congregation with his own ideas but with the authoritative word of God."[10]

1.2. God's Prophets Speak as God's Mediator (18:16–17)

The prophet not only speaks at God's initiative, he also speaks as God's mediator. Verses 16–17 take us back to the giving of the Torah as recorded in Deut 5:22–28. The people were terrified by the "glory and greatness" of Yahweh, by his voice and the fire out of which he spoke. They asked that Moses be allowed to serve as their mediator before God so that they would not die. The Lord commended them and honored their request, noting, "They are right in what they have spoken" (v. 17; cf. 5:28). God then said in 5:29, "Oh that they had such a mind as this always, to fear me and to keep all my commandments, that it might go well with them and with their descendent forever!"

As mediator, Moses served as Yahweh's spokesperson to reveal God's word and will to the people. Those who followed him in the prophetic calling would serve in a like manner, culminating in "the one mediator between God and humankind, the man Christ Jesus" (1 Tim 2:5). Warren Wiersbe was correct when he asserted: "Moses promised the people that God would raise up other prophets as the nation needed them," and he "was doing more than promise the whole line of proph-

---

8. Prophets and preachers alike are men under divine authority. God gives them His Word and their calling is simple: faithfully proclaim the Word (see 2 Tim 4:2).
9. H. Robinson, *Biblical Preaching* (2nd ed.; Grand Rapids: Baker, 2001) 20.
10. R. Brown, *The Message of Deuteronomy* (BST; Downers Grove, IL: InterVarsity, 1993) 186.

ets that the Lord would send; he was also announcing the coming of The Prophet, the Lord Jesus Christ."[11] This mediator would serve not only as God's prophet, but also as God's priest-king, as is clear from the book of Hebrews (see also Ps 110). Here in Jesus Christ is God's voice; through him we can hear and not die. In Jesus Christ is also God's face; through him we can see and not die. Indeed, here in Jesus Christ is the Word of God that "became flesh and dwelt among us, and we have seen his glory, glory as of the only Son from the Father, full of grace and truth" (John 1:14).

2. *God Speaks Through His Prophets and We Should Obey Them (18:18–19)*

Many students of the Bible have identified numerous parallels and similarities between the life and ministry of Moses and that of Jesus of Nazareth. That our Lord is portrayed as a second and greater Moses in the Gospel of Matthew, for example, is almost universally accepted. Samuel Schultz provides a helpful summary of these parallels when he says:

> In the New Testament era, Jesus was recognized as fulfilling the prediction by Moses (cf. Mt 21:11; Lk 7:16; Jn 5:46; Ac 3:22; 7:37; Heb 3:2–6). Jesus was like Moses in numerous ways. He was spared in infancy (Ex 2; Mt 2:13–23); He renounced a royal court (Heb 11:24–27; Phil 2:5–8); had compassion for the people (Num 27:17; Mt 9:36); made intercession (Deu 9:18; Heb 7:25); spoke with God face to face (Ex 34:29–30; 2 Cor 3:7); and was mediator of a covenant (Dcu 29:1; Heb 8:6–7). The greatest revelation of the Old Testament era came through Moses. This revelation was only surpassed in the coming of Christ, who not only revealed God's message but provided salvation through His death.[12]

In our text, the emphasis is on divine revelation and Moses as the prophet and mediator of that revelation. Those who follow him will also mediate God's word, and because it is God's word, the people who hear it have an obligation to receive and obey it.

2.1. God Gives the Prophets the Words to Proclaim (18:18)

Verse 18 parallels v. 15 with almost the same words. However, a new and specific observation is made concerning those who mediate

---

11. W. Wiersbe, *Be Equipped: Deuteronomy* (Colorado Springs: Christ Victor, 1999) 94–95.

12. S. Schultz, *Deuteronomy: The Gospel of Love* (Chicago: Moody, 1971) 64. See also M. Rosen, "A Prophet Like Unto Moses," *Issues: A Messianic Jewish Perspective* 11.4 (July 1997), accessed March 9, 2012, http://jewsforjesus.org/publications/issues/11_4/prophet.

the word of God at the Lord's initiative. God says, (1) "I will put my words in his mouth" and (2) "he shall speak to them all that I command him." The words the prophet proclaims are God's words, and they encompass all that God commands. As such, the prophet functions as his mouthpiece, speaking exactly and completely all that the Lord instructs him to speak. As J. A. Thompson observes, the idea that God placed his words in the prophet's mouth underlies the messenger formula that commonly introduces prophetic speech: "Thus says the Lord."[13]

God gives the prophets the word to proclaim. It is always to be his and never just theirs! Similarly, as Brown notes, the contemporary "preacher's task is not to confront the congregation with his own ideas but with the authoritative word of God."[14] How we need to hear and heed this admonition when so much modern preaching is void of biblical content and theological substance.

2.2. God Expects His People to Respond (18:19)

By speaking on behalf of God, the prophet's words have divine authority that demands our radical attention and obedience. Accordingly, "To reject the words that the prophet spoke was to reject God, and he would not permit such rebellion to go unchallenged."[15] Verse 19 is realistic in its assessment and ominous in its promise. The Lord acknowledges that there will be those who "will not listen to my words" that the prophet "shall speak in my name." However, as Eugene Peterson in *The Message* paraphrases, God declares that he "will personally hold [him] responsible." Psalm 19:11 tells us there is "great reward" in keeping and obeying God's word. On the other hand, there is great loss in disobeying and rejecting it. Christopher Wright is correct: "Those who heard the prophet heard God; whatever response they made to the prophet they made to God, and they would take the consequences."[16]

With this in mind, God's words about Jesus given on the Mount of Transfiguration gain great significance. In the presence of the prophets Moses and Elijah, the Lord spoke to Peter, James, and John concerning Jesus, "This is my beloved Son, with whom I am well pleased; *listen to him*" (Matt 17:5). God expects his people to respond in obedience to his word.

---

13. J. A. Thompson, *Deuteronomy* (TOTC; Downers Grove, IL: InterVarsity, 1974) 213.
14. Brown, *Message of Deuteronomy*, 186.
15. D. McIntosh, *Deuteronomy* (HOTC; Nashville: Broadman & Holman, 2002) 224.
16. C. J. H. Wright, *Deuteronomy* (NIBC; Peabody, MA: Hendrickson, 1996) 218.

3. God Validates His Prophets and We Should Trust Them (18:20–22)

While God raises up true prophets and puts his word in their mouths, we can be certain that Satan through his demons will raise up false prophets, putting deception in their mouths (see Deut 32:16–17). Moses had already warned the Israelites about false prophets in Deut 13:1–5. Jesus would do the same in Matt 7:15–23; 24:11, 24. Paul would follow suit in 1 Tim 4:1–5; Peter in 2 Pet 2:1–3; and John in 1 John 2:18–23; 4:1–6; and Rev 13:11–18; 19:20. Even to the end of the age, the evil one will oppose the truth of God and counterfeit that truth deceiving those who do not exercise spiritual discernment. Wolves do come in sheep's clothing, as Jesus warned (Matt 7:15). What test might we apply then to discern the true prophet from the false, the genuine article from the counterfeit? Moses highlights two guidelines for evaluation: false prophets speak lies for other gods and true prophets speak truth for the one true God.

3.1. False Prophets Speak Lies for Other Gods (18:20, 22)

Moses warns us that self-proclaimed prophets may come on the scene claiming to speak for God. However, he warns us that they are presumptuous in their claim to speak in the Lord's name. Their appearance and declaration may be bold and even persuasive, but in actuality their words betray them because they are not consistent with what God has plainly revealed ("I have not commanded him to speak"). Further, if their words lead to idolatry and allegiance to false gods, it is clear that they do not speak for Yahweh. In the Mosaic economy, "that same prophet shall die" (Deut 18:20; cf. 13:15).

In addition, if they make a prediction "in the name of the Lord" of a future event and that event does not come true, then (1) "that is a word that the Lord has not spoken," (2) "the prophet has spoken presumptuously," and (3) no matter how powerful the personality or how compelling the orator, "you need not be afraid of him." Consistency with the revealed word and complete accuracy in predictive pronouncements will expose false prophets for the liars that they are! Peter Craigie points out that these criteria "represent the means by which a prophet gained his reputation as a true prophet and spokesman of the Lord. Over the course of a prophet's ministry, in matters important and less significant, the character of a prophet as a true spokesman of God would begin to emerge clearly."[17]

---

17. P. C. Craigie, *The Book of Deuteronomy* (NICOT; Grand Rapids: Eerdmans, 1976) 263.

3.2. True prophets speak truth for the one true God (18:21–22)

Donna Ridge highlights at least four tests of a prophet gleaned from other texts in the Bible:

1. Do their predictions come true (Jer 28:9)?
2. Does the prophet have a divine commission (Jer 29:9)?
3. Are the prophecies consistent with Scripture (2 Pet 1:20–21; Rev 22:18–19)?[18]
4. Do the people benefit spiritually from the prophet's ministry (Jer 23:13–14, 32; 1 Pet 4:11)?[19]

These four criteria echo and expand what Moses wrote. Moses takes for granted that we want to benefit spiritually ("if you say in your heart, 'How may we know . . . ?'"). Deep within we want to know what the Lord has said as well as "the word that the Lord has not spoken." Again, the decisive factor is truth. Do the words of the prophet line up with divine revelation, which, for Christians, is the totality of Scripture, both Old and New Testaments? And, if there is a predictive component to their message, does it come to pass and is it true? Gene Tucker accurately says, "A true prophet is, quite simply, one who tells the truth."[20]

Conclusion

It is in Jesus Christ that we see the ultimate prophet of God in full truth, manifestation, and glory. The people present when he fed 5,000 (men) were correct when they said, "This is indeed the Prophet who is to come into the world" (John 6:14). He spoke truth and only truth for the one true God. He is indeed the Word made flesh who has made the Father known (1:18). This is how Peter saw him (Acts 3:22–23). This is how Stephen saw him (Acts 7:37). This is how we should see him too: Jesus "the Prophet who is to come into the world."[21]

In John 5:39, Jesus said, "If you believed Moses, you would believe me, for he wrote of me." The author of Hebrews would add, "Long ago, at many times and in many ways, God spoke to our fathers by the

---

18. Also, consider 1 John 2:18–27, 4:1–3.
19. D. R. Ridge, "False Prophets," *Holman Illustrated Bible Dictionary* (ed. C. Brand, C. Draper, A. England; Nashville: Holman Bible, 2003) 554. Similar to Ridge, Culver (in *TWOT*) lists "five certifying signs of a prophet" ("*nābîʾ*," 544–45).
20. G. M. Tucker, "Expository Articles: Deuteronomy 18:15–22," *Int* 41 (July 1987) 292–97.
21. J. D. Hays, "If He Looks Like a Prophet and Talks Like a Prophet, Then He Must Be . . . ," in *Israel's Messiah in the Bible and the Dead Sea Scrolls* (ed. R. S. Hess and M. D. Carroll R.; Grand Rapids: Baker, 2003) 57–69. Hays's article is a response to Block's article in the same volume, pp. 17–56 (see n. 1 above).

prophets, but in these last days he has spoken to us by his Son." The Baptist preacher in London, Charles Spurgeon, captured perfectly what all Scripture teaches concerning this prophet like Moses. He carefully and wonderfully informs us of what we need to *know* and what we need to *do* when confronted with this prophet raised up by God.

> The Lord knew that man would always be unable to hear his Maker's voice and He, therefore, determined not only to speak by Moses, but to speak by His servants, the Prophets, raising up here, one, and there, another. And then He determined, as the consummation of His condescending mercy, that at the last He would put all the words He had to say to man into one heart and that word should be spoken by one mouth to men, furnishing a full, complete and unchangeable revelation of Himself to the human race! This He resolved to give by One of whom Moses had learned something when the Lord said to Him in the words of our text, "I will raise them up a Prophet from among their brethren, like unto you, and will put My words in His mouth; and He shall speak unto them all that I shall command Him." We know assuredly that our Lord Jesus Christ is that Prophet like unto Moses by whom, in these last days, He has spoken unto us! . . . Hear the Voice of God by this greatest of all Prophets. . . . Brothers and Sisters, I beseech you not to reject the message which Jesus brings, seeing it is not His own, but the sure message of God! Trifle not with a single word which Jesus speaks, for it is the Word of the Eternal One! Despise not one single deed which He did, or precept which He commanded, or blessing which He brought, for upon all these there is the stamp of Deity![22]

---

22. C. H. Spurgeon, "The Prophet Like Unto Moses," in *Metropolitan Tabernacle Pulpit* (Pasadena, TX: Pilgrim, 1972) 25: 435–37.

Stealing Souls
Human Trafficking and Deuteronomy 24:7

Myrto Theocharous

1. Introduction

Deuteronomy "functions as a theological manifesto"[1] for the covenant community God envisages for the people of Israel, but it is not an ancient relic. Its reception history testifies to its lasting value and relevance for every generation. As Daniel Block has noted, "few OT books proclaim such a relevant word,"[2] a word that is not meant to be confined inside the four walls of a community of faith. Its principles are expressed "in the sight of the peoples," non-believing communities, whose ability to recognize and value the wisdom of its statutes is presupposed (Deut 4:6).

This essay seeks to highlight theological principles behind Deuteronomic legislation (the law against kidnapping, in particular) and show how Deuteronomy's wisdom is relevant and necessary in guiding how the Church thinks about crimes such as human trafficking—"in the sight of our world." Deuteronomy may be able to realign our lenses and to help us approach with appropriate seriousness parallel phenomena in our time, such as human trafficking.[3]

Author's Note: I dedicate this essay to my dear friend and mentor Dan Block whose life work has been so influential in the worldwide academic community and, more broadly, to the community of faith. Our acquaintance began in 2005 at Wheaton College when he first took up his post in the Old Testament department. His class on the book of Deuteronomy was a paradigm shift for me. Not only did it spur me on to the fascinating world of OT studies, but it began to form my vision of what justice in our world would look like. He is a regular visitor at the Greek Bible College in Athens, where his teaching is always a priceless contribution.

1. D. I. Block, "Deuteronomy," in *Theological Interpretation of the Old Testament: A Book-by-Book Survey* (ed. K. J. Vanhoozer; Grand Rapids: Baker, 2008) 67; repr. as "Deuteronomy: A Theological Introduction" in idem, *The Gospel According to Moses: Theological and Ethical Reflections on the Book of Deuteronomy* (Eugene, OR: Cascade, 2012), 1–20.

2. Block, "Deuteronomy," 71.

3. There have been many attempts by scholars to outline the basis of biblical Israel's ethics and to suggest adequate ways of appropriating those ethics to the Christian

2. Human Trafficking and Ancient "Kidnapping"

Human Trafficking was defined in 2000 by the United Nations' "Trafficking in Persons Protocol," article 3, paragraph (a) as

> the recruitment, transportation, transfer, harboring or receipt of persons, by means of the threat or use of force or other forms of coercion, of abduction, of fraud, of deception, of the abuse of power or of a position of vulnerability or of the giving or receiving of payments or benefits to achieve the consent of a person having control over another person, for the purpose of exploitation. Exploitation shall include, at a minimum, the exploitation of the prostitution of others or other forms of sexual exploitation, forced labor or services, slavery or practices similar to slavery, servitude or the removal of organs.[4]

On the basis of this dense definition, three constituent elements can be drawn out: the *act*, the *means*, and the *purpose*. The *act* is what is actually done: "recruitment, transportation, transfer, harboring or receipt of persons." The *means* refer to "how" it is done: "threat or use of force, coercion, abduction, fraud, deception, abuse of power or vulnerability, or giving payments or benefits to a person in control of the victim." Finally, the *purpose* reveals "why" it is done: "for the purpose of exploitation, which includes exploiting the prostitution of others, sexual exploitation, forced labor, slavery or similar practices and the removal of organs."[5]

Church (see an overview of various positions by C. J. H. Wright, *Old Testament Ethics for the People of God* [Leicester: InterVarsity, 2004] 415–40). While there are valuable elements in each of these views, I am particularly sympathetic to W. Janzen's emphasis on the primacy of stories in ancient Israel as a way of imparting ethical images for society. Janzen asserts that OT stories do more than simply serve the purpose of illustrating a timeless principle that, once discovered, can be extracted from the story thus making the story no longer necessary (*Old Testament Ethics: A Paradigmatic Approach* [Louisville: John Knox Press, 1993]. These emphases and concerns are shared by Wright (*Old Testament Ethics for the People of God*, 70–75), who understands Israel's society and laws as a paradigm designed by God for the nations to be understood in their historical context (62–65). In the framework of his "paradigmatic" understanding of Israel, Wright also gives emphasis to principles (320–21).

One should also be aware of the dangers of hermeneutical presuppositions when approaching ancient texts for the purpose of applying them to particular contemporary situations. See, for example, F. E. Deist, "The Dangers of Deuteronomy: A Page from the Reception History of the Book," in *Studies in Deuteronomy: In Honour of C. J. Labuschagne on the Occasion of his 65th Birthday* (ed. F. García Martínez; VTSup 53; Leiden: Brill, 1994) 13–29.

4. United Nations Office on Drugs and Crime, "What is Human Trafficking?" n.p. [cited 29 May 2012]. Online: http://www.unodc.org/unodc/en/human-trafficking/what-is-human-trafficking.html.

5. Ibid.

While the book of Deuteronomy has much to say about many of the concepts involved in this definition, we shall limit ourselves to exploring one particular law that seems most relevant for the trafficking of persons today. The law that seems to share something of all three constituent elements mentioned in the above definition is the law against "kidnapping," as is found in Deut 24:7: "If a man is found stealing a soul from his brothers from the sons of Israel, and he deals with him violently (or treats him as a slave), or sells him, then that thief will die and you will purge the evil from among you."

One does not naturally connect this biblical law with human trafficking because "kidnapping" today often refers to the practice of abducting a child and returning it on receipt of a ransom payment. "Kidnapping" defined this way is not equal to the biblical "peoplestealing".[6] The term may be misleading and make us miss the relevance of this biblical law to the problem of trafficking.

Further, kidnapping is only a subcategory of human trafficking. Kidnapping is usually understood to involve physical restraint and hiding of the victim, but victims of human trafficking are not necessarily bound in chains and hidden somewhere. Usually, "[t]hey are all around us and there is no reason to believe that their exploitation is somehow reduced because they are not hidden away. Violence is the central theme of how victims are controlled. The danger of relying on kidnappings is that it paints an image of victims who are physically restrained and hidden from view. The truth is most victims are not physically restrained and not hidden from view."[7]

However, the parallel between the situations envisaged by the law in Deuteronomy and human trafficking consists, broadly speaking, in the enslavement of persons against their will,[8] possibly under conditions of mistreatment, for the personal benefit/profit of the criminal. Therefore, the term "peoplestealing" will be used instead of "kidnapping."

---

6. The term "manstealing" is usually used as an alternative to "kidnapping." I will be using "peoplestealing" as a more gender neutral term.

7. The Palermo Protocol, "Human Trafficking Misunderstood," n.p. [cited 1 June 2012]. Online: http://www.palermoprotocol.com/general/human-trafficking-misunderstood.

8. Since the element of deception is commonly present in cases of human trafficking, the victim may become aware of her enslavement at a point following his/her recruitment. In biblical law (Lev 25:39–40; Deut 15:12) we find that Israelites did sell themselves as slaves to their fellow Israelites of their own free will. Moreover, fathers would sell their daughters as slaves (Exod 21:7–8), although some sort of marriage contract was probably envisaged (see G. C. Chirichigno, *Debt-Slavery in Israel and the Ancient Near East* [JSOTSup 141; Sheffield: JSOT, 1993] 244–55). Legislation required certain conditions to be met in each of the cases to limit the exploitation of these individuals.

The law of peoplestealing in the OT is significant for the way we think about human trafficking today because it demonstrates how seriously the authors of biblical law thought about the crime of "stealing a person"—a seriousness not always reflected in how traffickers are handled in our time. Recently, an Austrian newspaper described the results of a court case involving trafficking:

> [O]n 21 March, the sound of applause echoed in the halls of a Viennese courtroom, sending shivers down the spines of the victims who had just testified against the perpetrators. Six of the traffickers arrested that night in November had just received lenient sentences, handed down by a female judge. The prosecutor remained silent; he did not appeal. "He seemed to be happy with the verdicts," recalls a police officer who attended the proceedings.
>
> "Trafficking is torture," states the Helen Bamber Foundation, a British charity that works with "survivors of cruelty". In Vienna, the torturers, five men and one woman, got off lightly. One of them was convicted to four years because he was a repeat offender; the maximum could have been ten years. Others got a few months, and two walked out of the courtroom as free men. In the media, the case was largely ignored.[9]

This case is not an isolated incident. In Greece, from 2003 to the middle of 2005, the number of people convicted on charges of human trafficking was 284, but only two of them were actually incarcerated.[10] At the moment, the new rules set EU-wide maximum penalties of at least five years of imprisonment or, in particularly aggravating circumstances, ten years of imprisonment (i.e., where children are affected, or where life is endangered, or in the case of serious violence or harm to the victim and others).[11] In the light of the biblical treatment of peoplestealing, these measures seem particularly relaxed and, as a result, human trafficking continues to flourish as the third most profitable industry of our time, after gun and drug trading, with an estimate of 20.9 million victims according to the 2012 Trafficking in Persons Report.[12] Biblical law and the ideology behind it prove to be far from primitive in their

---

9. A. Rohrer, "A Licence to Torture," n.p. [Cited 1 June 2012]. Online: http://www.viennareview.net/news/special-report/a-licence-to-torture.

10. M. Delithanasi, "Human Traffickers, Unimplemented Convictions," n.p. [Cited 1 June 2012]. Online: http://news.kathimerini.gr/4dcgi/_w_articles_ell_1_25/02/2007_217254 [Greek].

11. Council of the European Union, "Press Release 16918/10," 21. [Cited 23 June 2012]. Online: http://www.consilium.europa.eu/uedocs/cms_data/docs/pressdata/en/jha/118183.pdf.

12. U.S. Department of State, "Trafficking in Persons Report 2012," 45. [Cited 23 June 2012]. Online: http://www.state.gov/documents/organization/192587.pdf.

treatment of peoplestealing, and they stand critically over against the way such crimes are handled in our secular culture.

3. Biblical Laws against Peoplestealing

A common practice in the ancient world, peoplestealing involved the forced enslavement of a person for the personal benefit (profit or labor) of the thief. In the Old Babylonian period slaves as well as free persons were stolen for enslavement.[13] Slave traders would prey on "stray children or unlucky adults."[14]

In the OT, the prohibition against peoplestealing is "hidden" in the Decalogue under the command not to steal. The word used for "steal," in both Exod 20:15 and Deut 5:19, is the Hebrew word גנב (gānab).[15] However, in the Decalogue there is no object for this verb. This apodictic prohibition is thus expounded further in casuistic forms.

In Exodus, the prohibition against stealing in 20:15 is applied to mundane cases, such as oxen and sheep (21:37) and money and goods (22:7), although the first object of stealing mentioned in Exodus is a human being, namely a man (21:16):[16]

| וגנב איש ומכרו ונמצא בידו מות יומת | And the one who steals a man and sells him or the man is found in his hand, he will surely die. |

In Deuteronomy, however, no other example of stealing is given, except the stealing of a human being (נפש). Deut 24:7, which is the only other place in Deuteronomy besides 5:19 where the גנב root is found, reads as follows:

| כי־ימצא איש גנב נפש מאחיו מבני ישראל והתעמר־בו ומכרו ומת הגנב ההוא ובערת הרע מקרבך | If a man is found stealing a soul from his brothers from the sons of Israel, and he deals with him violently (or treats him as a slave), or sells him, then that thief will die and you will purge the evil from among you. |

---

13. E. E. Carpenter, "Deuteronomy," in *Zondervan Illustrated Bible Backgrounds Commentary* (ed. J. H. Walton; Grand Rapids: Zondervan, 2009) 1:499, 501.

14. J. H. Walton, V. H. Matthews, and M. W. Chavalas, *The IVP Bible Background Commentary: Old Testament* (Downers Grove, IL: InterVarsity, 2000) 198.

15. In some cases it can mean "to deceive," especially when the object is someone's "heart," *DCH* 2:366–67.

16. The penalties show the hierarchy of value: death when the object is man (Exod 21:16); fivefold or fourfold restitution when the object is animals (Exod 21:37[22:1]); twofold for inanimate objects (Exod 22:6[7]).

There has been much discussion as to whether the apodictic form of the command "you shall not steal" was originally directed against stealing people, since the first two of the three brief homogeneous commands ("you shall not kill," "you shall not commit adultery," "you shall not steal") have to do with crimes against basic personal rights.[17] Anthony Phillips proposes that "all ten commandments concerned either an injury to God or to the person of a fellow Israelite, but never his property . . . [and] the penalty for breach of every commandment was death, the exaction of which was mandatory, but which was never required for a property offence."[18]

David Little evaluates Phillips' view and does not find a good reason why only peoplestealing would be "apodictically" prohibited. Certain forms of acquiring another's property without that person's knowledge or consent are also implied in the commandment.[19] Indeed, there is nothing in the Decalogue requiring that only capital crimes are included. We would need to look elsewhere for the penalties for each crime.

Deuteronomy shows interest only in the capital nature of stealing, and not in property theft. The fact that no example for the "do not steal" commandment is given in the book other than peoplestealing is significant and points to the primacy given by Deuteronomy to humanitarian concerns. Moshe Weinfeld observes that there is a general lack of interest in the book for offenses relating to property, with the main emphasis being the protection of humans, particularly those whose means of protection are limited.[20]

As we look at the biblical law against peoplestealing, especially the Deuteronomic version,[21] we shall attempt to extract various elements

---

17. V. Hamp, "גנב," *TDOT* 3:42. G. von Rad says, "It is today regarded as certain that the prohibition of stealing referred originally to the kidnapping of a free person" (*Deuteronomy: A Commentary* [trans. D. Barton; Philadelphia: Westminster, 1966] 59).

18. A. Phillips, *Essays on Biblical Law* (JSOTSup 344; London: Sheffield Academic, 2002) 12–13.

19. D. Little, "Exodus 20:15, 'Thou Shalt Not Steal,'" *Int* 34 (1980) 404. Also, D. I. Block, *How I Love Your Torah, O LORD!: Studies in the Book of Deuteronomy* (Eugene, OR: Cascade, 2011) 33 n. 50.

20. Damages or civil suits forming a large part of the book of the covenant are absent in Deuteronomy—e.g., laws of assault and battery (Exod 21:18–27), the goring ox (Exod 21:28–32), theft (Exod 21:37–22:3), damage to crops (21:4–5), and the four trustees of property (22:6–14) (M. Weinfeld, "The Origin of the Humanism in Deuteronomy," *JBL* 80 [1961] 243). Also, Weinfeld notes that in the realm of ritual, "the author is unconcerned with offerings wholly consecrated to God: he restricts his concern with ritual to individual offerings which extend benefits to those who lack adequate social standing" (p. 244).

21. For the differences between Exod 21:16 and Deut 24:7 see J. H. Tigay, *Deuteronomy* (The JPS Torah Commentary; Philadelphia: JPS, 1996) 224.

relevant for the way we think about human trafficking today. While we are fully aware of the historical and cultural differences between our contemporary world and the biblical world, it is a worthwhile exercise to scrutinize our worldview against the wisdom of this ancient book and to understand the ideologies at work behind its prescriptions.

4. Why Did Peoplestealing Carry the Death Penalty?

Peoplestealing constitutes one of the thirteen capital crimes in Deuteronomy 12–26,[22] and its penalty makes one wonder why the authors thought of this crime as so severe. Various reasons can be suggested for this.

4.1. Peoplestealing is a Reversal of the Exodus and Violation of God's Property Rights

Peoplestealing carries a negative symbolism with respect to Israelite identity. Stealing and enslaving a person who had participated in the exodus signifies a *reversal* of the exodus.[23] "And you shall love the sojourner, for you were sojourners in the land of Egypt" (Deut 10:19). Through peoplestealing, the criminal is undoing the defining historic act of God that brought the entire people into "existence": that of "taking people for himself" (see Deut 4:34). Thomas Mann points to this as a justification for the severity of the penalty: "Stealing for the purpose of selling into slavery was particularly reprehensible to the ancient Hebrews precisely because it *was* part of the communal history—they came from an enslaved people."[24]

From the divine perspective, peoplestealing is in effect a violation of God's property rights. When the LORD took the people of Israel out of Egypt, he was choosing his own "inheritance" (נחלה) out of all the peoples of the earth (Deut 4:19–20; 9:26, 29; 32:9). Therefore, one could deduce that the primary victim of peoplestealing is God himself whose inheritance is being taken from him. Under such crime, a human agent is acting in defiance of the LORD's property rights and claims possession

---

22. See their discussion in L. Stulman, "Encroaching in Deuteronomy: An Analysis of the Social World of the D Code," *JBL* 109 (1990) 616.

23. Similarly J. G. McConville asserts: "Israel's status is that of those who have been set free, legally from their status as slaves in Egypt. Their new situation is the opposite of such status and contradicts it. . . . All the commands that tend to protect the independence of families and individuals, especially the poor and the socially vulnerable, are designed to resist and defy the notion of slavery. The structure of society and economics must not be allowed to re-admit slavery, once abolished, by the back door" (*Deuteronomy* [AOTC 5; Leicester: Apollos, 2002] 364).

24. T. W. Mann, *Deuteronomy* (Westminster Bible Companion; Louisville: Westminster John Knox, 1995) 84.

of another person whose sole owner is God. Stealing from the LORD would thus be the worst form of violation of the "do not steal" command and would amount to a hubristic action of attempting to replace him.

However, one may go beyond Israel and extend the LORD's property rights over all humans. Deuteronomy itself declares God's ownership of the entire cosmos: "Behold, to the LORD your God belong the heavens and the heavens of the heavens, the earth and everything in it" (Deut 10:14). Other biblical writers did not hesitate to designate *every* nation as the LORD's "inheritance" (נחלה), not just Israel (e.g., Ps 82:8). Eugene Merrill seems to extend the application of this command beyond Israel, noting that humans as God's image are his most precious possession, therefore, "[a]s with murder or any such assault upon another, the heinousness of the deed lay in its victimizing of one who was the very image of God (cf. Gen 9:6; Deut 5:17)."[25]

The idea of humans as God's possession has wider implications that are determinative of the treatment of humans not just with respect to human trafficking, but with all ways of relating to one another. Possession of people can happen in the privacy of one's home and express itself in the form of domestic violence, but it can also happen at the national level where one nation may economically enslave another through national lending.

4.2. Peoplestealing is a Social Murder

Commenting on the clearest biblical example of peoplestealing and selling, that of Joseph's sale by his brothers to Midianite traders (Gen 37:22–28), Peter Craigie notes that the outcome of peoplestealing is the "cutting off" of a person from his/her family; it is a "social murder."[26] He asserts: "*Stealing the life*—the crime is social murder, for though the victim does not literally die, by being sold into slavery he is effectively cut off from the covenant family of God. Hence the penalty for the crime is severe—death! To cut a man off from the covenant community was to cut him off from sharing in the blessing of God for his people in the promised land."[27]

This remark on social murder is still valid even when one extends it beyond ancient Israelite society. Understanding this forced enslavement as "social murder" is an accurate description of the effects (social,

---

25. E. H. Merrill, *Deuteronomy* (NAC 4; Nashville: Broadman and Holman, 1994) 320.
26. P. C. Craigie, *The Book of Deuteronomy* (NICOT; Grand Rapids: Eerdmans, 1976) 161–62.
27. Ibid., 307.

physical, and psychological) incurred by victims of human trafficking today, particularly sex trafficking. Some sort of "cutting off" takes place in various ways and in different stages. Usually, the victims are cut off from their family and friends, and even their country. Moreover, if and when a person, usually female, manages to be freed, there are tremendous difficulties in being reintegrated back into her community, even her own family. The social stigma and the shame that accompany her experience poison both familial and social relations, resulting in the permanence of this "social death." At the moment, many countries lack reintegration resources such as shelters, educational and vocational training, job placement, and financial assistance.[28]

With sexual exploitation, this "cutting off" is much deeper than with other forms of exploitation. The victim is additionally cut off from his or her own physical body—it is no longer private. In other words, sexual exploitation removes the right of ownership of one's body. Usually, the criminal has to "condition" the victim into a state of servitude through a variety of methods including "starvation, confinement, beatings, physical abuse, rape, gang rape, threats of violence to the victims and the victims' families, forced drug use and the threat of shaming their victims by revealing their activities to their family and their families' friends."[29]

To this "conditioning," Roula Printezi adds numerous health risks faced by the victims: insomnia, drug and alcohol addiction, sexually transmitted diseases such as HIV/AIDS, hepatitis B and syphilis, unwanted pregnancies, various infections, severe psychological problems, psychoses, optical and aural illusions, disconnection from social reality, and others.[30] All of these social, physical, and psychological traumas inflicted on trafficked victims should justifiably be regarded as a form of "death" that calls for a penalty fitting the crime.

It is possible that Deut 24:7 adds something regarding the tyrannical treatment of the victim by the inclusion of the verb עמר in the Hithpael. It is difficult to know the precise meaning of this word because it is used in the OT only here and in Deut 21:14, the law against selling a former wife who was a foreign captive. Jeffrey Tigay translates this as

---

28. Human Trafficking, "Reintegration," n.p. [Cited 13 June 2012]. Online: http://www.humantrafficking.org/combat_trafficking/reintegration.

29. U.S. Department of Health and Human Services, "Fact Sheet: Sex Trafficking," n.p. [Cited 2 June 2012]. Online: http://www.acf.hhs.gov/trafficking/about/fact_sex.html.

30. R. Printezi, "Illegal Transportation and Human Exploitation" (M.A. diss., Panteion University, Athens, 2004 [Greek]) 67.

"enslaving," meaning that the thief uses the victim as his own slave.[31] Another possible meaning is "trade."[32] Peter Craigie, on 21:14, takes the word as parallel to מכר: "The man was not free to sell her as a slave for money, or to *treat her as merchandise*; that is, she could not be given in exchange for some other person or goods."[33] It is possible, however, that the word in 24:7 may have the sense of "dealing tyrannically"[34] with a person, as the LXX understands it (καταδυναστεύσας 'oppress').[35] Whatever the precise meaning of the word, it seems to say something about the act against the victim as well as the victim's treatment. Daniel Block notes that it highlights the humiliation of the victims, portraying them as "chattel property treated and sold like merchandise."[36]

4.3. Peoplestealing Disrupts the Community

Another reason for the severe penalty for this crime is the detrimental effects it has on the community as a whole. This is apparent in the use of the phrase "to purge the evil from among you" (Deut 24:7). This phrase is a "justification used to identify perversions of the social order."[37] Peoplestealing is thus to be seen as a perversion of the social order. It is a type of crime capable of polluting the entire community, disrupting the fabric of society and creating a destructive way of relating to one another that stands in stark contrast to the Deuteronomic aims: ensuring the well-being of everyone, especially the most vulnerable in society. People are not to live in constant fear of their lives being violently disturbed by abduction.[38]

Since this crime upsets the entire community its confrontation should be a collective concern. This is another element highlighted by the death penalty. "Purging" was indeed a *collective* responsibility (see Deut 13:6; 17:7, 12; 19:13; 21:21, 22, 24; 24:7). The death penalty was

---

31. Tigay, *Deuteronomy*, 224.
32. *DCH* 6:489.
33. Craigie, *The Book of Deuteronomy*, 282. Also, D. L. Christensen, *Deuteronomy 21:10–34:12* (WBC 6B; Nashville: Thomas Nelson, 2002) 474.
34. *DCH* 6:488.
35. J. A. Thompson takes the verb to mean "ill-treating," "dealing harshly or cruelly," *Deuteronomy: An Introduction and Commentary* (Downers Grove, IL: InterVarsity, 1974) 246.
36. D. I. Block, *Deuteronomy* (NIVAC; Grand Rapids: Zondervan, 2012) 567.
37. J. M. Hamilton, *Social Justice and Deuteronomy: The Case of Deuteronomy 15* (SBLDS 136; Georgia: Scholars, 1992) 128. Tigay notes that this expression refers to capital punishment in every case but one, and "it expresses the view that the punishment removes a palpable evil from the people's midst" (*Deuteronomy*, 131). In the same context he also notes that the connotations of this expression are graphically evident in 1 Kgs 14:10: "I will sweep away the house of Jeroboam utterly, as dung is swept away."
38. Hamilton, *Social Justice and Deuteronomy*, 128.

usually imposed at the city gates under the direct jurisdiction of the city/community elders.[39] In this paradigmatic manner the community publically declared its opposition to this way of relating to another human being.[40]

The expression ימצא in the passive voice ('is found') makes this point as well. This verb has an unspecified subject. The subject could be anyone from the community whose testimony would count. In other words, evil resides in the land until the people discover it and bring it to the surface, and thus the command is simultaneously a call to the community to be on the lookout for such practices among them.

Today we know such practices exist in the form of human trafficking. The responsibility lies with authorities worldwide to develop and implement necessary measures for bringing these crimes to the surface and for finding and punishing the offenders. But it is the responsibility of the global Church to go beyond state laws when they are not being applied. Members of the Church are the ones who seek to "do good to all people" (Gal 6:10) and they cannot be comfortable at the sight of a suffering "neighbor." Sometimes, "street" work is necessary for spotting cases of trafficking. New Life Ministries, for example, the organization with which I am involved, has regular visits to the Red Light districts of Athens and enters the city's brothels, bars, and other places where prostitution may be taking place—all in pursuit of trafficked victims that need to be rescued and cared for.[41] The church's role is not about better "police work," although the church may use secular means in the pursuit of justice. Just as in the book of Deuteronomy, the pursuit of justice by God's people is done in the context of a holistic redefinition of humanity in the light of God's historic acts. It presupposes a careful family catechesis and a collective memory formation that emphasizes the LORD's identity as the "slave freer," the one who brings people out of Egypt (Deut 5:6).

4.4. The Penalty Preserves the Distinctiveness of Humanity

When one observes how peoplestealing is treated in law codes outside the Bible, not much can be inferred. Like the biblical instruction, the Hammurabi code requires the death of the offender (*COS* 2:338), while the Hittite code appears much lighter, requiring simply the mere

---

39. Stulman, "Encroachment in Deuteronomy," 620.

40. The punishment in the case of peoplestealing is interpreted as strangulation according to m. Sanh. 11:2 and b. Sanh. 86b. Also, in Tg. Ps.-J. the death is understood as "strangulation with a scarf."

41. New Life (http://neazoi.org/) is part of International Teams (http://www.iteams.org/).

forfeiture of property (COS 2:108).⁴² However, one needs to look more broadly at laws concerning theft in general in order to get a clearer perspective.

In the code of Hammurabi, stealing things that belong to the temple or to the king is also punishable by death. A later stratum of the code offers the opportunity for thirtyfold restitution for things stolen from the temple or the king and tenfold for things stolen from a citizen, but capital punishment is required in the case of failure to repay. At an earlier time, however, all serious thefts and burglaries seem to have been punished by death. In Assyrian law, stealing in certain cases (e.g., stealing by a wife) was punished by death, and other penalties included mutilation. In contrast, in Hittite law the only kind of theft punishable by death was stealing a bronze lance on the palace gate.⁴³

It is only by looking at theft laws more broadly in the ancient Near East that one is able to see that humans and possessions could be treated indiscriminately. The fact that a human life can be given to cover the loss of a material object is indicative of the value of human life in a culture. This stands in contrast with biblical law. Christopher Wright points to the sharp distinction Deuteronomy's commandment against theft makes between the value of human life and material possessions:

> [I]n normal Israelite judicial practice (i.e., excluding exceptional cases like Achan, where laws of war were also involved), no kind of theft of property carried the death penalty. Only theft of persons (i.e., kidnapping, usually for slave sale) was a capital offense (Exod. 21:16; Deut. 24:7). This feature of Israelite law stands in sharp contrast to the laws of theft in other ancient Near Eastern law codes, where there was a wide range of penalties, including mutilations and death, for different kinds of theft, as well as a gradation of penalties according to the social rank of the victim.⁴⁴

He notes further that, for the Deuteronomic author, "material property and human life were not to be measured in terms of each other, or substituted for each other."⁴⁵ Stealing a person had to be punished much more severely than stealing cattle or other possessions so that the hierarchy of value would be clearly reflected. Today this hierarchy is not obvious. Article 380 and paragraph 1 of the criminal code concerning

---

42. G. T. Manley notes: "The Hittite code requires, not death, but ample restitution. Other slight differences between the Hittite and Babylonian codes show how in the patriarchal age custom already varied from place to place" (*The Book of the Law: Studies in the Date of Deuteronomy* [London: Tyndale, 1957] 77 n. 3).

43. Hamp, "גָּנַב," *TDOT* 3:40.

44. C. J. H. Wright, *Deuteronomy* (NIBC 4; Peabody, MA: Hendrickson, 1996) 81–82.

45. Ibid., 82.

theft in Greece issues the same penalty, if not more severe, for stealing material things (imprisonment for five to 20 years, while the most severe penalties for human trafficking range from five to 10 years).

For Deuteronomy, the penalty should not follow the mentality behind the crime. Removing a person from the covenant community and from all the blessings that accompany that status for the sake of profit is an act of "substituting" that person's life with money. It equates the person's value with an arranged "market" price. It treats him or her as a commodity. If money could be given to compensate for stealing a person, that would be another, more subtle, form of human commodification.

Victims of human trafficking today are removed from their normal, secure, and healthy way of life and from their protection networks, and their body—indeed their life—is given in exchange for material benefits. This is too high a price to pay. The victim's life simply should *not* be equated with any amount of profit. Human life is not measurable in material terms. Opposing human trafficking today is not simply an effort to protect the victims and secure a safe society. It is a declaration and a demonstration of an anthropology that says that humanity cannot have a price tag. People cannot be commodified, because they are of immeasurable value.

This idea was preserved in Judaism all the way to the turn of the era. Jews like the Jewish philosopher Philo (20 B.C.–A.D. 50) still considered death to be the appropriate penalty for such a crime (*Special Laws* 4.19). He says, "Everyone who feels any admiration of virtue is full of exceeding anger, and is utterly implacable against kidnappers, who for the sake of most iniquitous gain dare to inflict slavery on those who are free by birth, and who partake of the same nature as themselves" (*Special Laws* 4.14). The crime is mentioned in 1 Tim 1:10, where the author adds "manstealers" (KJV) (ἀνδραποδισταῖς) in his long list of vices, a condemnable practice of the time:

> In the Hellenistic world, "kidnappers" or "slave-traders" was a term of opprobrium. Their willingness to enslave free people, to exploit them sexually, whether they be young males or females, and to flout the Aedilician Edict (the law on selling slaves and beasts of burden) was legendary—if not always a matter of fact in a particular instance. Philostratus included kidnappers on a vice list along with adulterers, the sexually immoral, clothes-stealers, and pickpockets, all of whom he compared to rabble. (*Life of Apollonius of Tyana* 4.22)[46]

---

46. R. F. Collins, *I & II Timothy and Titus* (The New Testament Library; Louisville: Westminster John Knox, 2002) 33. Philostratus was a sophist from Athens, who lived from ca. A.D. 170–247.

Finally, the book of Revelation draws a shocking picture of a society where the commodification of "human souls" has become the norm. Babylon represents a society in which merchants profit from their global trade of various goods. In Rev 18:11–13 the author presents a long list of commodities traded by these merchants, such as jewels, linen, spices, etc. The cargo climaxes, or rather, hits the bottom of the merchants' degradation with the final "commodity," which is "bodies, even the souls of humans" (καὶ σωμάτων, καὶ ψυχὰς ἀνθρώπων).[47] As the author declares the final judgment of Babylon, he seems to share Deuteronomy's stance on the horrendous nature of the crime of commodifying humans. In a way, Revelation offers us the vision of the end of human trafficking, a bright light towards which we actively proceed.

5. Conclusion

In this essay we examined the law against peoplestealing (Exod 21:16; Deut 24:7), which is the most severe infringement of the command, "you shall not steal" (Deut 5:19). Mark Briddle says, "As Deuteronomy understood it, theft is less about the property stolen and more about the value of life lived well and fully."[48] The treatment of peoplestealing cases in Deuteronomy, which has relevance to the present phenomenon of human trafficking, shows an awareness of the severe effects on the individual and his/her community and presupposes an ideology that rejects the commodification of God's most precious possession: humans.

While there are many commonalities between human trafficking and Deuteronomy's law against the capital crime of peoplestealing, our attitude towards the former has not matched the seriousness with which this crime was treated in the biblical law code. The physical, psychological, and social effects human trafficking has on the victims do constitute a type of "death" that demands to be confronted with an analogous severity in the way we perceive it, and its graveness needs to be reflected in the Church's approach to this crime.

What does the death penalty for peoplestealing teach the believers of the Church? Is it a call for them to push towards introducing capital punishment? Or is it rather an exhortation that it is appropriate for believers to respond by dedicating their lives to seeking, rescuing,

---

47. While Ezek 27:12–24 puts "souls of humans" early in the list, the author of Revelation leaves it for the end, thus creating the sense of a descending order of value these items had in the empire. See the discussion of this by G. K. Beale, *The Book of Revelation* (NIGTC; Grand Rapids: Eerdmans, 1999) 910.

48. M. E. Briddle, *Deuteronomy* (Smyth and Helwys Bible Commentary 4; Macon, GA: Smyth and Helwys, 2003) 358.

protecting, and investing in the lives of these victims—life for life? If someone must "die" for this crime to stop, should it not be the Church that gives itself over as a living sacrifice (Rom 12:1) in the manner of their Lord (Luke 9:23; 1 John 3:16), thus making a public declaration of the pricelessness of humanity?

The Book of the Torah as a Gospel of Grace
A Synthesis of Daniel I. Block's Biblical Theology of Deuteronomy

Thomas H. McClendon Jr.

The professor stepped confidently to the chalkboard and wrote from right to left the Hebrew word חָכְמָה 'wisdom'. I sat frozen in fear. This third-year-level class was my first at Bethel Theological Seminary in St. Paul, Minnesota. It was a daunting place for me at that time, although I was excited to be attending "Wisdom Literature" taught by the esteemed Dr. Daniel I. Block. I sat anxiously until he turned to assure us that we did not have to know Hebrew to succeed in the course. With that encouragement I went on to complete one of the most challenging yet enjoyable classes I have ever taken. Later, after studying Hebrew for a couple of years, I became Block's teaching assistant and learned to admire even more this man who possesses the unusual combination of a commitment to exceptional scholarship and a true pastor's heart. To find these two extraordinary qualities combined in one man is rare indeed. Block has helped countless young seminary students to see the relevance of the Old Testament in our modern world, and it is indeed a privilege to write this article as an expression of gratitude on behalf of those students who are now serving in pastorates across the world.

The goal of this essay is to synthesize Block's biblical theology of Deuteronomy. According to Block, the book of Deuteronomy is the heart of the Torah, providing the theological base for virtually the entire Old (and New) Testament. He reminds us that if we are diligent in our study, we will discover in Deuteronomy the divinely breathed, living, and transforming Scripture of which the apostle Paul spoke about in 2 Tim 3:16. Block then admonishes us, like Paul, to find in "the Book

---

Author's Note: My friend Daniel Block has been my interim pastor, my professor, and my mentor. No other man played such a crucial role in my calling as a minister of the Gospel. He is an Ezra-type man who has set his heart to study, to practice, and to teach the Word of God. Few have his combination of an academic mind and pastoral heart. He has shared personally with me his knowledge, his time and advice, his dinner table, and even his love for hostas. It is indeed a great honor to contribute to this volume.

of the Torah of Moses" an effective instrument for teaching, reproof, correction, training in righteousness, and equipping for every good work for the glory of God.[1]

This essay is shaped around the four categories highlighted in Block's *Bibliotheca Sacra* articles: (1) A Theology of the Word; (2) A Theology of Worship; (3) A Theology of Leadership; and (4) A Theology of Missions.[2] This is a natural structure that captures most of Block's biblical theology of Deuteronomy. Very little departure is made from the essays themselves, and many lines are pulled almost verbatim. It is my hope that this synthesis will move the reader to delve more deeply into Block's writings and to love the God of Deuteronomy more (Deut 6:5).

1. A Theology of the Word

None can question the great privilege we have today in living after the death, resurrection, and ascension of Christ, the word made flesh. In Jesus, we encounter a glory permeated with grace and truth, "glory as of the only Son from the Father" (John 1:14). With such amazing grace in our foreground, it is often easy to think that ancient Israel, pre-cross, had experienced no real glory and grace. However, as the apostle Paul stresses: To them "belong the adoption, the glory, the covenants, the giving of the law, the worship, and the promises"; "to them belong the patriarchs, and from their race . . . is the Christ" (Rom. 9:4–5).

Block opens his article, "The Grace of Torah," by stating, "The power of God's Word is seen in the Old Testament in several ways."[3] Block's stress is on the fact that Old Testament Israel was truly a privileged nation. They knew that God had spoken the universe into existence and had determined the course of their history. They were aware that God's word is even powerful in calling people to life and declaring their

---

1. D. I. Block, "Recovering the Voice of Moses: The Genesis of Deuteronomy," *JETS* 44, no. 3 (2001) 385–408 (407–8); republished in idem, *The Gospel according to Moses: Theological and Ethical Reflections on the Book of Deuteronomy* (Eugene, OR: Cascade, 2012), 21–51.

2. The *Bibliotheca Sacra* articles, respectively, include the following: D. I. Block, "The Grace of Torah," *BSac* 162 (Jan–Mar 2005) 3–22; idem, "The Joy of Worship: The Mosaic Invitation to the Presence of God," *BSac* 162 (Apr–June 2005) 131–49; idem, "The Burden of Leadership: The Mosaic Paradigm of Kingship," *BSac* 162 (July–Sept 2005) 259–78; idem, "The Privilege of Calling: The Mosaic Paradigm for Missions," *BSac* 162 (Oct–Dec 2005) 387–405. These four articles can also be found, respectively, in idem, *How I Love Your Torah, O LORD! Studies in the Book of Deuteronomy* (Eugene, OR: Cascade, 2011) 1–20, 98–117, 118–39, 140–61.

3. Block, "The Grace of Torah," 3–22 (3); idem, *How I Love Your Torah*, 1–20 (1).

death.[4] But what about the power of his written word? In other words, how are we to understand the nature and significance of Israel's torah revealed through Moses?

Block reminds us that these stipulations, ordinances, and laws were to be passed from one generation to another. The assumption was that children would look to their parents for an explanation of their way of life, and the parents were to be able to answer them from God's word. The word of God was to affect how they lived in every area of their lives. It was to be an "all of life" experience.

Some may mistakenly feel sorry for the Israelites because of the supposed hardship of obeying the law. However, we must understand the great privilege the nation of Israel had by God revealing his will. If we were to take a poll today concerning the significance of the law for Israel, most would answer that the law was intended as the way of salvation. Many would argue that whereas after the cross people are saved by grace, God's people in the Old Covenant were saved by keeping the law. We can be thankful for Block's clarity that this explanation "flies in the face of Paul's explicit statements that even in the Old Testament people (like Abraham) were justified by faith rather than obedience to the law" (Romans 4; Gal 3:1–12).[5]

Others argue that the significance of the law lies in its power to enslave those under the law and to demonstrate their desperate need for a Savior. However, Block rightly asks, why would God rescue the Israelites from slavery in Egypt only to give them a heavier burden of the law, a law which they were unable to keep?[6]

1.1. Moses' First Answer

According to Block, Moses addressed the torah's significance in two ways, both of which stress that the law was a gift of honor for Israel and was neither burdensome nor a way of salvation. First, Block observes that "knowledge of the will of God is the supreme privilege of the covenant people of God."[7] He highlights this matter by observing three points Moses makes in Deut 4:1–8 regarding the significance of the law. First, total acceptance to God's will is the correct and reasonable response to the amazing grace shown by God in redeeming them, calling them to covenant relationship, and commissioning them to

---

4. Ibid.
5. Block, "The Grace of Torah," 6; idem, *How I Love Your Torah*, 5.
6. Block, "The Grace of Torah," 7; idem, *How I Love Your Torah*, 5.
7. Block, "The Grace of Torah," 7; idem, *How I Love Your Torah*, 5.

represent him in the world (vv. 1–2). Second, obedience to God's word is the key to life; it is a matter of life and death (vv. 3–4). Serving pagan gods brings death. In contrast, holding fast to Yahweh and his word is rewarded with life. Third, Moses affirmed that the knowledge of the torah was the highest benefit imaginable, for no other nation had a god so near or laws so clear as Israel (vv. 5–8).

This viewpoint may catch many people today by surprise. Most would see the commandments as obligatory duty rather than privilege and consider the nation of Israel as a sorrowful and burdened people. In contrast, however, this great nation had received a revelation of the will of God, a revelation that would make them a holy people, and bring them life, prosperity, and a promised land.

Citing the second millennium Sumerian "Prayer to Every God" (*ANET* 391–92), Block charges the reader to consider Israel's neighbors who did not have a revelation of God and thus were faced with three insurmountable obstacles—namely, they did not know (1) which god they had offended, (2) the nature of their offense, or (3) what would actually satisfy the gods. In contrast, Yahweh was near to Israel when they called on him, and they had a clear knowledge of his will (4:1–8). Because of divine revelation, Israel knew Yahweh as their God and knew what constituted sin and how that sin could be removed and peace established.

1.2. Moses' Second Answer

Moses' second statement regarding the meaning and purpose of the law comes in Deut 6:20–25. When children ask their parents about the law's significance, Moses calls them to respond:

> We were Pharaoh's slaves in Egypt. And the LORD brought us out of Egypt with a mighty hand. And the LORD showed signs and wonders, great and grievous, against Egypt and against Pharaoh and all his household, before our eyes. And he brought us out from there, that he might bring us in and give us the land that he swore to give to our fathers. And the LORD commanded us to do all these statutes, to fear the LORD our God [or, to practice all these ordinances as an expression of the fear of the LORD our God], for our good always, that he might preserve us alive, as we are this day. And it will be righteousness for us, if we are careful to do all these commandments before the LORD our God, as he has commanded us.[8]

Moses' point is clear: "Obedience to the will of God is the supreme delight of the covenant people of God."[9] The law is not a system of rules

---

8. Unless otherwise noted, all translations are from the English Standard Version.
9. Block, "The Grace of Torah," 13; idem, *O How I Love Your Torah*, 11.

but is designed to guide a proper response to the salvation that Yahweh graciously provided by his mighty power and grace. Following God through obedience is a mark of gratitude.

In Deut 6:20–25, the foundation of Israel's covenant relationship with Yahweh is detailed as follows: rescue from bondage, performance of signs and wonders, deliverance from bondage in order to gain the land of promise, and the revelation of God's will. Because of all this, Block rightly observes that the giving of the law was a climactic moment of divine grace. God freed his chosen people from slavery and claimed them as his own, giving them stipulations, decrees, and laws not as a burden but as a privilege. The Israelites were liberated from the bondage of Egypt that they might become the privileged servants—and even "sons"—of the Lord (Deut 14:1).

In support of this view, Block cites John 1:16–17: "For from his fullness we have all received, grace upon grace. For the law was given through Moses; grace and truth came through Jesus Christ." God's grace was mediated through Moses; personified in Christ. Significantly, the contrast here is not between law and grace, but between two ways in which grace has been communicated: the grace and truth given through Christ are built "upon" the grace of torah mediated through Moses.

So when our children ask us why we go to church, why we put money in the offering plate, or why we speak out against the evils of our day, can we speak as Moses did? The answer is emphatic: Such acts represent a glorious privilege. Our obedience to God's word is a way of saying "thank you" to God for delivering us from the bondage of sin. Obeying God's commandments for Israel was to be a delight, and so it should be for believers today.

To those who regard the law as a burden, Moses responds (Deut 6:24–25): Yahweh graciously gave Israel the law (1) as a visible means of demonstrating her fear of him, (2) for her own good, (3) so that she might live, and (4) that she might be confident of his approval. God makes it clear what it means to be righteous.

According to Deut 6:20–25, when a member of the covenant community obeyed the law, Yahweh accepted it as evidence of that person's righteousness. This text, therefore, clarifies one of the most fundamental questions concerning the relationship between human works and human righteousness. Moses in no way viewed obedience to the commandments as Israel's means of salvation, for her position as God's people rested entirely on Yahweh's saving actions, independent of human merit. Furthermore, Moses is clear that a relationship with God could only be enjoyed when his people followed him closely through obedience to his commandments.

Gen 15:6 provides us with a clear picture of Old Testament faith: Abraham believed Yahweh and it was reckoned to him as righteousness. We see the patriarch's trust in God and a demonstration of his loyalty in the way he obeyed the Lord's commands. Similarly, Moses' point was that Israel should demonstrate her loyalty by concrete acts of obedience. When these arose out of genuine faith, Yahweh accepted this obedience of faith as a proof of righteousness and responded with blessings of life. In contrast, with the absence of obedience, Yahweh responded with curses and death.

1.3. Applications

In light of the teaching in Deut 6:20–25, Block ends his theology of torah calling Christians to form deliberate strategies for transmitting our faith. The text highlights the absolute imperative of keeping our faith alive from generation to generation. Furthermore, Block notes that 6:20–25 teaches clearly the difference between law and grace within the divine plan of salvation and sanctification. The Scriptures consistently teach that no one may merit the saving favor of God by performing works of righteousness (Rom 3:23).

In the end, Block sees no conflict or gulf between law and grace. The law was a gracious gift to Israel. It was a constant reminder of Yahweh's deliverance, his power, his faithfulness, and the key to life and prosperity. The gospel of salvation is by grace alone through faith alone. God is gracious to give us a standard of righteousness by which his redeemed people may live and be confident of his approval.

In conclusion, Block asks the question, how can this perspective be reconciled with Paul's statements regarding the death-dealing effect of the law in contrast to the life that comes by the spirit (Rom 2:12–13; 4:13–15; 7:6, 8–9; 8:2–4; 2 Cor 3:6; Gal 3:12–13, 21–24; 5:18)? Block responds with several important considerations.

First, Moses has already made the point that the law gives life. It is an outward expression of an inner heart change. The basic Old Testament stance is summarized by Hab 2:4: "As for the proud one, his soul is not right on the inside; but the righteous in his faithfulness shall live" (Block's translation). Ezekiel also declares that the "righteous" person "shall surely live" but that the one who has committed abominations "shall surely die" (Ezek 18:9, 13). Thankfully, Ezekiel continues: "If a wicked person turns away from all his sins that he has committed and keeps all my statutes and does what is just and right, he shall surely live" (18:21). In Ezekiel's mind, forgiveness of the wicked and true reconciliation with God is possible.

Block believes that Paul was not correcting an earlier revelation. Instead, Moses and Paul were in perfect agreement. "Both Testaments attest to the same paradigm: (a) The Lord's gracious (i.e., unmerited) saving actions yield the fruit of a redeemed people. (b) A redeemed people yield the fruit of righteous deeds. (c) Righteous deeds yield the fruit of divine blessing."[10]

In conclusion, what follows is Block's summary attempt to capture the lasting relevance of Deut 6:20–25 for Christians:

> When our children ask us in days to come, what is the meaning of the ordinances and customs that we Christians observe, then we will say: "We were slaves to sin, but the Lord rescued us from the kingdom of darkness with a strong hand, through the work of Christ on the cross and by raising Him from the dead. Moreover He showed great and distressing signs and wonders before the prince of the powers of this world and his followers. He has brought us out from there in fulfillment of His promises and in accord with His glorious plan of salvation, in order to bring us into an inheritance eternal and imperishable. So the Lord commanded us to observe His commandments as an expression of our fear and love for Christ for our good always and for our survival as His people. And it will be righteousness for us if we are careful to show that we love God with all our hearts by doing all that He commanded us. Then we will hear Him say, "Well done, good and faithful servant. Enter into the joy of your Life."[11]

2. A Theology of Worship

Block opens his article, "The Joy of Worship,"[12] noting how many churches today continue to battle over worship styles—a topic that receives little direct guidance from the New Testament. He writes, "Nowhere does it tell us how to build churches, meet on Sundays, have morning worship services, open with a song and a prayer, have a sermon, or even close with a benediction."[13] The crisis, he argues, is due to the lack of a biblical theology of worship. Block believes that Deut 12:1–14 may help in this matter.

---

10. Block, "The Grace of Torah,"22; idem, *How I Love Your Torah*, 20.
11. Ibid.
12. Block, "The Joy of Worship," 131–49; idem, *How I Love Your Torah*, 98–117.
13. Block, "The Joy of Worship," 131–32; idem, *How I Love Your Torah*, 98.

While many scholars hear in the speeches of Deuteronomy the voices of a scribe or even a priest, Block maintains that the style of the speaker is better understood as a pastor nearing the end of his tenure as shepherd of God's sheep (Num 27:15–17). Moses was concerned with the future spiritual and physical well-being of the people, especially their relationship with God. Deut 12:1–14 represents Moses' specific instruction to his people on living a life of faith and godliness.

While the covenant relationship has its roots in the call of Abraham, it was formalized with Abraham's descendants at Mount Sinai, "the mountain of God." This was the divine palace to which the people were invited to meet with the Lord of all the earth and redeemer of all his people. Later they would be charged with building a tabernacle, which would operate as God's palace. These special places provided a context for the Israelites to maintain their covenant relationship with Yahweh.

The design and décor of the tabernacle was to reflect the glory and majesty of its divine resident. At the time of Moses, the tabernacle needed to be portable, but the travels of the shrine would not go on indefinitely. Someday Yahweh would identify a particular place where his name would dwell.

Block divides Deuteronomy 12 into three parts: Moses invitation to worship (vv. 2–7), Moses' description of the nature of true worship (vv. 8–12), and Moses' concluding exhortation (vv. 13–14). The purpose of his article, "The Joy of Worship," is "to explore the substance of this passage by noting the contrast between true and false worship."[14]

2.1. Who Is the Object of True Worship?

The gods of the nations surrounding Israel were the products of the futile imagination of depraved human minds.[15] They were simply the work of human hands and could not see, hear, eat, or smell; they were certainly not worthy of human homage (Deut 4:28). This worship of such an inferior creature is abhorrent to a living, eternal God.

In contrast, Yahweh had established himself as "the God of your fathers" (12:1), leading to his adopting the Israelites as sons, setting them apart as his holy people, and choosing them as his royal treasure. In Block's words, "A starker contrast between Israel's God and the gods of the nations can scarcely be imagined."[16]

---

14. Block, "Joy of Worship," 134; idem, *How I Love Your Torah*, 101.

15. For more on this, see D. I. Block, *The Gods of the Nations: Studies in Ancient Near Eastern National Theology* (Evangelical Theological Society Studies; 2nd ed.; Grand Rapids: Baker, 2000).

16. Block, "The Joy of Worship," 136; idem, *How I Love Your Torah*, 103.

2.2. Who Are the Subjects of True Worship?

Deuteronomy 12 speaks of two kinds of worship. On the one hand it speaks of "the nations whom you shall dispossess" (v. 2), whose worship Yahweh abhors. In contrast, Moses invites households to worship the LORD. Moses perceives Israel as a community of faith that was to gather regularly to worship in God's presence (Deut 12:7, 12, 18). They were "a chosen people in a chosen land gathered at the chosen place for worship of the One who had graciously chosen them."[17]

This is a remarkable statement. Moses is declaring that in the presence of God all believers are equal and have equal access to him. According to Block, when Paul wrote that "there is neither Jew nor Greek, slave nor free, male nor female, for you are all one in Christ Jesus" (Gal 3:28), he was not addressing an Old Testament problem but correcting a certain ethnocentrism held by some Second Temple Jews.

2.3. Where Is the Place of Worship?

Block maintains that Deut 12:5 is one of the most important verses in Deuteronomy for understanding the history of Israelite worship: "the place that the LORD your God will choose out of all your tribes to put his name and make his habitation there" represents one of twenty-one occurrences of "the place formula" in Deuteronomy.[18] Block makes four fundamental observations about "the place." First, it is a place that Yahweh would choose. Second, the place was to be chosen from "all your tribes." Third, the place would have Yahweh's name on it. The expression speaks of divine ownership where his name would be remembered (Exod 20:24). Fourth, the place would be a dwelling place for the LORD.

By not naming the location, Moses kept the focus on the person rather than the place. Later Jerusalem became the final resting place of the central sanctuary, but the important point for Moses was the presence of Yahweh himself. Access to Yahweh is not a privilege reserved for the few; it is for all.

2.4. What Is the Motivation for True Worship?

Block argues that Deuteronomy 12 provides reasons why future generations should be motivated to worship Yahweh. First, God would give them the land promised to their ancestors (vv. 1, 10). Second, he would bless the Israelites in all their economic activities (v. 7). Third, he would give them rest (v. 9). Fourth, he would give Israel the land of

---

17. Block, "The Joy of Worship," 137; idem, *How I Love Your Torah*, 104.
18. Deut 12:5, 11, 14, 18, 21, 26; 14:23–25; 15:20; 16:2, 6–7, 11, 15–16; 17:8, 10; 18:6; 26:2; 31:11.

Canaan as their special grant. Fifth, he would provide security for them (v. 10). Block summarizes, "Worship involves a glorious celebration of privilege and relationship, rather than fright and manipulation."[19]

2.5. What Are the Characteristics of True Worship?

Deuteronomy 12 includes hints of both the right and the wrong ways to worship. True worship does not take its cues from the world. It is designed not by the worshiper but by the one who receives worship.

Block sees five dimensions of the invitation to worship highlighted in verses 5–7. First, Moses invited the Israelites to come to where Yahweh would reside. This was an offer to fellowship with God on a regular basis. Second, Moses bade Israel to come and enter the place where Yahweh resides. This is the Old Testament equivalent to Jesus' invitations: "Come to me, all who labor and are heavy laden" (Matt 11:28), and "If anyone thirsts, let him come to me and drink" (John 7:37). True worship occurs in God's presence by his request. Third, Moses called the Israelites to bring all their offerings to God to the place where he would establish His name (Deut 12:6, 11). Fourth, Moses encouraged the Israelites to eat there in the presence of their God. Whereas at Sinai the elders of Israel observed the glorious presence of Yahweh as they ate and drank, here the privilege was for all believers. It is an invitation to be guests at a banquet prepared by the living God. Fifth, the Israelites were asked to celebrate God's blessings on their work.

Block writes that many Christians think of Israelite worship as simply boring and repetitive rituals, but Deuteronomy presents worship as a spontaneous response of all members who personally enter into God's presence. Moses set the mode of worship by using the verb "rejoice," which occurs in various forms seven times in connection with appearing before Yahweh.[20]

Although the privilege of access is extended to all individuals, this worship was not to be individualistic. True worship celebrates the vertical relationship that manifests itself in horizontal charity. The blessings that worshipers celebrate are to be shared (Deut 12:18; 16:11, 14; 26:11).

2.6. Concluding Reflections on Worship

What lessons on worship for today can be gained from this passage? Block lists six:[21]

---

19. Block, "Joy of Worship,"142; *How I Love Your Torah*, 110.
20. Deut 12:7, 12, 18; 14:26; 16:11, 14; 26:11.
21. Block, "The Joy of Worship," 148–49; idem, *How I Love Your Torah*, 116–17.

1. The only legitimate object of worship is Yahweh, who created heaven and earth, redeemed Israel, and appeared as the divine and incarnate Son, Jesus Christ. All other objects of worship are both illegitimate and abominable.
2. The only persons who may worship God legitimately are the redeemed, those who have experienced God's gracious redemption and enjoyed his mercy.
3. True worship involves an audience with the divine King. Entrance into the presence of God is a privilege to be accepted with humility and awe.
4. In true worship the location is less important than the presence of the divine Host. Jesus' conversation with the Samaritan woman in John 4:21–24 about worshiping "in spirit and truth" indicates that worship must be driven by the word of God and the spirit of God. Likewise, according to Moses, the object of worship has been more important than the place.
5. The redeemed anticipate worship with delight and sobriety. What God says is always more important than what the believers say to him (Deut 12:6–11). Worship is never to be entered into flippantly.

True public worship is communal rather than private. It includes all needy people. Those who are overwhelmed by their own unworthiness on the one hand and the grace of God on the other will be more concerned about pleasing Yahweh than about pleasing themselves. If God's people are united about anything, it should be about the joy and privilege of worshiping him together!

In light of these lessons, we pray with Block: "May the Lord renew in his church a passion to worship him in spirit and in truth. May those who have been redeemed answer his invitation to come and celebrate his grace for the glory of God."[22] Amen.

3. A Theology of Leadership

In his article, "The Burden of Leadership," Block states that the church in America is experiencing a crisis of leadership with respect to style and definition.[23] In response, Block directs readers to Deut 17:14–20, which he believes to be "the most eloquent presentation of servant leadership in the Old Testament."[24] Here Moses gives instructions concerning the conduct of Israel's future kings.

---

22. Block, "The Joy of Worship," 149; idem, *How I Love Your Torah*, 117.
23. Block, "The Burden of Leadership," 259–78 (259); idem, *How I Love Your Torah*, 118–39 (118); cf. idem, "Leader, Leadership, OT," in *New Interpreter's Dictionary of the Bible* (5 vols.; ed. K. D. Sakenfeld; Nashville: Abingdon, 2008) 3:621–26.
24. Block, "The Burden of Leadership," 260; idem, *How I Love Your Torah*, 119.

3.1. What Circumstances Call for this Paradigm of Leadership?

The opening clause of Deut 17:14 anticipates a future when Israel has entered, taken possession of, and established residence in the promised land. Deut 17:14a sets the *context*: "When you come to the land . . . and you possess it and dwell in it. . . ." Verse 14b announces the *key issue*: "and then [you] say, 'I will set [or install] a king over me, like all the nations that are around me." Verse 15 then declares the *divine response*: "You may indeed set a king over you whom the LORD your God will choose. . . . You may not put a foreigner over you, who is not your brother."

The present request catches the reader by surprise. Up to this point Israel had neither asked for a king nor raised the issue of a human monarchy. However, ancient Near Eastern kings were expected to fill several roles, and it makes sense that the broader ancient Near Eastern culture would influence Israel. First, as warrior, the king was to lead his nation in battle and protect them from outside threats. Second, as chief judge, the king was to guarantee justice within the nation. Third, as patron of worship, the king was to maintain places of worship, providing materials and personnel for religious rituals.

In Deut 17:16–20, Moses repudiated prevailing models of kingship for Israel. They were not to be like all the nations around them (v. 14). Moses had spoken repeatedly of the seductive attractions of the Canaanite religion, and here he specifies that they must not follow the political system of those whom they would displace.

Although one may question the motivation behind Israel's request for a king (see 1 Samuel 8), Moses' response was positive: "You may indeed set a king over you" (Deut 17:15). This statement represents a granting of permission to act according to the people's desire, showing that Israel's constitution was not opposed in principle to a monarchical system. Nevertheless, Moses narrowed the qualifications of candidates for kingship, and then he set limits on the conduct of any who would be installed as king (17:16–20).

3.2. What Qualifies a Person for this Kind of Leadership?

First, the king must be chosen by the LORD. The concept of divine election runs throughout Deuteronomy: Yahweh chose Israel as his people; he chose a place to establish his name; and he chose priests from the tribe of Levi. And now God is laying the groundwork for choosing a king from the people of Israel to govern the nation for him.

Second, he must be a fellow Israelite. This point was made emphatically by declaring that the candidate must be one "from among your brothers . . . not . . . a foreigner" (Deut 17:15). In Block's words, "According to Moses the people were to be ruled by a viceroy of the Lord chosen from their own ranks, not someone brought in as an expert from outside."[25]

3.3. How a True Leader Exercises True Leadership

Having expressed his fundamental support of the appointment of a king, Moses turned his attention to the manner in which the responsibilities of kingship were to be exercised (Deut 17:16–20). Moses described the duties of a future king in two parts: (1) proscriptions intended to prevent common abuses of the office (vv. 16–17) that could arise out of ambition and greed (vv. 16–17); (2) the spiritual and ethical prescriptions for the king, portrayed in his submission to Yahweh and his humility (vv. 18–20).

3.3.1. The Danger: Ambition (vv. 16–17)

Moses signaled his transition to a new phase of his instructions with the restrictive particle רק, "only, except." This emphatic particle applies to all four negative commands, although they may be considered as three prohibitions, for the first two relate to multiplying horses. Each of these commands has significant symbolic significance: multiplying for himself horses, women, and silver and gold.

Lust for Power: The Prohibition Regarding Horses. Moses' first proscription prohibited the king from multiplying horses for himself. Although horses were sometimes used to transport goods, they were used primarily for pulling chariots. Fleets of chariots gave a great military advantage over foot soldiers when battles were conducted on flat terrain (Deut 20:1, Josh 17:16–18, Judg 1:19). The kings of Israel were not to look to horses and chariots as guarantors of security (Ps 20:7, Isa 20:16). As Moses wrote elsewhere: "When you go out to war against your enemies, and see horses and chariots and an army larger than your own, you shall not be afraid of them, for the LORD your God is with you, who brought you up out of the land of Egypt" (Deut 20:1).

In addition to this basic prohibition against the multiplication of horses, the king must never send Israelites back to Egypt to acquire horses (17:16b). The prohibition seems to be based on the possibility that the king might reverse the exodus and lead his people back into bondage, thereby undoing the salvific acts Yahweh had accomplished through Moses.

---

25. Block, "The Burden of Leadership," 265; idem, *How I Love Your Torah*, 125.

The Lust for Status: The Prohibition Regarding Women. The second command prohibited the king from multiplying women in his court (Deut 17:17). According to Block, this statement is the closest the Old Testament comes to prohibiting having more than one wife.

In the ancient Near East, kings would amass large harems for numerous reasons. First, a harem gave the king unlimited opportunities to satisfy his sexual passions with the most beautiful women in the kingdom. Second, these marriages strengthened alliances with other states and many outside rulers. Third, the larger the harem the more impressed foreign visitors would be. In short, one of the functions was to enhance the status of the king amongst his international peers.

Instead of condemning these motivations, the prohibition is simply stated: "lest his heart turn away." As Block notes, "Like wine and strong drink, the lust for pleasure and status could lead to intoxication that would turn the king's heart away from God and his mind away from the rational exercise of his office (Prov 31:3–9)."[26] Instead, the king was to love Yahweh his God exclusively.

The Lust for Wealth: The Prohibition Regarding Silver and Gold. Moses' third prohibition pertained to the king's excessive accumulation of material wealth (Deut 17:17). According to Block, Moses probably had in mind the accumulation of private wealth by imposing heavy taxes on the citizens of Israel. In contrast, kings were to maintain a modest lifestyle and were never to consider themselves superior to their countrymen (v. 20).

Synthesis. These three restrictions address temptations common to people in leadership: the purchase of horses, the enjoyment of women, or the accumulation of worldly goods. What Moses bans specifically, however, was the king's accumulation of all of these *for personal gain*, as is highlighted by the threefold repetition of the prepositional phrase "for himself."[27] As Block asserts, "Persons are placed in positions of leadership for the sake of those they are called to lead, not for their own sakes."[28]

3.3.2. The Demand: Submission (vv. 18–20)

According to Block, "this torah" in Deuteronomy is best understood minimally as Moses' second address (5:1b–26:19 and 28:1–68) and maximally as the entire collection of Moses' speeches preserved in the

---

26. Block, "The Burden of Leadership," 268; idem, *How I Love Your Torah*, 128.
27. Block, "The Burden of Leadership," 269; idem, *How I Love Your Torah*, 129.
28. Ibid.

book.²⁹ Block observes three distinct commands in Deut 17:18–20 all related to this torah: the command to copy the torah, the command to wear the torah, and the command to read the torah.

The Command to Copy the Torah. Block writes that the charge for the king to produce a copy of the torah is remarkable on five counts.³⁰ First, it suggests that Moses recognized the canonical status of his teaching. Second, the king is not one who writes the laws, but one who receives them from a higher authority and is subject to them. Third, the charge assumes that the king can read and write, that he is literate. Fourth, the charge identifies the document to be copied as a copy of the torah (Deut 17:18). Block argues that calling Deuteronomy a second law "clouds the fact that the overriding tone of the book is homiletical, expository, and rhetorical, rather than legal."³¹ Fifth, God instructed Moses to copy the torah on a scroll in the presence of the Levitical priest. In this case one should think of a specially tanned leather scroll of sheep or goat skin that could be carried around and stored for protection.

The Command to Wear the Torah. The command for the torah to be with the king parallels how, in the ancient world of suzerain-vassal relationships, the vassal would receive a written copy of the covenant, which he then deposited in the temple of his chief deity who provided oversight of the document. As Block notes, the king was not to treat the torah as a museum piece or an object to be retrieved only periodically and have read before him. It was not to be treated as a good luck charm, but the king was to carry it with him as a constant reminder of his personal vassal status and as a guide of his conduct.³² A comparable teaching is picked up and applied to parental commands and instructions (Prov 1:8–9; 3:3, 21–22; 6:20–21).

The Command to Read the Torah. The command that "he shall read it all the days of his life" governs Deut 17:19–20. Following the prescription itself are four purpose clauses, all of which echo earlier injunctions to the people. According to Moses, faithful reading of the torah is the key to four things: (1) a proper relationship with Yahweh, the divine suzerain; (2) a proper relationship with fellow members of the covenant community; (3) staying on course in one's devotion to the Lord; and (4) a secure future for the king and his sons.³³

---

29. Ibid.
30. Block, "The Burden of Leadership," 270–72; idem, *How I Love Your Torah*, 130–32.
31. Block, "The Burden of Leadership," 271; idem, *How I Love Your Torah*, 131.
32. Block, "The Burden of Leadership," 273; idem, *How I Love Your Torah*, 131.
33. Block, "The Burden of Leadership," 273–74; idem, *How I Love Your Torah*, 133–34.

3.3.3. Synthesis

In at least six ways, the model of Israelite kingship stood in direct contrast to leadership models of other nations.[34] First, Israelite kings were not to gain power by sheer force, but in response to a democratic impulse and a favorable response to Yahweh. Second, Israelites were to be governed by one of their own, who was himself under the authority of God. Third, Israelite kings were forbidden to amass power and wealth for themselves whereas the kings of other nations used their positions to satisfy their lust for power, status, and wealth. Fourth, the role of Israelite kings was to embody the divinely revealed standard of covenantal justice whereas other kings were administrators of justice demanding absolute loyalty. Fifth, instead of interpreting or teaching the torah, the Israelite king could only demonstrate its intent by modeling it. Sixth, the Israelite king was to be a brother of his people and a model citizen whereas the kings of other ancient Eastern nations were elevated above their countrymen. The king's countrymen should be able to recognize that if they imitate him, their own well-being in the land would be secured. At the same time the consequences of not fearing and obeying Yahweh are clearly spelled out in the covenant curses (Deut 28:58–68).

3.4. Concluding Reflections on Leadership

In the concluding section of the essay, Block draws out a number of leadership principles for contemporary ministry from Deut 17:14–20.[35] First, the paradigm presented here suggests that the forms of leadership in the church need not necessarily follow a prescribed order. Kingship was not prescribed; it was permitted. Second, God's people must choose their leaders. In other words, churches today must be led by persons the congregation as a whole recognizes as being called by God. Third, church leaders exist for the well-being of the people they lead. They are not to exploit their position for personal advantage or selfish gain. The lust for power, the lust for status, and the lust for wealth remain temptations in every age. Instead of power or privilege, servant leadership is always about securing the well-being of those under the leader's charge. Fourth, for the sake of function in ministry, leaders may be perceived as above their peers, but they themselves must acknowledge their subordination to God. There is not a word said about administrative gifts or persuasive talent, but much is written concerning accountability for one's personal conduct. Fifth, few leaders in Israel's

---

34. Block, "The Burden of Leadership," 274–76; idem, *How I Love Your Torah*, 135–36.
35. Block, "The Burden of Leadership," 276–78; idem, *How I Love Your Torah*, 137–39.

history even came close to modeling the ideals of the torah presented here. Jesus the Messiah, who came not to bring an end to the torah but to fulfill it (Matt 5:17), is the one who performed this regal role perfectly. He serves as the perfect embodiment of the ideals of covenant relationship as represented in the torah. Sixth, before leaders presume to teach and create visions of growth, they must personally embody the ideals of covenant relationship to which the people have bound themselves. Church leaders must walk according to God's word in order to model for people the direct link between knowing the word and fearing and obeying Yahweh (Deut 31:9–13).

Block ends this article by calling church leaders, through the work of the Holy Spirit and the written word of God, to shepherd "according to God" (1 Pet 5:2). This means leading "with their own lives before they lead with their ideas and gifts."[36] Only when God's definition of leadership is affirmed will the Church find fruition in the mission to which the Lord has called it.

4. A Theology of Missions

In his article, "The Privilege of Calling,"[37] Block uses George W. Peters' distinctions for mission strategies. Two words are important here: centrifugal and centripetal. Centrifugal universality is the method of missions that acts in a direction away from the center or axis, as when a gospel messenger crosses frontiers to carry the good news to people of no faith. Centripetal universality proceeds or acts in a direction toward a center or axis. It operates like a magnetic force, drawing distant peoples to a central place, people, or person.[38]

The centripetal feature of God's mission strategy in the Old Testament is seen in Yahweh's rescuing Israel from slavery and drawing them into a covenant relationship in order that the world might be attracted to the light of his glory. The centrifugal feature of missions becomes more clearly illuminated in the New Testament as the disciples of the Lord Jesus are transformed and then sent out into the world with his transforming power.

With these features in mind, Block turns his attention to Deut 26:16–19, which he believes echoes Exod 19:3–6 and is vitally important for the shaping of a biblical perspective on missions. He outlines the passage as follows: (a) the basis of Israel's calling, (b) the essence of Israel's calling, and (c) the keys to the fulfillment of Israel's calling.

---

36. Block, "The Burden of Leadership," 278; idem, *How I Love Your Torah*, 139.
37. Block, "The Privilege of Calling," 387–405; idem, *How I Love Your Torah*, 140–61.
38. Block, "The Privilege of Calling," 387; idem, *How I Love Your Torah*, 140–41.

4.1. The Literary Context, Structure, and Style of Deuteronomy 26:16–19

In Block's perspective, the significance of these four short verses is quite out of proportion to their length, for they summarize several of the key theological issues of the book, function as a hinge within Moses' second address, and remind Israel of the primary goals of the covenant. Besides looking back, these verses also look forward, particularly to Deut 28:1: "And if you faithfully obey the voice of the LORD your God, being careful to do all his commandments that I command you today, the LORD your God will set you high above all the nations of the earth."

4.2. The Basis of Israel's Calling

Israel's missionary calling was based on God's previous gracious workings on their behalf (Exod 19:4–6). Israel should be eternally grateful (a) because God rescued them from the Egyptians, (b) because he cared for them throughout their history, and (c) because he brought them to himself. This last point supplies an important principle for missions: "God did not call Israel basically to a code of conduct but to a relationship to Himself."[39]

The covenant relationship provides the context for rightly understanding Deut 26:17–19, which reads:

> You have declared today that the LORD is your God, and that you will walk in his ways, and keep his statutes and his commandments and his rules, and will obey his voice. And the LORD has declared today that you are a people for his treasured possession, as he has promised you, and that you are to keep all his commandments, and that he will set you in praise and in fame and in honor high above all nations that he has made, and that you shall be a people holy to the LORD your God, as he promised.

These verses seem to presuppose an oral version of a covenant procedure used in the second millennium B.C.E. Block describes it as follows:[40] (1) Diplomats representing both states settled on the terms of the agreement. (2) Representatives of each side produced a version styled as the words of the respective monarchs. (3) These versions were inscribed in cuneiform in the Akkadian language (the language of international diplomacy) on tablets of precious metal (silver in this case). (4) These tablets were exchanged and taken home. (5) The texts were translated into the native language, providing the Egyptians and Hittites respectively

---

39. Block, "The Privilege of Calling," 390; idem, *How I Love Your Torah*, 144.
40. Block, "The Privilege of Calling," 393; idem, *How I Love Your Torah*, 148.

with constant reminders of the obligations to which the other parties had bound themselves.

In Deut 26:16–19, Moses' goal was to emphasize Israel's obedience driven not by duty but by an awareness of the special nature of their relationship with God. When Israel heard Yahweh declare orally his commitment to be their God and when Yahweh heard Israel make their declaration to be his treasured people, that generation standing before Moses became the privileged people of God as highlighted by Moses and the Levitical priests in 27:9: "Keep silence and hear, O Israel: this day you have become the people of the LORD your God." This special covenant relationship is the foundation of Israel's call to reach the nations with the good news of God's grace.[41]

4.3. *The Nature of Israel's Calling*

Having shown how the present generation confirmed their acceptance to the covenant relationship that God had promised Abraham and ratified with their parents at Sinai, Block turns and asks why this relationship was created. To what had Yahweh called Israel? The privileges and obligations that Israel and Yahweh heard affirmed to one another are detailed in vv. 17–19.[42]

Verse 17, What Israel Heard Yahweh Declare:

- *Privilege:* I promise to be your God.
- *Obligation:* You are to walk in my ways.
- *Obligation:* You are to keep all my commandments.
- *Obligation:* You are to listen to my voice.

Verses 18–19, What Yahweh Heard Israel Declare:

- *Privilege:* We accept our status as your treasured people.
- *Obligation:* We will keep all your commandments.
- *Privilege:* We accept our status above all the nations.
- *Privilege:* We accept our status as a holy people of God.

In these verses, Yahweh declares his commitment to be Israel's God, and Israel accepts their status of being a treasured people. Four privileges are shown to mark Israel: They were called (1) to be Yahweh's people, (2) to be Yahweh's "special treasure," (3) to be a light of God's grace to the nations, and (4) to be a holy people.

Israel bore a distinct relationship with Yahweh, filled with mutual commitment. While this relationship is often understood primarily as a covenant relationship between a suzerain and vassal, other passages

---

41. Block, "The Privilege of Calling," 393–94; idem, *How I Love Your Torah*, 149.
42. Block, "The Privilege of Calling," 394; idem, *How I Love Your Torah*, 149.

use more familial images to depict the makeup of the bond. For example, at times echo is made to the ancient Hebrew marriage formula: "I will be your husband, and you shall be my wife."[43] Or the language of adoption is used: "I will be your father, and you shall be my son" (Deut 14:1–2, Exod 4:22, Hos 11:1).[44] In all portrayals, stress is on the depth of the bond between Yahweh and his people.

4.4. Israel Had Been Called to be the Lord's "Special Treasure"

Deut 26:18 is the third and climactic occurrence of the expression "treasured people" in the book of Deuteronomy (Deut 7:6, 14:1). The word connotes valued possession, especially the treasure of kings, and according to Deut 14:1, Israel was granted this status through divine election. Of all the peoples in the world, Israel was chosen by Yahweh for this privileged status of being a "treasured possession" (26:18). Block writes, "Just as the crown jewels in London reflected the glory of the monarchs of England, so Israel was especially chosen to reflect the glory of God among the nations."[45]

4.5. Israel Was Called to be a Light of God's Grace to the Nations

The metaphor Isaiah used to describe the mission of the servant of Yahweh—"a light to the nations" (Isa 42:1, 49:6)—is missing in Deuteronomy, but the concept is certainly present in Deut 26:19. In spite of her insignificant size (7:6–7) and her moral discredits (9:1–24), God gave Israel a superior status above all the nations he had made. With the words "he will set you . . . high above all nations" (26:19), the mission strategy moved beyond Canaan to the world. Support for this interpretation is seen in the echo of 28:1, where God stresses that Israel's obedience will set them "high above all the nations of the earth." Although Moses does not specify how this superiority would manifest itself, he does give hints of economic blessing, political superiority, military power, and psychological superiority. "And all the peoples of the earth shall see that you are called by the name of the LORD, and they shall be afraid of you" (28:10).

God's promise to elevate Israel above the nations was for *Yahweh's* "praise and fame and honor" (26:19). While this interpretation is not certain, three factors move Block to support this rendering. First, Israel's standing was never to be a source of national hubris; Moses sought

---

43. Block, "The Privilege of Calling," 396; idem, *How I Love Your Torah*, 151.
44. Block, "The Privilege of Calling," 396–97; idem, *How I Love Your Torah*, 151–52.
45. Block, "The Privilege of Calling," 397–98; idem, *How I Love Your Torah*, 153.

to defuse any temptation to arrogance. Second, Israel was to praise Yahweh because of all he had done for her. Third, Jer 13:11 (and 33:9) echoes the present text that Israel's praise will bring honor to Yahweh among the nations. "For as the loincloth clings to the waist of a man, so I made the whole house of Israel and the whole house of Judah cling to me, declares the LORD, that they might be for me a people, a name, a praise, and a glory, but they would not listen."

4.6. Israel Had Been Called to be a Holy People

The fourth privilege of the Israelites is that Yahweh declared them to be a holy people belonging to him. Israel's holy status is associated with Yahweh's election of her as his treasured possession. As highlighted in Exod 19:5–6, if the Israelites would keep God's covenant and listen to his voice, they would be his special treasure, his kingdom of priests, and his holy nation.

The last of these—Israel's holy standing—bears great significance for grasping Israel's missionary role. God separated Israel not simply to lavish his attention on her but so that they might "serve as a link between God and the world."

4.7. The Burden of Israel's Calling

Although God's call of Israel to salvation was unconditional, the nation's effectiveness in fulfilling her call to mission was conditional, as seen in Exod 19:5–6: "If you will indeed obey my voice and keep my covenant, (then) you shall be my treasured possession . . . my kingdom of priests and a holy nation." Fidelity to the covenant was vital for mission success. In the words of Deut 26:16, Israel was to keep the statutes and rules "with all your heart and with all your soul." Moses' emphasis was on "doing" (Deut 26:16), and the purpose of the law was clearly to serve as a guide for conduct, not to nurture pride or to provide a resource for philosophical reflection.[46] Israel was to "walk in his ways, and keep his statutes and his commandments and his rules, and . . . obey his voice" (26:17). In doing so, they would fulfill their mission.

4.8. Concluding Reflections on Missions

According to Block, Moses' conclusions have profound implications not only for biblical theology but also for a biblical understanding of Israel's role in divine revelation and redemption. In Deuteronomy, the nations provide the context from which and before which Yahweh chose and redeemed Israel and set them as his treasured possession.

---

46. Block, "The Privilege of Calling," 401; idem, *How I Love Your Torah*, 157.

God supplied the law to Israel "in order to declare to the world what his glory and grace could accomplish in the lives of the destitute and the enslaved."[47]

Block pinpoints four critical factors that were to be a part of Israel's life and service as people of Yahweh.[48] First, as the products of Yahweh's gracious and unmerited saving actions, they were to show their gratitude by obedience. Second, their occupation of the land was contingent on their fidelity to God. Third, Israel was to declare to the world the righteousness of God's law and the righteousness and graciousness of their God. Fourth, the people's obedience was to demonstrate the glorious privilege of their status as Yahweh's special treasure and his holy people. As Israel followed closely God's instructions, they "would be the means of God's blessing the whole world."[49]

Block concludes that in Deuteronomy the pattern for missions is fundamentally centripetal. Nowhere does the Pentateuch include a missionary mandate like the great commission in Matthew 28. The prevailing formula for mission activity was to begin with obedient living as a demonstration of gratefulness for divine grace. The result would be experiencing Yahweh's blessings, which would then attract the attention of the surrounding nations. Those nations would in turn give praise and glory to Yahweh and would desire to join Israel in their covenant relationship with him.

Block observes that the New Testament strategy is in some ways similar but in other ways quite different. Like the ancient Israelites, New Testament believers have experienced God's grace and are to respond in gratefulness by living godly lives, thus proclaiming his marvelous light to a dark world (Matt 5:13–16). Living as "a chosen race, a royal priesthood, a holy nation, a people for his own possession," Christians are to "proclaim the excellencies of him who called you out of darkness into his marvelous light" (1 Pet 2:9). This is the same centripetal missionary witness described in the Old Testament.

Nevertheless, Jesus' Great Commission in Matt 28:18–20 shifts the New Covenant focus from centripetal to centrifugal. In Block's words, the strategy has shifted from "Come see what God has done for his people" to "Go tell the world what God has done for his people."[50] Paul and others were called to carry the gospel of divine grace to the Gentiles, and the Scripture closes with a glorious vision of people from

---

47. Block, "The Privilege of Calling," 403; idem, *How I Love Your Torah*, 159.
48. Block, "The Privilege of Calling," 404; idem, *How I Love Your Torah*, 159–60.
49. Block, "The Privilege of Calling," 404; idem, *How I Love Your Torah*, 160.
50. Block, "The Privilege of Calling," 405; idem, *How I Love Your Torah*, 161.

every tribe and nation redeemed and gathered around the Lamb to worship him (Rev 5:9, 7:4). May the passion of all believers be to see this mission accomplished.

5. Conclusion

It is my hope that this synthesis of the book of Deuteronomy has revealed its beauty as a mirror-image of Paul's epistles in the New Testament and that ministers of the gospel will be further equipped to preach the glorious riches of the golden nuggets of truth contained therein. It has already been mentioned that Deuteronomy provides the theological basis for the entire Old (and New) Testament. What Block did in only four articles is profound. If shepherd-leaders will only heed his advice, they will indeed have the building blocks for a great ministry. "The Word of God" is the prescription for life. "The Joy of Worship" is an invitation into the presence of God. "The Burden of Leadership" is a paradigm for godly oversight. And "The Privilege of Calling" is a mandate for missions.

Index of Authors

Aaron, D. H.   123
Aberbach, M.   161
Achtemeier, E.   464, 465, 472, 476
Ackroyd, P. R.   258
Albright, W. F.   20, 22
Alexander, T. D.   419
Allison, D. C.   368, 371
Alster, B.   315
Alt, A.   180
Alter, R.   108, 464, 467, 468
Altman, A.   48
Álvarez-Pedrosa, J. A.   43, 47
Amsler, S.   212
Andersen, F. I.   12, 103, 109
Anderson, C. B.   22
Anderson, G. A.   137
Andrew, M. E.   118
Arnaud, D.   33
Arnett, B.   94
Assmann, J.   321
Augustine of Hippo   100, 101
Aurelius, E.   156
Austin, J. L.   63
Avioz, M.   470
Avishur, Y.   30

Badenas, R.   404
Bahnsen, G. L.   455
Bahrani, Z.   169
Bailey, R. C.   21
Baker, D. L.   89, 448, 460
Baker, D. W.   110
Balentine, S. E.   446
Bandstra, A. J.   404
Barbour, J.   328, 340
Barker, P. A.   83, 148, 408
Barrett, C. K.   405
Barrett, R.   445, 446
Barstad, H. M.   14
Barth, K.   404, 430
Barth, M.   404
Bartholomew, C. G.   329, 336, 337

Bauckham, R.   220
Beale, G. K.   427, 428, 440, 508
Becker, J.   334
Beckerleg, C. L.   417
Becker, U.   258
Becking, B.   305
Beckman, G. M.   7, 10, 26, 44
Begg, C. T.   153, 155
Bekken, P. J.   409
Bellefontaine, E.   217
Bell, R. H.   401
Bennett, H. V.   444
Ben Zvi, E.   260
Berges, U.   259
Bergey, R.   256
Bergsma, J. S.   293, 297, 298, 301
Berman, J. A.   452
Bernabé, A.   43, 47
Biddle, M. E.   176
Bird, P. A.   184
Bjørndalen, A. J.   254
Blank, S. H.   315
Blenkinsopp, J.   146, 149, 153, 256, 257,
   259, 265, 266, 267
Block, D. I.   74, 76, 94, 108, 117, 119,
   121, 122, 127, 128, 130, 143, 165,
   166, 168, 170, 171, 210, 211, 229,
   231, 235, 244, 288, 295, 303, 308,
   323, 328, 373, 374, 375, 390, 416,
   418, 419, 424, 426, 428, 434, 435,
   436, 440, 446, 447, 448, 452, 460,
   463, 470, 472, 474, 475, 484, 485,
   492, 495, 500, 504, 511, 512, 513,
   514, 515, 516, 517, 518, 519, 520,
   521, 523, 524, 525, 526, 527, 528,
   529, 530, 531, 532, 533
Blomberg, C.   220, 455
Bock, D.   366, 372, 378, 380, 383, 384,
   387, 446
Boda, M. J.   30, 31
Boorer, S.   150, 151
Booth, W. C.   63

Borger, R.   12
Borowski, O.   54
Bovon, F.   367, 370, 377, 380, 381, 383
Bozkurt, H.   49
Braswell, J. P.   396
Braulik, G.   119, 162, 308, 480
Bray, G.   394
Brekelmans, C.   254
Breneman, M.   350, 358
Brettell, C. B.   441
Brett, M. G.   442
Breuer, M.   94, 95, 97, 98, 99, 100, 101, 106, 113, 114, 118
Brichto, H. C.   148
Briddle, M. E.   508
Brin, G.   180
Bring, R.   404
Brinkman, J. A.   5
Brockington, L. H.   352
Brown, J. K.   62, 63
Brown, R.   488, 490
Brown, W. P.   335
Bruce, F. F.   348, 395
Bruckner, J. K.   452
Brueggemann, W.   23, 136, 149, 159, 189, 204, 209, 213, 278, 313, 408, 472, 474
Brummitt, M.   284
Bryce, T. R.   44
Buber, M.   23
Bultmann, R.   366, 371, 409
Burton, E. de W.   395
Buttrick, D.   480, 482
Bystrom, R. O.   482

Caesar, L. O.   312
Cahill, L. S.   23
Cairns, I.   77
Calvin, J.   101, 407, 410
Campbell, A. F.   62
Campbell, W. S.   404
Camp, C. V.   317
Caneday, A.   396
Caquot, A.   32
Carasik, M.   132, 133, 134, 135, 136, 138
Carpenter, E. E.   237, 499
Carr, D. M.   271, 273, 275
Carroll, R. P.   189, 199, 275, 278

Carroll R., M. D.   323, 443, 444, 446, 458, 460
Carruba, O.   48
Carson, D. A.   437, 440
Castles, S.   441
Cazelles, H.   274
Charlesworth, J. H.   281
Chavalas, M. W.   43, 499
Chibici-Revneanu, N.   402
Childs, B. S.   113, 114, 117, 124, 327, 418
Chirichigno, G. C.   322, 497
Christensen, D. L.   169, 304, 463, 464, 465, 504
Chrysostom, J.   282, 283, 395, 400
Chung, Y. H.   147
Ciampa, R. E.   407
Cifarelli, M.   169
Çığ, M.   49
Clayton, P. B.   285
Clemens, D. M.   328
Clements, R. E.   256, 267, 327, 465
Clifford, J.   441
Clifford, R.   176
Clines, D. J. A.   315, 317, 318, 319, 321, 323, 358
Coats, G. W.   163, 296
Coggins, R.   150, 226
Collins, A. Y.   386
Collins, B. J.   10, 11
Collins, C. J.   419
Collins, J.   419
Collins, R. F.   124, 507
Collon, D.   11
Conrad, E. W.   258
Conzelmann, H.   385
Coogan, M. D.   446
Cook, P. M.   257, 260
Cooper, J. S.   14
Copan, P.   21
Cosgrove, C. H.   455
Cox, D.   313
Coxhead, S. R.   408
Craddock, F.   482, 483
Craigie, P.   168, 242, 273, 373, 374, 375, 491, 502, 504
Cranfield, C. E. B.   404, 410
Crenshaw, J. L.   327, 336, 337, 339

Index of Authors

Cross, F. M.   225, 304
Crüsemann, F.   446, 459, 460
Crystal, D.   109
Cuellar, G. L.   443
Culver, R. D.   487, 492
Cunchillos, J.-L.   32
Currid, J. D.   119
Curtis, J.   11

Daddi, F. P.   46
Dahood, M.   323
Dardano, P.   39, 40, 51
Das, A. A.   396, 399
David, M.   180
Davidson, R. M.   174, 440
Davies, E. W.   445, 455, 456
Davies, J. A.   418
Davies, W. D.   371
Davis, E. F.   447
Dawkins, R.   21, 22
Day, J.   20
Dearman, J. A.   271, 277
Deck, S.   253
Deist, F. E.   443, 496
Delithanasi, M.   498
Delitzsch, F.   100, 336, 337
Dell, K. J.   314
Dempsey, C. J.   469
Dempster, S. G.   103, 109
DeRouchie, J. S.   93, 102, 106, 109, 115, 121, 373, 417, 419, 421, 431
Dever, M.   486
Dhorme, E.   319, 321
Dick, M. B.   315, 317
Dietrich, M.   33, 34
Dodd, C. H.   372
Doll, P.   314
Domeris, W. R.   447
Donaldson, T. L.   370
Doxey, D. M.   320
Dozeman, T. B.   151, 158
Driver, S. R.   61, 147, 149, 169, 218, 223, 269, 273, 319, 408
Dufoix, S.   441
Duhm, B.   319, 325
Dumbrell, W.   67, 229, 396, 419, 430
Dunn, J. D. G.   395, 404, 405
Durand, J.-M.   25

Durham, J. I.   148

Edzard, D. O.   318
Ehrlich, E. L.   311
Eichrodt, W.   295
Eissfeldt, O.   31
Ellis, E. E.   389
Enns, P.   79
Erdman, C.   486
Eshkenazi, T.   350
Estelle, B. D.   408
Evans, C. A.   220, 367, 371

Fales, F. M.   5
Fee, G. D.   409
Feinberg, J. S.   455
Fensham, F. C.   352, 357, 358
Fidler, R.   341
Finkelstein, J. J.   42
Fischer, G.   275, 277, 278
Fishbane, M.   146, 296, 348
Fitzmyer, J. A.   368, 370, 371, 380, 383, 405, 407
Flückiger, F.   404
Flusser, D.   95, 110
Fohrer, G.   312, 314, 317
Forman, C. C.   328
Foster, B. R.   13, 307, 309, 314, 315
Fox, M. V.   310, 312, 314, 330, 331, 333, 336, 337, 429
France, R. T.   369, 380, 382, 384
Frankel, D.   152
Frankena, R.   9
Fretheim, T. E.   460
Friedrich, J.   46, 47
Frymer-Kensky, T.   180
Fuller, D. P.   404

Ganzel, T.   295
García López, F.   160
Garland, D.   366, 369, 371, 378, 380
Garlington, D. B.   367, 377
Garrett, D. A.   106, 109, 115, 336, 337
Garrett, S. R.   365, 367, 386
Garr, W. R.   422
Gathercole, S. J.   402
Gentry, P. J.   113, 117, 417, 418, 419, 420, 422, 430, 437, 439, 440

George, M. K. 138
Gerhardsson, B. 366, 368, 369, 371, 378, 379, 382
Gese, H. 334
Geus, C. H. J. de 54
Gilan, A. 40, 47
Gilbert, M. 276
Gile, J. 287, 289, 291, 296, 360
Ginsberg, H. L. 311
Glassner, J.-J. 5, 6
Godet, F. L. 410
Goetze, A. 10, 44, 49
Goldberg, A. M. 405
Gonçalves, F. J. 260
Gonzales, J. L. 368
Gordis, R. 312, 313, 348
Gordon, C. H. 128, 322
Gordon, T. D. 395
Gowan, D. E. 190, 448, 477
Grabbe, L. L. 19
Graves, M. 465
Gray, G. B. 319
Grayson, A. K. 11, 12, 305
Grech, P. 348
Green, A. 11
Greenberg, M. 100, 114, 296, 301, 302, 432, 473
Greenfield, J. C. 35, 36
Green, J. 385, 386
Greenman, J. P. 415
Greenspahn, F. E. 307
Greenstein, E. L. 12, 307, 310, 311, 314
Grillmeier, A. 284
Grisanti, M. A. 90, 228
Gundry, R. H. 396, 400
Güterbock, H. G. 44, 49
Gutridge, C. A. 341

Habel, N. C. 309, 312, 316, 317, 318
Hafemann, S. J. 220
Hagner, D. A. 368, 372
Hahn, S. W. 293, 297, 298, 301
Hallo, W. W. 71
Halpern, B. 216, 269
Hamilton, J. 419
Hamilton, J. M. 504
Hamilton, M. 321
Hamilton, V. H. 111, 114

Hamnuna, Rabbi 97
Hamp, V. 500, 506
Haran, M. 330
Harding, J. E. 312
Hardmeier, C. 254
Hardy, R. S. 43
Harrelson, W. J. 123, 124
Harrington, D. J. 220
Harris, M. J. 381
Hartley, J. E. 319, 321
Hartman, L. 94
Hasel, G. F. 219
Hatina, T. R. 189
Hatton, T. J. 441
Hauerwas, S. M. 23
Hayes, C. E. 150, 155, 156, 158, 162
Hays, J. D. 440, 455, 492
Hays, R. B. 23, 347, 393, 395, 396, 400, 409
Headlam, A. C. 407
Healey, J. F. 30
Heckel, U. 393
Heim, K. M. 31
Heimpel, W. 24, 25, 29
Heller, J. 405
Hendel, R. S. 146
Hertzberg, H. W. 54
Heschel, A. J. 281
Hess, R. S. 18, 19, 29, 31
Hester 380
Hill, R. C. 283, 284, 285, 286
Hillers, D. 20, 303, 305, 319
Hirshman, M. 281
Hitchens, C. 21
Hobbes, T. R. 168
Hodge, C. 407
Hoffman, Y. 311
Hoffmann, I. 43
Hoffmeier, J. K. 450, 457
Hoffner Jr., H. A. 41, 42, 43, 49, 50, 322
Holladay, W. L. 269, 270, 273, 275, 466, 468
Holland, T. 405
Hollifield, J. F. 441
House, P. R. 481
Houston, W. J. 448
Houten, C. van 446, 447
Houtman, C. 345

Index of Authors

Hout, T. P. J. van den 43, 44, 45
Houwink ten Cate, P. H. J. 44
Howard, G. E. 404
Howard Jr., D. M. 72, 74, 231
Hubbard, R. I., Jr. 455
Hübner, H. 395, 407
Huehnergard, J. 12, 184
Hugenberger, G. P. 440
Hummel, H. D. 94
Hurowitz, V. A. 33, 34
Husser, J.-M. 30
Hutton, R. R. 94
Hwang, J. 135, 159, 451, 201, 145, 460
Hyatt, D. 409
Hyatt, J. P. 269, 275

Isbell, C. D. 277

Jacobs, L. 282
Janzen, J. G. 130, 131
Janzen, W. 313, 440, 456, 496
Japhet, S. 345
Jastram, N. 94, 106, 115, 117
Jensen, J. 253
Jeremias, J. 405
Jewett, R. 443, 444
Joannès, F. 54
Johnson, E. E. 409
Johnson, L. T. 383, 384
Jones, L. G. 30
Jong, M. de 261
Josberger, R. 166, 169, 176, 187, 324, 436, 448
Josephus 95, 99, 101, 114, 383
Joüon, P. 179, 275
Joyce, P. 302

Kaiser Jr., W. C. 402, 439, 455, 458, 486
Kaiser, O. 254
Kalland, E. 487
Kaminski, C. M. 417
Käsemann, E. 401, 405
Kaufman, S. 84, 119
Keener, C. S. 368, 372
Keil, C. F. 100
Kellermann, D. 447
Kellermann, U. 345
Kelly, H. A. 366

Kelly, J. N. D. 284
Keydana, G. 33
Khanjian, J. 33
Kidd, R. 446, 447
Kierkegaard, S. 164
Killebrew, A. E. 442
Kimball, C. A. 366, 369, 380, 383
Kim, S. 395, 400, 409
King, P. J. 447, 448
Kingsbury, J. D. 64
Kitchen, K. A. 8, 9, 10, 62, 227, 235, 303, 304, 446
Klein, W. W. 455
Kline, M. G. 8, 62, 417
Klinger, J. 47
Klock-Fontanille, L. 39
Knauth, R. J. D. 447
Knierim, R. 111
Knight, D. A. 444, 447
Knoppers, G. N. 154, 224, 226
Koch, D.-A. 389, 393, 404, 409
Kohn, R. L. 290, 291, 295, 298
Konkel, A. H. 447
Koster, M. D. 94
Krašovec, J. 300
Kratz, R. G. 164
Krüger, T. 336, 337
Kuhn, K. A. 136
Kümmel, H. M. 43
Kustár, Z. 254, 256
Kynes, W. 328

Laato, T. 399, 401
Labahn, A. 254, 262, 263, 265
Lambdin, T. O. 108
Lambert, D. 134, 136, 138
Lambert, W. G. 33, 34, 307
Lapsley, J. E. 136, 137, 302
Laroche, E. 40
Larsen, T. 415
Lasine, S. 312
Lauha, A. 334, 341
Lawrence, J. S. 443, 444
Lawrence, P. J. N. 8, 9, 303
Lee, E. 461
Leichty, E. 12
Lemaire, A. 11, 14
Lemche, N. P. 18, 19

Lenchak, T. A. 157
Leuchter, M. 271, 276
Levenson, J. D. 304, 430
Levinas, E. 22, 23
Levinsohn, S. H. 106, 109
Levinson, B. M. 64, 149, 164, 446, 463
Levit, Rabbi 97
Levy, J. 272
Lichtheim, M. 315, 322
Lightfoot, J. B. 395
Lincicum, D. 411
Lindenberger, J. M. 35, 315
Lintz, R. 440
Lipiński, E. 320
Little, D. 500
Liverani, M. 8
Livingstone, A. 9
Lohfink, N. F. 77, 78, 84, 110, 118, 122, 125, 148, 156, 158, 159, 204, 302, 375, 471
Lohse, E. 404
Lombard, P. 100
Longenecker, B. W. 395
Longenecker, R. N. 389, 395, 400, 407
Longman III, T. 331, 385
Long, V. P. 232
Loretz, O. 30
Lowry, E. 482
Lucas, E. C. 75
Luckenbill, D. D. 11, 12
Lundbom, J. R. 274, 275, 465, 470
Lust, J. 288, 296, 297
Luther, M. 394, 395
Lyons, M. A. 287, 289, 291, 292, 293, 300

Macchi, J.-D. 252
MacDonald, N. 474, 475
MacIntyre, A. 450
Magnetti, D. L. 299
Maier, C. 276
Maier, F. W. 401
Maier, P. L. 94
Maimonides 84, 100
Malul, M. 308
Manley, G. T. 506
Mann, T. W. 501

Marazzi, M. 44
Marcus, D. 12
Marshall, I. H. 365, 366, 370, 372, 377, 378, 380, 383, 385
Marshall, J. W. 124
Martens, E. A. 440, 456
Matlock, B. 399
Matthews, V. H. 499
Mayes, A. D. H. 180, 208, 308, 465, 471, 482
McBride, S. D. 137, 459
McCarter, P. K. 138
McCarthy, D. J. 62, 303, 304
McConville, J. G. 72, 73, 83, 110, 130, 137, 140, 143, 145, 157, 174, 178, 190, 192, 197, 198, 199, 200, 201, 203, 204, 208, 212, 217, 224, 225, 228, 232, 240, 241, 243, 270, 275, 301, 308, 372, 373, 374, 375, 407, 408, 410, 411, 446, 447, 448, 452, 459, 465, 501
McIntosh, D. 490
McKane, W. 270, 279
McKenzie, S. L. 224, 225, 252
McNamara, M. 406
Melanchthon, P. 100
Mendenhall, G. E. 8, 61, 299
Merrill, E. H. 73, 141, 206, 229, 486, 502
Mettinger, T. N. D. 253
Meyer, J. C. 419, 439
Meyers, C. 171, 184, 448
Michel, C. 54
Michel, D. 331
Michel, O. 405
Mikoski, G. 450
Milgrom, J. 86, 92, 152, 205
Millard, A. 4, 10, 11, 14, 15
Millar, J. G. 73, 192, 200, 203, 204, 206, 209, 210, 211, 212, 213, 214, 215, 218, 301, 408, 447
Miller, C. L. 109, 115
Miller, J. M. 4
Miller, M. J. 441
Miller, M. P. 348
Miller, P. D. 124, 131, 200, 229, 236, 448, 459, 464
Miner, E. 346

Moberly, R. W. L.   129, 130, 141, 148, 464, 477, 478
Moo, D. J.   390, 391, 396, 398, 406, 407, 410, 412, 439, 440
Moor, J. C. de   30, 32
Mora, C.   44
Moran, W. L.   10, 27, 28, 94, 107, 108, 134, 136, 436
Muffs, Y.   137
Müller, M.   320
Murphy, R. E.   314, 327, 336, 337, 339
Murray, J.   405, 410
Mussner, F.   392, 395
Myers, J. M.   352
Mysliwiec, K.   320

Na'aman, N.   18
Naselli, A. D.   406
Nelson, R. D.   70, 79, 119, 121, 225, 304, 305, 374, 480
Neville, R. W.   321
Newsom, C. A.   309
Nicholson, E. W.   148, 277, 465
Niditch, S.   168
Niehaus, J. J.   157
Nielsen, E.   117, 303
Nihan, C.   252
Nissinen, M.   29, 252
Nolland, J.   365, 371, 372, 378, 380
Noth, M.   154, 224, 225, 226, 236, 303, 393
Notley, R. S.   18
Nougayrol, J.   33
Nurmela, R.   265
Nussbaum, M. C.   136, 137

O'Connell, R. H.   148
Oded, B.   67, 303, 304, 305
Oden, R. A., Jr.   21
O'Dowd, R.   314
Oeming, M.   314
Olmo Lete, G. del   32
Olson, D. T.   136, 214, 459
Origen   101
Osborne, G. R.   63, 368
Otten, H.   48
Otto, E.   148, 446

Palmer, C. E.   177
Pao, D. W.   383, 384
Pardee, D.   30, 31, 32
Parker, S. B.   30
Parpola, S.   9
Pate, M. C.   199, 205, 214, 215
Paton-Williams, D.   266
Patton, C.   296
Paul, S. M.   13, 263, 265, 266, 267
Pelikan, J.   285
Peobel, A.   111
Perdue, L. G.   314, 323, 340
Perlitt, L.   164, 254
Peterson, E.   490
Pfeiffer, R. H.   75, 314
Phillips, A.   500
Philo   95, 99, 101, 114, 402, 404, 409, 432, 507
Piper, J.   425
Pleins, J. D.   460
Plöger, J. G.   209
Poebel, A.   12
Pokorny, P.   371
Polzin, R.   157
Pressler, C.   174, 180, 186
Preuss, H.-D.   302, 328
Printezi, R.   503
Provan, I.   76, 270, 336, 337
Pury, A. de   252

Rad, G. von   146, 168, 176, 302, 303, 308, 310, 312, 314, 327, 463, 476, 500
Rainey, A. F.   18, 27, 29
Reeder, C. A.   82, 445, 446
Reicke, B.   94
Reid, D. G.   385
Remus, M.   309
Rendtorff, R.   447
Reventlow, H. G.   111
Rhyne, C. T.   401
Riches, J.   394
Richter, S. L.   72, 224, 225, 226, 237, 238, 270
Ridderbos, J.   173, 178
Ridge, D. R.   492
Rignell, L. G.   256
Ringgren   116

Robinson, H. 488
Rodd, C. S. 444
Rofé, A. 169, 299, 475
Rogerson, J. W. 61, 456
Rohrer, A. 498
Rollston, C. A. 269
Römer, T. 8, 224, 252, 302
Rom-Shiloni, D. 295
Rosen, M. 489
Ross, P. S. 437
Roth, M. T. 318, 322
Rowley, H. H. 313
Rowley, M. 435
Rubenstein, J. L. 282
Ruiz, J.-P. 443

Sailhamer, J. 408, 481
Salyer, G. D. 335
Sanday, W. 407
Sanders, E. P. 398, 401
Sanders, P. 32
Sanders, S. L. 12
Saporetti, C. 6
Schacter, D. 137
Schaff, P. 286
Schaper, J. 271, 273
Scharbert, J. 274
Schearing, L. S. 224, 252
Schiavo, L. 372, 386
Schmid, K. 148, 216, 277
Schmidt, B. B. 320
Schmidt, W. H. 254
Schmitt, H.-C. 148
Schnabel, E. J. 383, 384, 409
Schniedewind, W. M. 278
Schökel, L. A. 319
Schoors, A. 341
Schreiner, T. R. 395, 396, 401, 408, 439
Schultz, R. 348, 349
Schultz, S. 489
Schürmann, H. 380
Schwartz, R. 477
Schweizer, E. 405
Schwiderski, D. 11
Scobie, C. H. 327
Scott, J. M. 189, 216, 391, 396
Scott, W. R. 100
Seebass, H. 267

Segal, M. H. 236
Seibert, E. A. 445
Seifrid, M. A. 404, 409, 410
Seitz, C. 129
Seitz, G. 156
Sellin, E. 312, 314
Selms, A. van 323
Seminara, S. 33
Sénéchal, V. 163
Seow, C.-L. 330, 333, 338, 339
Sherwood, Y. 284
Shields, M. A. 328, 329, 331, 337, 339
Sicre Díaz, J. L. 319
Silva, M. 396, 400
Simpson, W. K. 71
Ska, J.-L. 154
Skweres, D. E. 152
Smelik, K. A. D. 259
Smend, R. 225
Smith-Christopher, D. L. 303, 304
Smith, D. E. 33
Smith, G. A. 305
Smith, G. V. 311, 348
Smith, L. 94
Smith, M. S. 20, 30, 147
Smith, S. 12
Smolar, L. 161
Sneed, M. 444
Soden, W. von 11
Soennichsen, J. 461
Sommer, B. D. 263, 265, 292, 347, 348
Sonnet, J.-P. 147, 271, 272
Southwood, K. E. 442
Sparks, K. L. 18, 33, 43, 46, 79, 442
Sprinkle, P. M. 402
Spurgeon, C. H. 493
Stager, L. E. 447, 448
Stamm, J. J. 117
Stanley, C. D. 392, 393, 396, 406, 407
Starling, D. I. 396
Steck, O. H. 216, 261
Stegner, W. R. 368, 371, 378
Steiner, R. C. 108, 109
Steinkeller, P. 6
Stein, R. H. 216, 370, 381, 387
Strawn, B. A. 164
Strickland, W. G. 438
Strine, C. A. 296

Stromberg, J.   251, 257, 260
Stuart, D.   69, 416
Stulman, L.   277, 278, 501, 505
Suggs, M. J.   409
Sutherland, R.   317
Swanston, H. F. G.   371
Swart, L.   66
Swartley, W. M.   459

Talmon, S.   195
Talstra, E.   148
Tarragon, J.-M.   32
Taschner, J.   156
Tate, M. E.   383, 384
Taylor, N. H.   366, 370, 380
Terrien, S.   312
Theocharous, M.   324, 448
Theodoret   283, 284, 285, 286
Thompson, J. A.   238, 490, 504
Ticciati, S.   313
Tigay, J. H.   84, 88, 91, 97, 111, 121, 136, 137, 165, 178, 198, 408, 464, 467, 472, 473, 500, 503, 504
Tillesse, G. M. de   154
Tita, H.   341
Tobin, V. A.   320
Toorn, K. van der   28
Tov, E.   72, 270
Towner, P. H.   121, 434
Tsevat, M.   325
Tsumura, D. T.   227
Tucker, G. M.   492
Turner, K. J.   190, 191, 192, 194, 196, 198, 205, 206, 208, 209, 218, 220, 301
Tur-Sinai, N. H.   311

Urbach, E. E.   282, 402

Vang, C.   65
VanGemeren, W. A.   383, 384
Vanhoozer, K. J.   63
Van Leeuwen, R. C.   307, 317
Van Seters, J.   5, 6, 147, 148, 149, 151, 153, 160, 161, 162, 163
Vaux, R. de   54
Venema, G. J.   157, 272, 277, 278
Vermeylen, J.   254, 255, 256, 260
Via, D. O.   410
Vieyra, M.   46
Vischak, D.   321
Vita, J.-P.   27
Vogt, P. T.   70, 72, 73, 78, 79, 168, 211, 237, 446, 452
Volf, M.   450
Vonach, A.   330

Wace, H.   286
Waltke, B. K.   328
Walton, J. H.   119, 422, 424, 429, 430, 431, 499
Wan, E.   442
Warrior, R. A.   21
Washington, H. C.   174, 177
Watanabe, K.   9, 10
Waters, G.   395, 397
Watson, F.   411
Watts, J. D. W.   112, 446
Watts, J. W.   446
Webb, B. G.   337
Webb, W. J.   459
Weinfeld, M.   6, 9, 62, 70, 73, 77, 108, 110, 111, 124, 132, 140, 141, 217, 227, 260, 264, 268, 269, 271, 273, 274, 297, 303, 313, 322, 328, 435, 464, 465, 500
Weiser, A.   325
Welch, A. K.   305
Wellhausen, J.   61, 164
Wells, T.   438, 439
Wellum, S. J.   113, 117, 417, 418, 419, 420, 422, 430, 437, 439, 440
Wenham, G. J.   61, 62, 73, 81, 86, 88, 150, 237, 238, 402
Westbrook, R.   25, 87, 91, 299
Westerholm, S.   400
Westermann, C.   85, 327, 328, 358
Wette, W. M. L. de   61, 465
Wevers, J. W.   95
Whedbee, W.   312
Widengreen, G.   288
Widmer, M.   148
Wiersbe, W.   488, 489
Wijk-Bos, J. W. H. van   442, 447
Wilckens, U.   401
Wilcox, J. T.   314

Wilcox, P. 266
Wildberger, H. 305
Wilde, A. de 319
Wilken, R. 283
Willems, D. 481
Willey, P. T. 265
Williamson, H. G. M. 251, 253, 255, 260, 261, 265, 267, 268, 345, 358
Williamson, J. G. 441
Williamson, P. R. 430
Wilson, P. S. 476, 481, 483, 484
Wilson, R. R. 227
Winthrop, J. 444
Wisdom, J. R. 395
Wiseman, D. J. 9
Witherington, B. 409
Wolde, E. van 180, 181, 182
Woods, E. J. 408
Work, T. 465
Wright, C. J. H. 21, 22, 65, 72, 124, 165, 185, 186, 211, 229, 237, 408, 422, 440, 447, 448, 452, 455, 456, 457, 459, 474, 475, 479, 490, 496, 506

Wright, J. E. 280
Wright, N. T. 189, 215, 216, 219, 220, 396, 404, 405, 408
Wyatt, N. 30, 31, 32, 320

Yadin, Y. 168, 169, 175
Yamada, F. M. 22
Ybarrola, S. 442
Yeivin, E. 100
Youngblood, K. J. 420
Youngblood, R. 94
Yung, J. 461

Zaspel, F. 438, 439
Zehnder, M. 10
Ziegler, Y. 299
Zimmerli, W. 116, 117, 302, 314
Zipor, M. A. 152
Zycha, J. 100

Index of Scripture

Old Testament

Genesis
1–3   328
1–11   85
1:2–3   85
1:3   437
1:6   437
1:9   437
1:11   437
1:14   437
1:20   437
1:24   437
1:26   437
1:26–28   417, 430
1:28   431
1:28–29   437
1:29–30   85
2:1–3   429, 430
2:5–3:24   417
2:22–24   82
3   417
3:6   367
3:15   85, 417, 419, 485
4:24   86
5:1   415
5:1–3   417
6:11   85
7:1   103
9:3–4   86
9:5–6   86
9:6   435, 502
11:28   422
12   208, 430
12:1–3   72, 485
12:3   417, 418, 430, 437
15:6   516
15:16   37
16:6   181
16:9   181
17:6   231, 233

Genesis (cont.)
17:16   231, 233
18:18   418, 430
19:30–38   454
20   20
22   367
22:12   334
22:17–18   417, 418, 419, 430
22:18   420, 485
23:3   422
24:16   110
24:38   103
24:60   419
26   20
26:4   418, 420, 430
26:5   440
27:41   136
28:14   418, 430
29–31   82
31:50   181, 182
32:22   422
33:17   103
34:2   181
35:4   423
35:22–23   95
37:22–28   502
38:7   234
38:8   110
38:14–15   177
39:5   108
41:42   177
42:18   334
43:18   157
43:32   90
46–47   454
46:34   90
49:8–10   419
49:10   233, 485

Genesis (cont.)
49:27   170
50:1   422
50:10   177

Exodus
1:21   334
2   489
2–3   367
2:23–25   449
3:7   253
3:12   129
3:14–15   129, 130, 424
4:22   369, 530
4:22–23   417
5   58
5:2   59
6:2   111
6:3   129
6:6   111
6:8   111
6:29   111
7–12   58
7:1   133
9:2   110
12:11   264
12:12   111
13:3   112
13:9   429
13:14   374
13:14–16   437
14:31   334
15–17   371
15:9   170
15:24   379
15:26   234
16   379
16:2–3   379
16:4–5   429

Exodus (cont.)
16:23–26 429
17 379, 382
17:1–7 151, 384
17:14 415
18 449
19–34 146, 148
19:1 164
19:3–6 527
19:4 265
19:4–6 114, 430, 440, 456, 528
19:5 418
19:5–6 233, 243, 416, 418, 430, 431, 437, 531
19:6 264, 353, 418
19:22 418
19:25 114
20 94, 95, 115, 117, 121, 123, 143
20–23 123
20:1 100, 115, 141, 418, 437
20:1–17 93, 94, 97, 123, 124, 125
20:2 12, 97, 99, 100, 111, 112, 113, 114, 115, 122, 421, 425
20:2–3 113, 116
20:2–6 97, 100, 121, 426
20:2–17 98, 100, 415
20:3–6 97, 318
20:3 99, 100, 101, 111, 112, 114, 115, 116, 117, 122, 421, 422
20:4 100, 111, 112, 116, 421
20:4–5 106
20:4–6 99, 101, 114, 122, 423
20:5 111, 115, 116, 117, 118, 424
20:6 114, 422
20:7 57, 100, 111, 112, 117, 128, 129, 426
20:8 111, 112
20:8–11 99, 117, 267

Exodus (cont.)
20:9 111
20:10 108, 111, 428
20:11 111, 429
20:12 111, 112, 117, 389, 432
20:13–16 99, 106
20:13–17 103, 107, 115, 389
20:14 110, 318
20:15 499, 500
20:17 97, 99, 100, 101, 103, 106, 107, 108, 110, 318, 389, 434
20:18–19 114
20:19 114
20:20 417, 416, 334
20:23 318
20:24 236, 237, 238, 519
21–24 205
21:2–11 322
21:4–5 500
21:7–8 497
21:15 433
21:16 499, 500, 506, 508
21:17 433
21:18–21 318
21:18–27 500
21:26–27 318
21:28–32 500
21:37 81, 499
21:37–22:3 500
22 88
22:6 499
22:6–14 500
22:7 499
22:16–17 318
22:21–22 181
22:22 434
22:26–27 114
23:2–8 318
23:4–5 318
23:9 442
23:20 423
23:20–33 374
23:24 116
24:12 124, 415

Exodus (cont.)
24:18 156
25:21–22 415, 417
31:13 429, 431
31:14–15 57
31:17 429
31:18 124, 415
32 150, 151, 152, 154, 158, 160, 161, 162, 164, 371
32–34 150, 151, 153, 154, 155, 158, 160, 163, 376
32:1–6 161
32:3 161
32:4 154, 161, 162
32:6 161
32:7–8 163
32:7–10 156
32:7–14 154
32:9 154
32:9–10 162
32:11 361
32:11–14 156, 158
32:13 154, 158
32:14 158
32:15–16 124, 415
32:20 152, 153, 155
32:21 153, 162
32:23–24 423
32:30 153
32:30–31 162
32:30–32 153
32:31 153
32:32 153
32:33–35 159
32:34 153
32:35 162
33:14 431
33:15–16 431
33:16 431, 437
33:19 422
34 123
34:1 124
34:5–7 128
34:5–8 129
34:6 129
34:6–7 477
34:7 153

Exodus (cont.)
34:9   153
34:11–26   93, 123, 124
34:14   117, 424
34:15_16   173
34:19   114
34:23   114
34:27–28   123, 415
34:28   93, 123, 124, 156, 368, 377, 378, 437
34:29–30   489
35:2   57
40:20–21   415, 417
40:34–35   361

Leviticus
1–16   92
1:16   274
2:6   112
2:13   110
4–5   340
4:12   274
6:3–4   274
6:7   112
7:1   55
7:19–20   87
9:24   56
10   47, 55
10:2   55, 56
10:3   422
10:10–11   291
11:44   111
11:44–45   417
12   354
14:8   176
15   354
15:41   111
16   32
17   86
17–22   86
17:2–5   86
17:8–9   86
18   90
18:2   111
18:2–6   114
18:4–5   111
18:5   111, 396, 401, 402, 408

Leviticus (cont.)
18:6–30   354
18:17   318
18:24–25   21
18:24–30   354
18:26–27   90
18:29–30   90
18:30   111
19   123, 354, 451
19:2   111, 417, 433
19:3–4   123
19:4   118, 318, 423
19:5   114
19:8   114
19:11–18   318
19:12   111, 114
19:13   323
19:14   111, 334
19:16   111
19:17–18   318
19:18   111, 439, 442, 451
19:19   114
19:28   111
19:32   111, 334
19:33–34   451
19:34   439
19:36   114
19:37   111
20:7   111, 417
20:8   111, 431
20:9   433
20:10   81, 318
20:22–24   21
20:22–27   354
20:24   111
20:26   417
21   292
21:5   176
21:8   431
21:12   111
21:15   431
21:23   431
22:2–3   111
22:8   111
22:9   431
22:13   179
22:16   431
22:30–33   111

Leviticus (cont.)
22:32   431
23–27   205
24:10–16   87
24:10–23   57
24:12–16   57
24:15–22   57
24:22   57
25:6–7   318
25:17   334
25:23   447
25:31   108
25:38   111
25:39–40   497
25:47   448
25:55   111
26   205, 207, 229, 289, 291, 292
26:2   111
26:12   233
26:14   111
26:18   300
26:19   10
26:21   300
26:22   292
26:23   300
26:27   300
26:33   289, 290, 292, 293, 300
26:38   292
26:40   207
26:40–45   205, 207
26:41   207
26:45   111

Numbers
3:4   55, 422
3:13   111
3:41   111
3:45   111
4:13   274
6:27   426
10:10   164
10:29   280
11:1–3   151
11:4–35   151
12   53
12:1   54
12:2   53

Numbers (cont.)
12:6–8   53
14   158
14:1–4   145
14:24   218
14:26–35   145
14:34   378
15   340
15:32–36   57, 88
15:35   58, 112
16   52, 56
16:1   56
16:2   56
16:3   56
16:8–11   56
16:11   57
16:19–35   56
16:23–27   57
16:30   56
17:3   57
17:17   103
19   354
20   379
20:29   177
21   58
22–24   454
24:7   419
24:17–19   419
25   297
25:1–9   297
25:1–15   480
25:17   112
26:61   55
27:1–11   448
27:15–17   518
27:17   489
30:14   181
32:13   234
35:25–28   89
36:1–12   448

Deuteronomy
1   52
1–4   58, 481
1–11   62, 108, 110, 111,
       124, 132, 140, 141,
       269, 297, 304, 435,
       464
1–30   417

Deuteronomy (cont.)
1:1   79, 145
1:2   145, 204
1–3   203, 224
1:3–4   125
1:5   272
1:6   145, 201
1:6–18   146
1:6–3:29   13
1:6–4:40   146
1:7   159
1:7–8   360
1:8   201, 206
1:9–18   201, 231
1:10–11   208
1:16   112, 447
1:16–17   449
1:17   335
1:19   145, 146
1:19–45   60
1:19–46   146, 163, 201
1:20   206
1:25   206, 209
1:26–33   145, 209
1:26–40   452
1:26–43   213
1:26–46   204
1:27   193
1:30   154
1:31   194
1:34   342
1:34–35   145
1:35   206
1:35–36   135
1:36   213, 217, 218
1:37   214, 219, 480
1:38   161, 209, 213, 217
1:40   206
1:44   191
1:46   204
2   67, 211
2:1   204
2:1–15   146
2:1–23   65, 70, 71, 76
2:2–4   202
2–3   60
2:4   65, 70, 159, 454
2:4–23   211
2:5   168

Deuteronomy (cont.)
2:5–8   454
2:7   202, 210, 342
2:8   65, 70
2:8–12   454
2:12   454
2:14   202
2:14–16   145, 297
2:15   201
2:16   135, 200
2:18   159
2:19–21   454
2:24   168
2:26–3:11   204, 208,
          213, 214
2:29   206, 454
2:30   168
2:34   85
3:2   209
3:2–5   128
3:6   85
3:14   128
3:15   128
3:20   84
3:21   134, 159, 161
3:24   341
3:25–26   214
3:26   219, 480
3:28   160, 209
3:29   297
4   162, 163, 207, 214,
    242, 243, 244, 463,
    464, 475, 479, 480
4:1   204, 206, 464, 466,
      473
4:1–2   474
4:1–5   356
4:1–8   373, 474, 513,
        514
4:1–32   233
4:1–40   464, 465, 467,
         471, 472, 474, 479
4:2   330, 468, 473
4:3   193, 201, 467
4:3–4   217, 474, 480
4:4   213, 218, 371, 467
4:4–7   136
4:5   353, 466, 468, 472,
      473, 474, 475

Deuteronomy (cont.)
4:5–8   418, 430, 437, 440, 451, 453, 456, 474
4:6   276, 333, 468, 495
4:6–8   208, 211, 243
4:7   371, 468, 471, 475, 482
4:8   452, 471, 473, 475
4:9   217, 450, 467, 468
4:9–10   204, 474
4:9–14   135
4:9–24   203
4:9–31   464
4:10   141, 145, 453, 454, 334
4:10–14   201, 334, 467, 474
4:10–15   146
4:12   134, 146
4:12–13   124, 125
4:12–14   471
4:13   93, 113, 123, 146, 203, 207, 272, 437, 472, 473
4:13–19   472
4:14   159, 354, 468, 473
4:15   134, 145, 468
4:15–16   467
4:15–18   424
4:15–19   318, 473, 475
4:16   163
4:16–19   482
4:17   341
4:19   116, 191, 320, 321, 470, 475
4:19–20   208, 501
4:20   136, 201, 204, 465, 467, 471, 472, 474
4:21   206, 219, 473
4:21–22   214, 470
4:21–24   480
4:22   159
4:23   201, 203, 207, 450, 468, 472, 475
4:23–24   424
4:23–28   207
4:24   56, 117, 473

Deuteronomy (cont.)
4:25   163, 195, 196, 201, 234, 241, 473, 474
4:25–26   479
4:25–28   190, 191, 195, 201, 202, 213, 298, 299, 301, 302, 303, 304, 472, 473, 482
4:25–31   240, 241, 247, 248, 249, 364
4:26   159, 195, 210, 299, 468
4:26–27   197
4:26–28   241, 299, 472
4:27   191, 219, 290, 293, 298, 360
4:27–28   290, 294
4:28   195, 219, 294, 475, 518
4:29   468
4:29–30   198, 211, 241
4:29–31   190, 195, 197, 198, 199, 201, 205, 211, 270
4:30   198
4:30–31   198, 437
4:31   198, 199, 203, 206, 207, 211, 241, 243, 471, 472, 477
4:32   210, 466, 468
4:32–35   471
4:32–38   208
4:32–40   474, 475
4:33   482
4:34   154, 471, 474, 475, 501
4:34–36   201
4:35   266
4:35–36   425
4:36   134
4:37   237, 267, 467, 472, 474
4:38   467
4:39   210, 266, 341, 424, 430, 475
4:39–40   452, 474
4:40   206, 334, 468, 472, 473, 474, 479

Deuteronomy (cont.)
4:41–43   330
4:44   373
4:44–26:19   373
4:44–30:20   224
4:44–49   297
4:45   373
4:45–46   125
5   95, 110, 114, 118, 119, 121, 122, 123, 125, 146, 159
5:1   12, 272
5:1–21   94
5:1–26:19   524
5:2   145
5:2–3   201, 202, 203, 373
5:2–31   203
5:2–33   201
5:3   135, 145, 200, 206, 452
5:4   114
5:4–5   115, 125
5:5   114
5:5–21   93
5:6   97, 99, 100, 111, 112, 113, 114, 115, 122, 204, 421, 425, 505
5:6–7   113, 116
5:6–8   382
5:6–9   163
5:6–10   97, 100, 121, 426
5:6–21   93, 94, 100, 123, 124, 125, 146, 157, 204, 373, 415
5:6–27   233
5:7   99, 100, 101, 111, 112, 114, 115, 116, 117, 122, 230, 421, 422
5:7–10   97
5:8   111, 112, 116, 421
5:8–9   106
5:8–10   99, 101, 114, 122, 423
5:9   111, 115, 116, 117, 118, 424

Deuteronomy (cont.)
5:10   114, 359, 422
5–11   373
5:11   100, 112, 117, 128, 129, 426
5:11–12   111
5:12   111, 112, 122, 125, 267
5:12–15   99, 117, 318
5:13   111
5:14   111, 428, 447, 448
5:14–15   322
5:14–16   111
5:15   89, 111, 117, 267, 429, 449, 450
5:16   112, 117, 122, 125, 184, 206, 389, 390, 432
5:17   109, 110, 122, 502
5:17–20   99, 106
5:17–21   103, 107, 115, 389, 390
5:18–21   108, 110
5:19   499, 508
5:21   97, 99, 100, 101, 106, 107, 108, 110, 121, 318, 389, 390, 434, 436
5:22   114, 125, 141, 272, 415, 453
5:22–28   488
5:22–33   146
5:23   114
5:23–29   204
5:24–28   213, 214
5–26   157
5:26   334
5:27   114
5:28   488
5:28–31   157
5:29   196, 197, 204, 213, 214, 334, 488
5:31   119, 204, 206, 360
5:32–33   204, 373
6–8   368, 369, 373
6–9   366
6:1   119, 159, 354, 360
6:1–3   204
6:2   334

Deuteronomy (cont.)
6:4   111, 127, 143, 330, 382
6:4–5   119, 130, 137, 141, 230, 374, 428
6:4–6   128
6:4–9   37, 373, 374
6:5   82, 128, 132, 137, 197, 273, 366, 426, 439, 512
6:6   127, 141, 143, 144, 428, 452
6:6–9   140, 272, 432
6:7   375, 437
6:7–9   142
6:8   428
6:9   130, 272
6:10   201, 206, 375
6:10–11   209, 356, 363
6:10–12   375
6:10–15   382
6:10–19   374, 382
6:11   329
6:12   209, 375, 450
6:12–15   114
6:13   334, 371, 334, 374
6:13–14   375
6:14   209
6:14–15   118, 193
6:15   117, 375, 384
6:16   201, 257, 366, 371, 384
6:18   201, 204, 206, 234, 356
6:20   373
6:20–23   201
6:20–25   201, 217, 373, 374, 433, 437, 474, 514, 515, 516, 517
6:21   201
6:22   154, 213, 214
6:22–23   201
6:23   201, 206
6:24   204, 334, 334
6:24–25   515
7   59, 374, 382, 445
7:1   173, 208, 353
7:1–5   209, 230, 352, 374
7:1–6   168

Deuteronomy (cont.)
7:1–7   355
7:2   85, 193, 203
7:3   173, 355, 362
7:3–4   173, 443
7:3–5   58
7:4   193, 230, 382
7:5   191
7:6   82, 194, 243, 264, 353, 530
7:6–7   237, 267, 530
7:6–11   208
7:6–16   206
7:7   200
7:7–8   452
7:7–11   480
7:8   201, 206, 361
7:9   203, 264, 334, 359, 375
7:11   119
7:12   203, 206, 207
7:13   206, 208
7:13–16   207
7:14   208
7:15–16   208
7:17   162
7:17–19   160
7:17–23   209
7:18   154, 267, 375
7:18–23   213
7:19   201
7:21   160, 359
7:22   193
7:24   193
7:25   354, 355
7:25–26   58, 90, 266
7:26   193
8   375, 379
8:1   206, 208, 375
8:1–6   375, 379
8:1–18   302
8:2   267, 334, 369, 377
8:2–4   201
8:2–5   202, 204
8:3   210, 366, 371, 378, 379, 380
8:4   210
8:5   208, 369
8:6   334, 335
8:7   209

Deuteronomy (cont.)
8:7–10   209, 356, 363, 375, 376
8:9   209, 210
8:10   329
8:11   334, 450
8:11–17   209, 376, 382
8:12   329
8:14   201, 450
8:15–16   201
8:17   162, 375
8:17–18   160
8:18   154, 201, 203, 206, 375
8:18–20   376
8:19   209, 450
8:19–20   193, 375
8:26   85
9   52, 148, 153, 154, 163, 202
9–10   135, 145, 147, 148, 149, 150, 151, 153, 154, 155, 157, 160, 161, 162, 163, 164
9–11   376
9:1   159, 208
9:1–4   356
9:1–24   530
9:1–10:11   159
9:2   159
9:3   56, 159, 160, 193
9:3–6   376
9:4   160, 162, 403, 404
9:4–5   17, 21, 36, 37, 201
9:4–6   19, 404
9:4–7   160
9:5   21, 133, 154, 201, 206
9:6   154, 160, 196, 202, 204, 206, 213, 217
9:6–7   452
9:6–21   192
9:6–10:11   217
9:7   19, 151, 154, 157, 196, 201, 202, 213, 217, 267, 450
9:7–8   193, 342

Deuteronomy (cont.)
9:7–10:11   146, 149, 151, 154, 155, 159, 160
9:7–10…11   147
9:7–21   152
9:8   145, 157, 159
9:8–19   201
9:8–21   213, 214
9:9   152, 156, 203, 369, 377, 378
9:9–10   156
9:10   152, 272, 415, 453
9:11   156, 203
9:11–17   156
9:12   152, 157, 163, 196
9:12–14   156, 157
9:13   154, 196, 213, 217, 452
9:14   193, 203
9:15   203
9:15–17   156
9:16   152, 157
9:17   154, 157, 159
9:18   153, 156, 157, 158, 162, 234, 465, 489
9:18–19   157, 159
9:18–20   193
9:18–21   156
9:19   156, 158, 342
9:20   151, 158, 162
9:20–21   52, 53
9:21   152, 153, 155, 159, 162, 163, 272
9:22   201, 342
9:22–23   193
9:22–24   151, 152, 156, 193, 202, 213
9:23   157
9:24   196, 213, 217
9:25   156, 157, 193
9:25–29   152, 157, 158
9:25–10:9   156
9:26   193, 361, 501
9:27   19, 153, 154, 158, 213, 452
9:28   193, 197, 211
9:29   208, 361, 501
10   148, 458

Deuteronomy (cont.)
10:1–2   157
10:1–5   152, 158, 415, 417
10:1–10   376
10:4   93, 123, 124, 125, 272, 437, 453
10:6   214
10:6–7   151
10:6–9   156, 158
10:8   203
10:10   156, 201
10:10–11   152, 156, 157, 158, 159
10:11   157, 159, 160, 206
10:11:1   376
10:12   159, 334
10:12–11:1   137
10:12–13   334
10:12–19   439
10:12–22   131, 233, 480
10:13   376
10:14   210, 502
10:14–22   376
10:15   137, 208, 237, 267
10:16   196, 197, 208, 213, 217, 376, 408, 451
10:17   359, 423, 425
10:17–18   90, 323, 434
10:17–19   442
10:18   137, 184, 335
10:18–19   434, 447, 451
10:19   201, 450, 501
10:20   334, 334
10:21   376
10:22   208, 213, 214
10:28–40   85
11:1   376
11:1–8   480
11:1–32   233
11:2   200, 452
11:2–7   213, 214, 376
11:3–4   201
11:4   191, 192
11:6   52, 53, 55, 56
11:8   159, 354, 356

Deuteronomy (cont.)
11:8–9 204
11:8–17 376
11:9 201, 206
11:9–12 209
11:10 353
11:11 159, 354
11:13 159, 452
11:15 329
11:16 209, 253, 319, 321
11:16–17 193, 272
11:17 193, 206
11:18–21 141, 272
11:18–25 376
11:19 433, 437
11:20 272
11:21 206, 208
11:23 208
11:25 208
11:26–27 207, 363
11:26–32 376
11:29 353
11:31 206
11:31–32 230
12 72, 73, 76, 77, 78, 86, 235, 236, 238, 518, 519, 520
12–26 37, 119, 166, 205, 217, 501
12:1 204, 518
12:1–4 230
12:1–14 517, 518
12:2 77, 236, 266
12:2–4 37, 48
12:2–5 239
12:3 191, 238
12:5 72, 236, 237, 238, 246, 361, 519
12:5–7 86
12:6 339, 520
12:6–7 73
12:6–11 521
12:7 343, 519, 520
12:8 196, 213, 234
12:9 84
12:9–10 206, 431
12:9–14 86
12:10 84
12:10–11 236

Deuteronomy (cont.)
12:11 236, 237, 246, 361, 519, 520
12:11–18 78
12:12 89, 322, 343, 434, 519, 520
12:14 236, 237, 361, 519
12:15 87
12:15–16 86
12:17 339
12:17–18 87
12:18 89, 236, 237, 322, 343, 519, 520
12:20–28 86
12:21 191, 236, 237, 519
12:25 234
12:26 236, 237, 361, 519
12:28 141, 234, 356
12:29–31 21
12:29–32 48
12:31 90, 354, 355
13 64, 85, 341, 389
13:1 330
13:1–3 257
13:1–5 491
13:2–6 341
13:4 201
13:5 272, 334, 335
13:6 87, 88, 191, 321, 504
13:6–18 230
13:7–11 82
13:7–12 445
13:9 201
13:10 64
13:10–31 362
13:11 87, 191
13:14 191
13:14–15 355
13:15 87, 90, 354, 491
13:17 318
13:18 206, 208, 318, 319
13:19 234, 334
14:1 194, 515, 530
14:1–2 48, 530
14:2 210, 237, 264, 267

Deuteronomy (cont.)
14:3 91
14:21 264, 447, 453
14:23 237, 334
14:23–25 236, 237, 519
14:24 191, 237
14:24–25 361
14:26 343, 520
14:29 184, 323, 329, 342, 447, 448, 451
15 83
15:1–18 140, 448
15:2 112
15:3 447
15:4 206
15:4–6 83
15:7 83, 206
15:7–14 83
15:9 90, 160, 339
15:11 83, 356
15:12 434, 497
15:12–15 322
15:12–17 318, 322
15:13–14 89
15:15 201, 267
15:20 236, 519
16:1 201
16:2 236, 237, 519
16:3 201, 264, 267
16:6 201, 237, 361
16:6–7 236, 237, 519
16:9–15 318
16:10 339
16:11 89, 236, 237, 322, 323, 343, 447, 449, 519, 520
16:12 201, 267, 450
16:14 89, 236, 322, 323, 447, 449, 520
16:14–15 343
16:15 342, 451
16:15–16 236, 519
16:16 237
16:18–18:22 121, 451, 459
16:18–20 70
16:19 89
16:20 168, 191, 206, 265
17 64, 85

Deuteronomy (cont.)
17:1   354
17:1–4   355
17:2   203, 234, 465
17:2–7   64, 321
17:3   320
17:4   272, 354
17:5   87
17:7   87, 88, 233, 504
17:8   236, 237, 361, 519
17:8–9   291
17:8–13   127, 231
17:10   237, 361, 519
17:12   88, 504
17:14   206, 522
17:14–20   78, 231, 233, 323, 419, 451, 452, 521, 526
17:15   231, 447, 522, 523
17:16   67, 157, 201, 523
17:16–17   231
17:16–20   522, 523
17:17   524
17:18   146, 272, 525
17:18–20   231, 277, 419, 525
17:19   334, 335
17:19–20   272, 525
18   488
18:1   233
18:5   237
18:6   236, 361, 447, 519
18:9   90, 206, 230, 354, 486
18:9–12   355
18:9–14   48, 253, 486
18:10–12   230
18:12   90, 354
18:15   127, 487, 488
18:15–17   485, 487
18:15–22   485, 486, 492
18:16   145, 453
18:16–17   487, 488
18:17–20   157
18:18   487, 489
18:18–19   486, 487, 489
18:19   338, 487, 490
18:20   87, 487, 488, 491
18:20–22   487, 491

Deuteronomy (cont.)
18:21–22   487, 492
18:22   487, 488, 491
19:1–2   206
19:1–13   84
19:5   89, 191
19:6   191
19:10   206
19:11–13   88
19:13   504
19:14   206
19:15   389, 390
19:18   272
19:19   84, 88
19:19–20   88
20   85, 169, 179, 445
20:1   168, 201, 523
20:1–4   209
20:3   257
20:4   168
20:5–7   84
20:7   434
20:8   301
20:10–12   84
20:10–15   85
20:10–18   85, 168
20:13   171, 302
20:14   169
20:16   302
20:16–18   84, 168, 209
20:18   90
20:19   168, 191
20:21   302
20:26–27   238
21   185
21:1   206
21:1–9   169
21:4   238
21:5   237, 291
21:7   428
21:9   234
21:10   168, 169
21:10–12   174
21:10–13   171, 178, 179, 186
21:10–14   89, 165, 166, 168, 169, 170, 171, 174, 178, 181, 184, 185, 187, 324, 436, 448

Deuteronomy (cont.)
21:10–17   434
21:10–34:12   169, 504
21:11   172
21:12   172
21:12–13   175
21:13   170
21:14   178, 179, 180, 181, 182, 184, 186, 187, 503, 504
21:15–17   82, 166
21:18   88, 218
21:18–21   166, 184, 434, 445
21:20   218
21:21   88
21:21–22   504
21:22–23   396
21:23   206, 389
21:24   504
21:25   233
21:33   390
22:1   191
22:1–4   448
22:5   354
22:6–7   448
22:8   89
22:13–19   184
22:13–21   166, 187, 434, 445
22:14   184
22:19   178
22:21   88
22:21–22   88
22:22   88
22:23–29   434
22:24   88, 181
22:29   178, 181
23   336, 338, 339, 340, 342
23:1   110
23:2–8   443
23:3–5   351
23:3–6   66
23:3–8   458
23:4   201
23:4–9   445, 453, 460
23:5   454
23:7   355
23:8   447, 454

Deuteronomy (cont.)
23:10–11   337
23:10–14   47
23:10–15   454
23:14   47
23:15   322
23:15–16   89, 448
23:19   90, 354
23:20   82
23:20–21   89
23:21   354, 447
23:22–24   332, 336
23:25   329
23:25–26   90, 337
24:1–4   91, 166, 178, 179, 187, 272, 435
24:4   184, 206, 354
24:5   166, 343
24:6   82, 89
24:7   88, 89, 180, 324, 448, 495, 497, 499, 500, 503, 504, 506, 508
24:8–9   54
24:9   201, 267
24:10   82
24:10–13   89
24:14   185, 447
24:14–15   82, 323, 449
24:15   90, 339
24:17   323, 434, 447
24:17–18   449
24:17–22   184
24:18   201, 267, 450
24:18–21   323, 434
24:19   342, 451
24:19–21   447, 448
24:19–22   82, 90
24:22   201, 267, 450
25:4   389, 390, 448
25:5–10   166, 435
25:13–14   112
25:13–16   91
25:15   206
25:16   354
25:17   201, 267
25:18   334
25:19   84, 206, 450
26:1   206
26:2   236, 237, 361, 519

Deuteronomy (cont.)
26:3   206
26:5   208, 447, 454
26:6–7   201
26:6–10   450
26:8   201
26:9   361
26:10   237
26:11   343, 449, 520
26:11–13   447
26:12   329, 434
26:12–13   323, 448
26:13   237, 450
26:15   206, 237, 341, 451
26:16   531
26:16–18   440
26:16–19   208, 211, 233, 243, 452, 472, 527, 528, 529
26:17   531
26:17–19   437, 528
26:18   530
26:18–19   418, 430
26:19   208, 210, 211, 264, 530
27–28   229
27–30   230, 392, 397
27–32   220
27   76, 77, 78, 91, 246
27:1–8   272
27:2–3   127, 206
27:4   78
27:4–5   73
27:6–7   78
27:7   343
27:8   272
27:9   529
27:12   207
27:15   90, 266, 321, 354, 355
27:15–26   123, 217, 364
27:16   433
27:18   448
27:19   184, 323, 441, 447, 449
27:26   389, 390, 391, 392, 393, 394, 399, 400, 412

Deuteronomy (cont.)
28   9, 62, 205, 214, 232, 294, 305, 443
28:1   208, 334, 528, 530
28:1–14   207
28:1–68   524
28:6   3
28:7   84
28:8   206
28:9   264
28:9–10   208, 211, 427
28:10   208, 210, 238, 354, 426, 530
28:11   206, 208
28:12   342
28:12–13   453
28:13   208
28:15   195, 334
28:15–66   364
28:15–68   19, 92, 190, 192, 335
28:20   195
28:20–68   230
28:21   354
28:22   191
28:23   9
28:25   211
28:27–33   9
28:30   319
28:36   230, 294, 295
28:36–37   290, 304
28:37   191, 211
28:41   191, 290
28:43   447
28:43–44   448, 453
28:45   191, 334
28:45–68   196
28:48   270
28:49   210
28:58   195, 273
28:58–68   195, 197, 201, 202, 213, 364, 526
28:61   127, 393
28:61–64   191
28:63   195, 197, 230, 354
28:64   191, 195, 210, 219, 290, 293, 294, 295, 298, 360
28:65–67   219

Deuteronomy (cont.)
28:65–68 202
28:68 195, 202, 219
28:69 145, 203
28:69–30:20 299, 407
29 211, 240, 242, 243
29–30 240, 241, 299
29:1 154, 201, 489
29:1–9 242
29:1–30:10 243
29:3 132, 196, 197, 213, 218, 389
29:4–5 201
29:5 111
29:8 203
29:9–11 443
29:9–14 218
29:10 447
29:10–14 242
29:11 203, 299, 453
29:11–12 452
29:12 206, 208
29:13 203, 299
29:15–16 297
29:15–18 241
29:15–20 242, 243
29:16 201, 294
29:16–28 249
29:16–30:10 241, 242
29:17–20 217, 219
29:17–27 240
29:18 203, 218
29:18–28 335
29:19 241
29:19–20 217, 241
29:20 203, 273, 393
29:21 218, 447
29:21–22 210, 241
29:21–23 211
29:21–27 197, 210, 218, 242, 300, 301
29:22–26 197
29:23 210, 241
29:24 195, 202, 203, 205
29:24–25 241
29:24–27 290
29:26 210, 393, 397
29:26–27 241

Deuteronomy (cont.)
29:27 202, 210, 342
29:28 197, 205, 307
29:29 324
30 199, 240, 242, 243, 404, 405, 406, 410
30–33 220
30:1 141, 191, 196, 198, 207, 290
30:1–2 198, 241
30:1–4 364
30:1–10 190, 196, 198, 199, 201, 205, 207, 208, 211, 219, 240, 241, 243, 244, 247, 270, 408, 452
30:1–14 408
30:2 203, 208, 360, 361, 437
30:3 191, 199, 241, 290
30:3–5 198, 241
30:4 191, 360, 361
30:5 208, 211
30:6 197, 198, 199, 201, 203, 207, 208, 211, 214, 218, 241, 302, 439, 440
30:7 208, 241
30:8 83, 198, 208, 241, 437, 440
30:9 83, 208, 342
30:9–10 241
30:10 208, 273, 334, 393
30:11 406
30:11–14 212, 307, 308, 325, 389, 390, 400, 403, 407, 408, 409, 410, 411, 412
30:12–14 391, 402, 404, 407, 410
30:13 405, 406
30:14 406
30:15 483
30:15–16 452
30:15–20 214, 233, 364
30:16 334, 354
30:17 116, 191
30:17–18 193, 335
30:18 159, 193, 290

Deuteronomy (cont.)
30:19 210, 299, 452, 483
30:19–20 230
30:20 201, 206, 212
31 157
31:1 141, 214
31:1–8 246
31:1–13 213, 214
31:3 159
31:3–5 208
31:6–8 209
31:9 127, 203
31:9–11 142
31:9–13 145, 273, 449, 527
31:10–11 127
31:11 236, 519
31:12 322, 447, 453
31:12–13 334
31:14 214
31:14–29 214, 398
31:16 202, 203, 205, 213, 214
31:16–20 300
31:16–21 196, 201, 335, 417
31:18–21 196
31:19–22 273
31:20 202, 203, 205, 213, 329
31:20–21 206
31:21 213, 450
31:23 206, 209
31:24–29 273
31:25–26 127, 203
31:26 417
31:27 196, 217, 300
31:27–29 417
31:28 141, 210, 299, 453
31:29 163, 196, 201, 214, 234, 300, 335, 465
31:30 453
31:50 181
32 196, 289, 291, 298, 320
32:1 210, 299
32:1–43 256

Deuteronomy (cont.)
32:4   335
32:6   201
32:6–14   208
32:8   443, 454
32:9   501
32:11–12   265
32:15   213, 264
32:15–25   335
32:16   117, 266
32:16–17   491
32:17   423, 424
32:18   450
32:21   117, 389
32:22   319
32:28   110
32:30   110, 191
32:35   389, 390
32:36   110
32:39   197, 264, 266, 424
32:40   298
32:40–41   298
32:40–42   335
32:41   335
32:43   208, 389, 390
32:45   141
32:48–52   214, 330
32:49   206
32:51   219
32:52   206
33:2   145, 146, 201, 281
33:5   231, 264
33:9   203
33:18   343
33:21   335
33:23   110
33:26   264, 341
33:27   208
33:29   208, 264
34   246, 331
34:1   123, 368
34:1–4   368, 381
34:1–12   214, 330
34:2   181
34:4   206, 368
34:8   177
34:10   127
34:10–12   213
34:12   201

Deuteronomy (cont.)
34:28   124
49:7   267

Joshua
1:1–9   246
1:8   246
1:13   431
2:12   429
4:24   334
6:2   133
6:17–18   58
6:21   58, 85
7   50, 58
7:1   58
7:2–5   58
7:10–26   58
7:19–21   58
7:24–26   58
8:30–35   233, 238, 246
9   85
9:25   234
9:27   236, 246
17:16–18   523
18:1   73
22:16   73
22:24–27   73
24:14   297, 334
24:14–28   233
24:15   103
24:19   117
24:23   423
24:29   246

Judges
1:1   246
1:17   85
1:19   523
2:5   238
2:8   246
2:10   74, 433
2:11   235
3:5–6   173
3:7   235
3:12   235
3:30   66
4:1   235
5:30   169
6:8–10   114
6:25   74

Judges (cont.)
6:26   238
8:33–34   74
10:6   74, 235
10:16   424
11   342
11:2   107
11:15   67
11:31   103
11:34   103
13:1   235
13:16–23   238
16:17   176
16:19   176
16:22   176
17:1–5   74
17:6   234, 246
18:1   246
19:1   246
19:24   181
20:5   181
20:27   74
21:25   234, 246

1 Samuel
4   74
4:4   470
4–6   420
6:14–15   238
7:3   424
7:9   74
7:9–10   238
7:17   238
8   232, 522
8:5   232
8:7–8   232
8:11–18   232
8:19–20   232
9:12–14   239
9:16   138
9:19   239
9:25   239
10:5   239
10:8   238
10:13   239
10:19   232
11:8–11   67
11:15   74, 238
12:2–5   315
12:14   334

Index of Scripture

1 Samuel (cont.)
12:20–21 425
12:24 334
13:8–15 232
13:9–14 74, 232
13:14 138
14:7 138
14:36 111
14:47 67
15:10–11 232
15:17–35 232
15:19 235
15:22 340
15:27 340
16:1–13 232
16–31 138
17:45 470
20:16 103
22:6 239
24:6 45
24:10 45
25:43 232
26:9 45
26:11 45
26:16 45
26:21 340
26:23 45
27:3 103
30:16 170
31:13 177

2 Samuel
1:14 45
1:16 45
6 74
6:2 470
6:13 238
7 233, 246
7:1 431
7:2 133
7:12–13 419
7:12–17 485
8:2 67
8:4 67
8:13 67
8:14 67
8:17 14
10–12 67
10:4 176
11:20–21 53

2 Samuel (cont.)
12:9 235
12:28 238
13:12 181
13:14 181
13:22 181
13:32 181
14:6 110
14:26 176
15:12 74
19:7 234
23:3 334
24:22 238
24:24–25 238

1 Kings
1–2 246
2:2–4 232
3:2 76
3:2–4 74, 239
3:4 238
3:5 341
3:7–14 232
3:15 341
4:3 14
4:20 343
5–10 20
7:7 54
8 236, 240, 241, 242, 243
8:10–11 361
8:22–53 240
8:23 359
8:23–61 274
8:28–29 359
8:43 238
8:46–53 239, 240, 241, 243, 244, 248
8:51 465
8:51–53 243
8:62–64 236
9:3 238, 246
9:6–9 232
9:7 422
9:9 116
11:1–2 173
11:1–10 230
11:2 173
11:4–11 232
11:7 74, 239

1 Kings (cont.)
11:8 173
11:29–30 232
11:33 234
11:34 232
11:38 234
12 147, 150, 151, 154, 160, 161, 162, 164
12:25–33 232
12:26 162
12:26–32 160
12:28 154, 161
12:30 162
12:31–32 74, 239
12:32–33 161
12:33 162
13:2 74
13:32–33 74
13:33–34 232
13:34 162
14:1–16 232
14:8 234
14:10 504
14:16 163
14:20 162
14:21 238
14:22–24 239
14:23 74, 77
15:5 234
15:11 234
15:14 74, 239
15:26 235
15:29 260
15:30 163
15:34 163, 235
15:35 74
16:2 163
16:19 163, 235
16:25 235
16:26 163
16:30 235
16:31 163
18:12 334
18:33–38 238
19:8 377
21:1–3 448
21:20 235
21:22 163
21:25 235
22:19 422, 470

1 Kings (cont.)
22:19–22   422
22:43   74, 234, 239
22:52   163
22:53   235

2 Kings
3   20, 67
3:2   235
3:3   163
3:24   68
3:36–37   19
5:2–3   169
8:18   235
8:20   68
8:22   68
8:27   235
9:36   260
10:10   260
10:29   163
10:30   234
10:31   163
11:6   235
11:18   154, 272
12:3   74, 234, 239
13:2   163, 235
13:6   163
13:11   163, 235
13:14   422
14:3   234
14:4   74, 239
14:7   68
14:22   235
14:24   163, 235
14:25   260
15:3   234
15:4   74, 239
15:9   163, 235
15:18   163, 235
15:24   163, 235
15:28   163, 235
15:34   234
15:35   74, 239
16:2   234
16:4   74, 77, 239
16:5   257
17   232, 252
17:2   235
17:6   305
17:7–12   230

2 Kings (cont.)
17:7–18   305
17:7–20   230
17:7–23   160
17:7–41   20
17:8   230
17:9   74, 239
17:10   77
17:11   239
17:12   230
17:13   260
17:15   230
17:17   230, 235
17:21–22   163
17:23   260
17:29   74, 239, 423
17:32   74, 239
17:35   116
18–20   232, 258
18:3   234
18:3–6   232
18:4   74, 154
18:7   232
18:13   258
18:14   239
18:22   74, 239
19:14–19   232
19:18   295, 423
21:2   235
21:2–16   232
21:3   74, 116, 239
21:4   238
21:6   235
21:7   236, 238, 246
21:8–10   260
21:15   235
21:16   235
21:20   235
22–23   157, 269
22:2   232, 234
22:3   276
22:3–20   275
22:3–23:24   277
22:8   277
22:8–23:27   235
22:11   277
22:11–13   232
22:15   20
22:19–20   232
23:2   277

2 Kings (cont.)
23:3   232
23:4–27   232
23:5   74, 239, 320
23:6   154
23:8–9   74, 239
23:13   74, 239
23:15   74, 163, 239
23:19–20   74, 239
23:32   235
23:37   235
24:2   260
24:9   235
24:19   235
25   246
25:10   358
25:27–30   228

1 Chronicles
6:3–15   55
10:12   177
16:39–40   74
21:1   377
27:32   14
29:1   130
29:15   447

2 Chronicles
1:1–3   74
1:3–6   238
6:14   359
6:20   238
6:40   359
7:14   238
7:15   359
7:22   116
12:13   238
25:12   68
26:8   68
27:5   68
29:5   354
33:3   116
33:15   424
34:6–7   71

Ezra
1:3–4   79
1:5   358
1:5–10   358
1:5–11   358

Ezra (cont.)
1:6   358
1:6–7   358
1:8–10   358
1:11   358
2:6–8   358
3:2   350
3:4   350
4:1–5   355
4:7–23   357
4:21   358
4:23   358
6:18   350
7:6   350
7:9   352
7:10   350
7:11   350
7:21   350
7:25   350
7:26   350
7:36   352
8:1–2   351
8:7–8   351
8:9   351
8:13   351
8:18   351
8:33   352
8:36   352
9   352
9–10   173, 442, 459
9:1–2   352
9:1–3   351
9:1–15   345
9:2   353
9:3   353
9:5   353
9:5–15   352
9:6–7   353, 362
9:6–10   353
9:6–15   189
9:7   357
9:8–9   353
9:9   357, 363
9:10   350, 353
9:10–12   353
9:11   353, 354
9:11–12   353, 357, 358
9:12   355, 356, 364
9:13   357, 363
9:13–14   351, 353

Ezra (cont.)
9:13–15   353, 362
9:14   350, 357, 363
9:14–15   357
9:15   353
9:16   351
9:26   351
9:29   351
9:34   351
10:1   157, 364
10:1–3   363
10:1–4   357
10:2   364
10:3   350
10:9   352
10:29   351
10:36   351
12:44   351

Nehemiah
1:2–3   357, 364
1:3   358
1:4–5   359
1:5   358, 363
1:5–7   362
1:5–11   345, 357
1:6   359, 360
1:6–7   358, 364
1:7   351, 360, 362
1:8   346, 360
1:8–9   358, 362
1:9   360, 361, 362, 363, 364
1:10   361, 362, 363, 364
1:11   359, 363
2:4   359
2:20   359
4:8   359
5:1–10   352
5:1–13   362
5:3   108
8   157
8:1–18   352
8:13   110
9:13   416
9:29   402
9:32   359
9:36–37   189
13   459
13:1–3   351

Nehemiah (cont.)
13:10–29   352
13:15–22   274, 352
13:23–27   173
13:25   362

Esther
6:1   5

Job
1–2   422
1:1   312, 335
1:6–12   422
1:8   312, 335
1:12   423
2:1–7   422
2:3   312, 335
2:6   423
2:10   312
3–31   308
4:2–6   315
4:7   309
4:8–9   310
4:10–11   309
4:12–16   311
4:12–21   311
4:15   312, 422
4:17   312
4:17–21   311
4:18–21   312
5:3   310
5:6–7   309
5:8–16   309
5:17–22   309
5:27   310, 312
6:5–6   310
6:10   316
6:30   310
7:1–2   310, 313
7:17–21   313
8:5–7   309
8:8–22   309
9:2–12   310
9:13–35   313
9:21   316
11:7–8   307
11:12   309
11:13–20   309
11:20   309
12:3   310

Job (cont.)
12:7–10   310
12:11   310
12:11–12   309
12:13–25   312
13:1–2   310
13:2   310
13:18   316
14:1–2   310
15:7–8   309
15:9–10   309
15:14–16   309, 311
15:17   310
15:18–35   309
16:2   310
17:5   310
19:9   177
20:4–29   309
20:19   309
21–37   315, 317, 318, 319, 321, 323
21:7–34   313
21:14   316
21:31   422
22:3   309
22:6–9   316
22:21–30   309
22:22   316
23:11–12   316
23:13   131
24:1–25   313
24:2–25   316
25:4–6   309, 311
26:5–14   310
27:5–6   316
28   307
28:20–21   307
28:21   308
28:28   335
29:2–25   315
29:11–17   316
29–31   321
30:1–31   315
31   314, 315, 317, 324
31:1   317, 318
31:1–40   315
31:4   316, 317
31:5–8   318
31:7   317, 318
31:9–12   317, 318, 319

Job (cont.)
31:12   319
31:13–15   318, 321
31:15   131
31:16–23   318, 322
31:24–25   317
31:26   320
31:26–27   319, 320, 321
31:26–28   318
31:28   321
31:29–30   317, 318
31:38–40   318, 322, 323
31:39   323
34:14–15   425
34:35   110
37:21   320

Psalms
2   485
2:7   365
2:8   381
2:11   334
7:3–5   317
9:20   422
15   315, 317
16   485
16:11   425
19:7–9   416
19:10   334
19:11   490
20:5   138
20:7   523
22   485
24   317
24:4   315
29:2   422
37:31   420
40:9   420
49:4   136
50:16–23   415
51–100   384
55:20   180
63:6   139
68:5   323
68:18   348
72   315
72:4   419
72:9   419

Psalms (cont.)
72:17   419
78   133
78:7   433, 437
81:9   415
81:10–11   114, 118
82:1   422
82:8   502
85:10–13   404
89:6   422
89:8   422
90   383, 384
90–106   383
91   383
91:1–10   384
91:11–12   366, 383
92   383
95:3   422, 423
95:7–11   431
97:7   116
101:4   133
103:1–5   139
103:20–21   422
105   371
106   371
106:13–15   371
106:13–43   371
106:19–23   371
106:26   403
106:26–27   296
106:32–33   371
107:26   403, 405
110   485, 489
111:10   334
114:8   379
119   137
119:11   420
119:20   137
119:35   137
119:71   180
119:97   137
119:131   137
128:1   334
132:7–8   429
132:13–14   429
137:7   71
145:3   307
145:9   477
146:9   323
148:2–5   422

Index of Scripture

Proverbs
1 328
1–9 317
1:8 433
1:8–9 525
1:20–33 328
3:3 420, 525
3:7 335
3:12 110
3:18 282
3:21–22 525
5:1–23 317
5:21 317
6:16 355
6:20–21 525
6:20–35 317
6:27–29 320
7:1–27 317
7:3 420
8:13 335
8:14–16 312
8:21–36 404
10:1–22:16 31
11:1 355
11:20 355
12:22 355
13:13 335
14:16 335
15:8–9 355
15:26 355
16:5 355
16:10 111
16:12 355
16:17 335
24:21 335
25:2–3 307
25:21–22 317
30:4 307
30:6 330
30:7–9 317
31:3–9 524

Ecclesiastes/Qoheleth
1:8 329
2–3 343
2:10 343
2:26 339, 341
3:12 343
3:14 330, 331, 332
3:15 332

Ecclesiastes (cont.)
3:16 332
3:16–17 332
3:17 332
3:22 343
4:1–16 342
4:6 338
4:8–9 329
4:13 338
4:17 337, 340
4:17–5:6 339, 340, 341, 342
5 329, 336, 338, 339, 340, 341
5:1 136, 338, 339
5:1–7 329
5:2 341
5:3 338, 340
5:3–5 334, 336
5:4–6 332
5:5 331, 332, 338, 340, 341
5:5–6 331
5:6 331, 334, 341
5:7 338
5:9 329
5:11 329
5:18 341
5:18–19 343
6:2 341
6:3 329
6:9 338
7:1–3 338
7:5 338
7:8 338
7:17 333, 338
7:17–18 335
7:18 331
7:20 339
7:26 339
8:2 332, 334
8:3 332
8:5 332, 334
8:5–6 332
8:12 334, 335, 339
8:12–13 331, 333, 343
8:15 341, 343
9:2 339
9:4 338
9:7 343

Ecclesiastes (cont.)
9:16 338
9:18 338, 339
10:5 340
10:19 343
11:7 320
11:8–9 343
11:9 333
12:2 320
12:7 341
12:9 328, 330
12:9–14 333
12:11 330
12:12 330, 331
12:13 327, 331, 333, 334
12:13–14 331, 335
12:14 333

Isaiah
1 256
1–5 253, 255
1–12 254, 305
1–27 253
1–39 256, 257, 262, 266
1:2 255, 256, 299
1:10 256
1:16–17 315
1:17 434
1:18–20 255
1:29 253, 267
2:2–4 255
2:3 420, 440
3:2–3 253
3:12 453
3:24 176
4:2–6 251
5:1–7 254
5:7 253
5:8 108
5:24 256
6 261, 422
6:1–5 253
6:3 470
6:9–10 261
7 258, 259, 261
7:1–17 257, 260, 261
7:3 258
7:4 257

Isaiah (cont.)
7:4–9 258
7:7–8 261
7:11 258
7:12 257
7:14 485
7:15–16 253, 267
7:15–17 258
8 259
8:1–2 261
8:1–15 261
8:5 261
8:11–12 261
8:18 259
9:2 170
9:6–7 419
11:1 485
11:3 334
11:14 68
14:1 253, 267
14:4–21 253
18:4 320
18–20 257
20 257, 259, 260
20:3 260
20:16 523
21:17 255
22:8–11 259
22:25 255
25:8 255
28 253
29:10 389
30:1–5 259
31:1–3 259
32:7 110
33:6 334
33:15 315
33:23 170
36:1 258
36:2 258
36–39 258, 259, 260
37:6–7 258
37:19 295
37:30 258
38:7–8 429
39:6–7 258
40–48 266, 267, 268
40–55 251, 262, 265, 266, 268, 328

Isaiah (cont.)
40–66 220, 262, 263, 265, 292
40:5 255
40:19–20 266
40:31 265
41:4 266
41:7 266
41:8–9 267
41:24 266, 425
42:1 267, 530
42:2 110
42:4 420, 440
42:8 425
42:17 116
43:10 267
43:10–11 266, 425
43:11 266
43:13 264, 266
43:18 267
43:20 267
44:1–2 267
44:2 264
44:5 426
44:6 266
44:12–13 266
44:14 266
44:19 266
44:21 267
45:4 267
45:5–6 266
45:8 404
45:9 404
45:16 266
45:17 264
45:18 266
45:21 266, 425
45:21–22 266
46:4 266
46:6 266
46:8–9 267
46:9 266
48':11 425
48:12 266
49:6 530
49:7 264
49–55 268
50:1 178
51:1 265
51:1–8 262

Isaiah (cont.)
51:4 420, 440
51:7 420
51:7–8 265
52:6 266
52:11–12 264
52:13–53:12 486
54:13 420
55 262
55:10–11 404
56:1–8 431
56:6 459
57:5 266
58:6–12 315
58:7 322
58:14 255
59:9 110
60:19–20 320
61:2 431
62:12 264
63:18 264
63:19 238
65:3 75
65:9 267
65:15 267
65:22 282
66:22–23 431

Jeremiah
1–20 274, 466, 470
1:2 284
1:4 284
1:4–10 470
1:11 284
1:12 279
1:13 284
1:18 275
2 269
2:8 275, 276, 279
2:26 275
2:35 474
3:1 178
3:8 178, 275
3:9 295
3:11–4:4 419
3:14 420
3:16–17 420
3:17 420
3:23 275
4:1–2 420

Index of Scripture

Jeremiah (cont.)
4:9   275
4:22   276
5:2   275
5:4–5   276
6:12   108
6:19   276, 279, 299
6:19–20   275
7   252, 274, 463, 464
7:1–5   479
7:1–11   315
7:1–15   275, 276, 464,
        465, 466, 470, 479
7:2   466
7:2–3   466
7:3   468, 470, 472, 479
7:3–4   468, 481
7:4   472, 474
7:5   474, 475
7:5–7   468, 473, 474
7:5–10   474
7:7   468, 472
7:8–10   468
7:8–11   474, 479
7:9   275, 415, 472, 475
7:9–10   469, 473, 474
7:9–11   478
7:10–11   238
7:11   469, 473
7:12   473
7:12–14   239
7:13–15   469
7:14   238, 480
7:15   472, 473
7:20   474
7:21–23   275
7:23   472
7:30   238, 465
8:1–2   320
8:1–3   275
8:8   275, 276, 279
9:3   276
9:6   276
9:13   276
9:24   276, 420
9:26   68
11:4   465, 472
11:15   275
11:21   467
12:14   420

Jeremiah (cont.)
12:16   420, 437, 440
13:11   531
13:12–14   275
13:18–20   275
14:9   238
15:14   474
15:15   275
15:19   282
16:5   31
16:6   176
16:11   276
17:1   275, 420
17:10   110
17:13   275
17:19   75
17:19–27   274
17:26   75
18:10   465
18:18   276
19:1–6   275
20:9   279
21:1–7   470
21–36   275
22:3–7   315
22:9   116
22:11–19   470
22:15–16   274, 420
22:24–30   470
22:30   275
23:5–6   274, 419
23:13–14   492
23:18   422
23:23   471
23:29   279
23:32   492
24   473
24:7   276, 472
25:1   277
25:11   346
25:13   275
25:15   474
25:21   68
26   479
26:1–15   479
26:4   276
26:14   234
26:17–19   274
26:18   346
26:20–23   279, 280

Jeremiah (cont.)
26:24   275, 280
27:3   68
27:15   275
28   270
28:9   492
28:16–17   470
29:3   275
29:9   492
29:10   346
29:16–20   270
30:1   275
30:8–9   420
30:22   472
30:23   474
31:1   472
31:8   420
31:9   369, 420
31:14   274
31:31   420
31:31–34   408
31:33   265, 275, 276,
        420, 437, 472
31:34   276, 420
32:9–16   275
32:12   276
32:12–16   275
32:15   108
32:23   276
32:30   465
32:38   131, 472
32:38–41   131
33:5   474
33:9   531
33:14–26   274
33:15–16   274
33:17–22   274
34:5   234
34:15   238
34:16   180
36   157, 271, 275, 276,
        277, 278, 279, 280,
        282, 283, 284, 285,
        286, 465
36:1   284
36:5   279
36:10   277
36:10–12   275
36:17–19   278
36:18   280

Jeremiah (cont.)
36:23   279, 280
36:24   277, 280
36:26   283
36:27   280, 281
36:27–32   279, 280
36:28   283
37   277
39:8   358
39:14   275
40:4–5   234
41:5   176
42:7   279
43:3–6   275
43:4   284
43:8   284
43:10   284
43:11   284
43:27   284
43:28   284
43:32   284
44:10   276
44:22   465
44:23   276
51:46   257
51:59–64   275

Lamentations
4:21–22   71
5:8   453
5:11   181

Ezekiel
1–20   296, 301, 302
3:1–3   275
3:15   110
4:1–3   429
4:25   301
5:2   288, 289
5:6–7   287
5:10   288
5:12   288, 289
5:16–17   291
6:8   288, 290
8:3   117
11:12   287
11:16   289
11:16–17   288
11:17   290

Ezekiel (cont.)
11:19   421
11:19–20   287, 302
12:14   289
12:14–15   288
12:15   290
16   289, 291
18:7   322
18:9   516
18:13   516
18:16   322
18:21   517
20   291, 295, 296, 297, 298
20:7–8   296
20:10–11   306
20:11   402
20:12   429
20:13   287, 402
20:16   287
20:20   429
20:21   287, 402
20:21–22   297
20:23   288, 290, 296, 297, 298, 299, 301, 302, 306, 360
20:24   287
20:25–26   293
20:32   295
20:34   288, 290
20:41   288, 290
21:31   177
22:10   181
22:12   288
22:15   288, 290
22:19   288
25:7   292, 293
25:12–14   71
26:16   177
27:12–24   508
27:31   176
28:7   289
28:25   288, 290
29:12   290
29:12–13   288
29:13   290
30:11   289
30:23   288, 290
30:26   288, 290
31:10   133

Ezekiel (cont.)
32:10   422
33:24   201
34:5–6   288
34:13   288
34:23–24   419
36:19   287, 288, 290
36:22–23   426
36:23   440
36:24   288
36:24–28   398
36:26–27   302, 421
36:27   287, 420, 437, 440
37:14   420
37:21   288
37:24   287
37:27   420
39:25   117
39:27–28   288
40–46   75
44:20   292
44:23–25   291
48:14   111

Daniel
5:23   424
7:13–14   381, 386, 486
9   189
9:2   346
9:4   359
9:11   398
9:18–19   238
9:19   426
9:20   360
10:13   381
10:20–21   381
12:1   386
12:7   264

Hosea
4:2   415
4:13   75
4:14–15   19
9:10   297
11:1   369, 530
13:4   114, 425

Joel
  2:18 117
  3:19 69

Amos
  1–2 19, 68
  1:6 69
  1:9 69
  1:13 169
  5:14–15 315
  5:18–27 464
  6:7 31
  7–8 261
  7:9–17 261
  9:12 238
  9:13–15 199

Jonah
  2:3–10 406

Micah
  1:2 299
  1:16 176
  2:2 108
  3:9–12 464
  3:12 346
  4:4 255
  5:2 486
  6:8 315

Habakkuk
  2:2 272
  2:4 516
  3:4 320

Zephaniah
  2:8–11 69

Zechariah
  1:14 117
  3:1 377
  3:4 177
  8:2 117

Zechariah (cont.)
  12:10–14 486
  14:9 130, 428

Malachi
  1:4 69
  1:4–5 69
  2:16 178
  3:5 323

New Testament

Matthew
  1–13 372
  1:1–7 370
  1:32–33 370
  2:11 370
  2:13–23 489
  2:26 370
  3:7 477
  3:15–18 370
  4:1 366
  4:1–11 365, 366, 368, 370
  4:2 378
  4:4 380
  4:8 368, 380
  5:13–16 532
  5:17 419, 527
  5:17–20 439, 455
  5:21 415
  6:10 432
  7:12 439
  7:15 491
  7:15–23 491
  7:24–27 439
  8:4 79
  9:36 489
  11:28 520
  11:28–29 431

Matthew (cont.)
  12 53
  12:40 406
  13:44 425
  17:5 439, 490
  19:7–8 79
  19:17–19 93, 113, 432
  19:18 415
  21:11 489
  22:4 79
  22:37 132
  22:37–38 119
  22:37–40 439
  23:23 455
  24:11 491
  24:24 491
  28 532
  28:1 431
  28:18 381
  28:18–20 532
  28:19 439
  28:20 420, 439

Mark
  1:1 370
  1:12 366
  1:12–13 365, 370
  1:44 79

Mark (cont.)
  2:27 428
  3:27 386
  7:9–13 433
  7:10 79
  9:2–8 368
  10:3–5 79
  10:19 415
  12:19 79
  12:26 79
  12:29–30 119, 132
  12:30–31 426
  16:2 431

Luke
  1–9 365
  1:1–9:50 366, 367
  1:15 366
  1:32 378
  1:35 378
  1:41 366
  1:67 366
  1:68–79 419
  2:22 79
  2:52 284
  3:22 365, 377, 378
  3:38 367, 378, 386
  4:1 366

Luke (cont.)
4:1–13   365, 367, 370, 377, 380
4:2   368, 378
4:2–4   377
4:5   368, 372
4:5–8   380
4:6   381
4:9   380
4:9–12   382
4:12   384
4:13   385
5:14   79
7:16   489
8:23   284
8:31   405
9:23   509
10:18   385
10:27   119, 132
10:28   402
11:18   385
11:21–22   386
13:16   385
16:17   439
18:20   415
20:28   79
20:37   79
22:3   385
22:31   385
22:42–43   284
22:53   385
24:1   431
24:27   79

John
1:1   284
1:14   285, 489, 512
1:16–17   515
1:17   79
1:18   492
1:21   486
1:25   486
1:45   79
2:19   285, 286
3:14   79
3:36   477
4:21–24   521
5:22–23   79
5:39   492

John (cont.)
5:46   79, 489
6:14   492
6:45–46   420
7:19   79
7:37   520
8:28   487
12:31   381
12:45   438
14:9   438
14:28   284
14:30   381
15:10–11   425
16:12–14   439
16:31   381
17:8   439
17:18   439
17:20   439
20:1   431
20:17   284

Acts
2:4   366
2:42   439
3:22   79, 486, 489
3:22–23   492
3:25–26   419
4:8   366
7   482
7:37   486, 489, 492
7:44–54   479
13:9   366
15:10   439
15:19   439
15:21   79
17:24–25   429, 430
17:25   424
20:7   431
26:22   79
28:23   79

Romans
1:21   424
2:1–3:20   401
2:8   477
2:12–13   516
2:13–14   440
2:15   421
2:20   416

Romans (cont.)
2:26   440
2:29   421
3:21   439
3:21–26   439
3:23   516
3:31   439, 440
4   513
4:4–5   399
4:13–15   516
4:23   439
5:14   440
5:18–19   419
7   398
7:6   516
7:7   389, 390
7:8–9   516
7:10   398
7:12   416, 440
7:14–25   398
8:2–4   516
8:3   398
8:4   412, 440
8:31–32   422
9:4–5   512
9:6–29   401
9–11   401, 404, 405, 409
9:15   79
9:20–21   404
9:24–29   401
9:30–10:3   401
9:30–10:13   400
9:30–10:21   400, 401
9:30–31   400
9:31   401
9:31–32   402
9:32   401
9:32–33   401
10   406
10:3   400, 401, 402
10:4   401, 404, 419, 439
10:5   79, 401, 402, 404
10:5–6   400
10:5–13   401
10:6–7   406
10:6–8   389, 390, 391, 400, 401, 402, 404, 412

Index of Scripture

Romans (cont.)
10:6–10 409
10:7 405
10:11–13 401
10:19 79, 389
11:8 389
11:36 424
12:1 509
12:1–2 37
12:19 389, 390
13:8 440
13:8–10 439
13:9 389, 390, 415, 426, 439
13:14 37
15:4 439
15:5–6 431
15:10 389, 390
16:20 485

1 Corinthians
2:6 381
2:13 420
8:4–6 423, 425
9:9 79, 389, 390, 439
9:20–21 439
9:21 440
10 52, 53
10:1–13 455
10:6 440
10:6–9 371
10:11 439, 440
10:13 386
10:19–20 423, 424
16:2 431
16:16 60

2 Corinthians
1:9 423
3:3 420
3:6 516
3:6–8 439
3:7 489
3:11 439
4:4 381, 419
4:6 438
12:7 423
12:9 423
13:1 389, 390

Galatians
1:4 399
2:12 395
2:15–21 391
2:16 391, 394
2:17 395
2:19 395
3 394
3–4 220
3:1 399
3:1–5:12 391
3:1–6 391
3:1–12 513
3:1–14 396
3:2 391, 394, 395
3:5 391, 394
3:6–14 395
3:7–9 391
3:7–29 391
3:8 419, 430
3:9 394
3:10 220, 389, 390, 391, 392, 394, 395, 396, 398, 399, 400, 412
3:10–13 396
3:10–14 392
3:12 395, 396, 402
3:12–13 516
3:13 389, 390, 396, 399
3:13–14 419
3:14 430
3:16 419
3:21–24 516
3:25 439
3:28 459, 519
5:1–12 391, 439
5:2 395
5:3 396
5:4 398
5:14 439
5:18 516
6:2 439, 440
6:10 434, 505

Ephesians
1–2 37
2:2 381

Ephesians (cont.)
2:14–16 439
2:15 419
2:20 439
4:8 348
4:11 60
6 37
6:1–3 432, 433, 439
6:2–3 389, 390
6:4 433

Philippians
2:5–8 489
2:5–11 286
2:6–8 381, 386
2:6–11 405
2:8 419
2:9 284
2:9–11 386
3:6 398
3:8–9 439
3:20 459

Colossians
1:15 438
1:16 419, 424
2:9 285
2:13–14 439
2:13–15 419
2:16–17 431, 440

1 Thessalonians
4:9 420

2 Thessalonians
2:15 439

1 Timothy
1:10 507
2:5 285, 488
3:16 405
4:1–5 491
5:1–2 434
5:3 121, 432, 433
5:4 434
5:8 434
5:18 389, 390, 439

2 Timothy
  1:5   433
  3:14–15   433
  3:15–17   455
  3:16   439, 511
  4:2   488

Titus
  1:16   433

Hebrews
  1:1–2   439
  1:3   419, 425, 437, 438
  3:2–6   489
  3:14   431
  4:8–11   431
  5:8   419
  7:12   439
  7:25   489
  8:5   440
  8:6–7   489
  8:13   439
  9:4   415
  9:24   440
  10:9   439
  11   53
  11:24–27   489
  11:39–12:1   455
  12:23   438
  12:28   438
  12:28–29   56
  12:29   56, 438
  13:14   459
  13:17   60

James
  1:25   439, 440
  1:27   434
  2:8   439
  2:10–11   110
  2:12   439, 440

1 Peter
  1:1   442, 459
  1:15–16   439
  1:16   417
  2:9   532
  2:11   442, 459
  3:21   440
  4:11   492
  5:2   527

2 Peter
  1:4   425
  1:20–21   492
  2:1–3   491

1 John
  2:18–23   491
  2:18–27   492
  2:20–21   420
  3:16   509
  4:1–3   492
  4:1–6   491
  5:21   439

Revelation
  2:13   426
  2:17   427
  3:8   426

Revelation (cont.)
  3:12   427
  5:9   533
  7:4   533
  9:1–2   405
  9:11   405
  11:7   405
  11:15   381
  12:7–9   386
  13:1   427
  13:3–4   382
  13:8   382
  13:11–18   491
  13:16–17   427
  14:1   427
  14:9–10   477
  14:9–11   427
  14:11   382, 427
  14:13   431
  16:2   382
  16:13   382
  17:8   405
  18:11–13   508
  19:20   382, 491
  20:1   405
  20:3   405
  20:4   427
  21:2   420
  21:4   432
  21:9   420
  22:1–2   381
  22:3   432
  22:3–4   428
  22:4   427
  22:18–19   492

Index of Ancient Sources

Inscriptions

Egyptian
Book of the Dead 125   315n25
Mesopotamian
Royal Inscriptions of the Assyrian Periods   12nn36, 37, 38
Statues of Gudea, Statue B   318n35
Story of Idrimi, King of Alalakh   12
Hittite
Political Testament of Ḫattušili I   39
Treaty Between Muwattalli and Aleppo   7–8
Treaty Between Šuppiluliuma I and Ḫukkana of Ḫayaša (*CTH* 42)   47–49
Treaty of Suppiluliuma I and Shattiwaza of Mitanni   10(n29)
West Semitic
Inscription of Zakkur, King of Hamath   3
Moabite Stone   3
Tel Dan Stele   3, 4

ANE Texts

Egyptian
Instruction Addressed to Kagemni   315n25
Instruction Addressed to King Merikare   315n25
Instruction of Amenemope   315n25, 318n35
Instruction of Any   315n25
Instruction of King Amenhemet I for His Son Sesostris I   315n25
Instruction of Papyrus Insinger   318n35
Instruction of Prince Hardjedef   315n25
Instruction of Ptahhotep   315n25, 318n35

ANE Texts *(cont.)*
Mesopotamian
Adapa Myth   34
Annals of Sennacherib
  150 VIII   11n36
  150 X   12n38
  151 XII   11n36
  151 XV   11n36
Babylonian Chronicle   4–5, 8
Babylonian Theodicy   309n5, 315n23
Counsels of Wisdom   34, 315n25, 318n35
Curse of Agade   14
Dialogue Between a Man and His God   314n23
Dialogue of Pessimism   34, 307n1
Laws of Hammurabi
  (whole)   62
  1:27–49   318n35
  1:50–53   11n36
  8:30–9:13   322n44
  35:37–36:5   322n44
  46:97–102   322n44
  47:9–10   11n36
  47:59–78   318n35
Epic of Tukulti-Ninurta I   13
Eponym Chronicle   6, 8
Esagila Chronicle   5–6, 13–14
Furious God   315n23
Gilgamesh Epic   34
Instructions of Shuruppak   34, 315n25
Laws of Lipit-Ishtar   318n35
Laws of Ur-Namma   318n35
Ludlul Bēl Nēmeqi, "I Will Praise the Lord of Wisdom"   307n1
Man and his God   309n5
Poem of the Righteous Sufferer   314–15n23
Sumerian King List   6

ANE Texts *(cont.)*
Mesopotamian (cont.)
  To Any God (Prayer to Every
    God)   315n23
  Vassal Treaties of Esarhaddon
    (whole)   9–10
    lines 419–430   9
    lines 528–532a   9
    line 576   10
  Who Has Not Sinned?   309n5
Hittite
  Apology of Ḫattušili III   43
  Instructions for Palace Personnel
    (*CTH* 265)   46
  Old Hittite law collection
    §§46–56   41
    §54   41
    §55   41
    §173   50
  Palace Chronicle (*CTH* 8)   39–40,
    40n4, 40n5, 47, 50–52, 55,
    59
  Song of Release   42–43
    §17   42
    §§18–19   42
  Telipinu Proclamation (*CTH* 19)   43–
    44, 43n16, 50–52
    §7   44
    §13   44
    §§20–21   44
    §§22–23   46n20
    §§30–33   44
    §30   44
    §31   44–45
    §32   45
    §33   45
    §49   45
West Semitic
  Royal Archives of Mari
    ARM 26.197   29n34
    ARM 26.199   29n34
    ARM 26.202   29n34
    ARM 26.438   29n35
    ARM 26.449   29n35
  Baal Cycle   386n76
  Dawn and Dusk (Birth of the
    Gracious Gods)   28
  Dialogue of Shupe-ameli   30, 32–35

ANE Texts *(cont.)*
West Semitic (cont.)
  El-Amarna tablets (EA)
    EA 147   10(n30)
    EA 252   29n33
  Emar documents   25–26
  Mari Letters   23–25
  Ugarit texts (*KTU*)
    (whole)   26–28
    KTU 1.17 (*Aqhat Legend*)   30(n37)
    KTU 1.23   28
    KTU 1.40   30, 31–32
    KTU 1.84   32
  Wisdom of Ahiqar   30, 35–36; cf.
    315n25

Apocrypha and Septuagint

Baruch
  3:9   409
  3:29–30   409
  3:29–4:1   307n1
1 Maccabees
  1:54–61   281
Sirach/Ecclesiasticus
  1:3   307n1
  1:8   307n1
  9:8   320
Tobit
  4:16–17   322
Wisdom of Solomon
  9:16–18   307n1

Old Testament Pseudepigrapha

1 Enoch
  40:7   377
  45–46   386n76
  54:6   377
4 Ezra
  4:8   409n58
Jubilees
  1:20   377
  17:15–18   377
  24:31   409n58
  35:17   381
Liber Antiquitatum biblicarum
  23:10   402

Old Testament Pseudepigrapha (cont.)

Psalms of Solomon
   14:1–2   402
Testament of Abraham
   16a   377
Testament of Job
   8:1–3   381

DSS and Related Texts

1QM (*War Scroll*)
   1:13–15   386n76
   17:5–8   386n76
4Q129 (Phyl B)   108n26
4Q134 (Phyl G)   108n26
4Q266   402
4QJer^c 274n20
11Q13
   2:13–25   386n76
11QT
   Col. 63:12, 13   175n29
Damascus Document (CD)
   3:14–16   402
   4:12–13   377
XQ3 (Phyl 3)   108n26

Philo

De decalago
   12.50–51   99n11, 432n37
On Rewards and Punishments
   80   409n57
On the Change of Names
   236–237   409n57
On the Posterity of Cain
   84–85   409n57
On the Preliminary Studies
   86–87   402
On the Special Laws
   4.14   507
   4.19   507
On the Virtues
   183   409n57

Josephus

Jewish Antiquities
   3.91   99n11
   3.101   99n11
   15:411–12   383

Mishnah, Talmud, and Related Literature

b. ʿAbodah Zarah
   35b   281
b. Megillah
   14b   280n42
   16b   280n42
   19a   280n40
b. Menaot
   34a   280n40
b. Moʾed Qaṭan
   26a   280n43
b. Sanhedrin
   89b   366n7
Baba Meṣiʿa
   59b   409n58
   85a   282n47
Horayot
   12a   99n11
m. ʾAbot
   3:6   282
   6:7   282
m. Peʾah
   1:1   282
Makkot
   24a   99n11
t. Šabbat
   15.17   402n37
y. Megillah
   4:1, 74d   280n41
y. Moʾed Qaṭan
   3:7, 83c   280n43, 281
y. Soṭah
   9:13, 24b   280n42
   21d   393n12

Targumic Texts

Targum Onqelos
   Lev 18:5   402n37
Samaritan Targum
   Deut 27:26   393n12
Targum Neofiti
   Deut 30:13   406n47
Targum Pseudo-Jonathan
   Lev 18:5   402n37

Other Rabbinic Works

Ecclesiastes Rabbah
  1.4.4   282
  5.11.5   282
Leviticus Rabbah
  11.7   282n48
  25   393n12
Deuteronomy Rabbah
  11:5   366n7
Mekilta de-Rabbi Ishmael, Pisha
  1   280n42
Pesiqta Rabbati
  36   383
Pirqe Rabbi Eliezer
  53   280n42
Seder Eliyahu Zuta
  ch. 2   282n48

Other Rabbinic Works (cont.)

Seper Torah
  1   280n40
Sipre Deuteronomy
  48   281n44
  307   366n7
  343   281, 282
Sipre Numbers
  78   280n42
  99   280n42
  112   99n11
Sipre Zuta
  Num 10:29   280n42
Soperim
  1   280n40

www.ingramcontent.com/pod-product-compliance
Lightning Source LLC
Chambersburg PA
CBHW052109010526
44111CB00036B/1583